CHRISTIAN WORDS

CHRISTIAN WORDS

by

Nigel Turner

T. & T. CLARK
36 George Street, Edinburgh

TO
MARY KATHLEEN TURNER
who helped me with this book

Contents

Preface

When one ends a task like this one is conscious only of imperfections. I apologize at once to the reader for the more obvious negligences and ignorances of which he will soon be aware. I have tried to hold all the reins firmly, but the book is necessarily crammed with a nightmare of detail.

I am very grateful again to my distinguished publisher, T. & T. Clark, and among the directors I am especially indebted to Dr. Geoffrey Green who has generously guided and corrected, warned and encouraged, most unobtrusively and with *chrēstotēs*.

I express my obligation to Mr. Kitney and the staff of craftsmen at Billing & Sons Ltd., who transformed an ugly manuscript, lengthy and most complex, into a visually attractive format. I owe a large debt to their uncomplaining patience and skill.

The book is dedicated to Mary, deeply beloved, who with a bright vision beyond the things of earth, has inspired and controlled it.

3 Palace Green,   NIGEL TURNER
Ely.
Lent 1980

Introduction

A Word Book deals with single words and may neglect their wider context in the Bible as a whole. For sound exegesis it is imperative to bring out the sense of the total environment. The paragraph determines the gist of the individual words within it.

Nevertheless, I am sure that the Word Book must still be the student's guide, for every syllable is important as long as its context is watched. The great exegete, C. J. Vaughan, found that when the microscope was applied to one single phrase, or even to *one word* of holy Scripture, something was always discovered which was interesting to the expositor and profitable to the student in a spiritual way.

> Oh Book! infinite sweetnesse! let my heart
> Suck *ev'ry letter,* and a honey gain
> Precious for any grief in any part,
> To cleave the breast, to mollifie all pain.

George Herbert well knew how 'all its lights' combine, how each verse and 'all the constellations of the storie' are luminant. How one verse marks a further verse, and how both turn our attention to a third, ten pages away, and then all three verses form a potion to guide some Christian's destiny! 'For in ev'ry thing Thy words do finde me out.'

The Church today is concerned about communicating with the contemporary world and especially about the need to speak in a new idiom. The language of the Church had better be the language of the NT. To proclaim the Gospel with new terminology is hazardous when much of the message and valuable overtones that are implicit in the NT might be lost for ever. 'Most of the distortions and dissentions that have vexed the Church,' observed the late Dean of York, 'where these have touched theological understanding, have arisen through the insistence of sects or sections of the Christian community upon using words which are not found in the NT.'[1]

True, we must in our preaching employ the speech of the 'factories and homes' of our century, or we will not preach at all. Here comes the clash of the two languages, the Biblical and the secular. We must translate. Else we shall continue to speak Greek. But our peril is that of succumbing to modern language and failing to preach the Gospel because we have made not only its language but its message 'modern'.[2] Resolving the clash of language is the whole art of preaching, and the Word Book is to help in that very thing. 'The Christian preacher and teacher stands in the middle of the clash.' If he will not accept the challenge he loses relevance and dies. If he rejects the language of the Gospel, again he dies by conforming to the world and by losing the power to preach. 'What a fascinating oscillation of Christian language!' cries Dr. Laeuchli. In the centre of the oscillation is the man in the pulpit: he may give his community true Christian roots, or he may distort the message and lead his congregation to betrayal.

St. Chrysostom warned that the Christian who does not know the Bible is a workman without tools. To read it with loving attention, he suggests, is to converse familiarly with God. The Scriptures, said St. Thomas, have an authority wholly their own. But the question of verbal inspiration of the NT autographs is beset by innumerable difficulties. We may ask whether the dictating author or his amanuensis is inspired.[3] We may ask which of the hundreds of manuscripts of the Bible is to be trusted. Guided by traditional views of inspiration, nevertheless, I cannot believe that the Scriptures enshrine any ultimate or essential error, any defect, any excess, anything except heavenly wisdom. In all instances the truth may be limited by the capacity of the authors or by the literary symbols which they used or by the intervention of amanuenses and copyists. Saintly and inspired men were given God's speech, but Biblical Greek is still a language of earthly symbols. One of the God-breathed authors was ready to confess that as yet he knew only in part. I have written with these presuppositions.

The NT authors belonged to their own age, were fallible and weak, of a different environment from our own, of a strange language, an alien culture. 'If God has condescended to address men in the full particularity of their peculiar historical and cultured environments, then we have got to immerse ourselves fully and sympathetically in those environments, with their customs and values, ways of thinking and patterns of imagery, before we can understand either his demand or their response.'[4] We must learn their peculiar language. Biblical Greek and its special content should be our diligent study.

More than fifteen years ago my studies in syntax led me to ask whether the Biblical language was not unique, and since then investigation of the style of Biblical Greek has confirmed that impression.[5] Now, in turn, the vocabulary of the same kind of Greek has come under discussion, only to strengthen it.

This book of Christian Words is but a sample of the speciality of Biblical and Christian language.

By 'Christian words' I have in mind Greek terms which so far as I know the first believers devised for themselves. The number of improvised "Biblical" words, in both LXX and NT, is now conceded to be much smaller than was once advertised, and the distinguished lexicographer, the late Dr. Walter Bauer, found that even among the words which were probably new there are traces of Hellenistic secular influence in such contingencies as spelling.

Although the newly coined Biblical words are quite few apart from transliterations, still their number is not negligible. Some are fresh compounds made out of old words, like 'little-faith' and 'eye-service', 'double-minded' and 'respect of persons'. Some are nouns altogether new, concocted from old verbs, or new verbs from old adjectives. However, I have extended the name 'Christian' to a group of words much more numerous.

There are certain terms, some common enough already in the language and some rarely appearing in general usage, which acquire a deeper sense and a new consecration within the Christian vocabulary. Pondered in their new contexts, they are felt to be peculiar words and I still cannot do better than follow Archbishop Trench who described them as 'words which the Church did not invent, but has assumed into its service, and employed in a far loftier sense than any to which the world had ever put them before' (p. 1). Such words are *Truth* and *Church, parable* and *way, covenant, Word, saint, angel.* Some of them had been infrequent, now becoming widely used, like *goodness* and *reverence, evangelist* and *Beloved.* Some had been used religiously before, in a quite different sense, like *Bishop, Presbyter* and *Deacon,* like *brother* and *gospel,* like *koinōnia, parousia* and *salvation.*

Some words, through their Biblical association, had deployed a new level of meaning in addition to their gist hitherto – *doxa* added glory, *homologō* added praise, *glōssai* added nations, *diathēkē* added covenant.

Some words too are 'Christian' because on the lips of believers they have quite changed their former meaning: 'hypocrite' is no longer an actor, 'peace' is longer the cessation of strife, 'tender mercies' no longer the entrails, 'parable' no longer a maxim, and (perhaps) 'powers' no longer the civil authorities. Many observers have already noticed this. 'Because Christianity revealed a new life,' says one, 'it required a new vocabulary to express the new conditions. Words, therefore, came into use which were, in some cases absolutely new inventions, in others so charged with new meaning as to be equivalent to new words.'[6]

How is one to define the new sense, and by what criteria to determine the meaning of Biblical words? F. C. Fensham indicated what I take to be an obligation of the first importance – to understand words by means of their context, that is, from their immediate linguistic environment. He prescribes the utmost care whenever non-Biblical material is brought into play in NT exegesis. Scrutiny must be made of the time and place in which the word was used in secular Greek, and of the different literary genre in which it appears. Even contemporary Jewish material must be received cautiously, for words gain a new specific Christian sense as they are taken over into Christian use. It is still more implausible to focus attention upon comparable contexts of Christian words in Judaism when the contexts are later than the NT.[7]

The event of our study, as I see it, has been disenchantment with Bishop Lightfoot's guess that 'if we could only recover letters that ordinary people wrote to each other without any thought of being literary, we should have the greatest possible help for the understanding of the language of the New Testament'.[8]

It happens that a towering mass of papyrus material of that very kind was recovered and yet I have been at pains to show how little of it has helped in understanding the weighty Christian words which first appeared in the NT and early Fathers, or were applied by these believers in a way different from that in which ordinary people exploited them. Always 'the greatest possible help' came to me, I confess, not by closely examining the papyri, which I have done, but from the immediate context and from the Greek Scriptures first of all. After examining the secular use of the following words, I will show repeatedly that it is seldom the same as the Christian use, and that we must always go elsewhere for a more assured and devotional understanding.

God may not after all have communicated 'absolutely in the language of the people, as we might surely have expected He would',[9] when the NT was written. From a liberal Protestant point of view we might well have expected it and yearned for it, but my own enquiries in the sphere of syntax, style, and now in vocabulary, have pleaded for caution. God seems not to have used the contemporary vernacular speech without revolutionizing it, whether in style (or lack of it), whether in sentence construction, or whether in vocabulary. The early Christians had their own form of speech, and I account it to be as 'sacred' in vocabulary as I found it in syntax and style.

Can it be that I have taken insufficient notice of the influences of secular Greek upon the Christian vocabulary? Truly there are many Christian words and expressions upon which the vernacular papyri shed light. Such words are *apechei* (Mk 14[41]) which in the business papyri abound in receipts for payment. So I would agree with the late Dr. William Barclay that the meaning is probably, 'You may rest and sleep now. Judas *has had his wages*.'[10] Likewise the word *arrabōn* is found in secular Greek to mean a first instalment, a pledge that in time the full amount of a debt will be repaid. To know this helps to see why the Holy Ghost is said to be a first instalment of the life in heaven, a guarantee that God will in time pay the full amount (2 Co 1^{22} 5^5; Eph 1^{14}).[11]

Sometimes indeed (but rarely, I find) the vernacular papyri exceed the LXX in the help they give for Christian exegesis. The word for false accusation (Lk 19^8 RV), used of tax-gatherers, meant sometimes different in the LXX (oppression). It suits the NT context far better to understand the word as it is found in contemporary secular Greek, i.e. false accusation, especially for the extortion of money. Tax-gatherers had power to 'accuse' defaulters to the high revenue officials.[12] The circumstance throws no light on Christian doctrine but it is interesting. So are several other examples: secular Greek suggests that Apollos should be described as 'eloquent', not learned (Act 18^{24}), that faith should be understood as the 'title-deed' of good things to come, not the assurance (Heb 11^1), and that the word *logizesthe* (Ph 4^8), being a term from accountancy in secular Greek, ought to be rendered, 'Reckon these things among your assets'.[13] I would not underestimate these examples and others, all of which I have already acknowledged. I am not 'out upon a witch hunt against Greek thought', and hope that I have never deliberately ignored the evidence from non-biblical Greek.

What we call Christian Greek is essentially the old Attic dialect of the secular language extended and popularized by contact with other dialects and by its employment among the conquered peoples of the Greek and Roman empires. So much was established long ago by the papyrus discoveries at Fayum, Oxyrhynchus, and other parts of Egypt. Vernacular scripts often came from the humblest grades of society and showed in some ways a remarkable similarity with the Christian language, so much so that many since the time of those discoveries at the beginning of the century have assumed that NT language is the speech of the lowliest classes. For many years the significant contribution of Deissmann and J. H. Moulton was their insistence that the early Christians did not create a specialized vocabulary but used some of the simplest words in Greek to express their Gospel and the ideas which resulted from it.

That was a long time ago and much study has occupied the intervening years. The following pages will indicate the directions in which research into the vocabulary has moved. My own strong feeling is echoed in the words of the late Biblical scholar, Dr. C. H. Dodd, that 'it is rarely safe to ignore the LXX in attempting to determine the meaning of Pauline language'.[14] Only I think it is true of other NT writers besides St. Paul. The contemporary secular Greek does help us to a limited extent. It throws light on the meaning of such words as 'milk' and such trivia as the height of a man's stature. It brings in a wealth of ideas from accountancy, wills, receipts, deposits, and beggars' collecting-bags. However, if we would get to the heart of the Christian message we need more than the help of secular Greek. The great Christian words which concern salvation and Christian living were not produced in a secular environment. They are rooted in the Greek OT, so that Septuagintal study is likely to forward Christian exegesis. Greek-speaking Jews, even before the advent of the Saviour, had worked wonders with the Greek language. The Greek of their Scriptures is very different from the uncultivated dialect of the market-place which you read in the secular papyri and which literary men scorn. Grecian Jews had imbibed their linguistic tradition in several ways – from religious experience, from the bilingual circumstances of their environment, and especially from devotion to their Scriptures and almost daily attendance at the synagogue liturgy. Christians being mostly Jews at the beginning, inherited this metabolized language, only to transform it still more remarkably.

I avow then that Christian words are often the ordinary vocabulary of ordinary people in the secular world. It is, however, important to recollect that when we are examining words in any given environment we need above all to be aware of the system of thought that lies behind their use – in our case, the Christian system of thought. Indeed, much of the difficulty in Christian communication today arises from the fact that the very vocabulary whose profound significance is familiar enough to the serious reader of the Bible so often conveys something quite different to all his secular contemporaries, simply because each philosophy of life has radically altered the meaning of words.[15] So the way in which each word is used in the Christian context is of the first importance.

The words which follow are arranged alphabetically for the sake of convenience, but I would observe that both new words and re-christened words tend to fall around certain specified themes. It is interesting to find that the largest number of these Christian words concern the Gospel, Salvation, the Jewish mystery, and Life within the Fellowship of the Christian Church.

Creativity is most marked within these spheres.

NOTES

[1] Alan Richardson, *Introduction to the Theology of the New Testament*, SCM 1958, p. 217.
[2] S. Laeuchli, *The Language of Faith*, Epworth 1965, pp. 238f.
[3] See G. I. Mavrodes in *Evangelical Quarterly* 41 (1969), pp. 19–29.

CHRISTIAN WORDS

[4] D. E. Nineham in *The Church's Use of the Bible Past and Present,* ed. D. E. Nineham, SPCK 1963, p. 161.

[5] Moulton-Turner, *Grammar* vol. 3 (Syntax) 1963, vol. 4 (Style) 1976.

[6] E. K. Lee, *Expository Times* 62 (1950), p. 28.

[7] F. C. Fensham *Nederduitse Gereformeerde Teologiese Tydskrif* (Stellenbosch,. R.S.A.) 15 (1974), pp. 268–273.

[8] J. B. Lightfoot in 1863, cited by G. Milligan, *Selections from the Greek Papyri,* CUP 1927, p. xx, and by J. H. Moulton, *Grammar* vol. 1 T. & T. Clark, 3rd ed., p. 242.

[9] J. H. Moulton *Grammar* vol. 1, p. 5.

[10] *The New Testament in Historical and Contemporary Perspective* (Festschrift for Macgregor), Blackwell 1965, pp. 75ff.

[11] Ibid., p. 79.

[12] *Expository Times* 71 (1960), p. 104.

[13] Ibid., p. 104.

[14] *Journal of Theological Studies* NS 5 (1954), p. 248.

[15] E. K. Lee, op. cit., p. 31.

Abbreviations

AV: The Authorized Version (King James' Version)

Aeschylus: plays, Oxford Classical Texts, ed. A. Sidgwick

Andocides: Teubner edition 1913

Appian: Teubner 1897–1905

Aristophanes: plays, OCT ed. F. W. Hall and W. M. Geldart

Aristotle: works, ed. I. Bekker, Berlin 1831–70.

Armitage Robinson: J. A. Robinson, *St. Paul's Epistle to the Ephesians*, 2nd ed. London 1904

Athenaeus: Teubner 1887–90

BFBS: British & Foreign Bible Society, Diglot, 1973

BDB: F. Brown, S. R. Driver, C. A. Briggs, *Hebrew and English Lexicon of the Old Testament*, Clarendon 1906

BGU: *Berliner griechische Urkunden*, Berlin 1895–1933

BS: A. Deissmann, *Bible Studies*, ET T. & T. Clark 1901

Barn: The epistle of Barnabas

Bauer: Walter Bauer, *Griechisch-Deutsches Wörterbuch zu den Schriften des NT und die übrigen urchristlichen Literatur*, Töpelmann, Berlin, 4th ed. 1952

Beginnings: *The Beginnings of Christianity*, ed. F. Jackson and K. Lake, Macmillan 1920–33

Burton: E. de W. Burton, *Galatians* ICC, T. & T. Clark 1921

CIG: *Corpus Inscriptionum Graecarum* (A. Boeckh) Berlin 1827–77

Clem: The epistles of St. Clement of Rome

Cremer: H. Cremer, *Biblico-Theological Lexicon of New Testament Greek*, ET 4th ed. T. & T. Clark 1895

Demosthenes: orations OCT ed. S. H. Butcher and W. Rennie

Did: the Didache

Diog: the epistle of Diognetus

Diogenes Laertius: ed. C. G. Cobet

Dionysius of Halicarnassus: *Antiquitates Romanae*, ed. C. Jacoby (Teubner) 1885–1905

Dittenberger: W. Dittenberger, *Sylloge Inscriptionum Graecarum*, Leipzig, 2nd ed. 1898–1901, 3rd ed. 1915–24, 4th ed. 1960

Euripides: plays, OCT ed. G. G. A. Murray

Field: F. Field, *Notes on the Translation of the New Testament*, CUP 1899

HDB: *Hastings' Dictionary of the Bible* (5 vols) T. & T. Clark 1898–1904

Hermas *Mand., Sim., Vis.*: The Shepherd of Hermas, *Mandates, Similitudes, Visions*

Herodotus: works OCT ed. C. Hude

Homer *Iliad, Odyssey:* OCT ed. D. B. Monro–T. W. Allen

ICC: International Critical Commentary (T. & T. Clark)

IG: *Inscriptiones Graecae,* Berlin 1873ff.

I. Eph, etc.: St. Ignatius to the Ephesians, Magnesians, Trallians, Romans, Philadelphians, Smyrnaeans, Polycarp

Isocrates: ed. Teubner (F. Blass) 1889–98

Jastrow: M. Jastrow, *A Dictionary of the Targumim, etc.,* Luzac 1903

Josephus *Ant. Jud.*: Antiquities of the Jews; *C. Apion.*: Contra Apionem; *Bell. Jud.*: Jewish War; *Vita:* Life – ed. B. Niese, Berlin 1890

Justin *Dial., Apol.*: St. Justin Martyr, *The Dialogue with Trypho, Apology*

Kittel *TWNT: Theologisches Wörterbuch zum Neuen Testament,* ed. G. Kittel 1933ff., G. Friedrich 1949ff., Kohlhammer, Stuttgart

LS: Liddell and Scott, *Greek-English Lexicon,* ed. H. S. Jones, Clarendon 9th ed. 1940

LXX: Septuagint (Hebrew text cited in brackets)

Lucian: Teubner ed. C. Jacobitz 1896–7

MM: J. H. Moulton and G. Milligan, *The Vocabulary of the Greek Testament,* Hodder 1930

M. Pol: the Martyrdom of Polycarp

Menander: Teubner 1912

NEB: New English Bible

NT: New Testament

OT: Old Testament

OCT: Oxford Classical Texts

OGI: *Orientis Graeci Inscriptiones Selectae,* ed. W. Dittenberger, Leipzig 1903–5

PG: J. P. Migne, *Patrologia Graeca,* Paris 1857–66

P. Philip.: the epistle of St. Polycarp to the Philippians

P. Amherst: *Amherst Papyri,* ed. B. P. Grenfell and A. S. Hunt, London 1900ff.

P. Cairo Zen.: *Zenon Papyri,* ed. C. C. Edgar, Cairo 1925–31

P. Fay.: B. P. Grenfell and A. S. Hunt, *Fayûm Towns and their Papyri,* London 1900

P. Flor: *Papiri Fiorentini, documenti pubblici e privati dell' età romana e bizantina,* Milan, I–III 1906ff.

P. Grenf: B. P. Grenfell, *An Alexandrian Erotic Fragment,* Clarendon 1896

P. Lille: *Institut papyrologique de L'Université de Lille: Papyrus grecs,* ed. P. Jouguet, Paris 1907–28

P. Lond: *Greek Papyri in the British Museum*, ed. F. G. Kenyon, H. I. Bell, 1893ff.

P. Mag. Leid. V: *Papyrus Magica Musei Lugdunensis Batavi*, ed. A. Dieterich 1888

P. Mag. Par: see Preisendanz

P. Masp: J. Maspéro, *Papyrus grecs d'époque byzantine*, Cairo 1911–16

P. Oxy: *Oxyrhynchus Papyri* I–XVII, ed. B. P. Grenfell, A. S. Hunt, London 1898–1927

P. Petr: *The Flinders Petrie Papyri*, ed. J. Mahaffy, Dublin 1891ff.

P. Ryl: *Catalogue of the Greek Papyri in the John Rylands Library*, ed. A. S. Hunt, etc., 1915ff.

P. Tebt: *Tebtunis Papyri* I–III, ed. B. P. Grenfell, etc., London and New York 1902–33

P. Tor: *Papyri Graeci Regii Taurinensis Musei Aegyptii* I and II, ed. V. A. Peyron, Turin 1826f.

Philo: ed. L. Cohn, P. Wendland, Berlin 1896–1915

Plato: works ed. OCT (J. Burnet)

Plutarch *Moralia:* Teubner (G. N. Bernadakis) 1888–96; *Lives: Vitae Parallellae* ed. Wyttenbach, Leipzig 1796ff.

Polybius: works ed. Teubner (Büttner-Wobst) 1882–1905

Preisandanz: K. Preisandanz, *Die griechische Zauberpapyri*, I and II 2nd ed. Teubner, Stuttgart 1973–4

Ps Sol: Psalms of Solomon

RSV: the Revised Standard Version

RV: the Revised Version

Selwyn: E. G. Selwyn, *The First Epistle of St. Peter*, Macmillan 2nd ed. 1947

Sophocles: plays ed. OCT (A. C. Pearson)

Strabo: ed. G. Kramer, Berlin 1844ff.

T. Abr: *Testament of Abraham*, ed. M. R. James, cited by page and line

T. Sol: *Testament of Solomon*, ed. McCown, cited by chapter and verse

T. XII P. *T. Jud: Testaments of the Twelve Patriarchs*, Testament of Judah, etc.

Thucydides: ed. OCT (H. S. Jones)

Trench: R. C. Trench, *Synonyms of the New Testament*, Macmillan 7th ed. 1871

UPZ: *Urkunden der Ptolemäerzeit*, ed. U. Wilcken, Berlin and Leipzig, I 1922, II 1935ff.

Vettius Valens: works ed. W. Kroll, Berlin 1908

Xenophon *Anabasis, Cyropaedia, Historia Graeca, Memorabilia;* ed. OCT (Marchant)

A

ABBA

ἀββά

Abba meaning 'Father!' is an indeclinable noun coined in Christian Greek and found subsequently only within the Church, where it is a respectful title of monks and abbots, bishops and priests.

It is a direct transliteration of the Aramaic *'abbâ*, which is in turn an emphatic form of the Hebrew word for father, often used as a title by rabbis but hardly ever applied to God. *Abba* was part of the prayer of Jesus in Gethsemane (Mk 14[36]), and the highly unusual way of addressing God doubtless reflects the extreme stress Jesus was under at the time. All four gospels record the word, and yet it was 'new and unheard of', as Professor Jeremias points out. It breaks through the limits of Judaism.[1] It also gives a new pattern for Christian prayer and a new word to the language.

With the Spirit's help believers too make the cry of *Abba* in the hour of their spiritual struggle (Ro 8[15]; Gal 4[6]), and it is a sign that they are truly by adoption the sons of God. Both of St. Paul's instances occur in adoption formulae. 'We have received the Spirit of adoption,' he says, 'the adoption of sons.' We seem to hear once more, in this Christian prayer, the cry of the old slave whose master adopts him and allows a new son to utter the joyous cry, 'Father!' From Nuzu the archaeologist finds that childless couples among the Semites customarily adopted a slave to serve them and to be designated their heir.[2]

By the same Spirit in which the believer cries, *Abba!* he mortifies the deeds of the body. The prayer is part of the battle of flesh against spirit, of the old man against the new, of the Law against grace, of the first Adam against the last.

The use of *abba* and *patēr* together, Aramaic and Greek (Ro 8[15]; Gal 4[6]), may well be liturgical in origin – the beginning of the Lord's Prayer as uttered by early Christians in the bilingual environment of Palestine and still maintained in churches further afield, in Galatia and in Rome.

ABOMINABLE: ABOMINATION

βδελυκτός : βδέλυγμα

Bdeluktos (adjective) and *bdelugma* (noun) occur occasionally in

1

secular writers of the post-Biblical period, but most likely the words were coined in Jewish Greek by way of the LXX.

The 'abomination' *(bdelugma)* which was foretold in the prophecy of Daniel and is mentioned by our Lord,[3] is the Hebrew *shiqqûṣ*, a contemptuous term for any object tainted by idolatry and heathen divinities. An Aramaic word, *bᵉdhal* (to keep away from) may itself be borrowed from the Greek words – they have three letters in common, B, D and L.

The Hebrew *tô'ēbhâ* (Pr 17[15]) is rendered by two Greek words together, *akathartos* (unclean) and *bdeluktos* which is evidently something that was shunned and abhorred in a ritual and ethical sense – the basis of *tô'ēbhâ*. 'Gather together our dispersion ... look upon them that are despised and abhorred *(bdeluktos)*': 2 Mac 1[27]. According to Hesychius *bdeluktos* meant 'hateful', 'set at nought' (citing Pr 17[5]; 2 Mac 1[27]), and, on his authority, he adds 'loathsome' *(bdeluros)*.[4]

Philo has the adjective *bdeluktos*. 'We find,' he says, 'that no person of good character is admitted to the Mysteries; but robbers and pirates and associations of abominable *(bdeluktos)* and licentious women, when they offer money ... are sometimes accepted.'[5]

Christian Greek. By both Daniel and Jesus *bdelugma* is linked with events at the end. Objects high in men's estimation are a *bdelugma* to God (Lk 16[15]). The word has connection with spiritual harlotry – idolatry (Rev 17[4f.]) – and perpetrators of a *bdelugma* will find no place in the heavenly Jerusalem (Rev 21[27]). It is part of that world which resists God.

To be *bdeluktos* is to be an unbeliever, for all his professions of religion. Known by his disobedient 'fruits', nothing he does will pass the Christian test (Tit 1[15f.]). St. Clement uses *bdelugma* of schism and adultery (1 Clem 2[6] 30[1]), and St. Justin has it in the OT sense of sacrifices which are unacceptable to God (*Apol.* 37[7]).

ACCEPTABLE (TO GOD)

δεκτός

The verbal adjective *dektos* was formed from the verb *dechomai* (to accept) and appears for the first time in Biblical Greek.

Subsequently the neuter of the adjective *(dekton)* forms an expression in the secular Greek of the first-century grammarian Erotianus: 'it is an accepted principle ...' (preface). Iamblichus, the fourth-century philosopher, used *dektos* of a hand *to be grasped*.[6]

Very often in the LXX it has a sacrificial context, usually

2

translating the Hebrew *rāṣôn* (good will, acceptance Pr 11[1], etc.). The most significant passage in the LXX for our purpose is Isai 49[8] where *rāṣôn* is rendered by *dektos* and the 'acceptable time' is explained as the 'day of salvation;' it is 'acceptable' in the sense that now the despised prophet is encouraged to see himself as approved of God in the proclamation he is making. Another significant passage is Isai 61[1f.], where the prophet is sent to proclaim the 'acceptable' year of the Lord, the age when God's favour is revealed. This is the passage which Jesus quotes during the preaching at Nazareth when He claimed to be anointed by the Spirit 'to preach the *dektos* year of the Lord'. He applied the phrase to the age of the Gospel (Lk 4[19]), and the Christian application is made clear in another citation by which St. Paul insists that the '*dektos* time' is this day of salvation (2 Co 6[2]) – a time of God's favour upon man, the proclaiming of His good will. It may incidentally be an acceptable, or welcome, time for men, too, but that is incidental and secondary.

The word is applied to persons who have feared God and walked righteously in every age (Act 10[35]). They are **acceptable to God** *(dektos)*. St. Paul appreciated the gift from Philippi's Church – a *dektos* sacrifice to God (Ph 4[18]). The words, 'to God', are actually expressed here, but even when they are not this seems to be included in the Christian meaning. Sabbath-observance is not *dektos* (Barn 15[8]), but Polycarp the martyr is (M. Pol 14[1]). It was not a rare word among Christians,[7] and usually means **acceptable to God**. The concept of human popularity appears only at Lk 4[24] and in an apocryphal saying of Jesus ('a prophet acceptable').[8]

ADOPTION

υἱοθεσία

Huiothesia is a distinctively Pauline term, defining the nature of God's salvation,[9] a part of the unique vocabulary of Christian Greek.

Secular Greek. The meaning of *huiothesia* was 'adoption as a son', usual in the formula which is found upon inscriptions, *kath' huiothesian* (by adoption), understood as the reverse of *kata genesin* (by birth).[10] Diodorus Siculus (XXXI 27) has the phrase, *eis huiothesian*, for giving sons 'to be adopted'. Diogenes Laertius tells how Bion at Rhodes would persuade sailors to don students' garb and follow him, so that when he was on his way to the gymnasium, attended by them, all eyes were turned. It was his custom to procure the 'adoption' of certain young men for the gratification of his appetite (IV 53).

Christian Greek. St. Paul was availing himself of a generally intelligible secular figure, according to Deissmann (BS p. 239), when he used *huiothesia*. Deissmann pointed out that 'adoption' was a word frequently found in inscriptions and papyri and represents no uncommon recourse in Roman law in the Hellenistic world. The term *huiothesia*, he argued, would be immediately intelligible to the ordinary man.[11] However, it should be noticed that in Christian Greek it is used as a technical term for God's new relationship with Israel and the Gentiles. To Israel had previously belonged the *huiothesia*, along with the covenants, the Law, and the *sh*khînâ* (Ro 9[4]). Now the situation has changed, for those who were under the Law may only receive *huiothesia* by the instrumentality of Christ (Gal 4[5]). Besides, the too hasty assumption of Deissmann has at last been questioned. The Pauline concept is Semitic and not Graeco-Roman essentially. W. H. Rossell, for instance, has shown from Nuzu evidence that adoption of slaves is well attested among Semites and has urged that the Apostle 'is appealing to the testimony of the Old in writing the doctrine of the New'.[12]

Christians, the new Israel, are adopted into the People of God and the individual believer receives 'the Spirit of *huiothesia*', granting him with full validity the enjoyment of the Fatherhood of God, for by that relationship he can cry, 'Abba Father' (Ro 8[15]). RSV is inadequate in the rendering, 'the spirit of sonship'. That is 'to blur Paul's meaning rather than to clarify it'.[13] The divine act of grace, the merciful 'adoption', in making us sons is important in St. Paul's thought.

See, 'Abba'.

ALLELUIA

ἀλληλουιά

Hallēlouia (or *Allēlouia*) is a Biblical Greek coinage, being a transliteration of the Hebrew *hal*lû-Jâ*, 'Praise ye the Lord!' The exclamation is found in the LXX titles[14] of certain psalms, at the close of Ps 150, and in Tob 13[18(23)], 3 Mac 7[13]. Its occurrence in the Psalms may indicate that the exclamation was chanted by Levitical choirs in the Temple as a kind of anthem before the psalm. At the end of the book of Tobit is appended what purports to be Tobit's prayer or psalm of joy, and part of it is a song about 'Jerusalem, thou holy City'. Tobit foretells that the gates of the New Jerusalem shall utter hymns of gladness, and all her houses cry, 'Alleluia!' In the Jewish history, the third book of Maccabees, we read of the Jews departing with joy from King Philopator who had become their patron. Triumphantly they cry, 'Alleluia!'

In a third-century magical text which is a rag-bag of charms and other Jewish and pagan ingredients, we find that a talisman against perturbation of the womb consists of the words, 'Alleluia Amen'.[15] The word was evidently sacred by that time.

Christian Greek reproduces the exclamation in the Song of heaven before the Lamb's marriage (Rev 19[1,3,4,6]): 'I heard a great voice of much people in heaven, saying, *Alleluia,* salvation, and glory, and honour, and power, unto the Lord our God. ... And again they said, Alleluia!' The unending smoke of Babylon ascended, while twenty-four elders and four beasts worshipped God with the words, 'Amen, *Alleluia.*' The Seer heard a voice like many waters, saying, '*Alleluia:* for the Lord God omnipotent reigneth.'

The Church adopted the Jewish exclamation in doxologies and hymns in both Greek and Latin. It was sung before the Gospel at the Eucharist.[16] David chants this cry of praise in Paradise, explains the angel in the apocryphal vision of St. Paul, and the Church on earth ought to follow, 'at the time of offering the Body and Blood of Christ', and *alleluia* is interpreted to mean, 'Let us bless Him altogether.'[17] That was in the fourth century. To sing Alleluia solemnly at certain periods was, according to St. Augustine, an ancient tradition of the Church.[18] The medieval Latin hymn warns of the approach of Lent, for

> Alleluia cannot always
> Be our song while here below;
> Alleluia our transgressions
> Make us for a while forgo.

In Christian vocabulary Alleluia is a heavenly song, a chant of saints in the bliss of Paradise, echoed on earth at joyful seasons.

ALMIGHTY

παντοκράτωρ

Pantokratōr is literally the All-controller, the Almighty, a name given to the victorious Christ and now consecrated in Christian art by long devotion in the Eastern Church.

The word seems probably to be a coinage of Jewish Greek, for there are comparatively few secular examples apart from the magical papyri, and these show Jewish influence. The great Paris papyrus of the fourth century AD calls upon a god who has the title *pantokratōr*,[19] and refers to the house the *pantokratōr* god, Albalal.[20] Another papyrus gives to the god Hermes the same title.[21] An inscription bearing a hymn of uncertain date gives this title to 'Mandoulis', an Egyptian sun-god.[22] Well within the Christian period the title is found on papyri and is applied to God.[23] As Bauer avows, the occurrences of the title are much more frequent in Jewish literature than elsewhere.

In the LXX the word renders the Hebrew *Ṣᵉbhâôth* (of Hosts) and *shaddhai* (almighty). Later the word occurs in Jewish books, the Testament of Abraham and the Testament of Solomon.[24]

There are indications that the title *pantokratōr* may go back to a very early date and they suggest that the title was adopted by the Jews rather than created by them. There is, for instance, an ancient Cretan inscription[25] in the form of a song inscribed at the top, 'Artemis daughter of Salvius', and the song addresses the *pantokratōr* Eriounious who is none other than the god Hermes.

St. Paul's phrase, *Kurios Pantokratōr* (2 Co 6[18]), is Septuagintal and means 'Lord of Hosts' (2 Km 7[8]). Elsewhere in the NT *pantokratōr* is confined to the vocabulary of the Seer of Patmos whose contexts again recall the OT, 'Lord God Almighty, which wert and art and ever more shalt be,' – the Lord God Omnipotent (Rev 1[8], 4[8], 11[17], 15[3], 16[7,14] 19[6,15] 21[22]). It denominates the Lord God Who is First and Last, past, present, future, Who takes His great power and reigns despite what earth and heaven can do, Who is just and true and King of the Ages, Whose wrath is fierce, Whose great day of battle is to come. He is the Lord of all power and might, at the same time Author and Giver of all good things, and Father of those who come out from Belial, who are separate and who touch not the unclean thing (2 Co 6[18]).

We shrink from the tremendous cipher, as Dean Farrer winced at Michaelangelo's depiction of *Christos Pantokratōr* in the Sistine Chapel, finding in it only 'the grim earnestness and sense of horror in the painter's soul'. Wrath and terror reign, though some contemporaries defended it. Defend it as we will, protested the dean, it enshrines something deplorable,[26] a nude and wrathful Giant, merciless and pitiless, facing a shrinking, terrified Virgin. To a large part of our imagination, such is the image of the *Pantokratōr*. Little wonder if we prefer our 'good' God to this almighty Potentate. Very easily we conceive Him as 'moral' and His precepts as 'righteous'; not so readily we see Him as strong, vital, wise, magnificent, glorious, beautiful. Yet the tremendous title is frequently on the lips of the ancient Church. *Pantokratōr* is a name of the Father, the almighty One of Whom we stand in awe, Whom we supplicate to be propitious to our sins, Who justifies us through faith and grace. This, cries the Church of old, is a title which compels our obedience both to Him and to His rulers and governors upon earth.[27] St. Polycarp cried with dying breath, 'O Lord God, *Pantokratōr*, Father of Thy beloved Son' (M. Pol 14[1] 19[2]). For the early Christians He was the all-sovereign Father, immortal, invisible, Who sent to our world the Artificer Jesus by Whom He made all things (Diog 7[2]). For them the Father was the *Pantokratōr* Who gives meat and drink, particularly of a spiritual kind, through His Servant Jesus (Did 10[3]).

The title is not reserved for the Father but comes to be applied also to Christ by simple reasoning. St. Paul looked forward to a time which he named the *telos* (End) when Christ, victorious at His appearing, shall be prepared to deliver the Kingdom to His Father, having quelled all opposing forces – likely to include angels of the grades of *archē*, *exousia*, and *dunamis* (see 'Principalities', 'Authorities', 'Powers'). The End comes after a period of *basileuein* (reigning), during which all foes are subjected (1 Co 15[24ff.]). What this evidently means is that, when Christ is 'all in all' and is truly, like His Father, the *Pantokratōr*, then the universe shall lie at His feet (Eph 1[22f.]).

Dodd pointed out that by derivation the word should mean 'one who has power of control over all things' rather than 'almighty', for the latter implies only the possession of might and is rather *pantodunamenos* in Greek. The verb *kratō*, within the compound *pantokratōr*, suggests the exercise of power, i.e. rule and control. The title, therefore, indicates the One Who *controls* all things.[28]

ALMS, ALMSDEEDS

ἐλεημοσύνη

In the vocabulary of the Bible this word stands for the practical virtue of charitable giving. In secular Greek *eleēmosunē* was 'mercy' and 'kindness'. The daughter of Coeus called to Peneius, 'Do not for my sake suffer evil for this thy *compassion*.'[29]

The LXX has it to render the Hebrew words for 'kindness' (e.g. *ḥesedh* at Gen 47[29]; Pr 3[3], etc.) and 'righteousness' (e.g. *ṣᵉdhāqâ* at Deut 6[25] 24[13]; Ps 23(24)[5]). In Biblical Greek,[30] however, it is more often alms or almsgiving (as Tob 4[7]), and so in the Christian language. The Sermon on the Mount gives direction about it (Mt 6[1ff.]; Lk 11[41] 12[33]). *Eleēmosunē* applies both to Jewish (Act 3[2,3,10] 10[2,4,31]) and Christian almsgiving (Act 9[36] 24[17]).

Thereafter the meaning passed into the secular Greek of Diogenes Laertius[31] and into modern Greek (charity, almsgiving).

The difficult phrase of Jesus (Lk 11[41]) probably means 'Give *alms* from the heart (sincerely),' warning of the Pharisees who were inclined to parade their almsgiving before the public gaze.[32]

ALTAR

θυσιαστήριον

Thusiastērion is a Christian word but the precise meaning is widely disputed. *Thusiastērion* is not a secular word. It belongs to the Jewish Greek of the LXX, of Aristeas, Josephus, Philo and the Testament of Solomon. Here and in Christian Greek it is used of the Jewish altar.[33]

To interpret *thusiastērion* as a metonym for 'God'[34] is gravely to misconceive Jewish thought. This is not what St. Paul means by his phrase, 'partakers of the *thusiastērion*'. He is not saying that Israelites were *koinōnoi* (sharers) of God. G. V. Jourdain sufficiently maintained that it never occurred to ancient Hebrews, or those of St. Paul's time either, that they were or could be *ḥᵃbhērîm (koinōnoi)* of God (1 Co 10[18]). Not even Philo had gone so far as to describe them thus.[35] The passage in Philo is in fact very close to St. Paul in expression and meaning: 'partakers of the Lord's Table' (1 Co 10[21]).[36] *Thusiastērion* cannot be anything else than the Jewish altar, the OT type of the Christians' *trapeza Kuriou* (Lord's Table).

St. Paul does not stand alone in the NT. The Jewish altar is seen by the Seer of Patmos and the writer to Hebrews as a type of something specifically Christian: we have an 'altar' and Jesus suffered 'without the camp' in order to sanctify His people with His own blood. To this 'altar' we must go, bearing His reproach (Heb 13[10ff.]) Where is the altar? Can we identify it? For many older commentators it was the Cross,[37] but for others[38] it is the Holy Table of communion which from early times has been known as the Altar. Still, 'altar' was not apparently used of the Holy Table before Tertullian[39] and possibly Irenaeus.[40] Although Lightfoot could not believe that the references in St. Ignatius and St. Irenaeus are to the Holy Table of communion, yet Irenaeus does speak of the Eucharist in the same context. Before the time of Tertullian, according to J. M. Creed, the use of *thusiastērion* was no more than figurative, but Creed did confess that among those who understand *thusiastērion* to be the Table at the Eucharist in Heb 13[10] are St. Chrysostom and Bishop Westcott. 'Our rites', urged St. Chrysostom, 'are not as the Jewish rites whereof it is not lawful even for a high priest to partake, for Christians do indeed eat a sacrificial feast: they partake of the Eucharist.'[41] The writer to Hebrews is emphasizing the difference between the type and the reality: the Jewish rites are the type, the Eucharist the reality. Westcott agreed with the interpretation and added, 'Our great sin-offering ... is given to us as our food. The Christian therefore who can partake of Christ, offered for his sins, is admitted to a privilege unknown under the old Covenant'.[42]

However, most recent commentators, such as Windisch and Moffatt, preferred to assume that the sacred writer is warning his readers against looking to regulations about food and is urging that our 'altar' is spiritual, not one where we consume foods of any kind but an 'altar' where we cleanse our heart and conscience. The Christian sacrifice is not one which involves any connection with a meal.[43] For such commentators *thusiastērion* is not the Holy Table or any other physical location. Creed preferred this view, for in the whole passage it yields one consecutive line of thought, in his opinion. Men like this see the epistle as mystical, not as sacramental, and cannot find that the Eucharist has anything to do with the passage.

Michel, too, felt that the general thesis of Hebrews was against the eucharistic concept of *thusiastērion*. 'If Heb 13, 10 speaks of an "altar" within the community, this would surely contradict the fundamental view of our epistle.'[44] The 'altar' is then no visible table, for the real things are not visible; the 'altar' is a heavenly offering-place. And so with A. S. Peake: 'the only Christian altar is in the heavenly sanctuary where Christ ministers'.[45] Moffatt went so far as to suppose that our text was definite polemic against a rising tide of sacramentalism, which Creed thought unlikely. The lucid writer would not have expressed himself so obscurely, and there is no evidence for controversy of this kind in the first century.[46]

J. E. L. Oulton, too, felt, as against St. Chrysostom's view, that the writer to Hebrews was on this interpretation saying in verse ten the very reverse of what he affirmed in verse nine – that the heart must be established with grace, not with meats. Oulton however would not accept that the sacred writer was arguing that in Christian worship there is no sacrificial meal.[47]

R. Williamson too takes the view that the writer to Hebrews has no involvement with his readers in eucharistic faith or practice. He bases his view not only on the absence of all explicit mention of the sacrament in the epistle, but on the general argument of the writer that the worshipper has direct access to the throne of grace without cultic or eucharistic mediation. 'In this present life the bliss of glory is still an object of faith and hope, though by faith the throne of grace may be approached even here.'[48] So our 'altar' is not here, it is in the heavens. We are on pilgrimage, and 'there is no word in the epistle to suggest that the conditions of pilgrimage are ever, on earth, suspended, or that man can ever, while a pilgrim, anticipate in the Eucharist the blessings of a future life'.[49] At best, that is an argument from silence, at worst it may be denying the reality of much Christian experience at the Lord's Table.

> How glorious is that Body now, throned on the throne of heaven!
> The angels bow and marvel how to us on earth 'tis given.
> O! to discern what splendours burn within these veils of His!
> That faith would into vision turn and see Him as He is!

The typology of the altar is seen at its height in the last NT book where heaven's golden *thusiastērion* guards the souls of Christian martyrs (Rev 6[9]), and on it are offered the prayers of all the saints (8[3ff.]). The archetypal altar stands inside the heavenly Temple (11[1]) and from within its area[50] fly angels with various messages (14[18] 16[7]).

In patristic Greek the word *thusiastērion* is prominent, although it is not the Holy Table. It means first the Jewish altar (1 Clem 32[2] 41[2]) and then a spiritual altar for personal self-sacrifice in the Flavian amphitheatre (I.Rom 2[2]). Widows are said to be God's 'altar', bringing perfect gifts (P. Philip 4[3]). Supremely the *thusiastērion* is Jesus Christ, the one Altar to Whom we all resort (I. Magn 7[2]). For St. Ignatius, according to Lightfoot, 'it symbolizes the congregation lawfully gathered together under its duly appointed officers'.[51] Christ must not be divided, for there is one Altar and there is one bishop (I. Philad 4[1]). The *thusiastērion* is the place of assembly of the whole Church (I. Eph 5[2]; Trall 7[2]). Here spiritual sacrifices are offered, and Christian prayers take the place of the old sacrifices. The 'altar' is the congregation of believers.[52]

Inserted after Tit 1[9] there is a passage which is found in a thirteenth-century minuscule manuscript (460), counselling Titus 'not to appoint twice-married men *(digamous)* and not to make them deacons ... neither may they go up to the *altar* to minister holy things'. But almost certainly the insertion is not of very early date.

ALTAR (TO BRING TO THE ALTAR)

ἀναφέρω

In Biblical Greek *anapherō* has sacrificial meaning.

Secular Greek. It means to carry up or carry back, for instance from Hades.[53] It is to refer to, to bring to the attention, to make a report,[54] to carry up the country (Herodotus VI 30), to 'spit up' a quantity of blood,[55] to bring back from exile (Thucydides V 16), to 'trace' a family to ancestors,[56] to 'ascribe' a fault,[57] to make compensation,[58] to transfer,[59] to 'register' a death,[60] as well as to notify.[61] Mr. Simpson[62] urged that *anapherō* had a religious application in pagan sources and cited Euripides. When, however, Euripides is supposed to ask, 'Hath the god no power to absolve *when I made sacrifice to him (anapheronti moi)*', the verb has no stated object and it is just as feasible to render, 'When I refer the matter to him.'[63]

Biblical Greek. The word received an additional special meaning, to **bring to the altar** for sacrifice. The LXX used it seventy-nine times to render several Hebrew words, chiefly the Hiphil of *'lh* (from which comes *'ōlāh*, a burnt-offering). In the Pentateuch it fairly often renders the Hiphil of *qṭr* (from which comes *qᵉṭōreth*, incense). In the NT the doctrinal sense is that based on the LXX (Heb 7[27] 9[28] Jas 2[21] 1 Pet 2[24]), even where there is no direct citing and even though in some contexts the LXX has a different word for *qṭr*. Undoubtedly the LXX is the basis of the Christian usage.[64]

If the meaning is, 'bring to the altar', there is a problem. Often the object of the verb in the LXX is *thusias* (sacrifices), denoting the offering of sacrifices first for the high priest's own sins, then for those of the people (Heb 7[27]), and referring also to the offering of metaphorical Christian sacrifices (Heb 13[15]; 1 Pet 2[5]) – spiritual sacrifices and the sacrifice of praise;[65] and once also of the victim Christ (Heb 7[27]). This presents no difficulty, but sometimes the object of the verb is 'sin', and what is the point of offering sins upon the altar? Christ 'bare our sins' in His own body (1 Pet 2[24], recalling Isai 53[4f.] LXX), and Christ was once offered to 'bear the sins' of many (Heb 9[20]). The concept of the Sin-bearer may well arise from the Greek OT but it has nothing to do with bearing sins to an altar. When the Hebrew source has *sbl* (bear a burden) and *nś'* (take away), the contexts are usually expiatory, as in Num 14[33] (children expiating their parents' idolatry), Ezek 36[15] (expiating the reproach of the people), and Isai 53[11f.] (expiating guilt). The NT meaning of *anapherō* may therefore be 'to expiate' – not 'to offer'.

The question arises, was Christ a Sin-*bearer* and if so, in what sense? It is not likely that the 'offering' of sins is acceptable to God whose wrath is provoked by them. The sacrifice which Christ offered was the sacrifice rather of Himself than other men's sins. Still, He is a Sin-bearer in this sense: that although the sins were in no way His who knew no sin, yet He did identify Himself with sin for our sake, so that He was 'made sin' for us and so carried our sins.

Nevertheless, to 'expiate' may be a more appropriate meaning.

11

St. Peter puzzled us by the use of *anapherō* with sin as its object but, if we suppose that expiation is the intended meaning, then St. Peter himself provides enlightenment in the same paragraph: the phrase, 'by whose stripes ye were healed' (2^{24}), takes us back to the Servant songs where One seems to stand, the Bearer (Expiator) of our griefs and sorrows, rejected and chastened, expiating the guilt of us all. St. Paul shares this figure, for he pictures Christ nailing to the Cross 'the handwriting of ordinances that was against us' – that is, bearing to the Cross the record of our sins (Col 2^{14}), expiating them, doing away with them.

Others have urged[66] that St. Peter used *anapherō* in a secular forensic sense, signifying the transfer of the debts of a second person upon a third, so as to free the second from need of payment. The case has merits, but when all is said, the weighty influence of the LXX upon all NT writers must indicate passages like Isai 53 and the Hebrew *nś'* (take away guilt or punishment).

Others again avoid the difficult concept of Christ offering sins to God by supposing that in this context, as in Lev 6^{25} (but nowhere else in the LXX), the word *hamartia* is not so much 'sin' as 'sin offering'.[67] If that is so, the difficulty goes and, as elsewhere in the NT, the object of *anapherō* will be, not the sin of others but the 'sin-offering' of His very self. The verb will not mean 'expiate', but 'bring to the altar'.

AMEN

ἀμήν

The word *amēn* abounds in the NT but had been coined already in the LXX as a transliteration of the Hebrew *'āmēn* (verily). It was the people's unanimous response after David's psalm (1 Chr 16^{36}). It was their response to Nehemiah's decree (Neh 5^{13}) and, accompanied by the lifting of the arms, to Ezra's public blessing of the Lord (Neh 8^6; 1 Esd 9^{46}B).

Even where the LXX uses *genoito* (so be it) instead (Deut 27^{15}), the later versions of Symmachus and Theodotion substitute *Amēn*.

After the prayer of Tobias before retiring, he and his bride say together, 'Amen' (Tob 8^8), and that is the word which ends the book of Tobit, as if to confirm Tobias's act of blessing God (14^{15}). It closes both the third and fourth books of Maccabees: 'Blessed be the Deliverer of Israel for ever. Amen.' 'God to whom be glory for ever. Amen.'

So when the exclamation began to enrich Christian worship there was ample precedent for it, and it becomes a stylized ending to

Christian doxologies (Mt 6[13] 28[20]; Lk 24[53]; Ro 1[25] 9[5] 11[36], etc.). It adorns the gracious speech of Jesus when He would make great emphasis (e.g. Mt 6[2]), so that the Greek Fathers interpreted it as a form of divine oath.[68] 'The Son swears by Himself saying, Amen, Amen, I say unto you.'[69] However, in the synoptic gospels Amen is never doubled in this way.

Jesus is very fond of the introductory Amen, '*Verily* I say unto you. ...' It is rendered 'verily' (AV, RV), 'truly' (Moffatt, RSV), 'in truth' (BFBS), 'solemnly' (Jerusalem Bible). It is indeed used like a particle, confirming a statement which is about to be made. It seems to be an innovation of Jesus Himself.[70] Were the Greek Fathers right in supposing it to be His own substitute for an oath? Dr. Daube thinks that, though it is not possible to show that such a form of speech has any complete parallels in extant Jewish works, nevertheless Jesus need not have created it. It was perhaps current in His time. He gives examples from Jewish literature of an Amen almost corresponding to the 'remarkable' Amen of Jesus. Thus, the Amen before the *Shema* is now connected not with the benedictions that it follows, but with the ensuing *Shema* itself. Perhaps, suggests Daube, this introductory Amen in the sense of 'verily', which is so characteristic of the idiom of Jesus and yet is almost completely suppressed in Jewish literature, was disliked by the rabbis and was confined mainly to eschatological utterances.[71]

It has been argued that the Amen-formula was used in the Church after the resurrection to lend authority to the Lord's teaching concerning situations in Gentile churches, and that the formula, 'Verily I say unto you,' originated with the charismatic prophets in Gentile Christian areas.[72] No doubt it was a formula for introducing a prophetic oracle.[73] The six Amen sayings in St. Luke's gospel were chosen deliberately by the author, according to Dr. O'Neill, 'to draw attention to the key points of Jesus' teaching, as Luke understood it'[74] – to form a body of 'faithful sayings' selected from our Lord's teaching, a guide to believers waiting for His Coming when it seems no longer imminent. It may be 'the beginning of Pastoral Theology'.[75]

Usually St. Luke rejects all foreign words – *hosanna, abba, eloi ..., talitha coum, rabbi, rabbounei* – and renders *amēn* by the Greek word for 'truly'. So, when he did retain the word he had doubtless good reason. St. Luke 'particularly wanted the six Amens to stand out', and an English translation should 'leave them untouched'.[76]

Use of *amēn* in Christian Greek as a name for God should not be overlooked. It arises in the Hebrew OT, where God is 'the God of '*Āmēn*' (Isa 65[16]). The version of Symmachus was later to render the Hebrew '*Āmēn* as *Amēn* in Greek where the LXX had used *alēthinos* (true). The use of *Amēn* for Jesus (Rev 3[14]), the faithful and true *(alēthinos)* Witness, the beginning of the creation of God, is thus a very significant feature of Christian Greek,[77] for it seems to give to Jesus the status of God. Moreover, the frequency of *Amēn* in the gospels raises the question whether it may not be a play on the title of Jesus: 'I, the *Amēn,* say unto you'.

The application of *Amēn* to Christ is the most striking usage of the word in Christian Greek. An unusual view[78] is that 'the Amen' of the Seer is an incorrect transliteration of the Hebrew *'āmôn* (artificer, master-workman, architect).

The word appears in Pr 8[30] where Wisdom states that, when God created the world, she was with Him as *'āmôn.* It appears in Jer 52[15] for the 'master-workmen' who were carried away by Nebuzar-adan. In the midrashic commentary on Gen 1[1] (Bereshith Rabbah), rabbi Hoshaiah in iii AD discusses Pr 8[30] and applies *'āmôn* to the Tōrâ, for the Law was the Architect by whom God created the world. When the Seer, therefore, gives to Jesus the title of Amen he may intend to say *'āmôn* and to designate Jesus as the heavenly Architect (Rev 3[14]), ' the Lord *(archē)* of the creation of God'.

THE ANGEL HIERARCHY

See 'Angel', 'Authorities', 'Dominions', 'Powers', 'Principalities', 'Thrones'.

ANGEL

1. ἄγγελος: ἀρχάγγελος: ἰσάγγελος

Nor angels, nor principalities, nor powers ... nor height nor depth ... shall be able to separate us from the love of God which is in Christ Jesus our Lord. – ROM 8[38]

Aggelos is a secular word which, with a new meaning, has assumed importance in Biblical Greek. The other words, *archaggelos* and *isaggelos,* are new.

Angel. In secular Greek *aggelos* had signified an envoy or messenger.[79] Far back in Homer it was occasionally an envoy of the gods, but not in the later secular language. The revival of Homer's special sense was left to Biblical Greek very much later and to texts which were under Jewish influence, like the magical papyri. The Biblical sense is not due to Homer. It arises from the use of *aggelos* in the LXX to render *mal'ākh,* a messenger of God.

Secular Greek had meanings for *aggelos* which were very different from the Biblical and the Jewish: a talkative person, in Menander (32), and one who gives information, like the birds of augury, in Homer.[80]

Although *aggelos* has sometimes the secular sense of 'messenger' (Mt 11[10]; Lk 7[24]; Jas 2[25]), the prevailing context in the NT in nearly all its one hundred and seventy occurrences requires a heavenly being, one who appears in the form of men but is made of spirit and clothed with 'glory', one who is sent out from His presence by God to declare His will – such a one as appeared to Zacharias, to Joseph, to Mary and others. Ministering beings of this kind visited Jesus in the desert. Angels figure extensively in His parables and at His resurrection – fifty-five times in the gospels. It must seem strange to anyone who thinks of the Bible as a text-book of anthropology to find so much about angels and heaven.

The Church today, seeking to solve her problem of communicating with modern society, is frightened of the charge of other-worldliness. Social concerns of the hour loom large. They were paramount to Marx and his disciples and have inspired much that is popular in our own age since Niebuhr. The modern Church is tempted to see heaven and those who dwell therein as less vital than the affairs here and now in which she is involved. Sometimes the Christian will cease even to mention the supernatural, when he knows that the Scriptures never tire of the subject. How miserable would we be if we could no longer cry, 'Our Father, which art in *heaven!*'

Barth has reminded us how readily the angels are dismissed as superfluous, absurd and comic. If we can no longer accept angels, how can we accept what is told us also about God in the Scriptures? 'Where God is, there the angels of God are. Where there are no angels, there is no God.'[81] It is comforting and good that the world should not be without God and His angels, and that our lower cosmos should not lose its contact with the higher cosmos. The angels wait to be perceived by us and they offer their services. 'The worse for us if we are not aware of it!'

Just as angels ministered to Jesus in His earthly days so, because of the intimate links between the Son of Man and His disciples, they shall always minister to the earthly needs of the disciples.[80] One of the last promises of Jesus was that the Son of Man would send His angels 'and they shall gather together His elect' at the Parousia (Mk 13[27]).

Angels appear too in the first days of the Church in converse with Peter, Philip, Cornelius and Paul. It is incautious to allege that St. Paul never pictured them in a good light.[83] Angels are prominent in Christian discussion in most of the epistles and are

15

mentioned by the Seer of Patmos over seventy times. The 'angels' of the churches (Rev 1[20]) raise interesting questions: were they a variety of church official, bishops perhaps? In the Seer's kind of literature they are more likely to signify supernatural beings – the Church's guardian angels.[84]

The doctrine of angels was developed in Philo and in the apocalyptic books of Judaism during the period of about 165 BC to AD 100, especially in the book of Enoch. Some have seen the growth as due to foreign contacts of the Jews, Babylonian and Persian, during this period, and perhaps also to the theological necessity of keeping God as far away as possible from direct intervention in human affairs. The apocalyptists did not invent the idea, however, for earlier Hebrew literature, though with less elaboration, accepts unquestioningly the existence of other beings of supernatural character besides God. The spectacular growth in angelology among the apocalyptists is a circumstance that no one will deny, and one of the forces that may have been behind the growth was the need to harmonize certain doctrines with the sad realities of history. I refer to the inconsistency that seemed to lie between the idea of God's supremacy and the relentless suppression of His people. It made it easier to reconcile oneself to such a devastating paradox if one took consolation in the belief that His people are not without mighty patrons, the angelic guardians.[85]

The thought was no less acceptable to Christians. Indeed, they sometimes went so far as to accord worship to good angels, certainly at Colosse (Col 2[18]). In his vision in Patmos the Seer twice fell adoringly at the feet of an angel (Rev 19[10] 22[8]). 'We worship angels,' said St. Justin Martyr, rebutting the charge of atheism.[86]

It is observed that in the NT, at least in Mk, Q, Paul (including the Pastorals) and Revelation, a kind of divine triad – Father, Son, and holy angels – is several times mentioned as a group. Moreover, in the passage I cited from Justin Martyr, the apologist has a similar triad: Father, Son, and the army of angels who follow Him and are like Him. Clearly, because of their inherited Jewish ideas, the early Christians pictured God surrounded in heaven by His angels, with Jesus on His right hand. Our Lord confirmed this conception. Though early Christians held to one God they believed in subordinate beings too. Very soon they thought of Father and Son as one, of the Logos in the beginning with God, and the Logos as God, and Jesus and the Father as one (Jn 1[1] 10[30] 17[11,21ff.]), but at first the Holy Ghost did not come into the picture for He was usually conceived as operating only within men. However, the common Christian experience of the Holy Ghost as sent by Jesus set Him in a unique relationship to Jesus and His Father. Very soon the doctrine of the Trinity was perceived and, from that time, the triad which included angels was largely banished from Christian thought.[87]

Archangel. Our second word, *archaggelos*, is a later Jewish development of *aggelos*, not appearing in the LXX. In a work by a Hellenistic Jew about the time of Christ, originally appearing in Greek,[88] now surviving in a Slavonic redaction, 'fiery hosts of great archangels' appear, together with dominions, principalities and powers, dwelling in the seventh heaven (Enoch 20[1]). Seven archangels are mentioned in this book; their names are Uriel, Raphael, Raguel, Michael, Sariel, Gabriel and Remiel (the same as Jeremiel elsewhere).

A Jewish apocalypse of the period mentions 'Jeremiel archangelus', the angel in charge of the souls of the righteous (4 Ezra 4[36]). Archangels, amongst whom is Michael, appear in the NT in an eschatological context (1 Thes 4[16]; Jude 9; Rev 12[7]). An archangel's voice proclaims our Lord's second Coming. Michael is so powerful that he disputes with the Devil and leads the war against him in heaven. Gabriel appears in the nativity story (Lk 1[26]) but is called simply, 'angel'.

In Church Greek the archangels who are named include Michael, Gabriel, Raphael, Uriel and Satan (a fallen archangel); they belong to the third and lowest hierarchy, together with 'Principalities' and 'Angels', only the choir of Angels being said to be beneath them.[89] Their names are taken over from Jewish angelology. Gnostic heretics likewise applied to their *aiōnes*, who were cosmic beings, the term *archaggelos*.[90]

Equal to the Angels. Our third word, *isaggelos*, is an adjective appearing first in Christian Greek. It describes the risen and glorified saints (Lk 20[36]). It continues in Church Greek,[91] where it appears on a Christian grave inscription from Sparta of uncertain date.[92] More important, the concept of being like the angels after death appears among the beliefs of the Dead Sea sectaries. 'They are not only to live like angels and consort with angels, but to become as angels.'[93] The word itself and the thought behind it are both characteristically Jewish. 'The Lord bless thee ... and make thee a crown of glory in the midst of the holy ones' (the angels). 'And thou shalt be as an angel of the Presence ..., sharing the lot of the angels ... for ever and ever.'[94]

2. δόξαι

Reference should be made to the article, 'Glory', where it is shown that 'splendour' is a new meaning of *doxa* within Christian Greek. Moreover, when the plural *doxai* occurs (2 Pet 2[10]; Jude 8) there would seem to be a further new meaning – 'angels', or other supernatural powers. An exception must be the plural of *doxa* in 1 Pet 1[11], where 'splendours' is meant – the splendours which follow the sufferings of Christ.

Evidently there were primitive heretics who blasphemed against angels. St. Clement of Alexandria, according to the Latin version of his commentary on the General epistles, understood *doxai* (plural) as 'angels'. On Jude 8 ('they despise dominion and speak evil of *doxai*'), he explains the first clause ('they despise dominion') as: 'That is, the only Lord, truly our Lord Jesus Christ.' St. Clement explains the second clause: 'That is, angels.'[95]

Of course, with Bigg, I find it difficult to see how the False Teachers can have blasphemed angels of any kind,[96] and concede that *doxai* may more probably have meant persons invested with the highest *doxa*, i.e. the rulers of the Church. But many interpreters have understood *doxai* as 'angels', including Alford ('celestial lordships and dignities ... the holy angels').[97] Besides, there are De Wette, Huther, Ritschl, von Soden, Kühl, Spitta, Hofmann, Brückner and Schott (bad angels). J. B. Mayor found no such difficulty as Dr. Bigg found, explaining that the angels *(doxai)* are blasphemed by the heretics in their teaching that angels had created the world in opposition to the will of the true God – a terrible doctrine and quite untrue, for even the great Michael submitted everything to the true God.[98] After all, immediately following the mention of the *doxai*, we have the introduction of Michael as a good example (Jude 9), as if he were one of the *doxai*.

I think it very probable that *doxai* are 'angels', splinters or rays from the brightness of God, the total *doxa*. Philo provides a helpful picture, for he understands 'Thy *doxa*' to be 'the powers which keep guard around Thee',[99] as if the complete *doxa* of God, His whole brightness (the *Shᵉkhînâ*), were divided into lesser rays and as if these lesser rays are the angels, the *doxai*.

Then we may surely pray that, 'as Thy holy Angels alway do Thee service in Heaven, so ... they may succour and defend us on earth'. (Michaelmas collect.)

> *The angels keep their ancient places,*
> *Turn but a stone and start a wing.*
> *'Tis ye – 'tis your estrangèd faces –*
> *That miss the many-splendoured thing.*

ἀντίχριστος

Antichristos is a new word, probably coined by St. John. In the singular it is the name of a personage who is expected to be in the world at the time of the Lord's Coming (1 Jn 2[18] 4[3]). He will deny that Jesus is the Christ (1 Jn 2[22]). He is the Deceiver (2 Jn 7). *Antichristos* is used also in the plural, as if in these times there were many antichrists (1 Jn 2[18]).

The compound word is formed with the preposition *anti*, which in composition means either 'against' or 'instead of'. Does then Antichrist derive his name from the fact of his being a pseudo-Christ ('instead of') or from his opposition to the true Christ ('against')? Does Antichrist say that he himself is Christ, or does he affirm that there is no Christ?

He is thought to be what St. Paul intends by the Man of Sin, an Imposter who 'as God' sits in the Temple of God, verily a pseudo-Christ (2 Th 2). He 'will do and speak like the Beloved', according to the contemporary Ascension of Isaiah (A 4[6]). He is therefore 'pseudo'. Moreover, according to the Didache, the Lord's Coming will be heralded, for all the uncertainty of the exact time, by the manifestation of Antichrist *disguised as* God's Son (Did 16). Indeed, he is 'pseudo'. On the other hand, St. Paul represents the Man of Sin as the 'opposer' (2 Th 2[4]) – 'against', rather than 'instead of' – and many of the Fathers have understood Antichrist's rôle to be not so much that of an imposter as that of the Enemy of God (Origen, Tertullian, Theophylact). 'Ambrosiaster' saw him in this light: the collapse of the Roman empire was a sign of the approaching end, when Antichrist should appear and be destroyed by divine power (in 2 Th 2[8f.]; in 1 Co 15[52]).

We may well conclude that Antichrist denies the existence of any Christ while the False Christ is a different figure who maintains that he himself is the Christ (Trench pp. 93–103).

Clearly he is not Satan, from whom the Man of Sin is distinguished (2 Th 2[9]), although St. Chrysostom observes that he is inspired by Satan. One would suppose that Antichrist is a bold political figure, 'the Prince of this world', a Beliar who slew his own mother, one who obviously reminded some Christians of Nero.[100] Jews, rather earlier, identified Antichrist with Pompey. The 'sinful man' and 'dragon' who, in his colossal 'hubris' would set his own puny puissance against that of God, defiling the Temple after Pompey's fashion, came to an end very like Pompey's, 'lying pierced on the borders of Egypt', without the decencies of burial (Ps Sol 2[1,30]). Antichrist by other Christians has been identified as the emperor Caligula and the magician Simon Magus. Heresy too has been thought to be the characteristic of Antichrist. St. Cyril of Jerusalem said he would be a magician who controlled the Roman empire and rebuilt the Temple, claiming to be Christ.

He has often been identified as some contemporary – Nero or Napoleon, or Hitler. St. Gregory Nazianzus warned that his own days were Antichrist's tremendous opportunity.[101] But we ought not to confine so significant a figure to the short lifetime of any particular generation. Cullmann and many another careful student have warned us against using the Bible to calculate dates, against seeking to put the ultimate secrecy of the divine plan at man's own disposal. Holy Scripture gives us the direction in which He is moving, and very cautiously we may dare to look on isolated historical incidents as signs of divine stirring. There is no harm in seeing Antichrist in a particular dictator or his self-deified government (Rev 13), for many antichrists shall appear. 'But we shall never venture to say, even in this case, that this is now the Antichrist.'[102]

In our own day we may already identify the increasingly unified world-spirit which exalts man as capable of establishing on earth his desired social order, an alternative saviour, an Antichrist. This force, as Bishop Newbigin sees it, is a secularized and distorted form of the Christian eschatology, a faith of this world, which builds on earth a new order of human society.[103]

Compared with the real Saviour of the world it is both 'pseudo' and 'anti'.

APOLLYON

See 'Destroyer'.

APOSTASY

ἀποστασία: ἀφίστημι

The words *apostasia*, the noun, and *aphistēmi*, the verb, have gained a religious meaning.

Secular Greek. *Apostasia* had been a political revolt or defection – a late form of *apostasia*. In Plutarch, *apostasia* was a revolt from Nero, and in Josephus a revolt from Rome.[104]

Christian Greek. Here *apostasia* is always religious apostasy. The LXX had prepared the way by associating *apostasia* with the Hebrew words meaning rebellion against God and transgression from His ways, such as *ma'al*, the 'transgression' of Ahaz and the 'trespass' of Manasseh, and *meredh* which was Israel's 'defection' from God (Josh 22²²; 3 Km 20 (21)¹³A; 2 Chr 29¹⁹ 33¹⁹A). It represents a word for the backsliding of Israel (*rā'ă*, Jer 2¹⁹) and Hellenizing apostasy from Judaism (1 Mac 2¹⁵). It came to occupy a large part in Jewish eschatology.

St. Paul was charged with raising **apostasy** among the Jews, inducing them to forsake Moses (Act 21²¹). He himself taught that before the Lord's Coming there would be an **apostasy** in conjunction with the manifestation of an evil personage, the Man of Sin (2 Th 2³). What was the nature of the apostasy? Was it a falling away of Jews, or of Christians, from their faith? St. Justin suggests that a 'Man of the apostasy' shall perpetrate 'lawless' deeds on earth against us Christians, which indicates that for him the apostasy is not Christian but probably Jewish (*Dial.* 110²). The use of the verb, however, indicates Christian apostasy.

To apostatize (aphistēmi). In secular Greek in intransitive tenses the meaning was depart, withdraw oneself, revolt from. Often in Herodotus it is to revolt (e.g. III 30, 162), as in Thucydides (VIII 35, 90). Sometimes it is to desist.¹⁰⁵ When Demosthenes offers to withdraw a claim, he says, 'I *stand aside*' (XIX 45). But Christian Greek has added an important metaphorical meaning, to become an apostate, as when disciples are said to have no root so that in time of temptation they fall away (Lk 8¹³). Such activity is a sign of the Last Times and involves departing from the faith (1 Ti 4¹). Already in the LXX it meant to 'fall away' from God.

In Church Greek the verb was sometimes even more specialized – to withdraw from communion with the Church.¹⁰⁶

APOSTASY (A CENTRE OF APOSTASY)

πορνή : πορνεία : πορνεύω

The meaning of *pornē*, *porneia* and *porneuō* in Greek bears upon prostitution and harlotry. *Pornē* is a harlot, *porneia* harlotry, and *porneuō* is to prostitute or practise prostitution. Of Alexander, the false prophet, Lucian uses the verb. 'While he was still a boy, and a very handsome one, he prostituted *(eporneue)* his attractiveness and sold his company to those who sought it.'¹⁰⁷ Bauer (col. 1263) professes that *porneuō* is used figuratively in secular Greek in the sense of practising idolatry and cites an epistle of Phalaris¹⁰⁸ – a citation which is not justified. Phalaris has the perfect participle of the verb to describe Conon's state, but Phalaris is not charging Conon with idolatry. He is using the verb rather in Lucian's sense,[109] to describe the acts of a very disrespectable fellow. 'You take the utmost care to preserve the life of that infamous wretch *(peporneukotos)* Conon; and none for Sameas and Nicarchus, men eminent for their merit and virtue.'[110] Conon is crafty and a villain,[111] but is not said to be idolatrous. The verb is metaphorical in Phalaris only to the extent of moral lewdness and stands in contrast with 'men eminent for their merit and virtue'. The concept of 'idolatry' in this verb appears in Biblical Greek and arises through Hebraic influence.

Pornē, a harlot, is used figuratively in Christian Greek to designate a certain city, whether Rome or, more likely, Jerusalem (Rev 17[1,5,15f.] 19[2]).

Porneia, too, is allusive harlotry and through Hebrew influence, translating in the LXX the stem *zānâ,* has come to mean 'idolatry'. The Hebrew stem for harlotry is used repeatedly in an allusive sense to denote intercourse with foreign deities in the OT. It may be that such idolatry often in fact involved prostitution.

A new sense for the Greek words, which has arisen through their OT references, is illustrated in Rev 2[21] (of the spiritual Jezebel), 14[8] 18[3,9] (of the spiritual Babylon), and 17[2,4] 19[2] (of the woman in purple and scarlet). The texts refer to the universal **apostasy** which precedes the Lamb's victory at the Millennium and first resurrection. The apostasy will centre on the place where Jesus died (Rev 11[8]). It points to Jerusalem rather than Rome. Many commentators assume that Rome is meant and that we are faced with an attitude to the state which is inconsistent with that of any other part of the NT. It is urged that whereas for St. Paul the state is God's *diakonos* (minister), for St. John the state is the Beast and Babylon and Mother of Harlots. Some, like Streeter, hold that 1 Peter was a deliberate correction of the attitude of St. John.[112] I do not believe that the Seer of Patmos stands apart in this respect, nor assume that he refers to the Roman state when he speaks of the Beast and the 'Harlot'.

In Revelation, I think, there is a studied contrast between the Church, which is the Bride in her purity, the Mother of us all, the new Jerusalem (Rev 21), and the *Pornē* in her harlotry which is faithless Sion. The latter will be the *old,* unbelieving Jerusalem, the 'children of the flesh', conversely with the 'children of promise' (Gal 4[25ff.]).

If this emended view of the Seer's intention be correct, there is a uniform attitude towards the state in the NT – and a very mild one.[113]

ἀπόστολος: ἀποστολή

In Christianity the two old words, *apostolos* and *apostolē,* are adopted to indicate a new institution which was without parallel.

Apostle. In secular Greek *apostolos* had many indefinite meanings. It was, quite rarely, a delegate or messenger.[114] By this word Josephus indicated the head of a delegation.[115] In later Greek it denoted a colony and even an export licence.[116] Hesychius in his lexicon defines *apostolos* as an admiral, as a 'general over a fleet'.

The general use of *apostolos* casts no light on its meaning in the NT. In no pagan literature is there an example of a technical usage of the verb which is in any way like the early Christian concept of an apostle. 'Both Hellenism and Hellenistic Judaism', says Walter Schmithals, 'appear to be eliminated as sources of the New Testament apostolate'.[117] Pagan Greeks would have understood the word to mean emissary, and it is not true to say that the Christian word would have been incomprehensible. It would however have been inadequately comprehended. H. Mosbech rightly observed that there is no connection between the term of Herodotus and the apostle of the NT. 'For this reason it is more likely that the Christian term appeared to the Greeks as something quite new.'[118] Among Christians *apostolos* became exclusively an apostle of Christ, one of His charismatic gifts to the Church. Once more a rather general pagan word is adopted to express idiomatic Christian concepts at a hint from the Greek Bible. In the Greek OT *apostolos* has denoted a divine messenger, translating *shālûaḥ* (3 Km 14⁶A), and an ambassador, translating *ṣîr* (Isai 18² Symmachus).

The word 'is not customary in non-Christian Greek'.[119] Doubtless it may already have been used religiously in certain quarters, but Christians endowed it with a sense quite new. 'Thus we have the extremely interesting linguistic fact,' wrote Lake, 'that a Pauline-Lucan branch of Christian literature seems to have popularized and given a technical meaning to a word which was otherwise scarcely used, except in a different sense, in the whole course of previous Greek literature.'[120]

As the term for a Christian leader *apostolos* may be based on the corresponding Jewish office,[121] the *sheliaḥ ṣibbhûr* (plenipotentiary of the congregation), a supposed official of the synagogue who led the worship,[122] but in actual fact in the early days of the synagogue the prayer was not said by any permanent officer; any member might be asked to do this in the name of the congregation by the ruler of the synagogue.

The *shālîaḥ* is mentioned also as an agent for betrothal pur-

23

poses.[123] The difficulty is, that it cannot be proved that *shālîaḥ* in any Jewish source before AD 140, 'in spite of the various far-reaching hypotheses with which Jewish scholars have filled the pages of their respective journals'.[124] Symmachus in the second century AD translated the Hebrew *ṣîr* by *apostolos*, so that the equivalence of *shālîaḥ* and *apostolos* was not stereotyped as yet.[125]

This is true. As we have seen, the word *apostolos* occurs but twice in the Greek OT: 3 Km 14[6]A is probably not the LXX version at all but Aquila's, and *apostolos* in Isai 18[2] is from the version of Symmachus. We must not assume too much from this meagre Biblical precedent. The noun may not be translated by *apostolos*, but *shālaḥ*, the verb, is constantly rendered by *apostellō* in the LXX.

There is a real connection, then, between *apostolos* and *shālîaḥ*. If our Lord conversed in Hebraic or Aramaic (and not, as I think, in Greek) it is reasonable to suppose that He would use *shālûaḥ* or *shālîaḥ* or *shᵉlûḥa*, and in fact He is reported as using 'apostle' or its Semitic equivalent of the Twelve: Mk 3[14]vl; Lk 6[13]. So far so good, but the term *shālîaḥ* (or its Aramaic equivalents) was not always a technical term among the Jews. Sometimes the person so indicated was simply an 'agent', and the connotation varies with the context in which it is found.[126] To Dom Gregory Dix, who had relied on the *shālîaḥ* to support the doctrine of apostolic succession,[127] Bishop Hunkin protested that 'plenipotentiary' was an unfortunate word, implying that our Lord had endued men with immense power on earth. 'The idea that He ever could have has been one of the besetting illusions of the Catholic Church.'[128] As Dom Gregory replied, Bishop Hunkin did at least concede that the Catholic Church has always taught this.[129]

Moreover, against Dom Gregory's plea for a parallel between *shālîaḥ* and apostolic succession, it should be noted that a *shālîaḥ* of a court (according to the Mishnah) lacked power to appoint his successor, and that if he could not perform his own function for any reason a new officer might be appointed only by the *beth dîn*, the court of magistrates, on the principle of *delegatus non potest delegare*.[130] His powers were not handed on by himself.

It is clear that *apostolos* represents something quite new, quite outside the Jewish or pagan sphere.

The earliest Apostles, summoned by Jesus, were twelve in number. The term occurs but once in Matthew (10[2]) where the number twelve is meant to restrict those who are called 'apostles' to the names that appear in the ensuing list.[131] Matthias is subsequently added to take the place of Judas. Then Paul is known as an apostle and apparently he himself includes also Andronicus and Junia, 'of note among the apostles' (an ambiguous phrase, Ro 16[7]).

Barnabas too is *apostolos* (Act 14[14]), and so are Silas and Timothy (1 Thes 2[6]) and the Lord's brother (Gal 1[19]). Moreover, St. Paul distinguishes between the Twelve and 'all the apostles' (1 Co 15[5ff.]). Primarily, the apostles' function was to witness to Christ's resurrection (Act 1[22]), but in the wider sense they were missionaries to the Jews and to the heathen.

The origin of the term may be as Mosbech suggests. The very first Christian missionaries were merely 'occasional workers' in the field and were simply called Gospel-preachers *(euaggelistai)*, but later on at Antioch some of the preachers sought the higher authority and honour of being sent by a local church, preferably Jerusalem, or by God Himself. So a simple evangelist is distinguished from the higher vocational missionary. In seeking a name, the preachers rejected *aggelos* (messenger) as already a technical term for 'angel', and so the special term *apostolos* emerged for a new type of missionary who was signally authorized.[132]

Apostleship. Similarly *apostolē* was in classical Greek a sending away, particularly an expedition,[133] while in the LXX the word denoted 'dismissal' (Eccles 8[8]) and 'gift' (3 Km 9[16]). In Christian Greek, however, it is reserved for the highest kind of ministry, the apostleship.

From this peak Judas fell (Act 1[25]). The high office was bestowed on Paul by the Son of God (Ro 1[5]), the seal of his *apostolē* being in part the believers at Corinth (1 Co 9[2]). St. Peter's *apostolē* was 'of the circumcision' (Gal 2[8]).

ASSURANCE, FULL

πληροφορία: πληροφορέομαι

The noun *plērophoria* is a Christian coinage which appears again in the second century – but with uncertain meaning, isolated in a fragmentary context.[134]

St. Paul writes of 'the *full assurance* of understanding' which is desirable for believers so that they have a thorough knowledge of the mystery of God (Col 2[2]). St. Paul's own preaching of the Gospel was with spiritual power and **full assurance** (1 Thes 1[5]). *Plērophoria* has to do with faith and hope, and tireless following of these virtues to the final point without wavering (Heb 6[11] 10[22]). Where better is **full assurance** realized than in contemplating the resurrection of our Lord (1 Clem 42[3])?

It is almost exclusively in Biblical Greek that the passive verb, *plērophoroumai*, appears and there it concerns the exemplary faith of Abraham who was **fully assured** that what God promised He would perform (Ro 4²¹). The verb denoted the confident faith with which brethren must be prepared to face such weighty questions as the observance of food laws and other mandates from Judaism (Ro 14⁵).

In the LXX the passive verb had meant 'to be fully bent on doing' (Eccles 8¹¹), as also in T. Gad 2⁴ ('assured we ought to kill'). In the NT the passive may mean to be fulfilled, a prophecy (Lk 1¹): 'those things which are most surely *fulfilled* among us'. More likely, I think, the idea conveyed by the verb is that of full assurance: 'those things which are most surely believed among us'.¹³⁵ And so in 2 Ti 4¹⁷ the Christian meaning is, 'The Lord strengthened me that the preaching might *be most surely believed*' – rather than the alternatives, 'fully proclaimed' (RV) or 'fulfilled' (De Wette), or the Vulgate's 'fulfilled' *(impleatur)*, Beza's 'made more certain' *(certioraretur)*, and AV's 'fully known'.

In the Fathers the active verb *plērophorō* is to fill up what is lacking: 'The poor ... *complement* their wealth by interceding for the rich' (Hermas *Sim*. II 8). It is to fulfil: 'The Lord will not desert you but will *fulfill* the petition of your soul' (*Mand*. IX 2). For St. Ignatius it means to *convince* the disobedient that there is one God (I Magn 8²).

ATONEMENT (AV. PROPITIATION)

ἱλασμός

Hilasmos is a controversial word. If we were to give much weight to secular influence in Christian vocabulary, we would say that it means, 'a way of propitiating the deity'. A glance at the LXX presents us with second thoughts.

Secular Greek. *Hilasmos* denoted both a means of appeasing the wrath of the gods and also the rites advocated by augurs to be carried out for hallowing a city.¹³⁶ Philo wrote of Israel's affliction in the wilderness. 'This affliction,' he says, 'is propitious *(hilasmos)*'.¹³⁷

Biblical Greek. In the LXX *hilasmos* seems, both from the contexts and from the Hebrew exemplars, to have two distinct senses – a 'means of appeasing' the wrath of God (i.e. a propitiation) by either prayer or sacrifice, and secondly the 'forgiveness' of the sin which has been committed against God. The two meanings, though interrelated, should not be confused. First then, *hilasmos* is a 'sacrifice for sin', an offering made in appeasement to bring about a happier situation (*ḥaṭṭâth*, Ezek 44²⁷), such as was

26

made by the high-priest Onias on behalf of Heliodorus (2 Mac 3³³), and meaning 'atonement' *(kippūrîm)* in the phrase, day of Atonement (Num 5⁸; Lev 25⁹). The second sense, though it arises from the idea of appeasement, is quite distinct in itself. It arises because *hilasmos* sometimes renders the Hebrew *sᵉlîḥa*. 'There is *forgiveness* with Thee' (Ps 129(130)⁴) and, 'To the Lord our God belong ... *forgivenesses'* (Dan Th 9⁹).

It is probable that the two concepts, sacrifice and forgiveness, are combined in the word *hilasmos* in the NT, so that it does at times include the thought of 'propitiation'. There has been some debate on its meaning at 1 Jn 2² 4¹⁰, where Jesus is said to be the *hilasmos* for our sins, sent on purpose from the Father.[138] The emphasis is rather on forgiveness than sacrifice, for the Father Himself 'sent His Son' and the Father takes the initiative in averting His own wrath. However that may be, yet the mention of 'sins' is there too.

Throughout Church history the death of Christ has usually been seen as a propitiatory sacrifice for sin offered to the Father. The concept is always softened, none the less, by realizing that God's own loving initiative provided the sacrifice by which His own wrath is appeased. Thereafter, in Christian Greek, *hilasmos* will be a means of propitiation, as in secular language, with the added concept of forgiveness and atonement and reconciliation with God, at His own initiative.

An interesting note[139] draws attention to the word *paraklētos* accompanying *hilasmos* (1 Jn 2¹ᶠ·): we have an 'Advocate' with the Father and He is the *hilasmos* for our sins. If the word *paraklētos* necessarily conveys the idea of advocasy, a brief on our behalf to appease or pacify the Father, then *hilasmos* here 'is likely to have propitiatory overtones'. There is every probability, however, that in Christian Greek *paraklētos* means Comforter (see 'Comforter'), one who may not necessarily involve Himself in any appeasing rôle. Is there any reason then why *hilasmos* (1 Jn 2²) 'should not bear the same expiatory, non-propitiatory meaning' as *hilasmos* in 4¹⁰, where God is said to have sent His Son to be the *hilasmos*?

Dr. C. H. Dodd has shown (see 'Be merciful') that this verb has a meaning which is quite foreign to secular Greek.[140] 'To be gracious', 'to have mercy', 'to forgive', is entirely new, is unknown outside Biblical Greek and is without pagan parallel.[141]

ἐξουσίαι

Often in the Greek of the Bible *exousiai* (plural) are rulers in the spiritual realm, both good and bad angels.

Secular Greek. The plural *exousiai* as well as the singular *exousia* might refer to civil authorities like magistrates, 'men in power'[142] – and so sometimes in the LXX, NT and the Fathers.[143] Plato has *exousia* for the 'liberty' of a man to do as he likes.[144] As *exousia poētikē*, it may be 'poetic licence' (LS). Aristotle uses the phrase, *en exousiais*, 'in high position'.[145] A writer, just before the Christian era began, has *exousia* for a 'period of office' and for a magistrate.[146]

Does exousia (Mk 1[22-7]) mean a 'licence' conferred on teachers of Jewish Law, and did Jesus astonish the public because He taught as one who had this special licence? The suggestion is nothing but guesswork, although it is received by LS (1968 Supplement). The misconception arises with those who suppose that the basis for *exousia* in this context lies either in the Hebrew *rāshûth* or in the Aramaic *rᵉshûthâ* (a licence to lay down binding decisions and doctrines).[147] In countering the misconception, it has been protested that in none of the fifty occurrences in the LXX does *exousia* once translate *rāshûth*.[148] In St. Mark's language *exousia* must refer to the highest possible power (1[22]).

Jewish Greek. The plural, however, acquires new meaning. *Exousiai* become 'rulers in the spiritual realm' – a Jewish conception.[149] In a Jewish description of the seven heavens God is said to dwell in the highest, the seventh, and the ministering archangels in the sixth. In the fifth are the angels who convey prayers to the angels of the Presence, and in the fourth are 'thrones' and *exousiai* ever offering praise (*T. Levi* 3). Another Jewish work conjoins the exousiai with Principalities and Powers (q.v.) who fly over the approach to heaven and carry out heaven's will, while demons have no admittance there (T. Sol 20[15]).

Christian Greek. For the Christians *exousiai* are still rulers in the spiritual realm, 'authorities' (AV) who dwell in heaven along with 'principalities' (Eph 3[10]). Believers have to wrestle with these spiritual entities (Eph 6[12]). *Exousiai*, as well as Thrones, Dominions and Principalities (q.v.), are all part of God's creation (Col 1[16]). Believers must obey and be subject to Principalities and *exousiai*.[150] Does St. Paul mean to counsel obedience to angels or does he have the secular meaning in mind – the ordinary magistrates? If angels are meant it may be difficult to reconcile inconsistent standpoints.

On the one hand, St. Paul counsels the Ephesians to wrestle with angels and, on the other, bids Titus obey them! The truth may be that some angels are evil and some good. The benefits of the Cross are said to extend to them (Col 1[20]) – as though some of them needed forgiveness of sin. They are placed closely with demons in the Christian phrase, 'Powers, authorities, lordships and demons.'[151]

It is better to understand *exousiai* as archangels than as 'magistrates' in Tit 3[1] because the context links them with Principalities. On the other hand, in Ro 13[1] the context is equally insistent that the *exousiai* are the civil magistrates. 'Rulers are a terror to evil-doers.' Some have therefore put forward the suggestion that the *exousiai* are not civil magistrates, even in Ro 13[1], but as elsewhere angelic powers – the powers that are the wicked cosmic forces lying behind the powers of this world. The suggestion is that *exousiai* has a double significance: both angels, and also the earthly powers which they inspire (Cullmann). However, a new Biblical meaning does not necessarily hold in every context, and sometimes the secular meaning should be retained. I cannot see that in Ro 13[1] a double meaning is required by the context.

Evil angels is certainly the new meaning of the word elsewhere. In the post-Christian book, the Ethiopic Ascension of Isaiah, the evil hierarchy is said to belong to the Prince of this world, probably Beliar, the Antichrist, the 'king of this world' who will descend in the form of a man to persecute 'the plant which the twelve Apostles of the Beloved have planted', and who is reminiscent of the Man of Sin (Asc. Isai 1[3] 4[2f.]). Sooner or later the whole hierarchy is to do homage to One who is 'so much better', to One who is temporarily made a little lower, but subsequently shall be set over all the works of God (Heb 1[4] 2[5–9]). St. Peter affirms that angels, *exousiai* and Powers were all made subject to Christ, who is gone into heaven (1 Pet 3[22]).

In another Ethiopic text, the book of Enoch – in the part known as the Similitudes – we find a list of angelic dominations corresponding with those in the NT: Cherubim, Seraphim, Ophanim, and all the angels of Power, all the angels of Principalities (LXI 10f.). St. Paul's lists are similar: Angels, Principalities, Powers (Ro 8[38]), and Principality, Power, Might, Dominion (Eph 1[21]). In a Slavonic redaction, the Secrets of Enoch, written originally by a Hellenistic Jew in Egypt about the beginning of the Christian era, the seventh heaven is given as the abode of the following: Archangels, Dominions, Principalities, Powers, Cherubim, Seraphim and Thrones (XX 1). Again we recall St. Paul's list: Thrones, Dominions, Principalities, Powers (Col 1[16]). The Jewish lists of 1 and 2 Enoch may not antedate those of the NT, but they do indicate that the angelology of St. Peter and St. Paul had parallels in Judaism, besides a popular response in subsequent Christian devotion.

> Oh, the depth of joy divine
> Thrilling through those Orders nine,
> When the lost are found again,
> When the banished come to reign.

The Church assumed this heritage and in her prayers cherished the hope that by virtuous living we might all rise to a likeness with those who are so far above us – Thrones *(thronoi)*, Dominions *(kuriotētes)*, Authorities *(exousiai)*, and Principalities *(archai)*.[152]

Where St. Paul is concerned, is each one of these terms a different expression for much the same thing?[153] Is a Dominion or a Principality or a Throne but another name for an Authority? We may find it difficult to distinguish the shades of meaning among the terms and be driven to suppose that the names were indiscriminately assigned to designate cosmic powers in general.[154] In addition to Angels, Archangels, Authorities, Dominions, Powers, Principalities, Thrones, it is suggested that there were further terms to represent cosmic powers in St. Paul's vocabulary: 'gods many', 'lords many', 'every name', 'things in heaven' *(epourania)*, *'things in earth' (epigeia)*, 'things under the earth' *(katechthonia)*, 'world-rulers of this darkness', 'astral deities' *(stoicheia)*, 'the god of this world' and 'the prince of the power of the air'.[155] Perhaps the devils whom Jesus cast out are the same as St. Paul's cosmic powers. Perhaps, on the other hand, the Gospel devils are such as inflict individual mortals rather than the impersonal and cosmic forces of St. Paul's understanding.

St. Paul does indeed place his cosmic forces in the context of personal renunciation and the personal sanctifying of the believer; for Christ is said to have spoiled them and triumphed over them (Col 2[15]), and the cosmic forces are seeking unsuccessfully to divide the believer from God's love (Ro 8[35ff.]). In what sense does the Apostle suppose that evil angels and powers hinder the believer's sanctification? We can only guess. Man appears to the Apostle to live under the sway of divinely appointed authorities – the power of the state, the power of legal religion, the powers of nature – which through sin have become demonic agencies. To expect that evil will be defeated by any of these powers is therefore to ask that Satan cast out Satan. The powers may be robbed of their influence and brought into proper subjection to God, only in the Cross. 'The final victory, then', says Dr. Caird, 'is the Parousia of him who once was crucified'.[156]

We may always resort to demythologizing the demonic element from our faith, if we do not like it, and suppose these powers to be no more than what is very well known to us – anxiety, care, death, secularization, 'distortion in the structure of existence', and other frustrating everyday things. Some would add public opinion, the modern state, technics, and capitalism.[157] By some it is felt, regarding these familiar nightmares, that 'as long as they separate us from the love of God in Christ Jesus our Lord, they are the cosmic powers'.[158] In our situation we clamour to bring St. Paul up to date and forget that, if the Apostle meant that these powers were nothing more objective than our fears and frustrations, he might have said so.

In the West perhaps we have a more insistent urge to demythologize than people in other areas of the globe where St. Paul's spirit-world is well understood. In the Philippines, for instance, it is felt that in teaching and preaching it is permissible to see the *archai* and *exousiai* of St. Paul as those spirits which are believed to exist in the islands.[159] An important issue in contemporary Biblical theology is that of the scope of redemption – is it cosmic, extending to all creation, or is it personal, centred on man, his sin and redemption? Do we take too small a view? Are not our own human sufferings, as joint-heirs with Christ looking for glory, only part of the earnest longing of the vast creation, of its hunger for restoration from cosmic corruption and decay (Ro 8[19ff.])? We may well reason that if there were problems in the Lycus valley long ago concerning the 'elements' and the cosmic powers, it is not likely that the author of Colossians would ignore all this when it came to discussing Christ's work, not likely that he would leave the creation out of all reckoning when he discussed man's redemption in Christ.[160]

This is not to establish that St. Paul was very precise in his detailed distinction between cosmic angelic powers of one kind or another. He does class the terms together without much differentiation and it is interesting to find that in Christian Gnosticism the *exousiai* are closely associated with the *archai*.[161] Basilides and Valentinian, famous Gnostics, refer to them as cosmic powers,[162] but among churchmen they become personalized as mighty watchers round the Throne of God, our majestic and beneficent guardians on earth.

> These keep their guard amidst Salem's dear bowers,
> Thrones, Principalities, Virtues and Powers,
> Where, with the Living Ones, mystical four,
> Cherubim, Seraphim, bow and adore.

St. Paul on three occasions has the terms in the singular with the same sense: principality, authority, power (1 Co 15[24]), principality, authority (Col 2[10]), principality, authority, power, dominion (Eph 1[21]). The singular may denote the various angelic orders, considered in an abstract way – 'authorityship', 'principalityship', etc.

What, however, of the singular in 1 Co 11[10]: 'the woman ought to have *exousia* upon her head because of the angels'? The difficult singular will probably be an instance of the secular use of *exousia*, unconnected with angelic hierarchy. If it is secular usage, then the woman has a veil upon her head to symbolize the man's 'authority' over her, and the whole context concerns the idea that the woman is created for the man. It may be worth noticing[163] that the same Hebrew word *ṣammâ* (a woman's veil) which the LXX of Isai 47[2] renders by *katakalumma* (veil) is rendered by a word which means 'silence' *(siōpēsis)* in Cant 4[1,3] 6[6(7)]. The keeping of silence in the Church is also a sign of the 'authority' under which the woman is placed, represented by the wearing of the veil. Westcott and Hort regarded the variant reading of 'veil' instead of *exousia* (1 Co 11[10]) as an interesting and notable variant, and 'veil' has good support. It is 'doubtless only a conjectural gloss',[164] but it may also give the obvious meaning of *exousia* on which it is a gloss, that is, the veil which involves silence.

An altogether different suggestion is that the woman's veil is described as *exousia* (power) because the Christian woman, contrary to Jewish custom, may now take part in prayer and prophecy. A new *exousia* has been given to her, although the differences of creation remain, as reflected in the different dress.[165] It is the secular meaning of *exousia*.

See also 'Angel', 'Principalities', 'Powers', 'Dominions', 'Thrones'.

NOTES

[1] J. Jeremias, *The Central Message of the New Testament*, ET SCM 1965, first lecture.
[2] W. H. Rossell, *Journal of Biblical Literature* 71 (1952), p. 234.
[3] Dan 12[11]; Mt 24[15]; Mk 13[14].
[4] *Hesychii Alexandrini Lexicon*, K. Latte, Hauniae 1953, I, p. 319.
[5] *De Specialibus Legibus*, I, 323.
[6] *Protrepticus*, ed. H. Pistelli (Teubner 21.19; page 117.27).
[7] Hermas *Sim*. V i 3, 5; V ii 7; V iii 8.
[8] *Kleine Texte* (ed. H. Lietzmann) 8[3], Logia Jesu 1[6].
[9] M. W. Schoenberg, *Thomist* (Washington) 28 (1964), pp. 51–75.
[10] Cremer, p. 563, also MW s.v.
[11] L. H. Marshall, *The Challenge of NT Ethics*, Macmillan 1946, p. 258.
[12] In *Journal of Biblical Literature* 71 (1952), pp. 233f.
[13] C. E. B. Cranfield, *Romans*, ICC T. & T. Clark 1975, p. 398, n. 1.

[14] In the psalm it is uncertain whether the alleluia is a title or the conclusion of a previous psalm. See H. B. Swete, *Introd. to the OT Greek*, CUP 1900, pp. 250ff. Alleluia may be a conclusion, for each of the Odes of Solomon ends with it.

[15] F. G. Kenyon, *Greek Papyri in British Museum*, London 1893, p. 93, line 271.

[16] *Martyrdom of Matthew* 25 (M. R. James, *Apocryphal NT*, Clarendon 1924, p. 461.

[17] *Apocylypse of Paul* 29, 30 (M. R. James, pp. 540f.).

[18] Migne *Patrologia Latina* XXXVII 1419.

[19] Preisandanz, vol. I, Teubner 1973, p. 80 (IV 272).

[20] Ibid., vol. I, p. 106 (IV 969).

[21] Ibid., vol. II 1974, p. 30 (VII 669).

[22] F. Preisigke, *Sammelbuch griechische Urkunden aus Aegypten*, vol. I Strassburg 1915, 4127.19.

[23] L. Mitteis, *Griechische Urkunden der Papyrussammlung zu Leipzig*, vol. I, Teubner 1906, p. 128 (40 II 13) iv–v AD, and p. 302 (103,12) Arabic period.

[24] T. Abr A 85^{12} $96^{2, 10}$ (James), T. Sol III 5,7, VI 8, III 3D, IV TD (McCown).

[25] CIG, vol. II, p. 423 (2569, line 12).

[26] F. W. Farrer, *The Life of Christ in Art*, Black 1894, p. 468.

[27] 1 Clem inscr. 2^3 32^4 60^4 62^2; cf. Hermas *Sim.* V 7.4.

[28] C. H. Dodd, *The Bible and the Greeks*, Hodder 1935, p. 19.

[29] Callimachus, *Hymnus in Delum* (Loeb 152) iii BC.

[30] Also in the apostolic Fathers: 2 Clem 16^4; Did 1^6 15^4.

[31] V 17 (giving alms to a bad man) iii AD.

[32] N. Turner, *Grammatical Insights*, T. & T. Clark 1965, p. 57.

[33] Mt $5^{23f.}$ $23^{18f., 35}$; Lk 1^{11} 11^{51}; Ro 11^3; 1 Co 9^{13} 10^{18}; Heb 7^{13}; Jas 2^{21}.

[34] 'Deckwort für Gott ist,' says F. Hauck in Kittel *TWNT* III, p. 805.

[35] Not even in *De Specialibus Legibus* I 221, a passage sometimes cited.

[36] *Journal of Biblical Literature* 67 (1948), pp. 122f.

[37] So J. B. Lightfoot, *Ap. Fathers* Pt. II, vol. II, p. 123. So also Bengel, Alford, W. F. Moulton, Bleek, De Wette, Delitzsch. H. W. Montefiore also understands the altar as Calvary – 'not some heavenly altar': *A Commentary on the Ep. to the Hebrews*, London 1964, p. 244.

[38] T. Haering, *Der Brief an die Hebräer*, Stuttgart 1925, p. 103. According to F. D. V. Narborough, the verse (Heb 13^{10}) 'must imply, in the eyes of unprejudiced criticism, some reference to the Holy Communion' (*Hebrews* Clarendon Bible 1930, p. 150). In earlier days, also J. H. A. Ebrard.

[38] *De Oratione* xix.

[40] *Adversus Haereses* xxxi 5.

[41] Homily on the Ep. to the Hebrews, xxxiii 304A.

[42] B. F. Westcott, *The Ep. to the Hebrews*, Macmillan 1889, p. 439.

[43] E.g. J. Moffatt, *Hebrews* ICC, T. & T. Clark 1924, p. 235.

[44] O. Michel, *Der Brief an die Hebräer*, Göttingen 1949, p. 342.

[45] *Hebrews* Century Bible, n.d., p. 241.

[46] J. M. Creed, *Expository Times* 50 (1938), pp. 13–15, and added note, 380ff.

[47] *Expository Times* 55 (1944), p. 304.

[48] *New Testament Studies* 21 (1975), p. 310. See also pp. 300–12.

[49] Ibid., p. 312.

[50] The *thusiastērion* is understood as the enclosure (place of sacrifice) within which the *bōmos* (altar proper) stands.

[51] J. B. Lightfoot, *Apostolic Fathers*, 2nd ed. Macmillan 1889, Part II, vol. II, p. 169.

[52] Clement of Alexandria *Stromateis* vii 6.31, 32, Origen *Contra Celsum* viii 17.

[53] Homer *Odyssey* XI 625. So also sometimes in Biblical Greek: T. Abr A 93^{15} 94^{10} 112^{19}; Mt 17^1; Mk 9^2; Lk 24^{51}.

[54] Herodotus III 80 and in Christian Greek, e.g. Justin *Dial.* 71^3.

[55] Plato *Cleomenes* 5.

[56] Plato *Alcibiades* I 120E.

[57] Euripides *Orestes* 76, *Bacchae* 29, etc.

[58] *Sammlung der griechischen Dialekt. Inschriften,* ed. H. Collitz, Göttingen 1884ff., 3537 (Cnidus), but the exact meaning of *anapherō* in the execration tablets of Cnidus is uncertain K. Weiss in Kittel *TWNT* IX, p. 62, n. 1). A. Audollent, *Defixionum Tabellae,* Paris 1904, 2,11; 3A 10f., etc.

[59] P. Lille I 7.17 (iii BC).

[60] P. Lond 281.1.5 (AD 66).

[61] P. Ryl 163.13 (AD 139).

[62] E. K. Simpson, *Words Worth Weighing,* Tyndale 1946, p. 10.

[63] Euripides *Orestes* 597.

[64] K. Weiss in Kittel *TWNT* IX, p. 63.

[65] In the Fathers, offering of prayer: 2 Clem 2^2; Barn 12^7.

[66] Deissmann BS pp. 88f., basing his case on P. Petr I 16 (2) 10 (237 BC).

[67] C. Bigg, *St. Peter and St. Jude* ICC, T. & T. Clark, 2nd ed. 1902, p. 147.

[68] Gregory of Nyssa, *Gregorii Nysseni Opera Ascetica,* W. Jaeger, etc., Leiden 1952, p. 88 (PG XXXIV 442A).

[69] Chrysostom, Homily 11,1 in Heb (de Montfaucon 12. 112B).

[70] H. L. Strack, P. Billerbeck, *Kommentar zum Neuen Testament aus Talmud und Midrasch,* Munich 1928, I 243f.

[71] David Daube, *Journal of Theological Studies* 45 (1944), pp. 27–31.

[72] V. Hasler, *Amen: Redaktions geschichtliche Untersuchung zur Einführungsformel der Herrenworte 'Wahrlich ich sage euch',* Zürich 1969, p. 171.

[73] E. E. Ellis, *The Gospel of Luke,* New Century Bible 1966, p. 98.

[74] In *Journal of Theological Studies* NS 10 (1959), p. 1.

[75] Ibid., p. 9.

[76] Ibid., p. 1.

[77] G.-M. Behler, *Vie Spirituelle* (Paris) 112 (1965), pp. 545–62.

[78] L. H. Silberman, *Journal of Biblical Literature* 82 (1963), pp. 213ff. See also W. D. Davies, *Paul and Rabbinical Judaism,* SPCK 1965, p. 172 quoting Burney.

[79] Homer *Iliad* II 26; Herodotus V 92B.

[80] *Iliad* XXIV 292, 296.

[81] Karl Barth, *Church Dogmatics* III 3, ET, T. & T. Clark 1961, p. 238.

[81] P. T. Coke, *Estudios Bíblicos* (Madrid) 32 (1973), pp. 283–9.

[83] D. E. H. Whiteley draws attention to Richardson's haste. *Theology of St. Paul,* Blackwell 1964, p. 27.

[84] R. H. Charles, *Revelation,* ICC T. & T. Clark 1920, vol. i, p. 34. See also G. M. Gwatkin in HDB vol. i, col. 97, and W. M. Ramsay, *The Letters to the Seven Churches of Asia,* London 1904, pp. 69–72.

[85] H. B. Kuhn, *Journal of Biblical Literature* 67 (1948), p. 230.

[86] *Apol.* I 6^2. See later, Clement of Alexandria *Stromateis* VI 5.39 and Origen *Contra Celsum* V 6.

[87] The argument is fully developed by G. B. Bernardin in *Journal of Biblical Literature* 57 (1938), pp. 273–9.

[88] A Greek version of some chapters of the book of Enoch was discovered in Egypt at the close of the nineteenth century. Of the extant fragment of this version, one verse has the word *archaggelōn* in the context, 'names of the seven *archangels*' (20^8), ed. L. Radermacher, 1901.

[89] Dionysius the Areopagite (v AD), *De Coelesti Hierarchia* VI 2 (PG III 201A).

[90] Clement of Alexandria, *Excerpta Theodoti* 38 (PG IX 677B).

[91] Clement PG VIII 293B, IX 328A; Origen *contra Celsum* iv (PG XI 1069B); Iamblichus (c. AD 300) and Hierocles (c. AD 450). See Kittel *TWNT* I, p. 86. Bauer col. 690.

92 *Epigrammata Graeca ex lapidibus conlecta*, ed. G. Kaibel, Berlin 1878, 542.6f. (p. 216).

93 Matthew Black, *The Scrolls and Christian Origins*, Nelson 1961, p. 139.

94 Cave 1 *Benedictions (1 QS b), col. III 25f., IV 25f.*

95 *Adumbrationes in Epistolam Judae* in loc.

96 C. C. Bigg, *St. Peter and St. Jude*, ICC T. & T. Clark 2nd ed. 1902, p. 279.

97 H. Alford, *The Greek Testament*, vol. IV, part II, Rivingtons 4th ed. 1871, in loc. Jude 8 (p. 534).

98 J. B. Mayor, *The Epistle of St. Jude and the Second Epistle of St. Peter*, Macmillan 1907, p. 35.

99 *De Specialibus Legibus* I 45.

100 Asc Isai 4²; Sib Orac 2¹⁶⁷ 3⁶³ 5²²²,³⁶¹.

101 *Orationes* XXII 7 (PG XXXV 1140B).

102 O. Cullmann *Salvation in History*, ET SCM 1967, p. 310.

103 L. Newbigin, *The International Review of Missions* 48 (1959). See the whole paper, 'The Summons to Christian Mission Today'.

104 Plutarch *Galba* 1; Josephus *Vita* 10.

105 Plato *Laws* 960E.

106 Hermas *Sim* VIII 8.2; Irenaeus *Haereses* I 13.7.

107 Lucian *Alexander* 5.

108 R. Hercher, *Epistolographi Graeci*, Paris 1873, ep. CXXI, p. 444 (vi BC).

109 So Hauck and Schutz in *TWNT* VI, p. 581, citing Lucian as parallel.

110 *The Epistles of Phalaris*, Th. Francklin, M.A., London 1749, pp. 122f.

111 *The Epistles of Phalaris the Tyrant*, tr. by W. D., London 1634, p. 183.

112 B. H. Streeter, *The Primitive Church*, Macmillan 1930, p. 133.

113 The argument in full, see *Journal of Theol. for Southern Africa* 2 (1973), pp. 41–52.

114 Herodotus I 21, V 38.

115 *Ant. Jud.* XVII xi 1.

116 Dionysius of Halicarnassus IX 59; see *Der Gnomon des Idios Logos*, ed. W. Schubart 1919, 162 (ii AD).

117 W. Schmithals, *The Office of Apostle in the Early Church*, ET SPCK 1971, p. 97.

118 *Studia Theologica* (Lund) 2 (1948), p. 167.

119 K. Lake in *Beginnings* I 5, p. 46.

120 Ibid., p. 47.

121 K. H. Rengstorf (*TWNT* I pp. 414–20) traced the origin of *apostolos* to *shālîaḥ*. He saw the formal coincidences as too close not to admit that this was the probable technical background of the word 'apostle'.

122 Tractate *Berachoth* V 5, *Rosh hashana* IV 9.

123 *Kiddushim* II 1.

124 A. Ehrhardt, *The Apostolic Succession*, Lutterworth 1953, p. 17.

125 Op. cit., p. 17, n. 1.

126 J. W. Hunkin, *Theology* 51 (1943), p. 168.

127 *The Apostolic Succession*, ed. K. E. Kirk, Hodder 1946, pp. 228–32.

128 Hunkin, op. cit., p. 169.

129 *Theology* op. cit., p. 256.

130 T. W. Manson, *The Church's Ministry*, Hodder 1948, pp. 36f.

131 G. Frizzi, *Revista Bíblica* (Buenos Aires) 22 (1974), pp. 3-37.

132 H. Mosbech, *Studia Theologica* (Lund) 2 (1948), pp. 187ff.

133 Euripides *Iphigenia in Aulis* 688; Thucydides VIII 9.

134 O. Eger, etc., *Griechische Papyri zu Giessen*, Leipzig 1910ff., 87.25 (time of Trajan or Hadrian). But see also *Rhetores Graeci*, C. Walz, Stuttgart 1832–6, VII 108.3.

35

[135] As understood by Origen, the AV and by K. H. Rengstorf, *Das Neue Testament Deutsch*, ed. P. Althaus and J. Behm, 1937, ad loc. Per contra RSV has 'accomplished' (following Creed's 'fulfilled', *The Gospel according to St. Luke*, Macmillan 1930, p. 3).

[136] Plutarch *Solon* 12.5, *Fabius Maximus* 18.3, *Camillus* 7; Orphica *Argonautica* 39.554.

[137] *Legum Allegoria* III lxi (III 174).

[138] C. H. Dodd, *The Bible and the Greeks*, Hodder 1935, pp. 94f. (a divinely supplied 'sin-offering', not 'propitiation'); Leon Morris, *The Apostolic Preaching of the Cross*, Tyndale 1955, pp. 178f. ('propitiation'); David Hill, *Greek Words and Hebrew Meanings*, CUP 1967, pp. 36ff. ('propitiation').

[139] T. C. G. Thornton, *Expository Times*, 80 (1968), pp. 53–5.

[140] C. H. Dodd, *The Bible & the Greeks*, Hodder 1935, p. 93.

[141] Ibid., p. 89.

[142] Plutarch *Philopoemen* 17.

[143] Est 8^{13}; Jer $28(51)^{28}$A; Dan LXX $3^{2f.}$ 7^{27}; Lk 12^{11}; Ro 13^1; M Pol 10^2.

[144] *Alcibiades* 1.135A.

[145] *Nicomachean Ethics* 1095 b 21.

[146] Dionysius of Halicarnassus VII 1.1; XI 32.1.

[147] Viz. D. Daube, *The New Testament & Rabbinic Judaism*, Athlone 1956, pp. 205ff.

[148] A. W. Argyle, *Expository Times*, 80 (1969), p. 343.

[149] T. Levi 3^8; T. Sol 20^{15}; Origen PG I 472D.

[150] Tit 3^1. There is no MS authority for the addition in AV: 'to obey magistrates' (the secular meaning of *exousiai*).

[151] Acts of John 98 (James, *Apocr. NT.*, Clarendon 1927, p. 255, E. Hennecke, *NT Apocr.* ET Lutterworth 1965, II p. 233).

[152] Origen *contra Celsum* IV 29 (PG I 1069C).

[153] As W. Foerster in Kittel *TWNT* II pp. 569f.

[154] As J. Y. Lee of Ohio, in *Novum Testamentum* 12 (1970), p. 55.

[155] 1 Co 8^5; Eph 1^{21}; Ph 2^{10}; Eph 6^{12}; Gal $4^{3,9}$; Col $2^{8,20}$; 2 Co 4^4; Eph 2^2.

[157] G. B. Caird, *Principalities and Powers. A Study in Pauline Theology*, Clarendon 1956, p. 101.

[157] H. Berkhof in *Biblical Authority for Today*, ed. A. Richardson and W. Schweitzer, SCM 1951, p. 255.

[158] J. Y. Lee in *Novum Testamentum* 12 (1970), p. 69.

[159] D. Schneider, *South East Asia Journal of Theology* (Singapore) 15 (1974), pp. 91–101.

[160] J. G. Gibbs in *Biblica* 56 (1975), p. 23.

[161] Irenaeus *Adversus Haereses* I 23.2f.

[162] Ibid., I 24.6; Epiphanius *Adversus LXXX haereses* XXXI 5.2.

[163] As by E. H. Blakeney, *Expository Times* 55 (1944), p. 138.

[164] Westcott & Hort, *The New Testament in the Original Greek*, Macmillan 1896, II, p. 116.

[165] M. D. Hooker, *New Testament Studies* 10 (1964), p. 416.

B

BAPTISM

βάπτισμα : βαπτισμός : βαπτιστής : βαπτίζω

The first three words *(baptisma, baptismos, baptistēs)* are probably of Jewish Greek invention, referring to special details of Jewish and Christian religion. *Baptisma* is peculiar to Christian Greek (Bauer), while *baptismos* is unusual there and was for the Jews a ritual washing. Josephus refers to the *baptismos* of John the Baptist.[1] In secular Greek, however, a medical writer of vi AD, Oribasius, used *baptismos* of 'dipping',[2] and that is evidently its meaning in the NT where it is simple washing (Mk 7[4,8]; Heb 9[10]), and only once may it be used of Christian baptism – and that is doubtful (Heb 6[2]). At Col 2[12] the better text has *baptisma*,[3] the usual Christian word for the rite (Act 13[24]; Ro 6[4]; Eph 4[5]; Col 2[12]; 1 Pet 3[21]), but in addition *baptisma* is John's baptism a dozen times and our Lord's baptism of suffering and consecration five times (Mt 20[22f.]; Mk 10[38f.]; Lk 12[50]). 'Ye shall be baptized with the baptism that I am baptized with' (Mt 20[23]).

Among Christians therefore the word for 'baptism' is *baptisma*, a special term of Christian Greek. Probably the etymological distinction between the two words (that is to say, *-mos* for the act, and *-ma* for the act as complete) has no great significance in the Christian vocabulary where *baptisma* represents both senses.

The 'Baptist' *(baptistēs)* is a name for St. John in Josephus (loc. cit.) and in the gospels, never occurring previously. Our last word, however, the verb *baptizō* is secular enough, meaning 'dip', and is peculiarly Christian only in the sense of 'baptize' whether of John in the gospels or of Christian baptism elsewhere (Acts passim, Ro 6[3]; 1 Co 1[13-17] 12[13] 15[29]; Gal 3[27]). In Biblical Greek as a whole, it has the further unusual sense of performing ablutions (middle voice in LXX) – once even in the NT (passive Lk 11[38]).

The word *baptisma*, then, is peculiar to Christianity. It represents a rite performed in water involving repentance and the remission of sins. It was administered both by John the Baptist and the Christians. The verb is more frequently used than the noun for the Christian rite and, though it was originally a pagan word, it has become peculiarly Christianized. The unique institution which these words indicate was carefully distinguished from that practised by St. John the Baptist.

We can only guess at the precise formula which was recited at the earliest Christian baptisms, but it was evidently a formula which distinguished the rite from that of the Jews and St. John.

From the end of the first century the Christian rite was administered in the three-fold name of the Trinity. It is true that probably even earlier, Mt 28[19] represents a command of Jesus to the disciples to baptize in the three-fold name, 'Father, Son and Holy Ghost', but that is not strictly a liturgical text and it throws no definite light on contemporary practice. The first baptisms are reported to have been 'in the name of the Lord Jesus' (Act 2[38] 10[48] 19[5]), and it cannot be said for certain that these passages are intended to indicate a baptismal formula. To be baptized in the Lord Jesus' name was perhaps no more than an indication of Christian baptism as distinct from John's. Whatever the formula, the rite was expressly distinguished from that of John. Nevertheless, however carefully the early Christians distinguished it, they used the same terms to express it – both *baptisma* and *baptizō*.

We gather, moreover, that the imposition of hands was part of the primitive Christian rite, for imposition is closely associated in one writer's words with 'the doctrine of baptisms' (Heb 6[2]). But here we should notice that the peculiarly Christian word *baptisma* is avoided and that the word which is used, *baptismos,* stands in the plural – perhaps distinguishing the baptisms (plural) of John and the Christians.

Elsewhere in the epistle and in the NT *baptismos* is a Jewish word and refers to a ritual cleansing. It still cannot be disclaimed that *baptismos* sometimes represents the Christian rite of baptism. Moreover, besides the hint in Heb 6[2], St. Paul is found laying his hands on disciples who were baptized at Ephesus (Act 19[5ff.]), and after baptism the Apostles' hands were laid on disciples in Samaria (Acts 8[14ff.]). The 'anointing' and 'unction' mentioned by two Apostles (2 Co 1[21]; 1 Jn 2[20, 27]) suggests that Chrism, as later described in the Apostolic Constitutions (vii 41) and by St. Cyril of Jerusalem (*Catech. Myst.* 2), and which took place during confirmation after baptism according to Tertullian (*de Baptismo* vii), was already a very primitive part of the Christian rite.[4] At any rate the first Christians evidently intended that their way of initiation should be marked as peculiar to themselves, distinct from John's, whatever its origin may have been and even though they used the same words to describe the rite.

The importance of the new rite was considerable. Our Lord made clear to Nicodemus that unless one be born of water and of the Spirit – surely a reference to the new rite – one cannot enter the Kingdom of God (Jn 3[5]). Christian baptism must be accompanied by faith and repentance (Act 2[38] 8[13]). 'Repent and be baptized,' cried St. Peter at Pentecost. The early Christians believed and then were baptized. Baptism admits to the Body of Christ (1 Co 12[13]). 'Arise and be baptized,' cried Ananias, 'and wash away thy sins'

(Act 22^{16}). In view of such a command to Saul, the new Christian, is it unreasonable to suppose that later St. Paul was referring to Christian baptism when he reminded the Corinthians that they were 'washed' (1 Co 6^{11}) and that he meant that the new rite cleanses from sin?

It is important to see that the word *baptisma* covers also the Jewish rite, although it is evidently a peculiarly Christian word, because the Christian rite is in fact now widely considered to be undoubtedly Jewish in origin. It is no longer thought to be a borrowing from pagan Mysteries. The relation between St. Paul and the contemporary esoteric ideologies was once a preoccupation of the 'History-of-religions' school of thought, notably of A. Loisy and R. Reitzenstein, but now the topic is out of fashion because at last we see how deeply the Apostle was rooted in Judaism.

Most scholars, including J. Jeremias,[5] affirm that Jewish proselyte baptism was of pre-Christian origin. Baptism as a rite came from Judaism and the same word *baptisma* expresses both John's baptism and that of the Christians. Although we ought to concede that St. Paul's interpretation of it is to some extent influenced by the religion associated with initiation in the Mysteries,[6] yet the Christian initiation in itself is quite unique and dependent neither on Jewish ceremonies nor the pagan mysteries. Moreover, when we examine St. Paul's interpretation of Christian baptism in Ro 6 we find that on the whole it is consistent with other NT passages which altogether form a unity in themselves and provide a concept which is unique.

The teaching of Ro 6 has been fully examined in Switzerland by Dr. G. Wagner who compares it carefully with the like teaching in various cults of the Mystery religions – the Eleusinian, the Osiris-Isis, the Tammuz, the Adonis and the Attis cults. Often more has been read into these cults than is actually there, while the more significant parts of St. Paul's teaching on baptism are not there at all. St. Paul's stress on the mystical union of the baptismal member with Christ by spiritual death and resurrection does not need the Mystery religions to explain it.[7] The early Christians themselves saw their rite of baptism to have been foreshadowed in the Flood (1 Pet 3^{21}), in the Red Sea crossing (1 Co 10^2), and in the rite of circumcision. 'Ye are circumcised ... buried with Him in baptism' (Col 2$^{11f.}$). Indeed, the rite was foreshadowed in Judaism, for baptism is the reality which the 'example' dimly reflects and is altogether more than that OT type. It is something wholly new and peculiar.

The uniqueness of Christian baptism is further emphasized by the expression, 'baptizing with the Holy Spirit'. St. Paul affirms, 'By one Spirit were we all baptized' (1 Co 12^{13}). St. John the

Baptist promised, 'He shall baptize you with the Holy Ghost and with fire' (Mt 3[11]; Mk 1[8]; Lk 3[16]; Jn 1[33]). Jesus gave to His disciples the assurance, 'Ye shall be baptized with the Holy Ghost not many days hence' (Act 1[5]), and they recalled the assurance when at last the Holy Ghost came upon them and upon the Gentiles (Act 11[16]).

There have been attempts to see two forms, both ritual baptism and Spirit baptism, and to distinguish them as two 'moments' of Christian initiation. The NT incidents disclose that scripturally every Christian who has received the gift of the Holy Spirit has the right to think of himself as baptized in the Holy Spirit, and we must regard every complete act of Christian initiation as including both forms, baptism by water and baptism by the Holy Ghost.[8] However, there have been attempts to refer the baptism in fire to the second Coming, so that the age of the Church is seen to be marked off by two baptisms, one at the beginning (Spirit baptism, which is Pentecost), and one at the end (fire baptism, at the Coming of the Lord).[9] That still leaves us with water baptism. Does it mean that the earliest Church thought that water baptism was not baptism in the Holy Spirit and that only by the laying on of hands was there baptism in the Holy Spirit (as Mason and Dix)? When the Church Fathers say that in baptism the Holy Spirit is given, so Dr. Mason argued, they meant that He is given 'in that part of the baptismal sacrament which we know by the name of Confirmation'.[10] It was one sacrament, yet each part of it had its special gift to convey. Mason distinguished the activity of the Spirit *ab extra* as the Agent in baptism from the Spirit's inward presence given in Confirmation, and he documented it by massive patristic learning. Professor Lampe, on the other hand, finds that the Fathers had no consistent doctrine. Nor does he agree with Bishop A. M. Ramsey that in the undivided initiation rite of the early Church it was through Confirmation that the indwelling presence of the Spirit was given.[11] The moment of laying on hands was not thought of as the moment of receiving the Spirit, claims Lampe, and as Dean Richardson said, too precise attempts to define what the Bible leaves undefined 'are rationalistic intrusions into the mystery of revelation and are almost always the cause of disunity amongst Christians'.[12]

An exact definition of *baptisma* is not possible. We may be sure, however, that the gift of the Holy Spirit – whether by the water rite or in a separate part of the one baptismal rite, call it Confirmation or what we will – is what distinguishes St. John's *baptisma* from the Christian version. It is a point which is strongly made by Cullmann,[13] when he insisted that during the present period until the Coming of our Lord, the peculiarity of Christian *baptisma* is that it imparts the Spirit, 'the eschatological gift which is even now realised', and Lampe agrees that St. John's baptism was only preparatory to that Christian rite which is now the means of pouring out of Holy Ghost.[14]

Christians by the verb *baptizō* and the noun *baptisma* mean to imply a water baptism which is, when administered in the name of Jesus, also a baptism with the Holy Ghost. The giving of that Spirit, though sometimes in the NT it took place at a different time from the water baptism, was really part of the same unique rite. It does not alter the fact that *baptisma*, the peculiar Christian word, sometimes has a wider connotation in Christian Greek. It includes the baptism of John, which was its forerunner. It includes our Lord's own spiritual *baptisma*, where the word is a figure of martyrdom. The Christian words, *baptisma* and *baptizō*, indicate more than the new rite itself. They include in one great concept the Jewish antecedents, the new rite of initiation and bestowing of the Spirit, as well as the theme of consecration and martyrdom. Christian disciples are to share the spiritual *baptisma* with Jesus Himself.

See 'Blood'.

BASENESS

αἰσχρότης

In secular Greek the meaning of *aischrotēs* was 'ugliness' and 'deformity',[15] but the concept of moral baseness was lent to the word by Christians. *Aischrotēs* is a failing which, like foolish talking and jesting, must not be once mentioned among saints (Eph 5[4]).

By the fifth century the word had come to mean both 'disgraceful conduct'[16] and 'shameful thoughts'.[17]

BEHAVIOUR IN THE CHURCH

περιπατέω

In Biblical Greek the verb *peripatō* has a new metaphorical meaning.

Secular Greek. The meaning was 'to walk around'. 'I *walked about* and stole a mess of pottage from the workshop,' boasts the Sausage Seller of Aristophanes.[18] The verb was used of peripatetic teaching – walking while giving instruction. Plato recalls, 'I was *walking* in the garden' (*Epistles* 348C). For Diogenes Laertius too it was peripatetic teaching. Zeno discusses relative duties: 'Dialectic

41

by question and answer or walking exercise *(peripatō)* are not at all times incumbent' (VII 109).

Biblical Greek. The additional meaning, 'to pass one's life', is due to LXX influence for it renders the Hebrew verb *hlk* which moves in the physical and metaphysical arenas.[19]

In the NT there is the metaphorical 'walk' (1 Jn 2⁶), and there are phrases like 'walk in darkness' (Jn 8¹² 12³⁵; 1 Jn 1⁶ 2¹¹), 'walk in the day' (Jn 11⁹), 'walk in the light' (1 Jn 1⁷; Rev 21²⁴), 'walk in truth' (2 Jn 4; 3 Jn 3f), and 'walk after His commandments' (2 Jn 6). The devil 'walketh about' (1 Pet 5⁸). The metaphor occurs thirty times in Paul, but never in the Pastoral epistles.

In addition to the great apostles, Peter, Paul and John, the metaphor is found in the apostolic Fathers and we have phrases like 'walk in strange doctrine' (I. Philad. 3³). Virgins must 'walk with a blameless conscience' (Pol. ad Phil. V 1.3). We must 'walk in innocence' (Barn 10⁴), 'walk in the way of light' (Barn 19¹), 'walk in the ordinances of the Lord' (Barn 21¹), 'walk in the straight path' (Hermas *Mand.* VI 1.4). The righteous man is said to 'walk in this world' and to look forward to the holy *aiōn* (Barn 10¹¹).

BELOVED

See 'Love'.

BESETTING (OF SIN)

εὐπερίστατος

The word's derivation is controversial, but 'clinging' is probably the best meaning. *Euperistatos* is a coinage of Christian Greek, occurring only once (Heb 12¹) and describing sin which must be laid aside in the Christian race.

The adjective might have been formed in one of a variety of ways, each suggesting a different meaning. It might, for instance, be derived from the verbal adjective *peristatos,* which means 'surrounding' (from the verb *periistēmi*) compounded with *eu* (well). In this case, if we assume an intransitive meaning of the verb (standing around), the meaning of *euperistatos* will be, as AV, 'easily surrounding', 'besetting'.

If, however, the term is derived from *peristamai,* the middle voice of the same verb, with the meaning, to avoid, then the verbal adjective, which may have a passive as well as an active sense, will signify, 'easily avoided' – which was the first choice of St. Chrysostom. The verb, *peristamai*, is used of 'shunning' errors.[20]

A further suggestion about the word's derivation is based upon a hint of Theophylact.[21] It may be derived from the noun *peristaseis* (distresses), thus having the sense of 'dangerous', by the reasoning that a sin through which one falls easily *(eu)* into distresses is a dangerous sin. In support of this suggestion, *peristasis* is calamity in a pre-Christian Ptolemaic papyrus,[22] as also in 2 Mac 4[16], to say nothing of the fact that Vettius Valens constantly expresses by it the concept of straits or embarrassments.[23]

The most generally accepted choice has been the first and in support of it we should observe that the word which is formed probably on the same analogy by a Hellenistic author,[24] viz. *aperistatos*, might most suitably be rendered 'unencumbered', since it was the chief boast of Diogenes that he was not hampered by circumstances. So if *aperistatos* is 'unencumbered', then *euperistatos* may be 'encumbering' (besetting),[25] since it may have an active sense.

Héring derives our word from *periistēmi* (surround), supposing that the prefix *eu* signifies that sin has a clear understanding of the advantage it may take of the situation in causing the Christian to fall.[26]

Besides, this meaning has the support of the Vulgate *circumstans*, and it is St. Chrysostom's alternative choice. Moreover, it suits the context, for the sins to which the author alludes might well be like a wrap which encumbers the runner by 'besetting' his limbs – 'sin with its clinging folds' (Moffatt), 'the sin which clings so closely' (RSV), 'so easily' (Jerusalem Bible).

However, if to suit the context be primary, attention should be turned to the entries in the ancient lexicons of Hesychius and Suidas. By Hesychius *euperistaton* is defined as *eukolon, eucherē* (easy-going, tolerant). No matter how he derived such a meaning it makes good sense of the context, for the writer to Hebrews is concerned that his readers press on to perfection, forsaking their smug contentment with elementary doctrines. The compiler of the Suidas lexicon has reached the same definition: 'foolish, quickly upset (or diverted)'.

The old lexicons are worth study. The sin which must be laid aside is probably the tolerant disinclination to perceive that times are late and that we must press on to perfection – a sin all too characteristic of Christians.

> *Hora novissima, tempora pessima*
> *Sunt. Vigilemus,* – sang Bernard of Cluny.

BISHOP

ἐπίσκοπος : ἐπισκοπή : ἐπισκοπέω

All three words, *episkopos, episkopē, episkopō,* indicated 'oversight' in secular Greek,[27] but they did also have a more specialized application, as secular inscriptions show.

Bishop. Deissmann[28] revealed that *episkopos* was not only a communal official, a municipal officer, in the last century BC,[29] but even a religious personage at the temple of Apollo at Rhodes. It is doubtful whether the existence of such an official was widely known among early Christians. He did not in any way resemble their own 'bishop'.

There are indeed superficial parallels with the bishop outside the Bible. For instance, there is a resemblance between the Christian *episkopos* and the Jewish *mᵉbhaqqēr,* the censor or inspector or superintendant of the general membership of the Dead Sea sectaries.[30] Jeremias argued that there was a relation between the episcopal office and the *mᵉbhaqqēr.*[31] Both were overseers and teachers, for what the parallel is worth. 'He is to bring back all of them that stray, as does a shepherd his flock,' says the Damascus Document.[32] Both exercised a fatherly concern over their people like that of a pastor and both managed discipline and funds.[33] There was but one *mᵉbhaqqēr* at Qumrân, just as later on there was in each local church one *episkopos.* 'The comparison of the hierarchy at Qumrân, however, with that of the Christian Church is largely superficial,' as Sir Godfrey Driver pertinently explains.[34] There is no indication that the Church followed the Dead Sea covenanters in arriving at monepiscopacy and in some ways indeed the *mᵉbhaqqēr* rather resembled the deacon than the bishop, for he cared for material needs in the fellowship.[35] He does not seem to have been the principal officer of the society, and most of his duties were quite secular, like the management of property.

Fr. J. A. Fitzmyer, S.J., rightly concludes from his judicious survey, that although *episkopos* and *mᵉbhaqqēr* have a common etymological meaning, as well as certain similar functions, yet no direct connection has been established between the Essene 'overseer' and the institution of the early Jewish Church in Palestine. He does not exclude the possibility of Essene influence on the early Christians in non-Palestinian areas, e.g. probably at Damascus and further afield in Asia Minor.[36] Dr. Bo Reicke too concludes that the Church did not derive *episkopos* from *mᵉbhaqqēr.*[37]

The truth is that the early Christians filled the words *episkopos, episkopē, episkopō,* with their own special content, and *episkopos* in their language was a church overseer or 'bishop' which in NT days was the same as a presbyter or elder (q.v.). The elders of the church at Ephesus at least are also called bishops (Act 20[17,28]).

There were *episkopoi* and deacons at Philippi (Ph 1[1]). *Episkopos* denotes a definite office, like that of the deacons (q.v.), from which indeed it is distinguished – as again in 1 Ti 3. The *episkopos* is not marked out, however, from the presbyter, as St. Jerome recognized.[38] It should, all the same, be noted that *episkopos* is placed in the singular where just previously *presbuteroi* (elders) appears in the plural (Tit 1[7]), raising the question whether in the Pastoral epistles we may not have an incipient 'monepiscopacy' before it was fully developed in the time of St. Ignatius early in the second century – one bishop presiding over presbyters in each church, like St. Polycarp at Smyrna.[39] Episcopacy was widely extended throughout proconsular Asia early in the second century,[40] although in Egypt at least the threefold ministry established itself somewhat later.

It may be, as some have suggested, that the deaths of Peter, Paul, and James who were pillars of the Church, together with the overthrow of Jerusalem, resulted in a Church council which took measures for the well-being of the Church, at which a system was organized involving episcopacy as its centre, compacting each individual local church into one undivided Catholic Church – a system which was everywhere accepted.[41]

One important qualification is called for. A forceful article of Dr. Glasson protests against the attempt to find modern diocesan bishops before the fourth century; the Ignatian letters show the bishop as the local pastor who was personally known to his flock, assisted by presbyters and deacons; and they are all functioned within one local church.[42]

On the analogy of the Seven one supposes bishops and presbyters to have been appointed with the help of fasting and prayer and by the imposition of hands. Timothy's ordination was by the hands of the presbytery (1 Ti 4[14]) but precisely to what office was he ordained, since Timothy is both deacon (1 Ti 4[6]) and apostle (1 Th 2[6]), and is never said to be either *presbuteros* or *episkopos*?

Jesus Christ is *episkopos* of our souls (1 Pet 2[25]), a phrase which suggests that *episkopos* was not yet in NT times exclusively a technical term for a definite office, as it became in the writings of the apostolic Fathers.

Office of a Bishop. *Episkopē* is a 'watching over' in secular Greek. Hermes was sent by Zeus for visiting (watching over) the child.[43] The word received its distinctive sense in the LXX.[44] It is God's eschatological 'visitation' in mercy or judgment (e.g. Gen 50[24]; Wis 3[7]; Lk 19[44]; 1 Pet 2[12] 5[6]A; P min 1 Clem 50[3]). But *episkopē* is also an 'office', rendering *pᵉquddhâ* (Num 4[16]; Ps

108(109)[8] quoted in Act 1[20] concerning Judas's office of apostleship, although one must hesitate to deduce from this alone a close relationship between Apostle and Bishop). From this second meaning in the LXX comes the Christian use of *episkopē* to denote 'the office of a bishop' (1 Ti 3[1]; 1 Clem 44[1,4]).

To be a Bishop. The verb *episkopō* was 'to examine'[45] in secular Greek, 'to inspect the ranks'.[46] A special meaning arises in Christian Greek: 'to be a bishop' (1 Pet 5[2]). In this way St. Ignatius uses it, assuring that Jesus alone will 'be bishop' of the Syrian church when her earthly bishop is taken from her (I. Ro 9[1]). Polycarp 'is a bishop' who has God and Jesus Christ as bishop over him (I. Pol insc). The verb means 'to serve as a bishop' in Hermas (*Vis* III 5.1).

BLASPHEMY

βλασφημία : βλασφημέω : βλάσφημος

In the Christian vocabulary the three words, *blasphēmia, blasphēmō,* and *blasphēmos,* represent one of the worst possible offences – apostasy and the treachery of him who knows the Gospel truth and treads it under foot.

Secular Greek. The words implied frivolous speech concerning matters like the gods which ought to be held sacred.[47] Ill-omened or unlucky talk about divinity is so denominated by Plato and Demosthenes. One might, for instance, chance to pray for something disastrous, instead of the good, and that was 'blasphemy'.[48] Reviling angrily against one's father was rated as *blasphēmia* against *to theion* (divinity), according to Menander the comedian of iv BC.[49]

Nevertheless, the words cover evil speaking generally for the orators of classical Greece,[50] and Lucian refers to 'whole cart-loads of abuse' under the word *blasphēmia*.[51] For Demosthenes, slander is *blasphēmia* (X 36, XVIII 95), and to blaspheme against a man *(blasphēmō)* is to speak ill of him or utter imprecations against him. The adjective *blasphēmos* was 'speaking in an evil way'.[52]

Biblical Greek. In the Bible the words represent a trait more execrable, contemptible and sacrilegious. They have acquired a special meaning in Judaism and Christianity which they never had before, as Thumb confessed.[53] A sin was envisaged which can have no repentance, according to one apostolic Father, for it was a treacherous backsliding. Having argued that turn-coats are worse than those who never made a Christian profession, Hermas proceeds: 'Apostates and *blasphēmoi* against the Lord and

betrayers of the servants of God have no repentance' (*Sim* IX 19.1).
Hypocrites and false teachers may be penitent but apostates and
blasphemers cannot be; the former, after all, did not deceive the
Lord nor betray the servants of God, and although they were
greedy for gain and although they taught wrong-headedly for sore
punishment, yet at least they did not become *blasphēmoi* and
traitors (*Sim* IX 19.3). Elsewhere Hermas had conceived the
Church to be purified by rejecting them – hyprocrites, *blasphēmoi*,
doubters and all gross sinners (*Sim* IX 18.3).

The Bible's worst instance of the verb *blasphēmō* depicts
Rab-shakeh's abusive clamour before Jerusalem (4 Km 19[4,6,22]),
rendering the Piel of *gdp*. The verb voices Sennacherib's profanity
(Tob 1[18]S) as well as the debasing of God's Holy Name (Isai 52[5]:
Hithpo. of *n's*). The verb expressed sacrilegious abuse directed
against Maccabaeus, the champion of God (2 Mac 12[14]).

In the Bible a *blasphēmos* is the worst kind of fellow (Wis 1[6];
Ecclus 3[16]) and the term includes Antiochus, the tyrant who cruelly
abused God's people, as well as the profane Gentiles in general
(2 Mac 9[28] 10[4]). To bless an idol is to be *blasphēmos* (Isai 66[3]), and
Maccabaeus is reported to have burnt such offenders alive (2 Mac
10[36]). Jesus was indicted as this kind of sinner when He claimed to
be God (Mt 9[3] 26[65]; Mk 2[7] 14[64]; Lk 5[21]; Jn 10[33,36]), and so was St.
Stephen for denigrating the Law and the Temple (Act 6[11,13]). St.
Paul reckoned himself the chief of sinners, a 'blasphemer' in his old
life (1 Ti 1[13]).

Christian Greek. In its less heinous aspect, 'blasphemy' is still, as
in secular Greek, malice, clamour, railing, slander, rudeness and
abuse,[54] but the three words now indicate a different kind of
impiety – the reviling of Jesus erstwhile upon the Cross and today
in the time of grace, the very sin which the unregenerate Saul had
urged Christians to, and for which they are rightly handed over to
Satan, the sin which their own persecutors commit, blaspheming at
Christ.[55] Our three words on the lips of Christians are constantly
linked with sin,[56] with derision of God and His name,[57] His word
and truth.[58] We saw that for Hermas in the sub-apostolic Church
the sin is that of apostasy.

The unforgivable sin is represented as contempt for, or 'blasphemy' against, the Holy Ghost.[59] As to what this unforgiven
blasphemy is, I think that Dean Richardson had pertinent things to
say. The context suggested for him that Jesus meant that the
unforgivable sin, which was *aiōnios* (against the coming Dispensation), was denial of the fact that the Kingdom, the new Dispensation, had already broken into history and rejection of the signs
that it was here, rejection of the miracles which demonstrated the
overthrow of Satan's kingdom. To refuse that, is to resist the

salvation which God offers.[60] Indeed, as Hermas suggests, the sin was apostasy: once to have known and then to have spurned, once to be enlightened and then to turn deliberately to darkness. This is blasphemy. It is the one-time believer's sin, 'wilful, strong-armed arrogant blasphemy of good as evil'.[61] To the later Church it was mortal sin.

Blasphemy is to be a sad characteristic of the Great Tribulation and of the last days. Men will be proud to disown Jesus Christ. Upon the heads of the Beast will be written 'the name of blasphemy' (2 Ti 3[2]; Rev 13[1,5,6] 17[3]).

BLESSING, BLESS, 'THE BLESSED'

εὐλογία: εὐλογέω: εὐλογητός

Eulogia, eulogō, and *eulogētos* in Christian Greek well illustrate the influence of their Hebraic heritage on believers' language.

Secular Greek. The meaning of *eulogia* was fair speech, fine language,[62] while the verb *eulogō* was to praise[63] – 'without any of the deeper thoughts which spring from the Jewish conception of the divine order and essence of things'.[64] In his funeral oration Pericles referred to his *eulogia* (panegyric) of the men over whom he was speaking.[65]

The verb *eulogō* is found in Egyptian inscriptions, both of a Jew praising God[66] and of pagans praising Isis and Pan.[67] In the Jewish letter of Aristeas, *eulogō* is no more than 'to speak well' (249). The noun *eulogia* is found in the expression, 'blessing God', but it is Jewish.[68] The adjective *eulogētos* appears only in Biblical and Jewish literature.

Biblical Greek. In the LXX these words render the Hebrew stem *brk* (to kneel, bless, prosper) without the characteristic Greek idea of 'praise', and 'speaking well'. *Berekh* is a knee, and the verb is the bending of the knee in homage (e.g. Gen 24[48]) but, when the knee is bent to God, when God blesses, the idea of granting prosperity is prominent.

Many of the concepts associated with *brk* were inherited by the Christians from the old Scriptures: the concepts included blessing God (Lk 1[64] 2[28] 24[53]) and being blessed by Him. In Christian Greek the verb *eulogō* is to bless God or our food before a meal (Mt 14[19]; Mk 6[41] 8[7] 14[22]; Lk 9[16] 24[30]; 1 Co 10[16]), it is the priestly blessing given by Simeon and Melchizedec (Lk 2[34]; Heb 7[1,6,7]), it is material prosperity and the eldest son's birthright (Heb 6[14] 11[20f.]), while the participle of the same verb describes the Messiah as 'blessed' (Mt 21[9] 23[39]; Mk 11[9]; Lk 1[42] 13[35]19[38]; Jn 12[13]). The church of Ephesus was greatly 'blessed' by God (I. Eph 1), and Jesus Christ is the Father's beloved and 'blessed' Son (M Pol 14[1]). As distinct from this participle, the adjective *eulogētos* indicates God the Blessed One (Mk 14[61]; Jn 12[13]D) and appears in the phrase, '*Blessed* be God' (Lk 1[68]; Ro 1[25] 9[5]; 2 Co 1[3] 11[31]; Eph 1[3]; 1 Pet 1[3]).

Eulogētos is used only of God in the NT and may imply that blessing is due, whereas *eulogēmenos* (participle) implies merely that the blessing has been received.[69] The noun *eulogia* is what the earth receives from God and is the birthright of the eldest son – material prosperity (Heb 6[7] 12[17]) in the OT sense, but it has also a new Christian sense. It may mean Christian generosity[70] (Ro 16[18]; 2 Co 9[5f.]; Jas 3[10]), for there is a similar use of *eulogia* in the LXX when Jacob says to his reconciled brother, offering him a gift, 'Take my *blessing*' (Gen 33[11]), and Caleb's daughter said, 'Give me a *blessing*. ... Give me springs of water' (Josh 15[19]; Jg 1[15]). Abigail takes a present to David saying, 'This *blessing* thine handmaid hath brought' (1 Km 25[27]).

Christian Greek. All these phrases and concepts come to the NT by way of Hebrew and the LXX. But other phrases which embrace the words express a more characteristically Christian idea of a believer's blessing, whether that of Christ upon His disciples (Lk 24[50f.]), or Paul's upon the brethren at Rome when he came to them in the fullness of the *eulogia* of the Gospel (Ro 15[29]). The Gospel brings the *eulogia* of Abraham to the Gentiles (Gal 3[14]). God has 'blessed' the brethren *(eulogō)* in heavenly places (Eph 1[3]).

The brethren 'bless' their persecutors *(eulogō)*, for they are themselves called to inherit a *eulogia* (Mt 5[44]; Lk 6[28]; Ro 12[14]; 1 Co 4[12]; 1 Pet 3[9]). They are the 'blessed' (participle) of the Father with faithful Abraham (Mt 25[34]; Gal 3[9]). Jesus was sent to 'bless' them (Act 3[26]).

Moreover, the words are special terms in the Church's worship. A believer will 'bless' *(eulogō)* with the Spirit (1 Co 14[16]; Jas 3[9]). *Eulogia* denotes the cup at Communion (1 Co 10[16]) and is part of the homage of the doxology (Rev 5[12f.] 7[12]; T. Abr 83[18]) – 'glory and *blessing*' – the bending of the knee.

> Thee we would be alway *blessing*,
> Serve Thee as Thy hosts above;
> Pray, and praise Thee without ceasing,
> Glory in Thy perfect love.

The secular meaning of fair speech is nowhere dominant in Christian Greek. To bless God is the bending of the knee in homage, and to bless man is to bestow prosperity, especially spiritual prosperity; to bless food and the cup of Communion is evidently to 'consecrate'.

'BLINDNESS' (SPIRITUAL OBTUSENESS)

πώρωσις

O'er heathen lands afar thick darkness broodeth yet;
Arise, O morning Star; arise, and never set!

Pōrōsis is now the special quality of a mind lacking in spiritual insight, incapable of appreciating the things of God.

In secular Greek it was a physical 'hardening' – a medical term in Hippocrates and Galen. Although Theodoret in v AD clings to the secular meaning, i.e. an extreme want of feeling, through deadness, yet in Christian Greek the word signified a pre-ordained **blindness of heart,** similar to the Hebrew concept of the divine hardening of Pharaoh's heart (Ex 7¹³), for which, however, the LXX uses a different word *(katischuō).*

At the healing of the man with the withered arm Jesus was grieved for His foes' *pōrōsis* (AV 'hardness') of heart (Mk 3⁵). C. H. Turner properly protested against the sense of moral hardness. 'Jerome, the greatest of all translators of the Bible, rightly gives *caecitatem* "blindness".'⁷¹ St. Jerome's rendering might, however, be due to his reading *pērōsei* instead of *pōrōsei* in his Greek text, as Swete thought,⁷² but Armitage Robinson pointed out that *pōrōsis* had by now acquired the sense of *pērōsis* (blindness).⁷³ Jerome may have read *nekrōsei* (deadness) with codex Bezae, supported by one manuscript of the Syriac version, but again *nekrōsei* may well be an editorial gloss to explain the true meaning of *pōrōsei.*

Israel suffered 'blindness' (AV) in part, so that the Gentiles might be saved (Ro 11²⁵). Ambrosiaster and St. Hilary rendered *pōrōsis* here by *obtusio,* not a hardening of the will but an intellectual obtuseness which codex Claromontanus (vi AD), the Vulgate, and St. Augustine with St. Ambrose, support by their rendering *caecitas.* The Syriac and Armenian versions have the equivalent of 'blindness'.

St. Paul refers to the spiritual blindness of hearts among the Gentiles⁷⁴ (Eph 4¹⁸). Again the Latin versions have *caecitas* and the Syriac and Armenian versions have 'blindness'. Armitage Robinson had already, before C. H. Turner, protested against the English renderings, 'hardness', and 'hardening'.⁷⁵

Pōrōsis in Christian Greek is 'intellectual obtuseness and not the steeling of the will'.⁷⁶ In some contexts, 'hardening' is quite out of place. Pagans have not deliberately shut their hearts to the life of God, nor are the foes of Jesus said to be obstinate. St. Paul is referring rather to 'dulness' of heart, to a *mind* which has grown hard rather than a hard *heart.* St. Paul's immediate context makes clear that he is concerned with the pagans' darkness of understanding (Eph 4[18]). Jesus finds His foes lacking spiritual insight rather than obstinate in heart, and it is doubtful whether 'obstinate stupidity' (NEB) was the quality which struck Him so forcibly.

BLOOD: (1) SHEDDING OF BLOOD

αἷμα: αἱματεκχυσία

The second term, *haimatekchusia*, is a coinage of Christian Greek, formed from current words, sometimes applied to the blood-spilling at the gladiatorial contests.[77] It is shedding of blood, more especially the blood of Jesus.

Although *haima*, the first term, is representative enough in the general range of Greek, itemizing blood, bloodshed, and natural generation – as sometimes in the NT – it may not properly be rendered 'blood' in a Christian context unless 'blood' be understood as a symbol expressing martyrdom. The day following Epiphany, St. John Chrysostom was preaching on the martyr Lucian and sighed, 'Yesterday our Lord was baptized in water and today His servant in blood.'[78] The phrase, 'blood of Jesus Christ', has overtones which transform *haima* into a new image, the **life laid down for a sacrificial purpose on the cross.**

The Greek Pentateuch prepared the way, especially in Exodus 24, from which it will be seen that a stark term like 'blood' fails to include the sacrificial association which *haima* acquired in the Bible. Much less was it merely 'life'. For the Israelite, *dām* was not only blood in the veins, it was life poured out in death, a symbol in particular of sacrificial dying.[79]

Leon Morris has counted Armitage Robinson, Denney, Moffatt, Behm, and F. J. Taylor (in Richardson's *Word Book*) as already prominent among those who explain *haima* as 'death' while, on the contrary, Milligan, Westcott, Hicks and V. Taylor preferred to look upon *haima* as meaning 'life'. Morris pleaded[80] that both in the OT and in the New 'blood' signifies essentially death, and that the few passages in which 'blood' may be interpreted as life yield better sense and a sense consistent with the wider Biblical usage, if understood to mean, 'life given up in death'. Behm was of the same opinion: ' "Blut Christi" ist wie "Kreuz", nur ein anderer, anschaulicherer Ausdruck für den Tod Christi in seiner Heilsbedeutung.'[81] The 'blood of Christ' is the sacrificial and saving death of Christ.

Moreover, blood and wound and water are conjoined in a mystical way. The very moment of the death of Jesus coincided with the Jewish sacrifices in the Temple. At His death Scripture

51

was fulfilled, even to the coincidence of the hour, and so its sacrificial nature was confirmed. Not only was no bone broken, but blood was poured out on that occasion. The outpouring effected by the soldier's spear ensured the efficacy of the sacrifice (Jn 19[31-7]). At the same time, the flow of water recalls the circumstance of Moses' establishing the old Covenant with blood and water, for 'Moses took the blood ... with water and scarlet wool and hyssop ...' (Heb 9[19]). It has been shown too that the emphasis on Christ's *effusio sanguinis* (Jn 19) has an eschatological force which is strengthened by the future tense of the verb *opsontai*. 'They *shall look* on Him whom they pierced.' St. John evidently expected that at the second Coming Christ's enemies would be terrified by the sight of the wounds.[82]

Those dear tokens of His Passion
Still His dazzling Body bears.

'Two Advents of His shall take place,' affirms St. Justin Martyr, '... a second when you recognize Him whom you pierced, and all your tribes shall lament, tribe over against tribe, the women alone and the men alone' (*Dial.* 32[2]). 'They who pierced Him shall see Him and lament' (*Dial.* 64[7]).

Every NT writer except St. James and St. Jude makes use of the term *haima,* and its most solemn point of reference is the chalice of Holy Communion which is identified as Christ's blood of the new Covenant shed for remission of sins.[83] To drink the chalice 'unworthily' is to be guilty of His blood (1 Co 11[27]) in the secular sense of *haima* (bloodshed) – to crucify Him afresh, like those who taste the heavenly gift and then fall away (Heb 6[4]). Believers must 'drink' His *haima* (Jn 6[53ff.]), and it eludes us whether St. John has in mind the sacramental 'blood' of the eucharist, of which we partake, in the way that *haima* often appears later in Church Greek,[84] or whether he reports Jesus as spiritualizing the word 'drink' into a personal participation in the life of Jesus by faith.[85] The whole discourse has been seen as a midrashic discussion on a verse from the Psalms: 'He gave them bread from heaven to eat' (Ps 78[24]). This is manifest by the characteristic repetition of phrases and by the division of the text on which the midrash is based into two parts: the first, 'He gave them bread from heaven', is dealt with in verses 32–48, and the second ('to eat') forms the basis of 49–58. Patterns for this kind of exposition are found in the Palestinian midrashim and in Philo.[86] Why has Jesus gratuitously added 'drink' and 'blood' in His exposition of the manna as 'bread' from heaven? No mention of it appears in the psalm-text, but the very addition of *haima* makes that word extraordinarily significant – eucharistic, without a doubt.

Belief in the Blood. A further problem is posed by *haima* in St. Paul's address at Miletus (Act 20[28]): 'the Church of God which He hath purchased with His own *blood*'. Apart from the unusually forthright declaration that Jesus is God, we remark the word, 'purchase', and recall that Origen debated whether the blood of Christ was paid as a ransom to the Devil.[87] The NT satisfies no curiosity in this respect and St. Paul fails to disclose from whom the Church was 'purchased' at the price of *haima*. St. Peter evaluates the *haima* as 'precious', as if it effected a redemption or made a weighty purchase (1 Pet 1[19]), as if it were a ransom which might be relied upon implicitly – *haima* in which we could trust (Ro 3[25]), *haima* to be 'believed in', as St. Ignatius found. Even angels 'believe in' the *haima* of Christ (I. Smyrn 6[1]).

Belief in the *haima* is part of Christian faith, for Christ's blood cleanses those who believe in it.[88]

Sanctification by the Blood. To 'believe in' the blood is not so much the experience of conversion or the act of commitment to Jesus. Efficacy of the blood reaches to sanctification and election too (1 Pet 1[2]). Blood must be 'sprinkled' upon us as upon Israel our exemplar and precursor. It 'cleanseth us' – and the tense is present – not only from sins of a former period of life but 'from all sin', every fall along our pilgrim way, including sins into which even the brother in fellowship falls (1 Jn 1[7]). True, we have the initial 'redemption through His blood' (Eph 1[7]; Rev 1[5] 5[9]), for 'without *haimatekchusia* (shedding of blood) is no remission' (Heb 9[22]), and by *haima* we were 'brought nigh' (Eph 2[13]) and reconciled to God (Col 1[20]). Nevertheless, the cleansing is continuous, not initial only. As the setting of Heb 9 is sacrificial it is but reasonable to take *haimatekchusia* there as 'the pouring out of sacrificial blood', but what is the special significance of 'pouring out'? T. C. G. Thornton drew attention to the phrase *ekchein haima* in reference to OT sacrifices to denote the pouring of the blood of a sin-offering upon the base of the altar. This, and not the slaying in itself, was the significant gesture. Whereas the shedding of blood in non-Jewish sacrificial contexts has reference to the killing of men and animals, sure enough, yet Thornton rightly suggested that this is not the meaning of *haimatekchusia* in the NT context, which is reminiscent of the OT.

Neither in the OT nor among Jews of the NT period was it believed that the mere slaughter of a victim was the essential ritual which effects the purpose of sacrifice. 'Once the blood has reached the altar, the owners are forgiven,' said the rabbis. The sprinkling on the altar is the important moment. So then, although a slaying is presupposed, the reference in sacrifice is primarily not to death but to the sprinkling of blood.[89]

The writer to Hebrews sees the symbolism of it all. *Haima* is 'the blood of sprinkling' (Heb 12[24]) and the blood wherewith we are *today* sanctified and have boldness to enter the Holiest (Heb 10[19-29]). The 'blood' signifies not the sacrificial death of Jesus on its own, but the death availing now, the constant appeal to the sacrifice, the daily sprinkling, the continuous cleansing. That great multitude which no man could number 'washed their robes and made them white with the blood of the Lamb' at their final tribulation (Rev 7[14]).

In the Fathers. St. Gregory Nazianzus underlined the place of the 'blood' in our spiritual life (*Orationes* 45.15). Church Fathers exult in the thought of being sanctified *(hagnizomai)* in the sprinkling of His blood (Barn. 5[1]). Rahab's scarlet thread was a type of the blood of the Lord, foreshadowed also in the paschal lamb and the blood of the covenant.[90]

Haima is ridiculed by pagans,[91] but it avails for all.[92] It is the blood that brings salvation.[93] Early Christians were soon alive to the devotional aspect of it. 'Thou, Lord, didst give Thyself for us,' they cried, 'and by Thy *blood* hast bought us and gained a precious possession! But what have we given to Thee, Lord, in exchange for Thy life which Thou didst give for us?'[94] Miss Havergal was not more contemplative:

'Thy life was given for me, Thy blood, O Lord, was shed,
That I might ransomed be and quickened from the dead;
Thy life was given for me: what have I given for Thee?'

It becomes Christians not only to believe in the blood, but to let their 'hearts be kindled in the blood of God', as St. Ignatius urged.[95] When greeting the Smyrnaeans he has the rare phrase, 'firmly grounded in love in the blood of Christ', as he thanks God for their immovable faith (I. Smyrn. 1[1]). Stranger still, but intensely earnest, is the contempt of St. Ignatius for earthly food set against the metaphorical draught of His blood, which is love incorruptible (I. Ro 7[3]).

St. Irenaeus reminds us that, in every letter, the Apostle plainly testifies that through the flesh of our Lord and through His blood, we have been saved and that Christ has redeemed us by His blood.[96] The concept spans the wide range of Christian thought: the precious blood of the dying Lamb never loses its power till all the ransomed Church of God is saved and is evermore free from sin.

We proceed to the Christian understanding of the term, 'sprinkling'.

(2) SPRINKLING OF BLOOD

ῥαντισμός: ῥαντίζω

Both *rantismos* and *rantizō* may be Biblical coinages, although the verb *(rantizō)* appears later in a secular author (Athenaeus, iii AD). In the NT and Fathers there are references to the OT sprinkling (Heb 9[13,19,21]; Barn. 8[1,3,4]) and to the contemporary Jewish rite (Mk 7[4] SB), which are considered as but types of the true *rantismos*, the sprinkling of the sanctified in the blood of Jesus. Their hearts are **sprinkled** thereby from an evil conscience (Heb 10[22]).

The sprinkling of Christ's blood was a Christian phrase.[97] 'The *rantismos* of the blood of Jesus Christ' guarantees the elects's sanctification and final victory (1 Pet 1[2]). The word for 'sprinkling' is absent but the same idea lies behind the picture of Christ, 'the Faithful and True' who is 'clothed with a vesture dipped in blood' which nevertheless has marks of victory upon it (Rev 19[13,16]).

Hort recalled that the 'sprinkling' in the old Dispensation was a means by which the People was consecrated and purified, followed by the People's promise of obedience (1 Pet 1[2]). So 'reception into the Christian covenant implied acceptance of an authoritative standard of righteousness: ... a Christian obedience took the place of the obedience of the Old Covenant'.[98]

In a type, therefore, overcoming believers can be said to have 'washed their robes and made them white in the blood of the Lamb' when they come from the great Tribulation (Rev 7[14]). In that way the Saviour's afflictions will have 'overflowed into' them (2 Co 1[5]), and by their deaths they will be 'conformed to His death' (Ph 3[10]). Hort's insights in this discussion are worth meditating.

On the other hand, some see a very obvious connection with baptism in the sprinkling which is mentioned in Heb 10[22] – our hearts sprinkled from an evil conscience. It is thought that this phrase and the next ('our bodies washed with pure water') describe two aspects of one and the same thing: as the body is washed with water (i.e. baptism), so the heart is cleansed and freed from a bad conscience. Some think, therefore, that the idea of sprinkling with the blood of Christ belongs to baptismal theology. If this is true of Heb 10[22] it will include also 1 Pet 1[2]: sanctification of the Spirit and sprinkling of the blood of Jesus probably belong also to the same theology. The epistle of St. Peter is full of references to baptism. Moreover, we recall that Christ imparted to Nicodemus the idea that man needs a re-birth in water and the Holy Ghost. If the hypothesis is correct, 1 Pet 1[2] shows that the idea of sprinkling with

Christ's blood is not peculiar to the epistle to the Hebrews but is part of a widespread baptismal tradition in the early Church.[99]

Baptismal cleansing is thought to be behind St. Paul's phrase, 'that He might sanctify and cleanse with the washing of water' (Eph 5[26]), and behind St. Peter's choice of Noak's Ark as a type of baptism, 'wherein eight souls were saved by water' (1 Pet 3[20f.]). St. John too sees the water from Christ's side as significant (Jn 19[34]). It is thought that by water he understands baptism and by the blood the eucharist.

See also 'Blood', 'Baptism', and 'Prayer' *(eperōtēma)*.

BROTHER, BRETHREN, AND BROTHERHOOD (CHRISTIAN)

ἀδελφός : ἀδελφότης

Adelphos and *adelphotēs* have become proper technical words among Christians to denote their sacred relationship.

Secular Greek. The word *adelphos* was used of brothers born of the same parents (as in Mt 1[2], etc.), or of neighbours (as Lev 19[17]; Mt 7[3]), or of members of the same nation (as Ex 2[11]; Deut 15[3]; Ro 9[3]). I cannot find *adelphotēs* in the vernacular or in secular literature before Dio Chrysostom and Vettius Valens of the Christian period, but *adelphos* appears occasionally in pre-Christian papyri in the religious sense of an associate of a pagan community – a member, for instance, of an embalming society.[100] Besides, Josephus applies *adelphos* to adherents of what he calls the Essenes: 'there is one patrimony among all the *brethren*'.[101]

In a papyrus letter which is adduced in evidence of its pagan religious association, the term *adelphos* seems rather to mean 'husband'; the man was in retreat at the Serapeum and evidently belonged to a society connected with the place, but the circumstance is incidental to his being 'adelphos' in his wife's affections.[102]

Christian Greek. To the first Christians *adelphos* was no fraternal relationship as understood in the pagan or Jewish world. It had a special sense which derives from divine revelation itself. A large group of such words, which do incidentally find themselves in a religious context elsewhere, have a very distinct and proper sense among Christians – e.g. apostle, deacon, bishop. The new meaning of *adelphos* is 'fellow Christian'.[103]

'Brethren' *(adelphoi)* becomes a term for Christians at an early date. Jesus says, 'Go to My *brethren*' (Jn 20[17]), and a report is said to circulate among 'the brethren' (Jn 21[23]). It may be that the current of St. John's thought is anti-Gnostic[104] – stressing union with the Father and knowledge of Him by means of a close relationship with Christ. The Son's love reflects the Father, and the brethren's love for one another reflects the Son: the united Church is a sign to the world, like the filial relationship of Jesus to the Father.

St. Paul links his own name with Sosthenes 'our brother' (1 Co 1[1]). The 'brethren' who brought Saul down to Caesarea and sent him on to Tarsus were fellow-Christians (Act 9[30]). Very much later, e.g. AD 335, *adelphos* relates to members of a monastic community. A monk who belonged to the Meletian schism writes to 'my beloved *brother* Apa Paieou', another monk, and says that 'certain *brethren* can inform you what occurred', referring to the harrying of the Meletians by St. Athanasius.[105]

Similarly, *adelphotēs* has changed its meaning in Christian Greek from that in the LXX (brotherhood, brotherly affection: 1 Mac 12[10,17]; 4 Mac 13[27]), and now refers to the Church. It is a collective term like 'the brethren'. The *adelphotēs* suffers afflictions and deserves our love (1 Pet 2[17] 5[9]), being identified by Hermas with the Church's fellowship which is worthy of preservation (*Mand.* viii 10). If a man will keep this fellowship he becomes blessed in his life. It is synonymous with the Church,[106] even the local church,[107] for Novatus was said to be disturbing the Roman *adelphotēs*; and it refers to religious communities.[108]

NOTES

[1] *Ant. Jud.* XVIII v 2 (Niese XVIII 117).
[2] Ed. U. C. Bussemaker and C. Daremberg, Paris 1851ff., 10.3.9.
[3] Despite the attestation of B and p[46] for *baptismos*, and the preference of Lightfoot (in loc.).
[4] G. Wainwright, *Studia Liturgica* (Rotterdam) 10 (1974), pp. 2–24.
[5] *Die Kindertaufe in dem ersten vier Jahrhunderten*, Göttingen 1958, where it is urged that as children were baptized with their parents in Jewish proselyte baptism, so baptism of household in the NT implies that the children of Christians were baptized with them.
[6] M. Simon, *Religious Studies* (CUP) 11 (1975), pp. 135–144.
[7] G. Wagner, *Das religionsgeschichtliche Problem von Römer 6, 1–11* (Abhandlungen zur Theologie des Alten und Neuen Testaments, no. 39), Zürich 1962.
[8] F. A Sullivan, *Gregorianum* (Rome) 55 (1974), pp. 49–68.
[9] H. Schlier, *Die Zeit der Kirche: exegetische Aufsätze und Vorträge*, Freiburg 1956, p. 114.
[10] A. J. Mason, *The Relation of Confirmation to Baptism*, Longman 2nd ed. 1893, p. xv.
[11] G. W. H. Lampe, *The Seal of the Spirit*, SPCK 2nd ed. 1967, p. xi.
[12] A. Richardson, *Introduction to the Theology of the New Testament*, SCM 1958, p. 355.

[13] O. Cullmann, *Baptism in the New Testament*, ET SCM Studies in Biblical Theology, no. 1 1950, pp. 9f.

[14] Lampe, op. cit., p. 10.

[15] Plato *Gorgias* 525A. Only 'ugliness' in secular writers (Bauer).

[16] Nilus Ancyrus, *Epistularium Libri Quattuor* i 129 (PG LXXIX 137C).

[17] Esaius, an abbot of AD 488, *Orationes* vi 7 (PG XL 1116C).

[18] Aristophanes *Knights* 744.

[19] Some have tried to find the Biblical meaning already in Philodemus (*Peri Parresias*, ed. A. Olivieri, Teubner 1914, p. 12, fragment 23) in i BC, but the passage is very fragmentary and the meaning doubtful.

[20] Philodemus (i BC) *Rhetorica* I 384S.

[21] MM s.v.; Moulton-Howard *Grammar* II, p. 282.

[22] P Lond 42.21 (168 BC).

[23] *Evangelical Quarterly* 2 (1930), p. 397; article on Vettius Valens by E. K. Simpson.

[24] Arrian IV 1.159 (c. AD 100). Cf. E. K. Simpson, op. cit.

[25] Such an understanding may have given rise to the early variant in the Chester Beatty papyrus *(euperispaston)* which is probably, on the analogy of *aperispastos,* 'easily distracting'. F. W. Beare *JBL* 63 (1944), pp. 390f.

[26] J. Héring, *The Epistle to the Hebrews*, ET Epworth 1970, p. 111.

[27] Overseers and agents, in Josephus *Ant. Jud.* X 53, XII 254. Moses was *episkopos*, Philo *Quis Rerum Divinarum Heres* 30.

[28] BS p. 230f. See H. W. Beyer in Kittel *TWNT* II, pp. 608f.

[29] IG I 2.12 (1), 49.42.

[30] Damascus Document (Zadokite Fragments) xiii 7–11; also *Manual of Discipline* vi 11f. T. H. Gaster, *The Scriptures of the Dead Sea Sect*, Secker 1957, pp. 60 and 90.

[31] J. Jeremias, *Jerusalem in the Time of Jesus*, ET Fortress, Pa, 1969, pp. 261f.

[32] Gaster, op. cit., p. 90.

[33] M. Black, *The Scrolls and Christian Origins*, Nelson 1961, p. 117; B. J. Humble, *Restoration Quarterly* (Houston) 7 (1963), pp. 33–8.

[34] G. R. Driver, *The Judaean Scrolls*, Blackwell 1965, pp. 521–3.

[35] *Manual of Discipline* vi 20.

[36] *Essays on the Semitic Background of the New Testament*, Chapman 1971, p. 294.

[37] In *The Scrolls and the New Testament*, ed. K. Stendahl, New York 1957, p. 154.

[38] Jerome *Epistola ad Ocean.* 73 (Ellicott, *Pastoral Epistles*, 39; Lightfoot, *Philippians*, 98f.).

[39] I. Pol intr.

[40] J. B. Lightfoot, *The Christian Ministry*, Macmillan 1901, p. 51.

[41] J. B. Lightfoot, *Philippians*, pp. 201–4, summarizing Rothe's theory. Lightfoot thought the development was not likely to have been so sudden, however.

[42] T. F. Glasson, *Expository Times* 79 (1967), pp. 52–4.

[43] Lucian *Dialogi Deorum* 20[6].

[44] H. W. Beyer in Kittel *TWNT* __ p. 602.

[45] T. Wiegand, *Milet. Ergebnisse der Ausgrabungen und Untersuchungen seit dem Jahre 1899*, Berlin 1906, 3.155 (ii BC inscription).

[46] Xenophon *Anabasis* II 3.2.

[47] Vettius Valens (58.12, 67.20), Herodian (vii 8.9), Dio Chrysostom (iii 53: 'something *blasphēmon* about the gods'). So also Diodorus Siculus, Philo and Josephus.

[48] *Republic* 381E, *Laws* 800C; *Alcibiades* II 149C. Demosthenes XXV 26.

[49] Menander 715 (*Comicorum Atticorum Fragmenta*, ed. T. Kock, Leipzig 1880ff.).

[50] Isocrates XV 2; Aeschines I 180; Demosthenes LI 3 – all orators of the fourth century.

[51] *Eunuchus* 2.

[52] Aristotle *Rhetorica* 1398 b 11; Plutarch *Moralia* 1100D.

[53] Albert Thumb, *Die griechische Sprache im Zeitalter des Hellenismus*, Strassburg 1901, p. 178.

[54] Act 13[45] 18[6] 19[37]; Ro 3[8] 14[16]; Eph 4[31]; 1 Co 4[13] 10[30]; Col 3[8]; 1 Ti 6[4]; Tit 3[2]; 1 Pet 4[14]; 2 Pet 2[10,12]; Jude 8, 9, 10.

[55] Mt 27[39]; Mt 15[29]; Lk 22[65] 23[39]; Act 26[11]; 1 Ti 1[20]; 1 Pet 4[14].

[56] Mt 12[31] 15[19]; Mk 3[28] 7[22].

[57] Ro 2[24]; 1 Ti 6[1]; Jas 2[7]; Rev 13[6] 16[9,11,21].

[58] Tit 2[5]; 2 Pet 2[2].

[59] Mt 12[31]; Mk 3[29]; Lk 12[10].

[60] Alan Richardson, *Introduction to the Theology of the New Testament*, SCM 1958, p. 108.

[61] HDB I, p. 306.

[62] Plato *Republic* 400D, linked with 'good nature' and 'grace of manner'. Lucian *Lexiphranes* 1, as perhaps Ro 16[18] – almost 'flattery', but see below.

[63] E.g. Aeschylus *Agamemnon* 580.

[64] B. F. Westcott, *Hebrews*, Macmillan 1889, p. 210.

[65] Thucydides II 42.

[66] OGI I 73.1.

[67] CIG 4705.

[68] A iii BC inscription, OGI I 74.1.

[69] Armitage Robinson, p. 142.

[70] B. F. Westcott, op. cit., p. 209.

[71] In *A New Commentary on Holy Scripture*, C. Gore, A. Guillaume, H. Goudge, SPCK 1928, p. 59b.

[72] H. B. Swete, *The Gospel according to St. Mark,* Macmillan 1902, pp. 52f.

[73] *Journal of Theological Studies* 3 (1904), pp. 81ff.

[74] B. Lindars, *Theology* 69 (1966), p. 121.

[76] Armitage Robinson, p. 274.

[76] Ibid., p. 266.

[77] Tatian *Oratio ad Graecos* 23.

[78] *Panegyricum in Lucianum martyrem* 2.

[79] The verdict of Armitage Robinson and others endorsed by Leon Morris, *Journal of Theological Studies* NS 6 (1955), p. 82.

[80] *Journal of Theological Studies*, NS 3 (1952), pp. 216–27.

[81] In Kittel *TWNT* I, p. 173.

[82] M. Miguens, *Studii Biblici Franciscani Liber Annuus* (Jerusalem) 14 (1964), pp. 5–31.

[82] Mt 26[28]; Cp. Mk 14[24]; Lk 22[20]; 1 Co 10[16] 11[25].

[84] I. Philad 4[1]; Acta Thomae 49; Acta Andreae 6, and everywhere in Christian history.

[85] Very few today reject the eucharistic significance. Barrett clearly does not. Bultmann acknowledged the sacramental character of the discourse, though he considered it a non-Johannine addition; yet the style is that of the rest of the gospel.

[86] P. Borgen, *Zeitschrift für die neutestamentliche Wissenschaft* 54 (1963), pp. 232–40.

[87] *Commentarii in Johannem* 6.53.

[88] Justin *Apol.* I 32.7.

[89] *Journal of Theological Studies*, NS 15 (1964), pp. 63–5.

[90] Justin *Dial.* 40[1] 111[4]; 1 Clem 12[7].

[91] Origen *contra Celsum* 1.66.

[92] 1 Clem 7⁴ 21⁶.

[93] Justin *Dial.* 24.

[95] Acta Thomae A 72.

[95] I. Eph 1¹.

[96] Irenaeus *contra Haereses* V ch. 14.3.

[97] Barn. 5¹. Literally: 'the blood of His *sprinkling*' (His sprinkled blood).

[98] F. J. A. Hort, *The First Epistle of St. Peter*, Macmillan 1898, pp. 23ff.

[99] C.-H. Hunzinger in Kittel *TWNT* VI, pp. 983f.

[100] P. Tor I i 20 (ii BC).

[101] *Bell. Jud.* II ii 3 (Niese II 122).

[102] *British Museum Papyri*, ed. F. G. Kenyon, vol. I, 1893, no. 42 (pp. 29ff.); G. Milligan, *Selections from the Greek Papyri*, CUP 1927, p. 8.

[103] 1 Clem 1¹; T. Abr 104⁵ (Christian ending). P. Grenf II 73 (iii AD, Christian papyrus) has: '*brother* in the Lord'.

[104] M. Bouttier, *Revue d'Histoire et de Philosophie Religieuses* (Paris) 44, 1964, pp. 179–190.

[105] H. I. Bell, *Jews and Christians in Egypt*, London 1924, p. 58 (1, 4, etc.).

[106] 1 Clem 2⁴, Irenaeus *Haereses* II 31.2.

[107] Eusebius *Historia Ecclesiastica* VI 45.1.

[108] E.g. St. Gregory of Nyssa *de Virginitate* 23 (PG XLVI 409B).

C

CALLING: CALLED

κλῆσις: κλητός

The words *klēsis* and *klētos* indicate the divine invitation to salvation.

Secular Greek. *Klēsis*, the noun, was the tone of voice which one employed. As Plato remarks, 'He called in a banting *klēsis*.'[1] It is a calling upon the gods,[2] a 'summons' from Cyrus,[3] a 'citation' which is issued,[4] an 'invitation' which is offered,[5] as when the Council sent invitations to dinner at the Town Hall,[6] or a 'call' for help (like *paraklēsis*) from the Achaean League.[7]

Further, it is a calling in the sense of an occupation or trade. Libanius tells us that Demosthenes' father received the *klēsis* (trade) of a maker of cutlery.[8] Again, *klēsis* is a title of 'naming' and Philo uses it for the name, 'god': the Alexandrians, he complained, pay little attention to the title *(klēsis)* of 'god', for they give this name to ibises, snakes and other beasts.[9]

One who is *klētos* (adjective) is one 'summoned' to Court.[10] As early as Homer, *klētos* meant 'welcome:' prophets, healers, builders and minstrels are 'welcome' all over the boundless earth.[11] In Homer too it means 'chosen'. 'Let us send for *chosen* men,' says Nestor, 'to go to Achilles.'[12]

Christian Greek. Christians have straitened the sense until it becomes the divine call to salvation, that is, the first point in the initiative of God's saving grace. The words *klēsis* (calling) and *klētos* (called) now indicate a **vocation** of which believers are urged to walk worthily, 'with all lowliness and meekness, with long-suffering forbearing one another in love' (Eph 4[1]). Our **calling** is an invitation to believe, to put all our trust in Christ, so that in fact a *klētos* (called person) is a Christian believer. Indeed, in the apostolic Fathers the *klētoi* are Christians (1 Clem intr.).

God in the first place 'called' Israel. St. Paul would make clear that, despite Israel's disobedience, He has not rejected her but will keep His word, for the gifts and *klēsis* of God are without change of mind (Ro 11[29]).

Gentiles are now invited by the Gospel, and to this *klēsis* St. Paul refers when he writes, 'Ye see your *klēsis*, brethren, how that not many wise men after the flesh, not many mighty, not many noble are called' (1 Co 1[26]). *Klēsis* here does seem to mean 'the *circumstances* attending your calling', rather than the calling itself. The circumstances are earthly class-distinctions, wealth and pedigree and privilege – or the lack of them.

K. L. Schmidt, however, rejects the sense of *externa conditio* as unnecessary, following Cremer (revised by Kögel). He admits that 'external circumstances' suits the meaning of *klēsis* in 7[20]: 'Let every man abide in the same *klēsis* wherein he was called.' He asks[13] why the word should have a different meaning in 7[20] from that in 1[26], but I do not think it has. In both places St. Paul would stress that the divine invitation is not a calling to improve our earthly estate. It is always a summons to riches of glory and an inheritance in the saints (Eph 1[18]) – a 'hope' uniting all saints in one Body and one Spirit (Eph 4[4]).

The *klēsis* has a prize for its goal, to which a believer must press (Ph 3[14]). Above all the believer must pray to be worthy of the 'invitation', by pleasing God, producing by His enabling the good results of faith, as He is good (2 Th 1[11]).

It is, then, 'an holy calling' and 'a heavenly calling', pursued not by our own goodness but only by His grace (2 Ti 1[9]; Heb 3[1]). Even the imperfect pilgrim is the 'called' *(klētos)* of Jesus Christ, and a 'saint', for whose good all things work (Ro 1[6f.] 8[28]; 1 Co 1[2,24]; Jude 1). He may be distinguished from the Elect, however, in the sense that 'many are the **called** but few are the Elect' (Mt 22[14] and some texts at 20[16]). However, it is not always so easy to particularize the Called from the Elect, for the Called are ranked with 'the Elect and the Faithful' as those who overcome at last (Rev 17[14]). See 'Elect'. In a strict analysis it may be that the Called are the initially justified while the Elect are the fully saved.

To our limited understanding, the doctrine of God's special 'calling' comes near to determinism, although it is true that by our own will we are able to make our **calling** sure – as also our 'election' (2 Pet 1[10]) – and the matter of vocation in Pauline terminology is made still more difficult when we consider what he has to say about **calling** as it concerns social assignment or sectionalism. Mentioning slavery in particular, he exhorts, 'Let every man abide in the same calling *(klēsis)* wherein he was called,' for if he became *klētos* (a Christian) while he was a slave, yet he is, despite his social status, 'the Lord's free man' (1 Co 7[20,22]). Evidently, to St. Paul, the hope and prize of Christ's high calling far eclipsed all the class-disadvantages suffered on earth.

It goes without saying that *klēsis* in these verses is not to be understood as a 'professional calling', an occupation in life, as in the later secular Greek of Libanius (see above), but as a **divine calling to salvation** while the believer was in a state of serfdom. Indeed, both here and in 1[26], we find St. Paul indulging in very compressed speech. Here and in 1[26] by *klēsis* he evidently means the *earthly circumstances* in which God calls us[14] – that is, serfdom or wealth, or nobility or the reverse – not the act of calling itself (as in Ph 3[14]).

'Ye see your *calling*, brethren,' is, 'ye see the *circumstances* ye were in when ye were called'. The slave is to abide in his *klēsis*, content with his earthly lot. The Christian servant is still to obey his master (Eph 6[5]; Col 3[22]; Tit 2[9]). The Christian Onesimus returns to his master, and the master must receive him.

When we ponder *klēsis* and election and predestination, we should observe their integrated setting in the history of God's relation with the Jews. A choice was offered to Israel. Israel received the call, but God did not at the same time premise an antecedently infallible and efficacious means of responding to it. St. Paul is at pains to show (Ro 11[7-25]) that even Israel fell under God's wrath for continual resistance. Take heed, Christian, lest He also spare not thee! St. Paul easily reconciled the truth that God's salvation is universal with the tragic paradox that not all men achieve salvation. God's call and His grace are conditional, depending upon human response.[15]

CHALICE: ORDEAL?

ποτήριον

In secular Greek *potērion* was a wine cup, a drinking vessel,[16] but in Christian Greek it peculiarly means the **chalice** of Holy Communion (1 Co 10[21] 11[25ff.]; I. Philad 4[1]).

Moreover, in Biblical (OT) and Christian Greek it stands in a figurative sense for 'the experience of God's providence', whether beneficial or the reverse. In the Greek of the OT it renders the Hebrew *kôs*, God's 'cup' whether of judgment or blessing. *Potērion (kôs)* is the cup of God's fury (Jer 32(25)[15,17,28]), meaning Babylon the conqueror (Jer 28(51)[7]). *Potērion (kôs)* is the cup of God's judgment (Ps 74(75)[9]; Isai 51[17,22]; Jer 29(49)[12]), and the cup of punishment (Ezek 23[31ff.]). Upon the ungodly He shall rain fire and brimstone: this shall be their *potērion* (Ps 10(11)[7]). Nevertheless, *potērion (kôs)* is also the cup of consolation offered to mourners (Jer 16[7]), the cup of God's highest blessings, the portion of mine inheritance and of my *potērion* (Ps 15(16)[5]), my salvation (Ps 115(116)[13]), my cup which runneth over (Ps 22(23)[5]).

Jesus asks whether the disciples can drink of His *potērion* (Mt 20[22f.]; Mk 10[38f.]) – a 'cup' which was part of the agony of the Passion (Mt 26[39]; Lk 22[42]; Jn 18[11]). In time of trial Christians have seen the *potērion* of Christ as their own martyrdom. St. Polycarp cried at the stake, 'I bless Thee, Almighty God, for letting me share with Thy martyrs the *potērion* of Christ!' (M Pol 14[2]).

In Christian Greek, as in the LXX, *potērion* is nevertheless still the indignation of God and His punishment, which all who have the mark of the Beast shall taste, and which spiritual Babylon must drink (Rev 14[10] 16[19] 18[6]).

CHASTENING

παιδεία

The general word for education and culture, *paideia*, finds in Biblical Greek the additional meaning of 'chastening'.

Secular Greek. *Paideia* was training,[17] including the ancient schooling at Athens.[18] It was the education a man had,[19] and the schooling which a father by his economies is able to provide for his boys,[20] defined by Plato as the process of guiding children to principles which are right as judged by the law and the experience of good and senior people.[21]

Compatible with this definition was the meaning, 'lesson', such as a man might be taught.[22] In Josephus *paideia* is the Greek 'learning' of which Manetho had made himself master.[23] It is what we might call 'culture' – no sum of abstract ideas, but Greek history itself in all its concrete reality.[24] 'The true representatives of paideia were not, the Greeks believed, the voiceless artists – sculptors, painters, architects – but the poets and musicians, orators (which means statesmen) and philosophers.'[25]

Biblical Greek. Only in the Bible and related literature has *paideia* the extended meaning of chastening. It is 'correction' whose rod drives foolishness from the heart (Pr 22[15]) and should not be despised when it comes from the Lord (3[11]). However, Bertram[26] points out that there is secular testimony to the sense 'chastise' in popular Hellenistic Greek of the second century AD,[27] when a prodigal son writes to his mother and uses the verb *paideuō*, 'I am suitably *chastened*.' In spite of that, as Bertram remarks,[28] the Greek terms acquire in the LXX a new and almost alien significance – the sense of discipline and chastisement.

Of course, the Biblical concept is but a development of the secular, for as education cannot stand apart from discipline and pain, so vice versa in the Biblical concept of chastening there lingers palpably the design of instruction – the learning which divine Wisdom affords (Pr 8[10]; Jer 39(32)[33] 42(35)[13]; Ecclus 1[27]). The Bible concept has passed into ordinary speech in many modern languages. The regular Rumanian word for 'penalty' is *pedeapša* (which is the Greek *paideusis*) and in modern English we have the colloquial saying, 'I'll *teach* you,' when we mean 'punish you'. In

New High German *zucht* is 'breeding' and 'education', and yet *züchtigen* is to 'censure', 'chastise', and 'punish'.[29]

Trench pointed to St. Augustine's distinction between 'eruditio' simple and 'eruditio per molestias', the latter being peculiarly the meaning of *paideia* in the singular Greek of the LXX, the NT and the Fathers (pp. 105f.).

The writer to the Hebrews quotes Pr 3[11] and here again *paideia* means 'chastening', the Lord's discipline (12[5,8,11]). It is to be expected that in Christian circles children were in mind when *paideia* was discussed, for God's tutelage is a longsome process, starting in infancy. Fathers among the faithful must bring up their children within its influence (Eph 6[4]), and mothers, too.[30]

Christian 'chastening' is for the young, but not exclusively since all brethren submit to the holy *paideia* of the Father (1 Clem 21[8] 56[16]). Scripture is for the *paideia* of the man of God (2 Ti 3[16]), being the oracles of His *paideia* (1 Clem 62[3]). Godly 'chastening' yields the peaceable fruit of righteousness to those exercised by it; such discipline is proof that they are God's children and are not spiritual misbegots (Heb 12[7,8,11]). As Bertram points out,[31] *paideia* and *lupē* (grief) go together in Christianity, as in the OT; *paideia* does not in the first instance bring joy, but strenuous discipline.

The scene in the vision of Hermas is an allegory of the believer's chastening. 'When they have been afflicted,' observes the Shepherd, 'then they are delivered to me for good discipline *(paideia)*.'[32]

CHRIST

Χριστός

Christos is a style or second name given to their Lord by believers (Mt 1[16]), sometimes used alone as a proper name in place of Jesus (Ro 5[8] 6[4,8] etc.). Probably it was pronounced like *chrēstos* (good) and that is why Gentile unbelievers confused Chrestus (the Good) with Christ and Christian (q.v.).

In secular Greek *christos* is a verbal adjective meaning, 'to be used as an ointment'; it was also 'ointment' itself. Prometheus, commending his own resourcefulness, prided himself that there was no food, 'ointment', or medicine, 'until I showed them how to mix soothing remedies'.[33] In Euripides Phaedra asks, 'Is this charm of thine a *salve* or a drink?'[34]

In Biblical Greek *Christos* renders the Hebrew *māshîah* and the Aramaic m^eshîhâ (anointed) which concerned the Messiah of Jews and Christians. Only St. John gives the transliterated form, *Messias* (Jn 1[41] 4[25]). The Biblical *Christos* differs in sense from the classical

– it is 'Anointed,' not ointment. Jesus uses it in the new sense, when He asks, 'How say the scribes that *Christos* is the son of David?' (Mk 12^{35}) and warns that many imposters shall appear under the name *Christos* at His Coming (Mt 24^5; Mk 13^{21}). His own disciples belong to *Christos* (Mk 9^{41}), their Master (Mt 23^{10}).

The early brethren devoted a full title of *Kurios Iēsous Christos* (Lord Jesus Christ) to One whom God made both *Kurios* (lord) and *Christos* (Messiah): Act 2^{36}; 1 Co 8^6. When the phrase 'Christ Jesus' is used the main emphasis is rather upon the glorified Christ than upon the historical earthly Figure, but by the time of St. Ignatius there is little difference between 'in Jesus Christ' and 'in Christ Jesus'.^{35}

CHRISTIAN

χριστιανός

A new coinage, the name *Christianos* was given to the disciples in Antioch (Act 11^{26}) as early as AD 44. It is generally assumed that disciples were so nicknamed by the people of Antioch or by the Roman governor's staff when the brethren were first registered under their legal name.^{36} However, E. J. Bickerman^{37} reasoned that the correct meaning of *chrēmatizō* (to call) in this context is 'to style oneself'. He quoted Patristic works for the verb's meaning, and so St. Luke is saying that at Antioch the disciples themselves started to take on the style of 'Christians' – not, 'they were called Christians'.

The weakness of Bickerman's ingenious argument is that *chrē-matizō*, as he admitted, *can* mean to bear a name as well as to adopt a title. 'Why not, then, in Acts xi.26?'^{38}

The Latin sound of the word *Christianos* need not imply that the nickname, if such it was, arose at Rome as some suppose rather than in Antioch. It does have a Latin termination meaning 'belonging to', but the termination was common enough in Greek words of the period,^{39} and so in common parlance the Christians are those who 'belong to Christ'. On the other hand, we may suppose that 'the Greek-speaking disciples of Antioch adopted the word because they regarded themselves as those who were anointed, as Jesus had been, with the Holy Spirit in the latter days'.^{40} That is to say, *Christianos* was derived from *chriō* (to anoint), like the noun 'Christ'. Certainly, St. Paul says, 'God has *anointed* us' (2 Co 1^{21}).

Whatever its meaning, St. Luke readily took the new word into his vocabulary. No doubt it significantly marked the flight of the fledgeling religion from the Jewish nest, one important stage of which was accomplished at Antioch. To be called 'Christians' opened a chapter in the believers' history.

At Caesarea, however, king Agrippa scornfully utters the word 'Christian' when he is commenting upon St. Paul's defence (Act 26[28]). Paul himself avoids it, both in his defence and in the epistles, having a preference for 'believer' or 'brother' or 'saint'.

For St. Peter, 'Christian' was a generic term for those in Christ, and perhaps it was associated with what their persecutors call them, especially when he writes of 'suffering as a Christian' (1 Pet 4[16]). Mommsen and Ramsay quite properly insisted that never were Christians punished merely for *flagitia* but always for the 'name'.[41] As soon as the name was known it became punishable, and it was not very long before Christians ceased to have the advantage of being passed for Jews.

Very soon it was obvious that they were in conflict with Jews. They had not accepted circumcision and the authorities could not fail to recognize the new sect as falling outside the protection accorded to Jews. 2 Ti 3[12] would indicate that all Christians, even if they commit no *flagitia*, will automatically endure persecution. The 'name' is enough.

Tacitus[42] has the Latin version of the Greek word about AD 64 and says that Christ was the origin of it. At the same period Suetonius, too, has the Latin name, *Christiani*.[43] The apparent occurrence of the name in an inscription at Pompeii, however, is not to be relied upon,[44] and the word in Josephus was rejected by his editor, Niese, as an interpolation.[45]

Mattingly has argued that the Greco-Syrian population of Antioch coined the name, modelling it on the term *Augustiani*, the para-military supporters of Nero who adulated him and accompanied him everywhere.[46] The witty Antiochenes felt that the disciples of Jesus were ludicrously like the *Augustiani* in their fanatical devotion to their Master, and by this new title they ridiculed both groups at once. 'Christ also has His claque at Antioch!' they were intending to say (p. 31). If so, it could not have happened before AD 59–60. Mattingly ingeniously suggested that in AD 60 Herod Agrippa visited Antioch and heard the nickname with which he later taunted Paul at his trial before Festus. That is a convincing part of Mattingly's thesis. From Antioch the name would pass to Rome and be current there where numbers of Christians lived. When Nero, therefore, made them his scapegoat for the fire at Rome he may have been venting his personal spite and exasperation at the thought of the miserable *Christiani* being given a similar name to that of his own élite *Augustiani*. 'Such innuendos', claimed Mattingly, 'would give Nero's temper extra edge, when he championed good order and morality' (p. 36). Nero's was indeed a personal and transient persecution, the first profound clash of the *nomen Christi* with the *nomen Augusti*, foreshadowing the later bitter conflicts of loyalties in the Empire.

Strangely, apart from St. Luke and St. Peter, every Church writer before Trajan's reign (AD c.112) follows St. Paul in avoiding the title. St. Clement lacks it and among the apostolic Fathers only St. Ignatius has it. The Church had other names for her members – *pisteuontes* and *pistoi* (believers), *adelphoi* (brethren), *mathētai* (disciples), *hagioi* (saints), *eklektoi* (elect), *hodos* (the Way). The Jews called them *Nazōraioi* (Nazarenes) and 'this sect' *(hairesis)*.

Despite Bickerman, 'Christian' may at first have been a contemptuous epithet, for to be persecuted as a Christian was to be treated as a criminal (1 Pet 4[16]). Possibly the name which was said to provoke blasphemy (Jas 2[7]) was that of 'Christian'. Not until the time of St. Ignatius were believers quite resigned to its use among themselves.[47]

The spelling of Christ and Christian, especially in Greek inscriptions, is often enough with the long ē, viz. *Chrēstos* and *Chrēstianos*, and the first hand of the Greek Bible codex, Sinaiticus, has *Chrēstianos*. Some early Fathers rejoiced in the connection of Chrēst and Christ, seeing that *chrēstos* and *chrēstotēs* denote in Greek the virtue of 'kindness'.

CHURCH

ἐκκλησία

From heaven He came and sought her
To be His holy Bride;
With His own blood He bought her
And for her life He died.

Ekklēsia is a singularly vital word, and the reasons for its particular choice are matters of interest and controversy.

The secular meaning is preserved even in the NT (Act 19[32, 39, 41]) where it indicates an invited concourse of people, whether organized tradesmen or citizens in a regularly convened conclave.

Among the Greeks *ekklēsia* was an assembly of all the townsfolk of Samos.[48] Sthlenelaidas put the vote to the *ekklēsia* of the Spartans,[49] and at Athens in classical times the parliament of all the citizens, summoned for law-making, was known as the *ekklēsia*. After the second invasion by the Peloponnesians, the people of Athens found fault with the great leader Pericles, who at once declared, 'I have called an *ekklēsia* for the purpose of evoking your memory upon certain points.'[50] From Andocides we learn that a public *ekklēsia*, a gathering, was held for the generals due to embark for Sicily.[51]

It was in St. Luke's earlier years as a Christian, while he was writing the diary which is thought to have been incorporated in the complete edition of Acts, that he used the word *ekklēsia* in the secular way to which he was accustomed (Act 19, above). I presume that his language subsequently suffered a change in the direction of a new dialect, in which Christians had made *ekklēsia* a special name for the believing brotherhood.

They contemplated it in two new ways.

Firstly, *ekklēsia* was for them the whole redeemed fellowship in heaven and earth – the word we render 'Church' (Mt 16^{18}; 1 Co 12^{28}) – persecuted by Saul (1 Co 15^9; Gal 1^{13}), the Body and fullness of Christ (Eph 1^{22}), purchased with His blood (Act 20^{28}), the House of God, pillar and ground of the Truth (1 Ti 3^{15}), the Assembly of the firstborn (Heb 12^{23}), the People of God in the unity of the Body of Christ. Our Lord says to Peter in the context of the *ekklēsia*, 'I will give thee the keys of the Kingdom,' implying a significant connection between Church and Kingdom. There is no wonder if St. Augustine and others identified the Kingdom with the Church, and the Church is in a sense the visible expression of the Kingdom of God. Although we ought not to apply directly to the Church all that Jesus said about the Kingdom, His teaching on discipleship touching the Kingdom is, of course, relevant also for the Church.[52]

Secondly, *ekklēsia* is realized in its local assemblies of believers (Mt 18^{17}), 'the churches of Christ' (Ro 16^{16}), such as 'the church which was at Jerusalem' (Act $8^{1,3}$), the churches in Syria and Cilicia (15^{41}), the church 'at Cenchrea' (Ro 16^1), or in the house of Priscilla ($16^{15,19}$), or in the house of Nymphas (Col 4^{15}), 'all the churches' and 'every church' (1 Co 4^{17} 7^{17} 14^{33}). Local assemblies of brethren are indicated by the further expression, 'when ye come together in the church' (1 Co 11^{18}), and by phrases which concern speaking and refraining from speaking 'in the church' (1 Co $14^{19,34f.}$). The conception of the house-church was a vital factor in first-century Christian history, assisting in the mental cleavage from Judaism before the break itself came, and helping to Christianize whole family groups. Partly it explains too the proneness of the apostolic Church to make divisions and take stances and it explains how well-to-do families were able to gain an initiative within a pilgrim Church. It reveals a situation in which leaders could arise to succeed them of the apostolic generation.[53]

Early Christians chose *ekklēsia* to express both the local and the universal concept. In making the term their own they did not necessarily have a LXX pattern in mind. It has been shown that in late Jewish books, such as the OT apocrypha, *ekklēsia* does not express anything so ideal as a holy community called to salvation. Schrage has suggested that Christians avoided *sunagōgē* (assembly) and preferred *ekklēsia*, not because they followed the LXX (for there *qāhāl* is often rendered by *sunagōgē*) but because in contemporary Judaism *sunagōgē* symbolized attachment to the *Tôrâ* and its traditions. *Ekklēsia*, on the other hand, was free to denote a fresh manifestation of the Holy Spirit and a break with the Jewish past and with the old Law.[54]

Sometimes in Church history Christian congregations have been known as 'synagogues' but very soon indeed the word 'synagogue' was confined almost exclusively to Jewish assemblies and the word 'churches' to Christian assemblies. See the article, 'Synagogue'.

Burton had already suggested that in the Greek-speaking world where Jewish congregations existed Christians found it necessary to distinguish their own congregation from Jewish ones much more boldly than from civil assemblies with which they were not likely to be confused. So Christians would reject the term *sunagōgē* and welcome *ekklēsia*, especially as the Jews had already discarded it.[55]

At all events there is no doubt that *ekklēsia* had indicated the *qāhāl*, the assembly of the People of God of the old Dispensation in parts of the LXX, and Christian readers of the Bible, seeing themselves as true Israel, made the term their own. So it happens that sometimes in the NT, as in the Greek Bible, *ekklēsia* signifies the *qāhāl* (congregation) of old Israelites assembled for a religious purpose, the ancient Church (Deut 4[10] 23[2] 31[30] etc.; Act 7[38]; Heb 2[12]). More often, however, it is the Church, which began at Pentecost and is conceived as the real successor of the ancient Church.

It should be observed how Christians avoided the cultic words, *thiasos, eranos, sunodos, sullogos*, etc., and preferred instead to fill a secular term with their own peculiar meaning,[56] making the term sacred for ever afterwards.

Christian Scriptures assure us that the Church is not confined in scope to this present earth and indeed the Church herself through all her history has believed that the larger part of her membership is in the unseen world. The true allegiance of believers is in heaven although they must reside here for a season. Earthly life is not the end but it provokes more immediate interest and the Church is constantly moved to make life more pleasant and fair and to reform man's society. To do so is not among her deliberate aims and such reforms as the Church witnesses are achieved incidentally – they are a by-product of her spiritual life.[57] St. Paul and the Seer assure us that the Church's destiny is not to be realized within the bounds of temporal society. At last, the Church will prove to be co-extensive with all humanity, but we have no reason to expect that the consummation happens upon this old earth nor evolves by any natural process. God's transcendent judgment, His mercy and grace, must achieve it.

CIRCUMCISION

ἀπερίτμητος: ἀκροβυστία: περιτομή: περιτέμνω

The first two words (aperitmētos, akrobustia) mean uncircumcised and uncircumcision, the latter two (peritomē, peritemnō) mean circumcision and to circumcise. All of them are rare in secular Greek and came into prominence only in the Biblical language. Indeed, the negative word, aperitmētos (uncircumcised), is a creation of the LXX.[58] Deissmann was prepared to concede that it was coined by Greek-speaking Jews of Alexandria to express contempt for Gentiles (BS p. 153), and the word is sometimes used in the papyri concerning the Egyptians. We learn from St. Justin that the scornful epithet was later thrown also at Christians (Dial. CXXIII 1).

Akrobustia (uncircumcision) is exclusively Biblical and ecclesiastical (Bauer col. 60). Despite its occurrence in Philo,[59] it would appear to be a Biblical creation,[60] through literal reproduction of the Hebrew 'orlâ (foreskin):[61] that which the Israelites were required to remove from the male child, Abraham being ninety-nine years old when he was circumcised in the flesh of his foreskin.

Such is the meaning in the NT – 'thou wentest in to men who have the foreskin' (Act 11[3]) – but usually akrobustia has the metaphorical meaning, 'uncircumcision' or simply 'Gentiles', and not 'foreskin', and it would seem to be St. Paul who has changed the meaning (Ro 2[25.27] 3[30] 4[9f., 12]; 1 Co 7[18f]; Gal 2[7] 5[6]; Eph 2[11]). St. Paul was accepted as preacher of the Gospel of akrobustia (i.e. the Gentiles), and St. Peter as preacher of the Gospel of peritomē (the Jews).

The third word, peritomē, used by secular writers, still has the Jewish sense. Regarding Moses and his people Strabo mentions peritomē (circumcision) and other observances of the kind (XVI 2.37). The verb peritemnō is to clip round, 'cutting round the head by the ears',[62] but usually to circumcise.[63] Herodotus notes that the Colchians and Egyptians and Ethiopians are the only nations that have from the first 'practised circumcision' (II 104), and Diodorus Siculus notes that the Colchians and the Jews have a long-established custom to circumcise their male infants (I 28).

71

Undoubtedly, Christian inventiveness was at work on the meaning of *peritomē*, for it ceases to be circumcision literally and is now a special term signifying 'Jewish Christians' in general. They of the *peritomē* (the Jewish Christian party) contended with Peter (Act 10[45] 11[2]) and alarmed him at Antioch (Gal 2[12]). Some of Paul's fellow-workers were of the *peritomē* (Col 4[11]) and some Jewish Christian heretics are denominated 'they of the *peritomē*' (Tit 1[10]).

Christian inventiveness added a quite new kind of *peritomē* – that made without hands, a *peritomē* of the heart, meaning people who worship God in the Spirit (Ro 2[29]; Ph 3[3]; Col 2[11]). The only valid *peritomē* is that of the heart (Barn. 9[1-9]). 'God has declared that true *peritomē* was not in the flesh' (Barn. 9[4]). Conversely, St. Stephen charges his judges with being *aperitmētoi* (uncircumcised) in hearts and ears (Act 7[51]).

COARSE JESTING

εὐτραπελία

Christians have given *eutrapelia* a bad sense.

Secular Greek. The word is innocent of a specially bad sense. It is wit or wittiness.[64] The young aped their elders in Plato's day and vied with them in speech and action, while the not so young, accommodating themselves, were full of *eutrapelia* and graciousness, imitating the young for fear of being disagreeable and authoritative.[65]

Isocrates defines the adjective (*eutrapelos*, turning well, nimble-minded) as 'those who had a turn for jesting' – wits, indeed.[66] In one of the best definitions Aristotle clarified the adjective in this way: 'Those who jest with good taste are called *eutrapeloi*,'[67] and there is his cynical defining of wit as 'cultured insolence' *(pepaideumenē hubris)*.[68]

A historian of Julius Caesar's vintage told how a certain Dionysius forgave a man's bold humour because joking took the edge off the censure and raised a smile at the *eutrapelia* (ready wit) of the words.[69]

Christian Greek. For Christians, on the contrary, *eutrapelia* evokes a sin of worldliness, the **coarse jesting** which, like idolatry and covetousness, may sadly characterize the saints on their wayfaring scene. It is linked with filthiness and foolish talking as not being 'convenient' for the faithful. 'Let it not be once named among you, as becometh saints' (Eph 5[4]). The 'jesting' of AV and RV is probably not forceful enough in modern English which requires something like 'levity' (RSV) or 'scurrilous talk' (Moffatt). The Christian word denotes something worse than 'flippant talk' (NEB) and 'smartness in talk' (Knox) and 'jokes' (Jerusalem Bible), something nearer to 'suggestive language' (BFBS).

COMFORTER DIVINE

παράκλητος: παράκλησις: παρακαλέω

The three words in the Christian language no longer refer to an Advocate in a law-court, or merely to a Helper, but now have the definition of divine consolation – 'a distinctive biblical meaning'.[70] *Paraklētos* is the Comforter, *paraklēsis* is comfort, and *parakalō* is to comfort. They all speak of divine refreshment.

Secular Greek. Philo preserves a well-recognized meaning of *paraklētos* when he reports Joseph as saying to his brethren, 'I grant you free forgiveness ... you need no other *intercessor*.'[71] Philo speaks of the Son in the same way as a *paraklētos*.[72] In secular Greek *paraklētos* was especially an advocate, a barrister,[73] but the word might denote an adviser in general. In the Jewish Talmud it becomes a loan word *(pᵉraqlît)* in the secular sense of 'advocate' and 'intercessor' when it is said, 'He that does a good deed, acquires an advocate for himself.'[74]

Paraklēsis was a summons, intreaty or exhortation. For instance, Thucydides uses the word for an 'appeal' for help to the Athenians by the Chalcedic people,[75] and Strabo for the appeal which he makes to his readers not to blame him for wordiness.[76] In classical Greek the verb *parakalō* is to 'call in' as an adviser.[77]

The Biblical meaning, 'consolation', does not appear in the secular language; nevertheless, under the word *paraklēsis* Bauer (1125) brings forward Epictetus and Dio Chrysostom[78] as evidence for 'comfort' (Trost) in secular Greek. The passages which Bauer cites will not bear his construction. Epictetus writes concerning an 'invitation', not *consolation*, of a physician and a philosopher to attend the consulting-room and the lecture, and the verb *parakalō* is used in the same way. In the passage which Bauer cites from Dio, Charidemus upon his deathbed dictates 'an address for our *paraklēsis*', and when we read this address we find it to be rather an 'exhortation' than a consolation. *Zuspruch* is possible in German, but not if we render it 'consolation', as Arndt–Gingrich do.

In a like dubious way, Plutarch[79] is cited for the verb's meaning, *ermuntern, zusprechen, trösten* (comfort, encourage, cheer up), giving the impression that *trösten* (console) was a secular meaning. That is not so. In Plutarch's passage at least, if *parakalō* is 'consolation' at all, it is a philosophical kind of refreshment: the dying emperor 'exhorts' his young nephew 'to be brave and not to fear Vitellius'. I am bound to agree with Otto Schmitz that in the very few instances where the verb and noun imply consolation in ordinary Greek, the consolation is at the level of exhortation or encouragement to those who sorrow.[80] Dr. Kingsley Barrett too is justified when he claims that *parakalō* and *paraklēsis* are used by St. John in a sense 'which seems to have little or no basis in Greek that is independent of the Hebrew Bible; they refer to consolation, and in particular to the consolation to be expected in the messianic age'.[81]

My contention will be that 'consolation' is a new meaning in the Bible. Nevertheless, it is very generally urged that *paraklētos* on the lips of Jesus does not mean Comforter. Hatch was content to have established from Philo that its meaning is Helper, both at court and in a wider sense, and was confident that Philo's meaning lay behind its use by St. John.[82] Field still welcomed the rendering, 'Comforter,' on the ground of long familiarity, but felt that the arguments for 'Advocate' were stronger (pp. 102f). A. E. Brooke, too, was sure that 'Advocate' was the most satisfactory translation in both the gospel and epistle of St. John, and would not believe that there was authority for the meaning, 'Comforter,' in either the sense of strengthener or that of consoler.[83] Westcott, too, affirmed that 'comfort' was no more than a secondary meaning of the words, merely an isolation of one function of the advocate who only incidentally 'comforts' when he is 'called in to help'. The original meaning (advocate), urged the bishop, is confirmed by the form of the word itself and by its secular usage.[84]

For Dr. Norman Snaith, comfort and sorrow do not appear very prominently in the concept and he suggests that Convincer is the more suitable rendering of *Paraklētos*. Christ convinces men of the things of God and accomplishes in them a change of heart.[85] Howard too advocated what amounts to the secular sense and he put it very neatly: in the epistle the *Paraklētos* is the 'friend *at* court', One who has been called to the side of another, while in the gospel of St. John He is the 'friend *from* court', the Holy Spirit given in Christ's stead to help believers and to bring them to God; in both places He is an intercessor, as the word indicates in secular Greek.[86]

All these are honoured names in the Bible's exegesis and one is reluctant to adhere obstinately to the rendering of *Paraklētos* by Comforter, as in AV and RV, but I find much force in Dr. Kingsley Barrett's remark that the early Christians chose *parakalō* and *paraklēsis* deliberately when other words might have been chosen to describe their preaching. The words 'were particularly appropriate because to those who knew the Old Testament in Greek they suggested the messianic consolation which was the central theme of the preaching'.[87]

It must be conceded forthwith that sometimes the Christian context requires the secular meaning of *paraklēsis* ('exhortation' in Heb 12[5] 13[22]) and of *paraklētos* ('advocate' or 'intercessor' in Barn. 20[2]; 1 Jn 2[1]; 2 Clem 6[9]). 'We have', urges St. John, 'an *Intercessor* with the Father', and, 'Who', asks the Alexandrian homilist, 'shall be our *intercessor*, if we are not found possessed with holiness?' In the Testament of Solomon, written by a Jew in the Christian era, there is still vacillation between the secular and Biblical meanings of *paraklēsis*, for now it is 'entreaty' (D II 5), and now 'comfort' (IV 11). St. Luke uses *parakalō* in the secular sense when Paul 'summoned' the Roman Jews (Act 28[20]), and St. Matthew too (8[5] 'a centurion beseeching Him').

Biblical Greek. In the Bible, however, these Greek words bear the additional sense of 'comfort', quite distinct from exhortation, invitation, and appeal. 'Blessed are they that mourn,' says Jesus, 'for they shall be *comforted*' (Mt 5[4]). Here the verb is *parakalō* and it cannot bear the secular meaning for it represents the consolation that the mourner needs, the wiping away of tears. It is what God gives to those in tribulation. Both *parakalō* and *paraklēsis* are used in that tremendous passage where St. Paul opens up the wealth of the 'comfort' which God can give, and we in turn can bestow on other sufferers (2 Co 1[3-5]).

The innovation first appears in the LXX where the words render the Hebrew *nḥm* stem, and *parakalō* is used sixteen times for Niphal and Hithpael of that verb. All Jacob's sons and daughters came to '*comfort* him, but he could not be *comforted*' (Gen 37[35]). *Mᵉnaḥēm* was a name for the Messiah in Judaism although it cannot be found before the fourth century.[88] A semantic survey of the Hebrew root leads to the conclusion that the basic meaning of *nḥm* is 'comfort, console'. It is to comfort *out of* sorrow, thinks Dr. Norman Snaith, rather than to comfort *in* sorrow, and the idea of sorrow should not, he thinks, be assumed unless the context demands it.[89] Yet the basic meaning is consolation and, by metonymy, nominal derivatives of *nḥm* may take also the meaning, 'compassion', denoting the emotional pain or sorrow felt by a comforter through sympathy with a mourner.[90]

Job acknowledges the consolation (*paraklēsis*) given by his friends (21[2]), who are incidentally called 'Job's *paraklētoi*,' his comforters, in the Greek versions of Aquila and Theodotion (16[2]). The psalmist delights in divine solace (*paraklēsis*) which refreshed his soul in the midst of sorrows (93(94)[19]). Isaiah too knows the sweetness: God's promises to the penitent include the restoration of comforts (57[18]), and Isaiah sings of the restored Jerusalem which to Christians is a type of the Church. 'Rejoice ... all ye that love her ... that ye may suck and be satisfied with the breasts of her *consolations*' (66[10f.]). He has the phrase, 'to comfort all who mourn' (61[2]). In Isaiah the 'consolation' is that which is to be expected in the Messianic age and so also in the NT where the rich are said already to have received their 'comfort'. St. Luke affirms that the devout priest was awaiting this 'consolation' when there was brought to him that Infant who later promised that the rich have already received their 'consolation' (Lk 2[25] 6[24]), and he writes of 'the consolation of the Holy Ghost' the Comforter (Act 9[31]).

> *O Source of uncreated heat,*
> *The Father's promised Paraclete.*

In Christian Greek, therefore, *paraklēsis* and *paraklētos* have become attached to Christ and to the Holy Ghost and, in the gospel but not perhaps in the epistles of St. John, *paraklētos* seems from the context to have the new connotation of 'comforter' (14[16, 26] 15[26] 16[7]). In that case, although in the secular language the formation of the word – the ending -*tos* – is passive, strictly speaking, denoting one who *is called* to the side rather than one who actively comforts or exhorts, the old rules no longer apply in Biblical Greek. Prof. J. G. Davies, who very carefully analysed the OT contexts of *parakalō*, concludes that despite the passive form of *paraklētos* St. John, who places the words in the same OT complex of contexts, has given to the word an active significance, and so he concludes that its primary meaning now is Comforter.[91] I note that the Johannine contexts speak of fear, trouble and bereavement (14[27] 16[17]). What more likely, therefore, than that the *Paraklētos* is the Comforter? *Paraklētos* meant Comforter for St. Chrysostom (*Hom. in Joh.* 75). 'He is called *Paraklētos*,' says St. Cyril, 'because He consoles and helps our infirmity.'[92] It was the way the Greek Fathers understood the word. Origen understood *Paraklētos* as Consoler, except in 1 John where it is 'intercessor'.[93] Wycliffe and Tyndale observed the distinction in their Bibles, rendering *Paraklētos* in the gospel by Comforter, but perhaps in the strictly etymological sense of Strengthener, and in 1 John by Advocate. Here they were following what they took to be the distinction in the Vulgate. At any rate, 'the dear old word', Comforter, as Schaff called it, may be right after all (Field p. 103, n. 1). In a part of the Acts of John (of the 3rd c.?), found in an isolated papyrus fragment,[94] Jesus is called *Paraklētos* and here it seems to mean Comforter, as Kingsley Barrett observes.[95]

We should note incidentally that the 'Spirit of Truth' is mentioned closely with the *Paraklētos* (14[17]), and throughout his book O. Betz[96] has shown that in writings from Qumrân the 'Spirit of Truth' struggles on Michael's side against Belial. The literary heritage of Jewish converts to Christianity included strains of Judaism such as we find in the Dead Sea Scrolls, influencing some groups of Jews and Christians more than others, especially in the spheres of angelology, soteriology and eschatology.[97] Too much is explained by an appeal to Qumrân and much of this extensive literature is doubtless not relevant for Christian exegesis.[98] However, it should be recalled that the Spirit of Truth enables the Teacher of Righteousness to explain the words of the prophets and to prophesy, just as the Christian *Paraklētos* abides with the disciples for ever and brings to their remembrance whatever Jesus had said (Jn 14[16, 26]). There is evidently a parallel between the late Jewish and early Christian *paraklētos*, and though Michael does not appear in the gospel of St. John, he does figure in another Johannine book in a struggle against the dragon (Rev 12[7]), a parallel figure to Belial who struggles on Michael's side in the Qumrân texts.

Paraklēsis is **consolation** in St. Paul's vocabulary, and the comfort is not exclusively for the future. God bestows it now and the Scriptures bring it now (Ro 15[4f.]). The Father of mercies **comforts** us in our tribulations to enable us to **comfort** our brethren, for He is the God of all *paraklēsis*. Salvation and **consolation** are but different sides of the coin: both have much to do with endurance of sufferings on the journey home. 'As ye are partakers of the sufferings, so shall ye be also of the **consolation** at the End' (2 Co 1[3-7]). Believers share together **comfort** in their tribulations. St. Paul is **comforted** by their **comfort** (2 Co 7[4, 7, 13]). He has **consolation** in Philemon's love (7) and can wish no richer blessing on the Thessalonians than that they may know God's everlasting **consolation** with which to comfort their hearts (2 Th 2[16]).

AV often renders *paraklēsis* by 'exhortation', and as to 1 Th 2[3], St. Paul's 'exhortation' (preaching) would seem from the context to be what is meant. 'We were bold to speak to you the Gospel of God with much contention.' However, after a careful investigation one may conclude[99] that St. Paul describes the Gospel as 'consolation' because of the struggle in which the preaching of the Gospel takes place, both for preacher and hearer. The whole epistle is designed to console in trouble and it is very likely that *paraklēsis* (2[3]) means 'consolation' rather than 'admonition'.[100]

The archangel bestows God's **comfort** upon Abraham during an awesome journey (T. Abr 86[4]). This blessedness is expressed by *paraklēsis* despite the consideration that from the pagan point of view there was already a religious word available *(eudaimonia)*. As Trench (p. 18) observed, there was a good Christian reason why the secular word must be rejected. The root of the secular word (i.e. *daimōn*) involved the undesirable concept of polytheism, and so Christians carefully avoid it in favour of *paraklēsis*.

COMPASSION

σπλάγχνα: σπλαγχνίζομαι: εὔσπλαγχνος: πολύσπλαγχνος

The new Jewish sense represents an important contribution to the Greek language.

Compassion (the noun). In secular Greek *splagchna* (plural) signified the 'viscera', the inward parts, as indeed sometimes in the Bible (e.g. Act 1[18]), but in the sacred language Semitic influence plays its part. The corresponding Hebrew word *(raḥam)* had not only the physical meaning of inwards, as in Greek, but also the sense of tender emotions of kindness and pity, the 'affections'. In the NT *splagchna* is the 'tender mercy' of our God (Lk 1[78]), the affection which St. Paul yearns for at Corinth (2 Co 6[12]), the love of St. Titus for the brethren (7[15]), and the 'heart of compassion' which emblazons God's elect (Col 3[12]; Ph 2[1]; Phm 7, 12, 20; 1 Jn 3[17]).

It is cited by the Apostle as 'the *compassion* of Jesus Christ' (Ph 1[8]) and by St. Ignatius as 'the tender sympathy' which we have in Christ Jesus (I. Philad. 10[1]), that is, 'Christian sympathy' (Lightfoot). St. Clement bids us store up His words carefully in our 'affections' (plural) and (in the singular) he refers *splagchnon* to the Father's compassion for those who reverence Him (1 Clem 2[1] 23[1]). The plural noun is a marked virtue of Abraham and others in the Testament of Abraham (80[7] 82[20] 83[2]).

This is something new in Greek. Even in the classical poets, though the words represent the 'heart' of a man as opposed to his external aspect,[101] the feelings are exclusively the rougher emotions of anger and fear[102] – the 'pang and pulse of groin and *gut*', as Vellacott has it.[103] It is the disquieted bosom.[104] It is 'wrath'.[105] It is the vehement 'heart' of youth.[106]

Perhaps on occasion the secular papyri have the compassionate sense for *splagchna*,[107] and the meaning may have reached the vernacular by way of Jewish Hellenistic influence.[108] The LXX had so used the word (e.g. Pr 12[10]), and in this wise also the versions of Aquila, Symmachus and Theodotion (e.g. Işai 63[15]; Am 1[11]), and the words completely replace the LXX words *oiktirmos, oikteirō*, and *oiktirmōn*, to render the Hebrew *rḥm* stem. The new rendering is the immediate background of NT usage.[109] That is why the common LXX words, *oiktirmos*, etc., are notably rare in the NT and why *splagchna*, etc., in early Christian writings express so clearly the sense of the Hebrew root *raham*.

To have compassion (the verb). The noun acquired new meaning, but the verb, *splagchnizomai*, was altogether a fresh coinage in Biblical Greek, and Lightfoot suggested that it arose perhaps in the Dispersion (op. cit.). The meaning in the LXX is quite literal, not 'to pity', but to eat the entrails (NEB): Pr 17⁵A; 2 Mac 6⁸. However, the new Christian meaning is found in other Jewish literature: T XII P Zeb 4² 7² etc. T. Abr 116³¹ᶠ. The new meaning is common in the gospels, especially for the compassion of Jesus, and in Church writers. Hermas has *splagchnizomai* when the Lord is said to show mercy (*Sim*. VII 4, VIII 6.3, IX 14.3, VIII 11.1). Symmachus uses it in his translation to express the Ziphites' sympathy with Saul (1 Km 23²¹), and in Ezek 24²¹ it is uncertain what it renders. From Jewish Greek the verb later came into secular circulation.¹¹⁰

Compassionate (the adjectives). Our third word, *eusplagchnos*, was a medical term applying literally to the stomach.¹¹¹ It acquired the moral connotation of tenderness in Jewish Greek and was a quality of the Lord most High which induced man's repentance (Prayer of Manasseh 6, T. Zeb 9⁷) and it describes also the good man Joseph (T. Sim 4⁴). The adjective occurs in the Gnostic magical papyrus of Leiden,¹¹² but as H. Köster observes, the magical papyrus is not a secular witness. It does not fall outside the sphere of Jewish and Christian Greek, and we should note the OT name of God within it. So although *eusplagchnos* is here used as a divine predicate, it is still as Jewish as in the Prayer of Manasseh and the magic stone which it qualifies represents the OT deity. It is evident that the word belongs to post-Christian Jewish Greek. In earlier Jewish Greek *eleēmōn* denoted the divine mercy, and by the time of the NT *eusplagchnos* was used as well.¹¹³

The word qualifies not only the Deity. Christian believers should be **tender-hearted** too, loving and forgiving one another (Eph 4³²). They must be **compassionate** as brethren (1 Pet 3⁸). A technical term has therefore been taken away from the surgery to become a peculiarly Christian virtue. The apostolic Fathers use it of God (1 Clem 29¹) but mainly of Christian compassion (1 Clem 54¹). Deacons and presbyters in particular must be **compassionate** (Pol. ad Phil 5² 6¹).

From the spheres of Jewish and Christian Greek the word came into the mainstream of the language,¹¹⁴ and in modern times retains the Biblical meaning – compassionate, merciful, pitiful, clement.

Our last word, *polusplagchnos*, is a coinage of Christian Greek made from the noun. 'The Lord is **very pitiful** and of tender mercy.'

(Jas 5[11]). He is **compassionate** to His creation (Hermas *Mand.* IV 3.5). The Lord is **compassionate** and gives rest (Act. Thom. 119).

Biblical Greek has made a notable contribution in respect of these words. It should be noticed that the noun, *eusplagchnia*, is apparently 'courage' in one instance in earlier literature,[115] but this is not the Biblical meaning of the adjective. The Biblical sense of the words continued in the language right up to the present day.

We see that a Greek word for the internal organs was early felt as the seat of various emotions, but later it connotated especially pity and compassion because it was used in the LXX and NT to translate the Hebrew word 'bowels', and so in English too 'bowels' means 'pity'.[116]

CONCISION

κατατομή

In Greek *katatomē* was an incision, a notch or a groove,[117] or a certain part of a theatre,[118] or a 'face' of a rock.[119]

In the Biblical Greek version of Symmachus, however, *katatomē* stands for 'mutilation' of the hands in connection with the judgment of Moab (Jer 31(48)[37] 86, Syrohexapla), and in Christian Greek too it suggests a mutilation. In this word Christians preserve an ironic reference to circumcision by changing only one syllable of *peritomē* (*peri* becoming *kata*). The new word is a derogative term of contempt, a stronger word than *peritomē*, for *Judaizing Christians*.

By adopting the English word, 'concision', AV has found a satisfactory equivalent for the Greek simply by manipulating a similar word, as St. Paul had done. 'Beware of dogs, beware of evil workers, beware of the concision' – i.e. the Judaizing Christians! (Ph 3[2]) 'The incision-party', Moffatt rendered it. The Jerusalem Bible has: 'Watch out for the cutters'!

Lightfoot cites many curious manipulations of language of the same kind. Our ambassador in Madrid complained that he was sent to Pain (not Spain!) Leicester reported that the Queen's poor subjects in the Netherlands were no better than *abjects*.'[120] So St. Paul similarly complains that Jewish circumcision is a 'gashing' – a 'disfigurement' (Knox), a 'mutilation' (NEB). The Greek word is a contemptuous Christian pun on the word 'circumcision'.

αὐτοκατάκριτος

The adjective, *autokatakritos*, likely to have been coined by Christians in dispute with false teachers, is a new compound formed from older parts. It had possibly occurred in a fragment of Philo[121] in the phrase, '*self-condemned* by your conscience', but it has been conceded as a genuine Christian coinage (MM).

It may have been a useful term in Christian debate with fringe teachers and unbelievers, for Titus is counselled to reject 'a man that is an heretick after a first and second admonition, knowing that he that is such is subverted, and sinneth, being *autokatakritos* (condemned of himself).' Tit 3[10f].

St. Chrysostom has the same sense of the word,[122] speaking of Jewish unbelief. Irenaeus applies it to heretics. As many, he says, as separate from the Church to give heed to such old wives' fables, are truly self-condemned.[123] The heretic condemns himself in this way: he may no longer plead ignorance. What was once unenlightened error has now become sin in the face of the Church's faithful teaching. The heretic has judged himself by declining to listen.

CONFLICT
ἀγών

The new meaning of *agōn* in Christian Greek is quite unique. It is the Christian life.

Secular Greek. Even in the secular language the word had occasionally meant something more intense than a 'contest'. Polybius reported that the Sinopean envoys were in great *agōn* (dread) lest Mithridates undertake the siege of the city (IV 56.4).

Usually however in secular Greek *agōn* is a gathering to see the games, or the place of contest (Homer), or the Olympus games themselves,[124] or some smaller contest in particular – the *gumnikos, hippikos*, and *mousikos*[125] – and more generally, any struggle or battle.

Christian Greek. The Christian meaning is distinctive, for the word is predicated of the Christian life as an urgent concern with a heavenly prize in view, as adumbrated in the spiritual anxiety of Isaiah 7[13] (LXX), where the Hebrew *lā'â (Hiphil)* is rendered, 'to bring *weariness* (upon God and upon man)' – quoted by Justin Martyr.[126]

The new meaning appears frequently in St. Paul. He speaks of *agōn* (suffering) for Christ's sake (Ph 1[30]), of the *agōn* (opposition) attending the preaching of the Gospel at Thessalonica (1 Th 2[2]), and of the good *agōn* (fight) of faith (1 Ti 6[12]; 2 Ti 4[7]).

Agōn is the 'race' that is set before us, to be run patiently (Heb 12[1]), but something wider than a race, like the Latin *certamen* (strife, contest).[127]

St. Paul gives to *agōn* still deeper overtones of solicitude, remote from secular Greek, when he could wish that the Colossians appreciated the *agōn* he had for them though they had never met (Col 2[1]).

The apostolic Fathers sustain the new meaning of godly solicitude (1 Clem 2[4]) and warfare of the elect (7[1]). The theme of 2 Clement is that we must strive hard to be crowned. The *agōn* is still the good fight, the straight race, the spiritual conflict (7[1.3ff.]). It includes intercession for the saving of others (1 Clem 2[4]). It is the Christian life in general,[128] and even martyrdom,[129] while Justin Martyr urges Trypho to 'enter on this greatest of all *contests*', the Christian life (*Dial.* 142[2]). *Agōn* is an eager striving for knowledge of the perfect God, by which we obtain a more complete approval in the day of wrath.[130] It is what Bernard of Cluny meant by the 'battle' which we fight before we win the crown.

CONSECRATION (SEPARATION)

1. ἁγνισμός : ἁγνίζω : ἁγνός

The secular words, *hagnismos*, *hagnizō* and *hagnos*, express the new Christian concept of separation from the world with its sacrificial overtones.

Hagnismos is purification or expiation, and to make *hagnismos* is to make expiation;[131] it was a purification rite for the women's festivals.[132] In the LXX also the vow of *hagnismos* is the Nazirite vow (Num 6[5]), a mark of separation for God, and the water of *hagnismos* is the water of *niddhâ* (impurity), that is, the water to remove impurity. It represents the sprinkling of water which purified the Levite (Num 8[7]) to serve the Lord in separation from the children of Israel.

Hagnizō (to consecrate) involves the purifying of the dead by fire,[133] but outside the Bible it is confined almost to the poets. In the LXX it renders chiefly the Hebrew word for ceremonial cleansing (*qādhash*) and it kept the sense in Christian Greek.

Hagnos (consecrated) is a secular word for chaste and virginal, applied by Homer to the maiden goddess Artemis (e.g. *Odyssey* V 123). For Plato and Demosthenes it signifies a virgin,[134] and for

Plutarch it is 'chaste'.[135] In the LXX it signifies a rather different purity, that of metals refined in the fire (Ps 11(12)[6]), lasting and durable (Ps 18(19)[9]), a quality which has a moral fibre (Pr 15[16]), straight like a heart that is *hagnos* (Pr 20[9] 21[8]). A free Greek book still has the secular concept of virginity (4 Mac 18[7f.]).

Christian Greek. *Hagnismos* keeps the OT sense, the purification of men in the Temple (Act 21[26]) in a LXX phrase, 'the day of purification'. The epistle of Barnabas, however, spiritualizes it and uses it of the heart (8[3]).

The verb *hagnizō* in NT Greek represents ceremonial cleansing, purification for the passover (Jn 11[55]) and purification of a Jew visiting the Temple (Act 21[24, 26] 24[18]). It is also moral purification, making the heart right (Jas 4[8]), and the soul guiltless (1 Pet 1[22]). It is sacrificial separation from the world, undertaken by every Christian who is looking for our Lord's Coming (1 Jn 3[3]). In the Fathers it denotes cleansing from sins (Barn 5[1] 8[1]), and St. Ignatius retains the sacrificial idea of *hagnizō* when he says, 'I *devote* myself *as a sacrifice* to your church', and so confesses his commitment (I. Eph 8[1] – a commitment which he repeats in the phrase, 'My spirit *is offered up* (passive of *hagnizō*) for you' (I. Trall 13[3]). After mentioning His death on the cross St. Justin speaks of Christ *sanctifying* us by water (*Dial.* 86[6]). Clearly it is a sacrificial word, transformed and elevated by its Christian spiritual content.

The *parthenos* who is *hagnos* is thus the girl who has offered her purity as a sanctified offering (2 Co 11[2]) – a figure of the Church, the Bride espoused to Christ. In the same way, Timothy is to keep himself *hagnos* (consecrated): 1 Ti 5[22]. He must be ready to be offered as a sacrificial self-offering. The picture of Christian womanhood includes besides conjugal and motherly devotion, a sacrificial aspect – *hagnos* is one of the qualities – for wives are to be 'keepers at home ... obedient' (Ti 2[5]).

A high moral content is involved, of course, but essentially the concept realises Nazirite and Levite separation – chaste, but especially 'separated'.

2. ἁγιασμός: ἁγιάζω

The Biblical noun *hagiasmos* and the verb *hagiazō* involve the same idea. Both are likely to have been coined in Biblical Greek and, like the other words for 'consecration', are used in the LXX conspicuously to render the verb *qādhash* in its simplex, intensive and causative forms. The Hebrew stem has the quality of taboo from profane use, of setting apart for God's purposes.

In classical Greek there had been the like-sounding verb *hagizō* (to hallow, make sacred), but only a fresh coinage could offset the pagan associations. The new verb, *hagiazō*, rarely appears beyond the Bible, and then chiefly in Philo the Jew: God 'hallowed' the seventh Day (*Leg. All.* I 18).

So too *hagiasmos*, to which the nearest secular word is *hagismos* (an offering for the dead), is peculiar to Biblical and Church literature. Together with the versions of Aquila, Symmachus and Theodotion, the LXX renders the *qādhash* root by means of *hagiasmos*. It should be insisted that holiness or consecration was for the Hebrew a relationship with God which involved segregation from ritual uncleanness and from moral unworthiness. The same association has passed with *hagiasmos* into the Christian language of St. Peter, St. Paul and the writer to the Hebrews. It is clear from the contexts that they intend separation from immorality – from moral uncleanness, iniquity, from fornication, lust and fraud (Ro 6[19,22]; 1 Co 1[30]; 1 Th 4[3f,7]; 2 Th 2[13]; 1 Pet 1[2]). On that account it is well translated 'holiness' (AV 1 Ti 2[15]; Heb 12[14]).

St. Clement of Rome paired *hagiasmos* with temperance – the same idea as in the LXX where *hagiasmos* renders not only *qādhash* but also *nazîr*, one who was consecrated to God by a vow⁻ to abstain from intoxicants, among other things – urging his readers to do everything that pertains to *hagiasmos*, designating the 'called' and 'sanctified' (participle of *hagiazō*) by the will of God (1 Clem intr. 30[1] 35[2]). St. Ignatius reminds his readers that Paul was sanctified *(hagiazō)* and they too must be sanctified, in all things (I. Eph 2[2] 12[2]).

So *hagiasmos* and *hagiazō* are terms with sacred overtones throughout their extensive Christian use. As the Temple makes sacred the gold of its furnishings (Mt 23[17,19]), so a Christian may, by purging himself from secular involvement, become a vessel of great honour, sanctified and set apart for the Master's use (2 Ti 2[21]). This was so with Jesus who was sanctified by His father and was sent into the world without being 'of' the world[136] (Jn 10[36] 17[16]). He sanctified Himself (17[17,19]).

Hagiazō is a verb which expressed the setting apart of Aaron and his sons (Ex 29[21]), the separation of the Levites (Ex 19[22]; 2 Chr 5[11] 31[18]), and general refusal to be defiled (Lev 11[44]), besides qualifying the firstling males which have no blemish, else they cannot be sacrificed (Deut 15[19]). Field aptly rendered the words of Jesus, *Morti me devoveo* (p. 105). 'I sanctify myself.'

To set apart is the immanent idea in all the contexts, and sometimes washing is mentioned (1 Co 6[11]; Eph 5[26]). Even an unbelieving partner may be sanctified simply by living the same Christian life as the believing spouse (1 Co 7[14]). The sanctifying of the 'people' was accomplished by the blood of Jesus Who suffered 'without the gate'. We are therefore to go forth unto Him 'without the camp', bearing His reproach (Heb 13$^{12f.}$). Separation, and the reproach which it entails, is the way of sanctification, the turning from darkness to light (Act 26^{18}). Jeremiah knew this kind of separation and reproach. The verb *hagiazō* is applied to him who was set apart for a sacred duty (Jer 1^5). When Aaron and his sons were set apart as sacred priests, the word is *hagiazō* (Ex 28^{41}). It does not always imply literal and physical death, but both here and when the verb is applied to Jesus and His followers, there is the thought of 'death' to the world and to self. The altar is not far to seek (Jn 10^{36} 17^{17}).

To be sanctified 'wholly' involves separation, the abstaining from all appearance of evil (1 Th 5^{23}). Opposite ends of two poles are made prominent by the Seer: to be 'filthy' and its antithesis, to be 'sanctified' (Rev 22^{11}).

Selwyn has suggested that *hagiasmos* was a mark of the style of Silvanus, St. Peter's scribe, and certainly there is a parallel between 1 Pet 1^2 on the one hand and Ro 5–8 on the other. By St. Peter *hagiasmos* is said to be at the Spirit's instigation ('of' is subjective genitive) and election is said to take place in the sphere of *hagiasmos*, that is to say, in the Church after baptism; in the same way St. Paul's argument is that after justification comes baptism and then sanctification, the Spirit Himself helping our infirmities.

At all events, both sanctification and justification stem directly from the sacrificial death of Jesus. He sanctified the people with His own blood. When Hermas observed that we are 'justified and sanctified' from all wickedness, his phrase was not tautologous, for after the first ascent of salvation there must ensue the second, that of sanctification.

All three degrees of salvation may have been present to St. Clement's mind when he wrote of a three-fold operation upon those who love God, 'through whom Thou didst *instruct* us, didst *sanctify* us, didst *honour* us', i.e. justification, sanctification, and glorification (1 Clem 59^3).

3. ἁγνότης

Hagnotēs may be a peculiarly Christian word, coined by St. Paul, although it denotes an ethical virtue, joined with 'righteousness', on an Argos inscription of the second century (c. AD 175: IG IV 588.15). It is part of the Christian language, where it is 'purity' in contrast with lust,[137] but Hermas is faithful to the wording of St. Paul, who by *hagnotēs* meant the high standard of consecration and devoted simplicity to be expected in ministers. He set *hagnotēs* alongside other virtues and spiritual gifts – love, patience, and spiritual insight or *gnosis* (2 Co 6^6). The Corinthian believers must not be corrupted from sincerity and *hagnotēs* which were marks of the life 'in Christ' (2 Co 11[3]: a textual addition of major manuscripts, including Vaticanus). See also 'Sanctify'.

CORNER-FOUNDATION (STONE) OR, PEAK OF THE PYRAMID

ἀκρογωνιαῖος

This significant word has exercised the ingenuity of commentators. *Akrogōniaios* is a Biblical adjective describing a stone which was part of a building. What part, is not so clear. The word may well be an expedient of the LXX (see MM). It is, however, found in the Testament of Solomon to indicate the stone laid by the King at the 'head of the corner to complete the Temple' (22[7]).

The prefix *akro-* (topmost) was added by the Jews to the already existing Greek adjective, *gōniaios* (at the corner). In that way the translators of Isaiah rendered the Hebrew word for 'corner' (*pinnâ* Isai 28[16]), describing the stone which was a 'sure foundation' and which probably had reference to the future Messiah. Hooke, in a learned paper which examines the OT passages and stops short of 'the extraordinary transformation of images which centres in Christ' – 'another world altogether' – denies that any of the OT passages about the Stone, except those in Zechariah where Jerusalem is a 'burdensome Stone', have a definite messianic significance. The Stone, he would argue, is rather the symbol of Israel, chastened and humiliated and exalted by such heroes as the Maccabees to a key position in God's purposes.[138]

At any rate, Isaiah's Stone was said to be a sure foundation and its position was at the *pinnâ* (corner). On the other hand, the Peshitta Syriac version of Isaiah suggests by its rendering that the stone was not in the foundations but was 'head of the wall'.

Our adjective, *akrogōniaios*, appears nowhere else in the LXX but it is found in the Greek version of Symmachus to render 'chapter', a brass capital surmounting the pillars in Solomon's Temple (4 Km 25[17]), and the phrase *rôsh pinnâ* (headstone of the corner) in the Psalms. The adjective denotes the exalted destiny of the Stone, probably the Messiah, which the builders had refused (Ps 117(118)[22]).

St. Peter (and Barn 6[2]) quotes the LXX version of Isaiah and sees the precious *akrogōniaios* Stone in Sion as a figure of Christ in His Church (1 Pet 2[6]). St. Paul also may have the Isaiah passage in mind when he pictures all the saints bonded together in Christ, the *akrogōniaios* Stone (Eph 2[20]). But both writers could have in mind the Psalms passage also where Symmachus renders the Stone which the builders rejected and which had become the Head of the Corner, as *akrogōniaios*. In his very next verse St. Peter refers to the text in the Psalms and he reverts to the LXX version, using instead of *akrogōniaios* two separate words, 'head' and 'corner'. St. Justin Martyr, nevertheless, has our word twice: he says that the *Akrogōniaios* is the Stone cut without hands (*Dial.* 114[4] 126[1]), applying the word to Christ as do later Church writers.[139]

The question is, what is the meaning of the Hebrew text which our word translates. There is no doubt that the Stone held all the Temple together, but it is not certain where precisely it is located in the building. Edwin le Bas brings to our notice that the Stone was a pyramidion. That shape alone would crown both a pillar and building, and 'is perhaps the most suggestive yet penetrative messianic symbol in Scripture'.[140] Traditionally, however, in Christian interpretation the Stone was the *angularis Fundamentum* (the Corner-Foundation Stone) of the ancient hymn. St. Chrysostom took *akrogōniaios* so, together with Theodoret and Theophylact and many moderns. 'Christ is our Corner-stone; on Him alone we build.'

> *Angularis fundamentum lapis Christus missus est*
> *Qui compage parietis in utroque nectitur.*
> *Quem Sion sancta suscepit, in Quo credens permanet.*

Although Jeremias may be right in urging that the Stone in question was not a foundation-stone at all but a coping-stone crowning a building – *Abschlusstein*, not *Grundstein*[141] – it is still not merely a key-stone in an arch, and it has recently been urged that at any rate the Stone is conceived as unifying the whole Temple. It may after all be a foundation-stone located at a corner of the building.[142] The AV, based on the traditional interpretation, will then be quite right. The Isaiah passage undoubtedly refers to a foundation-stone, 'a sure foundation' *(mûsādh)*, at the *pinnâ* (corner) of a building. The Psalms text, on the contrary, seems just as likely to refer to a coping-stone for it has the word *rôsh* (peak, head). Truly, a very mixed metaphor is presented by the word *akrogōniaios*. The complex picture vastly enriches the word, for Christ is the Antitype of both the Isaiah text and the Psalms text – He is both the Basis and the Peak of the Church, the sure Foundation, the Head and Cornerstone.

The question is, what the Greek translators had in mind to express by coining the compound adjective which embodies two elements – peak and corner. The Biblical Greek concept, evidently well understood by the Christian writers, was that of an important Stone which was both *akro-* (a Peak) and a *gōniaios* (a corner-stone). But there are four or more corners to a building, and a stone at a corner cannot be uniquely significant – unless the stone be at the apex of a pyramid where all corners meet and bond together. If Le Bas is right, all is clear and beautifully suggestive about the word *akrogōniaios*.

COSMIC DEMONS

στοιχεῖα

In *stoicheia* (plural) we meet an old scientific term, recalled in Christian Greek with a novel meaning.

Secular Greek. *Stoicheion* is found only plural in the Bible and generally it is plural too in secular writers where the meaning is 'elements' in both a physical and metaphorical sense, 'first principles', and sometimes 'the stars'.[143]

In Greek physics it stands for the smallest division into which matter may be analysed, found as far back as Plato, if not before, for he mentions the primary *stoicheia* of which the human frame is composed (*Theaetetus* 201E), and the physical *stoicheia* (fire, water, earth, air) of the universe (*Timaeus* 48B). For him too *stoicheion* is a letter of the alphabet (*Cratylus* 424D). Later Diogenes Laertius, a Stoic philosopher of the third Christian century, spoke of men like Plato who in philosophical discussion used the terms, 'antipodes', 'dialectics', '*stoicheion*', etc. (III 24), but it is Aristotle who supplies the most complete secular definition of the term. 'In the case of geometrical propositions we call those the *stoicheia*, of which the proofs are embodied in the proofs of all, or most of, the rest (*Metaphysica* 998a 23).' He says that the word means, first, the primary immanent component which is formally indivisible into another form, so that if a *stoicheion* is divided the parts are formally the same as the whole. For instance, a part of water is still water, and so water is an 'element', while a syllable is not. Secondly, a *stoicheion* is a part into which a body is ultimately resolvable and can be split no further. Thirdly, *stoicheion* is a term for a primary syllogism; thus it is the primary demonstration which is contained in a number of other geometrical proofs. Fourthly, it is any small unity which is indivisible or simple enough for various checks. Fifthly, the most universal things are *stoicheia*, each of them being present in many things. Lastly, a genus of the highest genera, which cannot be further analysed into genus and differentia, is a *stoicheion* (*Metaphysica* 1014 a 35, 1014 b 1).

88

Aristotle's comprehensive demarcation includes most of the ways in which the word occurs in the Bible, but not all. It satisfies the LXX, where *stoicheia* is a physical term. Solomon had acquired an accurate knowledge of philosophy, of the physical universe and of the operation of the 'elements'. These appear to be earth, air, fire and water, and are said to ring the changes with one another as God combines them in the way that a musician blends the notes of his psaltery (Wis 7^{17} 19^{18}). They are the 'elements' of which we are made (4 Mac 12^{13}). The Sibylline oracle foretells that the coming of Beliar 'in later time' will accompany the vengeance of almighty God's fiery energy, when the 'elements' of the world shall be shorn of living things as God burns up land and sea (III 80). For Philo too the *stoicheia* of the universe were the 'elements', earth, water, air and fire (*Life of Moses* 1.17). In the apostolic Fathers the natural elements (the stars, water, etc.) are intended by the word (Diogn. 7^2 8^2). The secular meanings survived also in the NT. The day of the Lord is to come as a thief, on which the *stoicheia* shall melt with fervent heat (2 Pet $3^{10,12}$). Briggs preferred the meaning, 'stars',[144] and so did Alford, but all that may be intended is 'physical elements'.

In the NT another secular meaning, 'elementary principles', appears. The recipients of the epistle to the Hebrews, for instance, are chided because they scarcely know the 'elementary principles' of the oracles of God (5^{12}). That will be the meaning of *stoicheia* in Galatians and Colossians, according to Tertullian,[145] Aquinas and Calvin. St. Thomas reasoned that *stoicheia* involves the old Law 'because, just as boys learning science are first taught the *elements* of it and through them are brought to the fulness of science, so to the Jews was proposed the old Law by which they should be brought to faith and justice'. Under *stoicheia*, therefore, St. Thomas held to be included 'the corporeo-religious usages which they observed, such as days of the month, new moons and the sabbath. But,' said the Angelic Doctor, 'one should not object that on this account they differed nothing from the pagans who served the elements of this world, for the Jews did not serve them or pay them worship; under them rather they served and worshipped God, whereas the pagans in serving the elements rendered them divine worship.'[146]

Concerning this same verse, Gal 4^3, Calvin like St. Thomas understood that St. Paul was making a distinction between the OT dispensation and the NT Church. The *stoicheia* are the OT laws, the observance of days, months, times and years, the customs of Jewish legalism (4^{10}). Commenting on Col 2, Calvin explained the *stoicheia* as rudimentary lessons for instructing children, by which however they are not aided in attaining to mature doctrines: he instances the external ceremonies of which circumcision is an example. The view that *stoicheia* are the 'rudiments', in fact, elementary instruction, has been popular through centuries of Bible study – subscribed by impressive names like De Wette, Meyer, B. Weiss, Ewald, Ellicott, Lightfoot, W. L. Knox, R. M. Grant, C. F. D. Moule – and it is the view which, after some discussion, Burton followed, 'rudimentary religious teachings possessed by the race'.[147] All supposed the *stoicheia* to be impersonal.

Christian Greek. In addressing the Galatian and Colossian Christians, however, St. Paul may not intend a secular meaning, but rather a notion connected with the deities of nature religion. 'We were', he says, 'in bondage under the spirits of nature *(stoicheia)*.' St. Paul's 'we' (Gal 4^3) is sympathetic, implying that he himself, less than his Gentile readers, had been under the spirits and would now go back and serve the weak and beggarly *stoicheia* (4^9). Clemen reasoned that what St. Paul intended were astral deities, the spirits dwelling in the physical elements and in the heavenly bodies. True it is that heavenly bodies were seen even by early Christians as personal: the moon's light is 'her' light (Mk $13^{24f.}$), and for St. Paul sun and moon are animated beings (1 Co $15^{40f.}$).[148] St. Paul's 'we' may well include Jewish readers who in fact practised astrology, even though it was forbidden them.[149]

St. Paul's *stoicheia*, then, far from indicating a simple animism, will be something more intellectually conceived than nature spirits, and in a similar phrase he bids the Colossians, 'Beware lest any man spoil you through philosophy ... after the *stoicheia* of this age ... If ye be dead with Christ from the *stoicheia* of the age, why, as though living in the age, are ye subject to ordinances?' (Col $2^{8,20}$). It seems likely that he has in mind the form of cosmic spiritual being that Deissmann proposed.[150] T. K. Abbott endorsed this view,[151] and in modern Greek our word still denotes spirit, angel, and demon. An apter parallel is the appellation ('the blameless *stoicheion*'), given to Hephaestus in the Orphic hymn, and the appellation ('the incorruptible *stoicheion*') given to the moon goddess in the great Paris magical papyrus, beside the fact that for Hermes Trismegistos the *stoicheia* indicate gods.[152] Christ took the servant's form, affirms the Apostle, and submitted Himself even to death when He emptied Himself. In doing that, he took part in a mythical drama of the metamorphosis of the Deity, in which He delivers man from demonic powers.[153]

We may now look again at the Pauline 'we' in this context. If St. Paul would inclose himself in the pronoun he may be speaking as a Jew after all and may well mean by *stoicheia* those angels by whom, in Jewish belief, the Law was ordained, rather than Gentile spirits of nature. After all, in the context he is speaking of subjection to 'ordinances', i.e. the Law.

St. Paul's phrase, 'the *stoicheia* of the *kosmos*' (cosmic spiritual beings) may belong to an earlier Judaism than his own, for a similar phrase, 'the *stoicheia* of the *kosmokratōr* (world-ruler)' appears in the Testament of Solomon, a Jewish book which perhaps antedates the Apostle, in which *stoicheia* are **demons** identical with those thirty-six world-rulers who are invoked as deities, namely Apate, Eris, Dunamis, etc.[154] One writer has noticed 'the juxtaposition of our two Pauline words' (*stoicheia* and *kosmokratōr*) in the Testament, 'which seems clear evidence that in Paul both are to be understood as referring to these cosmic elemental powers'.[155]

They might also be intended in 2 Peter, for spirits as well as the natural elements can be conceived as 'melting' (3^{10}). In the Testament of Levi (4), for instance, invisible spirits are said to 'dissolve' at the day of Judgment. The NT author, like St. Paul, may be referring to a kind of evil angel or demon, destined to perish in the day of the Lord.

Elemental spirits are indeed a feature of Jewish thought. In the Slavonic version of the Secrets of Enoch comes the phrase, 'spirits and *elements*[156] and angels flying' (2 Enoch 16^7). There were elemental angels of the stars (1 Enoch $82^{10f.}$), angels of the winds, clouds, cold, heat, hail and thunder (Jubilees 2), not however called *stoicheia*. In the Revelation of St. John there appear four 'angels' of the four winds, beside the 'angel' of fire, of waters, and an 'angel' with reference to the sun. These again are not called *stoicheia* but they are likely to be elemental spirits.

Perhaps in other places, too, St. Paul refers in philosophical terms to astral deities and to various cosmic operators, especially when he mentions the *hupsōma* (height) and the *bathos* (depth), the *enestōta* (things present), and the *mellonta* (things to come). It would scarce be by accident that a collocation of astrological terms like this is found. Probably all denote present and future positions of heavenly bodies, in esoteric jargon.[157]

COVENANT

διαθήκη

An old word has received a new meaning, not so much a bilateral 'covenant' as a unilateral disposition of God's grace.

Secular Greek. *Diathēkē* was usually a person's last 'will' or 'testament'.[158] However, occasionally it might be a compact between two parties, not necessarily to be fulfilled at their death and which, after the fashion of a will, was deposited in care of a third party; which, moreover, unlike a *sunthēkē*, which was a mutual covenant, was one-sided in its provisions, in the sense that one party laid down the conditions and benefits which the other might accept or reject but might not modify.[159] The birds of Aristophanes must bind themselves by a 'treaty' not to hurt Peisthetairos if he lays down his arms.[160]

Biblical Greek. A re-orientation takes place, for *diathēkē* was set apart by the LXX to render the Hebrew *bᵉrîth* (covenant) when secular writers might more naturally have preferred *sunthēkē*. Later Greek versions of the OT do in fact use *sunthēkē*.[161] The secular meaning, 'will', never attaches to *diathēkē* in the LXX, and the new meaning of 'covenant' was readily accepted by Christians, who marked the speciality of their covenant-conception by avoiding the ordinary word for it, viz. *sunthēkē*. As Church members Christians claimed to belong to the new Israel, the people of the new *diathēkē* (2 Co 3⁶; Heb 8¹³).

Westcott had translated *diathēkē* by covenant and had rejected 'will' everywhere in the NT,[162] but Deissmann, who strongly resisted the view that NT language was a special speech, preferred to assume that *diathēkē* everywhere meant 'will', as in the contemporary secular Koine. Even AV, influenced by the Vulgate's *testamentum*, sometimes has 'testament'.

Indeed, in Heb 9¹⁶ᶠ· it seems unnatural to take *diathēkē* as anything but 'testament', 'will'. Here the author reasons that where there is a *diathēkē* there must be the death of the *diathemenos* (the person making it), before explaining that Christ must die in order to put away sin. Alford pleaded that it is quite vain to deny the testamentary sense, and Field agreed. 'A covenant is out of the question', he proposed, 'partly because there must be two parties to it, and also because the validy of a covenant, unless otherwise expressed, depends rather upon the life than the death of the parties' (p. 229). These two circumstantial considerations – the necessity for a death and the inherent unilaterality – have doubtless disposed the Latin versions to choose *testamentum* at each NT appearance of *diathēkē*. However, the Hebrew *bᵉrîth* (covenant) had itself involved the shedding of blood. So *testamentum*, which necessarily presupposes death, was not wholly unsuitable to declare the Hebrew concept of *bᵉrîth*.

The difficulty was behind the reasoning of Fr. Spicq[163] when he suggested that *diathēkē* ('the first *diathēkē*' and 'the blood of the *diathēkē* which God had enjoined') in 9¹⁵ and 9²⁰ means 'covenant' (in the OT sense) while in 9¹⁶ᶠ· it means 'will' and 'testament' ('the *diathēkē* is in force after men are dead'). Fr. J. Swetnam, S.J.,[164] too felt that in verses 16–17 the sense required 'testament', but that it was impossible to read this meaning in verses 15 and 18 ('it was not dedicated without blood'). This way the dual aspect in *diathēkē* is better understood. Death cannot be eliminated from the *diathēkē*. So in fact 9[16f.] is by way of being an illustrative metaphor inserted into the main line of argument which runs through chapters 9 and 10, and so for a moment *diathēkē* has the secular meaning.[165] However, Fr. Swetnam urged that Christ's blood, inaugurating a new arrangement between God and His people, links both ideas, covenant and testament. The link 'is something altogether essential and central.'

What, then, the new sense of *diathēkē* expresses is not 'will' as in secular Greek, nor strictly a 'covenant', but a one-sided *depositio* which insists on the inevitability of a death before it is put into effect. It is 'covenant', truly, but only in the Hebrew sense, unilateral in benefit, and linked with a death. Though we use the word 'covenant', for the sake of hallowed usage, we have in mind a one-sided deposition of grace. We indicate by the word God's declaration of His sovereign and saving will in history, by which He orders the relation between Himself and man.[166]

St. Irenaeus has *diathēkē* in this sense for the four Biblical covenants – those with Noah, Abraham, Moses, and that of the Gospel.[167] The apostolic Fathers make clear that *diathēkē* in the Christian sense is still 'covenant'. 'Be not like some, heaping up your sins and alleging that our *covenant* continues for them also.' The Mosaic covenant was eclipsed, 'that the *covenant* of Jesus, the Beloved, might be sealed in our hearts by the hope of faith in Him'. 'It will happen when we ourselves also have been made perfect to become heirs of the *Covenant* of the Lord.'[168]

In St. Justin Martyr's phrase, Christ Himself is the Law of the coming Dispensation (*nomos aiōnios*) and is the new *Covenant* for the whole world (*Dial.* 43.1).

NOTES

[1] *Symposium* 172A.
[2] Menander Rhetor (iii AD) in *Rhetores Graeci* ed. L. Spengel, III Teubner 1856, p. 333S.
[3] Xenophon *Cyropaedia* III 2.14.
[4] Aristophanes *Clouds*, 875, 1189.
[5] Plutarch *Pericles* VII 4.
[6] Demosthenes XIX 32.
[7] Polybius II 50.7.
[8] Libanius (iv AD) *Argumenta Orationum Demosthenicarum* 2. See *Libanii Opera*, ed. Rich. Förster, Teubner, Leipzig 1915, vol. III, p. 601, line 6.
[9] Philo *Embassy to Gaius* 163.

[10] P Amherst 2.79.5 (II AD).

[11] *Odyssey* XVII 386.

[12] *Iliad* IX 165.

[13] K. L. Schmidt in Kittel *TWNT* III, p. 492.

[14] A. Robertson and A. Plummer, *1 Corinthians*, ICC T. & T. Clark 2nd ed. 1914, p. 147.

[15] A point well made by M. J. Farrelly, *American Benedictine Review* (St. Paul, Minnesota) 14 (1963), pp. 572–89.

[16] Herodotus II 37, III 148; Aristophanes *Knights* 120.

[17] Aeschylus *Seven against Thebes* 18; Plato *Phaedo* 107D; Aristotle *Politica* 1338 a 30.

[18] Aristophanes *Clouds* 961.

[19] Xenophon *Cyropaedia* I 1.6.

[20] Ibid., VIII 3.37.

[21] Plato *Laws* II 659D.

[22] Aeschines *Oration against Ctesiphon* III 148.

[23] *C. Apion.* I 14 (Niese I 73).

[24] W. Jaeger, *Paideia: the Ideals of Greek Culture*, ET Blackwell 1939, vol. I, p. xvi.

[25] Ibid., p. xxvii.

[26] G. Bertram in Kittel *TWNT* V, p. 600.

[27] BGU III 846.11f.

[28] *TWNT* V, p. 607.

[29] C. D. Buck, *A Dictionary of Selected Synonyms in the Principal Indo-European Languages*, Chicago 1949, pp. 1446f.

[30] Polycarp àd Phil. 4².

[31] G. Bertram in Kittel *TWNT* V, p. 622.

[32] Hermas *Vis.* II 3.1; III 9.10.

[33] Aeschylus *Prometheus Bound* 480.

[34] *Hippolytus* 516.

[35] W. Sanday, A. C. Headlam, *Romans*, ICC, T. & T. Clark 5th ed. 1902, p. 161.

[36] E. Petersen, *Miscellanea Giovanni Mercati* (Studi e testi, 121) Vatican 1946, I, pp. 362ff.

[37] *Harvard Theological Review* 42 (1949), p. 113. See the whole article, pp. 109–24.

[38] H. B. Mattingly, *Journal of Theological Studies*, NS 9 (1958), p. 28, n. 3.

[39] J. B. Lightfoot, *Apostolic Fathers*, part II St. Ignatius, vol. I, pp. 415–19.

[40] Alan Richardson, *An Introduction to the Theology of the NT*, SCM 1958, p. 357.

[41] *Encyclopaedia Biblica*, Black 1914, col. 752–63.

[42] *Annals* XV 44.

[43] *Nero* 16.

[44] *Encyclopaedia Biblica* col. 754f.

[45] *Ant. Jud.* XVIII iii 3.

[46] H. B. Mattingly, op. cit., pp. 26ff.

[47] I. Eph 11²; I. Ro 3²; I. Magn 4¹; I. Pol 7³; M. Pol 10¹ 12¹; Justin *Apol.* I 4.5; *Dial.* XXXV 2, 6.

[48] Herodotus III 142.

[49] Thucydides I 87.

[50] Ibid., II 59, 60.

[51] *de Magisteriis*, Teubner I 2 (Reiske §11).

[52] F. J. A. Hort, *The Christian Ekklesia*, Macmillan 1914, p. 19.

[53] For the house-church, see F. V. Filson, *Journal of Biblical Literature*, 58 (1939), pp. 105–12.

[54] W. Schrage, *Zeitschrift für Theologie und Kirche* (Tübingen) 60 (1963), pp. 178–202.

[55] E. de W. Burton, *Galatians*, ICC, T. & T. Clark 1921, p. 419.

[56] K. L. Schmidt in Kittel *TWNT* III, p. 519.

[57] E. G. Selwyn, *Theology* 14 (1927), p. 289.

[58] From thence to Josephus *Bell. Jud.* I i 2 and Plutarch *Moralia* 495C.

[59] *Fragmenta* (ed. J. R. Harris, CUP 1886) 49H.

[60] There is, of course, the rare word, *akroposthia*, in classical Greek and Hippocrates. Why then did Biblical Greek invent a substitute? LS suggest that *akrobustia* is from *akros* and a Semitic root – perhaps *bōsheth* (shame) which the Greek word resembles in sound.

[61] Gen 17^{11} 34^{14,24}; Ex 4^{25}; Lev 12^3, etc.

[62] Herodotus IV 64.

[63] P Cairo Zen. 76.13 (iii BC).

[64] Aristotle *Nicomachean Ethics* II 7.13.

[65] Plato *Republic* viii (OCT 563A).

[66] XV 296, VII 49.

[67] *Nicomachean Ethics* IV 8.3.

[68] *Rhetorica* 1389 b 11 (II 12).

[69] Diodorus Siculus *Bibliotheca Historia* XV 6.

[70] Alan Richardson, *An Introduction to the Theology of the NT*, SCM 1958, p. 114.

[71] *de Josepho* ch. 40.

[72] *de Vita Mosis* iii.14.

[73] Demosthenes XIX 1.

[74] *Aboth* IV 11; also other instances in Jastrow, s.v.

[75] Thucydides IV 61.

[76] Strabo XIII 1.1.

[77] Xenophon *Anabasis* I 6.5.

[78] Epictetus III 23.27ff.; Dio Chrysostom *Discourse* XXX 6.

[79] Plutarch *Otho* XVI 2.

[80] Kittel *TWNT* V, p. 774 (des mahnenden Zuspruchs).

[81] C. K. Barrett, *The Gospel according to St. John*, SPCK 1962, p. 386.

[82] E. Hatch, *Essays in Biblical Greek*, Clarendon 1889, pp. 82f.

[83] A. E. Brooke, *Johannine Epistles*, ICC T. & T. Clark, 1912, p. 26.

[84] B. F. Westcott, *The Gospel according to St. John*, Murray 1887, p. 212.

[85] *Expository Times* 57 (1945), p. 50.

[86] W. F. Howard, *Christianity according to St. John*, Duckworth 1943, pp. 74–80.

[87] *Journal of Theological Studies* NS 1 (1950), p. 13.

[88] *Sanhedrin* 98 b, etc.

[89] *Expository Times* 57 (1945), pp. 48f.

[90] H. Van Dyke Parunak in *Biblica* (Rome) 56 (1975), pp. 512–32.

[91] *Journal of Theological Studies*, NS 4 (1953), pp. 35–8.

[92] Cyril of Jerusalem, *Catecheses* xvi 20.

[93] In Rufinus *de Principiis* II vii 4.

[94] P. Oxy no. 850, verso 10 (Grenfell and Hunt, vol. VI, pp. 12–18). Translated, 'Jesus the Comforter' in E. Hennecke, *NT Apocrypha*, vol. II, ET Lutterworth 1965, p. 207.

[95] *Journal of Theological Studies*, NS 1 (1950) p. 9.

[96] O. Betz, *Der Paraklet*, Leiden 1963.

[97] As expounded in detail throughout J. Daniélou, *Théologie du Judéo-Christianisme*, Desclée, Paris, 1958.

[98] See the review by R. Schackenburg, *Biblische Zeitschrift* (Paderborn) 9 (1965), pp. 138ff.

[99] As does D. W. Kemmler, *Faith and Human Reason*, Brill 1975, p. 177.

[100] Ibid., p. 177, n. 142.
[101] Euripides *Medea* 220.
[102] 'Anger': Aristophanes *Ranae* 844, Euripides *Alcestis* 1009. 'Anxious desire': Aeschylus *Choephori* 413.
[103] Aeschylus *The Oresteian Trilogy*, Penguin 1956, p. 76.
[104] Aeschylus *Agamemnon* 995.
[105] Euripides *Orestes* 1201.
[106] Euripides *Hippolytus* 118.
[107] J. B. Lightfoot, *Philippians*, on 1[8].
[108] As suggested in *New Testament Studies* 1 (1955), p. 223.
[109] H. Köster in Kittel *TWNT* VII, p. 552.
[110] P. Flor 296.23 (vi AD).
[111] Hippocrates *Prorrheticon* 2.6. The noun, *eusplagchnia*, meant 'courage' in secular Greek.
[112] *Papyrus magica Musei Lugdunensis Batavi*, ed. A. Dieterich, Leipzig 1888 (Jahrb. f. class. Philol. Suppl. XVI 9), IX 3 (p. 810).
[113] See the discussion by H. Köster in Kittel *TWNT* VII, pp. 551f., and note 26.
[114] E.g. P Masp 20.11 (vi AD).
[115] Euripides *Rhesus* 192.
[116] C. D. Buck, *A Dictionary of Selected Synonyms in the Principal Indo-European Languages*, Chicago 1949, p. 1085.
[117] Theophrastus *Historia Plantarum* 4.8.10 (iv BC); IG vol. i ed. minor (F. H. von Gaertringen, Berlin 1924) 372.134; Artemidorus Daldianus (ii AD), R. Hercher, Leipzig 1864, 1.67 (plural).
[118] Hyperides (iv BC) *Adversus Demosthenem* 3 (OCT).
[119] Philochorus (iv BC). See G. Müller, *Fragmenta Historicorum Graecorum*, Paris 1841, vol. i, 138.
[120] J. B. Lightfoot, *The Ep. of St. Paul to the Philippians*, Macmillan 1891, p. 144.
[121] Ed. Mangey II 652.
[122] Homily in Mt 43.2, 67.2.
[123] *Adversus Haereses* I 16.3.
[124] Aristophanes *Plutus* 583.
[125] Herodotus II 91.
[126] *Dial.* 43[5] 66[2]. More often, however, the LXX displays secular usage: Wis 4[2] 10[12]; 2 Mac 4[18] 14[43] 15[9].
[127] An interesting note draws attention to the Spanish versions' *batalla*, and the German's *Kampf*: J. D. Robb, *Expository Times* 79 (1968), p. 254.
[128] Hippolytus *Refutatio* IX 17; Origen *Exhortatio ad martyrium* 5.
[129] Eusebius *Historia Ecclesiastica* V 1.11; Origen *Exhortatio ad martyrium* 4.
[130] Tatian *Address to the Greeks* 12.4.
[131] Dionysius of Halicarnassus III 22.
[132] SIG 1219.19.
[133] Sophocles *Antigone* 545; Euripides *Supplices* 1211.
[134] *Laws* VIII 840E; *adversus Neaeram* 1371; *Alcestis* 55.
[135] *Praecepta coniugialia* 44, *Roman Questions* 20.
[136] For *ek* in the sense of 'belonging to', see Moulton-Turner, *Grammar* III, p. 260.
[137] Hermas *Vis.* III 7.3, *Mand.* IV 4.4.
[138] S. H. Hooke, *The Siege Perilous*, SCM 1956, pp. 235–49.
[139] Gregory Nazianzus *Orationes* 22.4; Chrysostom *De Non Esse Desperandum* 3; Cyril of Alexandria *Comm. in Isai.* 3.2; John Damascene *Homilia* 4.30.
[140] *Palestine Exploration Quarterly* 78 (1946), p. 115. Cf. also pp. 103–15.
[141] *Angelos (Archiv für neutestamentliche Zeitgeschichte und Kulturkunde)* 1 (1925), pp. 65–70; *ZNW* 19 (1930) 264–80, 36 (1937) 154–7; *KTWNT* I, pp. 792f., IV, pp. 277–83. Accepted in Beginnings V, p. 374.
[142] As argued by R. J. McKelvey, *New Testament Studies* 8 (1962), pp. 352–9.

[143] Manetho IV 624; Diogenes Laertius VI 102. 'Planets' in a ii AD papyrus, P. Lond 1[130] 60. It is sometimes considered that this is the meaning of *stoicheia* in Gal 4[3] and Col 2[8] ('heavenly bodies', Theodoret). See also Justin *Dial.* 23.3, *Apol.* II 5.2.

[144] *Peter and Jude*, ICC T. & T. Clark 2nd ed. 1902, p. 297.

[145] *Adversus Marcionem* I 4.

[146] Thomas Aquinas, *Commentary on St. Paul's Epistle to the Galatians*, ET by F. R. Larcher, O. P., Magi, New York 1966, p. 111 (chapter 4, lecture one, verse 3).

[147] E. de W. Burton, *Galatians*, ICC T. & T. Clark 1921, p. 518.

[148] C. Clemen, *Primitive Christianity and its Non-Jewish Sources*, ET T. & T. Clark 1912, pp. 106f., 109.

[149] D. E. H. Whiteley, *The Theology of St. Paul*, Blackwell 1964, p. 25.

[150] In *Encyclopaedia Biblica*, Black 1914, col. 1261.

[151] *Ephesians, Colossians*, ICC T. & T. Clark 1909, pp. 247f.

[152] G. H. C. Macgregor, *New Testament Studies* 1 (1954), pp. 21f.

[153] For an exposition of this hypothesis, see R. P. Martin, *Carmen Christi*, CUP 1967, pp. 177–80.

[154] T. Sol XVIII, MSS P and L.

[155] Macgregor, op. cit., p. 22.

[156] So the translation of Charles and Forbes (*The Apocrypha of the OT*, Clarendon 1913, p. 439): 'creatures' in that of Morfill.

[157] D. E. H. Whiteley, op. cit., p. 24.

[159] Plato *Laws* XI 923C; Demosthenes XXVII 13; Aristophanes *Wasps* 584, 589, etc.

[159] Isaeus VI 27; Aristophanes *Birds* 435–61.

[160] Aristophanes *Birds* 445ff.

[161] Gen 6[18] (Aquila, Symmachus); 3 Km 6[19] (Aqu. Theod.); Ps 24(25)[10] (Aqu. Sym.).

[162] B. F. Westcott, *The Epistle to the Hebrews*, Macmillan 1889, pp. 263ff.

[163] C. Spicq, *L'épître aux Hébreux*, Paris 1952, in loc.

[164] *Catholic Biblical Quarterly* 27 (1965), pp. 373ff.

[165] C. de Villapadierna, *Estudios Bíblicos* (Madrid) 21 (1962), pp. 273–96.

[166] O. Schmitz in *Die Religion in Geschichte und Gegenwart* I (2nd ed. Tübingen 1927), pp. 1362ff., cited by J. Behm in Kittel *TWNT* II, p. 137.

[167] *Adversus Haereses* III 11.11.

[168] Barn 4[6,8] 13[1] 14[1] 6[19] 9[6] 13[6] and citations (e.g. 1 Clem 15[4] 35[7]).

D

DAILY (BREAD)

ἐπιούσιος

Nor by 'our daily bread' mean common food. – KEBLE

Some have suggested that *epiousios*, this new Christian word, is a mistranslation of Aramaic, or even a Greek corruption. It is not apparently of first importance, however it be understood, but it occurs in the Sermon on the Mount and in the Didache (Mt 6[11]; Lk 11[3]; Did 8[2]). It is doubtful whether the word survives elsewhere in any literature, papyrus, ostraka or inscription, other than gospel quotations.

Bauer claims that *epiousios* is found at least once in secular Greek, where the meaning is apparently *diaria* (daily portion), but that depends on Sayce's deciphering, and the papyrus evidently cannot be found.[1] Moulton and Milligan are still justified in seeing no clear light from the papyri and in supposing the word to be coined by the collector of Matthew's and Luke's common material (MM sv.)[2] It was not known in Origen's day, either in colloquial or literary speech.[3]

Several derivations have been suggested and each points to a different meaning. (1) It may be assumed with Origen and other Fathers that *epiousios* derives from *epi* and *ousia* and denotes bread 'which is necessary for our existence', our material needs. (2) One may derive it from *epi tēn ousan (hēmeran)* and may render the phrase, 'our bread (determined) for this day'.[4] C. G. Sheward found Blass-Debrunner's derivation unsatisfactory,[5] for the adjective *epimēnios* is not a true analogy, *mēn* (month) being a part of the composition, and there is no evidence that *hēmera* (day) was ever understood with *ousa*. Besides, before *ousa* the iota would probably be elided to form *epousios*. It was a rule of word-formation that the final iota of *epi* be elided when *epi* is prefixed to a verb beginning with a vowel unless the verb originally began with a digamma. Sheward preferred the next derivation.

(3) It is that favoured by Moulton,[6] by J. B. Lightfoot,[7] A. T. Robertson,[8] and others, and said by Matthew Black to be the 'natural' derivation,[9] from the participle *(epiousa)* of the verb *epienai* (to come).

This verb, unlike *eimi* (to be), originally began with digamma and so the iota of *epi* is not elided. Dr. Black suggests that a translator of the language of Jesus, unaware of Aramaic idiom and wishing to give a literal equivalent of every word of Jesus, may have

98

attempted to translate *yômāḥᵉrâ* (tomorrow) literally. For this purpose he coined the Greek word, *epiousios* (following) from the participle *epiousa*, of the verb *epienai*.[10] Greeks used the phrase, *hē epiousa (hēmera)*, to denote 'the morrow'.[11] In the LXX *epiousa* is 'the morrow' (rendering *yôm*, Pr 27[1]). On this derivation, the Lord's Prayer probably reads, 'Give us this day our bread for tomorrow'. It was the way it was understood in the ancient Aramaic gospel of the Nazarenes, according to St. Jerome commenting on Mt 6[11], a gospel which is now lost and which read *māḥar* (the morrow), but it does conflict with the known sentiments of our Lord who said, 'Take no thought for the morrow'. Even so, the interpretation has some long-standing authority: the Memphitic (Bohairic) version in Mt and Lk, the Thebaic (Sahidic) in Mt, and the Coptic service books.[12] The gospel of the Nazarenes was a translation of Mt into Aramaic and is probably an excellent guide to the language of some early communities of Christians who might be expected to know exactly what our Lord said. T. G. Sherman rejects the interpretation, 'bread for the coming *day*', on the ground that there is no justification for introducing 'day' or 'night' or anything else. The noun is wholly absent. Unfortunately, Sherman relies for his own interpretation upon the said papyrus which no one can trace (Preisigke 5224.20). From this elusive text he claims that the meaning is 'our ration of bread', 'our day's appointed portion'. Until the text turns up one must suspend judgment.[13]

'Daily' is still an adequate English translation, like the Itala's *cotidianum*, for even on the third derivation above, 'the bread for to-morrow' is yet in a real sense a 'daily' bread, though it be a day deferred.

The earliest Christian versions of the gospels in Syriac, Coptic, Armenian and Latin, present a similar diversity of interpretation and the early translators were perhaps as puzzled by the word as we are. The ancient Syriac, possibly in the third century, is divided between 'continual bread' (Sinaitic and Curetonian) and 'bread of our necessity' (Peshitta Syriac). The Peshitta evidently derived the word as Origen did, making it correspond with Pr 30[8] ('my needful bread', LXX *ta deonta*). The interpretation, 'continual bread', may be supported on the basis of the Armenian codices Sergii, according to Dr. Hadidian.[14] The Itala of the Old Latin has *cotidianum* (for each day), and Vulgate has *superstantialem* (Mt) and *cotidianum* (Lk). St. Jerome in the Vulgate was probably influenced, in rendering Mt by Origen's derivation, i.e. 'necessary bread', since *substantia* is a Latin equivalent of the Greek *ousia*. The Bohairic Coptic version has the interpretation, 'bread for the coming day', but there is no consensus among primitive versions.

In recent times one has tended to suppose a misunderstanding of the underlying Aramaic – perhaps Hebraic – report of a saying of Jesus. 'Certainly', affirms Matthew Black, 'in this word of Jesus, if in any other, we can be confident that a Semitic, and presumably an Aramaic, original underlies the Greek'.[15] *Epiousios* is widely supposed to be a literal rendering of a phrase like *leḥem ḥuqqi*, as in the Targum on Pr 30[8].

Why should *epiousios* have been coined when there was already a forceful Greek word to express each of the suggestions we have considered? The context requires a meaning like that in Pr 30[8] (needful bread) but for some reason Christian Greek has avoided the LXX word *deonta*. Are there eschatological overtones in the enigmatic phrase? Can the bread of the Lord's Prayer be that of the Messianic Banquet? The whole context is one of destiny: 'Thy kingdom come', 'in heaven', 'forgive us', 'deliver us'.

St Jerome indicates that the Aramaic gospel used *māḥār* (bread for tomorrow) but he added the interesting note: '*māḥār* means "for to-morrow"', and that is future'. It was not, then, the immediate and literal bread that St. Jerome had in mind and he well knew that for the Jews *māḥār* specified not the next day but the End of the Age. He probably understood the Bread to be that of the messianic Banquet.

'Give us this day our daily bread', is not after all a petition for man's daily needs but a hunger for the Bread of Life, for the Manna which descends from heaven. We sang as children at every meal,

> Thy creatures bless and grant that we
> May feast in Paradise with Thee!
> Let manna to our souls be given,
> The Bread of Life sent down from heaven.

We did not know that the words explained the Lord's Prayer. Jesus said, 'If any man eat of the Bread, he shall live for ever'. He appointed for us a Kingdom, that we may eat and drink at His Table in His Kingdom.

DEACON AND MINISTRY

διάκονος: διακονία: διακονέω

The words, *diakonos*, *diakonō* and *diakonia* have a twofold significance in Christian Greek, both the diaconate and ministry in general.

Secular Greek. Here *diakonos* is a servant,[16] and *diakonia* his status,[17] or the serving itself[18] or even a body of servants,[19] while the verb *diakonō* is to do service.[20] It has been urged that in secular Greek even a religious use of *diakonos* is found: the word appears among a list of temple officials on an inscription of the last century BC,[21] and there are other references to pagan officers known by the same title.

Christian Greek. Three words have been filled by Christians with a new meaning, and that without influence of the LXX:

(1) Diakonos is a Christian 'deacon', a member of a distinct order of ministry, evidently serving under the presbyter-bishops, and mentioned alongside *episkopos* (bishop) on two occasions (Ph 1[1]; 1 Ti 3[8,12]). The deacon was of some importance, His requisite character and qualifications being carefully defined. The office must not be too rigidly conceived, for Timothy, apostle though he was, is sometimes called a deacon (1 Ti 4[6]).

The name *diakonos*, unlike the verb, is not applied to the Seven. They are not 'deacons', but they 'serve as deacons' *(diakonō)*, and the Seven do bear a certain resemblance with the later order of deacons in their special ministry to the poor. The appointment of the Seven, and their ordination by prayer and laying on of hands was the Church's first step towards a hierarchy (Act 6). Frequently the office appears in the apostolic Fathers. In the epistles of St. Ignatius, deacons are mentioned along with bishops and priests; deacons are invariably in the third place.[22]

The feminine version, which is also *diakonos* is applied to Phoebe, a 'deaconess' of the church at Cenchrea (Ro 16[1]). From the time of the Didascalia there was an independent office of deaconesses for a few centuries.

(2) The verb *diakonō* appears in the official sense, to serve as deacon, in the NT and Fathers.[23]

(3) *Diakonia*. Christ Himself was *diakonos* (Mt 20[26f.]). The Son of Man came to minister *(diakonō)*. Then the Church which is 'in Christ', and is His Body, is also the *diakonos* and her function in the world is a *diakonia*.[24] Though the secular meaning appears (Lk 10[40]), *diakonia* is now Christian ministry, whether apostleship (Act 1[17,25]), ministration to widows (6[1]), ministration of the Word (6[4]), Paul's divine commission to the Gentiles (20[24] 21[19]; Ro 11[13]), his charitable ministry at Jerusalem (Ro 15[31]), the ministry of the house of Stephanas (1 Co 16[15]), the ministry of reconciliation (2 Co 5[18]), ministry to the saints (Ro 10[30] vl; 2 Co 8[4] 9[1,12]), the ministry of Timothy (2 Ti 4[5]), or the ministry of angels (Heb 1[14]). The special character of *diakonia* is charismatic (Ro 12[7]; 1 Co 12[5]; 2 Co 3[8] 4[1]).

The apostolic Fathers extend the use of *diakonia* from the diaconate[25] to general Christian ministry – that of God (I. Smyrn 12[1]), of giving your wealth (*Mand.* 2[6]) and spending it for Him (*Sim.* 1[9]), of looking after the poor (*Sim.* 2[7]), and the ministry of bishops (I. Philad 1[1]) who shelter the destitute and widows by their *diakonia* (*Sim.* IX 27.2).

DEBAUCHERY

ἀσωτία : ἀσώτως

The words receive a new and extremely evil connotation in Biblical Greek.

Secular Greek. The meaning of *asōtia* had been prodigality and wastefulness in Plato, Aristotle and the pre-Christian papyri. Of the adverb *(asōtōs)* the meaning was 'wastefully' in Lucian, Josephus and Philo.

Plato spoke of those who gave to 'prodigality' the euphemism, 'magnificence', to excuse their own excesses.[26] Aristotle had a different version. 'Meanness', he supposed, 'is invariably applied to those who care more than is proper about wealth, whereas *asōtia* (prodigality) is sometimes used with a wider meaning, for we name the unrestrained and those who waste money on debauchery prodigal, and therefore *prodigality* is thought to be extremely wicked'.[27]

Asōtia was at most the vulgar incapacity to save, prodigal and spendthrift expenditure, and at best generosity. To live *asōtōs* was no more than to live extravagantly. Hyrcanus was reported as coming with a request for a thousand talents, and the steward as angrily taxing him with living *asōtōs*, comparing him with his sire who had saved money. There was no thought of riotous living, only of failure to gather an estate as carefully as the father had done.[28]

In secular writers of a later date the words acquired the less desirable sense of profligacy, the wasting of goods, as seen in the second-century grammarian, Athenaeus.[29] In the third-century historian, Herodian, *asōtiai* (plural) is linked with undesirable *kraipalai* (drinking bouts).[30]

Biblical Greek. Already in the Greek OT *asōtia* rendered *zālal* (morally riotous) and it meant **debauchery**.[31] So the way was open for Christians to denounce it as a rather worse vice than a spendthrift's wastefulness. It now has to do with lust and revelry and dissolute bibation, to say nothing of 'abominable idolatries' (Eph 5[18]; 1 Pet 4[4]). In wine lurk four wicked desires, declares the (probably) Christian author or compiler of the Testament of Judah: lust, hot passion, filthy lucre, and *asōtia* (16[1]). If a word is known by the company it keeps, this is a bad one.

The prodigal son devours his money *asōtōs* (in debauchery), which included lavishing it on harlots (Lk 15[13, 30]). Worldly men

102

think it strange that Christians fail to 'run with them to the same excess of *asōtia*', which by the context embraces wine-bibbing, revelling and banquets (1 Pet 4⁴; cf. Tit 1⁶). Christian Greek bequeathed the meaning at last to the modern language where it expresses dissipation and debauchery. The influence began as early as Athenaeus and Herodian.

There is the following interesting comparison in the Testament of Asher, a book surviving in Jewish Greek. The author, who may have been a Christian, very timely discussed some specified sins, making a contrast with their virtuous counterparts. Covetousness he placed with wealth, drunkenness with innocent conviviality, grief with laughter and, most instructively *asōtia* is contrasted with 'wedlock' (5¹). *Asōtia* then is the degeneration of the love between man and woman which is seen at its best in marriage.

It is more than wastefulness, worse than prodigality, and nothing short of immoral debauchery and excessive lewdness.³²

DECEIT, SEDUCING ERROR

πλάνη

In Christian Greek the word *planē* is more than a mistake or a simple trick to deceive. Christians avoided what they called *planē*, a twist of the wicked mind of the Serpent himself.

Secular Greek. *Planē* had been a wandering, a going astray. It is quite literally understood by Herodotus who mentions 'travelling' far in search of knowledge (I 30). The classical use is more broadly metaphorical for it includes 'discursive treatment' of a subject, a 'devious passage' without which the mind cannot attain to the truth,³³ and the wandering course of an argument.³⁴

Planē is contemptibly joined with *anoia* (folly) when the soul is said to be freed from 'error' and 'folly'.³⁵ *Planē* is 'confusion of thought'³⁶ and the 'illusion' of colour vision.³⁷ Then again it is difference of opinion and uncertainty.³⁸ *Planē* is a plain 'mistake', as is shown by the wrong impression gained by the Indians before deserters from Semiramis enlightened them that her elephants were nothing but dummies. The historian explains how their *planē* (error) concerning the elephants was pointed out to them,³⁹ and so his meaning is not likely to be 'deceit', or any doubtful ethics of Semiramis, for the point concerned the Indians' error in a fair strategem of war. Only in Biblical Greek is *planē* deceit and subtle imposture.

Biblical Greek. In the Bible a change overtakes the word. It renders *sheriruth*, walking in the deceit of one's heart (Jer 23¹⁷) and *pesha'*, which is transgression of God's law (Ezek 33[10]), and *mirmâ*, the folly of fools who make a mock at sin (Pr 14[8]). *Planē* is departure from the Law's precepts (Tob 5[13]; Wis 1[12] 12[24]). It is cunning deceit (Mt 27[64]). It is condemned as gross sin, perverted passion (Ro 1[27]), the twisting of true doctrine (Eph 4[14]), the guile to which St. Paul would not resort (1 Th 2[3]) but which will characterise the regime of the Man of Sin (2 Th 2[11]). It is the 'deceit' of Balaam (Jude 11), the 'guile' of a sinner's ways (Jas 5[20]), the 'trickery' of seducing heresy (2 Pet 2[18] 3[17]).

The spirit of 'deceit' (1 Jn 4[6]) opposes the Spirit of Truth. St. Ignatius warns the believers to be stedfast in their faith against the 'deceits' of heretics (I Eph 10[2]). Magicians share the evil characteristic (Diog 8[4]). The world in which we live has *planē* (guile) and *apatē*) (deceit): Diog 10[7] Barn 12[10]. Behind all this seducing error is the *planē* of the Evil One, the serpent of Eden (Diog 12[3,3]; Barn 2[10]), assailing unregenerate hearts (Barn 14[5]; 2 Clem 1[7]).

A like warning appears in the Hermetic writings, in what is perhaps from its date a Christian addition (probably ii AD): 'Repent, ye who have journeyed with *planē* (guile) and joined company with ignorance.'[40]

DEDICATE

ἐγκαινίζω

In the LXX the meaning of *egkainizō* was to dedicate, or rededicate, especially the Holy Place and Sanctuary subsequent to the sacrilege which Antiochus committed (1 Mac 4[36, 54, 57] SR 5[1]). It renders the Hebrew verb *ḥānakh* (Deut 20[5bis]; 3 Km 8[63]; 2 Chr 7[5]).

The NT follows LXX precedent, for in Heb 9[18] *egkainizō* refers to the first covenant being 'dedicated' with blood and 10[20] looks to the new and living way which Christ has 'consecrated' for us through the Veil.

The verb is alleged not to be exclusively Christian but to occur in a speculative reconstruction of a defective papyrus dated 127 BC. However, no more than the letters *zein* remain to identify the verb for sure with *egkainizein*. Besides, the meaning in the fragmentary text does not look like 'dedicate' or 'consecrate', as in Biblical Greek, but rather 'innovate'.[41]

It is true that 'innovate' may be a Biblical meaning. In the LXX sometimes the verb renders Piel of *ḥādhesh* (renew, repair),[42] but the meaning which was carried from the LXX into the NT was 'dedicate'.

DELIVERANCE: REDEEMER

λύτρον: ἀντίλυτρον: λύτρωσις: λυτρόω: λυτρωτής

These words, all from the same stem (*lutron, antrilutron, lutrōsis, lutrō, lutrōtēs*) incurred a substantial change of meaning through influence of the LXX where, however, *antilutron* is absent. In place of the secular idea of 'ransoming', a new conception of divine deliverance is prominent.

Secular Greek. The first word, *lutron*, was ransom-money in classical Greek,[43] and later on the price required to free a slave.[44] According to Josephus, the high priest presented Crassus with a beam of gold from the Temple as a ransom *(lutron)* 'in place of' *(anti)* the whole Temple, that is, to spare the Temple; it was a price laid out to parry worse things, perhaps the forfeiture of the Temple itself.[45] Josephus has a different preposition when *lutron* is the price of redemption paid 'on behalf of' *(huper)* Herod's brother to procure his release from the Parthians.[46] The second word, *antilutron*, is the price of any release and, more specifically, a medical remedy, an antidote.[47]

The third word, *lutrōsis*, too is a ransoming of prisoners by paying for them.[48] The next word, the verb *lutrō*, is both 'to release with the help of ransom-money' and also 'to hold to ransom' for a certain sum.[49] In the passive voice it means to be ransomed or to be released from an obligation,[50] and in the middle voice, to release by paying a ransom.[51]

Biblical Greek. *Antilutron* does not occur in the LXX, but the idea of redemption by paying an appropriate price is evident in the use of simplex *lutron*, for it renders the Hebrew *kōpher* (ransom or compensation: Ex 21[30] 30[12]; Num 35[31f.]; Pr 6[35] 13[8]) and *g⁽e⁾'ullâ* (the price to redeem land or slaves: Lev 25[24, 26, 51]), and also *gā'al* (to redeem by payment of the assessed value: Lev 27[31]). *Lutron* further renders *m⁽e⁾ḥîr*, the price for letting captives go (Isai 45[13]) and the *pdh* stem, to ransom at a fixed price (Ex 21[30]; Lev 19[20]; Num 3[46, 48f., 51] 18[15]). The Hebrew stems were further rendered by *lutrōsis* and the verb *lutrō*.

Our final word, *lutrōtēs*, I cannot find in the secular language, but in Biblical Greek it is an important description of God our Strength and Redeemer, not a mere Ransomer but a divine Kinsman, the high God, the *Gō'ēl* who delivers Israel from Egypt (Ps 18(19)[14] 77(78)[35] – applied by the Christians to Moses and indirectly to Jesus (Act 7[35]).

Christian Greek. In the NT the thought of a ransom-price is involved, but it is never studied for a moment to whom it is paid – though Christ is said to give His life as a *lutron* 'in place of' *(anti)*

105

all (Mt 20[28]; Mk 10[45]). Christ was the *antilutron* 'on behalf of' *(huper)* all (1 Ti 2[6]). To whom was this *antilutron* paid? The recipient might conceivably be God or the Devil, and both have been put forward. Scripture, however, presses no details of the ransom metaphor.

One place where the verb *lutrō* appears is Tit 2[14] ('to *deliver* us from all iniquity') and the expression is reminiscent of the LXX (Ps 130[8]), where the psalmist speaks of deliverance: 'He shall *deliver* Israel from all his iniquities' – and assuredly not of ransom.[52] Of course, the idea of 'purchase' is prominent in *lutrō* in 1 Pet 1[18] but with no indication *from* whom the purchase is made, only that believers 'were purchased' with the precious blood of Christ – perhaps purchased from the slavery of sin, if that is not too fanciful an idea, rather than from the penalty of sin. If so, the relevant idea behind *lutrō* is deliverance rather than ransom.

General deliverance without reference to purchase or ransom, is the sense of *lutrōsis* in Lk 1[68] 2[38] – the extrication afforded by the Messiah. Zacharias and Anna refer to God's saving initiative and blessing. The only occasion when the verb *lutrō* is used by St. Luke, general salvation for Israel is intended without thought of a ransom. Two disciples on the Emmaus road (24[21]) had been disappointed in their hopes by the crucifixion.

In Heb 9[12] we are said to have *lutrōsis* through His blood, again without mention of a purchaser. The setting is the day of Atonement, and the animal sacrifices which were offered on that day were accepted not as a ransom, nor a gift of any kind, and they were not brought to the altar.[53] The phrase, 'through His own blood', cannot be understood as a price, it is argued, for the preposition *dia* ensures that 'through' is instrumental. It is not 'at the price of' His blood therefore, but 'by means of' it, that *lutrōsis* was obtained. The word is probably 'deliverance' rather than 'ransom'.

Deissmann suggested that the *lutron* words ought to be interpreted in terms of ransoming slaves, with the emphasis on payment to gain freedom, as in secular papyri. 'But', it has been observed, 'if biblical Greek provides a better source from which to investigate the words, then ... themes and ideas other than those related to commerce and the slave-market provide the background of meaning, the most important of these being the theme of Israel's deliverance.'[54]

Nevertheless, in later Christian Greek there is a return to the secular idea of purchasing power. There is mention of working with the hands 'for the *lutron* of thy sins', and God is said to have given up His own Son 'as a *lutron* for us' to get us out of the clutches of pleasures and lusts (Barn 19[10] Diogn 9[1,2]). Eusebius of Caesarea declares that the Lord surrendered Himself for our sins to become our *antipsuchos* (Substitute) and *antilutron*,[55] the latter being inevitably interpreted in the context as substitutionary payment. It was widely believed that the Devil had obtained powers over mankind and that, to deliver man, someone must 'pay' the Devil his rightful due.

In the Bible, however, the work of deliverance from beginning to end is on God's initiative, with no mention of speculative contracts or trafficking arrangements. He actively and most readily reconciles man to Himself. He takes away His own enmity. When the Highest stooped to the lowest, the Highest did not lose any of His splendour, nor did the divine nature cease to be divine. God in His might was behind everything from first to last. God entered the world to bring atonement, and the whole life of Jesus, not only His death, was reconciling. 'What impossibility is there in the mystery that teaches us that Purity has stooped down to them that were dead, the Guide to them that had gone astray, that the defiled might be made clean, the dead raised, and the wanderers led back to the right way.'[56]

Salvation is generous and positive, not legally conceived, not a compensation paid to aggrieved justice, not a ransom, not the remission of a sentence – but spontaneous forgiveness, new life, everlasting blessedness, divine creativeness. It is *justification*, **sanctification**, GLORIFICATION!

DESPISER OF THE GOOD

ἀφιλάγαθος

Aphilagathos is a coinage of Christian Greek that occurs only in the pastoral epistles, although an abstract noun *(aphilokagathia)* was coined after the same manner in the papyri of a century later.

In 2 Ti 3[1-3] our new word denotes a characteristic of perilous eschatological days. The catalogue in which this item occurs is grim: it lists a regime of arrogancy and irreverent blasphemers, so selfish as to seek nought but their own pleasures. They contribute to the passing-show before the Coming of our Lord and include the covetous, the truce-breakers, the incontinent, the fierce, and pleasure-lovers. All of them make a pretence of godliness. All are to be shunned.

DESTROYER

1. ὀλοθρευτής

Olothreutēs is a new noun in Christian Greek, coined from existing words. It may be a hapax of St. Paul,[57] found only at 1 Co 10[10] where the Destroyer in the wilderness is conceived as a type of the punishment which shall overtake unworthy pilgrims in the scramble of this world. Perhaps he is to be understood as Satan.

2. ἀπολλύων

Apolluōn, a proper name, is in form a present participle of the verb 'to destroy'. Apollyon is thus the Destroying One, whose Hebrew name is Abaddon in Rev 9[11]. Oepke points out that from the time of Grotius the name has often been taken as a play on the name of Apollo, the god of pestilence, whose creature was the locust.[58] Cassandra cries in the play: 'Apollo! ... my Destroyer! Thou hast destroyed me again the second time.'[59]

Indeed, in the Philoxenian Syriac version of Rev 9[11], 'Apollo' is actually read, points out Oepke,[60] who then suggests that Revelation was directed against the Roman empire since, after the battle of Actium Apollo was regarded especially as the god of the Roman empire.

3. ἀβαδδών

In Christian Greek *Abaddōn* is an indeclinable proper noun transliterated from Hebrew.

According to post-Biblical Jewish theology, the angel Abaddon presides over the Bottomless Pit (see 'Hell') which is the resting place of the lost departed. His Hebrew name, *'ᵃbhaddhôn*, is derived from the verb *'ābhadh* (to perish) and occurs in the Wisdom literature where in AV he is rendered 'Destruction' (Job 26[6] 28[22] 31[12]; Ps 88[12]; Pr 15[11]) and where he is the Abode of the Dead personified insomuch as he and Death 'speak' (Job 28[22]). In literature of the rabbis, Abaddon is the lowest compartment of the underworld.

By using the transliteration, early Christian language was making a new departure, uninfluenced by any previous Greek model for the LXX had freely rendered the Hebrew into *Apōleia* (see 'Hell').

When the fifth angel sounds in God's apocalypse of the End (Rev 9[11]), the Bottomless Pit is opened to emit a smoke which is full of locusts looking like scorpions and having as their king the Angel of the Bottomless Pit, 'whose name in the Hebrew tongue is *Abaddon*, but in the Greek tongue hath his name Apollyon' (Destroyer). Henceforth the Seer knows him as 'Abaddon' instead of the Greek name.

In guise of the Beast, Abaddon ascends from the lowest realms to fight against the Witnesses (11[7]) and then goes to perdition (17[8]).

THE DEVIL

διάβολος

Diabolos in the Bible denotes a personal power of evil, as when Jesus says, 'One of you is a *devil*,' (Jn 6[70]) but *diabolos* is supremely Satan, chief of the fallen angels.

Secular Greek. *Diabolos* was here an adjective, often used as a noun. As an adjective, coupled with 'old woman', it meant 'backbiting',[61] and so St. Paul directs that in the Church 'old women' must refrain (Tit 2[3]). He uses the secular sense. As a noun it meant an accuser, a calumniator, a slanderer.[62] As a neuter noun, *diabolon* sometimes signified slander itself, linked in the context with malice and meddling.[63] *Diabolos* in the NT is still used in the secular way of 'slanderer', something which a deacon's wife must not be (1 Ti 3[11]), and a characteristic of many in the perilous times which shall come. (2 Ti 3[3]).

Biblical Greek. A new meaning appears in the Bible, as seen first in the LXX where the word renders *shāṭān* more than a dozen times. *Shāṭān* was the Hebrew for 'adversary', but it was also a name given to the chief of fallen angels. *Shāṭān* is rendered by *diabolos* when he is said to provoke David to commit sin by numbering Israel (1 Chr 21[1]) and when he is permitted to test the patriarch Job (1[6,7,9,12] 2[1,2,3,4,6,7]); in the vision of Zechariah, *diabolos* (= *shāṭān*) stands at God's right hand, as an accuser resisting Joshua the High Priest (Zach 3[1-3]). The typology represents that Satan opposes the cleansing of the Church and that God promises to bring forth His servant the Branch (v. 8). In the Psalms Satan *(diabolos)* is the wicked Accuser ruling over men (Ps 108(109)[6(5)]). In NT Greek the name given to this fallen Angel is often the simple transliteration *Satanas* – nearly forty times. The LXX too had not always rendered *shāṭān* by *diabolos* (the Devil), but once used *Satan* (3 Km 11[14,23]) and once *Satanas* (Job 2[3]).

The Greek word *diabolos* is nevertheless ubiquitous in Christian and Church Greek, invariably indicating the Church's arch-enemy and arch-slanderer, Satan who dwells on high and who is probably the Prince of the power of the air (Eph 2[7]), said to have fallen like lightning from heaven (Lk 10^{18}). One would think he is to be distinguished in Christian thought from the other fallen angels who dwell by contrast in the lowest depths of hell, in darkness awaiting judgment (2 Pet 2^4; Jude 6). As Richardson remarks, 'this ambiguity about his habitat is one of the many indications that thoughtful Jews knew that they were using pictorial symbols which they did not themselves take literally.'[64]

There is a contemporary revival of interest in various sorts of black magic and Devil worship, for men are still tormented with the paradox of belief in Almighty God and acknowledgement of all the pain and futility of the world. Father Coulange suggested that our modern 'priests' have now largely exorcized the Devil by their social reforms, by the progress of science, and by other narcotics.[65] Nevertheless, the Bible affords no hope that Satan is so easily overthrown.

DEVILISH

δαιμονιώδης

The adjective *daimoniōdēs* was formed in Christian Greek from the noun *daimōn* (deity or devil) and appears in the Symmachus version of Ps 90(91)^6. Here it was an attempt to render the Hebrew *shādhadh* (or *shûdh*), to despoil, devastate, or ruin ('the sickness that *destroyeth* in the noon-day'), and so the meaning is 'destructive'.

It appears again in post-Christian secular Greek where there may be some Biblical influence: viz. a scholion on the Frogs of Aristophanes,[66] and a fifth-century commentary of Proclus on Plato's *Timaeus*, where the meaning is obviously derived from *daimōn* (deity or devil). In the latter it is used of Phaethon, burning up every place where he approached[67] – the meaning, 'destructive' again.

The Christian sense may only be gathered from the context, where St. James refers to a worldliness which, by contrast with the wisdom of God – the truth revealed in the Gospel – is *daimoniōdēs*, earthly and sensual, a wisdom of this world, aggressively ambitious, filling the heart with envious turmoil (Jas 3$^{14f.}$).

DEVOTION (CHRISTIAN DEVOTION)

εὐσέβεια: εὐσεβής: εὐσεβῶς

Here is a further example of pagan words adopted by Christians and made specially their own. *Eusebeia, eusebēs* and *eusebōs* appear rarely in the canonical books translated in the LXX, but in the apocrypha they are relatively abundant, especially in 4 Maccabees. 'The concept is Greek and not Hebrew', is a fair judgment.[68] Originally the words had to do with the externals of the cult, but in later Greek they were like our word, 'religious'. For the educated Greek *eusebeia* is reverent and wondering awe at the lofty divine world; it is worship in the cultus and respect for the orders sustained by it – parents, the authorities, and so on. The word does not represent a situation of submission to the claims of a personal divine power.[69] It was not the obvious term to express piety towards God.

Devotion (noun). *Eusebeia* occurs occasionally in a sense which suggests personal religious devotion in the contemporary inscriptions (MM) but its more general meaning in the popular Greek of the Roman period was 'loyalty'.[70] In the classics it had expressed reverence for parents as well as for the gods,[71] and Demosthenes uses the adverb *eusebōs* in the context of ethics. 'You cannot *conscientiously* acquit him' (XIX 212) – a matter of principle, not religion.

For Christians *eusebeia* is the highest kind of **devotion** to God, a characteristic disclaimed modestly by St. Peter as the cause of his healing power (Act 3[12]), but much elevated in the pastoral Epistles as a quality which kings and rulers should possess (1 Ti 2[2]). It springs directly from acceptance of the gospel (Tit 1[1]), assuming that 'truth' here is the Gospel (see 'Truth').

It includes special emphasis on worship, in the phrase, 'mystery of Devotion', for in the ensuing context a liturgical creed is at once rehearsed (1 Ti 3[16]), or a primitive hymn.[72] Timothy must refuse all preoccupation with heresy and instead engage himself in *eusebeia*, that altogether profitable pursuit (4[7f.]). Correct Christian teaching is 'in accordance with *eusebeia*,' and is its own reward, bringing no material gain, the very peak of a man of God's achievement – along with righteousness, faith, love, patience and meekness (1 Ti 6[3, 5f., 11]). Heretics parade in this devotional guise, as a mere form (2 Ti 3[5]).

Eusebeia is ranked highly in 2 Peter – along with faith, virtue, temperance, spiritual insight, patience and brotherly love – and is a proper activity in which to be engaged at the Coming of our Lord (2 Pet 1[3, 6f.] 3[11]). Deissmann compares an inscription from Asia

111

Minor of i BC, which mentions successively the faithfulness, virtue, righteousness and 'godliness' *(eusebeia)* of the person to be honoured.[73]

Once in the apostolic Fathers *eusebeia* recalls the 'godliness' of Lot (1 Clem 11[1]); elsewhere it has the special meaning of **devotion** (1 Clem 1[2] 15[1] 32[4]), a fine quality of the Christian life, an example which should be set to all the younger brethren (2 Clem 19[1]).

The verb *eusebō* in secular Greek was used of pious and reverent acts of worship of the pagan gods[74] as a result of which, for instance, the Greeks may hope to come home safely from Troy,[75] but not only worship of gods – it is also the dutiful treatment of guests.[76] St. Paul uses it of the Athenians' blind devotion to the Unknown God and for the cherishing by Christian children of their parents (Act 17[33]; 1 Ti 5[4]).

Devout (adjective). The adjective *eusebēs* similarly expressed a pagan piety for gods. Herodotus records that on a stone statue of Sethos, the Egyptian king, shown with a mouse in his hand, was the inscription: 'Look on me and be a *eusebēs* (god-fearer)'. A multitude of field-mice had swarmed over the enemy camp and devoured the Assyrians' quivers, bows, and shields, for Sethos had called upon the god to good effect! (II 141).

St. Luke applies the word to Cornelius, the God-fearer, and to one of his soldiers, as well as to Ananias who baptized Saul (Act 10[2,7] 22[12]). Believers, however, are **devout** in the new sense, while the unregenerate are 'ungodly' (2 Pet 2[9]). It has to do with Christian worship, and St. Clement applies it to the confidence in which the elect and sanctified stretch out their hands to Almighty God (1 Clem 2[3]).

The devout man, the man who is *eusebēs* in the new sense, must not grieve if he endures sorrow at the present time (2 Clem 19[4]). The neuter adjective becomes a noun *(to eusebes)*, signifying a **Christian devotion** which is contrasted with training in commercial activity. So it is at variance with 'gain' (2 Clem 20[4]).

In a devout Christian way (adverb). The adverb *eusebōs* in the pastoral Epistles describes a Christian mode of life, a walk leading to persecution (2 Ti 3[12]), involving the denial of worldly lusts (Tit 2[12]) and leading nevertheless to God's favour (1 Clem 61[2]). It indicates a way of guiding the brethren's steps. To help towards achieving it, St. Clement has written his epistle (62[1]).

DISPERSION (THE PILGRIM CHURCH)
διασπορά

Diaspora is a new word, a literal translation of the Hebrew *za*ᵃ*wâ* (Deut 28²⁵; Jer 41(34)¹⁷). It indicates the Israelites' 'removal' to foreign lands – and not only the dispersal itself,⁷⁷ but the dispersed people, the outcasts of Israel⁷⁸ – and *diaspora* sometimes stands for any one of the lands to which they went. The word is found applied to Israel in Plutarch and Philo and is probably taken from the LXX.

Contemporary with the NT are the Psalms of Solomon, a Pharisaic collection which prays for the gathering together of the *diaspora* of Israel (8³⁴). At the same time the Testaments of the Twelve Patriarchs warn that Israel shall be set at nought in the *diaspora* (Asher 7). It has an unusual meaning in Judith – not the Dispersion, but rather the Jewish exiles in one particular place (5¹⁹). The prayer of a nationalist leader was, 'Gather together our *diaspora*! Set at liberty them that are in bondage among the heathen!' (2 Mac 1²⁷).

St. John too by diaspora refers to Jews who resided outside Palestine (Jn 7³⁵). Elsewhere, Christian Greek has added its own special interpretation, for it has made *diaspora* a figure of the pilgrim Church absent from home until her temporary exile ends with the Coming of the Lord. So, in its religious sense, *diaspora* is now a specific term in Biblical theology.⁷⁹ As Meyer observed, no Christian would have applied to the twelve Jewish tribes the expression, 'the elect dwellers of the *diaspora*', for that was a title of honour for Christians themselves.⁸⁰ Referring to St. Peter's letter also, Spoerri rightly affirmed that there was no need to think that the recipients were Jews.⁸¹ St. James and St. Peter are one in their Christian use of *disapora*.

Some have supposed that the Christian *diaspora*, on a Jewish analogy, refers to the Church outside the Holy Land, but there are no grounds for making a contrast between the Church in Palestine and the Church abroad: the real distinction for Christians is between saints on pilgrimage and saints in heaven. That is why, for St. James, the whole Church on earth is figuratively 'the twelve tribes in the *diaspora*' (1¹) and, for St. Peter, 'the strangers of the *diaspora* in Pontus ...' etc. (1 Pet 1¹). St. Justin Martyr affirms that saints on earth are the true *diaspora*,⁸² and he finds it significant that Moses did not lead the Dispersion into the Promised Land; it was left for Joshua (Jesus), as it is now left for our Joshua (Jesus) to lead us into our promised possession for ever (*Dial.* 113³ᶠ·). The Church on earth is the *diaspora*.

Reference should be made to our entry, 'Pilgrimage' *(paroikia)*, which in Christian Greek has the same meaning. The difference is that *paroikia* is a local church in the exile of this world, whereas *diaspora* is the pilgrim Church worldwide.

DISPUTE

ἐκζήτησις

The noun *ekzētēsis* is not vouched for in secular Greek (Bauer). It is probably a Pauline invention, and its meaning would appear by the context to be a 'dispute', for Timothy is exhorted to give no heed to fables and endless genealogies 'which minister *ekzētēseis*', that is, which lead to debates that are unprofitable (1 Ti 1⁴). The Revisers in 1881 have given the meaning of the verb *ekzētō* as it is in secular Greek – to seek out – that is, 'questionings'. LS similarly lean on secular precedent for their rendering, 'research'. The context requires disputes, differences of opinion and controversies.

Ekzētēseis is the better reading, but the Received Text has simplex *zētēseis*. The latter is a secular word, meaning search, investigation (as in the phrases, 'the *investigation* of truth', 'in *search* of supplies', 'the *search* for the murderers'),[83] or in the plural, controversies,[84] which is probably the Christian meaning of *ekzētēseis*.

DISPUTING, PERVERSE

παραδιατριβή, διαπαρατριβή

Paradiatribē is a coinage of Christian Greek, a hapax legomenon, formed however from the secular word *paratribē*, which Polybius uses for 'friction'. The better text at 1 Ti 6⁵ reads *diaparatribē*, but perhaps both forms of the word were in circulation among Christians, denoting the heretical discourse of arrogant men of crooked intellects who engaged in wordy strife contrary to the teaching which St. Paul handed down to true believers (1 Ti 6⁵).

Field (p. 211) observed that the prefix *dia-* has been thought to give a sense of continuance to the action, suggesting that the disputes never end. He himself preferred the idea of reciprocity, rather than continuance, on the analogy of similar words of this formation. So *paradiatribē* and *diaparatribē* will be 'mutual irritation', close to what the Revisers suggested in their margin, 'gallings of one another'.

DO GOOD

ἀγαθοεργέω

The new Christian verb, *agathoergō*, is apparently a coinage of St. Paul, made up from existing words. The adjective *agathergos* (doing good) is used by Plutarch, and the noun *agathergia* (good deed) by Herodotus, but both are rare.

Wealthy members of the Church are encouraged by St. Paul to do good *(agathoergō)*, which specifically means 'to be generous' and 'to have fellowship' (q.v.) with other believers (1 Ti 6[18]). A contracted form of the verb is *agathourgō* (Act 14[17]: God does good and sends rain from heaven), which is another new word.

In addition, Christians had the usual verb *agathopoiō* but they reserved them both for the peculiarly Christian virtue of showing kindness in a practical way.

DOMINIONS

κυριότητες

Singular. Probably the singular form, *kuriotēs*, and almost certainly the plural, *kuriotētes*, found new colouring in Jewish Greek. In the secular language, the singular occurs in the phrases, '*dominion* over many things',[85] and 'the *authority* of the law'.[86] In time it came to designate the proper or legitimate use of a term and the peculiar nature of a thing.[87]

The secular meaning, 'dominion', 'authority', was accepted by Christians and applied to Christ. The Didache, in common with the Apostolical Church Order (12), speaks of the 'lordship' of Jesus (4), and Hermas of the 'lordship' of the Son of God (*Sim.* V 6.1). The divine 'lordship' or 'majesty' may be the meaning of the singular form on two ocasions in the NT when heretics who despise *kuriotēs* are noticed.[88] It will not indicate civil power in these contexts, for whereas heretics were unlikely to resist the civil rule, they may very well have been resisting 'Church authority'.[89] In view of the use of the word in Jewish and Christian Greek, it is more likely that it denotes the majesty of God and thus even God Himself.[90] On one occasion, though standing in the singular (Eph 1[21]), it marks an order of superior angels, the 'Dominions'.

Plural. In the plural the word finds a new meaning of angelic 'Dominions' in Jewish and Christian Greek. Reference should be made to the article, 'Authorities'. The *kuriotētes* were an order of angels, like the Thrones, the Principalities, and the Powers (q.v.),

115

created for God's service (Col 1[16]). The hierarchy may be arranged in ascending order when rehearsed (in the singular) in Eph 1[21] (Principality, Authority, Power, Dominion), and in descending order in Col 1[16] (Thrones, Dominions, Principalities, Powers). The order of Dominion, then, is high on either list. Such beings probably appear in a list of angels who occupy the seventh heaven, surrounding God's throne, along with Principalities, Powers, Thrones, Cherubim and Seraphim, in a Jewish book which is perhaps a little older than the NT books.[91] No one can be sure of the original Greek words in this instance in the Secrets of Enoch but the translated list of the supernal beings resembles those of St. Paul quite closely.

The Testament of Solomon, probably appearing within the first four centuries, is evidence for the use in Jewish Greek of the plural form to indicate an order of angels. At the close of manuscript D, the wisdom and glory of Solomon are extolled, and it is said that in his temple were the Cherubim, the Seraphim, and the six-winged angels, while behind the altar were the creatures of many eyes, the *thronoi* (Thrones) and the *kuriotētes* (Dominions).[92] A hierarchy of celestial beings is intended, of which Thrones and Dominions were apparently the two chief.

Almost simultaneously perhaps, Origen was writing of the same hierarchy of *thronoi, kuriotētes*, etc., affirming that though Christians were below them, they may entertain the hope that by a virtuous life they will rise to a likeness with them.[93]

The sum of the angels in this group is represented by the plural form, *kuriotētes*, and it may well be that when the singular form is used in the NT, the word becomes, not a member of the group but a collective designation for this particular order of angels, the status of 'Dominions', as it were. St. Paul says that Christ is exalted above all 'principalitiship', 'authoritiship', 'powership', and 'dominionship', referring to each status in the hierarchy (Eph 1[21]). That may be the meaning in 2 Pet 2[10] Jude 8, where the heretics despise 'dominionship', but one may still feel the force of Biggs' objection – 'it is not possible to suppose that the False Teachers treated any particular class of Angels with contempt'[94] – and after all the divine majesty may be intended here.

See also 'Angels', 'Principalities', 'Authorities', 'Powers', and 'Thrones'.

DOUBLEMINDED

δίψυχος

Dipsuchos is a novel expression of early Christians. Though it occurs in later Christian writers, Moulton and Milligan allow the likelihood of St. James' coinage. The noun, *dipsuchia*, occurs in the lexicon of Hesychius where it is equated with *aporia* (distress, difficulty). Our adjective occurs in Philo.[95]

Whether or not it is a new Christian word, it means 'wavering' and 'lacking in faith'. A *dipsuchos* man is unstable in his ways (Jas 1[8]). His remedy is to draw nigh to God and to cleanse his heart (4[8]). Lot's wife is a lesson to believers, not to be *dipsuchos*, and not to doubt God's power. A doubting man is set for judgment (1 Clem 11[2]). The *dipsuchoi* are coupled with the *distazontes*, the doubters. Hermas gives frequent warnings about their character. They are those who dispute in their hearts. The message to them is plain: 'Believe, ye that are *dipsuchoi*.' (*Vis.* III 4.3, IV 2.6). In Hermas a consistent meaning is 'doubter'. (*Mand.* XI 2, 4, 13, etc.).

The three words, the adjective *(dipsuchos)*, the verb *(dipsuchō)*, and the noun *(dipsuchia)* occur altogether about sixty times in the *Shepherd* of Hermas. Hermas is evidently the writer most concerned with the concept, and Dr. W. Colebourne[96] has an interesting contribution to make upon his use of these words. The document forming the eighth Similitude, he believes, reflects a time of persecution in the last years of the first century when sometimes Christians would deny their faith, and it is this vacillation under pressure which seems to underly some of the *dipsuchos* words. Coleborne suggests that 'these words acquired a use, not necessarily exclusively, in relation to persecution and the attendant renunciation that some Christians made of their faith'. He agrees that the observation reflects on the date of the epistle of St. James, the only NT book to use this stem, and indicates a time of persecution, probably like that of the eighth Similitude, the end of the first century. Coleborne's felicitous suggestion is confirmed by the context of the word when St. James (4[11]) cautions, 'Speak not evil one of another'. As we know from Pliny's letter to Trajan, Christians were willing to inform on other Christians during the persecution.[97]

A remarkable concurrence has been observed between the Christian Hermas and the Jewish thanksgiving scroll from Qumrân which contrasts human fickleness and insincerity with God's fidelity. 'They enquire of Thee with double heart' *(dārash bᵉlēbh wālēbh)*.[98] What was probably the reasoning behind the coining of *dipsuchos* was the well-known Jewish and Christian conviction that man had to choose between two ways which are set before him.[99] There were two spirits in man, two inclinations, one to evil, the other to good.[100] Prof. Seitz suggests that here and in other ways there are parallels of thought and expression between the Dead Sea

Scrolls and Christian documents like James, the Didache, Barnabas, 1 and 2 Clement, and Hermas.[101]

TO DOUBT
διακρίνω

An additional meaning for the old verb *diakrinō* is found in Christian Greek.

Secular Greek. The meaning is wide. In the active voice it is to separate one party from another, like the parting of combatants or the distinguishing of one thing from another.[102] It is used of judges 'deciding'. It is to judge or discern. In the middle or passive voice, the verb means 'to contend' or 'to be partial'.

The active senses of discerning and judging are found sometimes also in the NT and in later Jewish Greek.[103] We have 'discerning' the face of the sky (Mt 16[3]) and the Body (1 Co 11[29]). We have 'judging' (1 Co 11[31] 14[29] 6[5] and 'distinguishing' (Act 15[9]; 1 Co 4[7]; Jude 22). So also in the apostolic Fathers: 'consider' (Hermas *Sim.* II 1), 'examine' (Did 11[7]), 'separate' (I. Eph 5[3]), 'distinguish' (Diogn 5[1]), 'dispose' (Diogn 8[7]).

As in secular Greek, the middle voice with the meaning 'contend' is found (Act 11[2]; Jude 9), and the passive voice with the meaning 'be partial' (Jas 2[4]).

Christian Greek. A meaning which is not found hitherto even in the LXX arises among Christians. It is the meaning, 'to doubt', and usually it is confined to middle and passive voices, but not always.

Our Lord promises that if His disciples have faith and 'doubt' not (passive), anything they ask shall be granted (Mt 21[21]; Mk 11[23]). It was St. Paul's certainty, and not his doubts, that made him a great servant of God. 'Uncertainty', says Mr. Stacey, 'may be commendable for its honesty and reserve, but doubters do not carry the gospel across continents or turn the world upside down.'[104] Simon Peter (Act 10[20]) was bidden to rise and go with the messengers, 'doubting' nothing (middle or passive voice). When later he reports on the matter, St. Peter turns the verb into the active with no change in meaning (11[12]). 'The Spirit bade me go with them nothing *doubting*' (AV). The Revisers, often not sensitive to the peculiarities of Biblical Greek, supposed that St. Peter lapsed into secular usage and said, 'making no distinction' (RV).[105]

Further examples of the new meaning abound. Abraham 'staggered' not at the promise of God (passive), that is to say, he did not 'doubt' (Ro 4[20]). The weak brother who 'doubts' (middle or passive)

118

ought not to eat the idol-meat, 'because he eateth not of faith' (Ro 14²³). The brethren at prayer must have faith and may not 'doubt' (middle or passive) like a wave of the sea (Jas 1⁶). The Church must have compassion in cases about which she is in 'doubt' (middle or passive): 'Have compassion on some, as you are *doubtful*' (Jude 22).

The new meaning appears in Hermas[106] and is undoubtedly 'a Christian coinage' (MM sv). Sanday and Headlam suggested that the word and the similar term *dipsuchos*, belong to the same circle of ideas.[107]

DRIVEN WITH THE WIND

ἀνεμιζόμενοι

Anemos (wind) is common enough and the Christians created a verb *(anemizō)* from it, of which *anemizomenoi* is the passive participle.

St. James in particular inclines to *-izō* verbs, in place of the more secular *-oō*. However, *anemizō* is found nowhere else but in an obscure scholion on the Odyssey.[108] By means of it Christians express an utter horror at the infusion of doubt into prayer. 'Let him ask in faith, nothing wavering. For he that wavereth is like a wave of the sea *driven with the wind* and tossed.' (Jas 1⁶). Doubt and hesitancy are natural feelings and not Christian virtues.

DUMB

μογιλάλος

Mogilalos may be a Biblical achievement, formed from two existing words: *mogis* (with difficulty) and *lalia* (speech). By secular derivation it would mean, not 'dumb', but 'speaking with difficulty'.[109] That such a sense was intended by St. Mark (7³², ³³) seems to be implied in that, after the cure, the man 'spoke plainly' (verse 35).

Tyndale, moreover, rendered, 'one that ... stumbled in his speech', and AV, 'had an impediment in his speech'. However, the derivation of words is often not at all decisive in reaching a Biblical meaning, and the Vulgate *(mutum)* proved acceptable to Wycliffe *(doumbe)*. It is more to the point to say that *mogilalos* renders the Hebrew *'illēm* (dumb) in the messianic prophecy (LXX Isai 35⁶). Besides, other Greek versions of the OT understand *mogilalos* in the sense of 'dumb' (Aquila Isai 56[10]; Aquila, Symmachus, Theodotion Ex 4[11]), despite the few later writers who attest the sense, 'speaking with difficulty'.[110]

Vettius Valens (73.12) in the second century, and a late second-century papyrus, have the sense 'dumb'. An astrological calendar which includes portrayals of presiding deities, reads: 'This deity causes long old age, till a man becomes bent by senility; he produces hunchbacks and makes men bent with sickness, he causes dwarfs to be born and monstrosities shaped like a beetle, and persons with no eyes and beastlike, *dumb* and deaf and toothless'.[111]

The importance of the word in Biblical Greek, as Hoskyns noticed,[112] is that our understanding of St. Mark's narrative (7[31–37]) depends upon the detection of the OT allusion (Isai 35[3–6]): the healing of the dumb is a messianic claim and a proof that Messiah is at work. Isaiah's words, 'the tongue of the dumb shall sing', were written for the disciples' learning, and now they are fulfilled. 'They brought to Him one that was deaf and *dumb* ... He touched the tongue of the *dumb* man.' (Mk 7[32f.]).

A word with slightly different spelling, *moggilalos* (hoarse of speech), might be preferred. It has good authority and appears in some manuscripts in the LXX passage (Isai 35[6]), but the force of the messianic argument remains.

NOTES

[1] F. Preisigke, *Sammelbuch griech. Urkunden aus Ägypten*, Strassburg 1915–50, I. 5224, 20; read ἐπιουσί[ων] according to Sayce, but see B. M. Metzger, *Expository Times* 69 (1957–8), pp. 52–4.

[2] Moulton-Howard *Grammar* II, p. 313.

[3] Origen *de Oratione* 27.7 (Library of Christian Classics, vol. II, Philad., 1954, p. 298).

[4] Blass-Debrunner *Grammatik* §123, 1.

[5] *Expository Times* 52 (1940), p. 120.

[6] Moulton-Howard *Grammar* II, p. 314.

[7] *On a Fresh Revision of the English New Testament*, 3rd ed. 1891, pp. 217–60.

[8] *Grammar* 3rd ed., p. 159.

[9] *An Aramaic Approach to the Gospels and Acts*, Clarendon 3rd ed. 1967, p. 204, and in *Journal of Theol. Studies* 42 (1941), pp. 186–9.

[10] *Journal of Theological Studies* 42 (1941), p. 189.

[11] Polybius II 25.11; Act 16[11] vl.

[12] For details see *Journal of Theological Studies* 35 (1934), p. 379).

[13] *Journal of Biblical Literature* 53 (1934), p. 116.

[14] *New Testament Studies* 5 (1958), pp. 79–81.

[15] *An Aramaic Approach to the Gospels and Acts*, Clarendon 3rd ed. 1967, p. 203.

[16] Herodotus IV 71, 72; P. Flor 121.3 (iii AD).

[17] Thucydides I 133, as Act 6[1].

[18] Demosthenes XVIII 69 (206).

D

[19] Polybius XV 25.21.

[20] Demosthenes XIX 69; P. Oxy 275.10 (i AD).

[21] *Die Inschriften von Magnesia am Maeander*, ed. O. Kern, Berlin 1900, 109 (100 BC).

[22] I. Pol 6[1]; I. Eph 2[1]; I. Magn 2[1] 6[1] 13[1]; I. Smyrn 8[1] 12[2]; I. Philad intr. 4[1] 7[1] 10[2]; 1 Clem 42[4ff.]; Did 15[1].

[23] 1 Ti 3[10,13]; Hermas *Sim.* II 10, VIII 4.1, IX 26.2; *Mand.* II 6; *Vis.* III 5.1.

[24] As developed challengingly and with Biblical emphasis by H. Kraemer, *A Theology of the Laity*, Lutterworth, Hulsean Lectures 1958.

[25] I.Magn 6[1]; I. Philad 10[2]; Hermas *Sim.* IX 26.2.

[26] *Republic* 560E.

[27] *Nicomachean Ethics* IV 1.3.

[28] Josephus *Ant. Jud.* XII iv 8 (Niese XII 203).

[29] Teubner iv 59–67.

[30] Teubner ii 5.1.

[31] LXX Pr 28[7]; 2 Mac 6[4].

[32] As seen in Tatian *Oratio ad Graecos* 17.4, 23.1; Palladius *Lausiac History*, ed. C. Butler, Texts and Studies, CUP (1904) 3 (lasciviousness).

[33] Plato *Parmenides* 136E.

[34] Plato *Laws* 683A.

[35] Plato *Phaedo* 81A.

[36] Plato *Republic* 505C.

[37] *Republic* 602C.

[38] Aristotle *Nicomachean Ethics* 1094b 16.

[39] Diodorus Siculus II 18.

[40] W. Scott, *Corpus Hermeticum*, Clarendon 1929, I libellus I 29.

[41] P. Par 16.24 (UPZ 185.II 6). See LS (1948) I, p. 469, for the meaning, 'innovate'.

[42] As in 1 Km 11[14]; 2 Ch 15[8]R; Ps 50(51)[10], and without corresponding Hebrew in Isai 16[11] 41[1] 45[16]; 2 Mac 2[29]A.

[43] Herodotus V 77; Demosthenes LIII 11.13.

[44] P Oxy 48.6 (AD 86); Josephus *Ant. Jud.* XII 2.5 (Niese XII 46); Philo *de Specialibus Legibus* ii 22.

[45] *Ant. Jud.* XIV vii 1 (Niese XIV 107)

[46] Ibid. XIV xiv 1 (Niese XIV 371).

[47] *Orphica Lithica*, ed. Abel, 593.

[48] Plutarch *Aratus* 11.

[49] Plato *Theaetetus* 165E.

[50] Demosthenes XIX 170; P. Eleph 198 (iii BC).

[51] Polybius XVIII 16.1.

[52] David Hill, *Greek Words and Hebrew Meanings*, CUP 1967, p. 70.

[53] Hill, op. cit., p. 68.

[54] Hill, op. cit., p. 67.

[55] *Commentarius in Isaiam* 53[6ff.] (PG XXIV 457C).

[56] St. Gregory of Nyssa *Great Catechism* XXIV 2.

[57] It is read by Cyril of Alexandria at Ex 12[23], but clearly under the influence of St. Paul's locution.

[58] R. H. Charles, *Revelation*, ICC T. & T. Clark 1920, vol. I, p. 246.

[59] Aeschylus *Agamemnon* 1081.

[60] In Kittel *TWNT* I, p. 396.

[61] Menander 878.

[62] Aristotle *Topica* 126a 32 (coupled with 'sophist'); Athenaeus 11.508d (ii-iii AD).

[63] Plutarch *Moralia* 61D.

[64] Alan Richardson, *Introduction to the Theology of the New Testament*, SCM 1958, p. 209n.

[65] Louis Coulange (J. Tourmel), *The Life of the Devil*, ET, A. A. Knopf 1929, especially p. 294.

[66] Ed. W. Dindorf, Oxford 1835ff., 29.3.

[67] Teubner 1903, ed. E. Diehl, vol. i, p. 113C.

[68] B. S. Easton, *The Pastoral Epistles*, Scribner 1947, p. 218.

[69] Foerster in Kittel *TWNT* VII, p. 477f.

[70] P. Lond 3.1178.14, 814.2 (i AD).

[71] Plato *Republic* 615C.

[72] See M. O. Massinger, *Bibliotheca Sacra*, 96 (1939), pp. 481f.

[73] OGI no. 438. A. Deissmann, *Light from the Ancient East*, Hodder 1910, p. 322; Hodder 1927, pp. 317f.

[74] P. Ryl 112 a 4 (iii AD).

[75] Aeschylus *Agamemnon* 338.

[76] Euripides *Alcestis* 1148.

[77] Jer 15[7] ('I will scatter them in the *diaspora*'); Neh 1[9] ('though your *diaspora* were to the uttermost part of heaven'). So also Dan LXX 12[2].

[78] Isai 49[6]: 'the *diaspora* (i.e. the dispersed) of Israel'. Ps 146(147)[2]: 'the *outcasts* of Israel'.

[79] K. L. Schmidt in Kittel *TWNT;* II, p. 104.

[80] A. Meyer, *Das Rätsel des Jakobsbriefes*, Giessen 1930, p. 78.

[81] T. Spoerri, *Der Gemeindegedanke im ersten Petrusbrief*, 1925, p. 52, n. 2.

[82] *Dial.* 113[3] 121[4]: 'You suppose it was of [the Jews]. In reality it was said of us who have been enlightened through Jesus' (122[1]).

[83] Thucydides I 20, VIII 57, 66. So Plato *Cratylus* 406A.

[84] OGI 629.9 (Palmyra, ii AD).

[85] Memnon (i AD historian), Fragment 4.7 in C. Müller.

[86] Achmes 229.17 (AD 900).

[87] Damascius *de Principiis* 306 (vi AD); Dositheus (H. Keil's ed. *Gram. Lat.* vii p. 376) 1.1 (iv AD).

[88] Jude 8 (Sinaiticus has the plural), 2 Pet 2[10].

[89] C. Bigg, *St. Peter and St. Jude*, ICC T. & T. Clark 2nd ed. 1902, p. 279.

[90] W. Foerster in Kittel *TWNT* III, p. 1096 (St. Clement: 'hoc est, solum dominum qui vere dominus noster est, Jesus Christus').

[91] The Secrets of Enoch, which survives in a Slavonic redaction, XX 1 (Morfill, p. 25).

[92] T. Sol (ed. McCown) D VIII 6.

[93] *Contra Celsum* IV 29 (PG I 1069C).

[94] Bigg, ICC, p. 279.

[95] Cohn and Wendland, Berlin 1896ff., 2.663.

[96] Unpublished thesis, *A Linguistic Approach to the Problem of Structure and Composition of the Shepherd of Hermas*, Newcastle, N.S.W., 1965.

[97] Ibid. pp. 609f.

[98] Cited by O. J. F. Seitz, *New Testament Studies* 4 (1958), p. 328.

[99] Hermas *Mand.* VI; T. XII P., *Asher* 1[3ff.]; Did 1–6; Barn 18–20; Qumrân *Manual of Discipline* 3.20f., 4.2; Jer 21[8].

[100] T. XII P., *Jud.* 20, *Asher* 1[3ff.]; *Benj.* 6[1], *Manual of Discipline* 3.13ff.

[101] See the interesting papers, 'The Double-Minded Man in the Light of Essene Psychology', by W. I. Wolverton, *Harvard Theological Review* 38 (1956), pp. 166–75, and 'Afterthoughts on the Term "Dipsuchos"', by O. J. F. Seitz, *New Testament Studies* 4 (1958), pp. 327–34.

[102] Herodotus III 39: Polycrates harried all men alike, *making no difference.*

[103] E.g. T. Abr 81[14,25]: 'thou shalt *interpret* the vision'.

[104] W. David Stacey in *Expository Times* 69 (1958), p. 178.

[105] The whole phrase is omitted in D and some old Latin and Syriac versions, no doubt because it was thought to duplicate 10[20]. However, the voice is active.

[106] *Mand.* II 6, *Vis.* I 2.2 – active.

[107] *Romans*, ICC T. & T. Clark, 5th ed. 1902, p. 115.

[108] *Scholia in Homeri Odysseam*, ed. W. Dindorf, Oxford 1855, 12.336.

[109] A. S. Wetherhead's note assumes that the meaning is, 'speaking with difficulty', *Expository Times* 23 (1912), p. 381.

[110] E.g. Aëtius 8.38 (ed. J. Hirschberg 1899), a medical writer of the sixth century.

[111] P. Oxy 465, 222–9.

[112] E. Hoskyns and N. Davey, *The Riddle of the New Testament*, Faber 1958, pp. 119f.

E

πρεσβύτερος : πρεσβυτέριον

The words denote a special order of the Church's ministerial hierarchy.

Priest. *Presbuteros* is the comparative form of the adjective *presbus* (old), which is a poetic version[1] of the prose word *presbutēs* (old man). The comparative form is found in pagan texts to denote a senior official, an alderman, of the village – a community magistrate, perhaps.[2] 'We were judged by Numenius and the elders.'[3]

Not many agree with J. Jeremias that *presbuteros* always in the pastoral Epistles is an old man and never a Christian technical terms,[4] but some think, on the other hand, that *presbuteros* was a technical term even outside Christianity. According to Deissmann (BS pp. 154ff, 233ff), who quoted Krebs, priests of pagan temples in the Mediterranean world were sometimes designated *presbuteros*. An inscription from Lower Egypt (c. 40 BC) mentions 'priests of the great god Amonrasonthēr, both the *presbuteroi* and all the others.'[5] Nevertheless, despite this instance of religious application in Hellenistic Koine, it was more important for Christians that *presbuteros* was found in the sacred Greek of the Bible, where it denoted elders of Israel (Ex 17[5] 18[12] 19[7] 24[1,9,14] Josh 24[1]; Num 11[16] etc.). The word signified throughout the gospels and Acts the members of the council who presided over every synagogue (e.g. Act 4[5,8,23] 6[12] 23[14] 24[1] 25[15]). More peculiarly it is used of 'presbyters' or 'elders,' a definite order of ministry, set alongside apostles in the Church (Act 15[2,4,6,22f.] 16[4]).

St. Paul urges Timothy not to rebuke a *presbuteros*, but to intreat him as a father and to intreat the *neōteroi* (younger men) as brethren (1 Ti 5[1]). Here *presbuteros* may not be an official term but may simply have the usual sense, an older man, for he is contrasted with *neōteros* (a younger man). On the other hand, why may not *neōteros* too be understood as a technical term, viz. a 'newly baptized person'?[6]

There is some reluctance to see *presbuteros* (1 Ti 5[1]) as a Christian technical term. C. Spicq,[7] for instance, saw it simply as 'older man' (as Moffatt, RSV and Knox, and 'a man older than yourself' in Jerusalem Bible). The rendering 'elder' (NEB) has been criticized.[8] Several have taken it in the secular sense,[9] as long ago even as Bishop Ellicott who found that the parallel, 'as a father,' and the contrast, 'younger men,' made this interpretation nearly certain[10] – indeed, as long ago as St. Chrysostom and the Vulgate (*seniorem*).

St. Paul nevertheless made a practice of ordaining *presbuteroi* (obviously a technical term) in every local church (Act 14[23]; Tit 1[5]). It is not certain how such elders first came to be appointed and they figure quite incidentally in the church at Jerusalem, receiving visitors and gifts from another community (Act 11[30]); they, with apostles, greeted Barnabas and Saul when they came to discuss the admission of Gentiles (Act 15). Evidently the office of an elder was eminent: the decrees of the meeting were issued partly in their name. Perhaps the office represented a synagogue pattern which St. Paul reproduced within the churches which he founded. One cannot, however, be sure that synagogues in the Gentile world, the Dispersion, knew their elders by the name of *presbuteros* at this period.

A. E. Harvey in any case will not assume that Christians borrowed the presbyterate from the Jews. Elders in the synagogue had no more than judicial and administrative functions and the name 'elder' would be no more than honorific.[11] Rather than look for Jewish precedent, why not suppose that Christians named their leaders 'elders' because they were accustomed to the term from the Greek Bible, especially Num 11? 'The archetypal "elders" of the OT were of course the Seventy ... to whom God imparted a share of Moses' spirit. ... They were the model, according to Alexandrian legend, for the seventy who translated the Torah into Greek; they were the origin, according to the Rabbis, of the Jerusalem Sanhedrin; and quite possibly they were looked upon by Christians as the spiritual ancestors of their own ministers.'[12]

The origin of the term 'elder' may well be much more literal than that. Apart from OT precedents, there is the probability that in the earliest days authority naturally rested in the hands of older members of the Church. Age was respected. Younger men are exhorted to submit themselves to the senior (1 Pet 5[5]). The exhortation to let no one despise his youth was a tacit reminder to Timothy of the respect in which mere age was held (1 Ti 4[12]).

The name of 'bishop' (*episkopos*) is sometimes given by St. Luke to the *presbuteroi* (elders), as will be seen by comparing *episkopoi* (Act 20[28]) with *presbuteroi* (20[17]). We must suppose that in some churches at least – Ephesus and Jerusalem certainly – there were several elders or bishops. We find the phrase, 'presbyters in every church', on the first missionary journey (Act 14[23]). What is known as monepiscopacy or the monarchical episcopate – only one bishop presiding in a church – probably did not develop until after the NT period,[13] but perhaps its beginnings are there in 2 and 3 John and the Pastorals. Two letters are addressed from 'the Presbyter' (2 Jn

1, 3 Jn 1), and the position of Timothy and Titus appears to be something special in the local church. However, 'the idea of one bishop – one see ... is a late concept which did not develop until the third century'.[14]

An interesting viewpoint is to see the Seven, not as the first deacons but as early *presbuteroi*, embryonic Elders in the Jerusalem church, assisting the Apostles in various duties and constituting a pattern for St. Paul to follow in his churches. It is suggested that after AD 57 – for deacons do not appear before St. Paul wrote Ph 1[1] – the duties of the *presbuteroi* were divided and specific names were given to those fulfilling them: *episkopoi* were concerned with teaching and worship, *diakonoi* with charity and other administration.[15]

Although it is common practice for Irenaeus (c.AD 130–200) to use *episkopos* as all but interchangeable with *presbuteros*,[16] yet the rise of the monarchical episcopate, a tripartite structure developing from the two-fold structure of 'bishop/elder-deacon', had been accomplished by about AD 185 and seems to have developed east of the Aegean earlier than in Europe.

It has been observed in an interesting study that the monarchical system follows closely upon the rise of Docetist and Gnostic heresies and that the threat of them was the immediate cause of the monarchical style of Church government. It has been further observed that Church organisation tended to follow the pattern of political organisation. The earlier rise of the monarchical episcopate in the east is understandable because in the west collegiality was a mark of Roman political administration.[17]

Right up to the time of Irenaeus, *presbuteros* indicates a *state*, *episkopos* a *function*. The 'bishops' were less dignitaries than functionaries.[18]

Elderly persons. An advance in Church hierarchy may be the presence of aged men, *presbutai*, and aged ladies, *presbutides*,[19] in the church of Crete (Tit 2[2f.]). They may be Church officers or nothing more than elderly persons. We cannot tell.

Presbytery. *Presbuterion* is a Biblical word denoting the honour or estate of presbyters (elders).[20] It may be a term of Christian adoption, if not of special coinage, but it does occur in the Alexandrinus text of a late book of the Greek Bible (Dan Th Su 50). Christians apply it to the Jewish sanhedrin (Lk 22[66]; Act 22[5]) and to the collective body of Christian elders or bishops (1 Ti 4[14]).

In Ephesus, therefore, there is already a 'college of presbyters' (*presbuterion*) and it seems that some specialisation has set in, for a bishop's office and its qualifications are discussed, including his aptness to teach (1 Ti 3[1-7]). It may be that, in the abode of St. Timothy, an *episkopos* was a specialised *presbuteros*, that a bishop was one of the elders who had special functions – still, however, a long way from the monarchical bishop of St. Ignatius and St. Polycarp.

Perhaps we should distinguish between the *presbuteros* in 1 Ti and the *presbuteros* in Titus, i.e. between the elders in the churches of Ephesus and Crete respectively.[21] The church in Crete is evidently the less developed. There Titus probably has to establish 'elders' for the first time and they are at the moment simply overseers, not officially 'bishops' (*episkopoi*) in a specialized way.

By contrast, in the church at Ephesus, a small group of teaching elders, the *episkopoi* in a special sense, is already coming to the fore and assuming a position of leadership within the body of the *presbuterion*, the general committee of elders – a state of development not reached in Crete. Crete had not yet a functional specialization, not yet an inner leadership within the larger group. Whereas the situation in Ephesus is that elders who rule well are counted worthy of double honour, especially if they labour in the Word and in doctrine, and whereas to desire the office of a 'bishop' is good, yet in Crete we find no comparable differentiation: the office of bishop and elder is the same. We should contrast 1 Ti 3[1f.] 5[17] where the qualifications of the 'bishop' are set out and where it is urged that certain elders be promoted, with Tit 1[5,7] where no distinction is drawn between 'bishop' and 'elder', and the implication is that both are one and the same person: 'Ordain *elders* ... for a *bishop* must be ...' (Tit 1[5,7]).

In the apostolic Fathers, *presbuterion* is a body of the local elders, the second of the three orders of Bishops, Presbyters and Deacons (I. Eph 2[2] 4[1] 20[2]; I. Magn. 2[1] 13[1]; I. Trall. 2[2] 7[2] 13[2]; I. Philad. 4[1] 7[1]; I. Smyrn. 12[2]). St. Ignatius declares that the Bishop must be honoured as representing Jesus Christ, and the Presbyters as representing the apostles (I. Philad. 5[1] I. Smyrn. 8[1]).

ELECT

ἐκλεκτός : ἐκλέγομαι

Many a blow and biting sculpture polished well those stones elect,
In their places now compacted by the heavenly Architect.

The words, *eklektos* and *eklegomai*, lie at the very heart of the Bible, expressing God's plan of salvation for His people.

Secular Greek. The adjective *eklektos* is 'select' or 'picked out',[22] and the verb *eklegomai* (middle voice) is to 'choose,'[23] but in Biblical Greek they become powerful and special waymarks.

The same statement is shared by other words – 'foreknow', 'predestinate' (q.v.) Israel in the old dispensation was the special object of God's 'election'. 'Because He loved thy fathers He chose their seed,' said Moses to the chosen people (Deut 4[37]). 'The Lord did not choose you because ye were more than other people, but because He loved you, and because He would keep the oath which He sware to your fathers' (Deut 7[7]). Moreover, within Israel itself God made further special elections, Levi, Aaron, Judah, David. So the Christian is 'an elect race', a new chosen people.

'Elect' is perhaps better than 'chosen' as an English equivalent, for it is itself more sacred in English in the formal sense of 'God's people'.

The LXX has many references to God's 'elect', denoting not only those who are destined to a good end: Saul's seven sons were 'the Lord's elect' (*eklektoi*), and they were intended to be hanged (2 Km 21[6]). More often the word denotes a blessed election. 'Mine *elect* shall inherit My holy mountain' (Isai 65[9]). The children of Jacob are 'His elect' (Ps 104 (105)[6]). The Servant is 'mine elect' (Isa 42[1]). Grace and mercy are towards His elect (Wis 4[15]).

Christian Greek. The contrast between *eklektos* (elect) and *klētos* (called) is marked, for the *klētoi* are many and the *eklektoi* few (Mt 20[16] 22[14]). On the other hand, the Called and the Chosen are not elsewhere contrasted.[24] In the language of the Seer they are one and the same: the conquering saints, fighting on the Lamb's side, are '*called* and *chosen* and faithful' (*klētoi, eklektoi* and *pistoi*, Rev 17[14]).

Whereas the old people of God were **elect**, the seed of Abraham, Israel and His servant Jacob whom He delivered with joy and gladness, yet at the present time it is the Church which, as the people of God, is **elect**. It is not possible for the *eklektoi* to be deceived but they are constantly in the care of God, their Avenger and Protector, to Whom they are precious and by Whom they were fore-ordained (Mt 24[24]; Lk 18[7]; Ro 8[33]; 1 Pet 1[2] 2[4]). The **Elect** are few in number (Mt 22[14]) but they are safe from the Accuser, Satan.

It surprises some that St. Paul makes little use of the term *eklektoi*.[25] Schrenk wonders whether the ex-Pharisee may have been afraid of using a word which in later Judaism was often misapplied in a nationalistic direction. St. Paul's use of the word in Ro 8[33] ('who shall lay anything to the charge of God's elect?') is a climactic summary of all he has said in the chapter about the sons of God. In the one word, elect, is summed up the whole of God's work of salvation, dating from before the beginning of time, on behalf of those whom He foreknew and predestinated, who are now clear from all condemnation, who are justified and finally glorified. Rufus is called *eklektos* (Ro 16[13]), not because he is an outstanding or choice Christian – which would be the secular sense of the word – but because every believer is *eklektos* in the new sense: called, justified, sanctified, and destined to be glorified.[26]

Among the apostolic Fathers, too, *eklektos* is a technical term for a Christian: a believer is an **elect** one[27] and the Church is **elect** (I. Trall intr). St. Clement[28] and Hermas[29] speak often of God's **elect**.

The verb **eklegomai**, no less, acquired the special definition of divine **election**. It rendered for the most part the Hebrew *bāḥar* in the Greek versions: God **elected** the holy Seed because He loved them (Deut 4[37]). He did not **choose** the tribe of Ephraim, but **chose** the tribe of Judah (Ps 77 (78)[68]). Constantly in the LXX *eklegomai* expresses the concept of divine **election** and in Christian Greek the precedent is followed. Christ promised that God would mercifully shorten the days of tribulation, 'for the **elects'** sake whom He had **chosen**' (Mk 13[20]). The **choosing** of an apostle to succeed Judas was a matter of divine election (Act 1[24]), as well as the selection of the children of Israel 'when they dwelt as strangers in Egypt' (Act 13[17]). Now God has **chosen** once more, in that Gentiles by the mouth of Peter hear and believe the Gospel (Act 15[7]) 'Foolish things' are the objects of His **choosing**, weak and base things (1 Co 1[27f.]). **chosen** in Christ before the world began, destined to be holy (Eph 1[4]), the poor of this world, rich in faith, and heirs of His promised kingdom (Jas 2[5]). These has God elected.

By this verb the Fathers, too, refer to the **Elect** of God,[30] **chosen** from among all other men (1 Clem 59[3]). Hermas refers to 'those **elected** by God for eternal life' (*Vis.* IV 3.5). St. Polycarp sees the connection with persecution – what the Latin hymn calls 'the blow' and 'biting sculpture' – for he says, 'Chains are the diadems of those who have been **elected** by God' (ad Phil 1[1]).

We must take good care to conceive **election** in no mechanical way, for it can only become a reality if there is belief in the Gospel. The choice between God and mammon is decisive and the individual himself alone can make it. Whether he passes the narrow gate or the wide is for him to say.

See also, 'Called', and 'Predestination'.

ELECTION

ἐκλογή

Eklogē is the noun corresponding with *eklektos* and *eklegomai*. See 'Elect'.

Eklogē was originally a secular word and it meant choice or selection.[31] It was adopted by early Christians to denote divine **election**, God's will exercising itself on certain of His creatures in preference to others.

Election is not dependent upon deserts, and Rebecca's two children were not yet born when Jacob's **election** was made. **Election** is a part of God's inscrutable purposes by which He selected Israel, the Chosen people, and especially the faithful Remnant among them: 'Jacob have I loved, but Esau have I hated' (Ro 9[11]). Because the Gentiles (Esau) have been brought in, He has not broken His word to Jacob. The Remnant of Israel has inherited the promises. To the believing Remnant His election and promises are binding. This Remnant is 'according to the **election** of grace' (Ro 11[5,7]). God's promises confirm that His ancient **election** of Israel remains. 'As touching the **election**, they are beloved for the Fathers' sakes,' (Ro 11[28]) and when the fulness of the Gentiles is gathered in all Israel shall be saved.

The writer to Diognetus refers to 'the Jewish **election**' (4[4]), but in Christian Greek **election** is a word which may be used of Gentile believers as well (1 Th 1[4]). It is once at least equated with 'calling' or 'vocation' (*klēsis*). 'Give diligence to make your *klēsis* and *eklogē* sure' (2 Pet 1[10]).

The word occurs in a special Christian sense in patristic Greek. 'We are an **elect portion**' (1 Clem 29[1]).[32] We are indeed the true Israel. St. Ignatius declares that 'the Lord makes **election** from His own servants' (M. Pol 20[1]). The martyrs are an inner selection chosen from the whole Christian community.

Difficult as it is to reconcile the concept with the axiom of free Will, the two need not be inconsistent, since Almighty God knows beforehand what man of his own volition will do. We should not push our thoughts too far.[33] Many Christians have held that **election** by God is entirely without relation to faith or works (Calvinism), and others have held that God's **election** is of those who believe and who persevere by grace in faith and good works (Arminianism). We may be sure that we owe everything to God's grace.

ELECTION (DIVINE PLEASURE AND DIVINE WILL)

εὐδοκία

For some reason sacred writers have avoided the secular word for good pleasure, *eudokēsis*, and either invented *eudokia* or else recruited it from obscurity. *Eudokia* is almost confined to Jewish and Christian literature (MM, Bauer, Kittel *TWNT*), occurring for the first time in the Greek Bible.[34]

Eudokia is divine good will and pleasure in some well-known phrases of the Bible: '*acceptable* in Thy sight' (Ps 18 (19)[14]), 'with *favour* wilt Thou compass him' (Ps 5[12]), 'do good in Thy *good pleasure* unto Sion' (Ps 50 (51)[18]), 'O Lord, in an *acceptable* time' (Ps 68 (69)[13]), 'in Thy *favour* our horn shall be exalted (Ps 88 (89)[17]), 'remember me, O Lord, with *favour*' (Ps 105 (106)[4]), 'upon us and upon our children be Thy *good pleasure* for ever' (Ps Sol 8[39 (33)]). Thus, God's 'good pleasure' was a well-established meaning in any synagogue community.

The Hebrew original (*rāṣôn*) is the good will or favour of God. However, in the OT it is sometimes applied to humans (1 Chr 16[10]; Ps 144 (145)[16]; Ecclus 18[31] etc.), and in Ps Sol 3[4] 16[12] *eudokia* does not signify divine pleasure: it belongs to the righteous man and to Solomon's soul. It is indeed St. Paul's own 'heart's desire' (Ro 10[1]) and is a human motive for preaching the Gospel in contrast with envy and strife (Ph 1[15]). If the Neutral text is followed, *eudokia* may be man's good will in the angels' message to the shepherds (Lk 2[14]). But elsewhere in the NT *eudokia* signifies God's good will: as shown in His works of grace (Ph 2[13]; 2 Th 1[11]) and in His **good pleasure** manifested to us at the incarnation (Lk 2[14] Received text). *Eudokia* is the smile which lies 'behind a frowning Providence', working at the behest of divine Wisdom for, as the Son confessed, to reveal His mysteries was the Father's *eudokia* (Mt 11[26]; Lk 10[21]). Our predestination as children of God was according to the **good pleasure** of His will (Eph 1[5]). *Eudokia* is the grace and favour of God, unfathomable and sovereign,[35] the smiling face behind the wrath.

The angels' Christmas message to the shepherds will most excite our interest. It is doubtful whether the text which we all know so well, the Byzantine tradition which is supported by Koridethi and Syriac and Bohairic versions – although it goes back to the second century – is the earliest text of Lk 2[14]. Field was persuasive in its defence (p. 49) and Westcott admitted that it 'claimed a place in the margin'.[36] This is the familiar reading, 'good will towards men'. But the better attested text, supported by the Vulgate, has the addition of a tiny letter which, as Field urged, need have been intended for no more than a punctuation point. It reads, 'peace on earth to men of *eudokia*' – seeming to indicate that the blessings of the incarnation are confined to 'contented men!' However, 'men of *good will*' may rather mean, 'men of God's good will',[37] i.e. men in whom He is well pleased (as RV, RSV) – but not because they deserve it. Then to understand the phrase as indicating God's will is to bring *eudokia* into line with its regular meaning in Christian

Greek – God's good pleasure, His absolute and incomprehensible favour towards the people of His election,[38] the special 'people' mentioned by St. Luke when he says, 'Good tidings to all the people' (that is, of Israel) in 2^{10} (RV).

Moreover, Dr. Vogt of the Pontifical Biblical Institute pointed out[39] that the Qumrân tests now challenge the acceptance of *rāṣôn*, the Hebrew behind *eudokia* in the LXX, as meaning God's 'good pleasure in man's conduct'. He reminded us that C.-H. Hunzinger has shown that the phrase, 'sons of His *rāṣôn*', occurs in the Qumrân hymns (1 QH iv 32f) and he added also 1 QH xi 9. He is probably right in claiming that there is no reason why sincere Israelites like the Bethlehem shepherds, like Simeon, Zacharias, John the Baptist, and Christ's future apostles, could not have been acquainted with the hymns and have esteemed them highly.[40] *Rāṣôn* in these hymns refers to God's will as electing and predestinating rather than to the divine pleasure. The phrase, 'the sons of *rāṣôn*', designates those whom the divine will has chosen, those to whom God will give eternal peace (1 QH ii 24) when the times of peace shall come (1 QH iii 15) – a conspicuous parallel with the angels' song. 'Peace to men of God's *rāṣôn*.'

The hymns, coming from the same terrain and almost the same antiquity as the angels' song, make it fairly clear that after all the reading *eudokias* in Lk 2^{14} is probably correct, while the Byzantine text which AV follows is probably wrong. We should understand the passage to mean: 'Peace on earth to men who are His chosen ones.' It is most unlikely that it means that God is well pleased with men, which is positively not the sense of the phrase from Qumrân. God's pleasure in His elect does not arise from anything that they have done; His pleasure consists in His electing them. The hymns indicate that *rāṣôn/eudokia* in the Christmas song refers more naturally to the will of God to confer grace on His chosen ones, than to God's delight in approving whatever there is of goodness in man.

On the other hand, exception has been taken[41] to this way of looking at the word, first, on the ground that one would expect 'His' to be added in conjunction with *eudokias* if it is to mean God's good pleasure. Moreover, the view we have commended may conflict with the purpose of the angels, which was to offer messianic glory and peace to *all* people ('which shall be to all people'), not merely to one group – to which it must be replied that 'all the people' is in fact one group, the chosen People of God, as the angels intended.

Thirdly, however, one must admit that prior to this passage St. Luke has supposed (in Lk $1^{7, 51ff., 76ff.}$) that salvation involves not so much God's arbitrary 'good pleasure in electing them' as the necessary accompaniment of a certain moral disposition from the side of man. That is true. Hearts must be turned to obedience, pride must be scattered, sins be confessed and forgiven. Man has a responsible part. Too much emphasis on the election of a single group may take away the force of the necessary co-operation on the part of man's own will.

For all that, the arguments from the Judaistic background are telling.

ELECTION (SPIRITUAL INHERITANCE)

κληρονομία: κληρονόμος: κλῆροι

For these words, *klēronomia, klēronomos,* and *klēroi,* the idea of 'inherited property' was discarded in Biblical Greek in favour of the sense of spiritual inheritance by God's free disposition in the Kingdom of Messiah. The old meaning persists in places[42] but the Biblical content, derived through the LXX, is established. The Christian sense comes near to 'Election'.

Inheritance. *Klēronomia* is the *naḥªlâ,* apportionment among the tribes, which was the joy of every Israelite, and denoted also the *yᵉrushâ,* a name for the land which he was to enjoy as a gift from Moses. The Israelite was a *yārash* (inheritor), rendered in the LXX by *klēronomos.* In the Psalms *klēronomia* is plainly identified with the People of God, as indicated by the following parallelism: 'For God will not reject His people (*laos*) and will not forsake His *klēronomia*' (Ps 93 (94)[14]).

In the NT the Church is conceived as Israel, taking the place of faithless Jews, and like the Israelites of old, believers now enjoy membership of the *klēronomia* (Col 3[24]; Eph 1[14,18]). The membership is, however, 'among them that are sanctified' (Act 20[32]) and has to do with promise in contrast with Law (Gal 3[18]). It is not now an inheritance in the land of David but in the Kingdom of Christ from which all immorality and foolishness which does not become saints is excluded (Eph 5[5]). Moreover, the inheritance is future – described as *aiōnios,* belonging to the Dispensation to come (Heb 9[15]), and heavenly (1 Pet 1[4]). The old inheritance in Canaan was its type. We are the people of the *klēronomia* (Barn 14[4]), the *klēronomia* of the Beloved which lies ahead and to which the days are hastening (Barn 4[3]).

St. Paul quotes the first half of Ps 93 (94)[14] in Ro 11[1]. Most manuscripts of the epistles give the quotation correctly according to our LXX text, but two Greek-Latin manuscripts of the ninth century, Augiensis and Boernerianus, substitute *klēronomia* for *laos* (people). To read *klēronomia* for *laos* would plainly not be correct;

it is a replacement by copyists. But the substitution goes further back than the ninth century, the verse being quoted by the fourth-century Donatist heretic, Tyconius, by St. Ambrose, and Ambrosiater in the fourth century, and by Pelagius and Sedulius in the fifth, all having the word, *hereditatem*. The substitution is in fact very early, as the Chester Beatty witness of c. AD 200 shows (p[46]), indicating that *klēronomia* was thought to be equivalent to the *laos*, the People of God, the Church.

The **heirs** (*klēronomoi*) in this new sense have God's promise, but not the Law, to support them (Ro 4[14]; Gal 3[29]). If those who rely on the Law are 'heirs', then faith is made void. Our whole religion is nonsense. But we share with Christ the privilege of being joint-heirs, looking forward to glory (Ro 8[17]). Having obtained justification, the 'heirs' now look forward to the life of the future Dispensation (Tit 3[7]). They are the elect of God, poor in this world's wealth, rich in faith, *klēronomoi* of the Kingdom and loved by God (Jas 2[5]).

The word *klēros* was in secular Greek a quota obtained by casting lots.[43] Thucydides describes the dividing of the Lesbians' land into three thousand *klēroi* (allotments),[44] and Herodotus speaks of apportioning an equal *klēros* (parcel of land).[45] Sometimes *klēroi* (plural) are title deeds,[46] but in Christian Greek *klēroi* has gained a new connotation, the cure of souls, the oversight of a part of the People of God. St. Peter cautions elders not to be lords over the *klēroi* but to be examples to the flock (1 Pet 5[3]). The *klēroi* will be various parts of the Christian body, 'assigned' like lots to the presbyters.[47] There is a conjectural emendation by Bunsen in Diogn. 12[9] which, if accepted, would provide an example of *klēroi* (clergy).[48] However, *klēroi* does not elsewhere mean 'clergy' until Tertullian.[49] In the singular *klēros* later on refers to the Christian clergy (Code of Justinian and Novellae) and the concept probably sprang from the LXX – Israel as God's People and God's *klēros* (Deut 9[29]). 'Possibly', suggested Bigg, 'this verse may have been in St. Peter's mind'. Both he and the LXX have a phrase in common, 'His mighty hand'.[50]

ENABLE (SPIRITUAL STRENTHENING)

1. ἐνδυναμόω

Endunamō is a Jewish and Christian word, found first in the LXX where it denotes the supernatural strengthening of Gideon (Jg 6[34]), then in Aquila's version, the NT, the apostolic Fathers, and

Poimandres (iii AD). Plotinus uses the passive in the technical sense of scientific theorems (IV 9.5).

It expresses in the passive voice the spiritual power of the newly converted Saul of Tarsus, who was **spiritually strengthened**, when he confounded the Damascus Jews, proving 'that this is very Christ' (Act 9[22]). St. Paul confessed that his preaching was ever in demonstration of the Spirit and of power, that the weapons of his warfare were mighty through God, spiritual and not carnal. He renounced all this world's widom; the Spirit was his well of strength. He was *enedunamouto*.

Moreover, he applies the passive to Abraham too, who **was strong** in the faith (Ro 4[20]), and, in this spiritual way Christians must **be strong** (Eph 6[10] passive). Christ is the **Strengthener** (Ph 4[13] active), who **tempers** them for the ministry (1 Ti 1[12] active). Timothy is exhorted to **be energized** in the grace that is in Christ Jesus (2 Ti 2[1] passive).

Face to face with the ordeal of his trial, when nearly all had left him, St. Paul confessed that the Lord stood with him and **spiritually energized** him (2 Ti 4[17] active).

In this special sense the apostolic Fathers affirm that Christ **enables** (I. Smyrn 4[2] active), and that the grace of God **gives spiritual strength** (1 Clem 55[3] passive). For Hermas the word represents **spiritual strengthening** in God's commandments, leading to the breaking of the Devil's power (*Mand.* XII 5.1; XII 6.4).

2. δυνατέω

Dunatō is rare in secular Greek, with a meaning like that of *dunamai* (can, be able). It occurs in Philodemus who speaks of being 'able' to resist one's lot.[51] In Christian Greek it has the stronger meaning, **to be spiritually effective**.

No less than *endunamō* (passive) it emphasizes the power of Christian preaching, for Christ speaking through Paul **is mighty**, not weak (2 Co 13[3]). Here again the thought of **divine strengthening**, especially for the work of the ministry, is in the verb.

AV follows the less well-attested reading, *dunatos* (able), at 2 Co 9[8] but the Neutral text, with Chester Beatty and other MSS reads the verb *dunatei*: 'God **is mighty** to make all grace abound.' Moreover, AV follows the Byzantine text and reads *dunatos* (able) at Ro 14[4] where again the best authorities have our verb *dunatei*: 'God is mighty to make him stand.'

3. κραταιόω

The middle voice of *krataiō* in secular Greek was to 'control'. In

Philo it was to 'curb' one's desires by reason.[52] But in the active and passive it is almost exclusively Biblical.[53] In the Bible it refers specially to the supernatural enabling of the Spirit. It is **divine strengthening** in the LXX,[54] and other texts of Jewish Greek. As Naphthali glorified the Lord he **grew strong** (T Naph 1[4] passive).

In the NT the verb is closely concerned with the Holy Spirit: the child Jesus **waxed strong** in the Spirit (Lk 1[80] passive) and the child Jesus **waxed strong**,[55] filled with wisdom and the grace of God (2[40] passive). St. Paul's exhortation to **be strong** (1 Co 16[13] passive) is finely woven into a context of faith and Christian love. Christ dwells in our hearts and we **are strengthened** (Eph 3[16] pass.) by His Spirit in the inner man.

> *And every virtue we possess,*
> *And every victory won,*
> *And every thought of holiness,*
> *Are His alone.*   (HARRIET AUBER)

ENLIGHTEN SPIRITUALLY

φωτίζω

Secular Greek. The meaning of *phōtizō* was literally to give light and shine,[56] as the sun illumines the world, and metaphorically to bring to light or make known, like the 'clear stating' of views in Polybius.[57] *Phōtizō* was indeed already used in Hellenistic Greek in a religious sense, of granting heavenly light to one who is an initiate. This was so in Gnostic magic and Hermetic literature. In the Paris magical papyrus comes the phrase, the god of gods 'der alles erleuchtet' (editor).[58] In the Hermetic literature, the prophet prays that supernatural power be given him to 'enlighten' his fellow men as he himself has been 'enlightened', and so obey the injunction of Poimandres.[59] The Christian meaning is little like that of Polybius, but it cannot be denied that Christians may have been acquainted with the use of the verb among the pagan Mystery devotees. 'Light,' in Hellenism, meant salvation.

Christian Greek. *Phōtizō* is for Christians a revealing of God's hidden Mystery – never a manifestation to the natural understanding. Only by *pneuma* (spirit) are mysteries grasped.

When the Lord comes He will bring to light (*phōtizō*) the hidden things of darkness (1 Co 4[5]), and in the meantime Gentile missions are for 'making all mean know' (*phōtizō*) the fellowship of the Mystery (Eph 3[9]) because Christ through the Gospel 'has brought to light' (*phōtizō*) life and immortality (2 Ti 1[10]) and the true Light which 'gives spiritual enlightenment' (*phōtizō*) is the Logos (Jn 1[9]).

The spiritual enlightening denoted by the verb in the passive, is given to the eyes of Christian understanding to appreciate their calling's hope and the rich glory of their inheritance (Eph 1[18]). Partakers of the Holy Ghost who know the power of the world to come, are those who have been 'spiritually enlightened', a notion expressed by the passive (Heb 6[4]). Theirs is no ordinary insight, for *phōtizō* indicates the re-birth (enlightening) of the believer (Heb 10[32]). The beginning of the Christian life is meant, perhaps baptism, for *phōtizō* is a technical term for baptism in St. Justin (*Apol.* 61[12]).

The Church at Rome is beloved and 'spiritually enlightened', a phrase expressed by the same passive in St. Ignatius (I. Ro intr) – an enviable title, implying that love and enlightenment were the two gifts rightly prized by a church which had presidency over all others, a church worthy of God, worthy of honour, worthy of praise.

ESCHATOLOGICAL

ἔσχατος

Eschatos has a new and important meaning for Christians. The usual secular meaning was 'the most extreme', whether in space, time, or degree. *Eschatos* was the farthest, the lowest, the innermost and last. It qualifies the meanest of people. Typical phrases which include the word are: 'the *worst* misfortune', '*extreme* democracy', and 'the *last* scion of the race'. At times the meanings are found in the NT, especially in the Synoptic gospels. However, *eschatos* for Christ's disciples indicates the hope of His Coming, and in the light of this meaning there is derived from it in English the word 'eschatology', i.e. contemplation of the closing events of the present dispensation (q.v.).

Christians therefore had a new meaning when they referred to Christ as 'the *eschatos* Adam' – not the 'last Adam', as if there were several, but rather the 'eschatological' or messianic Man, the Lord from heaven Whose *icon* (q.v.) we shall bear. In the same breath St. Paul speaks of the change from corruption to incorruption 'in the twinkling of an eye' at the *eschatos* (eschatological) Trump – not the 'last' Trump (1 Co 15[45]).

So the Day of Judgment and of general Resurrection (Jn 6[39] 7[37] 11[24] 12[48]) is not the last day in space, time, or degree – for after it there follow endless days in a new Jerusalem. Perilous times belong to the eschatological days (2 Ti 3[1]) and the NT period itself is part of these 'eschatological' days (Heb 1[2]), but worse 'eschatological' days are to come for which some have heaped up treasure (Jas 5[3]). In one sense the time in which we live is not the 'eschatological' time, wherein salvation is ready to be revealed, but in another sense it is, for the Lamb without blemish has already come (1 Pet 1[5,20]), [60] and 'He was revealed in the *eschatological* days to save us' (2 Clem 14[2]).

Both the NT authors and the apostolic Fathers see salvation under more than one aspect; it is not only past, and present; it is in part future, it is eschatological. Mockers and scoffers are not yet here in full force but they shall come (2 Pet 3[3]; Jude 18). The present day is nevertheless the eschatological time wherein are already many antichrists (1 Jn 2[18]).

It is likely then that the seven plagues of the Apocalypse (Rev 15[1] 21[9]) are not 'last', but rather 'eschatological' plagues. The meaning, however, must not always be pressed in the apostolic Fathers. Although St. Ignatius speaks of 'eschatological times' (I. Eph 11[1]) and the Didache refers to 'eschatological hours' and days (16[2f.]), yet in these writers *eschatos* sometimes means 'inferior' and 'uttermost', as in secular Greek.[61]

ESCHATOLOGICAL 'DAY'

ἡμέρα

The word for 'day' (*hēmera*) has rather a strange emphasis in Biblical Greek, specifically eschatological.

Secular Greek. The accepted understanding of 'day' as opposed to night is common enough but sometimes *hēmera* was concerned more metaphorically and poetically, as a time in one's life such as old age, or as a 'kind' of life, like a 'day' of misery. *Hēmera* may be poetically devised as a period of time. Sophocles can say, 'Until this *hēmera*,' meaning until the present era,[62] and he has the phrase, 'A day can prostrate and a day can raise up,' when he means that sometimes we are cast down, sometimes elated.[63] However, *hēmera* need not be so vague and often means a birthday,[64] a wedding day,[65] or a fixed day. 'The senate adjourned, *day* after *day*.'[66]

It seems at first as if there were secular precedent for St. Paul's use of *hēmera* as 'judgment'. A reminiscence of his phrase, *anthrōpinē hēmera* (human judgment, 1 Co 4[3]), appears in a charm which is incised upon a Roman silver denarius. The coin was converted to use as an amulet before AD 300 and its inscription, translated, appears to read: 'I invoke the holy and greatest name

138

that it may help me to accomplish all that I wish, that it may give me the upper hand in every *human judgment.*'

We cannot argue from this that in secular Greek *hēmera* had come to mean 'day of judgment'. Campbell Bonner, who gave his attention to the matter, declares that there is nothing to show that *hēmera*, standing alone, is a Greek way of expressing 'day of judgment', 'court', or 'tribunal', and he is led to conclude that the amulet designer knew St. Paul's letter and was probably a Jewish Christian who had not given up the language, nor even perhaps the practice, of magic.[67] It is not that we have a secular precedent for St. Paul's usage. Rather, his usage is the precedent for this little charm.

Biblical Greek. Under hebraic influence, *hēmera* means 'period' much more regularly and less poetically than in secular Greek. *Yôm* in Hebrew readily signifies both 'day' and 'time', and was traditionally associated with Yahweh's coming in judgment. Abraham rejoiced to see the *hēmera* (times) of Jesus (Jn 8[56]). The present age in the world's history is the *hēmera* (period) of salvation (2 Co 6[2]). The *Hēmerai* (times) are evil (Eph 5[16]). 'From ancient *hēmerai*,' is 'a good while ago' (Act 15[7]). 'Former *hēmerai*' means a period recently past (Heb 10[32]).

In Christian Greek particularly *hēmera* is eschatological, referring either to this present day of grace in which the Gospel is preached, or to events taking place at the second Coming and thereafter. The *hēmera* which we see approaching (Heb 10[25]), the *hēmera* of the Son of Man (Lk 17[24]), the *hēmera* of our Lord (1 Co 1[8] 5[5]; 2 Co 1[14]; Ph 1[6,10] 2[16]; 1 Th 5[2]; 2 Th 2[2]), and that *hēmera* in which Christians hope to find mercy but which overtakes them like a thief (1 Th 5[4]; 2 Ti 1[18]) – all are referring to the Parousia, the second Coming. *Hēmera* applies further to the *hēmera* of Judgement, the Last Time, the 'day' of wrath when solemn words shall be said (Mt 7[22]) and a fate pronounced worse than over Sodom and Gomorrah, Tyre and Sidon (Mt 10[15] 11[22,24]), when each idle word shall be accounted for (Mt 12[36]). But it is a *hēmera* of resurrection as well (Jn 6[39f.,44,54] 11[24] 12[48]) – portentous, great and notable (Act 2[20]). A risen Man presides over it (Acts 17[31]; Ro 2[16]), and it consigns us all either to life or to anguish (Ro 2[5-9]).

Who shall be able to stand in the *hēmera* of His wrath (Rev 6[17])? It is certain that all the beloved shall have boldness in the *hēmera* of Judgment (1 Jn 4[17]) – a boldness which fallen angels cannot share (Jude 6).

1. ἀποκαραδοκία

Whereas the corresponding verb had been in secular use, for instance by Polybius, the noun *apokaradokia* was evidently coined by Christians. Probably it was based upon the verb, which denotes 'a patient waiting' for the Lord when used by Aquila in his version of Ps 36 (37)[7]. The noun in Christian Greek had its own proper eschatological connotation, but later it finds a place in the lexicon of Hesychius, and in Suidas it appears that its meaning was very near to the secular *prosdokia* (expectation).

In the NT *apokaradokia* does in fact indicate the 'earnest expectancy' that lies behind the anguish of ruined nature from the blighting of the ground and the perversion of all natural things which is somehow involved in the Fall of man. It is an anguish which looks forward with longing to restoration and release from vanity and corruption, from the creed of killing in order to live, and from living only in order to die. 'It was not man alone, but the world in which he lives that was subjected to death. The ground is cursed because of him. The whole existence in which we are involved stands in bondage to corruption.'[68] The brute creation and the earth which is cursed for man's sake, is to share the benefit of salvation (Ro 8[19]). The lichen shall no longer consume the vigour of the stalk nor, to echo Thomas Hardy, shall the ivy slowly strangle the promising sapling, nor shall the cruel earthquake ravage. In its present condition, every created thing is doomed to futility, subjected to 'vanity' (see *mataiotēs*). As man has fallen, so Nature which was flawlessly made by God, has fallen too and man has dragged the animals down, just as the head of a house might involve the servants in his own iniquitous affairs.[69] And now those dependants are enemies and the fields are full of weeds.[70] Yet Nature awaits eagerly (*apokaradokia*) the Coming of Christ. When the new Man is revealed the whole Creation will find liberation and see the end of travail. Man brought it to bondage but a Man will deliver it.

The word has one other context in the NT and it, too, is eschatological. *Apokaradokia* indicates our own aspiring hopes and particularly those of the Apostle when he cries, 'My *apokaradokia* is that in nothing I shall be ashamed, but Christ shall be magnified in my body, whether it be by life or by death' (Ph 1[20]). The 'judgment-seat of Christ' is here foreshadowed when the fruit of every Christian's service shall receive its due reward.

See also 'Wait for', and 'Creation'.

2. ἐκδοχή

The old word *ekdochē* receives in Christian Greek a context of future judgment which essentially changes its meaning.

Secular Greek. In classical Greek *ekdochē* meant a 'succession', Aeschylus using it of beacon flares blazing one after the other,[71] and Euripides of God bringing fresh evils in succession.[72] Other accepted meanings, extracted from Polybius, are 'interpretation' (III 29.4) and 'inference'. From a letter of the senate it was easy to make the 'inference' that it was displeased (XXII 7.6).

Christian Greek. *Ekdochē* becomes virtually a new word, a synonym of *prosdokia*, as the lexicon of Hesychius records, and of *apokaradokia*. The vernacular offers no instance (MM), but the Christian context is that of believers sinning wilfully, and it is warned that there is for such people 'a certain fearful *ekdochē* of judgment and fiery indignation' (Heb 10^{27}).

Apparently, therefore, it is an expectation of the future judgment-seat of Christ when saints will account for themselves and receive what they deserve for the things done in the body (Ro 14^{10}; 2 Co 5^{10}).

The Vulgate rendering by *expectatio* gives the new meaning, and so does the Philoxenian version which has a Syriac word which is elsewhere interchanged with *prosdokia* (expectation).[73] Alford's suggestion, '*reception* of judgment', certainly reflects Josephus's use of *ekdochē*, for the Jewish historian speaks of 'a lake for *reception* of rain' – meaning a reservoir,[74] but the point is that, more recently than Josephus, Christian writers allowed a new scope to the old word.

ESCHATOLOGICAL MOCKERY

ἐμπαιγμονή : ἐμπαίκτης : ἐμπαιγμός

These three words, *empaigmonē*, *empaiktēs* and *empaigmos*, appear first in the Bible, formed from the rare secular verb, *empaizō*, to mock.

Not a LXX word, *empaigmonē* (mockery), occurs in the best texts of the NT (2 Pet 3^3). It is omitted by the Byzantine text which simply has *empaiktai* (mockers) in place of *empaigmonē empaiktai* (mockers with mockery), a rather stronger expression. The advent of the **mockers** is said to be a sign of eschatological days (Jude 18). Individuals who will play this prominent part before the Coming of our Lord would seem from the Hebrew equivalents of the Greek Bible, to be men of persecuting disposition. Theodotion used *empaigmos* for the 'rigour' with which Egypt afflicted the Israelite slaves (Ex 1[13]); other versions used it for the 'rigour' forbidden to a master over his Israelite bondman (Lev 25[43, 46]). The LXX and Theodotion have the plural of *empaiktēs* in the phrase, '*Persecutors* shall rule over them.' (Isai 3[4], *ta ⁵ᵃlûlîm*).

In the LXX *empaigmos* renders *niqlê* (burning, reproach) in Ps 37(38)[8] BS[1], and *qallāsâ* (Ezek 22[4]) where Jerusalem is said to be made a 'mockery' to all countries. *Empaigmos* has this sense too in the free Greek books. It refers to God's contemptuous mockery of Israel's disobedience (Wis 12[25]), and the context of severe persecution is implied when the word is used for the cruelty which the Jews suffered from maddened elephants in the hippodrome (3 Mac 5[22]). In the NT *empaigmos* refers to the suffering of the Maccabees (Heb 11[36]; cp. 2 Mac 7[7]). It appears for the first time in secular Greek in Herodian[75] where it signifies 'scorn'.

Within the limits of Biblical Greek, eschatological 'mockery' is almost certainly 'persecution'.

EVERLASTING (WITHOUT GENEALOGY)

ἀγενεαλόγητος

Agenealogētos belongs to Christian Greek and appears nowhere else. The writer to Hebrews describes Melchizedec (and hence the Son of God, the type's Fulfilment) as 'without father, without mother, *agenealogētos*, having neither beginning of days nor end of life; but made like unto the Son of God' (7[3]).

On the face of it the term seems as if it must have reference to the Virgin Birth, meaning that He has genealogy only on His Mother's side. He is born of Mary and born of God. In Keble's words,

> *When wandering here a little span,*
> *Thou took'st on Thee to rescue man,*
> *Thou hast no earthly sire.*

Nevertheless, both by St. Matthew and St. Luke a genealogy is in fact attributed to Christ through Joseph, the supposed father. As to His earthly existence, He cannot be said to be 'without genealogy', for both evangelists supply Him with one. The term *agenealogētos* must have, then, a rather different application. It seems to Origen, as to all Christians, that the Word-made-flesh, although He is the son of Abraham and son of David, was truly *agenealogētos* nevertheless, for He was in the beginning with God and was very God.[76] He has no antecedents, no forbears.

142

By c. AD 319, Arius started to teach that the Son of God had come into being out of nothingness, and that once He was not; at some very remote period He was created by the Father. A favourite Arian phrase was, 'There was once when He was not', and the Arians assumed that because the Father was *agenētos* (Unoriginate), therefore the Son was *genētos* (Originate). No wonder that St. Athanasius rejected 'Unoriginate' and insisted on the name, 'Father', as the divine title authorized by Scripture.[77]

To affirm that He is *agenealogētos* is not to say that the Son is not begotten, rather that He is *eternally* begotten – 'begotten of His Father before all worlds'.

'The Son is of the Father alone', states the Athanasian Creed (*Quicunque vult*): 'not made, nor created, but begotten'.

EXAMPLE OR PROTOTYPE

1. ὑπογραμμός

Hupogrammos was a rare word in secular Greek, used for a child's writing-copy which contained the Greek alphabet.[78] In the LXX it is the outline or abridgement of a book (2 Mac 2^{28}), and the same kind of thing for Philo who referred to 'shadow and *hupogrammos* (outline)'.[79]

In the NT and apostolic Fathers, however, it denotes characteristically the scrupulous pattern of Christian suffering which Christ bequeathed (1 Pet 2^{21}). St. Paul departed this world, writes St. Clement, 'having been found a notable *hupogrammos* (pattern) of patient endurance' (1 Clem 5^{7}). Our Lord's good works were a *hupogrammos* to which we should conform ourselves (33^{8}). St. Polycarp too urges us to be imitators of the sufferings of Jesus, 'for He gave this *hupogrammos* (pattern) to us in His own person' (ad Philip. 8^{2}).

2. ὑποτύπωσις

Hupotupōsis too in secular Greek was an outline or sketch,[80] like Strabo's 'sketch' of the inhabited world, the 'draft' of a book,[81] or the 'outline' of a subject, a specific title for a book, as 'Outlines of Philosophy' (by Sextus Empiricus) or 'Outline of Astrological Hypotheses' (by Proclus). Very rarely it came near to the idiomatic meaning in Christian Greek, 'pattern' of virtues.[82]

In the NT it is both an 'example' of behaviour to be copied, like the longsuffering of Christ Himself (1 Ti 1^{16}), and a doctrinal 'prototype' or tradition or formal creed like that handed on to

Timothy (2 Tim 1¹³). The Fathers maintain the moral meaning, an example to encourage others, as St. Theophylact and St. Chrysostom, in 1 Ti 1¹⁶, but in 2 Ti 1¹³ they insist 'upon the full force of the metaphor drawn from the art of the painter or architect'.[83] That is to say, in 2 Ti 1¹³ the *hupotupōsis*, as in secular Greek, is an 'outline' (NEB). In the Christian interpretation, it is a fixed form of sound teaching, a prototype by which Timothy is to construct his own programme of teaching.

EXASPERATION

παροργισμός

Parorgismos is found first in Biblical Greek where it renders *ka'as* (God's anger, 3 Km 15³⁰; 4 Km 23²⁶), *nᵉ'āṣâ* (provocation by God, 4 Km 19³; 2 Esd 19¹⁸, ²⁶), and *qeṣeph* (Jer 21⁵A, God's wrath).

In Christian Greek, however, it has altogether a derogatory meaning. St. Paul indicates that its absence is a Christian virtue. 'Let not the sun go down upon your *parorgismos*' (Eph 4²⁶: AV 'wrath'). It is not mere anger, which often may be a righteous passion. Trench (p. 127) suggested that *parorgismos* is 'the irritation, the exasperation, the bitterness', which often mingles itself with anger, the Latin *exacerbatio*. It is probably, as Alford and T. K. Abbott (ICC) suggested, 'irritation'.

See 'Divine Wrath'.

EXCOMMUNICATION

ἀνάθεμα : ἀναθεματίζω : καταθεματίζω : κατάθεμα

All these words, *anathema*, *anathematizō*, *katathematizō*, *katathema*, represent censure and abuse in Christian Greek.

The noun. *Anathema* is a Hellenistic form of *anathēma*, which in older Greek was a votive offering in a temple[84] or, in Homer, an ornament. In Biblical Greek *anathema* was an object devoted to God exclusively, often destroyed and in that sense 'accursed', or else an object under a ban, that is, not for common use (Hebrew *ḥērem*).[85]

Moulton and Milligan urged that Deissmann's discovery of *anathema* in the Biblical Greek sense in a source quite free of Jewish influence, 'is a remarkable confirmation of his general thesis' – presumably his thesis that there was no peculiarly Biblical Greek (MM p. 33). The discovery is that of a curse which includes both noun and verb,[86] and so there is apparently secular as well as Biblical evidence for the meaning 'cursed' in connection with *anathema*.[87] However, St. Paul's use of the word doubtless derives from the LXX, and the curse tables from Megara may show the same ultimate influence. Such a meaning of *anathema* is rare indeed outside the Scriptures.

St. Paul could go so far as to wish himself *anathema* (accursed) from Christ to forward his kinsmen's salvation – a desperate dreadful gesture (Ro 9³). To call Jesus *anathema* is also a fearful thing (1 Co 12³). Indeed, those who love not the Lord are declared *anathema maran-atha* (16²²) – possibly a bilingual censure, once in Greek and once in Aramaic.[88] The preachers of heresy are *anathema* (Gal 1⁸ᶠ·). It is clearly a term of censure of some weight, and in Church Greek, commencing from the council of Elvira, c. AD 306, it came to mean 'excommunication' rather than a curse.[89] However, from the sixth century *anathema* was distinguished from excommunication as a more serious ban.

St. Luke's meaning, a 'curse' (Act 23¹⁴), is thus rather different from St. Paul's peculiar Christian use – an extreme form of censure and expulsion. Theodoret later defined *anathema* as, 'alien to the communal body of the Church',[90] but whether excommunication or not, *anathema* was no longer simply a curse.

According to Lightfoot, however, the Fathers attempted 'to force upon St. Paul the ecclesiastical sense with which they were most familiar',[91] but which was not St. Paul's own meaning. He intended 'curse', not the later ecclesiastical 'excommunication', in Bishop Lightfoot's opinion.

What then is the meaning of the phrase cited by St. Paul, 'Anathema Jesus' (1 Co 12³)? What Christian might ever utter so dreadful a sentiment? Cullmann held that it was a formula reflecting the presecution to which Christians were subjected by pagans,[92] and a phrase which was tantamount to a deliberate denial of the faith. That is convincing enough, but there is no reason why it should not have been a persecution by Jews. It may have to do not so much with persecution as with the ecstatic language of believers under the influence of spirit-possession. Kingsley Barrett cites the view of Allo as 'probably right'.[93] It is paralleled by pagan ecstatics who tried by a similar formula to resist the influence they felt coming upon them.

However, there may rather be an incipient Gnostic connection, for to call Jesus 'anathema' is perhaps distinguished from calling 'Christ' anathema, and may be contrasting the earthly Jesus with the heavenly Christ. Gnostics would impose such a test to ensure that the candidate for their rites was 'spiritual'.[94] By uttering the anathema on 'Jesus' the Corinthian Gnostics would be stressing

145

their devotion to the 'spiritual' Christ and their contempt for earthly corporeal existence. Origen did indeed mention some Ophite Gnostics who tested all who would join their congregation by a readiness to pronounce a curse against 'Jesus';[95] but whether we ought to claim Origen's words as a true parallel with St. Paul's is doubtful.[96]

Perhaps, alas! some Jewish Christians found a way to gain re-admission to their old synagogue by the simple device of renunciation.[97]

The verb. The verb *anathematizō* (to devote to evil) occurs but rarely in pagan Greek.[98] In the LXX it renders *ḥāram* (to devote wholly to God).[99] The concept of devoting wholly to God, that is, of utter destruction, applies to the ruthless acts of Judas Maccabaeus (1 Mac 5[5]). It comes to mean, to bind oneself under an oath, a verb put into the mouth of the evil angels who lusted after the comely daughters of men, binding themselves under oaths not to abandon the wicked plan (Enoch 6[4]). It was similarly put into the mouth of the Jewish conspirators who made the oath to murder Paul (Act 23[12, 14, 21]). Then, like *katathematizō*, (Mt 26[74]), it came to mean uttering curses, the desperate speech that was attributed to Simon Peter in the porch of the high priest's palace (Mk 14[71]).

The *kata* compounds. *Katathematizō* and *katathema* are creations of Christian Greek based on the *ana* words, and they have the same two regular meanings: 'censure' – as when there is said to be no more *katathema* in the heavenly Jerusalem (Rev 22[3])[100] – as well as 'abuse' or 'profanity', as when Peter was distraught (Mt 26[74]) and when the men of Ananias 'cursed' their master as the cause of their blindness (*Acta Philip.* II 17).

The verb applies to godly women abhorring and 'execrating' Marcus the magician for seeking to seduce them under the guise of prophecy (Irenaeus I 13.4). St. Irenaeus detests and 'execrates' the dreadful opinion that God came into being by means of what he calls a 'defect' (I 16.3).

The connection between the two meanings, censure and profanity, is evidently this: men sometimes invoked an *anathema* or *katathema* (censure, curse) upon themselves to take effect should their allegation prove false. 'Damn me if it is not', provides an instance of the profanity in English.

EXPELLED FROM SYNAGOGUE, OR FROM THE CHURCH

ἀποσυνάγωγος

Aposunagōgos is a Christian word, perhaps St. John's own

coining. It was 'just the sort of word that would have to be coined for use in the Jewish community' (MM). Still, it is not found in the LXX. St. John twice keeps to a Jewish sense of expulsion from the synagogue (9^{22} 12^{42}), but one passage suggests that *aposunagōgos* was a Christian term indicating excommunication not from the synagogue but from the Christian Church during the time of final Tribulation when a believer must expect to be *aposunagōgos*, and when those who put him down will do so ostensibly in the service of God (Jn 16^2). It seems unlikely in that context to refer to Jewish expulsion, for the Lord's warning applies not to days prior to the breach with Judaism but to days just before His expected Coming. At the same time it is true that the 'Test' or 'Heretic' Benediction (the *birkath hammînîm*) came into the synagogue service with the motive of driving Jewish Christians from the Jewish fellowship, c. AD 90. 'It is probable', suggests Dr. Barrett, 'that among the readers of John were Jewish Christians who had been put out of the synagogue, being regarded, not improperly, as apostates'.[101]

Cremer (p. 64) supposed that *aposunagōgos* meant excommunication from 'the commonwealth of the people of God', and was synonymous with the Lord's words, 'Men shall hate you, and ... shall separate you from their company ... and cast out your name as evil' (Lk 6^{22}).

The ecclesiastical historian[102] used the term for expulsion from Church, referring to the excommunicated Lucian of Antioch, heretical protector of Paul of Samosata. So it is used by Origen,[103] and so by the fifth canon of the Council of Nicaea, AD 325, by the fourth-century *Apostolic Constitutions* (2.43.1, 4.8.3), and by Euthalios the Deacon.[104]

EXPOUND SOUNDLY

ὀρθοτομέω

Orthotomō is evidently a coinage of Biblical Greek and in the LXX renders *yāshar* (Piel: make plain, Pr 3^6 11^5). The meaning reappears in St. Paul's words (2 Ti 2^{15}) where, as Ellicott reminds us, the simile is that of 'laying out' a road, and Timothy is to show himself a workman who lays a plain track for others to walk by, and is to shun heresies and unprofitable discussions. Ellicott points to Pr 3^6 where God is represented as directing our paths. The Fathers tend to avoid the word but it does appear in the Apostolic Constitutions in a citation from 2 Ti 2^{15} which nevertheless is made to apply to bishops, presbyters and deacons.[105] Eusebius too speaks of the Church 'expounding soundly' the royal way.[106]

EXULTATION

ἀγαλλιάω, -ομαι, ἀγαλλίασις

Verb (*agalliō*) and noun (*agalliasis*) are new words, appearing only in the Bible and Church Greek (Bauer). The nearest classical form had been *agallō*, with the different meaning, to honour. Moreover, the lexicographer Hesychius indicates that for him the words *agalliazō*, *agallios* and *agalmos* had the bad sense of *loidoroumai, loidoros, loidoria* (reviling, abuse).

Our verb does not bear this sort of meaning for Christians but reflects the LXX rendering of several Hebrew words. They are *gîl*, which the Greek words resemble in sound, specially frequent in the psalms, expressing joy in God's salvation (e.g. Ps 9^{14} $12(13)^5$ $13(14)^7$ $20(21)^1$ $34(35)^9$ $52(53)^6$; Isai 25^9 61^{10}); '*ālaz* (exult); *rānan* (give a ringing cry in joy or praise), again most frequent in the psalms; *shîsh* (to exult, like a strong man running a race, and especially to exult in God's salvation); and *ṣāhal* (to cry shrilly in joy).

Our noun, *agalliasis*, often represents in Christian Greek the Hebrew nouns formed from the verbs above: *gîl, rinnâ, śāśôn, rᵉnānâ*. They all indicate highly excitable animation, often noisy, with clapping of hands and shouting (e.g. Ps $46(47)^1$ $131(132)^{16}$).

In general the feeling suggested by the Hebrew is that of **exultation** expressed firmly and with enthusiasm. In the psalms superlatively, the Hebrew words convey joy in worship and an eschatological or messianic thrill, especially, '*Rejoice* before the Lord ... He cometh to judge' ($95(96)^{13}$), 'The Lord reigneth; let the earth *rejoice*' ($96(97)^{1,8}$), 'in that day *cry* shrilly, ... thou inhabitant of Sion' (Isai 12^6). Outside the LXX in Jewish Greek, *agalliō* has an eschatological context: 'He shall open the gates of Paradise. ... Then shall Abraham and Isaac and Jacob *exult*.' It expresses a part of the resurrection experience on the present earth (T Levi 18^4; cp. T Jud 25^5; T Benj 10^6); and *agalliasis*, the noun, refers to the future lot of the righteous: 'the years of their *exultation* shall be multiplied' (Enoch 5^9). The two words echo the ecstasy of God's elect, their eternal gladness and peace.

Though they came, by way of Greek-speaking Jews, into the Christian language, yet St. Paul avoids the words. They are full of emotion, as in the LXX, and we may render our Lord's language as strongly as it was uttered: '*Make loud exultation*, for great is your reward in heaven' (Mt 5^{12}). St. Luke makes good use of the verb: Mary's spirit **exults** in God the Saviour (Lk 1^{47}). Jesus **exulted** spiritually (10^{21}). St. Peter quotes the psalms, 'My heart *exulted*' (Act 2^{26}). The believing gaoler **exulted** in his salvation (Act 16^{34}).

Men **exulted** for a season in the light of John the Baptist (Jn 5^{35}). The context is eschatological when Jesus declares, 'Your father Abraham *exulted* to see My day' (Jn 8^{56}), and St. Peter encourages the saints to rejoice when the Coming of our Lord seems near – the plainest indication of the eschatological setting of the word: in the Last Time 'ye *greatly rejoice*, though now for a season ... ye are in heaviness through manifold temptations' (1 Pet 1^{6,8}). The fiery trial, he affirms, is to test us, but partaking in Christ's sufferings brings **exceeding rejoicing** (verb) when His glory shall be revealed (4^{13}).

Not unnaturally the verb, established so firmly as an eschatological emotion, occurs in the great multitude's song in the apocalypse, 'Let us be glad and *exult* and give honour to Him: for the marriage of the Lamb is come' (Rev 19^7).

> *What an anthem that will be, ringing out our love for Thee,*
> *Pouring out our rapture sweet, at Thine own all-glorious feet!*

The noun *agalliasis* too expresses the eschatological **joy** of the first believers at their Breaking of Bread (Act 2^{46}) – 'till He come'. **Exultation** (ecstatic joy) was to be Zacharias's portion at the birth of Messiah's forerunner (Lk 1^{14}). Elisabeth vowed that the Babe leaped in her womb for *agalliasis* at Mary's salutation (Lk 11^{14,44}). The word comes in St. Jude's doxology: 'Now unto Him that is able ... to present you faultless ... with *agalliasis*' (24). It is a fruit of Christian love and its source is Christ (Barn 1^6). It is the spiritual exaltation of St. Clement when his people are obedient (1 Clem 63^2), and nevertheless is meekness (Acta Thom. A 86).

The verb occurs fifty times, the noun eighteen, in the psalms. Its rich excitement usually concerns salvation (Ps 50(51)^{12} 117 (118)^{15}) and the glorious End: in the everlasting rest of Sion the saints shall rejoice and sing (literally, 'shall **exult** with **exultation**', 131(132)^{16}).

> *They stand, those halls of Sion,*
> *All jubilant with song.*

The emotion is inspired by spiritual fervour, aptly accompanying prophecy. When Agabus prophesied at Antioch, the Western text adds that there was **great exultation** (Act 11^{28}D).

It is to be expected that in subsequent sacred Greek these ebullient words will express the exultation of martyrs even in the hour of supreme sacrifice. After St. Polycarp's death it was said, 'Now he *exults* with the apostles and all the righteous' (M. Pol. 19^2). In Church Greek the verb is used of God rejoicing in His creatures, of the Son sharing His joy and rejoicing in the Church. It was used of angels and Christians – especially at Eastertide and in the hour of departure.[107]

It can defy even the starkness of death, for Christians gathered round Polycarp's bones in gladness and exultation (M. Pol 18[2]).

NOTES

[1] E.g. Aeschylus *Agamemnon* 184, 530.
[2] BGU 195.30 (ii AD).
[3] P. Cairo Zen. 59520.4 (iii BC).
[4] E.g. *Zeitschrift für die Neutestamentliche Wissenschaft*, 48 (1957), pp. 127–32.
[5] OGI 194.3 (CIG 4717.2f.). BS, p. 233, n. 2.
[6] J. Elliott, *Catholic Biblical Quarterly* 32 (1970), pp. 369–91.
[7] *Revue Biblique* 76 (1969), pp. 508–27.
[8] J. N. D. Kelly, *The Pastoral Epistles*, London 1963, in loc.
[9] E.g. Guerra y Gomez, *Episcopos y Presbyteros*, Burgos 1962, p. 272; W. Michaelis, *Das Ältestenamt der Christlichen Gemeinde im Lichte der heiligen Schrift*, Bern 1953, p. 51.
[10] C. J. Ellicott, *The Pastoral Epistles of St. Paul*, Longman 5th ed. 1883, p. 67.
[11] A. E. Harvey, *Journal of Theological Studies* NS 25 (1975), pp. 318–32.
[12] Op. cit., p. 320.
[13] Such was St. Jerome's understanding. 'The Apostle plainly shows that presbyters are the same as bishops' (Epistle cxlvi). 'The one is a term of dignity, the other of age' (Epist. lxix). Lightfoot, *Philippians*, pp. 95–9.
[14] J. G. Soboson, C.S.C., *Scottish Journal of Theology*, 27 (1974), p. 132, n. 1.
[15] S. Nagy, *Roczniki Teologiczno-Kanonicze* (Lublin, Poland) 11 (1964), pp. 55–79.
[16] Sobson, op. cit., p. 132.
[17] K. A. Strand, *Andrews University Seminary Studies* 4 (1966), pp. 65–88.
[18] Soboson, op. cit., p. 134.
[19] Aeschylus *Eumenides* 731, 1027.
[20] It may be the collegiate body of the presbyters, as H. Schlier, *Le Temps de l'Église*, Paris 1961, p. 154.
[21] J. P. Meier, *Catholic Biblical Quarterly* 35 (1973), p. 344.
[22] Thucydides VI 100; Plato *Laws* 938B.
[23] Herodotus I 199.
[24] See J. B. Lightfoot on Colossians (in loc. 3[12]).
[25] G. Schrenk in Kittel *TWNT* IV, pp. 194f.
[26] See Schrenk, op. cit., p. 195.
[27] 2 Clem 14[5]; I. Philad 11[1].
[28] 1 Clem 1[1] 2[4] 46[4] 49[5] 58[2] 59[2].
[29] *Vis.* I 3.4, II 1.3, II 2.5, II 4.2, III 5.1, III 8.3, III 9.10, IV 2.5, IV 3.5.
[30] I. Eph intr., 1 Clem 50[7] 64.
[31] Plato *Republic* 414A, *Laws* 802B.
[32] Literally, 'a portion of election' – probably a genitive of the same kind as that in Act 9[15] ('a vessel of election') and Irenaeus I 6.4 ('seed of election'). It means a portion, a vessel, a seed, 'set apart' by election. Cf. Lightfoot, *Apostolic Fathers*, pt. I, vol. II, p. 93.
[33] D. E. H. Whiteley, *The Theology of St. Paul*, Blackwell 1964, p. 96.
[34] For secular instances, see IG 5960; Philodemus *de Pietate* 25 (i BC).
[35] G. Schrenk in Kittel *TWNT* II, p. 748.
[36] B. F. Westcott and F. J. A. Hort, *The NT in the Original Greek*, London 1896, vol. II, p. 56. 'Good will toward men', was preferred also by Mc Neile, Scrivener, and Ropes, beside Field.

[37] Cremer (215) urged that even if we accept the non-Byzantine text ('men of good will') we should have to take *eudokia* in the same sense as the Byzantine text and explain the genitive as in the phrase, 'children of wrath' (i.e. *God's* wrath).

[38] Schrenk, op. cit.

[39] Ernest Vogt, S.J., in Krister Stendhahl, *The Scrolls and the New Testament*, Harper 1957, pp. 114–17.

[40] Op. cit., p. 114.

[41] A. Feuillet, *Bulletin de l'association Guillaume Budé* (Revue de Culture Générale, Paris) 4th series (1974), pp. 91ff.

[42] E.g. Mt 21[38]; Mk 12[7]; Lk 20[14]; Act 7[5]; Gal 4[1]; Heb 6[17] 11[7f].

[43] As often in NT, e.g. Mt 27[35].

[44] III 50.

[45] II 109.

[46] P. Grenf 1.14.11 (ii BC).

[47] Bauer, s.v., col. 790.

[48] See E. G. Selwyn, p. 231.

[49] 'The *clergy* are assembled … in order'. But the MS has *kēroi* (candles, used by Christians at night). Sylberg conjectures *kairoi* (seasons). See H. Meecham, *The Epistle to Diognetus*, Manchester 1949, p. 142.

[50] C. Bigg, *St. Peter and St. Jude*, ICC 2nd ed. 1902, p. 188.

[51] *Peri Sēmeiōn* 11 (ed. T. Gomperz, *Herkulanische Studien* i, Leipzig 1865, pp. 53ff.).

[52] *de Confusione Linguarum* 101, 103.

[53] But passive in Philo *de Agricultura* 160, and *Quod Omnis Probus Liber Sit*, 27.

[54] Ps 88(89)[13]; Jg 3[10]B; Ps 104(105)[4]; 2 Km 22[23], etc.

[55] 'In the Spirit' added in Byzantine text, with Koridethi, harmonizing with 1[80].

[56] Theophrastus *de Igne* 30; Diodorus Siculus III 48 (Teubner) i BC.

[57] Teubner XXII 5.10.

[58] Preisandanz (2nd ed. Teubner 1973) vol. I, p. 106.

[59] W. Scott, *Corpus Hermeticum*, Clarendon 1924, I, libellus i §32.

[60] Thus it is beside the point for Hort to render verse 5, 'in a season of *extremity*', and we should bear the new Christian meaning of *eschatos* in mind. As Selwyn observed, there is no instance of *eschatos* bearing Hort's meaning ('extreme') in the NT (p. 125).

[61] I. Eph 21[2]; I. Trall 13[1]; I. Ro 9[2]; I. Smyrn 11[1]; Did 1[5].

[62] *Oedipus in Colonus* 1138.

[63] *Ajax* 131.

[64] Diogenes Laertius IV 41.

[65] UPZ 66.5 (ii BC).

[66] Dionysius of Halicarnassus VI 48.

[67] *Harvard Theological Review* 43 (1950), pp. 165–168.

[68] Anders T. S. Nygren, *Commentary on Romans*, ET London 1952, p. 331.

[69] Theophilus of Antioch, *ad Autolycum* ii 17.

[70] E. Stauffer, *New Testment Theology*, ET London 1955, p. 73.

[71] *Agamemnon* 299.

[72] *Hippolytus* 866.

[73] Field, p. 231.

[74] *Bell. Jud.* V iv 3 (Niese V 164).

[75] Grammarian of ii AD, ed. A. Leutz, 1867ff., I 166.7, II 119.6.

[76] Origen *In Johann.* I 4 (6) (PG XIV 29C). A. E. Brooke, *The Commentary of Origen on S. John's Gospel*, CUP 1896, vol. i, p. 6, line 18; C. Blanc, *Origène, Commentaire sur Saint Jean*, Paris 1966 (Sources Chrétiennes 120), pp. 68ff.

[77] *De Decretis Nicaenae Synodi* 28–32.

[78] Referred to by St. Clement of Alexandria (*Stromateis* V 8.49), but much older in invention. E. K. Lee, *New Testament Studies* 8 (1962), p. 173.

[79] *Fragmenta* 7H.
[80] Strabo II 5.18; Philo 2.12.
[81] Galen XV 760.
[82] In i BC Philodemus *de Musica*, Teubner p. 77, line 14.
[83] E. K. Lee, op. cit., p. 172.
[84] Herodotus I 14.92; Sophocles *Antigone* 286; Plutarch *Pelopidas* 25.7.
[85] Lev 27^{28}; Deut 7^{26} 13^{17}; Josh 6 $^{16(17)}$; Ro 9^3; 1 Co 12^3, etc.
[86] *Defixionum Tabellae*, ed. A. Audollent, Paris 1904, 41A and B (IG III 3, App. XIII, XIV 6.17) from Megara.
[87] See Johannes Behm in Kittel *TWNT* I, pp. 356f.
[88] The Aramaic *Maran-atha* is literally, 'Our Lord comes!' and has some very solemn significance.
[89] See the many citations in *A Patristic Greek Lexicon*, G. W. H. Lampe, Clarendon 1961, pp. 102f.
[90] Comm. on 1 Co 16^{22}.
[91] J. B. Lightfoot, *St. Paul's Epistle to the Galatians*, Macmillan 10th ed. 1890, p. 78.
[92] O. Cullmann, *Les premières confessions de foi chrétiennes*, 2nd ed. Paris, pp. 22f.
[93] C. K. Barrett, *1 Corinthians*, Black 2nd ed. 1971, p. 270. See also Lietzmann, in *Zeitschrift für die Neutestamentliche Wissenschaft* (Berlin) 1923, p. 262.
[94] W. Schmithals, *Die Gnosis in Korinth*, 2nd ed. Göttingen 1965, pp. 117–22.
[95] *Contra Celsum* vi 28.
[96] B. A. Pearson, *Journal of Biblical Literature* 86 (1967), pp. 301–5.
[97] J. D. M. Derrett, *New Testament Studies* 21 (1975), pp. 544–54.
[98] *Defixionum Tabellae*, ed. A. Audollent, Paris 1904, 41A (i–ii AD). Cf. above.
[99] Num 21^2; Deut 13$^{15(16)}$ 20^{17}; Josh 6$^{20(21)}$; Jg 1^{17}A 21^{11}; 1 Km 15^3; 4 Km 19^{11}; 1 Chr 4^{41}; 2 Esd 10^8; Dan Th 11^{44}.
[100] By contrast the Didache uses *katathema* of Christ, in the same way that St. Paul uses *katara* (Gal 3^{13}). By Him we are saved in the great Tribulation, by Him Who became *katathema* (excommunicated) for us (Did 16^5).
[101] C. K. Barrett, *The Gospel according to St. John*, SPCK 1962, p. 300.
[102] Theodoret *Historia Ecclesiastica* I 3. Cp. Alexander of Alexandria's *Epistles* to Alexander of Constantinople, 9 (PG XVIII 561A). Field, p. 96.
[103] Commentary on 1 Co 4^5 (§ XVIII 75). Text printed in *Journal of Theological Studies* 9 (1910) p. 356.
[104] *Editio Epistularum Pauli* (PG LXXXV 772D).
[105] Book VII ch. 31.
[106] *De Ecclesiastica Theologia* lib. 1, ch. VIII (PG XXIV 837A).
[107] *A Patristic Greek Lexicon*, ed. G. W. H. Lampe, Clarendon 1961, p. 6.

F

FAITH

πίστις : πιστεύω : ὀλιγοπιστία : ὀλιγόπιστος : πιστός

Secular Greek. All these words, *pistis, pisteuō, oligopistia, oligopistos, pistos,* denote trust of some kind, often the confidence that what one is doing is right. For instance, with regard to the noun, Creon says, 'In that *pistis* (confidence that I was right) I hunted down the quarry.'[1] *Pistis* may be 'trust' in someone's word.[2] It is confidence or persuasion about a matter. 'I have *pistis* (confidence) in his probity', affirms Demosthenes (XVIII 15). Aristotle refers to arguments which carry some degree of *pistis* (conviction),[3] and Euripides' words are said to have received *pistis* (confirmation) from facts.[4]

Our samples indicate that the noun meant trust, a feeling of assurance in a person or circumstance. Other instances will show that *pistis* refers more definitely to the object of the trust or to the reasoning that has inspired the confidence, such as a guarantee or pledge of good faith. Readers of Herodotus will recall that the Samians made a *pistis* (pledge) with an oath (IX 92). Men make personal 'pledges' to one another.[5] A lady may make a pledge of widowhood, which is a determination not to marry again.[6] A political guarantee is meant when the Chians obtained *pisteis* (pledges) from the Athenians to keep on the same terms as before.[7] Argument or reasoning may be *pistis*, for it gives confidence. The term means 'reassurance' when it is said, 'Much argument and *pistis* is required.'[8]

Again, *pistis* was a responsibility entrusted to another. Seleucus gave the government in 'trust' to his son Antiochus.[9] Like the Latin *fides* it had the special meaning of political 'protection', and Polybius reports that the Aetolians committed themselves to the *pistis* of the Romans (XX 9, 10).

It is not difficult to see how the special Biblical sense of complete trust in God arose for the word. Indeed, it had been sometimes used religiously in secular Greek. On an inscription from Setos about 120 BC are the words, 'choosing those who kept the *faith* reverently and justly'.[10] Still, it is doubtful whether this is quite the NT usage in the Christian phrase, 'I have kept the *faith*', and it is more likely to mean 'keeping one's word' or 'trustworthiness' in a purely ethical sense. Though Plato uses *pistis* of belief in the gods' existence, he never intends such personal faith in gods as would entail any sort of commitment.[11]

The verb *pisteuō* too indicates the placing of reliance or the

153

entrusting of one's affairs,[12] like the placing of special trust in the men of a certain city,[13] or the feeling of confidence. Regarding Socrates it was said that he would not have given counsel if he had not 'been confident' that what he said would come true.[14] The feeling of assurance is prominent, but it is not in itself a religious sentiment, even where it accompanies prayer, e.g. 'Pray to the gods, *trusting* them.'[15] The verb is no more religious than when it is used with any other object. 'I *trusted* thee and the gods.'[16] Such phrases express confidence in the word of the gods, but hardly more. 'I would have thee *trust* the gods and my words.'[17] A text of the Byzantine period has the religious meaning, 'We *believe* in the Lord of all things.'[18]

In secular Greek *pisteuō* is to 'believe', in the sense in which Creon says to Oedipus, 'I see you will not *credit* me,'[19] and the Melians say to the Athenians, 'We *believe* in the good fortune by which the gods have so far saved our city.'[20] There is the phrase, 'This is what I *believe* to be true.'[21]

A rather different meaning was that of entrusting something to someone. 'Do not *trust* your life to a woman!'[22] and, 'Whom would anyone *trust* as guardian of his money?'[23]

The verb is sometimes used of belief in the gods, which is more than simple credence in the power of some deity, or simple acceptance of the fact that divine beings exist. When Xenophon speaks of '*believing in* the gods',[24] we have something more obviously religious. 'It is confidence in God, displayed in the acceptance of His revelation as true,'[25] urged Dodd who claimed that the most we can say of the difference between Greek and Hebrew in this respect is that the intellectual moment of 'belief' is somewhat stronger in the Greek, while the moral element of 'trust' is more characteristic of the Hebrew.[26] Nevertheless, I cannot trace that, more than very occasionally, the use of the word in the secular language ever approaches the special religious sense which the word enjoys in Biblical Greek – that is, the *confidence* in God to help out of distress and the assurance one receives, through trust in God, to believe that one's conduct is correct (Ro 14[2]).

The noun *oligopistia* (little faith) is a coinage of Christian Greek (Mt 17[20] SB), and the adjective *oligopistos* (of little faith) likewise (Mt 6[30] 8[26] 14[31] 16[8]; Lk 12[28]; Acta Thom. 28). The adjective occurs occasionally, perhaps only once, in later secular writers, and it may be due to Christian influence. The new words may be a formation from Aramaic and much less probably from Latin.

Biblical Greek. As Burton observed, the words are Greek but 'the roots of the thought are mainly in the experience and writings of the Hebrew prophets and psalmists'.[28] Even in their use of Biblical Greek the Christians break new ground and seem to me (though not to some others) almost wholly to dispense with the passive sense which is characteristic of the OT word, 'faithfulness', preferring the active sense, 'faith'. It is true that the passive sense of *pistis*, e.g. 'the faithfulness of God', may sometimes be found in the NT (Mt 23[23]; Act 17[31]; Ro 3[3]; Gal 5[22;] Tit 2[10]; Heb 12[2] for Westcott), for it suits the context, but it seems to me to be rare.

Still many have argued persuasively in favour of 'faithfulness' in certain NT contexts, whether it is the faithfulness of God or of man. Urging that the Hebrew verb means both 'to have faith in' and 'to be faithful to', and that the Hebrew noun means more often 'faithfulness' than 'faith', A. B. Curtis long ago[29] concluded that in Biblical Greek the same is true of *pistis*. He appealed to the American RV in six important passages and added Mt 23[23] where *krisis* is the Hebrew *mishpat*, *eleos* is the Hebrew *ḥesed*, and *pistis* is the Hebrew, *ᵇᵉmunâ* (faithfulness). His final point is not without weight: the Seer records, 'Be thou faithful (*pistos*) unto death, and I will give thee the crown of life' (Rev 2[10]).

In more recent times, too, it has been proposed that in St. Paul's letters, the word *pistis* more often designates 'faithfulness' than 'trust'.[30] That we should understand the passive sense in such passages as 2 Th 2[13] (*pistis alētheias*), whether it is 'faithfulness of truth' or whether 'faith in truth', has been disputed in recent years.[31] Prof. Torrance is one who takes the passive sense. 'It is clear from the Old Testament background that for St. Paul neither *pistis* nor *alētheia* will express what he is after, and so he puts both words together to convey what the Old Testament means by *'emeth* and/or *'emunah*'.[32] Torrance urges what is true, that Jesus Christ is the incarnate 'faithfulness' of God. But are we justified in thinking that the earliest Christians followed the characteristically Hebrew sense of *pistis*, as found in the LXX? It seems to me more probable that the Christians have broken new ground and all but dispensed with the passive sense. Moreover, Moule urged Torrance to consider whether the genitive, *alētheias*, is not likely to be objective and whether the phrase does not mean, 'God chose you ... unto salvation in sanctification ... and faith in *alētheia*.'[33] I would add that *alētheia* seems to mean the Gospel in Biblical Greek (see, 'Truth') and would suggest that St. Paul refers here to belief in the Gospel, as indeed he does at Ph 1[27] where 'faith of the Gospel' is really, 'belief *in* the Gospel'.[34]

Nevertheless, on the other side, a strong case is made out for the passive sense, divine 'fidelity', even in the epistle to the Romans where human 'faith' (active) plays a large part. For instance, in 1[17] ('the just shall live by *pistis*'), when we ask whose is this quality, God's or man's, we may turn to the original language of Hab 2[4] and find it is man's. In the LXX, however, it is God's,[35] and *pistis* is passive in sense, meaning 'faithfulness', for God says, 'The just man will live because of My fidelity.' It is true that some MSS, perhaps deliberately, omit 'My', and others transpose the word (as in Heb 10[38]), so that we have, 'My just man.' Prof. O'Rourke has some ground for observing, 'If the apostle had the Septuagint's understanding in mind here he is teaching once more that justification comes from God.' But the professor has to admit that his proposed exegesis falls to the ground in Gal 3[11] where St. Paul makes the same citation of Habakkuk.[36] I cannot think that the argument in Romans is so different from that in Galatians, where our own active 'faith' is in mind, 'the hearing of faith' (Gal 3[2]). Moreover, the real sense of the LXX, any more than the original Hebrew, is not so very important for St. Paul. In regard to this particular citation, we must say that both he and the writer to Hebrews quite neglect the historic occasion and immediate reference of the text. G. B. Stevens long ago demonstrated that the writer to Hebrews cites the LXX in its mistranslated context, so that the 'shall live' of Habakkuk (i.e. 'shall be preserved in safety') becomes, 'shall inherit the messianic kingdom in the life to come'. For St. Paul it becomes, 'shall be acquitted and forgiven'. The citation illustrates the fact that NT writers often cite the LXX with little regard to verbal accuracy and the immediate reference in the original.[37]

It remains true all the same that in Ro 3[26] ('the justifier of him *that believeth* in Jesus') the meaning of *pistis* may not be active ('his faith *in* Jesus'), but rather passive ('because of God's *fidelity* to Jesus') or, 'because of the *fidelity* of Jesus'). I think that grammatically either interpretation is latent and that we may legitimately follow Prof. O'Rourke.[38] Moreover, in 10[6] ('the righteousness which is of faith'), the righteousness spoken of is contrasted with 'righteousness which is of the Law' – external to man is the Law, and so presumably is the parallel, 'faith', and therefore not man's 'faith'. Quite correct, therefore, will be the rendering of the phrase, 'the righteousness which comes from God's *fidelity*'.[39]

We ought indeed to be wary of viewing *pistis* in Romans in the light of the Pelagian and semi-Pelagian controversies,[40] where much turns on the question of human faith. Sometimes, then, but of course not invariably, *pistis* may be taken as referring to a quality of God's or of Jesus'. The greatest probability of this perhaps is Ro 3[22,25] ('divine faithfulness', proved by the death of Jesus), and to a less extent in 4[14,16]. Often the choice between active and passive senses is difficult, but the professor's conclusion is valid: 'If even some of the proposed interpretations of the use of *pistis* in Rom be correct, Paul stresses even more than has usually been thought God's part in man's justification.'[41]

To a large extent, however, the NT shuns the association which in secular Greek links the *pistis* words with intellect and morals and rejects the exclusive preoccupation with ethics which we find in the LXX and Jewish Greek. The words have rather what Hatch[42] called a 'theological meaning'. The sense resembles that of Philo. The object of 'faith' is always God, and 'faith' is a state of mind transcending ordinary knowledge, a conviction with a firmer basis than sense or reason, confidence in what God says without further evidence, 'the basis of what is hoped for, the evidence of things not seen' (Heb 11[1]).

It should be noticed that in many ways the verbs *pisteuō* and *ginōskō* (to have divine insight) in St. John's gospel are synonymous, although Jesus Who is said to 'know' God is never said to 'believe' in Him. However, to 'believe' (11[42]) and to 'know' (17[3]) are used in the same context. Clearly the words are synonymous in a passage like this: 'they have *known* ... that I came out from Thee and they have *believed* that Thou didst send Me' (17[8]). Faith is a deep insight, sure and divine knowledge.

Christians make 'faith' almost exclusively religious and they usually, to my mind, understand it in an active sense – belief or trust in God and in His promises, in Christ or in some promise or claim, or word of God and Christ. 'Faith' may also mean the 'content' of faith, the matter which is believed, as in the phrases, 'the good news of the *faith*' (Gal 1[23]), and 'one Lord, one *faith*' (Eph 4[5]). This was a common meaning for 'the Faith' in later Church history, this was the *fides quae creditur*, 'the Faith which is believed in', i.e. the Christian Faith, expressed in creeds, in decrees of Councils, the teaching of doctors and saints, and revealed in the Bible.

Again, it may mean 'the faith' in the sense of 'piety', as in the phrase, 'I have kept the *faith*' (2 Ti 4[7]); and when St. James contrasts faith and works (Jas 2[14]) he may not be understanding *pistis* in the usual Christian sense but as a mere piety, a 'hearing' of the Word without 'doing' (1[22]), a selecting of parts of the Law to keep and a neglecting of others (2[10]). It is then what has been called a *Gesetzesfrömmigkeit*, an attitude of pious devotedness towards the Law, which is effective for nothing and cannot save.[43] St. James, on this view of his use of *pistis*, is not at variance with the position of St. Paul.

In Christian Greek, the preposition *en* (in) often follows *pistis* through the influence of the Hebrew preposition b^e: Ro 3[25]; Gal 3[26]; Eph 1[15]; Col 1[4]; 1 Ti 1[14] 3[13]; 2 Ti 1[13] 3[15]; 2 Pet 1[1]. The verb too occurs with *en* (Mk 1[15] cf. Swete in loc.), but it occurs also with *epi* (Lk 24[25]; 1 Ti 1[16]), and more often with *eis*: Mt 18[6]; Acts; Paul;

1 Pet 1[8]; 1 Jn 5[10,13], and 33 times in Jn. This again is not a secular usage and arises from a parallel with Hebrew b^e.

A Believer (*pistos*). Relatively less often than *pistis*, the adjective *pistos* has the active sense in the NT. Moreover, commonly the context is not sufficient to determine whether the sense is active or passive. On the other hand, the following examples of *pistos* are clearly active in sense: 'be not faithless but *believing*' (Jn 20[27]), 'they of the circumcision which were *believers*' (Act 10[45]), 'a *Christian* Jewess' (Act 16[1]), 'a *believer* in the Lord' (16[15]), 'mercy of the Lord to be a *believer*' (1 Co 7[25]), 'a believer' (2 Co 6[15]), 'believing Abraham' (Gal 3[9]), '*believers* in Christ Jesus' (Eph 1[1]), 'saints and *believing* brethren' (Col 1[2]), '*believers* which know the truth' (1 Ti 4[3]), 'believers' (1 Ti 4[10,12] 5[16] 6[2]), '*Christian* children' (Tit 1[6]). In Revelation however, the context does not allow us to decide. At least, we can say that in Christian Greek 'the *pistoi*' has become a special term for the Christians: Act 10[45] 12[3]D; 1 Ti 4[3,12]; I. Eph 21[2]; I. Magn 5[2]; M. Pol 12[3]; I. Smyrn 1[2].

Although *pistos* may have an active sense in secular Greek ('relying on' a person),[44] yet the special Christian use is entirely new.

Our conclusion must be that 'faith' in the vocabulary of Christians is not only belief and trust, but also faithfulness and loyalty. Put technically and linguistically, 'faith' is both active and passive in sense. It is not only the inspiration of all religion but is also a moral excellence. We have gone further and seen that it signified a corporate body of doctrine, as the Christian vocabulary developed, and even a kind of piety. It is the means of entering into mystical fellowship with Christ, and at the same time is the mystical state itself in which the believer lives. It is indeed the Christian life – 'a social bond among those who are Christ's, as well as an individual gift'.[45] It is the channel which conveys a saint's distinctive blessings, peace with God, hope, joy, forgiveness and salvation. From it, all the graces spring to adorn the life of the Christian fellowship. It is an eclectic word and not easy to define, for it has quite cast off the old semantic garments of secular Greek.

FALSE BRETHREN

ψευδάδελφοι

Christian Greek will have coined *pseudadelphoi* (plural) to denote some kind of early heretic who had Judaistic leanings and who was persuading the brethren to surrender their 'spiritual liberty' (Gal 2⁴), to revert to Judaism. St. Paul was in some kind of danger among the false brethren (2 Co 11²⁶).

St. Polycarp refers to them. 'Abstain from *pseudadelphoi* who lead foolish men astray.' (Pol. ad Philip. 6³) – precisely in what direction we can but guess.

FALSE CHRISTS

ψευδόχριστοι

Pseudochristoi is a word of early Christian coinage. It refers to personages appearing in 'these days' – during what are known as the 'pangs' of Messiah's coming – who will do more than oppose the true Christ and will themselves claim to be Christ. Their very appearance is the sign that He is near (Mt 24³,⁸). They will work marvels and will all but deceive the elect (Mt 24²⁴; Mk 13²²).

They may be distinguished from Antichrists (q.v.) who oppose the true Christ without necessarily making such a claim themselves. Trench (p. 102f.) suggested that the False Christs do in fact make this claim, and he observed that 'there is a sense in which the final "Antichrist" will be a "pseudochrist" as well', for though he does not take the name it is expected that he will assume His offices.

FALSE MINISTRY

ψευδαπόστολος : ψευδοπροφήτης : ψευδοδιδάσκαλος

The three words, *pseudapostolos, pseudoprophētēs,* and *pseudodidaskalos,* appear as special terms in Christian Greek, signifying a false apostle, a false prophet and false teacher.

False Apostle. *Pseudapostolos* is a coinage of Christians and denominates certain teachers at Corinth, opposed to St. Paul, who made groundless claim to be apostles of Christ (2 Co 11¹³).

Were the *pseudapostoloi* legalistic Judaizers? E. Käsemann took them to be envoys from the Jerusalem church aiming to bring Gentile churches under the authority of the mother of all.⁴⁶ The opponents of St. Paul have by others been taken to be Hellenistic Jews who may have worked from a base in Palestine – possibly they were early Gnostics (see, 'Grecians') who adhered to St. Stephen and the Hellenists (Act 6).⁴⁷ It is all conjecture. Nevertheless the appearance of men with such high claims so early in the Church's story, is evidence of the dispatch with which the Evil One sows his tares.

False Prophet. *Pseudoprophētēs* is probably a coinage of Biblical Greek, rendering *nābhî* in the LXX, and appearing in extra-Biblical Jewish writers.[48] In the Testaments of the Twelve Patriarchs we hear of 'false prophets' who in the Hasmonean period persecuted 'all righteous men' (T. Jud. 21[91]). In the OT sense, 'false prophets' are mentioned also in the NT (Lk 6[26]; 2 Pet 2[1]).

Bar-Jesus, a Jew in Cyprus, was a 'false prophet' encountered by Barnabas and Saul on their first missionary journey (Act 13[6]). Our Lord had warned His disciples in the sermon on the Mount to be ware of 'false prophets' who appear in sheep's clothing with hearts of wolves (Mt 7[15]). He suggests that at His next Coming they will profess to have prophesied in His name, but He will disown them. The test of the falsity of a prophet is his 'fruits' (works). Dr. David Hill suggested[49] that in this passage the evangelist contrasts two distinct groups of false prophet – a body of charismatics *within* the Church, not worthy to accomplish the will of God and enter the Kingdom (v. 21), and a group of Jewish adversaries (grievous wolves), coming into the Church *from without* to threaten, deceive, and subvert (v. 15). He supposed it most likely that this group comprised Jewish teachers, none other than the Pharisees. That the prophets were the Pharisees, a faction *within* St. Matthew's local church, is a slightly different view advocated by Baumbach.[50]

Before the Coming of our Lord we are to expect the appearance of **false prophets** who will deceive many with miracles, all but deflecting the very elect (Mt 24[11,24]; Rev 16[13]).

In the Church **false prophets** are active already. They may be identified for they fail to confess that Jesus the Messiah is come in the flesh (1 Jn 4[1]). They corrupt the understanding of God's servants. They speak what they are desired to, however wicked those desires (Hermas *Mand.* XI 1, 2). No one but an 'idolator, empty of the truth', would enquire of a false prophet (XI 4, 7). The way to identify him is by the life he lives. An 'apostle' who seeks hospitality for more than two days is a **false prophet** or, if he asks for money, and does not live up to what he preaches (Did 11[5,6,10]).

False Teacher. *Pseudodidaskalos* is a further coinage of Christians. False teachers are to appear in the Church and are likened to the false prophets of the OT (2 Pet 2[1]). *Pseudodidaskalia* (false teaching) appears in the apostolic Fathers (Pol. ad Phil. 7[2]).

A survey of the false teaching referred to by SS. Peter and Jude, John and Paul, prompts the conclusion that the *pseudodidaskaloi* taught a form of the antinomian heresy,[51] which led to a corruption of morals and disbelief in God and Christ. It was likely to be a misrepresentation of St. Paul's doctrine of God's free grace which 'the unlearned and unstable' distort (2 Pet 3[16]). What the **false prophets** and the **false teachers** impart is 'heresy' (2 Pet 2[1]), and the heretics are plausible, disputatious and irreverent. They scoff at the idea of a second Coming. 'How naturally this might be connected with lax morality is evident.'[52]

TO FAVOUR

1. ἐπιβλέπω

Secular Greek. The meaning of *epiblepō* was to look upon, as when Socrates 'glanced at us'.[53] It was to gaze upon,[54] to look with envy, to look carefully at, to observe,[55] to 'view' the labour of workmen,[56] to take into consideration,[57] and, with a double accusative, to regard as, consider as.[58]

Biblical Greek. Now appears the additional meaning, to regard with favour, for in the LXX the verb renders the Hebrew *pānâ* (to have respect to, regard graciously).[59] The new Biblical meaning seems to be implicit in a magical papyrus[60] of the second or third century AD but, whatever the explanation, the text provides at best a lone example of what is frequent enough in the NT.

As applied to God's favouring of His lowly handmaid (Lk 1[48]), *epiblepō* is not merely to notice or to regard – the secular meaning – but to look graciously.[61] When *epiblepō* is used by the boy's father asking Jesus to 'bestow favour'[62] upon his son (Lk 9[38]) – not simply to have a look at him – the verb has acquired a new usage. One more example: it is not to be supposed that Christians were doing no more than 'gaze' at the well-dressed man who had entered their assembly (Jas 2[3]). The context makes it clear that *epiblepō* involves 'treating with respect and favour'.[63]

2. χαριτόω

Charitō is a verb of rare occurrence in secular Greek. The letter of Aristeas has it (225) but he is a Jew. His meaning is: 'To *be gracious* to all men is the best gift to receive from God.' In the Testaments of the Twelve Patriarchs (Joseph 1[6]), God is said to have 'shown favour' to Joseph in prison. The same use is made by Hermas: 'He *bestowed His grace* upon us in the Beloved' (*Sim.* IX 24.3).

A post-Christian papyrus of the fourth century has the verb in the middle voice, still with the active sense of bestowing favour upon (BGU 1026 xxiii 24). *Chariotō* is as frequent in Jewish writings as anywhere. Ben Sirach has the same participle as that which St. Luke applies to the Virgin, *kecharitōmenos*, and Aristeas has the same (perfect) tense, *kecharitōsthai*, but Ben Sirach's meaning, like that of Aristeas, is 'gracious' (active), not 'highly favoured' (passive): Ecclus 18[17]. The Syriac version confirms the active sense by its rendering, 'saintly'. Moreover, the Symmachus version (Ps 17(18)[26]) provides what seems to be the active sense, 'gracious'.

When St. Paul uses the verb it appears in the active voice and there is no doubt of the active meaning. 'He has *bestowed favour* upon us' (Eph 1[6]).

At the Annunciation, however, the form is middle or passive and the sense is passive – 'thou that art *highly favoured*', rather than, 'thou that art gracious' (Lk 1[28]). The context makes this clear. 'Thou hast found favour', says the archangel a little later (1[30]). A parallel has been noted with other similar annunciations, made by angels to Gideon (Jg 6[12]), to Daniel (Dan 10[11]), and to Zacharias (Lk 1[13]). The meaning then is correctly claimed to be 'blessed' and 'greatly beloved',[64] rather than 'gracious'.

Christians have made much of a very rare word, expressing the rich bestowing of God's most gracious favour. Subsequently it reached the secular language.[65]

FELLOW-IMITATOR

συμμιμητής

A coinage of Christian Greek,[66] based on existing words, *summimētēs* is known only at Ph 3[17]. A difficult question of interpretation is presented to commentators. Are the Philippian saints exhorted to be fellow-imitators (*summimētai*) of Christ together with Paul, or are they collectively to be fellow-imitators of Paul? Alford, Meyer, Weiss, Ellicott, Lightfoot and Vincent favoured the second interpretation – fellow-imitators with one another, all imitating Paul. They are probably right, but Bengel preferred the first interpretation – 'be imitators along with me, all imitating Christ'. It should be noticed that St. Paul immediately adds, 'Mark them which walk so as ye have us for an example.' Elsewhere he claims to be 'an example unto you' (2 Th 3[9]). 'You became followers of me', he notes (1 Th 1[6]). He besought the Corinthians to be followers of his example (1 Co 4[16]), 'even as I also am of Christ' (1 Co 11[1]). As Lightfoot noticed, St. Paul has the Judaizers in mind when he presents himself as a *tupos*.

St. Paul himself, then, is envisaged as the *tupos* to be followed, and the present context says nothing of Christ. It is taken for granted that all imitate Him, but in this instance the imitation is of Paul. Holy Scripture abounds in 'types' (i.e. examples).

FELLOWSHIP (CHRISTIAN FELLOWSHIP)

κοινωνία: κοινωνός: συγκοινωνός: κοινωικός: κοινωνέω: συγκοινωνέω

The words were familiar enough in Greek but early Christians made them properly their own, finding distinctly new meanings.

Secular Greek. In secular Greek the noun *koinōnia*, and the verbs *koinōnō* and *sugkoinōnō*, and the adjectives *koinōnos, sugkoinōnos* and *koinōnikos*, all denoted partnership in some sense.

1. The noun *koinōnia* had been a communion, association, or partnership – a military alliance,[67] or God's partnership with Moses.[68] The latter sense, that of religious sharing between God and man, is indeed not a common one and is quite distinctive to the Jew, Philo, and is in contrast with LXX usage.[69] The idea of partnership in a religious sense was sometimes thus indicated in secular Greek, a *koinōnia* with Zeus,[70] for instance. More usually, *koinōnia* expressed lower relationships – joint-ownership of property,[71] and carnal knowledge.[72] For instance, in a marriage contract of AD 170, one Menidorus gives his daughter 'for *koinōnia* of marriage'.[73] In secular Greek, co-education was described as '*koinōnia* of females with males'.[74]

This profoundly evocative Christian word was taken from Greek literature, and over large areas retained its general usage. Nevertheless, we must allow that in Christianity the original meaning 'had become invested with a spiritual content of such a unique enlargement and application as enabled it to reflect the transcendence of St. Paul's concepts and beliefs concerning the relationship of Christ to his faithful ones and their relationship to him'.[75]

2. The adjective *koinōnos* in secular Greek described a companion or partner, like *sugkoinōnos* which scarcely appears until the sixth century AD.[76] 'My tongue mutters in darkness,' cries the Greek chorus, 'sharing (*koinōnos*) the heart's distress. ... I share (*koinōnos*) your feeling.'[77] Thucydides writes of sharers or partners (*koinōnos*) in the empire of Athens (VII 63, VIII 46), and Sophocles of an accomplice (*koinōnos*) in wickedness.[78] In a Fayûm papyrus of the first century a father remonstrates with his son because he has no help on his smallholding. 'Our *koinōnos* (partner)', he says, 'has taken no share in the work.'[79] In a papyrus libellus of the time of the Decian persecution we may read a

certificate testifying that a Christian has duly sacrificed in a heathen manner to escape punishment. It runs thus: 'I, Aurelius Syrus, as a *koinōnos* (colleague) have certified Diogenes as sacrificing along with us.'[80]

3. The adjective *koinōnikos* meant, 'belonging to society'. Aristotle said that man was a 'gregarious' (*koinōnikos*) animal.[81] For Polybius too the word meant 'sociable' (II 44.1) and Lucian records that Timon was a plain man, 'ready to share' (*koinōnikos*) what he has,[82] while the verbs, *koinōnō* and *sugkoinōnō*, similarly mean to share, and to share jointly.

Christian Greek. The words are specially frequent in Paul, and two special meanings are added in the language of Christians:

(1) *Koinōnia* is 'life in the Body of Christ'. The first Christians continued steadfastly in the apostles' *koinōnia* (Act 2[42]), which is the fellowship of God's Son (1 Co 1[9]), while the pledges of fellowship were extended to Barnabas and Saul before the first missionary journey (Gal 2[9]). The *koinōnia* was not only a share in the 'mystery' of the Gospel, long hidden and now revealed (Eph 3[9]; Ph 1[5]), but also a share in the sufferings of Christ (Ph 3[10]). *Koinōnia* is more than a common experience with one another as Christians: it is communion with the Triune God (2 Co 13[14]; 1 Jn 1[3,6]). Our fellowship is with the Father and Son (1 Jn 1[3,6]) and Holy Ghost (2 Co 13[14]). *Koinōnia* is our 'communion' with other believers which depends on our 'communion' with God (1 Jn 1[7]). 'Abide in Me', says Jesus, 'and I in you' (Jn 15[4]).

St. Paul, however, does not venture to speak of a direct '*koinonia* of God'; indeed, in the NT this *koinōnia* is mediated through Christ, just as in the OT *koinōnia* with God was mediated through the altar (1 Co 10[18]).[83] The *koinōnia* of His sufferings (Ph 3[10]), like that of His Body and Blood (1 Co 10[16]), may refer to the communion of Breaking of Bread, for Christian *koinōnia* centres round the Table,[84]

> *Where remembering hearts Thou meetest*
> *In communion clearest, sweetest,*
> *Earnest of our coming bliss.*

C. Anderson Scott believed that the word *koinōnia* was a self-designation by the early Christian community, indeed the earliest of such self-designations to be adopted (Act 2[42]). He noted that in contemporary Judaism, *ḥᵃbhûrâ* was a group of comrades or a society, especially those united for eating the Passover lamb.[85] He supposed that Jesus' disciples would have some name by which they were collectively known and knew themselves, and he thought it not unnatural that they would be known as the *ḥᵃbhûrâ* of Jesus of Nazareth. The company might well have been described, even in our Lord's earthly lifetime, by a word of which *koinōnia* is the exact equivalent in Greek. He observed that the great Talmudic scholar, Israel Abrahams, had remarked that the Talmudic word *ḥᵃbhûrâ* occurs specifically in relation to the company united for the partaking of the paschal lamb,[86] and Anderson Scott concluded that subsequently to the Last Supper the name, *ḥᵃbhûrâ/koinōnia* became a natural self-designation for the disciples as a community. It is quite likely, as Anderson Scott declared with some insight, that the name had a new significance for those who were present at the Last Supper. His conclusion has the more force when we recollect that in his gospel St. John implies that the Last Supper was the occasion of instruction on the subject of the unity of the disciples one with another and with the Lord. That is to say, it was instruction on the *ḥᵃbhûrâ* – or, to give its Christian Greek form, the *koinōnia*.[87]

In *The Common Life*,[88] Fr. Thornton observed that Hauck hesitates to link *koinōnia* in Act 2[42] with the community in concrete form, the fellowship of Christians, and supposes it to be rather an interior spiritual reality, a bond of brotherly concord.[89] Yet despite a failure to link *koinōnia* in Act 2[42] with the Hebrew *ḥᵃbhûrâ*, nevertheless Hauck does quote Act 2[46] for the early Christian counterpart of the Jewish *ḥᵃbhûrâ* meals,[90] and he points out that in the post-exilic period the custom arose of meeting with friends for a common meal to introduce the Sabbath Day (quoting Oesterley) – times of table-fellowship which were called *ḥᵃbhûrâ*.

The same idiomatic meaning may be seen in the adjective *koinōnikos* which no longer, I believe, has the secular definition of 'sharing' and 'sociable', but now marks a believer who is **in fellowship**, an active constituent of the local church, rich in good works, ready to be generous (1 Ti 6[18]). The point is not generally conceded, however, and St. Chrysostom explained *koinōnikos* as 'affable, gentle', and Theodoret as 'having no arrogant disposition'. The Vulgate, too, gives rise to AV's 'willing to communicate'. RV has the alternative, 'ready to sympathise'. Moffatt has 'generous', and RSV follows him. The rendering of Knox, 'ready to share the common burden', makes a bridge between the secular and the Christian meanings. However, 'willing to share', in the Jerusalem Bible is, I believe, the secular meaning. NEB too takes this meaning. I would commend BFBS's rendering (p. 349) as nearest to the usage of Christian Greek, namely, 'to share freely with others in fellowship'. Although 'sociable' is the interpretation of *koinōnikos* in modern Greek, and although in the contemporary paraphrase of 1 Ti 6[18] which seems to be officially put forward by the Synod of the Church of Greece[91] the word is explained as 'affable' (katadektos), yet in the Christian Greek which follows that of the

NT *koinōnikos* came to have a proper ecclesiastical sense, 'in communion with'.[92] This I conceive to be its sense in early Christian language.

Another adjective, *koinōnos*, has a rather wider use in Christian Greek, for the secular example of 'partner' still appears.[93] However, the connotation of a Christian **in fellowship** applies to *koinōnos*, as I think it applies also to *koinōnikos*. Titus is Paul's *koinōnos* and so is Philemon (2 Co 8[23]; Phm 17). As a contrast, one may be a *koinōnos* of demons (1 Co 10[20]). A Christian may look forward to being *koinōnos* of the glory beyond the sufferings of earth, the highest fellowship of all (1 Pet 5[1]). Deissmann, noting the resemblance between *koinōnoi phuseōs* (2 Pet 1[4]) and the phrase on a contemporary inscription, *phuseōs koinōnountes anthrōpinēs*, urged that moreover these Commagenian inscriptions from Asia Minor 'afford other materials for the history of the language of early Christianity'.[94] The resemblance, however, is superficial and only verbal. In sentiment and context the phrases are far apart.

The notion of **fellowship** with God and with the Church and of separation from the *kosmos* (the hostile world), occurs in the verbs *koinōnō*[95] and *sugkoinōnō*, the former in 1 Pet 4[13] (to have fellowship with Christ's sufferings and then with the glory), the latter in the warnings against involvement in the unfruitful works of darkness and in wicked Babylon (Eph 5[11]; Rev 18[4]). Further, the adjective *sugkoinōnos* is much more than a 'companion'. It indicates a **member of the believers' fellowship**, nourished upon the richness of the divine Olive, sharing in the grace of Gospel-preaching and in the tribulation of those who belong to the kingdom and patience of Jesus Christ (Ro 11[17]; 1 Co 9[23]; Ph 1[7]; Rev 1[9]). In this sense one may be in **fellowship** with martyrs (M. Pol. 17[3]).

The *koinōnia* of the Spirit (2 Co 13[14]; Ph 2[1]), probably not to be understood of the human 'spirit', is likely to be the regular phrase in Christian Greek for possession by the Holy Spirit, through deliberate avoidance of pagan expressions for spirit possession.

(2) The other proper Christian meaning of *koinōnia* is derived from the foregoing, i.e. a brother's **contribution** to other brethren in money or kind. Perhaps it is not far from the secular interpretation, but rarely in secular Greek do these words signify 'to give a share'.[96] It is a token of one's living within the Body of Christ if one shares a temporal increase with one's brethren, and so the churches of Macedonia and Achaea made a *koinōnia* for the poor saints in Jerusalem (Ro 15[26]). Ministering in this way is a *koinōnia*, and the poorer saints glorify God for the liberal *koinōnia* of their brethren (2 Co 8[4] 9[13]). Probably Philemon had exercised such a ministry (6). 'Forget not *koinōnia*', urges the writer to Hebrews in context of sacrificial giving (13[16]).

L. S. Thornton well illustrates how the *koinōnia* in the sense of a 'collection', was in origin a symbolic gesture declaring the new fellowship between Christian Jew and Christian Gentile. The obstacles to such a fellowship had been alarmingly great, humanly speaking, and the two groups could not even eat together. Their leaders could not agree. In this situation deeds count for more than words. So the secondary *koinōnia*, the collection, was the outward pledge of the primary *koinōnia*, an inward understanding which at first was very fragile. 'It was a practical attack upon the age-long barriers of exclusiveness.'[97] No wonder that a gesture like this was called a *koinōnia*!

The verb *koinōnō* may have the same sacred meaning in Christian Greek. The life of sanctification, as outlined towards the close of Romans, involves the act of contributing, expressed by *koinōnō*, to the necessity of saints (Ro 12[13]). Those believers who are taught in the Word have this involvement with the teacher to **have fellowshop** by material things (Gal 6[6]), and the Philippians **had fellowship** with Paul by a gift (Ph 4[15]). Thus **fellowship** in the first special sense inspires **fellowship** in the second. The Gentiles of Rome are brought into the Church that they may share the spiritual things of Christ (Ro 15[27] *koinōnō*), and now they ought to share the *koinōnia* of carnal things (15[26]). However, the Christian *koinōnia* is nowhere better illustrated than in St. Paul's relationship with Philippian believers.[98]

All in all, it is little wonder if a term so rich in Christian content as *koinōnia* must needs be translated by no less than six English words in RSV in order to do it justice.[99] The transliterated symbol, 'koinonia', is perhaps the best of all translations.

The same double interpretation pertains in the apostolic Fathers. The Christian must **have fellowship** (*koinōnō*) and not plead that his things are his own (Barn. 19[8]). He must **have fellowship** in all things with his brother (*sugkoinōnō*); Christians **have fellowship** (i.e. are *koinōnoi*) in eternal things, which means they must **have fellowship** also in the perishable things (Did. 4[8]).

An occasional synonym with *koinōnō* is the verb *metechō* which in secular Greek is to 'partake', to share in, to be an accomplice. In contemporary papyri and inscriptions, *metechō* is the more common, but in Christian Greek the *koinōnia* group is more frequent and more prominent. In Christian Greek *metechō* sometimes has the special sacramental sense[100] of partaking in the Breaking of Bread (1 Co 10[17, 21]) as well as partaking in a church contribution (1 Co 9[10, 12]). It is **Church fellowship** in the apostolic Fathers, a partaking of God (I. Eph 4[2]), of His blessings (Diogn 5[5] 8[11]), of repentence (1 Clem 8[5]). Ellicott reminded us that the distinction between *metechō* and *koinōnō*, in the sacramental sense, is that *koinōnō* 'implies more distinctly the idea of a community with others'.[101] *Koinōnia* at the Table is the Church gathered at the Table.

FIGURE (TYPE)

Types and shadows have their ending. – ST. THOMAS

1. ἀντίτυπον

A religious meaning of much significance arises in Christian Greek. *Antitupon* refers to a type or figure of which the fulfilment is in the Christian revelation.

Secular Greek. The secular meanings of this many-sided adjective, used in the neuter as a noun, were 'resisting', 'reflecting', or 'striking back'. Herodotus graphically puts *tupos antitupos* together to mean thrust and counterthrust. 'There is a place', he says, 'where two winds ever blow. Thrust makes answer to thrust (*tupos antitupos*), and anguish is laid on anguish' (I 67). *Antitupon* denotes sound which answers back. The concept of a sigh, caused by a blood-reeking wound, being 'echoed' (*antitupon*) by no friend standing by, is the poignant image of Sophocles which soon he caps with another. 'To me, storm-tossed, Mount Hermaeum echoes back a responsive (*antitupon*) groan.'[102]

On the other hand, it means 'corresponding', but, turned the other way about, it means 'opposed to' – as a stamp corresponds in reverse to the die.[103] In describing the lay-out of a camp, Polybius has the word in the plural for 'opposite to': certain troops are 'back to back (*antitupoi*) with the cavalry' (VI 31.8).

The sense of antithesis is that of the passage in the Lucianic edition of the LXX where the Jews are said to be 'diverse from' or 'in contrast to' (*antitupon*) those of other people in the matter of their laws (Est 13[4] ASkz (3[8])). Significantly in this passage the Vatican manuscript (B) reads *antitheton* (opposed to), which may be pre-Lucianic but, even if it is not, indicates that the editors understood *antitupos* as having the sense of 'contrary'.

Christian Greek. Among Christians a further meaning emerges. *Antitupon* is now an exact copy or corresponding object which resembles another by a true likeness without being the real thing. The holy objects in the Temple are the 'figures' (*antitupa*) of heaven (Heb 9[24]). The water on which Noah floated and which saved him and his family while it drowned others, is seen as an *antitupon* (figure) of holy Baptism which now saves us (1 Pet 3[21]).

The word in its new semantic livery passed into later Christian

Greek. The apostolic Fathers saw flesh as *antitupos* of the Spirit. The Spirit, by contrast, is 'authentic'. No one who has corrupted the *antitupon*, the type, shall receive the reality' (2 Clem 14³). Thence it seems to have passed into secular use until in modern Greek *antitupon* is a 'copy' of a book. In the third century, Plotinus identified it as a Gnostic term, but the meaning is vague. 'What', asks he, writing against the Gnostics, 'ought one to say of the other things they introduce, their *paroikēseis* (Exiles), their *antitupoi* (Figures), and their *metanoiai* (Repentings)?' (II 9.6).

There developed, too, the rather different sense – correspondence in a deceptive way, the merely apparent likeness of something, an object counterfeit or feigned.[104]

In early Christian Greek, *antitupon* was what we would call a 'figure' – a symbol, a type, rather than an antitype or archetype. On occasion, however, there was some confusion and the adjective *antitupos* was the fulfilment and perfect reality, as when subsequent Christians described the Blessed Virgin as the antitype of Noah.[105] This was unusual and on the whole *antitupos* is a 'symbol' rather than the Reality of which it is symbolical. Melchizedec is a symbol of the Lord's body,[106] and Abraham's sacrifice is the symbol of a perfect one to come.[107]

OT allegories were *antitupa* (Heb 9²⁴) and the offspring of Achamoth was an 'antitype' of the Church above.[108] The elements at the eucharist were 'antitypes' of the Body and Blood.[109]

Everything in the OT was conceived by the first Christians as an *antitupon* of good things to come. The Scripture was pregnant with later significance, and it was all written for Christian learning – for believers upon whom the ends of the dispensations are come (Ro 15⁴). *Antitupon* may be expressed therefore as *allēgoroumenon* (allegory) and that is how St. Paul refers to Agar and Sinai – symbols of the earthly Jerusalem, types of unbelieving Judaism (Gal 4²⁴). 'Which things are an allegory.'

'Types' and 'allegories' should not be too nicely distinguished. Traditionally, however, typology is seen as giving more importance to the historic event, and allegorization (labelled sometimes as Greek, while typology was Hebraic) as giving less attention to historicity and more to the higher significance of the upper world. Typology in effect is what may be called a 'horizontal' approach, and allegorization a 'vertical'.

Bishop Westcott distinguished between the typical and the allegorical, the one resting upon a real and historical correspondence, the other on points arbitrarily taken.[110] The distinction drawn by R. P. C. Hanson[111] is similar: typology is the interpreting of an event which is present or recently past, as the fulfilment of a similar situation which Scripture records or foretells. Typology is the establishing of historical connections between certain events or persons or things in the OT and parallel events, persons or things in the NT.[112] On the other hand, allegory is the interpreting of a person or object as in reality meaning some later person or object, with little attempt to look for a similar context or for any relationship. It is quite arbitrary, in fact. But it has been observed that the separation of the two forms of exegesis is really superficial, and both are essential in Christian thought.[113]

It is Dr. R. P. C. Hanson's thesis that typology tends to pass over into allegory proper. Nevertheless, typology is an essential element in the early Christians' interpretation of the OT,[114] and there is nothing arbitrary in the NT authors' interpretation – unlike that of the rabbis and Christian Fathers. The normative approach of the NT writers, claims Dr. A. T. Hanson, is not that of typology so much as what he calls the view of the 'real presence' of Christ in OT history. Christ was not merely the constant subject of prophecy; He was really there all those years ago. 'The NT writers', he says, 'were extremely anxious to find the presence of Christ in OT history, challenging men to faith or unfaith.' A. T. Hanson's theme is moving and, I think, convincing. He regrets, 'Moderns cannot fail to find their methods of exegesis bizarre and startling at times, but it meant that again and again they found in the pages of the OT the living God speaking to them, meeting men face to face in mercy and judgement, demanding from them decision. ...'[115]

2. τύπος

Whatever the relation between typology and allegory, at least *antitupa* (figures) and *tupoi* (types) would seem to be synonymous. Adam is a *tupos* of Christ (Ro 5[14]), and events in the Scriptures are said to be our *tupoi* (types, 'ensamples' AV) in 1 Co 10[6] and in the Bezan text of 1 Co 10[11]: 'these things happened unto them as *tupoi*'. The cloud is an appropriate type of holy Baptism; the manna and the water prefigure the Eucharist; the rock prefigures Christ. It may be that in this mighty passage St. Paul did not mean that the cloud, the manna, the water and the rock were themselves types, for his wording strictly demands that the penalties inflicted on sinful Israel were the types.[116] Nevertheless, the historic objects in question correspond too closely not to be seen as types.

In secular Greek *tupos* was the 'impression' of a seal, the stamp on a coin, any kind of imprint and engraving or outline in relief, even a fully carved image, a pattern for reproduction, and therefore a model or example to be imitated, even a rule of life. *Tupos* is much the same as *antitupon* – the thrust of which *antitupon* is the counter-thrust. From the time of Philo, however, we find for *tupos* the new meaning of a 'pattern' given by God concerning the future,[117] and that is the main interpretation of the word in Christian Greek. It is idle to consider whether or not the term is 'technical'. One writer examines the Biblical evidence and concludes that the *tupos* word-group, like the *deigma* word-group,[118] has the meaning 'example' or 'pattern' in almost every instance.[119] Nevertheless, *tupos* is an example or pattern provided by God for our instruction. In its new sense the word came in by way of St. Paul, as we have already seen, and the epistle of Barnabas and the Shepherd of Hermas.

The first Christians most energetically searched the Scriptures. They found significance everywhere. Though he did not use the word 'type' or 'figure', in the particular context of Aaron and Abel, the writer to Hebrews clearly sees Aaron, founder of the Levitical priesthood, as a type of Christ for he alone offered incense in the Holy of Holies, mediated between God and the people, and was anointed and crowned like a king.

Aaron is replaced by Christ but he foreshadows Him, and his animal sacrifices look forward to the perfect oblation at Calvary. The Church sees Abel too as a type or figure of Christ, for his innocent life as a shepherd, his acceptable sacrifice and his violent death look forward to the Good Shepherd who died. Indeed, the blood of Christ speaketh better than that of Abel (Heb 12^{24}). St. Paul sees the relations of Church and Synagogue prefigured in Isaac's relation to Ishmael. He sees Christ as a 'last' Adam. He sees Him prefigured in Israel's paschal lamb. All these types were more than rhetorical figures, according to St. Augustine. They were God's fore-ordained prophetic announcements of future events. These examples are but a few of the types or patterns or figures which abound in the OT. On Ascension Day we sing with Bishop Wordsworth:

> Now our heavenly Aaron enters, with His Blood, within the veil;
> Joshua now is come to Canaan, and the kings before Him quail;
> Now He plants the tribes of Israel in their promised resting-
> place;
> Now our great Elijah offers double portion of His grace.

Outside the NT, allegory and typology are continued in the epistle of Barnabas, for it was in the author's Egyptian city of Alexandria that allegorizing became most popular. The author of this letter relies upon the allegorical method to undermine the defences of Judaism in Christian controversy. The Jews by taking the Scriptures in the literal sense had become ship-wrecked upon their own Law (3^6). By the method of allegory this author finds the Gospel in the Law. The *tupos* (prefiguring) appeared in Isaac (7^3).

The *tupos* of Jesus is manifested in the goat on the day of Atonement (7^7). 'See then the *type* of Jesus Who was destined to suffer' (7^{10}). Wool being placed in the midst of thorns is 'a *type* of Jesus, which is put there for the Church' (7^{11}). The whole house of Amelek being torn up by the roots is a type, manifesting Jesus as Son of God in the flesh (12^{10}). Moses provides 'types' of Jesus ($12^{2, 5, 6}$). Jacob, 'crossing' his hands in blessing over Ephraim and Manasses, 'saw in the Spirit a *type* of people that should come' (13^5).

St. Ignatius sees the unity of the Church under the care of her ministers as a *tupos* of the harmony of heaven (I. Magn. 6). For St. Clement the dove was the *tupos* of the Holy Ghost (*fragmentum* VIII). For St. Cyril of Jerusalem the bread and wine offered at the Eucharist are the *tupos* of Christ's Body and Blood (*Catechesis* IV), and the sacred elements were so represented in Latin by *typus* (St. Ambrose) and by *figura* (St. Augustine).[120]

To modern taste it is all quite outlandish, but St. Augustine found his way from Manichaeism to the Church because he felt that in St. Ambrose's use of allegorism was the answer to one difficulty after another in the OT. Texts were explained in a figure, 'which when I understood literally, I was slain spiritually'.[121]

A man may easily ridicule this attitude to the old Scriptures and will soon underscore the excesses which give full rein to mental ingenuity and the fertile imagination which he sees as only limited by what pious Christians will tolerate. I mean that for some Latin Fathers Susanna's bath symbolized the waters of Baptism, and the two servants who helped Susanna were Faith and Charity, while the two lustful elders in the garden were the two groups of Jews and Gentiles who united in vicious onslaught against the Church.[122] As C. S. Lewis readily conceded, we can go much too far, and often, when we think we are looking into the depths of Scripture, what we see may sometimes be nothing more than the reflection of our own silly faces. We see what we want to see. Even so, to commend reverence and reticence in looking for types and examples is no excuse for its neglect. Alexandria and Antioch may be reconciled without condemning either. Besides, it is hard to see how to maintain a doctrine of the inspiration of the Bible if we are not to take certain parts allegorically, such as the 'cursing' Psalms. Scripture often has for the Church quite a different sense from that which the original author intended. Take the love lyrics in the Song of Solomon: the Church finds in them spiritual grandeur when they are seen to concern the Bridegroom and His Church.

It may be that the study of the OT as a source of 'types' will tend to deprive it of any significance of its own. The old Scriptures are indeed the written record of God's dealing with men, bringing them to salvation in their own days. Still, the things written there were written for *our* learning and they point forward to Jesus. Without Him the OT record of history, though interesting in itself, is not as significant. It becomes but the record of a Mesopotamian religion, and the Prophets in particular become social reformers rather than Heralds of the Saviour.

Father Hebert has urged us to read the OT in the light of its fulfilment in Jesus the Messiah. 'When we sing of "Zion" or "Jerusalem" in the Psalms', he says, 'we give those words the meaning that they bear in St. Paul's Epistles and in the Book of Revelation; when we sing of "sacrifice", we think of Christ's Sacrifice and the eucharistic offering; when a psalm speaks of "the King", we shall in most cases refer it to Christ. Clearly, in this general sense the mystical interpretation of the Old Testament is for Christians a matter of obligation.'[123]

Nevertheless, one critic asks, 'Is not the Lord Jesus Christ the supreme "example" and "pattern" for Christians?' and adds, 'Perhaps those interested in typology should concern themselves less with looking for types *of* Christ and more with presenting Christ *himself* as the supreme "type" for Christians and the world?'[124] This ought we to have done, and not to have left the other undone.

The whole Bible, declared Karl Barth, speaks 'figuratively' (vorbildlich) and prophetically of Jesus Christ. Even in the early chapters of Genesis, at the very beginning, when it announces the Creator, the creation and the creature, the Scripture bears witness to Jesus Christ.[125] 'Its word in all words is this Word.' He is the Messiah, expected by Israel, coming according to the promise given to Israel. He is Emmanuel, the Head of the People of both Old and New Testaments, the Representative of each believer before God. We cannot see Jesus without seeing also His Israel and His Church. David Aune affirms that the validity of the typological method lies in the Bible's essential unity which is manifest in Christ Himself. That, at least, was the conviction of the early Church.[126] The works also of Amsler, Ellis, and France, all confirm that the NT cannot be understood unless typology first is understood.[127]

'When the Law is read by the Jews,' said St. Irenaeus, 'it is like a fable because they have no explanation. ... But when it is read by Christians, it is the treasure hid in a field ... made plain by the Cross of Christ, enriching the minds of men. ...'[128]

See 'Testify beforehand'.

ἀσχημοσύνη

In Christian Greek *aschēmosunē* is a term denoting utter baseness, the lowest stage of moral degradation.

Secular Greek. The meaning had been scarcely that of a gross misdeed. It was a mere lack of form, the ungracefulness and awkwardness[129] suggested by the very derivation of the word – schēma (form) with the negative alpha. Aristotle used it for 'want of form' and for the graceless contortion of the face which some people contrive while playing the flute.[130]

The word carries moral overtones occasionally. When Herod's sister, Salome, and a visiting Arabian politician fell in love, it soon became obvious to all heads and eyes that they had made love, too. The court ladies brought news of the scandal to the king, amused by the indecency (*aschēmosunē*) of it.[131] The same slightly indelicate meaning is found in the second-century astrologer Vettius Valens.[132] Another moral nuance for the word appears in Aristotle who gives the suggestion of disgrace or discredit.[133] At most, however, it was something a little unwholesome or dishonourable.[134]

Biblical Greek. In the LXX, on the other hand, it is a euphemism for the privy parts of men and women (Hebrew 'erwâ, Lev 18[7], etc.) and for human excrement (Hebrew ṣē'â, Deut 23[13]). St. Paul was likely to be influenced by these associations when he had in mind a certain discreditable conduct which ought to be kept outside the camp – in the OT sense of Deut 23[14]: 'Therefore shall thy camp be Holy that He see no *aschēmosunē* in thee.' One of the Hebrew words, ṣē'â, may also mean the drunkard's vomit, and so the Greek term became a Christian symbol for the very lowest reach of immoral indulgence.

The outrageous behaviour represented by *aschēmosunē*, which the apostle declares to be awaiting God's wrath (Ro 1[27]), is rendered 'unseemly' in English – probably inadequately, in view of the LXX background.

Philo has the same sense. 'Examples of shamelessness are all those nakednesses (*aschēmosunai*) when the mind uncovers shameful things which it ought to hide from view and prides itself in them.'[135] 'Soul, bring reason to bear on everything, wherewith all nakedness (*aschēmosunē*) of flesh and passion is put out of sight, for everything unreasonable is unsightly.'[136]

The Seer, too, is close to the LXX (e.g. Hos 2[9]), using the term for 'privy parts' or 'nudity'. He says, 'Blessed is he that watcheth and keepeth his garments, lest he walk naked, and they see his *privy parts* – or *nakedness*' (Rev 16[15]).

πρωτότοκος

By progression of meaning *prōtotokos* ceases to apply to a first-time expectant mother and becomes predicated of the Messiah, the Beloved.

In secular Greek the word is an adjective assignable to a heiffer bearing her first calf.[137] The meaning is, 'pregnant for the first time'. Plato speaks of the anger of *prōtotokoi*, women bearing their first child.[138] In an inscription about 200 BC a sacrificial inventory is given: 'To Demeter a pregnant sow, carrying for the first time (*prōtotokos*), to Kore a perfect boar, to Zeus Counsellor a porker.'[139]

However, in Biblical Greek the word appropriates the additional meaning of the Hebrew *bᵉkhôr* (first-born) and is a style of the Messiah. It is not, however, invariably a messianic title in the LXX. Sidon is the first-born of Canaan (Gen 10¹⁵) and Huz the first-born of Nahor (Gen 22²¹), and there are others. Moreover, *prōtotokos* carries the Biblical meaning of 'first-born' (and not the secular meaning, 'bearing her first') also in Philo, where Cain is said to be *prōtotokos*, 'who was the beginning of human generation through two parents'.[140] Josephus, too, has the Biblical Greek meaning, a man's 'first-born'.[141] The Sybilline oracles list among sacrificial animals, 'lambs *first-born*' (III 627). Nevertheless, in the LXX, it is pre-eminently the Messiah who is *prōtotokos*. 'I will make Him My First-born, higher than the kings of the earth' (Ps 88(89)²⁷).

Although the meaning of *bᵉkhôr* is 'first-born', yet in certain situations the Hebrew word comes to have a special sense – Israel as God's *bᵉkhôr* among the nations, His greatly Beloved, as was made plain to Pharaoh (Ex 4²²), the only one to be loved. Just as the '*bᵉkhôrê* of the poor' are the poorest of the poor, so the *bᵉkhôr* among the nations is the chiefest and most special of them all. 'My *bᵉkhôr*' in the psalms (88(89)²⁸) is the seed of David, and the only one to call God his Father. In Zach 12¹⁰ and Jer 38(31)⁹ similarly *prōtotokos* renders *bᵉkhôr* and the parallelism of the verses suggests that the meaning is 'beloved'. God causes the *prōtotokos* to walk by the rivers and not to stumble. All the tender feelings for a 'first-born' are prominent, and one must agree with Michaelis that *prōtotokos* shifts its meaning from 'first-born' to 'beloved' in certain instances in the Greek OT.[142] It is, therefore, in Christian Greek very likely to be the equivalent of the title *agapētos* (Beloved, q.v.).

Early Christians assigned both titles as a distinction of their Messiah. They affirmed that God brought the *Prōtotokos* into the world (Heb 1⁶). St. Paul entitles Jesus, the *Prōtotokos* among many brethren, the *Prōtotokos* before every creature[143] (Ro 8[29]; Col 1[15]) and, in common with the Seer, hails Him as *Prōtotokos* from the dead (Col 1[18]; Rev 1[5]).

An early editor of the NT had added the title at Mt 1[25]. St. Matthew explains that Joseph knew not Mary till she had brought forth a son, and the textual editor made the alteration, 'till she had brought forth her Son, the *Prōtotokos*'.[144] Evidently the title was already current in Biblical Greek, for it is used by St. Luke who reports that Mary brought forth her Son, the *Prōtotokos* (2[7]). The supposition, therefore, that it is a Biblical Greek dignification with the meaning, 'born before all mankind', is more probable than to suppose that it refers simply to Mary's 'first-born', as if she subsequently bore others. If St. Luke used the dialect of the Christians,[145] then by *Prōtotokos* he must understand the First-begotten of all creation, God's Beloved Son. The question whether St. Luke by implication denies St. Mary's perpetual virginity does not any longer arise.

We recall that in the LXX the term indicates the first-born of the Egyptians who perished in the last plague (Ex 12[29]; Heb 11[28] 12[23]). The sacred writer rejoices in 'the church of the *prōtotokoi*' whose names are written in heaven, and so the Christian *prōtotokoi* perhaps recall those of Exodus. Believers, therefore, share Christ's own distinction and are known as *prōtotokoi*.

'FLESH', 'FLESHLY', 'CARNAL' (AV)

σάρξ : σαρκικός

The world, the flesh and Satan dwell
Around the path I tread. (ISAAC WILLIAMS)

Secular Greek. *Sarx* is flesh in the familiar sense, often including the whole body; it is applicable to pieces of meat and membrane and sometimes to the pulpy parts of fruit. It is nearer to the Biblical sense when it is metaphorically conceived as the seat of affections and lusts, especially in the phrase, 'the pleasures of the *sarx*'.[146]

Christian Greek. Christians give to it and the cognate adjectives an evil sense. *Sarkikos*, from meaning flesh-like, made of flesh, lapses to a less desirable sense (1 Co 9[11]; Ro 7[14] vl). So with *sarkinos* (Ro 7[14] vl; Heb 7[16]), only in this case the unsavoury premise is found also in some secular writers – Epictetus, Maximus of Tyre, Dio Cassius.

Through Hebrew influence *sarx* finds various new styles: (1) people in the mass, as in the phrase, 'all flesh', which denotes every individual, and (2) an undesirable colouring, the seat of lust and gross appetites. The second implication is most easily to be discovered in St. Paul's letters where *sarx* is the reverse of mind (*nous*) and spirit (*pneuma*). Moulton and Milligan admitted that the theological implications in the Christian use of *sarx* 'are due partly to the influence of the LXX and partly to the language-forming power of Christianity by which old terms were "baptized" into new conditions' (MM p. 569). Agonizing turmoil within the regenerate believer is expressed feelingly by *sarx*: 'With the *nous* (mind) I myself serve the law of God; but with the *sarx* (flesh) the law of sin' (Ro 7[25]). The struggle is tense enough to arrest the Christian from doing the things he would (Gal 5[17]), but he will make no advance in saintliness until he walks after the Spirit, for they that are in the *sarx* cannot please God (Ro 8[8, 12f]; Gal 5[16]).

Only the Word Who became *sarx* (Jn 1[14]) was the exception, for by Him the *sarx* was cleansed and transformed. Our Lord Jesus was able to say that He gave His *sarx* on behalf of the world's life (Jn 6[51]), represented by the Bread of Holy Communion.

The *sarx* is mortal and St. Paul held it to be sinful, doomed to corruption. He does not quite say, with St. John, that the Word became *sarx*, but says rather that Christ came 'in the *likeness* of sinful *sarx*'. For St. John *sarx* as such is not evil: it stands for humanity as distinct from God, as in the OT and Jewish phrase, 'flesh and blood'.[147] St. Paul, however, uses the Greek word *sarx* 'in a way no Greek in his senses would ever dream of doing, though Plutarch on occasion comes near to it when he regards the flesh as the seat of the affections and the lusts'.[148] *Sarx* is not a common word in the pre-Christian philosophical vocabulary and has hardly any ethical significance there.

By contrast, the *pneuma* in Christian Greek is that constituent of a man which is implanted by God, representing God's power and presence within him. In the saint *pneuma* is where the risen Christ comes and dwells. This side of him has kinship with God and has power to win the victory of holiness (Ro 8[1-17]).[149]

The victory is not easy and the child of God who is in the way of salvation is in a cleft between serving both *sarx* and *pneuma*. The first master will foster fruits of adultery, fornication, lasciviousness, witchcraft, strife and drunkenness (Gal 5[19ff]). Holiness is separation from these. A crop of corruption will be his who 'sows to his *flesh*' (Gal 6[8]). Depicting appetites against which the child of God must be ware, St. Paul has the word *sarkikos*. 'I am *sarkikos*, sold under sin' (Ro 7[14]). The carnal brethren at Corinth are rated for their envious party spirit (1 Co 3[1,3f]), for the fleshly weapons which they use (2 Co 10[4]). Pilgrims must abstain from fleshly lusts (1 Pet 2[11]) which war against the *psuchē* (soul) and against the 'new man', the re-created servant of God, when the 'old man' is left to die (Ro 6[6]).

Sarkikos in the apostolic Fathers is contrasted with the spiritual, the higher side of man,[150] for man comprises two natures, one *sarkikos* and the other *pneumatikos*.[151] The catechumen shuns 'fleshly' desires, named also 'bodily'.[152]

We see, then, as Burton saw,[153] that *sarx* through the influence of Hebrew *bāśār* is no longer for Christians simply 'material', as it was in the secular language. There is another difference. Plato, Seneca, and Plutarch, followed to some extent by Gnostics and Mani-chaeans, had insisted that true happiness is achieved only by leaving the body, which is mean and wretched. The principle of evil for St. Paul, on the other hand, is not identified with the body, for the life of faith and victory may still be lived this side of the grave (Gal 2[20]). The principle, for St. Paul, is not the body but the *sarx*.

To translate *sarx* by the word 'body', as RSV does (e.g. 2 Co 7[1,5]), is quite unhelpful and is one of several instances where AV is closer to St. Paul's meaning and where RSV glosses over important words.[154] Being 'in the flesh', moreover, is not the same as being 'in the world' (RSV 2 Co 10[3] etc.), and the student of St. Paul will not necessarily find AV to be out of date, for all its seniority.

For St. Paul *sarx* is the principle of a certain type of evil and so, strictly, 'flesh' is not the right word. We share the word with AV, for none better comes readily to mind.

FOREKNOWLEDGE

πρόγνωσις : προγινώσκω

The Christian meaning of the noun *prognōsis* and the verb *proginōskō* is extraordinary and deeply theological.

The secular meaning of *prognōsis* was 'prediction', and of *proginōskō*, 'to perceive beforehand' by human forethought and shrewdness.[155] From the time of Hippocrates, *prognōsis* was a term in medicine.

God's foreknowledge of an event or report is said to be *prognōsis* in Biblical Greek (Jdt 9[6] 11[19] AB), and St. Clement alludes to the *prognōsis* (foreknowledge) of the apostles (1 Clem 44[2]). As to the verb, divine Wisdom both foreknows (Wis 8[8]), and is foreknown by, those desiring her (6[13] 18[6]). Here the sense is the same as 'know' in Biblical understanding, that is, to take favourable notice of, and to favour, as a prelude to selecting for a special purpose.[156]

Following these precedents, the new Christian meaning is that of **predestination** (foreordination) or **election**, that is, as Hort expressed it, 'virtually prerecognition, previous designation to a position or function'.[157] It was by the *prognōsis* of God that Christ was taken by wicked hands and crucified (Act 2[23]), and He was *proegnōsmenos* (perf. ptc.) – '*foreordained* before the foundation of the world' (1 Pet 1[20]). According to this *prognōsis* the brethren are the 'elect' of God (1 Pet 1[2]).

Those whom God foreknew (verb), them did He 'predestinate' (*proörizō*) and 'call' and 'justify' and 'glorify' (Ro 8[29f]). There is no indication that the context refers to the Jewish people, as in Ro 11[2], and Christian predestination seems to be in view. At all events, the meaning of *proginōskō* is similar to the OT 'know', as when God 'did know' Israel in the wilderness (Hos 13[5]). So Godet understood the verb *praediligere*, and St. Clement of Alexandria as a conformation to the image of His Son, which is rather a futuristic and anticipatory way of looking at the action, as if we might include the inevitable results in the word itself. But, 'If God has *destined* them beforehand to a future fashioning in the likeness, etc., He must also have already *known* them beforehand as those who should one day be thus fashioned.'[158] We cannot exclude the anticipated result from the mention of the act, and foreknowledge must itself imply glorification. God would not 'call', unless He were also going to save and sanctify.

The sense is evidently not far from predestination and election, and so is used by St. Paul of the Jewish nation (Ro 11[2]), of Israel as God's peculiar people which now includes the Church. AV once indeed translated the verb as 'fore-ordained' (1 Pet 1[20]).

The 'foreknowing' of the prophet (Jer 1[5]) is intended to be a **predestination** of Jeremiah to the Lord's service, and **predestination** is the sense of *prognōsis* and its verb in Christian Greek. In this special sense the words are peculiar to St. Paul and St. Peter (in his speeches and in his epistle). *Prognōsis* in their language is not a function merely of the speculative intellect but of God's benevolent will by which certain of His creatures are set apart to Himself, those who love God, those who respond to His call, the members of His Church.

Hermas uses the words differently, of God's knowing beforehand (*Mand.* IV 3.4) and of man's (*Sim.* VII 5), and so St. Luke (Act 26[5]) and 2 Pet 3[17].

See 'Predestination'.

FRUIT (IN THE MORAL SENSE)

καρπός

The secular meaning of *karpos* is fruit from the earth (from Homer on), seed (Xenophon), offspring (Euripides), and profits (Xenophon). However, there were metaphorical outgrowths from that – the fulfilment of an oracle,[159] the reward or 'compensation' of a danger,[160] the 'curses' of a tongue. 'Let persuasion check the *fruit* of foolish threats', is the advice of Athena to the Furies.[161]

The emphasis in the Bible is otherwise, for the LXX had rendered *pᵉrî* by *karpos*, and the Hebrew word denoted the consequences, whether of wisdom or of sin – indeed, a good or a bad character – much more readily than in secular Greek, where the moral sense is comparatively rare and exclusively poetic. The OT sense is relatively frequent in Christian language.[162] Even in instances where *karpos* manifests the literal sense, fruits of the earth, as in the reference to the Fig Tree, it is the figurative sense of good works which is intended (Mt 21[19]).

John the Baptist and Jesus consistently resort to the figurative sense, the good or bad fruit of a corresponding heart,[163] as does St. Paul too,[164] and St. James (3[17f.]), and the writer to Hebrews (12[11]). Moreover, praise is 'fruit of the lips' (Heb 13[15]), children are 'the fruit of the loins' (Act 2[30]), souls added to the Church are the 'fruit of labour' (Ro 1[13] 15[28]; Ph 1[22]).

The same note applies to the verb *karpophorō* (produce fruit), rarely metaphorical. Only the Jew Philo remarks that some bear virtue as their fruit (*karpophorō*).[165] Jesus introduced the verb in this sense into the parable of the Sower,[166] and St. Paul used it of Christian living (Col 1[6,10]), exuberance unto God as opposed to proliferation unto death (Ro 7[4f.]).

NOTES

[1] Sophocles *Oedipus Coloneus* 950.
[2] Sophocles *Oedipus Tyrannus*, 1445.
[3] *Nicomachean Ethics* 1179 a 17.
[4] Polybius I 35.4.
[5] Xenophon *Historia Graeca* I 3.12.
[6] Demosthenes XXIX 26.
[7] Thucydides IV 51.
[8] Plato *Phaedo* 70B; Isocrates III 8.
[9] Polybius V 41.2.
[10] OGI 339.47.
[11] *Laws* 966D.
[12] Polybius II 43.2.

F

[13] Herodotus I 24.
[14] Xenophon *Memorabilia* I 1.5.
[15] Pseudo-Plato *Epinomis* 980C.
[16] 'Ich Dir und den Göttern vertraut habe' (editor). U. Wilcken, *Urkunden der Ptolemäerzeit*, I, Berlin 1922ff., 144.12 (c. 164 BC).
[17] Sophocles *Philoctetes* 1374.
[18] BGU 874.11.
[19] Sophocles *Oedipus Tyrannus* 625.
[20] Thucydides V 112.
[21] Plato *Gorgias* 524A.
[22] Menander *Monostichoi* 86.
[23] Xenophon *Memorabilia* IV 4.17.
[24] Xenophon *Memorabilia* I 1.5.
[25] C. H. Dodd, *The Bible and the Greeks*, Hodder 1935, p. 67.
[26] Ibid., p. 67.
[27] Sextus the Pythagorean *Sententiae* (ed. A. Elter, Bonn 1892) 6.
[28] E. de W. Burton, *Galatians*, p. 478.
[29] *Bibliotheca Sacra* 65 (1908), pp. 755–9.
[30] G. Howard, *Harvard Theological Review* 63 (1970), p. 230.
[31] N. Turner, *Grammatical Insights*, T. & T. Clark, 1965, p. 110.
[32] *Expository Times* 68 (1957), p. 113.
[33] Ibid., p. 157.
[34] I agree with R. Bultmann, *Theology of the New Testament*, ET SCM 1952, I, p. 318.
[35] Dodd suggested that the LXX rendered perhaps a slightly different Hebrew original. *The Bible and The Greeks*, Hodder 1935, p. 69.
[36] J. J. O'Rourke, *Catholic Biblical Quarterly*, 35 (1973), p. 189.
[37] G. B. Stevens, *The Biblical World* 23 (1904), p. 271. See pp. 267–71.
[38] Ibid., p. 190.
[39] Ibid., p. 192.
[40] Ibid., p. 193.
[41] Ibid., p. 194.
[42] E. Hatch, *Essays in Biblical Greek*, Clarendon 1889, pp. 83–8.
[43] R. Walker, *Zeitschrift für Theologie und Kirche* 61 (1964), pp. 155–92.
[44] Theognis 283; Thucydides II 40; Aeschylus *Prometheus Bound* 917, *Persae* 55.
[45] W. H. P. Hatch, *The Pauline Idea of Faith*, Harvard Theological Studies II, 1917, p. 82.
[46] *Zeitschrift für die Neutestamentliche Wissenschaft* (Berlin) 41 (1942), p. 48.
[47] E.g. G. Friedrich, in *Abraham unser Vater: Festschrift für O. Michel*, ed. O. Betz, etc., Leiden 1963, pp. 181–215.
[48] Philo *de Specialibus Legibus* IV 51 (the false prophets is fraudulent and guesses; he adulterates true prophecy and by his spurious inventions throws the genuine into the shade); Josephus *Ant. Jud.* IX vi 6 (Jehu promised that the *false prophets* and false priests ...).
[49] D. Hill, *Biblica* (Rome) 57 (1976), pp. 327–48.
[50] G. Baumbach, *Das Verständniss des Bösen in den synoptischen Evangelien*, Berlin 1963.
[51] J. B. Mayor, *The Epistle of Jude and the Second Epistle of Peter*, Macmillan 1907, pp. clxxiiiff.
[52] C. Bigg, *Peter and Jude*, ICC T. & T. Clark 2nd ed. 1902, p. 271.
[53] *Phaedrus* 63A.
[54] Plato *Laws* 811D.
[55] Aristotle *Nicomachean Ethics* 1147 a 24, *Metaphysica* 991 a 8.
[56] Josephus *Ant. Jud.* XII ii 7 (Niese XII 58).
[57] Galen 15. 673.

58 Philodemus *Peri Theōn* 3 (ed. Diels, Berlin 1917) fr. 39.
59 2 Km 9[8]; 2 Ch 6[19]; 4 Km 13[23]; Ps 39 (40)[4].
60 P. Leid W xiv 23.
61 The way Knox renders the Vulgate *respexit.*
62 Vulgate *respice.*
63 Vulgate: *si... intendatis.*
64 M. Cambe, *Revue Biblique* 70 (1963), pp. 193–207.
65 BGU 1026 xxiii 24 (iv AD), Cat. Cod. Astr. XII 162.14, Achmes 2.18 (a Christian writer c. AD 900).
66 But the verb occurs in Plato's *Politicus* 274D.
67 Thucydides III 10.
68 Philo *de Vita Mosis* I 158.
69 F. Hauck in Kittel *TWNT* III, p. 803.
70 Arrian *Epicteti Dissertationes* (Teubner II 19.27).
71 P. Lond 2.311.2 (ii AD).
72 Euripides *Bacchae* 1276; the comicus Amphis (iv BC) *Commicorum Atticorum Fragmenta*, Leipzig 1880–8, 20.3 (ed. T. Kock).
73 P. Oxy VI 905.
74 Plato *Republic* 466C.
75 George V. Jourdan, *Journal of Biblical Literature* 67 (1948), p. 124.
76 P. Masp 158.11.
77 Aeschylus *Agamemnon* 1037, 1352.
78 Sophocles *Trachiniae* 730.
79 BGU II, p. 174.
80 BGU I, p. 282 (no. 287).
81 *Eudemian Ethics* VII 10, 1242 a 25.
82 *Timon* 56; so Strabo XVII 1.36 ('sharing in').
83 F. Hauck in Kittel *TWNT* III, P. 804, n. 51.
84 H. Lietzmann, *Messe und Herrenmahl*, Bonn 1926, pp. 223ff., A. Schweitzer, *Die Mystik des Apostels Paulus*, Tübingen 1930, pp. 260ff., J. G. Davies, *Members One of Another*, Mowbray 1958.
85 M. Jastrow, I, p. 416.
86 I. Abrahams, *Studies in Pharisaism and the Gospels*, CUP, second series 1924, p. 210.
87 C. Anderson Scott, *Expository Times* 35 (1924), p. 567.
88 L. S. Thornton, *The Common Life in the Body of Christ*, Dacre, 4th ed. 1963, pp. 450f.
89 Kittel *TWNT* III, p. 809f.
90 Ibid., p. 803.
91 Η Καινή Διαθήκη, μετὰ Συντόμου Ερμηνείας, N. Trempelas, Athens 1973, p. 868.
92 Origen *Hom.* 5.14 in Jer. (PG XIII 317A), Gregory Nazianzus *ep.* 102 (PG XXXVII 196A), Basil *ep.* 120, Council of Constantinople (381), *epistula* apud Theodoret *HE* V 9.9.
93 Mt 23[30]; Lk 5[10]; 1 Co 10[18]; 2 Co 1[7]; 2 Pet 1[4]; Heb 10[33].
94 BS, p. 368, n. 2 (i BC).
95 A secular meaning survives in 1 Ti 5[22]; Heb 2[14]; 2 Jn 11.
96 F. Hauck in Kittel *TWNT* III, p. 808.
97 L. S. Thornton, op. cit., pp. 8-10.
98 P. Hinnebusch, *Bible To-day* (Collegeville) 1 (1964), pp. 793-8.
99 B. Vassady, *Theology and Life* (Lancaster, Pa.) 8 (1965), pp. 245ff.
100 More usually it will bear the secular sense: 1 Co 10[30]; Heb 2[14] 5[13] 7[13].
101 A. Robertson and A. Plummer, *1 Corinthians*, ICC 2nd ed. 1914, p. 212.
102 Sophocles *Philoctetes* 694, 1460.
103 IG 14. 1320.
104 Nonnus *Dionysiaca* I 423 (iv-v AD).

F

[105] St. John Damascene *Homily* 5 (perhaps spurious).

[106] Epiphanius *Adversus Haereses* 55.6.

[107] St. Gregory Nazianzus *Orationes Theologicae* 28.18.

[108] Irenaeus *Adversus Haereses* I 5.6.

[109] St. Cyril of Jerusalem *Catecheses* 23.20; St. Gregory Nazianzus *Orationes* 8.18; Macarius of Egypt *Homiliae* 27.17, etc. (spurious, v AD).

[110] B. F. Westcott, *The Epistle to the Hebrews*, Macmillan 1889, pp. 200ff.

[111] R. P. C. Hanson, *Allegory and Event*, SCM 1959, p. 7.

[112] G. H. W. Lampe and K. J. Woolcombe, *Essays on Typology*, Studies in Biblical Theology no. 22, Allenson, Naperville 1957, pp. 39ff.

[113] H. Crouzel, *Bulletin de Littérature Ecclésiastique* (Toulouse) 65 (1964), pp. 161-74.

[114] The argument also of the late Fr. J. Daniélou, *Sacramentum Futuri*, Paris 1950.

[115] A. T. Hanson, *Jesus in the Old Testament*, SPCK 1965, pp. 8, 178 and throughout.

[116] As E. K. Lee protests in *New Testament Studies* 8 (1962), p. 170.

[117] *De Opificio Mundi* 157.

[118] Ex 25^9; Mt 1^{19}; Col 2^{15}; Jude 7, etc.

[119] D. L. Baker, *Scottish Journal of Theology*, 29 (1976), pp. 144ff.

[120] E. K. Lee, *New Testament Studies* 8 (1962), p. 171.

[121] *Confessions*, V 24.

[122] J. N. D. Kelly in *The Church's Use of the Bible Past and Present*, ed. D. E. Nineham, SPCK 1964, p. 47.

[123] A. G. Hebert, S.S.M., *The Throne of David*, Faber 1941, p. 256.

[124] D. L. Baker, op. cit., p. 157.

[125] K. Barth, *Church Dogmatics* III, part i, ET T. & T. Clark 1958, p. 23.

[126] D. E. Aune in *Evangelical Quarterly* 41 (1969), pp. 89–96.

[127] S. Amsler, *L'Ancien Testament dans l'Église*, Neuchâtel 1960; E. E. Ellis, *Paul's Use of the OT*, Edinburgh 1957, pp. 126–35; R. T. France, *Jesus and the OT*, pp. 38–80.

[128] *Adversus Haereses* IV xl. 1.

[129] Plato *Symposium* 196A, *Republic* 401A, *Theaetetus* 174C.

[130] *Physica* 190 b 15, *Politica* 1341 b 5.

[131] Josephus *Ant. Jud.* XVI vii 6 (Niese XVI 223).

[132] Ed. Kroll, p. 61, line 31.

[133] *Nicomachean Ethics*, 1126 b 33.

[134] Epictetus (Teubner II v 23).

[135] *Legum Allegoria* ii 66.

[136] Op. cit., iii 158.

[137] Deissmann's secular examples meaning 'first-born' are either post-Christian or else undated, *Light from the Ancient East*, ET p. 88.

[138] Plato *Theaetetus* 151C.

[139] Dittenberger 3rd ed. 1024, 17.

[140] *De Cherubim* 54.

[141] *Ant. Jud.* IV 71 (iv).

[142] *Sprachgeschichte und Wortbedeutung: Festschrift Albert Debrunner*, Francke (Bern) 1954, contribution by W. Michaelis.

[143] For a discussion of the precise grammatical implications of the phrase in Col 1^{15}, whether the genitive is objective or whether a genitive of comparison, see *Grammatical Insights*, pp. 122–4.

[144] *Prōtotokos* is added to the better text by codex Ephraemi, codex Bezae, the Byzantine text, the Vulgate and some old Latin MSS – probably a very early addition.

[145] The development of this thesis in the case of all NT authors may be seen in Moulton-Turner *Grammar* IV.

F

[146] Epicurus *Sententiae* 18; Plutarch II 107f.

[147] C. K. Barrett, *The Gospel According to St. John*, SPCK 1962, p. 137.

[148] Norman H. Snaith, *Interpretation* (Richmond) 1 (1947), p. 323.

[149] The point is developed clearly throughout the late Dr. William Barclay's study, *Flesh and Spirit*, SCM 1962.

[150] I. Magn 13^2; I. Eph 7^2 8^2; I. Smyrn 3^3 12^2 13^2.

[151] I. Pol 2^2.

[152] Did 1^4.

[153] E. de W. Burton, ICC, p. 494.

[154] P. Parker, *Anglican Theological Review* (Evanston) 46 (1964), pp. 251–60.

[155] Euripides *Hippolytus* 1072f; Thucydides II 64.6; Plutarch II 399D; Lucian *Alexander* 8.

[156] W. Sanday and A. C. Headlam, *Romans*, ICC T. & T. Clark 5th ed. 1902, pp. 217, 310.

[157] F. J. A. Hort, *1 Peter*, Macmillan 1898, p. 80.

[158] H. A. W. Meyer, *Critical and Exegetical Handbook to the Epistle to the Romans*, ET, T. & T. Clark, 2nd ed. 1879, p. 93.

[159] Aeschylus *Seven Against Thebes* 618.

[160] Diogenes Oenoandensis 27 (Teubner) (ii AD).

[161] Aeschylus *Eumenides* 831.

[162] The literal sense is rare: Lk 12^{17}; 1 Co 9^7; 2 Ti 2^6; Jas 5$^{7, 18}$; Rev 22^2.

[163] Mt 3$^{8, 10}$ 7$^{16ff.}$ 12^{33} 13$^{8, 26}$ 21$^{19, 34, 41, 43}$; Mk 4$^{7f., 29}$ 11^{14} 12^2; Lk 3$^{8f.}$ 6$^{43f.}$ 8^8 13$^{6f., 9}$ 20^{10}; Jn 4^{36} 12^{24}.

[164] Ro 6$^{21f.}$; Gal 5^{22}; Eph 5^9; Ph 1^{11} 4^{17}.

[165] *De Cherubim* 84.

[166] Mt 13^{23}; Mk 4$^{20, 28}$; Lk 8^{15}.

G

GENEALOGY

See 'Everlasting'.

GENEROUS

εὐμετάδοτος

Eumetadotos was coined from existing words. It occurs as 'generous' in later secular writings: those of Vettius Valens, M. Aurelius Antoninus, and in *Vitae Aesopi*. Christians are first to use it.

Wealthy believers are encouraged not to trust in their riches but to be generous, 'ready to distribute' (1 Ti 6[18] AV). The word has not survived in the apostolic Fathers, but St. Clement of Alexandria discussing wealth observes that the man who gives away is rich, and that the fruit of the *psuchē* is 'generosity' (*eumetadoton,* neuter used as a noun).[1]

St. Paul joins the word with *koinōnikos* which is, rather, 'generous' towards other Christians, indicating practical fellowship with fellow-believers in material things, while *eumetadotos* probably implies generosity to all and sundry. See 'Christian Fellowship'.

GLORY AND GLORIFICATION

δόξα: δοξάζω: ἐνδοξάζομαι: συνδοξάζομαι

Glory (the noun). Use of *doxa* in the Bible displays a sharp difference from the use in secular Greek where *doxa* meant glory in the sense of praise, but not in the sense of beauty and brightness, it was honour, repute, praise, opinion, judgment, expectation.

For Herodotus *doxa* had meant 'opinion' (VIII 132). Plato refers to 'false *doxa*' (opinion) and uses the verb *doxazō,* our second word, in the sense of having an opinion.[2] For Thucydides, too, *doxa* is belief or opinion, contrasted with sure knowledge (V 105). Indeed, Plato correlates it with *pistis* (belief).[3] For Xenophon *doxa* means a supposition: 'he gave the enemy the *impression* that he would not do battle that day.'[4] In secular Greek *doxa* might be a fundamental belief, an 'axiom' – like the *koinē doxa* (common opinion) of Aristotle.[5] For Thucydides it had the added meaning of fame or reputation (II 11). Socrates declared, 'In my *doxa* (opinion) ...'[6] It may also mean 'expectation' and 'pride'[7] – but never brightness or beauty. *Doxa* is a conspicuous example of a word adding a new meaning in Christian Greek through LXX influence.

Doxa had never signified 'brightness' until it was linked with the Hebrew words *hôdh* (splendour) and *kābhōdh* (splendour, honour). A striking instance of *doxa* translating *kābhôdh* in its sense of splendour is Isai 60[1f]. 'The light is come and the *doxa* of the Lord is risen upon thee.... Darkness shall cover the earth ... but His *doxa* shall be seen upon thee.' *Doxa* is bright light, contrasted with darkness. Here is a force quite foreign to the secular word.[8]

Doxa is 'the other-worldly splendour in which the Old Testament envisages the immediate presence of Yahweh'. No finite being may behold the naked *doxa* of God in its full blaze. Normally it is veiled behind a cloud, so that even Moses sees only the reflection.[9] As Dr. Moule insists, the Biblical *doxa* renders *kābhôdh* and gains a new sense thereby. The NT writers 'filled it with more besides, for by their time the glory of God had become closely associated with the famous rabbinical word for the divine *presence,* or God's *act of dwelling* among his people – *Shekinta* or *Shekina*'.[10]

By such association *doxa* found its new meaning – 'brightness' of the light at Saul's conversion (Act 22[11]), 'brightness' of the *Sh^ekhînâ* glory[11] (Ro 9[4]; 2 Co 3[18]) of which Jesus Christ is the reflection (Heb 1[3]), indeed the Glory itself (Jas 2[1]),[12] 'beauty' after mortal corruption and decay (Ro 8[18, 21] 9[23]), 'brightness' of the constellations (1 Co 15[40ff.]), 'beauty' of God and of His grace and Gospel (Ro 1[23]; 2 Co 4[6]; Eph 1[6, 12, 17] 3[16]; Jas 2[1]) and the final stage of salvation, our own 'eternal glory' (2 Ti 2[10]).[13] *Doxa* is the hope of every saint (Col 1[27]), who is called to this 'eternal glory' (1 Pet 5[10]).

> *When the last dread call shall wake us,*
> *Do not Thou, our God, forsake us,*
> *But to reign in* **Glory** *take us,*
> *With Thee on high.*

We may hope and trust that our ultimate 'glory' is like that of Christ's at His brief transfiguration on earth, for which the same word *doxa* is used (Lk 9[32]; 2 Pet 1[17]). That was the brightness of another world, bursting through, like the *doxa* shining round the shepherds at the nativity (Lk 2[9]), appearing briefly in this world. The *doxa* from another world shines on earth once again at Christ's Second Coming, for we are told that He arrives with His Father's 'glory' (Mk 8[38] 13[26]).

How literally and materially may we take the 'glory' of Biblical Greek? Physical light seems certainly intended by the 'glory' that surrounded the shepherds (Lk 2[9]). The 'glory' of Jesus transfigured was visible to Peter, James and John upon the mount (Lk 9^{32}). *Doxa* was visible to the first Christian martyr at his despatch. St. Stephen 'saw the glory of God, that is, Jesus standing at the right hand of God'. Jesus Himself, the *eikōn* of God, is also the *doxa*.[14] On the road to Damascus *doxa* was clearly a brightness which sent Saul to the ground in blindness. It was 'the *doxa* of that light' (Act 22^{11}). We must distinguish the literal from the freely symbolical. When St. Paul speaks of our eternal glory, we should be cautious, for a difficulty must naturally arise when, in an old vocabulary, new thought struggles for expression. The word in the OT had indicated literal theophanies but it cannot be held to define mechanically the new Christian thought, and we may not be justified in chaining St. Paul to the concrete idea of a literal light substance. It is wiser perhaps to suppose that he took *doxa* simply as a symbol for the manifestation of perfected human nature, the most significant symbol known to him for God's perfection as revealed to mortal sight.[15]

Glorify, be glorified, be glorified together (the verbs). In the same way the relevant verbs, our second, third, and fourth words *(doxazō, endoxazomai, sundoxazomai)*, which in secular Greek meant the holding of an opinion and the uttering of praise, now gain a new sense, viz. to clothe with brightness and splendour. Indeed, one of the verbs *(endoxazomai)* may itself be a coinage of Biblical Greek. Moulton and Milligan resisted Grimm's contention that the new Biblical meaning of *doxazō* (glorify) fails to appear in profane writers, but they should not have adduced the text, P. Lond. 121.502ff., against Grimm, for in any event it is post-Christian (iii AD). Moreover, the inscription, OGIS 168.56, should not have been adduced, for though it dates from BC 115, the meaning of *doxazō*, directed towards a temple on this inscription, might very well be 'praise', 'hold in honour' (or any of the secular meanings), and is by no means a parallel with its new sense in Biblical Greek – to 'shine', 'be radiant' (passive), like the face of Moses (Ex 34$^{29f.}$).

St. John reports Jesus as affirming that the Father is 'glorified' (13$^{31f.}$ 14^{13} 15^{8}), and that the Son 'glorifies' the Father (17^{1,4} 21^{19}), using the verb *doxazō*. God is 'glorified' in Jesus by His passion and His death of perfect obedience. By LXX precedent, for God to 'be glorified' in the Son it would be understood that God showed forth His glory in the person of Jesus,[16] and LXX background is of first importance. Moreover, it has been shown that to 'glorify' God meant to recognize His presence and to react to it by showing forth His praise.[17] That at least is the Pauline understanding of the phrase, and the Johannine is not so different: in both writings, one of the ways in which God's glory manifests itself in Christ is in His divine power (Col 1^{11}), in His miracles (Jn 2^{11}) – i.e. in visible beauty and grace. If we are to distinguish the new peculiarly Christian meaning of *doxazō*, we will think of glorifying God less as praise and rather as reflecting something of the beauty and grace of God.

St. John records that Jesus was 'glorified' at the Ascension (7^{39}). He would have in mind the great Psalm of the Ascension, 'Who is the King of Glory?' (Ps 23(24)). Triumph is depicted in that word, Glory. The gates and everlasting doors are lifted up; the procession of a strong and mighty Lord comes in. Yet at the same time St. John represents our Lord as 'glorified' at Judas's exit to betray Him ($13^{31f.}$). In the passion and death St. John brings out the **glory** and royalty of Jesus.[18] So antithetical a use of the *doxa* words is foreign to secular Greek and is very idiomatic. It is probably the same meaning as in another Christian context, where it is said that all the predestinated elect shall be 'glorified' (Ro 8^{30}). The noun *doxa* is used of the elect in the same paradoxical way to denote a splendour belonging to the future Dispensation reserved for those who were once of little account, the 'eternal' glory and the hope of every saint.

In St. John's gospel there is something subtle in the use of noun and verb in what is apparently the secular sense of 'praise' ($5^{41, 44}$ 7^{18} 8^{50} 9^{24} 12^{43}) – as if there were some play on the two meanings, secular and Biblical. Origen may assist at this point,[19] and his connecting these words with 'knowledge' has been remarked on.[20]

The Son is 'glorified' because He 'knows' the Father. Sometimes glorification seems to involve contemplation, 'knowing'. Perhaps we should distinguish the glory that consists in knowing God, from the glory that consists in God's being 'praised'. The former kind of glory transforms men, divinizes them, and brings them to full salvation when, as a result of holiness, they shall know God and reign in glory. The second glory, the extrinsic kind, comes very close to the secular meaning, 'praise'.

For the believer 'glory' in the first sense, the eschatological culmination of his holiness and contemplation, to know the Father, is a destiny devoutly to be followed.

St. Paul himself has a play on the two senses of *doxa*, which the Vulgate, unlike the Greek, is able to distinguish by two separate words (1 Co 15^{40-43}). St. Paul speaks of a *doxa* (brightness) of the sun, the moon, and the stars. 'One star differeth from another star in brightness *(doxa)*.' But when he uses *doxa* in verse 43 he has it in the secular sense: 'it is sown in dishonour, it is raised in honour *(doxa)*'. For the special Biblical sense of *doxa*, the Vulgate has *claritas*, for the secular sense (honour) it has *gloria*. The Latin translator felt that *gloria* was not a satisfactory equivalent of the Hebrew *kābhōdh* and its Biblical Greek translation.[21]

The *doxa* is a visible badge, an *eikōn,* a bright vesture or tent, with which we shall be surrounded hereafter (1 Co 15[41ff.]; 2 Co 3[18] 5[1-4]). The hoped-for splendour is like the radiant *sh^ekhînâ* (2 Co 3[7-12]), and the anticipation of heavenly joy comes on account of that splendour (1 Pet 1[8]). To suffer here with Christ, as Christ Himself did when Judas betrayed Him and He was said to be glorified, is to **be glorified with** Christ hereafter (*sundoxazomai* Ro 8[17]).

> *Thou shalt see My Glory soon*
> *When the work of grace is done,*
> *Partner of My Throne shalt be. ...*

For the plural, *doxai,* see 'Angels 3'.

GOODNESS

ἀγαθωσύνη

Agathōsunē belongs to Biblical Greek and is formed from the adjective for 'good', as if current pagan words for 'goodness' were deliberately avoided.

The new coinage would probably suggest the kindlier and softer aspects of virtue, just as 'righteousness' indicated the sterner.[22] However, the new word is not entirely synonymous with *chrēstotēs* (kindness), for it is more active and is the equivalent of *beneficientia* rather than *benevolentia,* according to Lightfoot.

In the Greek of the OT *agathōsunē* served to represent the Hebrew *tûbh, tôbh* and *tôbhâ* (a pleasant or excellent thing). In Christian language it is an active virtue, something more than *benevolentia,* for by St. Paul it is distinguished from the pagan virtue, *chrēstotēs,* among the fruits of the Spirit (Gal 5[22]), as he also distinguishes it from 'righteousness' and 'truth' (Eph 5[9]). In the NT, St. Paul alone has it, encouraging the Romans to be filled with it (15[14]). He extends the quality to God, after the manner of the LXX, praying Him to fulfil in the Thessalonians all the good pleasure of His **goodness,** consistent with their faith and high calling (2 Th 1[11]).

The word is continued in use by the apostolic Fathers. From them comes the phrase, 'the *goodness* of our Father' (Barn 2[9]), recalling 2 Esd 9[25,35] (Neh 9[25,35]). A rare LXX word was apparently adopted deliberately by the first Christians in preference to an accepted pagan word like *chrēstotēs,* for goodness and virtue. Were they hunting a special symbol to denote their ideal? It is thought that as the suffix *-sunē* was commonly added in the Hellenistic period to denote an abstract, the absence of secular attestation for this particular word signifies nothing that could carry any weight (MM). However, that is only to remark that Christians were capable of following Hellenistic practice in coining new words. It does not follow that they did not coin this word of which there is no pagan instance, although there is plenty of Christian attestation.

Later Christians applied it to God,[23] especially to His goodness towards penitents.[24] They applied it to Christ.[25] Demas and Hermogenes flattered Paul but he, 'looking only to the *agathōsunē* of Christ, did them no evil'.[26]

They applied it also to the 'goodness' of men.[27] It was a quality of Abraham, meritting his elevation from 'this vain world', in what is probably a Christian book.[28]

GOSPEL

εὐαγγέλιον: εὐαγγελίζω: εὐαγγελιστής

Early Christians reserved these words, *euaggelion, euaggelizō,* and *euaggelistēs,* to be vehicles of a new special insight – the Gospel of salvation.

The Gospel *(euaggelion).* The plural, *euaggelia,* in secular Greek was 'good tidings'.[29] True, the word already had for pagans a religious sense. An inscription at Priene, almost contemporary with Christ's nativity, is religious to the extent that it explains that the birthday of divine Augustus marks the beginning of *euaggelia* (good tidings) for the world.[30] The first Christians would not be aware of so definitive a use of the word and would be likely to avoid the association even if they were. One may be sure they were no strangers to the Hebrew *bśr*-root, rendered in the LXX by *euaggelion(-ia)* and its verb, especially in Isaiah where it proclaims the new and greater Exodus – the ending of warfare, the liberty of captives, tidings of salvation, the great Messianic Day, and the Lord's praise heralded by camels bearing gold and incense from Midian, Ephah and Sheba (Isai 40⁹ 52⁷ 60⁶ 61¹).[31]

The opening words of St. Mark, 'the beginning of the Gospel', probably gave rise to a later meaning for *euggelion,* viz. a book in which the Christian Gospel was set forth. So we speak of the four 'Gospels' which have unique authority as established by the Church, i.e. books which signal the true Gospel.

To evangelize. The verb *euaggelizomai* – the active voice is confined to later Greek – meant 'to bring good news'.[32] In the NT it is to preach the Gospel, but sometimes the verb is passive, to be evangelized (of people) and to be preached (of the Word and

Gospel).[33] St. Clement noted that the apostles 'were evangelized' by our Lord Jesus Christ (1 Clem 42[1]).

A Gospel-preacher *(euaggelistēs).* Had the first Christians been content with contemporary terms to express their significant ideas, doubtless they would have found *kerux* (herald) all ready to hand, but *kērux* had undesirable associations with Cynic preachers and with some kind of partaker in the Mysteries,[34] of which, however, *kērugma* was innocent. The less obvious *euaggelistēs* was untainted by pagan overtones. Early believers could not have been aware that *euaggelistēs* had indeed been used of a pagan priest on a faraway inscription.[35]

The charismatic ministry of the Gospel-preacher was one of the gifts of the ascended Lord to His Church (Eph 4[11]), but Philip and Timothy are the sole Gospel-preachers mentioned as such (Act 21[8]; 2 Ti 4[5]). Perhaps no separate ministry is intended by the word, and the Gospel-preacher may have represented simply another function of the primitive presbyter-bishop and deacon. At least, Philip was both deacon and Gospel-preacher (evangelist). Every believer will be anxious to spread the News of salvation at all times, but *euaggelistēs* is rather a full-time or travelling missionary. See, 'Apostle'.

GRACE

χάρις

Charis has a characteristically Christian meaning, though it is an old Greek word.

Secular Greek. Derived from *chairō*, to rejoice, *charis* already had a wide implication in Greek, for essentially it is what created joy either in the hearer or the observer. It embraces beauty, the 'grace' of the physical form, favour, gratification, homage, gratitude, gracefulness – all things which delight.

Secular meanings persist even in the Christian context where our Lord's preaching is said to be 'words of *grace*' (Lk 4[22]) in the sense that it delighted the hearers,[36] and where St. Paul cries, '*Thanks* be to God'.

Aristotle defines *charis* as that which is conferred guilelessly for pure joy, with generosity and open-heartedness,[37] and by Plutarch[38] *charis* is contrasted with *misthos* (reward), just as St. Paul sets it against debt and work. Is there, then, any substantial difference between the contemporary pagan and the Christian view of *charis*? It is true that in Hellenistic inscriptions the meaning of the word had developed so that it closely resembled, at least superficially, the

Christian view. *Charis* might describe a ruler's favour.[39] Inscriptions proclaim 'the grace of Caius Caesar' (Caligula). *Charis* was a 'gracious disposition' and a 'gracious gift', and the Stoics ascribed it to God. But, as in Christian Greek, the matter went further. It denoted 'power' of a supernatural kind, springing down from realms above.[40] Euripides had already used the word in this way when he exclaimed, 'O Love, Love! Thy sweet *potency*. ...'[41] His chorus sings sweetly of Love's almighty *charis* – Love, the son of Zeus. *Charis* in Greek was a divine power, right enough, but how different the Christian point of view! The primitive Church affirmed the unity of two truths, as Dr. Moffatt showed, the truth of God over all and the truth of God graciously entering human life, and although contemporary Graeco-Roman religion abounded in divine heroes, bringing salvation, 'the cult-heroes of salvation, on the other hand, were not supreme. Above these deities there was Someone or Something higher; the "saving" god might be commissioned to carry out his good work, but between him and the Supreme Power there was not the vital union that Christians saw in their God and Father with the Lord Jesus Christ His Son'.[42] As Moffatt said, the NT shows almost no signs that the first Christians were sensible of the cults as serious rivals of their faith. The vogue of the cults, and the grace they were supposed to give, was not felt by Christians until the second century. 'A throb of new life beats in every syllable about grace uttered in the first century.'[43] The Christian idea of salvation was not that of the cults; its conception of *charis* was something quite apart. Let us see what it was.

Biblical Greek. Among those who were familiar with the diction of the later books of the LXX, *charis* becomes God's grace, His supernatural assistance, 'the blessed condition of human life which resulted from the divine favour', because it translates chiefly the Hebrew word *ḥēn*.[44] On the other hand, *ḥesedh* and its group of words are translated by *eleos* (mercy), although it is true that when *ḥēn* and *ḥesedh* occur together in Est 2[17] they are together translated by *charis*. God's 'loving-kindness' and 'mercifulness' is there represented by *charis*. So a further transformation of meaning occurs in Christian Greek, unknown in the vernacular tongue, 'God's favour which is quite undeserved',[44] the mercy shown in offering salvation to the Gentiles, and the supernatural means by which a Christian is sanctified. We cannot do without *charis*.

No doubt, we are responsible for our actions: His words are there for us to hear, and yet we may not believe (Jn 12[47]) and the fault is ours. Nevertheless, try as we will, we cannot do what is good without God's aid. We cannot come except the Father draw us. It must be given to us. The Vine must vitalize us. I am what I am, only by the *charis* of God (Jn 6[44,65] 15[4f.]; 1 Co 15[10]). Through no

merit of our own, not because we willed or ran, we met God's mercy
revealing the riches of His glory – simply because He called us and
we became His people (Ro 9^{16-24}).

Apart from the gospels, the new sense of *charis* appears in every
NT book except 1 and 3 John, and it is a most characteristically
Christian word. Barnabas at Antioch, witnessing the Church's
increase, saw the *charis* of God and rejoiced *(echarē)* – a gentle
Lukan pun (Act 11^{23}). To 'continue in the *grace* of God' is to
persevere as a Christian (13^{43}). 'The Word of His *grace*' will be the
Gospel (14^3 20^{32}) of the '*grace* of God' (20^{24}). To 'recommend to
the *grace* of God' will be another way of indicating Christian prayer
(14^{26} 15^{40}). To be 'saved through the *grace* of Jesus' is the goal of
Jewish and Gentile believers (15^{11}). We cannot so much as 'believe'
without the assistance of grace (18^{27}). It is 'granted to' us to believe
in Him (Ph 1^{29}). St. Augustine tells how once before he became a
bishop, he took the view that the faith by which we come to God is
no gift of His but a thing of our own. But on this showing, he later
realized, grace would come after faith, and he was led to abandon
the error, he says, chiefly by the text, 'What hast thou that thou
didst not receive?' (1 Co 4^7).

Faith, then, is to be included in what we have received. It is one
of those works which follow the grace of God and cannot precede it.
All of us do not have God's gift of faith, and we are brought to the
question of predestination. By His foreknowledge God foresees the
things which He means to do. Grace is predestination taking effect,
in the opinion of St. Augustine. Grace makes us do what He
commands.[46]

Charis becomes something more than 'favour' in the Christian
vocabulary, even more definitive than 'God's favour'; it becomes a
special gift freely bestowed on believers, furthering them to
ultimate glory in heaven. 'Final perseverance', said St. Augustine,
'is a gift of God.'[47]

To 'fall from *grace*' (Gal 5^4) is to become detached from the
Vine, to have no life and to wither. *Charis* is 'grace abounding'
(*huperbalousa charis* 2 Co 9^{14}), 'super-abounding' (*huperpleonasen*
1 Ti 1^{14}), flowing over the Christian's head. *Charis* is 'a blessing
brought to man by Jesus Christ'[48] (Jn 1^{17}), comparable with mercy
and peace (2 Jn 3; 1 Ti 1^2; 2 Ti 1^2; Tit 1^4).

In the Johannine prologue both Truth[49] and Grace are prominent
(verses 14 and 17) and stand out from the provision of the Law by
Moses. Several commentators have remarked on the parallel
between these verses and Exodus 33 and 34, where God talks with
Moses, and the making of the Covenant and presenting of the Law
are described. These chapters depict God as full of Grace and
Truth, and the Johannine phrase is seen to be a studied citation of

rabh-ḥesedh we'emeth (abundant in goodness and truth, Ex 34[6]). The LXX, however, renders the Hebrew by *poluëleos* (merciful) and *alēthinos* (true), and indeed the LXX rarely has *charis* to render *ḥesedh*. It has been represented that *charis* and *alētheia* are never found in the LXX as a rendering of *ḥēsedh we'emeth*.[50] Dr. A. T. Hanson did, however, put forward several examples from the LXX and other versions, of *charis* as a rendering of *ḥesedh*,[51] and argued that Jn 1[14ff.] is best understood against the background of Ex 33, 34, the theophany to Moses and the presenting of the two tables of stone, which is all a foreshadowing of Jesus, the Lord Who is full of Good Tidings and Grace.

As Dodd remarked, in the version of Symmachus so far as we may judge from extant fragments *charis* was the preferred rendering of *ḥesedh*, 'and it is evident that the associations of that word have had influence in moulding' the special use of *charis* in the Christian vocabulary, 'which is different from any ordinary Greek use'.[52]

Moreover, J. A. Montgomery assured us that he had long held that the NT *charis* rendered the idea of the Hebrew word *ḥesedh*, 'and this without Septuagintal or other literary background'.[53] The beautifully evocative Hebrew word for the stork, the 'pia mater', because of her tender care for her young, is *ḥasîdhâ*.[54] As Montgomery noticed, one would never imagine that such was the Biblical meaning of *charis* unless one had the parallel word *ḥesedh* as a guide. 'The word is not to be understood primarily from the Greek but from its lively Semitic background.'[55] *Charis* in secular Greek fails to exhaust the whole of *ḥesedh* – that which by nature we do not have.

Charis in the NT, I believe, is best understood in comparability with the Hebrew *ḥesedh* and *ḥēn*, the divine attribute of 'loving-kindness' and God's 'favour' bestowed on man. It is a distinctive Jewish Christian concept and is closely connected with *Alētheia* – the Gospel.

Grace has everything to do with our salvation, everything to do with the Gospel, but we may not leave it at that. St. Paul owed everything to grace and yet he did not leave it there. The grace was not bestowed 'in vain', and St. Paul proceeded to labour 'more abundantly than they all', God helping him (1 Co 15[10]). The divine energy works in us, coersive and powerful, as Tertullian found, but we ourselves have a heavy responsibility.[56] Still grace is needed. We cannot perform worthy actions without it, although Pelagius sought to teach the Church to think so, saying only that grace made it *easier* to be good.[57] God endues us with goodness, He has such power over our wills that He turns us whither and when He wills, inclining us to do good of His free mercy.[58] Free-will is really a state of bondage to righteousness. The state of grace is the service of God which is true freedom.

Article X of the Church of England is based on the NT: man's fallen condition is such that we cannot by our natural strength and good works turn to faith, nor can we do anything acceptable to God unless His grace, by Christ, goes before us. 'O Almighty God', cried Cranmer in the beautiful collect for All Saints' Day, 'who hast knit together Thine elect in one communion and fellowship, ... *Grant us grace* so to follow Thy blessed Saints in all virtuous and godly living. ...' We must follow the blessed saints, we must be virtuous, we must live godly lives. Give us grace to do it!

GRAVITY (REVERENCE)

σεμνός : σεμνότης

The words express a Christian quality. They belong to a new ethical vocabulary.

In secular Greek the adjective *(semnos)* and the noun *(semnotēs)* signified at best a godlike majesty, at most a haughty pomposity. Early Christians could not have accepted the words at their face value, however plausible, and would have interpreted them in the light of the Greek Bible.

The words may bear, however, a worthy meaning in secular Greek. A man who is *semnos* 'has a grace and dignity not lent him from earth; but which he owes to that higher citizenship which is also his', and Trench stressed that the meaning of the word in the secular language prepared the way for the Christian context, since in pagan Greek it qualified things which belong to the heavenly world (p. 327). A closer look at the pagan contexts reveals that the resemblance with the Bible is superficial. The solemnity of *semnos* and *semnotēs* is very much the gravity and dignity of the externally august and revered. *Semnos* is freely applied to gods and goddesses like Hecate and Apollo.[59] The '*semnai* goddesses' were the Erinys at Athens.[60] The word was applied to the holy rites, the mysteries.[61] Truly, in a pagan sense, *semnos* belongs to the heavenly world, but the haughtiness which the pagans imported into their heaven and then took for their own pattern finds no place in the use of *semnos* and *semnotēs* in Biblical Greek.

O *semnoi* thrones!
You deities who watch the rising sun![62]

These imposing statues of Zeus, Apollo and Hermes stood on the eastern facade of Atreus' palace, each with an altar before it. So

195

when the term is applied to human beings a certain style and majesty is understood. 'A man who is not *semnos*' (stylish) is a nobody.[63] Plato contrasted the word with *chaunos* (frivolous),[64] Xenophon with *kompsos* (subtle).[65] 'Nothing *semnos*,' means nothing very wonderful.[66] So it may stand for what is repellently haughty,[67] and Heracles asks, 'Why do you look *solemn*?' believing such a look to be a bad omen.[68] We recall Aristotle's definition of *semnotēs:* 'Gentle and graceful arrogance.'[69]

Supposedly the first Christians had not read Aristotle or Xenophon or the dramatists, but be sure they knew their Greek Bible. Now, there was scarcely a context where *semnos* did not have a reference to the Law. The author of 4 Maccabees will not have his *semnos* mouth sullied after lifelong devotion to the Law (5^{36}). 'O *semnos* grey head', he cries, 'O life faithful to the Law!' (7^{15}). Perhaps the author's most pathetic passage concerns a brave mother of seven martyrs who had honoured the Law to the end. 'Not so *semnē* stands the moon ... as thou, having lit the path of thy seven starlike sons unto righteousness, steadfast in honour with God' (17^5). The struggle on behalf of nationalism and the *Tôrâ* is evident in contexts where *semnos* applies to that most 'solemn' Day, the Sabbath (2 Mac 6^{11}), to the 'venerable' and holy laws of the Jews (2 Mac 6^{28}), and to God's 'reverend' and glorious name (2 Mac 8^{15}). It occurs in close connection, not only with *Tôrâ* but with Wisdom and her 'princely' things, rendering Hebrew *nāghîdh* (Pr 8^6). Comparing a moral and upright walk with thoughts of those who are an abomination to God, the writer of Proverbs applies *semnos* to righteous works (*nō'am* Pr 15^{26}). The Law possesses *semnotēs* (gravity), according to the letter of Aristeas (171).

No less in Christian Greek, the new meaning is rigidly ethical and still has relation to the Law and the righteousness of God's people. Among qualities which St. Paul specially commends is the virtue of the *semnos*, along with truthfulness, justice, purity, loveliness and good report (Ph 4^8). Aged men, and deacons, and their wives, must have this quality (1 Ti 3^{8-11} Tit 2^2), and it was no superficial venerability.

Indeed, *semnotēs* is linked with godliness to mark a quiet life. To foster it the brethren pray for order and discipline in the state (1 Ti 2^2). Bishops must rule their households with *semnotēs* – with respectability, that is, or moral gravity (1 Ti 3^4). Titus must be a pattern of it (Tit 2^7). The word means seemliness in ministering. 'For each one of us', says St. Clement, 'must have a good conscience, not transgressing the appointed rules of his ministration, with all reverence *(semnotēs)*'.[70] Hermas intends it for moral purity and bears witness to its concern for the Law, as in OT

Greek. 'Where *semnotēs* lives, there lawlessness ought not to enter the heart of a righteous man' (*Mand.* IV 1.3). It denotes quiet patience, a contrast with ill-temper (*Mand.* V 2–8). Like St. Clement, Hermas sees it as 'reverence' (*Mand.* VI 2.3).

In modern Greek it is respectability, decency, coyness, decorum,[71] going sometimes to 'prudishness'. We may say that in the Bible there was already a close relation between *semnotēs* and 'chastity' (as Chrystostom and Estius render it) and 'propriety'. Luther rendered, *Ehrbarkeit*.[72]

GRECIAN (OR HELLENIST)

ἑλληνιστής

Hellēnistēs is likely to be a coinage by Christians, in spite of the employment by secular writers of the adverb *hellēnisti* which means, 'in the Greek language'.[73] The new adjective possibly denotes a Jewish Christian who was Greek-speaking.[74] Prof. Moule suggested that, to be precise, the 'Grecians' were Jews who knew only Greek while the 'Hebrews' may possibly have had Greek but in any case spoke a Semitic language.[75]

The Hellenists or 'Grecians' (AV) may have been a party in the Church opposed at one point to the 'Hebrews' (Act 6[1]). It looks as if there was also a party of that name outside the Church, with which the newly-converted Saul was in dispute and which sought to take his life (9[29]). Perhaps 'Grecians' is the name of a nonconforming group within Judaism which was opposed especially to worship at the Temple. The word may represent an opposition to the Temple or a spiritualizing of its worship, such as was shared by St. Stephen and St. John the evangelist within the Christian Church. Perhaps the 'Grecians' were an incipient esoteric movement, a Jewish form of Gnosticism originating earlier than the Christian variety.[76]

When the Gospel spread to Phoenicia, Cyprus, and Antioch, it was preached to 'Grecians' there (11[20]). We should notice that *hellēnistas* is textually better supported than *hellēnas* (Greeks), despite RSV and NEB. It is stated explicitly (Act 11[19]) that the preaching was to the Jews exclusively and in fact no controversy about the Gentiles was aroused on this occasion.[77] 'Grecians' are not simply 'Greeks', and 'Grecians' was a Jewish and not a Gentile party.

Apparently there were Jerusalemites who had Greek for their mother tongue, as distinct from Aramaic-speaking Jerusalemites who were termed 'Hebrews'. It is suggested that within the Church the Grecians were a distinct community, electing the Seven as their own equivalent for the Hebrews' Twelve.[78] There were perhaps other parties too, for instance, a Jerusalemite faction and an Antiochene, the factions at Corinth, as well as St. Paul's versatile opponents.[79]

Some writers suggest that only the Grecians were harassed by Jews while the Apostles and all the Hebrew Christians were unmolested (Act 8[1]). When St. Stephen and the Grecians suffered it was not as Christians but as those who rejected the authority of Law and Temple. The Church as a whole in Jerusalem was preserved because most Christian Jews could claim to be loyal to Law and Temple.[80] Walter Schmithals insists that the Grecian was a man who was committed to the Greek way of life; the word *hellēnistēs* derives from the verb *hellēnizō*, 'to live like a Greek'.[81] St. Luke gives no hint of this commitment in Acts. It is alleged that he was concerned to hide all traces of tension in his story of the early Church, but the theory about the Grecians is still speculative.

NOTES

[1] *Paedagogus* book III, ch. iv (84), PG VIII 605C.
[2] *Philebus* 40C, D.
[3] *Republic* 543A.
[4] *Historia Graeca* VII 5.21.
[5] *Metaphysica* 996 b 28.
[6] Plato *Gorgias* 472E.
[7] Herodotus I 79, V 91.
[8] C. H. Dodd, *Expository Times* 72 (1961), p. 272.
[9] R. P. Martin, *Carmen Christi*, CUP 1967, pp. 110f.
[10] C. F. D. Moule, *Colossians and Philemon*, CUP (CGT) 1957, p. 83.
[11] LXX had rendered *kᵉbhôdh YHWH* (glory of the Lord), where it indicated the bright cloud of Ex 16[10], etc., by *doxa*. Later the rabbis named it *shᵉkhînâ*. Cf. Talmud tractates, *Yoma* 9b, *Bᵉrakhôth* 6a, *Sabbath* 12b, *Baba Bathra* 25a, *Rosh hash-Shanah* 31a.
[12] According to Bengel and Mayor and Hort, taking 'Glory' in apposition to Christ, but Ropes thought the evidence for this was inadequate (*James*, ICC, p. 188).
[13] In the Gnosticism of the second and third centuries, *doxa* appears to have the new Biblical meaning, 'brightness'. Among the Leiden magical papyri is a text which refers to the *doxa* of the sun (p. 4, line 13). References are to A. Dieterich, *Abraxas: Studien zur Religionsgeschichte des spätern Altertums*, Leipzig 1891.
[14] I agree with R. P. Martin that the *kai* is epexegetical. Op. cit., p. 111, n. 3.
[15] J. Massie in HDB II, pp. 186f.
[16] G. B. Caird, *New Testament Studies*, 15 (1969), pp. 273–5.
[17] E. Lákatos, *Revista Bíblica* (Buenos Aires) 27 (1965), pp. 869–93.
[18] J. Riaud, *Bible et Vie Chrétienne* (Paris) 56 (1964), pp. 28–44.
[19] On John, tom. XXXII 28, 29. A. E. Brooke, *The Commentary of Origen on St. John's Gospel*, CUP 1896, vol. II, pp. 202ff.

[20] *Miscelanea Comillas* (Santander) 42 (1964), pp. 173ff.

[21] I should say, however, that in the phrase, 'star differeth from star in *glory*', some Latin versions and citations have *gloria:* viz. the sixth-century fragments, Fragmenta Frisingensia, now at Munich, four citations of Tertullian, c. AD 200, five of Origen, c. AD 230, and citations by St. Ambrose, Ambrosiaster, St. Hilary, St. Jerome, and St. Augustine.

[22] Armitage Robinson, note on 5[9].

[23] Theophilus of Antioch *ad Autolycum* 1.3 (PG VI 1028C) AD ii; Clement *Stromateis* vii 3 (PG IX 325B, 430B).

[24] Hegomonius *Acta Disputationis* v 4 (PG X 1436A) AD iv; *Apostolic Constitutions* ii 21.8, ii 22.12.

[25] Gregory of Nyssa *contra Eunomium* 1 (PG XLV 340B); Leontius of Naples, *Sermon* 2 (PG XCIII 1592B) AD vii: Clement *Paedogogus* i 9 (PG VIII 352C).

[26] *Acts of Paul & Thecla* 1 (ed. M. R. James, p. 272).

[27] Clement *Stromateis* vi 12 (PG IX 325A); Eusebius *Praeparatio Evangelica* xii 2 (PG XXI 953C).

[28] T. Abr p. 78, line 4.

[29] Aristophanes *Knights* 647, *Plutus* 765.

[30] OGI 458.40 (9 BC).

[31] D. J. McCarthy, 'Vox *bśr* praeparet vocem "evangelium",' *Verbum Domini* (Rome) 42 (1964), pp. 26–33.

[32] Josephus *Ant. Jud.* VI iv 2, XVIII vi 10.

[33] Heb 4[2,6]; 1 Pet 1[25] 4[6].

[34] *Novum Testamentum* 16 (1974), p. 154.

[35] IG XII 1.675.

[36] Also secular are 'thanks' (Lk 6[32ff.] 17[9]), 'favour' (Act 24[27] 25[3,9]), perhaps 'thank-offerings' (1 Co 16[3]; 2 Co 8[1ff.]), perhaps 'thanks' (1 Co 10[30]).

[37] *Rhetorica* ii 17.

[38] *Lycurgus* 15.

[39] OGI II 669.28f. (AD 68).

[40] Scott, *Corpus Hermeticum* I 32, XIII 12.

[41] *Hippolytus* 527.

[42] J. Moffatt, *Grace in the NT*, Hodder 1931, p. 61.

[43] Op. cit., p. 392.

[44] Armitage Robinson, pp. 221f.

[45] Burton, p. 424.

[46] *De Praedestinatione Sanctorum* 7–19 (PG XLIV).

[47] *De Dono Perseverantiae* 1 (PG XLV).

[48] Armitage Robinson, p. 223.

[49] See 'Truth', for the connection of *alētheia* with the Gospel.

[50] I. de Potterie, in *Jesus und Paulus* (Festschrift) ed. E. E. Ellis and E. Grässer, Göttingen 1975, p. 258.

[51] *New Testament Studies* 23 (1977), p. 93.

[52] C. H. Dodd, *The Bible and the Greeks*, Hodder 1935, pp. 61f.

[53] *Harvard Theological Review* 32 (1939), p. 96.

[54] Op. cit., p. 97.

[55] Op. cit., p. 101.

[56] *Adversus Marc.* II 9.

[57] St. Augustine *de Gratia Christi* 30.

[58] St. Augustine *de Gratia et Libero Arbitrio* 41.

[59] Hecate, in Pindar *Pythian Ode* III 79; Apollo, in Aeschylus *Seven against Thebes* 800.

[60] Thucydides I 126.

[61] Sophocles *Trachyniae* 765.

[62] Aeschylus *Agamemnon* 519.

G

[63] Aristophanes Fragmenta 52D.

[64] Plato *Sophista* 227B.

[65] Xenophon *Oeconomicus* VIII 19.

[66] Aristotle *Nicomachean Ethics* 1146a 15.

[67] Sophocles *Ajax* 1107; Andocides IV 18.

[68] Euripides *Alcestis* 773.

[69] Aristotle *Rhetorica* II 19.

[70] 1 Clem 41[1].

[71] A. Kuriakides, *Modern Greek-English Dictionary*, Athens 1909, 2nd ed. s.v.

[72] See C. J. Ellicott, *The Pastoral Epistles of St. Paul*, Longman 5th ed. 1883, pp. 27ff.

[73] Plato *Timaeus* 21C; Philo II 546; Josephus *Ant. Jud.* XIV x 2; P. Tor I v 4.

[74] Jackson and Lake, *The Beginnings of Christianity*, V, pp. 59, 74. The T. Sol mentions *Hellēnistēs* as a speaker of Greek by contrast with *Hebraios*, but MS P reads instead *Hellēn*, the ordinary word for a Greek.

[75] C. F. D. Moule, *Expository Times* 70 (1959), pp. 100ff.

[76] O. Cullmann, *Expository Times* 71 (1959), pp. 8–12.

[77] P. Parker, *Journal of Biblical Literature* 83 (1964), pp. 165–170.

[78] M. Hengel, *Zeitschrift für Theologie und Kirche* (Tübingen) 72 (1975), pp. 151–206.

[79] R. Pesch, *Concilium* (Nijmegen) 88 (1973), pp. 26–36.

[80] See the argument of Schmithals, *Paul and James* (46, SCM Studies in Biblical Theology) 1965, pp. 16–37.

[81] Op. cit., pp. 18f.

H

HEAD (OF THE CHURCH) AND ARCHETYPE

κεφαλή

The secular meaning of *kephalē,* in a literal sense, is 'head', and then metaphorically an extremity and a consummation.

Plato supplements his story with a conclusion *(kephalē)* in harmony with what has gone before, and elsewhere he speaks of coming to a *kephalē* as to a 'climax',[1] while for Aristotle wisdom is superior to knowledge in the sense that when knowledge has its *kephalē* (consummation) it becomes wisdom.[2]

However, the changes in meaning that developed in Biblical Greek are too radical to be considered as only metaphorical. Christians gave the term to Christ, not as the Head or Consummation, but as the active Director or Ruler, the *kephalē* of all Principality and Power, with everything under His feet, the *kephalē* over all things, the Director of the Body, the Husband of the Bride (Col 1[18] 2[19]; Eph 1[22] 4[15] 5[23]). Already the LXX had used *kephalē* to render *rôsh* which had the double meaning of 'head' and 'ruler'. The phrases, '*head* over all the inhabitants of Gilead' (Jg 10[18] 11[8]) and, 'Jephthah said, "Shall I be your *lord?*" ' (11[9,11]), show *kephalē* as 'ruler'.

Christ is seen by St. Paul as more than Head in a figurative Body, not merely the highest Member among many brethren, but rather as Director of the whole Church, the *Pantokratōr,* the Almighty, the victorious One 'Who filleth all in all' (Eph 1[22]).

Moreover, as Fr. Bedale pointed out.[3] *rôsh* was sometimes translated in the LXX also by *archē,* the Origin or Principle of Being – a fact which becomes immediately significant in Col 2[19] where heretics are said to make a man puffed up, not holding the *kephalē* which is the mainspring of his being. In this light it is possible to see how Christians can be said to 'grow up into Him', into the Archetype, the *kephalē* (Eph 4[15]), as into the archetypal image of the Second Adam which is progressively realized in them.[4] The visionary at Patmos sees Christ as the *archē* of creation (Rev 3[14]), not (as Swete and Charles) the Source of creation but its Archetype, its Beginning, its Sum-total, Head and First-fruits. *Kephalē* must be understood as having all the richness of meaning which may be extracted from *archē,* the equivalent of *rôsh* and *rêshîth.*[5]

HEART-SEARCHING ('WHICH KNOWETH THE HEARTS', AV)

καρδιογνώστης

Kardiognōstēs is a coinage formed from existing words. It probably belongs to an early liturgical vocabulary, forming part of believers' prayer. At a meeting before the day of Pentecost Christ is addressed as, 'Thou, Lord, *which knowest the hearts* of all men' (Act 1[24]), and Peter at the council of Jerusalem testifies concerning 'God *which knoweth the hearts*' (15[8]). Hermas with the same word indicates the Lord Who also has appointed repentance (*Mand.* IV 3.4).

'HEAVEN' OR 'HEAVENS'

οὐρανός, οὐρανοί

O world invisible, we view thee,
O world intangible, we touch thee,
O world unknowable, we know thee,
Inapprehensible, we clutch thee!   (FRANCIS THOMPSON)

For Christians, 'heaven' is a home in the future, and 'in heaven' is our citizenship even now. Secularists in St. Chrysostom's time craved a satisfaction which the material world did not provide and fed their superstition on amulets, spells and fortune-telling. Unreasoning credulity seems to be the nemesis of irreligion, and a world which has rejected the true supernaturalism has become a prey of the false,[6] looking only at the things which are temporal.

Bible images picture our future life as a 'heavenly' city which has streets of gold, for the life hereafter is beyond comprehension and we can but think in terms of earthly conceits. Eyes and ears and minds cannot know what God has prepared, and heaven and its scenes are but a glimpse of the life beyond.

In Greek the word which for Christians denotes 'heaven', whether singular *(ouranos)* or plural *(ouranoi)*, had various meanings – a 'tent',[7] a vaulted 'ceiling' (Hesychius), the 'sky',[8] and the gods' dwelling-place, identified with Olympus,[9] so that Aeschylus refers to 'the gods from *heaven.*'[10] It was the proper name of Uranos, one of the gods.[11]

It is not surprising if the student wonders whether there is significance in the difference which the Bible affords between 'heaven' *(ouranos)* and 'the heavens' *(ouranoi)*. In the secular language the word is found comparatively less frequently in the plural, and even in the Bible it is less often plural than singular.

Still the plural has a far greater use in Biblical Greek than it has in the secular. So can there be significance in its use? In the LXX the word is mainly singular and it nearly always renders the Hebrew *shāmayîm,* which is either 'sky' (as Gen 1⁸) or else the dwelling-place of God (as Ps 32(33)¹³) – which is probably the same thing, seeing that God looked down from thence.

The plural in Biblical Greek derives no doubt from the plural form of the Hebrew equivalent, *shāmayîm.* In the LXX, however, the plural of *ouranos* is almost confined to poetic books in such phrases as, 'Sing, ye heavens!' (Isai 44²³ 49¹³) and 'Rejoice, ye heavens!' (Deut 32⁴³), and to Hannah's song (1 Km 2¹⁰; 2 Km 22¹⁰), and so through all the poetry in phrases like, 'the heaven of heavens', 'exalted above the heavens', and 'let the heavens rejoice'. The plural is found also in later books which may even be post-Christian in translation, and so influenced by the use of the plural *ouranoi* in Christian Greek.¹²

In the LXX the use of the plural makes little difference to the intended meaning. One might well, however, suspect that the use of the plural affects the meaning as far as the NT is concerned, for here the plural is relatively more prominent. We recall that in the Hebrew cosmogony which the early Christians may have inherited Heaven as a whole consisted of seven heavens.

> *Above the clear blue sky, in heaven's bright abode,*
> *The Angel host on high sing praises to their God.*

A charming hymnographer, John Chandler, falls naturally into using the singular for this series of heavens in which the graded hierarchy of angels dwell. It might seem to the early Christians more natural to use the plural, *ouranoi,* for the seven heavens unless there was good reason to use the singular. St. Paul no doubt has all the heavens in mind when he points to the God who created everything in the *heavens* (Col 1¹⁶) and who is above *all the heavens* (Eph 4¹⁰). The writer to Hebrews assumes that our High Priest ascended through all seven *heavens* (Heb 4¹⁴). Both writers use plural in those instances.

There might, on the other hand, be special occasions on which use of the singular was called for. We would expect it when only one of the seven heavens was intended, as when mention is made of the waters above the firmament of 'heaven', that is, the blue sky, the lowest of all the heavens, indeed the 'heaven' in which the birds fly (Mt 6²⁶ 8²⁰ 13³²; Mk 4⁴,³²; Lk 8⁵ 9⁵⁸ 13¹⁹; Act 10¹² 11⁶), which gives rain (Jas 5¹⁸), to which men look up (Mt 14¹⁹; Mk 6⁴¹ 7³⁴; Lk 9¹⁶ 12⁵⁶ 18¹³; Jn 17¹; Act 7⁵⁵) and which is sometimes red (Mt 16²ᶠ·), where are the clouds (Mk 14⁶²) and the lightning (Lk 10¹⁸ 17²⁴) and the stars (Heb 11¹²; Rev 6¹³ 8¹⁰ 9¹ 12⁴; Mt 24²⁹, but the same verse has also the plural). *Ouranos,* the singular, indicates the sky in which signs appear (Mt 16^1; Mk 8^{11}; Lk 11^{16} 21^{11}; Mt 24^{30} 26^{64}; Act 2^{19}), from which fire descends (Lk 9^{54}) and brimstone (Lk 17^{29}), the sky which is 'far distant' (Mk 13^{27}) and 'shut up' (Lk 4^{25}). Capernaum is said to be exalted to the sky (Lk 10^{15}), and nations are said to live beneath it (Act 2^5; Col 1^{23}). At the Ascension Jesus was seen to be carried into the sky (Lk 24^{51}; Act 1^{10}). At Pentecost the sound was as the wind in the sky (Act 2^2). At the conversion of Saul a light shone in the sky (9^3 22^6), and in Peter's vision the sky opened ($10^{11,\,16}$ 11^{10}) and God's voice came from it (11^9). It is in the sky that the Lord will one day appear (1 Th 4^{16}; 2 Th 1^7). I think it reasonable that *ouranos* (sing.) should be used of the sky, which in Jewish thought was the first heaven (T. Levi 2^2 3^8). The first heaven was the place of the rulers of the stars (2 Enoch 3–6). Rakia, above the empty Vilon, was the 'heaven' in which are sun and moon and stars.[13]

Moreover, there is the third heaven (singular) mentioned by St. Paul (2 Co 12^2), which is one of the seven separate heavens. Another circumstance which might require use of the singular is the need to indicate the heavens collectively as one totality. There is, for instance, the phrase, 'Heaven and earth' (Mt 5^{18}; etc.).

What then of the phrase, 'the *heavens* were opened' (Mt 3^{16})? We would have supposed that, being plural, 'heavens' cannot mean the sky but, in the context, it must do so. Apparently the various NT writers have their own caprice in this respect, and some of them, the Seer, St. John and St. Luke, prefer the singular when indicating the totality of heaven, giving weight to its unity, while on the other hand St. Paul takes up the plural, perhaps with the plurality of the seven heavens in mind. The second epistle of Peter selects the plural too ($3^{5,\,7,\,10,\,12,\,13}$). St. Matthew and St. Mark are plainly at variance: the sky is but one of the heavens and should not logically be plural, as indeed Mk 13^{27} confirms, but the parallel surprises us with the plural (Mt 24^{31}). Such contradictions are few and some are only apparent. Thus, Mt $3^{16f.}$ (and Mk parallel) have plural *ouranoi* as the venue of the voice and of the Dove at Jesus' baptism, but St. Luke's parallel has the singular; perhaps it seemed to the bystanders that the sky only, rather than all the heavens, was affected. Again, St. Stephen's vision (Act 7^{56}) may have involved all the heavens and not the sky alone – hence the plural.

Concerning other ostensible breaches of the canon,[14] it must be said that it is a sphere where scribal activity is noteworthy: in Mk 13^{27} the majority of MSS read singular in the phrase, 'uttermost part of heaven', but if the seven heavens, rather than the sky, is intended, then the Old Latin with some Greek MSS are correct in reading the plural. NT editors had some hesitation whether singular or plural should indicate God's dwelling-place, but they seem to have felt that a rule of some kind was involved, for there are many textual corrections. In Lk 11[13] only p[45] has plural (correctly?) in the phrase, 'Father in heaven', while in Eph 6[9] only Sinaiticus has singular (wrongly?) in the phrase, 'Master in heaven'. In Col 4[1] only ℵ* BAC have singular (wrongly?) in the same phrase. In 1 Pet 1[4] only ℵ has the apparently correct singular in the phrase, 'reserved in heaven for you'.[15]

For Christians, heaven is a home (Diogn 10[7]) where their names are inscribed (Lk 10[20] plur. Heb 12[23] plur.). A glorified body awaits them there (2 Co 5[1f.] plur. and sing.), together with their reward and inheritance (Mt 5[12] plur.; Lk 6[23] sing.; Mt 6[20] sing.; Lk 12[33] plur.; 1 Pet 1[4] plur.). The question is whether, conceived as the Christian's home, heaven is regarded as a totality. Heaven, in its sevenfold entirety, is not the dwelling-place of the righteous dead in Jewish thought at least:[16] the souls of the departed righteous dwell only in the seventh heaven. Insofar as some Christians identified the eternal resting-place as Paradise (q.v.), it would appear that the third heaven was their home. In the third heaven was the Tree of Life in the place where God rests 'when He comes into Paradise'.[17] Later the Church rejected the idea of a plurality of heavens.[18] At any rate, there is no evidence that Christians ever believed that more than one of them was their final destiny, and it is not easy to see why the plural *ouranoi* is sometimes used to denote their reward and inheritance (Lk 12[33] plur.; Mt 5[12] plur.). It should be observed that at Mt 5[12] the singular is read, correctly it would seem, by many authorities.[19]

St. Paul in a curious way varies plural with singular at 2 Co 5[1f.]: 'We have a building of God, an house not made with hands, eternal *in the heavens* (plur.). For in this we groan, desiring to be clothed upon with our house which is *from heaven* (sing.).' Some nice difference may be implied. The Vulgate maintains the distinction: *in caelis ... de caelo.* Perhaps it is all a matter of compression and punctuation: 'We have an house not made with hands, a building of God (Who is) *in the heavens.*' The Christians' own house, on the other hand, belongs only to *one* heaven.

To be explained on the same lines is a similar change from plural to singular within one verse (Diogn. 10[7]): 'God lives *in the heavens* (plur.) ... the true life is *in heaven* (sing.).' God's dwelling is plural also at Mt 5[16]; Lk 11[13] p[45]; Eph 6[9]; Col 4[1] DG itala.

One may be tempted to dismiss the change in number as without significance, but I hesitate to do this, especially as the frequent corrections in the MSS suggest that a rule was involved.

1. ἀπώλεια

Secular Greek. *Apōleia* was a fairly rare word, both in its active sense of 'destruction' and its intransitive sense of 'loss'. It was a perishing[20] and a wearing out.[21] It was 'loss': to retire from a bath without clothes, remarks Aristotle, is troublesome for the laughter is much more unpleasant than the actual 'loss' of the clothes.[22] St. Mark's use of *apōleia* is therefore not strange – 'waste' of ointment (14[4]) – but generally the NT use of the word depends upon that of the OT.

Biblical Greek. In the vocabulary of Jews and Christians there is added to *apōleia* the special meaning of **eternal loss, perdition.** In the Paris magical text, it is true, a demon is handed over to the black chaos 'in the *apōleiais*',[23] but it should not be cited as a secular instance of the Biblical meaning for, as Oepke points out,[24] the text has suffered Jewish-Christian influence. Christians applied the old word to the absence of God, and they saw *apōleia* as the abnegation of all that salvation promised (Ph 1[28]), as the reverse of eternal life. Often in the LXX it denoted loss of the good life, for it translated the Hebrew *'êdh* (calamity, especially distress of the wicked), in the special context of the vengeance and judgment of God. Moses warned, 'The day of their *apōleia* is at hand' (Deut 32[35]). A time of *apōleia* is said to be reserved as punishment (Job 21[30] 30[12] 31[3]), coming like a whirlwind upon supercilious sneerers at divine Wisdom (Pr 1[26] 6[15]). The word describes the turning of God's back upon Judah (Jer 18[17]) and his devastation of Egypt (Jer 26(46)[21]).

Besides *'êdh,* our dreadful word renders the yet more solemn expression, *'ābhadh,* to perish, which indicates the banning of faithless Israelites from their portion in the Land (Deut 4[26] 8[19] 30[18]) and the fate of idolatry in Canaan (Deut 12[2]), as well as Judah's absolute overthrow (Obad. 12). *Apōleia* is synonymous with hopeless death: 'Is Thy mercy in the grave? Is Thy faithfulness in *apōleia*?' (Ps 87(88)[11]).

Moreover, *apōleia* renders that fearful Hebrew word, *'ªbhaddhôn* (Abaddon), Hell itself. Job retorts to Bildad, '*Sheʾôl* is naked before Him, and *'ªbhaddhôn (apōleia)* hath no covering' (Job 26[6]). *Apōleia,* the Biblical technical term, has travelled far from the mild word of secular Greek and still more remarkable Christian contexts are just round the corner. For Christians *apōleia* means **Hell,** the destiny of materialism (Ph 3[19]; 1 Ti 6[9]). It is the **Hell** which is to become the end of vessels of wrath (Ro 9[22]), the awesome antithesis of heaven and glory, which are the blessed destiny of the elect (9[21]).

The Saviour warned against a broad way which has **Hell** (*apōleia*) at its end (Mt 7¹³). He must have known the meaning of the word in the Greek Bible – the utter perishing of the wicked (e.g. Pro 11¹⁰ 28²⁸). Satan is *Apōleia* and Judas is his child (Jn 17¹²). Jesus thought of Abaddon as the angel of the Abyss, the Prince of Hell, the Man of Sin whom St. Paul expected at the Apostasy. Sometimes St. Paul designates him, 'son of *Apōleia*' (2 Th 2³), which recalls the words of Jesus concerning Judas Iscariot.

Although ultimate safety is their bright future, yet behind all believers if they tarry on their journey, looms dread *apōleia* (Heb 10³⁹) – no mere nominal horror, as we find to our cost at the day of Judgment, for 'our damnation *(apōleia)* slumbereth not' (2 Pet 2³ 3⁷·¹⁶). As if to crown all, St. John visualizes the Beast with the Whore upon his back, ascending from the bottomless pit, his tarrying place for a thousand years before going on to **Hell** *(apōleia)* for ever (Rev 17⁸·¹¹). The finality is awful.

Early Christian thought links *apōleia* with punishment belonging to the future Dispensation – *aiōnios* punishment (T. Abr 90⁷). It is linked with Gehenna (see below), too. The enemies of Jesus are 'the children of *Gehenna* and of *apōleia*' (Acta Thom. 74).

2. γέεννα

Geënna is a Christian transliteration of the Hebrew *gêhinnôm* (valley of Hinnom), a place in the Kedron valley southwest of Jerusalem where children were once sacrificed to Moloch.

More fully expressed as 'the *geënna* of fire', the expression denotes for Christians a form of damnation affecting both soul and body, of which the scribes and Pharisees were in danger, along with any disciple who charges his brother with atheism – with being a 'fool' in the Psalmist's sense – or who fails to mortify the flesh (Mt 5²²·²⁹ᶠ· 18⁹; Mk 9⁴³ᶠᶠ·). Our Lord's warning, stern and loving, was that it is better to fear God who may well wield this punishment, than men who cannot (Lk 12⁵).

Our Lord's kinsman is the only NT writer, outside the gospels, who ventures upon the dread word (Jas 3⁶), and the apostolic Fathers do so only in citation.

The association of 'this accursed valley'²⁵ with fire inspired the concept of Gehenna as a purgatorial process in later Judaism, by which Jews who failed to keep up the Law's requirements were reformed and made ready for Paradise.²⁶ It is 'sixty times as hot as the fire of earth', warns the Talmud, but some Jews held that very near to the furnace of Gehenna *(clibanus Gehennae)* was the Paradise of delight.²⁷

HELL (THE BOTTOMLESS PIT)

ἄβυσσος

Descendit ad inferna. – APOSTLES' CREED

Devouring depths of hell their prey
At His command restore. – ST. FULBERT OF CHARTRES

There is a new Christian meaning for the word *abussos:* it is the place of departed spirits, the underworld, the abode of Christ's spirit from the time of His death to that of His rising.

Secular Greek. In classical Greek *abussos* was an adjective. Herodotus speaks of the springs of the Nile which are 'unfathomed' (II 28). The word means bottomless and boundless, like that sea of ruin upon which a certain king was launched,[28] and the 'unfathomable' mind of Zeus. The chasm of Tartarus a place even lower than Hades, was 'bottomless'.[29] *Abussos* applies to 'inexhaustible' wealth.[30] It means 'without bottom', like the lake in Heracles' directions to Dionysus.[31]

Secular magical papyri adhere to the meaning but they have the word as a noun, the 'infinite void'.[32] Of the same late date (iii AD) is Diogenes Laertius, who uses *abussos* of the world of the dead (IV 5.27) – a meaning which came into the secular language perhaps through Biblical influence.

Biblical Greek. The LXX uses *abussos* to render *T^ehôm,*[33] the primaeval Ocean the Deep, personified.[34] Before the world was created (Gen 1²), primaeval darkness was upon the face of *Abussos (T^ehôm),* and when God drowned the world He opened *T^ehôm's* fountains (Gen 7¹¹ 8²). *T^ehôm (abussos)* was conceived as crouching beneath the earth's foundations like a monstrous giant, grimly evil (Deut 33¹³). Moreover, he was the Underworld, in stark contrast with the place of resurrection. 'Up to heaven, and down to *T^ehôm (abussos)!*' cries the Psalmist (106(107)²⁶). He personified the place where the dead rest and where demons reside. *Abussos* is with the dragons (Ps 148⁷). 'Thou shalt quicken me again', aspires the Psalmist. 'Thou shalt bring me up again from *T^ehôm/Abussos.*' (Ps 70(71)²⁰).

Abussos represents more than the place of gloomy repose. He was the dark Power who confessed, 'Wisdom is not in me' (Job 28¹⁴). He is not everlasting, for Wisdom is older (Ps 8²⁴) and God's commandment is ultimate. But he is the sea personified, and the sea was traditionally the home of evil spirits. God's way was in the sea when Moses and Aaron went safely through, and *T^ehôm/Abussos* was troubled (Ps 77(78)¹⁵). Every time the Lord sends down dew, *T^ehôm/Abussos* is broken up (Pr 3²⁰), for God placed the Ocean,

208

$T^e hôm/Abussos$, to cover the earth as with a garment (Ps 103(104)^6). When God rebuked the Red Sea He led His people victors through $T^e hôm/Abussos$ (Ps 105(106)^9). The arm of the Lord dried up the personified Ocean that His ransomed might pass (Isai 51^{10}). The Red Sea-crossing made the Lord's name glorious, for He took His people through the monster as one leads a horse through pasture-land (Isai 63^{13}).

The Lord God's punishment of Tyre is the more terrifying because He used $T^e hôm/Abussos$ to accomplish it. 'I shall bring $Abussos$ upon thee and great waters shall cover thee.' (Ezek 26^{19}). $Abussos$, the ship-bearing ocean, had made Assyria great (Ezek 31^4), but in the vision of Amos the Lord's fire devours $Abussos$ (7^4).

In the NT the devils who possessed Legion are understandably anxious to keep out of the underworld, out of their master's direct power. The irony of the sequel, their going into the swine, is that they did not escape $Abussos$ after all (Lk 8^{31}).

Elsewhere in the NT $abussos$ is the realm of the dead, the place where Christ was confined in His death, the 'deep' where He descended (Ro 10^7). The 'Angel' of this grim hell of devils is called Abaddon (see, 'Destroyer') and, in the revelation of future events, a Beast is seen to ascend from his domain to make war against the two Witnesses (martyrs), slaying them to the satisfaction of all who resented their preaching (Rev 9$^{1f., 11}$ 11^7). Here Satan shall be consigned at the Second Coming for an incredibly long time before his last warfare (Rev 20^{1,3}), when the very Deep itself, $T^e hôm/Abussos$, shall be destroyed and there is no more sea (Rev 21^1).

Christ descended into the $abussos$ between the crucifixion and ascension, in the belief of early Christians. The Ascension of Isaiah foretells that when He has plundered the Angel of death, He will ascend on the third day, and then many of the righteous will ascend with Him (19^{16}). St. Matthew tells us half the later story of the harrowing of hell – some saints left their graves at His resurrection – inferring perhaps that Jesus had released them (Mt 27$^{51ff.}$). 'The Lord went down to the $abussos$,' said Methodius.[35] It was believed that by descending thither He opened a way of escape for other souls (Acta Thom. 32). 'He went down to Hades ... and raised the dead,' says the Acts of Thaddai.[36] At the same time early Christians supposed that 'the unsearchable places of the $abussoi$ and the lower world are controlled by God' (1 Clem 20^5). St. Paul may have in mind this act of divine mercy and grace by his phrase, 'led captivity captive' (Eph 4$^{9f.}$), and St. Peter hints that Jesus preached in the depths (1 Pet 3^{19} 4^6). It is denied, however, by W. J. Dalton[37] who finds a parallel in Enoch 12–16 which indicates that the preaching was to evil spirits who dwelt on high in the lower heavens, and so the preaching took place *after* the Resurrection, not when Christ descended to the *abussos*.

It may not be that Jesus Himself preached in the 'depths', and a textual emendation of 1 Pet 3[19], unsupported by any MSS, has been suggested. Instead of the reading, 'in which He went', it is suggested that we read, 'in which Enoch went', by the addition of a few letters. However, it is an unlikely guess and it is not the traditional Christian interpretation.

The words, 'in which', are sometimes held to mean, 'on which occasion',[38] or, 'in which process' (Selwyn), but there is no reason why they should not mean, 'in which spirit', for 'spirit' has just been mentioned and appears to be the antecedent of the relative. Then, Jesus is said to have preached to the imprisoned ones, not in His resurrection state but in a 'spiritual'. His body is presumed to be still on earth in the grave or on the Cross. As a spirit He came to the spirits in prison.[39] 'But', as Leivestad insisted, 'it was certainly as a spirit capable of giving life both to the body of Christ and to the bodies of the departed' (p. 173).

Nevertheless, very early the belief arose that God sent His Son with a mission in three different spheres – heaven, and earth, and the *abussos* (Diogn. 7[2]) – and with it came the elaborated legends of the *descensus ad inferos* and the 'Harrowing of Hell' which in the Middle Ages stood for the conquest of evil powers at Christ's descent into the underworld between Good Friday and Easter Day, and which was a popular theme in drama and art.

'Thou hast preached to them that sleep,' declares the Gospel of Peter (ix). One component of the Acts of Peter is the Descent into Hell, an older document which became attached to the Acts, and in it Christ greets Adam and takes all the saints out of Hades.

The prophets of old were waiting for Him, and 'when He came He raised them from the dead'. With these words St. Ignatius bears early testimony to the Christian belief that Christ preached to the saints of the old dispensation (I. Magn. 9[3]).

At the same time, not only is Christ Himself represented as preaching to souls in prison, but so are apostles and teachers who had fallen asleep, and in the underworld are said to have had a message for those who fell asleep before them (Hermas *Sim.* ix 16.5ff.).

HELL, TO CAST DOWN TO

ταρταρόω

Tartarō is the Christian formation[40] of a verb based on Tartarus, a personified name for the lower world which in Jewish apocalyptic was presided over by an archangel named Uriel.[41] Fallen angels 'were cast down to hell' (passive) to await judgment (2 Pet 2[4]).

HERESY, HERETICAL

αἱρετικός : ἑτεροδιδασκαλέω : αἵρεσις

The words, *hairetikos, heterodidaskalō* and *hairesis*, if they have not yet become, are rapidly becoming technical Christian terms.

Heretical. In secular Greek the meaning of the rare adjective, *hairetikos,* was 'capable of choosing', 'careful to avoid'. It is found in Pseudo-Plato,[42] and also in Hierocles.[43]

The sense of schismatical, factious, and creating divisions, will be an invention of Christians, not found in the LXX.

Titus should reject, after two warnings, 'a man that is an heretick' (Tit 3[10]), and the context explains that such a teacher transgresses the Church's norm of doctrine because of his 'foolish questions', his debates, his reversion to Judaism with its emphasis on 'genealogies'. The adjective has this meaning quite consistently in ecclesiastical Greek and is notably applied to Arius, the heresiarch.

To teach heresy. The second word, the verb *heterodidaskalō,* is a coinage from existing words, literally 'to teach otherwise', that is, contrary to the Church. It is exclusively Christian (Bauer). Timothy's task in Ephesus was to forbid the dissemination of heresy – to prevent doctrine that was at variance with the Church's wholesome accepted tradition as St. Paul had delivered it to him, including, in one specific instance, the directions about servants (1 Ti 1[3] 6[3]). St. Ignatius wrote to St. Polycarp, 'Let not those who seem to be plausible and yet teach heresy *(heterodidaskalō)* dismay you. Stand firm, like a smitten anvil.' (I. Pol. 3[1]).

Heresy. The third word, *hairesis,* had in secular Greek indicated a philosophical tendency, a school or party. Nowhere perhaps in the NT does *hairesis* have the later technical meaning of 'heresy', that is, teaching which is opposed to the doctrine of the Church as a whole.[44] Nevertheless, *hairesis* stands listed among the works of the flesh (Gal 5[20]) and elsewhere St. Paul uses it in a bad sense (1 Co 11[9]), recognizing the incompatibility of *haeresis* and *ekklēsia.* 'There must be heresies among you,' if only to show up those who are 'approved', the *dokimoi.* It is despising the Church of God, this harbouring of heresies, for they harm the Church. Moreover, heresies are 'damnable' and deny the Lord (2 Pet 2[1]). Heresy in the

NT seems to be 'obstinate persistence in self-opinionated views contrary to revealed truth'.[45]

Because *hairesis* appears without explanation in the midst of a catalogue of vices, Dibelius assumed that the pejorative sense was not first created by St. Paul.[46] Such a sense is not suggested by the LXX, where it means 'free will' and 'choice', but if the pejorative sense was not coined by St. Paul it may well have been devised by other elements within the Church at a very early time. In 2 Pet 2[1] *hairesis* means false opinion, not mere schism (Spitta, von Soden, Weiss, Mayor, Bigg). Bigg observed that as early as 1 Co 11[18f.] *hairesis* and *schisma* were the same thing, and possibly St. Paul was quoting a saying of our Lord (p. 272). Now *hairesis* 'is changing its meaning with the change of circumstances'. No longer mere schism, it is hardening into the 'denial of the fundamental articles of the Christian creed'. It is a denial of the Lord and a bringing upon oneself swift destruction (2 Pet 2[1]). For St. Ignatius, *hairesis* is 'a rank weed' to be avoided; it is 'poison' mixed with Jesus Christ, a deadly drug (I. Trall. 6[1]), and he praises the Ephesians because no 'heresy' has a home among them – that is, 'aught else save concerning Jesus Christ in truth' (I. Eph. 6[2]). 'Heresy' is the equivalent of 'evil teaching' (I. Eph. 9) Simon of Samaria was the first heresiarch, according to St. Justin (*Apol.* 26).

HIGH-MINDED (TO BE)

ὑψηλοφρονέω

Christian Greek will have coined[47] the verb *hupsēlophronō* from existing components. A secular writer might use *megalophronō* in this situation, but Christians preferred a word which manifestly was in contrast with *tapeinophronō* (lowliness of mind), as *hupsēlos* (high) and *tapeinos* (low) are in evident contrast.

Timothy is to charge the rich 'in this present age' not to **be highminded** (1 Ti 6[17]), as if the temptation to this sin came from too much contentment with earthly pleasures. The wise Chrysostom bids his congregation to note St. Paul's phrase, *in this present age.* 'For,' said the preacher, 'there are also riches in the Age to Come!'

The Suidas lexicon (s.v.) equates the verb with *hupsauchō*, which is to carry the neck *high* like a proud bird. It was the reverse of the fear of God, as the Byzantine reading at Ro 11[20] shows: 'Be not highminded but fear'. The better text has two separate words *hupsēla phronei)*, but still the semantic point is not lost. *Hupsēlophronō* is the reverse of reverent fear.

ἐλπίς: ἐλπίζω

All the reserve and nervous fear which lurked in the words, *elpis* and *elpizō*, have disappeared in Christ.

Secular Greek. *Elpis,* the noun, is anxious and cautious optimism about what is to be. *Elpis* is a shadow of doom when the chorus in Euripides cries: 'Upon me and upon my children's children may *elpis* never come!'[48] At best, *elpis* is a rosy look into a sad tomorrow. In the play of Aeschylus the kindly herald trusts that by the providence of Zeus, who cannot yet be resolved to destroy the royal house, 'there is *hope* that Menelaus will arrive home safely'.[49] Plato remarks that each man entertains about the future opinions which go by the name of 'expectations' *(elpis).* Of these, that which precedes pain has the special name of 'fear', and that which precedes pleasure we call 'confidence'.[50]

There are two kinds of *elpis* in secular Greek, one nervous, the hoping against hope, and one optimistic. Sophocles gives the sum of the matter when he makes his chorus say, '*Hope* brings profit to some, emptiness to others, and no one knows how it will turn out'.[51] *Elpis* is man's comfort, for it is his nature to have optimism. Gods were supposed to have given man a casket filled with all good things, and when Pandora opened it from curiosity its contents fled back to the gods, and only *elpis* was trapped beneath the lid, to be man's comfort here below.[52] Plato had great *elpis* (optimism) that when he reached his destination he would attain his chief object.[53] *Elpis* is a mere 'assumption' in some contexts. Plato has the phrase, 'There is a strong *elpis* (presumption) that this class of thing ... is an object of reason alone'.[54] As in English, 'hope' signifies also the object of hope. With the words, 'You are our only *hope!*', the Plataeans addressed Sparta.[55] Orestes was 'the hope'.[56]

So in the verb *elpizō* pessimism and optimism mingle; the dark cloud is edged with silver. It is said that, 'a man of prudence can *hope* for greater things'.[57] In the narrative of Herodotus we read that there was strong optimism, when Maeandrius's brother 'thought it likely' (*elpizō* – he hoped!) that Maeandrius would die.[58] But, in the tragedy of Sophocles, there is almost despair when Teucer 'expected' *(elpizō)* that catastrophe would result from Ajax going abroad.[59] Hope's vitality is seen again when Demosthenes looked on the bright side and 'hoped' in his luck because he had met with no opposition.[60] By contrast, the pessimistic side of *elpizō* appears when a boy writes to his mother in the second century AD: 'I did not *venture to hope* that you would come to town'.[61]

There is little point in searching further through the secular instances of the words, *elpis* and *elpizō*. 'The NT concept of hope is essentially determined by the OT,' observed Bultmann.[62] 'Only where it is a matter of secular hope do we see the element of expectation characteristic of the Greek world, and always in such a way that it is expectation of something welcome. ...'

Biblical Greek. In the LXX noun and verb render in the main the Hebrew *bṭh* stem (seventy-five instances), which is 'trust', mostly trust in God, His name, His mercies, His word and salvation. It is security. In life there is 'security' in the sense that a living dog is better than a dead lion (Eccles 9[4]). The implication is quiet and secure confidence, and not desperate optimism. It is the act of confiding. 'Blessed is the man that maketh the Lord his *hope.*' (Ps 39(40)[4]). Such confidence in God is *elpis,* for He is the God of salvation Who is the *elpis* (confidence) of all the ends of the earth (Ps 64(65)[5]). 'Thou art my Confidant *(elpis)* from my youth' (Ps 70(71)[5]). Only once is *elpis* said to be evil *(ponēros),* and then it means 'fear' (Isai 28[19]). In the OT *elpis* is distinguished from dread. *Elpis* is a yearning, a patient waiting, a fleeing for refuge.[63]

'But,' observed Bultmann, 'hope is not a consoling dream of the imagination which causes us to forget our present troubles, nor are we warned of its uncertainty, as in the Greek world'. If hope goes, all is lost; to have hope is to have a future (Pr 23[18] 24[14] 26[12]; Job 11[18]; Lam 3[18]; Job 6[8] 7[6]). Death takes away all hope (Isai 38[18]; Ezek 37[11]; Job 17[15]). In LXX and NT '*elpizō* has come closer in meaning to *pepoitha* and *pisteuō,*' and has moved away from 'the secular Greek world'.[65]

Christian Greek. For Christian believers hope is a present virtue with future reference. It is their forward look at a distant goal. For Christians, hope is neither optimism nor fear, and doubt has no part in it. Hope is based on religious faith. Hope is very much a Pauline word, never tinged with nervousness or alarm, as in secular contexts. It is not the hoping against all hope, because Christian hope looks forward with joy to the Second Coming (Tit 2[13]; 1 Jn 3[3]), to glory (Col 1[27]), to eternal life (Tit 1[2]), to heaven (Col 1[5]). It has every relevance for faith and living. In 'hope' we believe despite appearances, and rejoice. Insofar as salvation belongs not to the world of visible things and is not yet fully achieved, salvation is matter for 'hope' (Ro 8[24]) – but no less certain for that.

Hope is built on Christian experience (Ro 5[4]). The Scriptures give us hope (Ro 15[4]) and, with faith and love, hope is one of the three 'theological virtues', one of the believer's present endowments (1 Co 13[13]). It is a characteristic which the non-believer does not share (Eph 2[12]; 1 Th 4[13]). But there is a sense in which, whereas faith refers to the past and reposes on the cross of Christ, and love belongs to the present, hope look ahead.[66] The event of the cross cannot, of course, be confined in time; its meaning is ever new. Yet faith must look back to that historic event and stand beside the cross. Hope, on the other hand is centred in what God will do with us and with the world in days to come. Christian hope is always out in the front looking at something good which lies ahead. The Christian believer has hope for the life beyond. Our calling is our hope (Eph 1[18] 4[4]). The Gospel is our hope (Col 1[23]) – the Gospel as proclaimed at Colosse and Ephesus. When we believed the Gospel, 'we at first placed our *hope* in Christ' (Eph 1[12]).

All this we find in Paul, but for the writer to Hebrews too 'hope' brings confidence and joy (Heb 3[6]). 'The Christian hope', wrote Bishop Westcott, 'is one of courageous exultation'.[67] The 'hope' is set before us (Heb 6[18]) as a prize to be awaited for running the race with patience. St. Luke reports the word on St. Paul's lips before the sanhedrin, closely linking it with resurrection, for he claims that the charges made against him concern the 'hope' and the resurrection (Act 23[6] 26[6]). St. Peter makes the claim. In his sermon on the day of Pentecost he quotes David, saying, 'My flesh shall rest in *hope*' (Act 2[26]). Moreover, in his epistles he blesses the God and Father of our Lord Jesus Christ that through the resurrection of Jesus He has begotten us again unto a lively 'hope' (1 Pet 1[3]). He adds that we must always be ready to give an answer to every man that asks a reason for the 'hope' that is in us (3[15]). St. Paul shared with the Pharisees this 'hope toward God' – the future resurrection (Act 24[15]). It is the 'hope' of Israel (Act 28[20]).

Christian hope concerns tomorrow above all things. St. Clement looks to the resurrection and exclaims, 'With this *hope* let our souls cling to Him' (1 Clem 27[1]). Christians, writes St. Ignatius, attained to newness of hope, fashioning themselves after the Lord's Day on which their lives rose through Him (I. Magn. 9[1]).

HOSANNA

ὡσαννά

Hosanna is a coinage of Christian Greek through transliteration either of Hebrew or of Aramaic.

It may be the Hebrew word *hôshî'ânnâ* (Ps 118[25]), which is a strongly expressed imperative of the verb *to save*, rendered in the LXX by *sōson de* (Save now!). The Hebrew expression, *'ānnâ YHWH hôshî'ânnâ*, was a prayer for rain, offered up at the Festival of Sukkoth.[68]

Alternatively, 'hosanna' might be the Aramaic word, *'ûsh'nâ*

215

(power, praise). To suppose a Hebrew derivation, that is, to involve the salvation concept, is to assume that the earliest Christians misapplied a prayer as a cry of greeting. 'The language of the psalm is supplicatory, that of the Gospels is jubilant.'[69] It happens that the Hebrew derivation, with the assumption that Hosanna is a prayer for salvation, is feasible when Hosanna is used in Mk 11[9]; Jn 12[13]. Here the meaning may well be, 'Save us now! The Blessed One comes in the name of the Lord.' Indeed, the cry may have some reference to the glorious name of Jesus (*Y^{e}hôshûa'* or *Yēshûa'*) which is derived from the salvation-stem in Hebrew. Very likely it was a popular cry for national deliverance, as if the poor people were pleading, 'Live up to Thine honoured name, Joshua!'[70] It is suggested that we reconstruct the confused cries of the crowd as: 'Save us now!' 'Blessed is He who comes!' 'Our Father's is the kingdom!' 'The kingdom is David's!' 'Up with your palms!'[71]

However, consider Hosanna in Mt 21[9,15]; Mk 11[10] and the Hebrew derivation is no longer feasible. Here Hosanna cannot be a prayer, it must be a shout of praise. 'Hosanna in the highest! Hosanna to the Son of David!' Such exclamations are not feasible if Hosanna is supposed to be derived from the Hebrew, but they may well reflect the Aramaic *'ûsh^{e}nâ* (Praise!).

At any rate, it is in this latter sense that the glad cry has passed into Christian liturgical use. Outside the Scriptures the sense begins very early with the Didache, 'Hosanna to the God of David!' (10[6]).[72] Hosanna is for Christians a shout of praise rather than a prayer. In the Sanctus (Anglican B.C.P.) is the cry, 'Hosanna in the highest', which derives from the medieval Latin rite, where it is, 'Hosanna in excelsis!'

> Our *glad* hosannas, Prince of peace,
> Thy welcome shall proclaim!

I suppose the Christian word to be a transliteration of Aramaic, rather than Hebrew.

HUMILITY OF MIND

ταπεινοφροσύνη : ταπεινός : ταπεινόφρων : ταπεινόομαι

Secular Greek. The words, *tapeinophrosunē, tapeinos, tapeino-phrōn*, and *tapeinoumai*, were not generally employed in Greek to express lowliness of heart or mind, and that may be why they became characteristic of the vocabulary of the first Christians, for their own *tapeinophrosunē* (humility of mind) was of a different quality and sprang from other motives than the 'mean-spiritedness' indicated by the secular word. As the late Dr. William Barclay observed, *tapeinophrosunē* is the term in which the essential difference of the Christian ethic is collected.[73]

Tapeinophrosunē does not mean for Christians a puny personality,[74] for that would be expressed by something like *oligopsuchos* (feebleminded 1 Th 5[14]) and *asthenō* (weak, Ro 4[19] 14[1]). The counter-sense of *tapeinophrosunē* is in a verb like *hupsēlophronō* (Ro 11[20]; 1 Ti 6[17]). Only in the NT is *tapeinophrosunē* lowliness of mind. Josephus has the typically secular sense of mean-spiritedness when he reports the emperor Galba as charged with this failing by the soldiers.[75] See, 'High-minded, to be.'

Tapeinos in secular Greek was the physically lowly, like flat ground and low-lying rivers[76] but, on the personal side, it was 'humbled' or 'abased'. Clearchus reassured Tissaphernes, 'The Mysians who are troublesome to you, with our present troops I think I could render *tapeinos* towards you.'[77] It is small, poor, weak or submissive,[78] and sometimes, in low estate or obscurity.[79] 'Your mind is too much *depressed* to persevere in your resolves', Pericles informed the people of Athens at the second Peloponnesian invasion,[80] and often the word indicates what is mean or debased.[81] Seldom outside the NT is it 'humble' in a noble sense.[82]

Nor do the remaining words fare better. *Tapeinophrōn* is 'base' or 'mean-spirited'. Plutarch lists it with 'petty' and 'timorous', in a poor light,[83] and only in the Bible (Pr 29[23]; 1 Pet 3[8]) has it the good sense of 'lowly in mind'.

The verb *tapeinō*, besides being physically to lower or make smaller in size,[84] has among the several metaphorical usages very few which are good, for they generally amount to disparagement and abasement.[85] The dejection of Tiberius (expressed by the perf. pass. ptc.) at the loss of the money he once had, represents Josephus's use of the verb.[86] A new sense in the LXX is that of the violation of women (Gen 34[2]; 2 Km 13[12,14]; Ezek 22[10f.]).

It is clear that when the words were used in secular Greek they had a craven or at least a mean-spirited connotation. That sense survives when St. Paul echoes the taunts of foes at Corinth who had mis-termed his appearance as *tapeinos* (2 Co 10[1]).

Biblical Greek. But, as often, the early Christians enhanced a word of diminished meaning to the rank of a new virtue. *Tapeinos* is no longer base. For Christians its opposite, pride, is base. Jesus was *tapeinos* in heart (Mt 11[29]), and God resists the proud, giving grace to the *tapeinos* (Jas 4[6]; 1 Pet 5[5]; cit. LXX Pr 3[34]). So with the Christian verb: '*Be humble* ... that He may exalt you' (1 Pet 5[6]; Jas 4[10]).

Christians have found a contrast with pride in the *tapeinos*-stem

217

of the Greek Bible, commonly rendering the Hebrew *spl*-stem, and *tapeinophrōn* renders *shᵉphal rûaḥ* (humble in spirit). 'A man's pride shall bring him low: but honour shall uphold the *tapeinophronas*' (Pr 29[23]). In the Greek Bible, *tapeinos* is used of the oppressed *(dakh)* whom the Lord will champion (Ps 9[39] (10[18])) and of the afflicted *('ānî)* and needy *(dal)* to whom the Lord is a strength (Ps 17(18)[27]; Isai 14[32] 25[4]). God accepts the *tapeinoumenos* (pres. ptc. pass.)[87] – the **humble-minded** man.

Christian Greek. All the Biblical precedent was at hand for early Christians when they rejected the pejorative sense of the secular words. The new virtue was 'not merely a grace, but the casket in which all other graces are contained'.[88] God exalted the Virgin, the *tapeinos* (Lk 1[52]), for He condescends to and comforts the *tapeinos*, giving him grace (Ro 12[16]; 2 Co 7[6]; Jas 4[6]; 1 Pet 5[5]). Let the brother who is *tapeinos* rejoice, he has a very high estate (Jas 1[9]). Only twice is *tapeinophrosunē* intended in a bad sense (Col 2[18, 23]); the heretics at Colosse had gone too far. However, even in these instances, the paraded humility of mind was indeed a 'show of wisdom' – one of the few good things about the heretics.

Everywhere it is Christian virtue adorning all service within Christ's Body (Act 20[19]). However the heretics paraded, the Colossian believers must put on *tapeinophrosunē* (3[12]). No 'walk' worthy of the Christian vocation, is complete without it (Eph 4[2]). It is the well-seen contrast to strife and vainglory (Ph 2[3]). No man acts as master in the Christian assembly, everyone is subject to his brother, everyone has *tapeinophrosunē* (1 Pet 5[5]). Everyone **humbles himself** (verb: Mt 18[4] 23[12]; Lk 14[11] 18[14]; Jas 4[10]; 1 Pet 5[6]), as Christ **humbled Himself** (Ph 2[8]). The verb, with its suggestion of abatement and deprivation (LXX Isai 58[10], NT Ph 4[12]), comes in later Jewish Greek to have the meaning 'to fast'.[89]

The noun appears as lowliness of mind in the apostolic Fathers,[90] and the adjective *tapeinophrōn* has the same sense.[91] St. Clement notes that Esther, with fasting and *tapeinōsis* (humility before God) besought that all-seeing Master and He rescued the people when He saw the humility *(to tapeinon)* of Esther's soul (55[6]); he notes that Jacob departed from his country in *tapeinophrosunē* (31[4]). St. Clement commends ministers who with *tapeinophrosunē* tend the Flock (44[3]). This quality, with eager gentleness, leads to enrolment within the number of the saints (58[2]). 'Thou shalt not exalt thyself,' writes another Father, 'but shalt be *tapeinophrōn* in all things' (Barn. 19[3]) Christian converse must be with the *tapeinos* and the righteous man (19[6], Did 3[9]). According to Hermas, such a virtue goes closely with fasting: 'every prayer needs *tapeinophrosunē*. Fast therefore'. (*Vis.* III, 10.6). The Christian who is *tapeinophrōn* and who is meek and gentle, has the Spirit from above (*Mand.* XI 8).

HYPOCRISY

1. HYPOCRITE, WICKED

ὑποκριτής

Hupokritēs has changed its meaning in a perceptible way. In secular Greek it was often an 'interpreter', for Plato speaks of a tribe of prophets who are to pass judgment upon inspired divinations, not being diviners themselves but 'interpreters' of the mysterious voice and apparition.[92] Besides, Lucian uses the word for an interpreter of dreams.[93]

More often in classical Greek *hupokritēs* is an actor, that is, an interpreter on the stage. Plato speaks of 'actors', along with rhapsodists, chorus-dancers, and others.[94] 'Upon the platform with your *actors:*' these are the words of Socrates to the dramatist, Agathon.[95] Xenophon refers to 'actors' in a tragedy, abusing one another without harm.[96]

In the Biblical language the new meaning is profane and godless, for *hupokritēs* renders the Hebrew *ḥānēph* (Job 34[30] 36[13], and elsewhere in later versions). Jesus applied the epithet to the scribes and Pharisees, who 'sound trumpets' before they give alms (Mt 6[2]), annulling the law of God by their traditions (15[7]), unable to discern the signs of the times (16[3]), devouring widows' houses and making long prayers (23[13f.]), fussing at small things and forgetting the momentous (23[23]). Does the diction of Jesus reflect the later meaning of the Hebrew *ḥānēph*?

An indignant synagogue official, aggrieved because Jesus broke the sabbath, is called *hupokritēs* (Lk 13[15]). The disciples, when they condemn their own faults in their brethren, earn the same reproach (Mt 7[5]; Lk 6[42]). It amounts incidentally to being a 'hypocrite', but only incidentally, for *hupokritēs* was used by Christians – as in the LXX – of ungodliness in general. U. Wilckens has pointed out that in virtually the whole of Jewish Greek literature a use of *hupokrinomai/hupokrisis* is found which essentially differs from that of classical and Hellenistic secular writers. The word in Jewish Greek represents a form of wrong-doing and there is no question of presenting a good appearance so that the true character is disguised. Hypocrisy is only incidental. What is meant is opposition to God. Wilckens observes that the Greek word is remarkable as a translation of the Hebrew, insofar as nothing in secular Greek tradition suggests that the 'evil doer' (the *ḥānēph*) ought to be translated into Greek by *hupokritēs* (actor), and nothing in the Hebrew words for 'evil doing' suggests that it ought to be regarded as 'acting'.[97] It should be noticed, however, that the same stem *ḥnp* (Hiphil) in later Hebrew does indeed bear the meaning of flattery

219

and insincerity.[98] Perhaps that late meaning itself arose from the fact that *hupokritēs* had been used to render the Hebrew stem. If so, it is testimony to the power of the Greek Bible to influence the course of the language subsequently. Besides, it has given a new word to our own language, 'hypocrite'. In later Greek, and in the modern language, *hupokrinomai* is to dissemble and *hupokritēs* is a hypocrite.

It still holds good that 'hypocrisy' is only incidental to the NT meaning of the word. In the Servants' parable there was one who was not ready for his Lord's Coming: his portion was set to be with the *hupokritai* (Mt 24[51]). These are not 'hypocrites'. They must be the 'wicked' for, as Hatch observed, it would be mere 'bathos' to render the word 'false pretenders'.[99]

It is the meaning 'wicked' which continues in the apostolic Fathers, for certain teachers who introduced strange doctrines were *hupokritai*.[100] There is the compound phrase, '*hupokritai* and teachers of wickedness' (*Sim.* IX 19.2), and Hermas collates the wicked, the blasphemers, and *hupokritai* (IX 18.3). The Didache classes them with the covetous and extortionate (2[6]) but later, as in the gospels, Jews seem to be in mind, for the *hupokritai* are those who fast on Mondays and Thursdays, whereas Christians fast on Wednesdays. His readers must recite the Lord's Prayer and not pray as the *hupokritai* (8[1,2]). Both meanings, **hypocrite** and **wicked,** were evidently current in Christian Greek but the latter is more prominent.

The noun *hupokrisis* (iniquity), moreover, came to lose the denotation of acting. Again we stand on the reasoning of Hatch (op. cit. p. 93): 'In the denunciations of the Scribes and Pharisees which both precede and follow this verse [i.e. Mt 23[28]], the point seems to be not merely that they were false pretenders but that they were positively irreligious.' In Mk 12[15] *hupokrisis* is the equivalent of malice and wickedness, as the parallels in Matthew and Luke reveal. The disciples are to be ware of the *zumē* (bad influence) of the Pharisees which is *hupokrisis* (Lk 12[1]). Some[101] see this bad influence indicated passively in verses 13–40 (i.e. covetousness and general worldliness), and actively in verses 41–59 (i.e. persecution).

2. EYE-SERVICE

ὀφθαλμοδουλεία (-ία)

Ophthalmodouleia is a Christian coinage to distinguish the characteristic virtue of seeking to please the Lord Jesus rather than men. It is a word peculiarly St. Paul's. Servants are to obey their masters, but as if they were serving Christ, 'not with *eye-service* as men-pleasers' (Eph 6[5f.]; Col 3[22]).

The association with the 'eye' may be interpreted either as referring to the time when the master's eye is upon the servant, or as referring to what the eye can or cannot see, in fact, to external matters as opposed to sincere service.[102]

3. MEN-PLEASER, FLATTERER

ἀνθρωπάρεσκος

Anthrōpareskos is a formation of Biblical Greek from existing words. The LXX has it to render *ḥnp* (profane), a reading for *ḥnk* (him that encamped against Thee, Ps 52(53)[6]). We recollect that *ḥnp* is rendered also by *hupokritēs* (impious, Job 34[30] 36[13]), and so in Biblical Greek *anthrōpareskos* is a near synonym of *hupokritēs*. The Hiphil of *ḥnp* in later Hebrew means to flatter or to be insincere.[103]

Our word appears in the Psalms of Solomon. The men so signified, probably the Sadducees, are held in scorn (4[8]), for they interpret the Law deceitfully. In our parlance, they are 'hypocrites'.

For the Deissmann school the coinage had little significance. 'If this is a "Biblical" word it is only an instance of the fact that every Greek writer made a new compound when his meaning required one.' (MM). Nevertheless, only Biblical and Jewish authors did make this particular compound.

The meaning, hypocrite, well suits St. Paul's words: servants must obey their masters, not as 'pleasing men', but primarily as servants of Christ (Eph 6[6]; Col 3[22]). They must not strive to please those who are in superior authority.[104]

Discussing the impression made by Christians on the outsider the author of 2 Clement says, 'Let us not be *anthrōpareskoi*; let us wish to please by our righteousness not ourselves alone but also outsiders, that the Name be not blasphemed' (13[1]).

The Apostolic Constitutions lay down that a bishop must be 'gentle, gracious, mild ... not *anthrōpareskos*, not timorous' (II 21.1).

The connection with *hupokritēs* is clear when St. Cyril of Jerusalem qualifies the *anthrōpareskos* as seeking favour of men and making a pretence of piety without believing from the heart.[105] St. Chrysostom sees the quality as 'vainglorious', contrasted with what is 'merciful' and 'kind'.[106] The apologist, Theophilus of Antioch, in the second century says that Jesus taught the do-gooders not to boast, not to be *anthrōpareskoi*.[107] It has the same meaning as Chrysostom's – to make a boast of piety.

The idea of 'flattery' lingers in the abstract noun, and for St. Justin Martyr *anthrōpareskeia deisidaimonōn* is a 'desire to flatter' the superstitious (Apol. 2[3]). The verb, a hapax, is used by St. Ignatius. 'I would not have you *to be men-pleasers* but to please God.' (I. Rom 2[1]). Lightfoot was aware that 'this family of words seems to be confined to biblical and ecclesiastical Greek'.[108]

NOTES

[1] *Timaeus* 69B, 39D.

[2] *Nicomachean Ethics* 1141a 20.

[3] S. Bedale, S.S.M., *Journal of Theological Studies*, NS 5 (1954), pp. 211ff. See also ch. 5 in F. L. Cross, *Studies in Ephesians*, Mowbray 1956.

[4] Bedale, op. cit., p. 214.

[5] C. F. Burney, *Journal of Theological Studies* 27 (1926), pp. 16ff., esp. p. 177.

[6] PG LXI 38, LXII 412.

[7] Themistius *Orationes* XIII 166b (iv AD).

[8] Which is 'wrapped in clouds', Homer *Iliad* XV 192, *Odyssey* V 303.

[9] *Iliad* I 497, VIII 394, XIX 129.

[19] *Prometheus Bound* 897.

[11] Hesiod *Theogonia* (Teubner 127).

[12] The other instances of plural in LXX are: 2 Chr 28[9]; Neh 9[6]; Tob 8[5]; Jdt 9[12] 13[18]; Job 16[20(19)AB]; Ps 2[4] 8[1,3] 32(33)[6] 49(50)[6] 56(57)[3,10,11] 67(68)[8] 68(69)[34] 88(89)[2,5,11] 95(96)[5,11] 96(97)[6] 101(102)[25] 107(108)[4f.] 112(113)[4] 135(136)[5] 143(144)[5] 148[4] (heaven of heavens); Pr 3[19] 8[26]B; Wis 9[10,16] 18[15]; Hb 3[3]; Isai 34[4]B; Ezek 1[1]; Dan LXX 3[17,59]; Th 3[17(59)]; 2 Mac 15[23]; 3 Mac 2[2]. See F. Torm, *Zeitschrift für die Neutestamentliche Wissenschaft* (Berlin) 33 (1934), pp. 48–50, who argues that the plural is poetic.

[13] See the rabbinical tractate, *Chagigah* 12.

[14] Other examples of plural, where only one of the heavens is involved, are very few: Mt 24[31] (but sing. in Mk's parallel), Lk 21[26] (and Mk 13[25]: are they the stars?).

[15] For the grammatical considerations of number, see Moulton-Turner, *Grammar* III, p. 25.

[16] *Bereshith rabba* c. 6, *Bammidhbar rabba* c. 17, *Chagigah* 12 b.

[17] Slavonic Enoch 8.

[18] Chrysostom *Hom. in Gen.* iv 3.

[19] D 258 1093 1241 abdhk Syr[cur.sin.pesh.hark].

[20] Aristotle *Nicomachean Ethics* IV 1 A.

[21] Polybius VI 11 A; BGU 1058.35.

[22] *Problemata* 952 b 27.

[23] Preisendanz 4. 1247f.

[24] A. Oepke in Kittel *TWNT* I, p. 395.

[25] Ethiopic Enoch 27[2].

[26] Talmud tractate *Erubin* 19a, *Succah* 32b, *Sotah* 4b, *Rosh hash-Shanah* 17a.

[27] 4 Ezra 7[36] (Bensley).

[28] Aeschylus *Supplices* 470. Also 1058: 'How shall I scan the mind of Zeus, a sight *unfathomable*?'

[29] Euripides *Phoenissae* 1605.

[30] Aeschylus *Seven against Thebe* 948; Aristophanes *Lysistratus* 174.

[31] Aristophanes *Frogs* 137.

[32] P Mag Paris I 1120.

[33] The LXX has it besides to render the Hebrew *Raḥabh*, the sea-monster broken in pieces by the Lord of Hosts, and also *mᵉṣûlâ* and *ṣûlâ*" the depths of the sea: Job 36[16] 41[22]; Isai 44[27].

[34] As T. Sol 2[8] BC.

[35] Fragm. 11 in Job. Also in Origen *Homily 6, in Luc.*

[36] Eusebius, *Historia Ecclesiastica* I 13.20.

[37] *Verbum Domini* (Rome) 42 (1964), pp. 225–40.

[38] Bo Reicke, *The Disobedient Spirits and Christian Baptism*, Copenhagen 1946, p. 113.

[39] Ragnar Leivestad, *Christ the Conqueror*, SPCK 1954, pp. 172f.

[40] But the compound with *kata-* appears in Sextus Empiricus (ii AD).

[41] Enoch 20[2]. LXX of Job 41[23] refers to Tartarus of the *abussos*. See 'Hell (the Bottomless Pit)'.

[42] Pseudo-Plato *Definitiones* 412A.

[43] *Ethische Elementarlehre nebst den bei Stobäus erhaltenen ethischen Exzerpten aus Hierokles*, ed. H. von Arnim, Berlin 1906, p. 40f.

[44] R. Falconer, *The Pastoral Epistles*, Clarendon 1937, p. 117.

[45] A. S. Wood, *Theological Student Fellowship Bulletin* (London) 67 (1973), 9–15, 68 (1974), 1–6.

[46] M. Dibelius and Hans Conzelmenn, *The Pastoral Epistles*, ET, Fortress, Philadelphia, 1972, p. 151.

[47] Pollux is post-Christian (AD ii): ix 145.

[48] *Iphigeneia in Aulis* 786.

[49] *Agamemnon* 679.

[59] *Laws* 644C.

[51] *Antigone* 615ff.

[52] Hesiod *Works and Days* 94ff.

[53] *Phaedo* 67B.

[54] *Laws* 898D.

[55] Thucydides III 57.

[56] Aeschylus *Choephori* 776.

[57] Xenophon *Memorabilia* IV 3.17.

[58] Herodotus III 143.

[59] *Ajax* 799.

[60] Thucydides III 97.

[61] BGU 846. See Deissmann LAE, pp. 176ff.

[62] R. Bultmann in Kittel *TWNT* II, p. 527.

[63] Ibid., pp. 518f.

[64] Op. cit., p. 519.

[65] *Encyclopedia of Biblical Theology* ed. J. B. Bauer, ET Sheed and Ward 1970, vol. I, p. 377.

[66] Emil Brunner, *Faith, Hope and Love*, Lutterworth 1957, passim.

[67] B. F. Westcott, *The Epistle to the Hebrews*, Macmillan 1889, p. 78.

[68] J. J. Petuchowski, *Vetus Testamentum* 5 (1955), pp. 266–71.

[69] J. H. Thayer in HDB II, p. 418b.

[70] F. D. Coggan, *Expository Times* 52 (1940), pp. 76f.

[71] F. C. Burkitt, *Journal of Theological Studies* 17 (1916), p. 145.

[72] See H. B. Swete, *The Gospel according to St. Mark*, Macmillan 2nd ed. 1902, p. 251.

[73] *Expository Times*, 70 (1958), p. 6.

[74] See the interesting note by D. Fyffe, *Expository Times* 35 (1924), pp. 377–9.

[75] *Bell. Jud.* IV ix 2 (Niese IV 494). Same meaning, Arrian *Epictetus* III 24.56.
[76] Herodotus IV 191; Pindar *Nemean Ode* 3.82; Polybius IX 43.3.
[77] Xenophon *Anabasis* II 5.13. Same meaning Herodotus VII 14.
[78] Isocrates IV 95; Xenophon *Hiero* V 4.
[79] Isocrates V 64; Plutarch *Theseus* 6.
[80] Thucydides II 61.
[81] Plato *Laws* 791D.
[82] Plato *Laws* 716A; Xenophon *Cyropaedia* V 1.5.
[83] *Moralia* 336E.
[84] E.g. passively of a river, Diodorus Siculus I 36.
[85] Polybius VI 15.7; Xenophon *Anabasis* VI 3.18.
[86] *Ant. Jud.* XVIII vi 2 (Niese XVIII 147).
[87] *Letter of Aristeas* 257.
[88] Trench (p. 140), quoting St. Basil.
[89] SIG 1181.11 (ii AD).
[90] 1 Clem 21^8 30^8 56^1.
[91] 1 Clem 19^1 38^1; I. Eph 10^2.
[92] *Timaeus* 72 B.
[93] *Somnium* 17.
[94] *Republic* 373B.
[95] *Symposium* 194B.
[96] *Memorabilia* II 2.9.
[97] In Kittel *TWNT* VIII s.v. B.3.
[98] Jastrow, pp. 481f.
[99] Edwin Hatch *Essays in Biblical Greek*, Clarendon 1889, p. 97.
[100] Hermas *Sim.* VIII 6.5.
[101] D. Bertrand, in *Christus* (Paris) 21 (1974), pp. 323–33.
[102] *Expository Times*, 59 (1947), p. 250.
[103] Jastrow, pp. 484ff.
[104] W. Foerster in Kittel *TWNT* I, p. 456.
[105] *Catecheses* III 7.
[106] *Homily* XXI 4 in Matth.
[107] *Against Autolycus* III 14.
[108] J. B. Lightfoot, *Apostolic Fathers*, part II, vol. II, p. 197.

I

ICON

εἰκών

Here is an old Greek word transformed into a significant term of
Christian theology, that Image of God which Jesus bore, which
man had lost at the Fall.

Secular Greek. In classical Greek *eikōn* signified the likeness of a
person, whether in the form of picture or statue or bust.[1] Readers of
Medea will remember the irony of the girl smiling at her lifeless
eikōn in the mirror.[2] The word was used sometimes of a verbal
image, a similitude or comparison. 'To speak by *eikōn*', was to use a
parable.[3] However, even in some of its pagan references, *eikōn*
signified rather more than mere image; it included the notion of
derivation from an archetype, especially when it was the portrait on
a coin, the parent's likeness on a child, or the Emperor's image on a
banner. The Jews very much resented the Roman banners, as in
some cities such icons had been placed among the rest of the local
gods.[4]

By banners and rings, like that engraved with the *eikōn* of Caius
Caesar,[5] it was felt that in some way the Emperor was really
present. In certain instances the *eikōn* was reported not to have
been made with mortal hands but to have descended straight from
heaven, like those of Artemis at Ephesus and Tauris.[6] In some sense
the *eikōn* was 'alive' *(zōsa)*, for on the Rosetta Stone, of second
century BC, Ptolemy Philopator is said to be 'the living *eikōn* of
Zeus'.[7] That is how Philo had described the Word – the *eikōn* of
God.[8]

Christian Greek. Into this ready pagan mould St. Paul poured the
wealth of his own Biblical Greek heritage and affirmed that Christ
was the *eikōn* of God (2 Co 4[4]; Col 1[15]), by which he intended God's
very being, expecting also that man was to be transfigured into, or
would wear, the *eikōn* of God or of the Son of God (Ro 8[29]; 2 Co
3[18]; Col 3[10]). He thus re-orientated the word, and so *eikōn* in
Christian Greek has a fuller definition than in the classical and
Hellenistic languages. The Christian increment is explained by the
use of *eikōn* in the Greek Genesis to render *ṣelem* and *dᵉmûth*,
where the Hebrew words express the 'image' of God infixed on man
at creation. The link between *eikōn* and creation is absent from
secular contexts, not even appearing in Philo, while it has much
prominence in the sacred Greek which is St. Paul's linguistic
milieu. It enters because of the Biblical premise that man, lost, or
rather defaced and corrupted, the *imago dei* which graced his

creation – a Pauline emphasis, quite alien to pagan ideas. In the Pauline letters, *eikōn* has acquired a novel definition.

The *eikōn* and the *doxa* (glory) which were man's initially and were lost subsequently, to be regained in progressive degrees through sanctification, illustrate the close association of the two words (1 Co 11[7]; 2 Co 3[18] 4[4]); for *doxa* too acquired new meaning in Biblical Greek (i.e. visible brightness) through LXX influence. *Doxa* was something in the nature of a visible badge to be shared hereafter by Christians (Ro 8[18-21]; 2 Ti 2[10], etc.) – a bright vesture or resurrection body (1 Cor 15[41]; 2 Co 3[18] 5[1-4]), the lost *imago dei*.

Church Greek. In this rich ground the early Christians sowed the seeds of a subtle theology which was to animate Byzantine art.[9] Significantly, even in its buildings and ministers the later Church revealed herself as the Icon of God. The portative portrait images of Orthodox liturgical painting were to be known by the very name which St. Paul had used both of Christ as the perfect Icon of God (2 Co 3[18]; Col 1[15]) and of the divine Icon which His saints shall one day bear (Ro 8[29]; Col 3[10]).

The Christian image-theology may not derive exclusively from St. Paul. As E. M. Sidebottom demonstrated, St. John also 'moved in circles where the Image was a common idea', howbeit avoiding the word *eikōn* itself. A similar use of *eikōn* 'appears in the Gnostic systems which are related to Christianity, for instance the Barbelo-gnostics, for whom the Ennoia, Barbelo, was the Image of the Invisible'.[10] But its full flowering is Christian.

The subsequent Church adopted the Pauline *eikōn*, rather than the word *charactēr* (Heb 1[3]), as the more significant term. The former traces a direct descent back through Philo and Wisdom ultimately to Genesis and, besides, *charactēr* was basically unsuitable in that it suggests a graven image, by derivation from *charassō*, to engrave, i.e. a statue, rather than a linear represen-tation. Its use would therefore give the unfortunate impression that the material from which the image is graven – man's potentially fallen nature – has material likeness to divinity. *Eikōn* leaves more room for a spaceless, etherial and linear interpretation than does the grossness of *charactēr*.

It is not so easy to see why the synonym *morphē* was not adopted for 'image'. Dr. R. P. Martin has shown that *morphē* in Ph 2[5-11] is a synonym of *eikōn*.[11] 'It would seem clear,' he writes, 'that the two concepts, "image", "likeness", must be taken as synonyms.' The simple expedient of so taking them, he notes, 'cuts through a veritable jungle of complexity by opening up a straight path', in the Philippian passage. So, 'Christ, being in the *image* of God, did not consider equality with God something to be seized'. Both words in the LXX, *morphē* and *eikōn*, had rendered the Hebrew words, *ṣelem* and *d^emûth*. It is just that the Church preferred *eikōn* when she might have chosen *morphē*.

Eikōn has many resemblances, too, with the word *antitupon*. Both are exact copies, identical correspondences; only *antitupon* has a more direct reference than *eikōn* to the details of holy Scripture as prefiguring the real Archetypes which were to come. See also 'Figure'.

IDOL

εἴδωλον

In the Bible *eidōlon* is both the image of a pagan deity and often the god himself.

Secular Greek. Whereas *eidōlon* had been only a phantom or a semblance, like a corpse when the soul has departed, the soul making us what we are and the body being but a likeness *(eidōlon)*,[12] nevertheless *eidōlon* became a different word in holy Scripture. Certainly in a late inscription it is used of images of heathen gods, but not until the sixth century when there had been plenty of time for Jewish and Christian influence to work on secular vocabulary.[13] Polybius uses *agalma* for an 'image' of the gods, but in the same passage he has *eidōlon* for a 'likeness' of gods and spirits and heroes, draped in garments and moulded according to the various myths of the gods. 'Following them came a representation *(eidōlon)* of Night and Day.' These are scarcely 'images' of pagan deities in the Biblical sense. *Eidōlon* here is rather a 'semblance' or a 'depiction'.[14]

Biblical Greek. The new meaning was that of an 'image' of heathen deities – an **idol.** In some contexts it is not apparent whether *eidōlon* signified also the deities themselves. What is true of *eidōlon* is true too of the several compounds, all bearing the new sense. See, 'Idol's temple', 'Idolatry', and 'Taint of idolatry'.

In the Greek OT the word translates the Hebrew *gillûlîm* (images) in the situation of idolatry, as when God warns Israel, 'I will cut down your *idols*', and forbids Israel to 'serve *doll-images*' (Heinrich Ewald's rendering).[15] The word translates also *t^erāphîm*, a kind of **household god** which Rachel stole from her father (Gen 31), and also *'āṣābh*,[16] especially the graven **idols** of silver and gold.

In the NT *eidōlon* embraces both the image of the pagan god and the god itself.[17] In the secular sense of 'image' St. Stephen uses *eidōlon* of the golden calf (Act 7[41]). In the same sense, the Corinthian believers were in former days 'carried away unto these dumb *idols*', when they were pagan Gentiles (1 Co 12[2]). In the

227

same sense, the Seer foresees idols – wood, brass, stone, gold and silver – as part of man's idolatrous heathenism at the End (Rev 9[20]). They all refer to the material 'image', but the idol-pollution mentioned at the council of Jerusalem is a reference to personal 'Deities' (Act 15[20]). The Jew seeking justification by his own merits is challenged: 'Thou that abhorrest *idols,* dost thou commit sacrilege?' (Ro 2[22]). St. Paul may infer that when Jews raided temples to topple idols under cover of the second Commandment, their hatred was not for images as much as for false 'gods', and he may understand *eidōlon* to mean a deity. The apostle has the same turn of thought again, reasoning 'that an *idol* is nothing in the world, and that there is none other god but one' (1 Co 8). An idol is very real to some weak brethren who suffer in conscience by eating an idol's offering. *Eidōlon,* in these instances, means the 'god'. Even St. Paul, who confesses that an idol is nothing, has the strong feeling that a Christian must not eat at the table of devils (1 Co 10[20]). On a further occasion he refers to idols as personal (2 Co 6[16]), from whose worship one turns to God (1 Th 1[9]), and it is against something decidedly personal and devilish that St. John warns his 'little children' to keep themselves from *eidōla* (pagan deities): 1 Jn 5[21].

IDOLATROUS

κατείδωλος

There are no secular examples of this exclusively Christian word (Bauer, MM). *Kateidōlos* was coined from existing material, but it reflects the new Biblical meaning of *eidōlon* (see above). It may be the expression of St. Luke's horror at Athenian superstition (Act 17[16]), for he reports St. Paul as troubled to see the city 'full of idols' (RV, RSV, NEB). The word's meaning may well be stronger: 'wholly give to idolatry' (AV), 'given over to idolatry' (Knox, Jerusalem), 'given over to idols' (BFBS).

TO BE IDOLATROUS

σεβάζομαι

In Homer *sebazomai* meant to fear, but later it meant to worship. It was, however, a rare word, taking the place of the more regular *sebomai,* and is almost exclusively Jewish and Christian. It is a forceful word.

The Sibylline oracles mention 'worshipping' of gold ornaments to lead souls astray (5^{405}) and mention 'worship' of the gods of Rome (8^{46}), using *sebazomai*. Elsewhere, apart from St. Paul's application to pagan 'idolatry' (Ro 1^{25}), it is used by Aquila (Hos 10^5) for the 'worshipping' of calves, by the Christian apologist Aristides for the 'worshipping' of sheep by certain pagans (xii 7), and by the oracle of Apollo as quoted by Eusebius of Caesarea,[18] to the effect that only Chaldeans and Hebrews 'worship' the true God in a chaste fashion. The oracle, however, did not use the word in the strongly pejorative sense favoured by Christians and Jews.

IDOLATRY, IDOLATOR

εἰδωλολατρία: εἰδωλολάτρης

Eidōlolatria and *eidōlolatrēs* are words coined in Christian Greek.[19] *Eidōlolatria* (idolatry) is one of the works of the flesh contrasted with the fruits of the Spirit, along with witchcraft, adultery, drunkenness and many others (Gal $5^{19ff.}$). It was a hurtful sin at Corinth, defiling the Lord's Table (1 Co $10^{7,14}$). It includes not just the worship of idols but, more subtely, covetousness (Eph 5^5 vl; Col 3^5), since twice for the Corinthians the Apostle links idolatry and avarice together as sins of this world – not to be tolerated, and for which a brother must be put out of Christian fellowship (1 Co $5^{10f.}$ $6^{9f.}$).

St. Chrysostom suggested a reason why the apparently lesser evil is closely linked with the apparently grosser: idolatry may appear to be the worse sin but idolaters do at least worship the handiwork of God; on the other hand, covetousness can have no plea of that kind and is without excuse.[20] Idolatry and covetousness were two notorious sins, at all events, in the Gentile world; they appalled St. Peter too for he classes 'abominable idolatries' along with lusts and carousings (1 Pet 4^3). The apostolic Father places *eidōlolatria* alongside adultery, murder, witchcraft, magic and covetousness (Barn 20^1; So Did 5^1).

The idolater *(eidōlolatrēs)* has his fearful lot in the 'second death' in contrast with the Christian overcomer. The idolater is excluded from heaven's Jerusalem along with other gross sinners, sorcerers and whores (Rev 21^8 22^{15}).

Little wonder if some lexicographers suggest that in this sort of Greek the words refer to a sin of Christians, not so much a worshipping of idols but a scorning of chastity,[21] one of the evils that destroy the soul (Barn 20^1; Did 5^1).

εἰδωλεῖον: εἰδωλόθυτον

There are no instances of *eidōleion,* an idol's temple, or of *eidōlothuton,* an idol's offering, in profane Greek. They arise from the LXX (1 Esd 2[10]; Dan LXX 1[2]; Bel 9; 1 Mac 1[47] 10[83]; 4 Mac 5[2]) and become significant for Christians.

It was evidently the practice of some early believers from time to time to 'sit at meat' in the idol's temple; in itself clearly not harmful, for an idol had no real existence, the indiscretion had nevertheless scandalized some 'weak' brethren (1 Co 8[10]), and Gentile believers had already been forbidden by the meeting at Jerusalem to partake of the *eidōlothuton* (Act 15[29] 21[25]). St. Paul counsels the brethren at Corinth to give no offence in this matter, even if they think they have 'knowledge'. Better to exercise Christian love and avoid upsetting the conscience of other believers (1 Co 8, 10[19]). See, 'Offence'.

These other believers, the 'weak' brethren, are probably Jewish Christians who could not conscientiously abandon the observance of the Law in such matters as clean and unclean foods, blood, the sabbath and special days.[22] Many take this view, but the matter is seen differently by others. The distinction of weak and strong, so it is thought, rests rather on social differentiation, the 'weak' being the lower orders within the local church who would not in the normal way, apart from religious feasts, have flesh in their diet, and the 'strong' being the better-off at Corinth who might often enjoy meat. It is thought that Gnostics of a later period affirmed their emancipation by eating sacrificial meat, such Gnostics being among the social élite at Corinth, for whose benefit St. Paul may have wished to ease a difficulty and so distinguishes between meals partaken in official cultic settings (e.g. 'in the idol's temple' 1 Co 8[10]) and meals consumed in private houses to which one may be invited and where sacrificial joints may be served (10[25f.]). St. Paul permits the eating of *eidōlothuton* in the latter circumstance, but in the former directs that care be taken not to scandalize the 'weak', the lower class, brother.[23]

Members of the churches at Pergamum and Thyatira were taking this meat and were strongly condemned for it (Rev 2[14, 20]). Dinners might be given by city trade guilds, and some church members might find it beneficial to attend. Perhaps the animals sacrificed to idols in temples were then sold cheaply on the market, the 'shambles', and poorer brethren were glad to pitch upon a bargain. It has been observed[24] that the Life of Aesop, probably AD i in Egypt, described Aesop as buying the tongues of sacrificial pigs at the butchers' shops (*Vita Aesopi* 51). Whatever the practice, it was condemned by the Seer.

Some have suspected that St. Paul's attitude was rather different, not wholly condemnatory since an idol was already stripped of power. Still he felt that excessive liberalism went too far and he maintained a middle position – 'the tight-rope between the legalism of Jewish Christianity and the false liberalism of gnostic rationalism'.[25]

At all events, the practice continued to give offence. The Didache used the word *eidōlothuton* when enjoining strict abstention 'from *that which is offered to idols,* for it is the worship of dead gods' (6³).

IDOL-POLLUTION

ἀλίσγημα

Alisgēma is a new word in Christian Greek, and the verb *alisgō* (to make ceremonially unclean) is a LXX creation referring especially to food. *Alisgēma* is found in the apostolic decrees formulated at Jerusalem to the effect that Gentile Christians should abstain from *alisgēmata* (pollutions) of idols (Act 15²⁰).

What is meant? Perhaps it was the meat sold on the market cheaply, having previously been offered up in an idol's temple. The lexicons of Suidas and Hesychius define the word as 'pollution from sacrifices to idols'.

Ritual pollution, not the moral kind, is meant. Nevertheless, it was a moral issue among early Christians. A 'weak' brother might damage his tender conscience through involvement with such **idol-pollutions.**

IMPENITENT

ἀμετανόητος

Ametanoētos, like the positive word 'repentance' (q.v.), has acquired a new direction in Christian Greek and in the Testaments of the Twelve Patriarchs. Its secular meaning is the same as *ametamelētos* (irrevocable, unregretted),[26] but in the NT it has gained the active sense of 'unrepentant' (Ro 2⁵), of which there are very few instances elsewhere. There is one in a *good* sense, 'free from remorse', very different from that of St. Paul.[27]

The NT context speaks of the unbeliever whose impenitence

invites God's wrath. The Testament of Gad, too, warns that 'the *impenitent* is reserved for eternal punishment' (7⁵). The new active sense of impenitence, arising in the NT and Jewish Greek, appears later in the Church.[28]

The religious understanding of Judaism and early Christianity gave a novel sense to *metanoia* and *metanoō* and in the same way a new meaning has come for the negative, *ametanoētos* (impenitent). We observe how different was the Stoic conception from that of the Jewish-Christian, in whose belief the goodness of God brings man to *metanoia* whereas, for the Stoic, on the other hand, it was good to be *ametanoētos*.

TO INSTRUCT IN CHRIST

1. κατηχέω

In secular Greek *katēchō* had indeed the meaning, to inform, to instruct,[29] but for this idea a more obvious stem was *didaskō*, *didaktos*. A fairly rare word, *katēchō* does not appear in the LXX but gives the impression of being a technical term among Christians, with the possible implication that instruction in the faith was a discipline wholly distinct from other education. For similar reasons Christian Greek had taken rare words like *agapē* and made them characteristic.

True that the verb *didaskō* has a wider use than *katēchō* in the NT, but already as early as Act 18²⁵ it seems that *katēchō* denoted elementary instruction in the Christian faith, so elementary that it did not include the distinguishing of Christian baptism from John's, while *didaskō* too denoted teaching constantly given to believers.[30]

Katēchō then has a specific Christian meaning. We may venture to depart from AV and render the verb more particularly 'give elementary Christian instruction', in the context of instructing Apollos (Act 18²⁵) and in the context of the 'initially instructed' brother having fellowship with his catechist (Gal 6⁶).

The verb is used in the apostolic Fathers in the phrase, 'We have commandment to tear men away from idols and to *give them Christian instruction*' (2 Clem 17¹). It lends point to St. Paul's statement that he should rather utter five words of 'elementary Christian instruction' than ten thousand in a tongue (1 Co 14¹⁹).

Our view requires us to suppose that Theophilus is being instructed as a Christian (Lk 1⁴), but H. J. Cadbury interpreted the verb *katēchēthēs* in the secular sense. 'You have received information', the Roman gentleman was reminded. That is, he had received incriminating reports about the brethren. Cadbury concluded that 'Theophilus was not a catechumen but an influential non-Christian'.[31] Certainly the secular meaning is envisaged by St. Luke at Act 21[21,24] ('laying information' against Paul), despite 18[25], but St. Luke often resorts to secular usages in the narrative sections.[32]

St. Paul's use, too, is rather different at Ro 2[18], the word attaching to a Jew 'instructed out of the Law'.

2. συμβιβάζω

In secular Greek the meaning of *sumbibazō* was to unite,[33] compare, examine,[34] literally, 'to cause to step with'. In a philosophical sense it meant to draw conclusions (Aristotle), but in the NT comes the important additional meaning, 'to give instruction in the faith'. Christians avoided the more obvious *embibazō*.

The concept of divine instruction had entered the word in the LXX.[35] Whereas in non-Biblical usage the verb had originally denoted a concern for logical deduction, in the LXX it refers exclusively to authoritative direction,[36] and the distinction is confirmed by syntactical structure; whereas secular Greek has the dative of person, the LXX has accusative of both person and thing (Ex 18[16]; Lev 10[11], etc.). In the NT, therefore, we should perhaps revise familiar translations. It is not that the whole Body is 'compacted' by that which every joint supplies, but the Body is 'instructed in Christian teaching'; it refers to the edification of the Body (Eph 4[16]). It will not be that the saints are 'knit together' in love (Col 2[2,19]), but they are 'instructed' in love – 'even as ye are taught' (Col 2[7]). Dr. R. P. Martin points out that though 'knit together' is one way in which the verb may be taken, nevertheless it can carry a didactic meaning, with the sense of the Vulgate *instructi in caritate*. Dr. Martin urges that the didactic meaning paves the way for the transition in the context into 'understanding' and 'knowledge' which follow.[37] Still, on balance, he prefers, 'knit together'. Fr. Spicq, on the other hand, rendered, 'étant instruits dans la charité', and saw it as a technical term for the Church's teaching ministry.[38] Moffatt had already appreciated this and had rendered, 'May they *learn the meaning* of love'. Dibelius, too, rendered, 'Sie sollen innerlich durch Belehrung in Liebe. ...'[39] Dibelius refers to Philo's use of the verb: 'Thou hast *taught* me to say what should be said. ... I will open thy mouth and *teach* thee what to speak'.[40]

The Vulgate's *instructi* accommodates both senses, for both 'equipped' and 'instructed' accord with Ciceronian usage (verse 2). In verse 19 the instruction is the 'nourishment' which is administered. Alford[41] preferred 'knit together' in verse 2, whereas Armitage Robinson allowed the LXX meaning, 'instructed', in verse 2, rejecting it in verse 19 and at Eph 4[16] (p. 186).

If then *sumbibazō* has a new content of meaning, it is likely that Saul did not so much 'prove' that Jesus was the Christ as that he 'gave instruction' to that effect. The Vulgate may intimate as much with its word, *affirmans* (Act 9[22]).

So Christians have taken a LXX word and have directed its new meaning, of divine instruction, to instruction in the faith.[42] It should be observed that at 1 Co 2[16] where St. Paul recalls the LXX of Isai 40[13], the AV renders correctly according to the meaning of Biblical Greek: 'For who hath known the mind of the Lord, that he may *instruct* Him?' (Hebrew: *yādha'* Hiphil).

INTEGRITY

ἀφθαρσία

Aphtharsia is an old word with a new sense. Its meaning in secular Greek was 'immortality', 'incorruption', freedom from disease.[43]

Christian Greek retained the word but brought in the additional connotation of moral **integrity** and sincerity, such as becomes the saint. The LXX does not exemplify the new meaning but keeps the secular sense of 'immortality' (Wis 2[23] 6[19]).

St. Paul usually retains the secular (Ro 2[7]; 1 Co 15[42, 50, 53f.]; 2 Ti 1[10]) but once has the new meaning:[44] 'Grace be with all them that love our Lord Jesus Christ in **integrity**' (Eph 6[24]). Commentators who are reluctant to concede the peculiar Christian meaning, reject the AV rendering (sincerity) and, insisting on secular usage (immortality), translate: 'with a love that will never change'. Bauer explains that this verse refers either to the believers who, by loving the Lord, are already partakers of 'immortality', or else to the Lord Himself who reigns in 'immortality' (col 228). But *aphtharsia* may well have changed its meaning from 'immortality', under some influence or other. As our own word, 'incorrupt', in English may mean both 'undecayed' and 'morally uncorrupted', so comparably there has appeared a two-fold meaning in Greek. Perhaps the influence which brought the change was Christian.

One circumstance suggests that Hebrew and Christian influence was at work on the Greek word: in Symmachus' version (Ps 74(75)[1]) *aphtharsia* renders the Hebrew *'al tashḥîth*, and the Hebrew verb *shaḥath* is not only to destroy but also to be corrupt, morally.

Once in the apostolic Fathers we find the new Pauline meaning, where believers are exhorted to be united with the Bishop as an example and lesson of integrity (I. Magn 6[2]). Moreover, St. Ignatius, having just previously dealt with evil heresy which corrupts faith and defiles the heretics themselves, writes, 'The Lord received ointment on His head that He might breathe *aphtharsia* on His Church' (I. Eph 17[1]). It is integrity of doctrine in such a context, not immortality. In Origen it is the same as virginity,[45] and it is an aspect of spiritual life for St. Irenaeus.[46]

NOTES

[1] Herodotus II 130.143; Aeschylus *Seven against Thebes* 559; Lucian *Alexander* 18.

[2] Euripides *Medea* 1162. For 'image' in a mirror, see also Plato *Republic* 402B.

[3] Plato *Republic* 487E. See also Aristophanes *Clouds* 559.

[4] Josephus *Bell. Jud.* II ix 2, II x 3 (Niese II 169, 194).

[5] Josephus *Ant. Jud.* XIX ii 3 (Niese XIX 185).

[6] Act 19[35]; Euripides *Iphigeneia in Tauris* 87f., 1384f.

[7] OGI 90.3.

[8] *De Confusione Linguarum* 97, 147.

[9] I sought to develop this in, *The Art of the Greek Orthodox Church*, University of Rhodesia 1976.

[10] E. M. Sidebottom, *The Christ of the Fourth Gospel*, SPCK 1961, p. 61.

[11] R. P. Martin, *Carmen Christi: Phil. ii. 5–11*, CUP 1967, pp. 107ff.

[12] Plato *Laws* 959B.

[13] OGI 201.8.

[14] Polybius XXX 25, 13ff.

[15] Lev 26[30]; 4 Km 17[12].

[16] Throughout Hosea, 1 Km 31[9]; Mic 1[7]; Ps 113[12] (115[4]) 134(135)[15].

[17] In these very new, non-secular senses, the word continued in Jewish and Christian use: e.g. T. Sol XXVI 5H, 6, 7B; C XII; 2 Clem 17[1]; Barn 4[8] 9[6].

[18] *Praeparatio Evangelica* IX 10.4.

[19] T. Nägeli, *Der Wortschatz des Apostels Paulus*, Göttingen 1905, p. 51.

[20] Homilies on 1 and 2 Corinthians, in loc. (Oxford Library of the Fathers, 1848).

[21] Cremer, p. 709.

[22] C. E. B. Cranfield, *Communio Viatorum* (Prague) 17 (1975), pp. 193ff.

[23] G. Theissen, *Evangelische Theologie* (Munich) 35 (1975), pp. 155–72.

[24] M. Isenberg, *Classical Philology* 70 (1975), pp. 271ff.

[25] C. K. Barrett, *New Testament Studies* 11 (1965), pp. 138–53.

[26] Lucian *Abdicatus* 11; Plotinus VI 7, 26; Vettius Valens (ed. Kroll) 263.16; *Corpus Papyrorum Raineri* clxvi 5 (Deissmann BS 257); Acts of John 9; Clement *Stromateis* II 13.

[27] A scholion on Arrian's Dissertations of Epictetus 25 – to represent the Stoic ideal of never repenting.

[28] Ephraim Syrus (J. S. Assemani *Opera Omnia*, Rome 1746, 3,517F); Chrysostom *Homilies* 29.4 in 2 Corinthians.

[29] P. Lips. I 32.1; Philo II 575; Josephus *Vita* 65 ('I will inform you of a great many things which you do not know').

[30] H. W. Beyer in Kittel *TWNT* III, p. 640.

[31] Beginnings part I, vol. II, p. 510.

[32] When penning these sections he was not so well acquainted with the Christian dialect. See *Studies in NT Language and Text*, ed. J. K. Elliott, Brill, Leiden 1976, pp. 387–400.

[33] Thucydides II 29: 'he *reconciled* them with Perdiccas'.

[34] Plato *Hippias Minor* 369D.

[35] Ex $4^{12,15}$ 18^{16}; Lev 10^{11}; Deut 4^9; Jdg 13^8; Ps $31(32)^8$; Isai $40^{13f.}$; Dan Th 9^{22}.

[36] Delling in Kittel *TWNT* VII, p. 763.

[37] R. P. Martin, *Colossians: the Church's Lord*, Paternoster 1972, pp. 68f.

[38] C. Spicq, *Agape* II (1959), pp. 202–4.

[39] M. Dibelius, *An die Kolosser, Epheser, an Philemon* (Handbuck zum Neuen Testament, 12) Tübingen 2nd ed. 1927, p. 18.

[40] *Quis Rerum Divinarum Heres* 25.

[41] Vol. III, p. 214.

[42] If we are right συνεβίβασαν would not be the correct reading at Act 19^{33}, but rather the κατεβίβασαν of the Western text, for the new Christian meaning of *sumbibazō* is irrelevant to the context. However, it may still mean, to instruct: some of the crowd were able to *inform* Alexander; the majority (v. 32) did not know. See Delling, op. cit., VII, p. 765.

[43] Philo *de Opificio Mundi* 153. So Epicurus *Epistula* 1; Philodemus *Peri Theōn* III 9.

[44] The inferior text (Tit 2^7) has *aphtharsia* in the context of moral sincerity: 'in doctrine showing *uncorruptness*'. However, we ought to read *aphthoria* (q.v.) rather than *aphtharsia*.

[45] Origen *Comm.* Eph 6^{24}.

[46] Irenaeus *adversus Haereses* IV 38.3.

J

κρίμα: κρίσις: κρίνω

Secular Greek. Already the meaning of *krima*, *krisis* and the verb *krinō*, was some kind of judgment, and yet by no means the judgment envisaged in the Bible.

Krima was an everyday decision.[1] 'When you are grieved by some external irritation,' writes Marcus Aurelius, 'it is not the thing itself that worries you, but your decision *(krima)* about it'. For Philodemus,[2] a philosopher contemporary with Jesus, *krima* is a finding of literary criticism; it is a decree for Dionysius of Halicarnassus, a Greek historian early in the reign of Augustus,[3] and a legal decision in papyri and inscriptions.[4]

Krisis too is transformed. It was in secular Greek the power of deciding,[5] the distinguishing of one thing from another, as the smaller from the greater, the decision of a ruler or of the gods.[6] It was the verdict of a court,[7] even the trial itself,[8] as well as its result, i.e. a verdict or condemnation.[9] Apart from anything legal, *krisis* was a trial of skill,[10] a dispute,[11] an issue to be decided in war.[12]

The verb *krinō* has a threefold extension in secular Greek. 1. It is to separate, to distinguish. 2. Often to choose, to decide disputes and contests (in middle and passive: to contend), to interpret in a particular way, to form a judgment. 3. Particularly, to accuse, to bring to trial, to pass sentence.

It is true, there are a few Christian instances where *krima* and *krisis* manifest the general meanings of opinion, decision, legal condemnation in a human court, going to litigation, simple justice, and railing accusation,[13] but on the whole the words are recast. The verb, much more often than the nouns, has the secular meanings of suing or judging at law,[14] and making a decision for oneself.[15]

Biblical Greek. While the concepts of just vindication and righteousness did no more than hover on the pens of pagan writers,[16] in our variety of Greek the words *krima* and *krisis* specially indicate God's judgment through Christ.

St. Clement firmly states, 'God is righteous in all His *krimata*' (1 Clem 27[1] 60[1]). St. Polycarp avers that whoever will say there is neither resurrection nor *krisis* (future judgment) is the first-born of Satan (ad Phil. 7[1]), and at his martyrdom the mention of fire prompted him to round on the proconsul, 'Thou art ignorant of the fire of the future *krisis*' (M. Pol. 11[2]). It means the future judgment for St. Ignatius, too, when he declared that even angels, if they fail to trust in the blood of Christ, await the *krisis* (I. Smyrn. 6[1]).

237

Another Father places it in the same eschatological context: 'I myself am altogether sinful and have not yet escaped temptation ... but am striving to follow righteousness that I may have strength ... in fear of judgment *(krisis)* to come' (2 Clem 18[2]).

The Day of *krisis* is a prominent phrase (Mk 6[11]; 2 Pet 3[7]; Jude 6; 1 Jn 4[17]; 2 Clem 16[3] 17[6]; Barn 19[10] 21[6]), and the future *krima*, the judgment in the Dispensation to come, is an element of Christian teaching, a constant topic of warning (Act 24[25]; Heb 6[2]; Rev 20[4]). *Krima* involves the divine damnation of sin. 'Thinkest thou this, O man, that thou shalt escape the *krima* of God?' (Ro 2[2f.] 3[8] 5[16] 13[2]; 1 Co 11[29, 34]; 1 Ti 5[12]). *Krima* will take in the Church, will begin at the house of God (1 Pet 4[17]). For *krima* Christ came into this world (Jn 9[39]). In Christian thought it recalls, like *krisis,* the Judgment to come. 'Those that are *dipsuchoi* (doubters) and are sceptical of God's power ... incur *krima,*' warns St. Clement (1 Clem 11[2]). 'Let us fear Him and desist from foul desires of evil deeds, that we may be sheltered by His mercy from the *krimata* (plural) to come' (28[1]). 'These are the last times', warns St. Ignatius; 'therefore let us be modest, let us fear the patience of God, that it may not become our *krima*' (I. Eph 11[1]).

Does *krisis* differ at all from *krima* in Biblical Greek? Generally in the LXX both render the Hebrew *shāphaṭ*-stem and a distinction is hard to find. *Krisis,* nevertheless, sometimes renders the *rîbh*-stem[17] and whereas *shāphaṭ* is to judge and govern, *rîbh* is to strive and contend and conduct a suit and find a fault: *rîbh* is the more querulous and less detached. Applied to *krima* and *krisis,* the distinction has little relevance in the NT, but the idea of strife or contending for God's cause, implicit in *rîbh,* is firmly understood in many instances of *krisis:* e.g. when God shows it to the Gentiles (Mt 12[18]) and sends it forth to victory (12[20]), when Nineveh and the south rise up in *krisis* (Mt 12[41f.]; Lk 11[31f.]). *Krisis* is the contention against this world because it prefers darkness to God's light (Jn 3[19]) and the Cross itself brings *krisis* (Jn 12[31]), so that men are already judged by the way they react to Jesus. 'Still, a future judgment is not excluded by the fact that its decision – and in part its effects – are already realized,' observed Dr. Kingsley Barrett.[18]

Krisis is, then, rather a merciless judgment (Jas 2[13]) – and 'fearful' (Heb 10[27]; 2 Clem 10[5]). To some extent that is no less true of *krima,* which again is damnation and the avenging hand of God (Mt 23[14]; Mk 12[40]; Lk 20[47]; Ro 2[3] 3[8] 13[2]; 1 Ti 5[12]; Jude 4; Rev 17[1] 18[20]). But Jesus makes it clear that those who hear this word and believe shall not come into *krisis.* As St. Paul expressed it, they are 'justified'.

Formations which are based on the *dikaios*-stem are examples of secular words advisedly made symbols for new meanings in Christian Greek.

1. δίκαιος: δικαιοσύνη

The renderings of *dikaios* in AV, 'just' and 'righteous', and of *dikaiosunē* as 'righteousness', fail to reflect all the iridescence of thought illuminating their Christian usage.

In the general way of Greek, *dikaios* was a man who satisfies ordinary legal norms but, first, a change of emphasis was wrought in the Greek of the OT when *dikaiosunē* involved 'righteousness' in the theocratic sense of meeting God's claims and observing the Law of Moses, while a *dikaios* was a 'righteous' man who strives to keep it, for the Greek words usually rendered the Hebrew *ṣdq* root.

It is urged that the *ṣidhqath JHWH*,[19] the 'righteousness of God' (Deut 33[21]) became a technical term in late Jewish apocalyptic for God's sovereignty and merciful vindication of His people, based on His covenanted faithfulness and associated with His demand of obedience. The 'righteousness' of the Head of Days forsakes not the Son of Man (Enoch 71[14]). Those who walk in the path of His 'righteousness' shall be saved (99[10]), and yet against His 'righteousness' are proud and insolent words spoken (101[3]). Cleave to it and the race will be saved for ever (Testament of Dan 6[10]). Now it is not impossible that St. Paul took over the apocalyptic term, understanding by it, God's sovereignty over all things by means of Jesus Christ.[20]

However, in Christian Greek a still more distinctive facet enhanced the spectrum when *dikaiōsis* affirmed God's merciful act of declaring sinful souls no longer the objects of His wrath – an act accomplished by the obedience of Christ when He perfectly fulfilled the Law of God and became supremely the *dikaios* (righteous) Man. The *dikaiosunē* (righteousness) of Christ – in the OT sense of fulfilment of the Law – initiated therefore the *dikaiosunē* (imputed righteousness) of God in the new sense found in Christian Greek: that is, the result of His 'justifying action' in declaring mankind to be pardoned, to be exempt from His wrath, His treating men as if they were righteous.

'The declaring of His *dikaionunē*,' writes St. Chrysostom,[21] 'is not only that He is Himself righteous but that He doth also make them that are filled with the putrefying scars of sin suddenly righteous. ... When the Judge's sentence declares us just, and such a judge too, what signifieth the accuser'?

239

Dikaiosunē has acquired a Christian sense. The word no longer means personal righteousness as such, but a derived righteousness, or an imputed righteousness, for the remission of sins that are past (Ro 3^{25}).

As for the logical and moral difficulty, how God could Himself be virtuous and yet pardon all this accumulation of Law-breaking on man's part, its solution lies in seeing Christ as a representative Man having fulfilled the Law perfectly, and in seeing all the rest of mankind as identifying themselves corporately with Him by an act of faith (Ro 3^{26}). Thus God treats mankind, in Christ, as actually righteous, having Christ's own righteousness. That is a fundamentally Hebrew concept.[22] The Israelite mind saw individual life as part of the life of the race. Not that St. Paul did no more than repeat the idea from Judaism. Rather did the idea provide a background for a truth which was already real to him – the total human implication in sin. On the two truths he based his doctrine of human redemption. Jesus is the representative Man, and all that He accomplished belongs to every man. He died, but in that representative death upon the cross all men died with Him; He rose from the grave, He ascended into heaven. All mankind rose and ascended with the representative Man, the 'Federal Head of all mankind' (Wesley). St. Irenaeus named this, His work of recapitulation. 'He summed up all things', said Irenaeus, 'in order that, as our species went down to death through a vanquished man, so we may ascend to life again through a virtuous One'.[23]

Redemption then is not fragmentary, but every human being is born again. Everyone is justified, sanctified, and has the hope to be glorified. A believer differs from a non-believer in one very important point. He knows what has happened, thanks God for it, rejoices in it, and lives in the grace and strength of it.

It is a pity that Catholic and Protestant interpreters tend to be divided on the meaning of *dikaiosunē*, the former holding that it is 'justice' (Vulgate's *justitia*) in the sense of uprightness, not forensic justice but part of an ethical vocabulary.

Protestants tend to regard *dikaiosunē* as a righteousness, coming from God to man, but they understand it forensically. To them, man does not become sanctified straight away but is treated by God as righteous because he stands clothed in the righteousness of Another.[24] In time he achieves righteousness in the OT sense of the term, when he becomes progressively sanctified. Men do not do penance in order to be forgiven, but they are forgiven in order that they might do penance. Forgiveness is initial; it is God's initiative. To divide Catholics and Protestants on this point is perhaps to make an abstract distinction rather than a real one, not fully to appreciate a difference of approach – the ontological versus the experiential.[25]

In Christian experience the imputed righteousness becomes real righteousness.

In what sense is the word used by Jesus when He declares, 'Blessed are they which are persecuted for the sake of *dikaiosunē*, further by St. Peter when he too speaks of suffering for the sake of *dikaiosunē*, and further by St. Polycarp when he follows the same expression?[26] Do they share the new Pauline sense and do they refer to persecution which is incurred 'because of justification' (i.e. because they are regenerate believers)? Justification inevitably leads to persecution, for without tribulation the sanctified may not be glorified, may not arrive at complete salvation to which justification was only the first step. Although a more acceptable explanation is probably that disciples are blessed when they suffer because they are fulfilling the Law,[27] the OT sense of *dikaiosunē*, it is still tempting to wonder whether, in a Christian context, the word will not appear with its special Christian sense – God's act of initial forgiveness.

2. δικαίωσις: δικαιόω

Dikaiōsis and *dikaiō* are special terms in the Christian language to express a part of God's gracious saving and sanctifying act.

Secular Greek. *Dikaiōsis* was the process of setting right or doing justice; often it was a just claim in law, a plea of legal right, and a punishing.

Dikaiō, the verb, was to set right, to deem right,[28] or else to think something fair, as in the compiling of a contract,[29] or else to make a decision in a legal action in court.[30] It was, then, to pass sentence, to punish, and to claim as right. In Herodotus it was to deem it right (I 89, 100, 133), to argue or reason (IX 42). In Thucydides it was both to deem it proper (V 26), and to bring about a just condemnation (III 40). But in none of the occurrences of *dikaiō* in St. Paul's letters, 'can it be at all tolerably explained on the basis of the word's use in secular Greek'.[31]

Biblical Greek. In the LXX *dikaiōsis* occurs but once, rendering the Hebrew *mishpāṭ* (judgement, decree, manner of law, Lev 24[22]). In St. Paul's letters, however, it may be no other than a merciful act of God in legally pronouncing certain sinners to be righteous – God's own declaration that believers are acquitted or 'justified' (in the sense of 'declared just') through the obedience of Christ, Who was delivered to death and raised from the dead, His merits being imputed to the sinner (Luther). That work of Christ is said to be our *dikaiōsis* and a *dikaiōsis* of life (Ro 4[25] 5[18]). It is an interpretation of St. Paul's term which is generally associated with Protestant theology.

In the LXX the verb *dikaiō*, rendering the Hebrew stem *ṣdq* some twenty times is not so obviously legal in function but still implies vindication in accordance with a code: to do a person justice, to give judgment in a controversy, to vindicate from heaven.[32] There is ample enough evidence in the LXX for the Pauline meaning, to **show to be innocent, declare to be innocent.**

So the Biblical sense differs from the secular by its much stronger concept of vindication. 'Hear Thou in heaven, ... justifying *(dikaiō)* the righteous, to give him according to his righteousness.' The believer in Jesus is 'justified' by the grace of God, deemed righteous, and treated as such (Ro 3[24, 26, 28] 5[1, 9] 6[7] 8[30]; 1 Co 6[11]; Gal 2[16f.] 3[24]; 1 Ti 3[16]; Tit 3[7]).

The Vulgate's translation, *justificatio,* from which comes our word 'justification', assumes that *dikaiōsis* means, 'making just' *(justum facere)* and suggests the Catholic view that *dikaiōsis* is the act whereby God sends his sanctifying grace to man's soul and makes him righteous in a real and not merely a juridical sense (St. Thomas, as distinct from Luther).

Canon viii of the Council of Trent made it clear that *justificatio* is not merely the forgiveness of sins but also 'sanctification' and the renewal of the inner man by the voluntary reception of grace and gifts; 'justification' involves a man's becoming *dikaios,* righteous, from being unrighteous, so as to be heir according to the hope of eternal life. Any real difference between Catholic and Protestant at this point is illusory, a matter mainly of terminology, especially when we give to this aspect of *dikaiōsis* (justification) the name of 'sanctification'.[33] 'The older Protestant theologians distinguished between Justification and Sanctification', and 'on the whole St. Paul does keep the two subjects separate from each other'.[34] Nevertheless, in experience they cannot be separated.

Karl Barth's teaching on Justification has been examined from the Church's point of view,[35] and much is found to be in harmony with Catholic doctrine – to Barth's own pleasant surprise! Dr. Küng recognizes difference of view and sees that it is not the same language that is spoken between Catholic and Protestant. Nevertheless, differences in terminology account for much of the confusion.

There is no call to underestimate differences in these matters, especially that between the doctrine of justification by faith alone (Protestant) and justification by faith with love, *fides caritate formata* (Catholic). Such conflicts must loom large in present ecumenical debate. However, to cherish the doctrine of justification by faith *alone* (Luther) does not necessarily involve disparagement of the Church and sacraments.

That would seem to be one of the conclusions of Catholics and

Protestants when they meet with understanding. At a joint con-
ference between members of the Community of the Resurrection
(Anglican) and a group from the Evangelical Fellowship of
Theological Literature,[36] the main heads of agreement were found
to be 'very considerable'. The paper of the late Dom Gregory Dix
showed that the Reformation battle-cry *sola fide* was rather a
protest against the notion of justification as a reward for human
effort than a disparagement of the validity of sacramental grace. At
all events, God is a holy Judge, to Whom man the sinner is
responsible, and with Whom a reconciliation has to take place.
From the work of Christ accrues both what the Protestant stresses
as 'forensic' righteousness *(justitia imputata)* – the initial forgiving
act of God – and what the Catholic particularly stresses, 'subjective' righteousness or new life in Christ through the Spirit
(justitia infusa). Both benefits flow from the Cross. It is still true
that *dikaiōsis* is primarily, when considered from the sinner's point
of view, God's act of forgiveness rather than the long process of
sanctification. 'It is forgiveness', exclaims Jeremias; 'nothing but
forgiveness for Christ's sake'.[37] It is not fair to Protestant devotion
to describe this view of the term as coldly 'forensic', as a mere act
of declaration, as a fiction. It is the extending of a waiting Father's
arms. When God justifies the sinner He absolves and acquits him of
all the past, and the erstwhile sinner is not merely 'regarded as if'
he were righteous. He is actually righteous, for God regards him
so.[38] God is the Lawgiver and the Judge. Those whom He declares
righteous actually *are* righteous. All the sanctification of the
coming days is made inevitable by that one gesture of acquittal and
the gift of grace that goes with it. So confesses the Protestant, and
the Catholic agrees that grace for salvation is already assumed
along with the forgiveness.

> *Rejoice in hope, rejoice with me!*
> *We shall from all our sins be free.*

Having determined what is the theological meaning of the new
Christian words, a difficult question arises how we are best to
translate them into English. The Christian words based on *dikaios*
include the idea of 'acquittal', God's wiping of the slate, but as a
translation 'acquittal' is too juridical on its own, too negative, and
gives no hint of the change of character which will inevitably
follow. Nor may we happily translate by 'sanctification', for
dikaiōsis is not in itself the final stage, but only the first step in an
unremitting process. The late Director of the New English Bible
explained the disquiet which his translators faced when they
pondered this group of words. They felt that the translation, 'Get
right with God', was good but unnatural and liable to be misun-

derstood for it confuses the idea in question with that of reconciliation. All the translators could do was to keep the words,
'justify', and 'justification', which are at least current English
words, but they had to understand them in a sense which is not
current and to take them as technical terms which either explain
themselves from the context or else await the commentator. They
were little better than symbols.

These words illustrate how formidable is the task of putting the
Greek of the NT into current English speech.[39]

3. δικαιοκρισία

Dikaiokrisia may not be a coinage of Jewish Greek, being found
in the late vernacular which probably suffered no Jewish or Biblical
influence. In the fourth century an appellant was hopeful to obtain
'fair justice' *(dikaiokrisia)* from the prefect, and in the fifth century
another appellant pleaded that 'the purity of your fair justice
(dikaiokrisia) will surely pity me, an old man'.[40]

It occurs in the Quinta column of Origen's Hexapla as a variant
from the LXX *krima*. The Hebrew is *mishpāṭ* (judgment). 'My
judgment goeth forth as the light' (Hos 6[5]). It occurs twice in the
Testament of Levi where in the lowest heaven fire, snow and ice are
said to await the day of Judgment in the *dikaiokrisia* of God (3[2]),
and lawless Jews are promised everlasting shame by His
dikaiokrisia (15[2]). The concept is still that of *mishpāṭ*.

The first Christians, on the other hand, had a special way of
applying the word, for the context links it with the dikaiosunē of
God (Ro 2[5]), suggesting that *dikaiokrisia* means 'justification' in
the Christian sense. In the very next chapter St. Paul will expound
the truth that no man is *dikaios* enough to escape the Judge's
condemnation unless he have upon him the *dikaiosunē* that is in
Christ Jesus (Ro 3[22]).

The question would be quite decided by the word's
appearance in 2 Th 1[5] ('it is a token of *dikaiokrisia* that ye are
counted worthy ...'), were it not for the uncertainty caused by the
presence of a variant reading there. The best text has *dikaiokrisia*
as two separate words – *dikaia* and *krisis* – and the reading
dikaiokrisia as a single word, vouched for by the minuscules[41] and
the Patristic commentators mentioned by von Dobschütz[42] may be
no more than an attempt to harmonize the verse with Ro 2[5].
Nevertheless, the variant palpably confirms this much: that to the
mind of the Patristic harmonizers, aware of contemporary
meanings of words, *dikaiokrisia* suited the context of 2 Th 1[5] very
well. The context concerns admission to the kingdom of God and
the persecution and sufferings which will afflict the saints. It is a

token of God's *dikaiokrisia* – so runs the reasoning in its context – that 'ye are counted worthy to enter'. No one is counted worthy by his own good works, but only by the justifying act of God.

That is evidently what the Patristic harmonizers conceived *dikaiokrisia* to mean, 'justifying act' or 'decision to justify'.

NOTES

[1] Chrysippus, in H. von Arnim, *Stoicorum Veterum Fragmenta*, Leipzig 1903, 3.58 (Teubner); Polybius 23.1.12; Arrian *Epicteti Dissertationes*, ed.. H. Schenkl, Leipzig 1894, 2.15.8 (Teubner).

[2] *Peripoiēmatōn*, ed. C. Jensen, *Philodemos über die Gedichte*, book 5, Berlin 1923.

[3] *Antiquitates Romanae*, ed. C. Jacoby, Leipzig 1885ff. (Teubner) 4.12.

[3] A iii BC papyri and a Delphic inscription of ii BC (P. Petr III 26.2, OGIS 335.100).

[5] Polybius XVIII 14.10.

[6] Herodotus III 34; Aeschylus *Agamemnon* 1289 ('by heaven's *decree*').

[7] The orator Antipho (Teubner 4.4.2), fifth century BC.

[8] Thucydides I 34.

[9] Xenophon *Anabasis* I 6.5.

[10] Sophocles *Trachiniai* 266.

[11] Herodotus V 5, VII 26.

[12] Thucydides I 23; Polybius XXXI 29.5.

[13] *Krima*: Mt 7^2; Lk 24^{20}; 1 Co 6^7. *Krisis*: Act 8^{33} cit.; 2 Pet 2^{11}; Jude 9; Pol. Phil. 6^1.

[14] Mt 5^{40}; Jn 18^{31}; Act 3^{13} 23^6 24^{21} $25^{9f.,20}$; 1 Co 5^{12} $6^{1,6}$.

[15] Lk 7^{43} 12^{57}; Jn 7^{24}; Act 4^{19} 13^{46} 15^{19} 16^{15} 20^{16} 21^{25} 25^{25} 26^8 27^1; Ro 2^{27} $14^{5,13}$; 1 Co 2^2 7^{37} 10^{15}; 2 Co 2^1; Tit 3^{12}.

[16] In an inscription at the end of the second century BC, *krisis* gets near the moral sense of Biblical Greek, *Receuil d'Inscriptions Grecques*, ed. C. Michel, Paris 1900, 542, 6.

[17] Ex $23^{3,6}$; 1 Km 24^{16} 25^{39}; 2 Ch 19^{10}; Job 13^6 39^{22} (40^2); Ps $118(119)^{154}$; Pr 15^{18} 22^{23} 23^{11} 24^{68} (30^{33}) 26^{17}; Hos 4^1 $12^{2(3)}$; Mic 6^2; Hab 1^3; Isai 1^{23} 41^{21} 49^{25} 58^4; Jer $32(25)^{31}$; Ezek 44^{24}.

[18] C. K. Barrett, *The Gospel according to St. John*, SPCK 1962, p. 190.

[19] *Sidhqath ēl*, in Qumrân scrolls.

[20] E. Käsemann, *New Testament Questions Today*, ET London 1969, pp. 172, 178, 180.

[21] Homily VII on Ro $3^{24f.}$.

[22] As developed by R. P. Shedd, *Man in Community*, Epworth 1958, and by J. de Fraine, *Adam et son lignage: études sur la notion de 'personalité corporative' dans la Bible*, de Brouwer (Bruges) 1959. Before them, see the work of the late Dr. Wheeler Robinson.

[23] *Adversus Haereses* V 21.1.

[24] J. A. Ziesler, *The Meaning of Righteousness in Paul*, CUP 1972, p. 8.

[25] J. Swetnam, *Biblica* 55 (1974), p. 145.

[26] Mt 5^{10}; 1 Pet 3^{14}; Pol. ad Phil. 2^3 3^1.

[27] 'The reference is quite obviously to the saints who were down-trodden and despised because of their fidelity to the will and law of God.' David Hill, *Greek Words and Hebrew Meanings*, CUP 1967, p. 128.

[28] P. Giss I 47.16 (AD ii): 'I *thought it right* to buy a girdle'.

[29] P. Tebt II 444 (AD i).

[30] P. Ryl II 119.14 (AD i).

[31] C. E. B. Cranfield, *Romans,* ICC T. & T. Clark 1975, p. 95.

[32] Gen 38[26] 44[16]; Ex 23[7]; Deut 25[1]; 2 Km 15[4]; 3 Km 8[32]; Job 33[32]; Ps 18(19)[9] 50(51)[4] 81(82)[3] 142(143)[2]; Isai 5[23] 42[21] 43[9,26] 45[26(25)] 50[8] 53[11]; Jer 3[11]; Ezek 16[51f.].

[33] As pointed out by W. M. Smyth, *Evangelical Quarterly* 36 (1964), pp. 42–8, especially p. 47.

[34] W. Sanday and A. C. Headlam, *Romans,* ICC T. & T. Clark 5th ed. 1902, p. 38.

[35] H. Küng, *Rechtfertigung: die Lehre Karl Barths und eine Katholische Besinnung,* Einsideln 1957.

[36] *The Doctrine of Justification by Faith,* Mowbray 1954.

[37] J. Jeremias, *The Central Message of the New Testament,* ET SCM 1965, third lecture.

[38] R. Bultmann, *Theology of the New Testament,* ET 1951, I, p. 276.

[39] C. H. Dodd, *Expository Times,* 72 (1961), p. 274.

[40] P. Oxy I 71 i 4; VI 904 ii. Also P. Flor 88.26 (AD iii). See Deissmann LAE 89f.

[41] Another minuscule, 87, feeling that it should be one word, has supplied a compromise, with *dikaiokriseōs*.

[42] E. von Dobschütz, *Kommentar zu die Thessalonicherbriefen,* 7th ed. 1909, Göttingen, p. 242.

K

KIND, TO BE

χρηστεύομαι

While *chrēsteuomai* is almost certainly a coinage of Christian Greek (Bauer), some have mentioned Harnack's suggestion 'that Paul may have derived it from a recension of Q, which was used and quoted by Clemens Romanus' (MM). As Q is still no more than a hypothesis, especially if understood as a written document, the suggestion is but a supposition based upon a supposition.

The new word indicates an aspect of Christian love (1 Co 13⁴). 'Love *is kind*.' The verb may be derived from the adjective *chrēstos*, useful, worthy, honest, but the Christian contexts suggest that compassion is an element of it. 'Be *chrēstos* and merciful', counsels Justin. 'Almighty God is *chrēstos* and full of pity' (*Apol.* 15¹³, *Dial.* 96³).

St. Clement's use of *chrēsteuomai* is suggestive of the word's underlying gentleness. 'Let us *be good* one towards another according to the compassion and sweetness of Him that made us' (1 Clem 14³) – perhaps a play on His gracious name. Justin has this play on the words *chrēstos* (kind) and *Christos* (*Apol.* 4⁵). Popular pronunciation of chrēstos as *christos*, as in modern Greek, would assist the pun.

St. Clement quotes a saying of Jesus, 'As you *are kind*, they will *be kind* to you' (13²) (MM).

KNOWLEDGE (OF SPIRITUAL TRUTH)

γνῶσις

Open the eyes of our hearts that we may know Thee.
– ST. CLEMENT OF ROME

'Knowledge of spiritual truth' and 'perception of God' were the higher extensions of *gnōsis* which accrued in Jewish and Christian Greek. The secular meanings were investigation and cognition in general – the reverse of ignorance[1] – a recognizing, as it might be in the darkness, by a watchword.[2]

Moreover, in Hellenistic Judaism *gnōsis* was a technical term. Like *phōs* (light), *alētheia* (truth), and *sōtēria* (salvation), it was part of the Way of Life.[3] In late books of the LXX the righteous man is said to have *gnōsis* of God (Wis 2¹³). Theological ideas spread into the Hermetic writings of pagan mysticism which themselves were originally Jewish. Technical terms like *gnōsis* and *sōtēria*, together with *metanoia* (repentance), appear in Judaism in the last pre-Christian century (T. Gad 5[7]). They were developed by the Jew Philo, teaching that human minds crave a *gnōsis* of God which is the height of happiness and age-long life.[4]

The term went into Gnosticism,[5] but for the heretics of the second century it signified a special kind of esoteric illumination, not the same as that intended by the Church, and anyway for Christians *gnōsis* had not quite the same priority as it enjoyed in Gnosticism. *Gnōsis* was indeed a hazard for those saints who were most blessed with it at Rome and Corinth (Ro 15[14]; 1 Co 1[5]; 2 Co 8[7]). It puffed up where *agapē* edified (1 Co 8[1]), and the *gnōsis* affected by the 'strong' brother may well 'embolden' the conscience of a 'weak' brother and compass his ruin (1 Co 8[10ff.]). A more excellent way than *gnōsis* is Christian love without which a brother boasting of *gnōsis* is nothing at all (1 Co 13[2]). The love of Christ surpasses *gnōsis* (Eph 3[19]), which has its day (1 Co 13[8]). Nevertheless, sadly though it may be abused, it is still a beneficial gift, indispensible for Christian teaching (1 Co 14[6]) and for growth towards maturity of understanding (1 Co 8[7]; 2 Pet 1[5f.] 3[18]).

It was generally argued by the 'History of Religions' school that St. Paul was acquainted with technical terms of the Mysteries – words like 'initiated', 'pneumatic', 'psychic', 'perfect', 'illumination', and *gnōsis* – but the caveats which he so often expressed show where he really stood. Very far indeed from St. Paul is the sentiment expressed by the Gnostic guide, Poimandres:[6] 'This is the blessed issue for those who have attained *gnōsis,* to be deified!' The desire for *gnōsis* among the seekers in the Hellenistic world, contemporary with St. Paul, was not a quest for rational understanding of natural phenomena. Their notion of *gnōsis* was not so much intellectual. It was rather a reaction against cool intellectualism. *Gnōsis* was thought of as the vision of God, an experience of direct insight into ultimate reality, warm and emotional. The possessor of *gnōsis* felt illuminated, in possession of 'salvation', at one with God, deified.

True, the term was tremendously important for St. Paul. The minister of God must not lack *gnōsis,* even though he be rude in speech (2 Co 6[6] 11[6]). *Gnōsis* of the Christian kind unlocks treasuries, allowing one to attain to salvation (Lk 1[77] 11[52]; Ro 11[33]; Col 2[3]), whereas devotion to the Law is but a form of *gnōsis* if God will not give inward light (Ro 2[20]; 2 Co 4[6]). Directed towards Jesus Christ it is an excellent faculty, a gift of the Holy Ghost (1 Co 12[8]; Ph 3[8]). Nevertheless, heresies parade under its name (Tit 6[20]) – perhaps Gnosticism?

Christian *gnōsis,* as conceived by St. Paul, is too rational and impassive to have much resemblance with the *gnōsis* of the heretics. For St. John, too, who avoids the suggestive term, perhaps deliberately, and instead prefers the verbs *ginōskō* and *oida,* knowledge is severely practical; it is not ecstatic nor even properly mystical, and is far from that understood by the Gnostics. It expresses itself in Christian love.[7] As St. Clement of Alexandria, the Christian gnostic, was to say later, 'The more a man loves, the more deeply does he penetrate into God'.[8] Besides, for St. John, man's wretchedness is due not so much to ignorance as to sin.[9]

A difficulty arises because it looks as if St. Peter somehow connected the term with matrimony. Husbands are cautioned to dwell with their wives according to *gnōsis* (1 Pet 3[7]). Can *gnōsis* be intercourse, understood as carnal 'knowledge'? The Hebrew *yādhâ* has this sense (Gen 4[1,17,25] 19[8] 24[16] 38[26], etc.) and St. Peter might be urging couples not to abstain, despite St. Paul's advice (1 Co 7[5]). However, that would be to involve *gnōsis* in two very different senses in Christian Greek. More likely, St. Peter is giving to *gnōsis* the meaning which St. Paul gives (1 Co 8) – the penetrating understanding that there is nothing sinful either in meats or in marital intimacy. *Gnōsis* gives freedom in both respects, but freedom should be exercised in a spirit of *agapē.* There was a tendency among Christian gnostics, at least of a later date, to allow Stoicism to cast 'the chill shadow of Apathy over the sweetest and simplest of Christian motives'. For St. Clement Christ, like God, is absolutely passionless and the Gnostic will be so absorbed in the divine Love that he will no longer love his fellow-creatures in the ordinary sense of the word. 'This was the price he paid for his Transcendental Theology.'[10] This may throw some light on the problem of 1 Pet 3[7] concerning conjugal affection. St. Peter means that *gnōsis* is not inconsistent with conjugal enjoyment.

In the apostolic Fathers true *gnōsis* of God comes through Christ, as in the NT.[11] *Gnōsis* and 'life' are connected,[12] as they are in Hellenistic Judaism, just as the Trees of knowledge and of life are connected (Diogn. 12[4]). *Gnōsis* has some relevance to immortality[13] (1 Clem 36[2]). It belongs to God and is bestowed on believers (40[1] 41[4]). It is perception of spiritual truth (Barn 6[9]), often by revelation.[14]

NOTES

[1] Demosthenes XVIII 224; Plato *Republic* 478C; P. Hib 1.92.13 (iii BC).
[2] Thucydides VII 44.
[3] C. H. Dodd, *The Bible and the Greeks,* Hodder 1935, pp. 183ff.

[4] *Quod Deus Sit Immutabilis* 142f., *de Specialibus Legibus* I 345.

[5] R. Reitzenstein, *Die hellenistischen Mysterien religionen*, 3rd ed. Leipzig and Berlin 1927, pp. 113ff.

[6] W. Scott, *Corpus Hermeticum*, I.26. See *Expository Times* 41 (1929), p. 423; C. H. Dodd, op. cit., p. 169.

[7] A. Skrinjar, *Verbum Domini* (Rome) 42 (1964), pp. 3ff.

[8] *Quis Dives Salvetur* 27.

[9] C. K. Barrett, *The Gospel according to St. John*, SPCK 1955, p. 68.

[10] C. Bigg, *The Christian Platonists of Alexandria*, Clarendon 1886, pp. 93ff.

[11] 2 Clem 3[1].

[12] Did 9[3]: 'we thank Thee for that life and *gnōsis* which Thou didst make known to us through Jesus'.

[13] Did 10[2]: 'we thank Thee for the *gnōsis* and faith and immortality which Thou didst make known to us through Jesus'.

[14] Hermas *Vis.* II 2.1: 'the *gnōsis* of the writing which was revealed to me'.

L

LAMB

1. ἀμνός

Amnos is a term for lamb which occurs only in poets in classical Greek – Aristophanes who speaks of 'lamb-like characters'[1] and Sophocles – and in Theocritus of iii BC.

Though rare, *amnos* was adopted by Christians as a special figure of Christ, the Lamb of God. It has to be understood in a sacrificial way, for in the LXX it rendered chiefly *kebheś*, and the Christian *amnos* too takes away sin (Jn 1[29, 36]). When the Ethiopian, reading Isai 53[7f.], comes on the words, 'like a *lamb*, dumb before his shearers', *amnos* is interpreted by Philip of Christ (Act 8[32]). He is 'a lamb without blemish', whose precious blood redeemed us (1 Pet 1[19]).

One recalls the suggestion of Dr. Ball which was cited by Dr. Burney,[2] that the Aramaic *ṭalyâ* meant 'servant' and 'child' (Greek *pais*) as well as 'lamb', so that if there is an Aramaic source behind the Baptist's words in Jn 1[29], then John's reference to Jesus, which may well originally have been *ṭalyâ dhêlāhâ*, is not only a reference to Jesus as a 'lamb', but to Jesus as the Servant of Isaiah 53[11, 12]. Burney concluded 'that the fact that our Lord was to fulfill the rôle of the ideal Servant, though not understand by the Apostles, *was in some measure realized by the Baptist*'.[3]

Burney did not think it improbable, therefore, that the words, 'which beareth the sin of the world', giving a picture of the atoning work in Isai 53, were indeed the words of John the Baptist. Dr. Kingsley Barrett[4] objects that we should expect, if there are Aramaic sources, not the word *ṭalyâ* but rather the word *'abhdâ* as the natural equivalent of the Hebrew for Servant. Burney himself anticipated that very objection and met it by pointing to the play of meaning involved in the choice of *ṭalyâ* in preference to *'abhdâ* – the *lamb-like* and *child-like* or sinless character of the ideal Servant.[5] I think there is a great deal to say for the suggestions of Ball and Burney, which incidentally Jeremias appears to support.[6]

Amnos betokens Christ again in the Testament of Joseph. 'From Judah was born a Virgin and from her was born a *Lamb*, and the Lamb overcame the beasts.'[7]

2. ἀρνίον

'Lamb' occurs also in Revelation, and though it is a different word, *arnion*, the sacrificial connotation is there (5[12] 6[16] 7[14] 13[8],

251

etc.), as in the LXX too where Jeremiah (11[19]) sees himself as a lamb sacrificed (*arnion*). It is a rare word in classical Greek, a diminutive of the more regular *arēn*.

By the Seer, however, the *arnion* is represented as risen from the dead,[8] the horned Lamb (5[6]) enthroned in heavenly splendour, the Ruler, the Judge, the Shepherd and object of our adoration, the Bridegroom of the Church, the Source of life and light in heaven's Jerusalem (21[24, 27]). The *arnion* is mentioned nearly thirty times in the last book of the Bible. But the messianic horned Lamb *(arēn)* figures in the book of Enoch (89[45] 90), signifying Samuel, David, and the Chasids, great champions of Israel. When St. John reports Christ as charging Peter to 'feed My lambs', he uses the word *arnion*, not *amnos*. Is this deliberate? Are the converts conceived as those victorious lambs who share the risen life of the Saviour-Messiah, entitled to share with Him the victory over Satan's works?[9]

LAW OF GOD

νόμος

Nomos has a technical meaning in the Bible.

In secular Greek *nomos* was a law in the sense of a rule or statute, a usage or a custom – by derivation, what is 'assigned' (from *nemō*). Plato couples *nomos* with decrees (*Theaetetus* 173D). He sees ruin pending for the state which is not subservient to *nomos*; he foresees salvation for the state in which magistrates are servants of the *nomos*. Here Plato refers to 'usage' and 'custom' (*Laws* 715D) and that is the sense of Herodotus when he says that Spartans are not quite free, for *nomos* is their master. That is to say, it was not their 'custom' to flee from the battle (VII 104). We find the same sense in Aristotle. He laments that there is a kind of democracy where the multitude is sovereign rather than the *nomos*, where the decrees of the assembly over-ride the *nomos* (*Politica* 1292a 7).

Nomos signifies all this in Biblical Greek, too, where however an extraneous meaning has appeared, i.e. the divine *Tôrâ*, the gracious revelation of God's will for Israel. 'This is the *Nomos* which Moses set before the children of Israel' (Deut 4[44]).

Often it is difficult to determine whether St. Paul refers to the *Tôrâ* or to 'rule' in general, especially when *nomos* is anarthrous.[10] The Apostle says that the Gentile is under a *nomos* or principle, which is distinct from the *Tôrâ* although it too produces a sense of guilt in its breach. At all events, for Paul, every form of *nomos* is

God's law; they all show up sin as disobedience to God. St. Paul insists that all men have sinned, the Jews against the Tôrâ, the Gentiles against the nomos of nature. He does not allege that neither kind of law has power to justify. All nomos is divine,[11] and the doers of nomos shall be justified (Ro 2[13]). St. Paul sometimes uses nomos in a secular sense, meaning 'principle'. For instance, he speaks of a nomos 'of the flesh' and 'of sin', and 'of the Spirit'. Often, of course, it is certain that he means the Tôrâ, in the way Tôrâ was extended in Rabbinical Judaism – the Mosaic Law, the Pentateuch, and the OT as a whole. St. John does not share this ambivalent usage. Unlike St. Paul's, his nomos has always and only the consecrated Jewish sense.[12]

So far we have discovered two meanings among Christians: the Jewish Law and the secular sense of 'principle' and of natural law. But we are to see that Christians sometimes departed still further from the general interpretation. They used it for Christian teaching – the nomos of faith (Ro 3[27]) and the nomos of Christ (Gal 6[2]). Jesus Christ is indeed the innermost meaning and goal of nomos, and there is no dichotomy between Jesus Christ and nomos, as if nomos belonged to one dispensation and Grace to another. God's word in Scripture is one,[13] and there is an essential unity between the Old Covenant and the New. The Elect will always see Christ as their Saviour, but let them remember that He is no less their Sovereign. 'This being so, the continuance of moral obligation follows as a necessary corollary and, far from being reduced by God's grace, the obligation to obey the Law of God is increased.'[14] Let us remember that 'Jesus had been no iconoclast' and had spoken of the Law in the most appreciative terms. He had confined His work to the people of Israel and urged publicans and sinners to become again 'children of Abraham' (Lk 19[19]). Following Him, the first Christians made no attack on the Jewish Law. If any of them offended against it, 'they justified their lax standard on no theoretic grounds'.[15]

The apostolic Fathers use nomos in the secular sense of the civil laws which all must obey (Diogn. 5[10]). Moreover, they give to it the Biblical sense of Tôrâ (Barn 3[6]; Diogn. 11[6]; I. Smyrn. 5[1]; I. Magn. 8[1] vl.), and the specially Christian sense of 'the new nomos of Jesus Christ which is without yoke of necessity, taking the place of the old ordinance' (Barn 2[6]). Hermas has nomos in the sense of a commission which Christ received from His Father, having cleansed the sins of His people (Sim. V 6.3). What St. Ignatius calls the nomos of Jesus Christ (I. Magn. 2[1]) is placed by Michael into the hearts of Christians, according to Hermas (Sim. VIII 3.3, 4, 5) who conceives that martyrs suffer for the sake of such a nomos (Sim. VIII 3.7).

This is not quite the Law that some of the English Puritan divines meant when they affirmed, 'Let the Law of Moses ... keep its own place, and be the result of our sanctification: but in our justification it hath no room at all' (Robert Traill)[16]. The 'law of Christ', in Christian language is not the same as 'the Law of Moses'. The phrase in Christian Greek has come to mean the Church's rule of life.

> Earth that long in sin and pain
> Groaned in Satan's deadly chain
> Now to serve its God is free
> In the **law** of liberty. – J. B. DE SANTEUIL

LAWLESS

ἄθεσμος

Athesmos is found comparatively rarely in secular Greek. Plutarch has it for the sacrilege of Clodius who scandalized the mystic devotees of Bona on being discovered in ladies' clothes.[17] It appears in esoteric texts, including the Paris Magic papyrus where it means godless or sacrilegious.[18] But it is essentially Jewish (LXX, Philo, Josephus, the Sibyllines, the Testament of Solomon).

Its etymology suggests the sense of lawless – violation of the moral law[19] and breach of the Tôrâ. Hesychius in his lexicon equates the adverb, athesmōs, with 'contrary to the Law' (paranomōs) on the basis of the LXX (3 Mac 6[26]). Diodore is convinced that fear of punishment by the laws of Isis restrains men from illegal (athesmos) violence.[20] The Jewish criminal, Gischala, had unlawful (athesmos) food served at his table,[21] and in his dirge on godless Rome the maker of the Sibylline oracles accuses the city of being conspicuously athesmos. 'Make thine home in Hades', he cries, 'where laws are not!' (V 177).

The close connection with law may indicate the meaning. It was the lawless purpose of Antiochus to liquidate Jews in the hippodrome (3 Mac 5[12]). Justin Martyr uses the word for a breach of the Tôrâ (Dial. X 1). As late as the sixth century, the first discernible vernacular instance concerns athesmata pragmata (illegal practices) as excuses for a broken engagement.[22]

In Christian Greek it specially indicates Lot's contemporaries who violated the law of conscience and probably also the antinomian heretics of the NT period (2 Pet 2[7] 3[17]). Among the Apologists it means sexually 'immoral'. Condemning adulterers and pederasts, Athenagoras says, 'They have made a business of

254

harlotry and have established *immoral* houses of every base pleasure for the young'. He considers adultery to be 'immoral' because it is against the Law of God Who decreed one man for one woman.[23]

LEAVEN, UNLEAVENED

ζύμη : ζυμόω : ἄζυμος

'Leaven' as applied to bread was the meaning of the words in secular Greek (e.g. Hippocrates) and in the OT. The Hebrew *maṣṣâ* was in the Greek Bible invariably rendered by *zumē* and this sense of *azumos* (unleavened) appears in the NT (Mt 26[17]; Mk 14[12]; Lk 22[1,7]; Act 12[3] 20[6]). However, the language is influenced by a Christian typological interpretation of the Scriptures: Noah's ark, leaven, the Red Sea, the cloud, the rock, Canaan, Jordan, the tabernacles, Israel, the Covenant – all are figures of what is to come. So Christian Greek has given *zumē, zumō,* and *azumos* a metaphorical sense of **moral influence,** invariably on the evil side except in the parable of the Leaven and except for one instance of St. Ignatius (I. Magn 10[2]: the new leaven, Jesus Christ).

The Christian sense of 'leaven' denotes a corrupting influence when applied to the brethren. The troublesome brother is 'a little leaven' influencing the whole lump (Gal 5[9]). Such is the corrupting activity of the brother who is flagrantly immoral, who is a drunkard, who is a swindler (1 Co 5[6ff.]). 'Purge out the old *leaven* that ye may be a new lump, as ye are *unleavened.* ... Let us keep the feast, not with the *leaven* of malice and wickedness but with the *unleavened* bread of sincerity and truth.'

St. Justin Martyr follows St. Paul is seeing *leaven* as covetousness, envy and hatred – thinking of things in a carnal way (*Dial.* 14[2]).

Some are inclined to see *zumē* in the NT as a neutral word, not necessarily indicating a bad influence. Rather, every man has a leaven and every teacher exerts an influence whether for good or ill, and the following genitive must indicate the kind of influence, e.g. 'of the Pharisees'.[24]

LEVITY

ἐλαφρία

Although *elaphria* (alleviation) appears as a medical term in the second-century Aretaeus, the word nevertheless is likely to be of Christian coinage, at least in a non-medical and moral sense. Aretaeus discusses the cure of diabetes and recommends getting at the prime cause rather than simply the 'alleviation' *(elaphria)* of the distress.[25] On the other hand, in the Pauline context (2 Co 1[17]), the Apostle renounces *elaphria,* that is, any suggestion of laziness or convenience, as a motive for his not coming to Corinth. The true reason was rather that he wished to spare his readers.

Elaphria in this environment is associated with the 'flesh' and is contrasted with the faithful purpose of the Apostle whose manner of speech was an artless, Yea yea, nay nay. The Christian *elaphria* is close to our word, levity. So the lexicon of Hesychius summarizes the meaning as *mōria* (folly) and, with special reference to 2 Co 1[17], *kouphotēs* (levity). Hermas uses the adjective *elaphros* with the meaning 'impetuous' (*Mand.* V 2.4) and 'frivolous' (*Mand.* XI 6, XII 4, 5). Much later, AD x, the lexicon of Suidas defines it as *oligotēs* (scantiness and feebleness).

LIBERTY, SPIRITUAL

ἐλευθερία

No longer 'freedom' as the world knows it, *eleutheria* has become in Christian Greek a different word.

Basically, *eleutheria* in the secular language was liberty, usually democratic 'freedom', by contrast to bondage under the Assyrians or some other power and the bondage of rule under one man.[26] By the death of Aegistheus, the house of Atreus passed through the fire to win *eleutheria.*[27] It means the 'liberty' of Athens[28] and of Greece.[29] In our literature sometimes we find the ordinary Greek meaning: freedom for a bondmaid (Lev 19[20]), national independence for the Jews (1 Esd 4[49,53]; 1 Mac 14[27]), and a servant's freedom (Ecclus 7[21] 30[34] (33[25]); Hermas *Sim.* V 2.7).

Christian Greek, however, in the language of St. Paul, St. Peter and St. James has brought new significance to an old word, which is now a 'glorious liberty', a stage in the full salvation of God, not only liberty from sin's bondage (Ro 6[17f.]), from the Law (Ro 7[3f.] 8[2], etc.), and from death (Ro 6[21]), but also the final glorification of believers (Ro 8[21]). So *eleutheria* assumes an eschatological aspect, all creation's future splendour.[30]

The eschatological is not the sense when the word is applied to believers' conduct – 'freedom' to eat polluted food if need be (1 Co 10[29]), the 'freedom' which the Holy Spirit gives (2 Co 3[17]), 'freedom' wherewith Christ has emancipated us from the thraldom

of the Law (Gal 2⁴ 5¹), a 'freedom' which must not be brought to
the level of lust (Gal 5¹³) and malice (1 Pet 2¹⁶). The rabbis held
that study of the Law, what they called the 'yoke of the Law', did
not enslave but it made a man 'free'.[31] Much less does the Christian
Law enslave, the body of teaching which is a perfect law of **liberty**
(Jas 1²⁵ 2¹²), for that is the yoke of the Lover of concord, 'whose
service is perfect freedom'.[32] To Him we declare:

> *Yet dearly I love You, and would be lov'd faine,*
> *But am betroth'd unto Your enemie.*
> *Divorce mee, untie, or breake that knot againe,*
> *Take mee to You, imprison mee, for I*
> *Except You entrall mee, never shall be free,*
> *Nor ever chast, except You ravish mee.* – JOHN DONNE

The Christian sense is that of St. Ignatius. 'Let slaves endure
slavery', he says, 'to the glory of God, that they may obtain from
God a better **freedom**' (I. Pol 4³). His meaning, and that of St.
Paul, differed radically from the 'freedom' of antiquity which was
as political and philosophical as that of our own day. It was not that
aspect of *eleutheria* which they had in mind. It was rather the
freedom that consisted of a change of service. The term *eleutheria*
was appropriate enough for their vocabulary, for it had associations
with slavery. To be a Christian was to exchange one ownership for
another and relationship with Christ involves the abnegation of all
self-interest.[33]

See 'Law'.

LORD

κύριος

The meaning of *kurios* in secular Greek, apart from religious
contexts, is a 'master',[34] or a 'guardian' and 'trustee'.[35] In the
vocative it is a courteous form of address ('Sir!').[36]

In Biblical Greek, however, *kurios* is a divine title, the LXX
rendering of JHWH (God's holy Name) and of 'ᵃdhonai, (my
Lord). We may expect to find the earliest Christian use of *kurios* in
the Acts of the Apostles, reflecting the life and worship of the first
believers. But in the earlier part of the book it is often difficult to
determine the reference of *kurios,* whether it is to Jesus or to the
Father. For instance, when the first believers prayed, 'Thou, *Lord,*
which knowest the hearts', were they addressing Jesus (Act 1²⁴)?
The title seems to apply equally well to both Jesus and the Father,

and the reading varies often enough within the Western and Neutral texts (e.g. 2^{38} 10^{48} 5^{42} 7^{55} 13^{33}). A title, once the prerogative of God the Father, is rapidly coming to be applied to Jesus, His Son. 'The fact is that we can almost see the Church's faith growing before our eyes.'[37] We are quickly approaching a point where *Kurios* is a technical word with only one meaning, the 'Lord' Jesus. Burton was of opinion that the use of Kurios in the gospels, meaning 'Master' (a secular sense of the word), originated in Christ's own lifetime and in His own teaching, while as a divine title *Kurios* was not applied until later on, perhaps originally in this sense with St. Peter, but more likely with St. Paul.[38]

It opens the question whether the assertion, 'The *kurios* has need of him,' (Mk 11^{3}) has reference to the 'owner' of the animal, which is the secular use of *kurios*. Jesus might have been the owner and His words could be taken in that sense in Mark and Matthew. However, St. Luke mentions other owners of the colt (19^{33}).[39] I would think that *Kurios* is therefore intended as a divine title when Jesus says, 'The *Lord* hath need of him' (Mk 11^{3}; Mt 21^{3}; Lk $19^{31, 34}$). In one and the same passage St. Luke can make use of both secular and Christian vocabulary. The point has not yet come when *kurios* in Christian Greek has but one meaning, and to confuse the issue, scribal activity has been busy over the word *kurios*. Dr. Kilpatrick provides a table of variant readings which concern fifteen passages in Luke where *kurios* (absolute) is used of Jesus, by which he shows that we cannot study Gospel problems properly without taking into account how the textual variants may determine our understanding.[40] Dr. Kilpatrick himself agrees that 'the Lord', as a title of Jesus, occurs in John and apparently in Luke but finds it questionable whether it occurs in this way in Matthew and Mark. He will not assume that 'the Lord' is necessarily Jesus in the phrase, 'how great things the Lord hath done for thee' (Mk 5^{19}), and there are other explanations of the Greek word in Mk 11^{3} ('owner') and $12^{36f.}$. The textual variants may reflect some uncertainty about the title on the part of early editors, but despite that, we can truly say that the title *Kurios* is accorded to Jesus by St. Luke and St. John.

Although *kurios* as applied to Roman emperors is not to be taken to indicate their divinity,[41] yet it is true that *kurios* was a divine title in some secular papyri.[42] In a papyrus of the last century BC appears the phrase, 'as Soknebtunis, the *kurios* (mighty) god wills it'.[43] Later on, a papyrus of the second century AD refers to another Egyptian god, the '*kurios* Serapis', in an invitation to dinner: 'Chaeremon requests your company at dinner at the table of the mighty Sarapis in the Serapeium tomorrow'.[44] A marble tablet of the same period at Tivoli refers to the goddess, '*Kuria* Artemis'.[45]

Even earlier, in the first century BC in Egypt, we have evidence that Isis was graced by the title of *Kuria*.[46] When Nero is hailed as *kurios* of the whole world it may well connote divinity.[47]

Perhaps, therefore, the Christian title, 'the Lord', came from the same Hellenistic pagan inspiration rather than from the LXX.[48] It was Bousset's claim that the use of *kurios* by the earliest Church, probably first in Antioch, was due to secular influence. Because *kurios* was the contemporary designation for a saviour god, Bousset saw a parallel to pagan cults in the worship of Jesus as 'Lord'.[49] It appears that in the pagan world of St. Paul's day, 'gods' and *kurioi* were pretty well related, for he mentions 'gods' many and 'lords' many (1 Co 8[5]).

If the Christian title did come from Hellenistic paganism, then pagan influence seeped into the brotherhood at a curiously early stage, for the title was used in the first days of the Church – as witness St. Paul's letters to the Thessalonians. Is it conceivable that, so soon, pagan influences from Egypt were affecting a primitive and largely Jewish community? Bousset's claim has been resisted with particular vigour by those who see the currency of the prayer, *Maranatha* (Aramaic for, 'The *Lord* is coming!') in early Christian worship as significant. Moreover, it is interesting that Dr. O'Neil, after a full survey of the material, finds that there is a conclusive number of places in Acts where the connotation of *kurios* is that of the Hebrew *'adhonai,* behind which lies the name JHWH, and yet at the same time there is no suggestion that the connotation is affected by any other religion than the Jewish, already itself touched by Hellenism, of course. And so it must be unlikely that *kurios* as a name of Jesus either originated outside Palestine or drew its meaning from a secular source.[50] The LXX of Ps 109 (110)[1] will be sufficient origin.[51]

We may be sure that already in the Palestinian Church there was a firm consolidation between preaching, confession of faith, and Baptism. *Kurios* was the link. 'Jesus is *Kurios*', was a major theme in the preaching (e.g. Act 2[36] 10[36] 11[20]). 'Jesus is *Kurios*' was the professed faith of the first disciples, for St. Paul refers to 'confessing' that Jesus is *Kurios* (Ro 10[9]) and speaks of 'every tongue' confessing Jesus Christ as Lord (Ph 2[11]). We know there was a link between this early confession and Baptism, for the initiation rite was 'in the name of Jesus'. Which among all His names? It is very probable that the confessional formula required of the catechumen at Baptism was none other than the primitive affirmation of the believer's faith, i.e. 'Jesus is *Kurios*', which is thus the earliest of all baptismal creeds.[52]

In Jn 20[28] St. Thomas confesses Jesus as *Kurios* and God. His confessional expression is not so different from the formula, 'Jesus is *Kurios*. The expanded formula was close at hand when we remember that in the OT *Kurios* is the equivalent of Yahweh God. Dr. Kingsley Barrett suggests that the fuller formula, 'Lord and God', may have been taken from a liturgical setting and that the whole passage of St. John was liturgical in origin. The occasion is the Lord's day, a blessing is given, and absolution is pronounced.[53]

THE LORD'S

κυριακός

In secular Greek the adjective *kuriakos* meant 'of a lord' or 'of a master'. The *kuriakos logos* was the 'imperial treasury'.[54] In Christian Greek the adjective refers to what peculiarly belongs to Christ, Who in the beliefs and preachings of early believers was 'Lord'. The adjective applies to His Day (Sunday) – the *kuriakē hēmera* (Rev 1[10]) – and to the *kuriakon deipnon,* the Lord's Supper which is celebrated upon that day (1 Co 11[20]).

A little later the adjective becomes a noun on its own, and St. Ignatius about AD 112 speaks of living according to the *kuriakē* (I. Magn 9[1]), that is, making the Lord's Day the centre of one's life. By this early period then the Lord's Day (Sunday), and not the Sabbath, is the Christian day of worship. However, someone has pointed out that even in the third century, when the Lord's Day was firmly rooted, the Apostolic Constitutions were still having to regulate for observance of the Sabbath, the Saturday. Still, the Lord's Day (Sunday) increased in importance as the years went by, until at last the emperor Constantine decreed every Sunday to be a national holiday, in AD 321.[55] In Egypt, however, and the east observance of the Sabbath as well as of Sunday continued to be common.

The Didache coins a quaint phrase, 'the Lord's Day of the Lord' (*kuriakē Kuriou*) to denote the day on which Christians came together to break bread (14[1]). Later, the 'Great *Kuriakē* ' was Easter Day, and it has been suggested that it was upon Easter Day that St. John received his vision, rather than upon an ordinary Sunday.[56]

Similarly, in the later language of Christians, a *kuriakon* was the Lord's house, a church building.[57] In his history Eusebius records how, after persecuting the Christians, the emperor Maximin now allows them to build *kuriaka*,[58] churches.

πάθος

In secular Greek the meaning of *pathos* included emotion, experience and calamity in a general way. Anger and fear were examples of it.[59]

A strongly ethical turn, in a downward way, was given in the NT where it represents evil desire, rather different from the secular force of ills and sicknesses, such as are invoked on men who disturb a tomb.[60] The secular gist of sickness and suffering does appear in later Christian Greek, supremely of the sufferings of Christ. St. Ignatius speaks of 'the *pathos* (Agony) of my God' (I. Rom 6³) and refers in this way to our Lord's passion on several occasions,[61] but in the NT the word is pejorative always, and 'affections' (AV) is too mild a term in modern English to express the pagan enormity which will bring God's wrath on fallen mankind (Ro 1²⁶). St. Paul thinks of homosexuality – a characteristically pagan perversion, which he twice associated with the depraved desire of *epithumia* (Col 3⁵; 1 Th 4⁵).

Hermas condemns the adulterous wife who continues her *pathos* (lust), and the ill-tempered man who gives satisfaction to his *pathos* (temper).[62] For Theophylact, *pathos* is an immoral fury which burns the body like a fever, like a wound, like a disease.[63] It is no longer the innocent emotion of the secular language.

LOVE, BELOVED

1. LOVE

ἀγάπη : ἀγαπάω

In Christian Greek the noun *agapē* and the verb *agapō* denote a proper Christian affection, the love of the faithful to God and man, and the love of God for us and for Christ, as well as the love of Christ for us. It is then the perfect compatibility of God and man – a supernatural grace.

Dr. Kingsley Barrett notices that in St. John's gospel the two words come much more frequently in ch. 13–17 than elsewhere, which indicates that while God indeed loves the whole world, His love is more effective among those who believe in Christ.[64]

The words are a notable example of the unique character of Biblical diction. 'Thirty years after the death of Christ,' wrote Fr. Ceslaus Spicq, O.P., 'the Church already had its own language, its own full and precise theological vocabulary. The word *agapē*, in particular, had acquired so specialized and rich a meaning that it seemed almost a neologism'.[65] Moreover, Fr. Spicq's profound study of Christian Love had induced Nygren to declare, 'Agape comes to us as a quite new creation of Christianity. It sets its mark on everything in Christianity. Without it nothing that is Christian would be Christian. Agape is Christianity's own original basic conception.'[66]

It was a regular presupposition of pagan thought that gods are not to be expected to love mortals. Indeed, the best of pagans, Aristotle himself, thought it was out of the question. God has no object of thought outside Himself, least of all can He love. God is *noēsis noēseōs* (Thought of Thought) and so cannot return our feelings.[67] We have no personal intercourse with Him. If I say that the revelation of a God Who does love is peculiarly Biblical, perhaps the generalization is too sweeping, but at least we will never expect a pagan to endorse the words of Herbert.

> Who knows not Love, let him essay
> And taste that juice, which on the crosse a pike
> Did set abroach; then let him say
> If ever he did taste the like.
> Love is that liquor sweet and most divine,
> Which my God feels as bloude; but I, as wine.

The world does not see God loving like that. Hell, said Dostoievsky, is the punishment of being unable to love, whereas 'God is Love'. *Agapē* is the very nature of God Himself.

Agapē, confesses Dr. Norman Snaith, 'is essentially a Christian word standing for something that is essentially Christian. It was this love, none other and nothing less, that brought the Lord Jesus into this world to die upon the Cross. It is a love that does not depend upon any worth at all in the object of it; it is God's love showered freely upon all men, and to be realized by every man who turns to God in repentance and faith'.[68]

The word *agapē* itself was not quite strange to secular writers, although it was extremely rare before the Christian language exploited it. Already in earlier Biblical Greek there were three words for 'love' and *agapē* was one of them. Yet *agapē* was gaining the ascendancy over *philia* and *erōs*, the other two. Indeed, *agapē* had begun with a disadvantage, and before the appearance of the Greek Bible it is so rare that we may almost affirm that there are no clear pre-Biblical instances in the secular world. It follows that if we seek the exact meaning of *agapē* outside the Bible we are driven to the expedient of reconstructing it from analogy with the meaning of the verb *agapō*.

Generally *agapō* is distinct from the warm liking implied by *philō* (be fond of) on the one hand, and the physical attraction of *erō* (be in love with) on the other. There are grounds for thinking that *agapō* may involve the sense of mutual respect in secular Greek ('to welcome with a courteous greeting'), and may indicate a preference for one object over another, with a difference from the other two verbs corresponding to that between *diligō* and *amō* in Latin.

On the analogy of the verbs, then, we may suppose that whereas *erōs* tends to indicate a feeling that is physically passionate, and *philia* to be warm and spontaneous affection, *agapē* will, like its verb, tend to choose its object deliberately. *Agapē* will come nearer to 'esteem' than 'love'. Employed religiously, *erōs* may rather indicate an aspiration or involuntary feeling for God and one's fellows, while *agapē* is a calculated disposition of regard and pious inclination.

Pre-Christian instances of *agapē* are few indeed outside Jewish Greek. Three only bear investigation and even they amount to little – barely enough to show that the noun was in some kind of circulation.[69]

Secular examples at a later period than the NT are hardly less difficult to find.[70] Quite certainly *agapē* was rare and it is probable that Christians availed themselves of it because, like the cognate verb, its very novelty made it acceptable. It provided a neutral vehicle, innocent of previous associations, free to convey the Christian ideal of disinterested love. 'The fact that its use was very restricted made it easier to annex for a special purpose' (MM).

Jews, however, may have been impressed rather by homonymous qualities of the *agapē* consonants, that is, the verbal resemblance between Greek *agp* and Hebrew *'kb* (divine and human affection), for it should be observed that Greek-speaking Jews, as seen in the LXX and Josephus, observed little apparent distance in meaning between all three verbs. In the LXX *agapō* chiefly renders *'hb* and only occasionally *yādhîdh* (as participle, in the prophets), while *philō* has declined to thirty instances – chiefly for *'hb* and *nsq* (to kiss) – and *erō* (and *erōmai*) is virtually extinct. There cannot be said to be a distinction. *Agapō*, being a homonym of *'hb*, is simply gaining ascendancy over the other two.

In the NT *erō* has fallen out altogether, while *agapō* and *philō* appear interchangeably, even in Christ's conversation with St. Peter (Jn 21[15ff.]), where the verbs really must be synonymous since Jesus is represented as asking Peter a third time whether he loved Him *(philō)*, whereas He is represented as using *agapō* on the first two occasions, and Peter had replied with *philō* no matter which of the two verbs Jesus had used. Reluctantly one must say, it is difficult to see any 'subtle and delicate play of feeling here' (Trench p. 41), and much easier to suppose that the evangelist, who has inherited the LXX's indifference over the two verbs, is varying the vocabulary simply to avoid monotony. St. John is indifferent, too, to the distinction between other synonyms beside *agapō-philō*, namely *pempō-apostellō* (send), *phulassō-tērō* (keep), and *horō/idein-theōrō* (see). The Vulgate, it is true, tries to do justice to the Greek by keeping *diligō* for the one verb and *amō* for the other.

Moreover, it is no more reasonable to find in the Greek Bible any clear distinction between the nouns, *agapē*, *philia*, and *erōs*. Although *agapē* is the usual rendering of *'ahᵃbhâ*, nevertheless the respective contexts show that it is usually connected with amorous love and is not at all a 'higher' kind than *philia*.[71] Indeed, when a higher kind is meant – Jonathan's love for David, love towards enemies, love for Wisdom, or God's love for man – the word in the LXX tends to be *agapēsis*, of which indeed *agapē* may eventually have become a curtailment (Souter).

It should not then be supposed that the Greek Bible was instrumental in giving *agapē* the special meaning it came to enjoy in the Christian environment. The Greek Bible did, however, bring the word prominently forward in the Jewish circles of Aristeas, Philo, and the various Testaments, and it left the way open for its special Christian adoption.[72]

The Greek Bible may be said to have rescued *agapē* from oblivion and to have dismissed *erōs* almost altogether as a religious word, retaining it only twice in the whole of its length. We cannot claim that *erōs* never came back as a Christian word. Indeed, it is interesting to find it instead of *agapē* in the third century, in a parallel passage or gloss on 1 Co 13[13], where four elements particularly about God are mentioned: they are, 'faith, truth, *erōs*, hope'.[73] There is too some more evidence for suspecting that *erōs* was soon re-adopted by Christians. St. Ignatius exclaims, 'My *erōs* is crucified,' (I. Rom 7), but he may not be thinking of divine love, and perhaps he means, 'My *love of the world* is crucified'. Faber's hymn certainly seems to accept St. Ignatius' *erōs* in an objective sense, Jesus the divine Beloved. Hymns Ancient and Modern in 1861 altered Faber's line, 'Jesus, our Love, is crucified'. Origen rendered the Ignatius-phrase as, 'Meus autem *Amor* crucifixus est',[74] and St. Clement calls Christ *erastos*.[75] In the context, St. Ignatius will by *erōs* mean Jesus, i.e. divine Love, rather than his own 'love' of the world and other idols.[76]

At all events, we may be satisfied that as yet no clear instance of *agapē* has come to light in pre-Christian secular Greek, and although it may not always be possible to affirm with Trench that the word was 'born within the bosom of revealed religion', for some new text may come to light, yet we may believe that it was baptized and consecrated within the Church.

In the NT, as far as the synoptic gospels go, *agapē* is deep-rooted affection, consciously reaching out for its object, always seeking to prove itself. Man receives God's *agapē* as an unmeritted bounty and feels the same emotion to Him in gratitude. In the teaching of Jesus '*agapē* implies being unconditionally available; it may demand the sacrifice of all that is humanly dear'.[77]

St. Paul sees *agapē* as consecration to Christ, and even when our *agapē* reaches out to other men, it continues to devote itself to the service of Christ. He sees the whole of our religion, and every virtue of it, as really being *agapē*. The Christian has no other thing to do but love. At the End, when there shall be a general cooling-off of *agapē* (Mt 24[12]), still the Elect will have but one concern, that their love for one another burns more intensely. In the Tribulation they will need 'mercy, peace and love' (Jude 2), but in all their frailty they may be of good cheer, for '*agapē* covers a multitude of sins' (1 Pet 4[8]) even when the End of all things is nigh.[78]

J. C. Fensham makes a study of 'love' in three types of writing: Qumrân, the Johannine literature, and the apocrypha-pseude-pigrapha.[79] In all three, he finds that much is made of man's love for God and that love to one another is fully worked out. What is unique in the Johannine literature is the Christian application of brotherly love as a new commandment because it reflects God's love in Jesus Christ. Moreover, nowhere in the Johannine literature is brotherly love contrasted with hatred to enemies.

Brotherly *agapē* is widely advocated in every type of Jewish and Christian literature, but it is not necessary to conclude that there has been direct borrowing from the Jews on the part of Christians. Brotherly love was indeed a general characteristic of contemporary Jewish thought.

The plural word, *agapai*, in the sense of 'love feasts', is indeed an additional Christian meaning (Jude 12; 2 Pet 2[13]). The Love Feast lingered on[80] in parts of the Church, especially in Egypt. In the time of St. Ignatius the Eucharist formed part of the *agapē*. 'It is not lawful', he declares, 'apart from the Bishop either to baptize or to hold a Love Feast' (I. Smyrn. 8[5]). The parallel with Baptism makes clear that the Eucharist is included in the *agapē*.[81] The Eucharist was not yet distinguished from it at Alexandria in St. Clement's time,[82] and as a newly ordained presbyter St. Augustine wrote to his bishop at Carthage about the scandals taking place at the Love Feasts in the cemeteries and martyrs' chapels.[83] The following year the council of Hippo banned them but they still went on and were held even in church, until the matter of discipline was finally taken in hand in 397 by the council of Carthage.

Later still the singular *agapē* denoted 'charity' in the sense of alms.[84] It is noteworthy that in modern Greek *agapē* is the regular and practically the only word for 'love' in all its senses.[85] Can this be due to Christian influence upon the Greek secular language?

2. BELOVED

ἀγαπητός

The adjective *agapētos* is derived from the verb and is another instance of a secular word acquiring its own peculiar meaning in Biblical Greek through LXX influence: beloved, or dearly beloved.

It involves the relation of Christian to Christian. Those at Corinth were Paul's 'beloved sons' and his 'dearly beloved'. Even the Jews are 'beloved', as touching the election, for all Israel shall be saved (1 Co 4[14] 10[14]; Ro 11[28]). It is contrasted with *echthros* (hostile).

The meaning becomes more disputable when Jesus at His baptism and transfiguration is hailed as *agapētos* (Mt 3[17] 17[5]; Mk 1[11] 9[7]; Lk 3[22]; 2 Pet 1[17]). Some still look to secular Greek and suppose the title not to be Beloved (the messianic title) but 'unique' or 'only', as in secular reference. So also in the parable of the Vineyard (Mk 12[6]; Lk 20[13]) the title appears, and here also some take the secular sense: not his 'well beloved' but his 'only' son.[86] C. H. Turner declared that from Homer to Athanasius the history of the Greek language bears out that the phrase is rightly rendered, 'only Son'.[87]

It accords with secular use in a later period to see *agapētos* as the equivalent of *monogenēs* (only). The lexicon of Julius Pollux in the second century defines '*agapētos* son' as, 'he whose father has only one',[88] i.e. *monos*, and that of Hesychius defines it as *monogenēs* (only-begotten). Though the lexicons reflect a relatively late Greek, one presumes that 'only' was the original secular meaning of *agapētos*.

In the classical language the word was applied to only-begotten children and was basically 'that wherewith one must be content'. The nurse of Telemachus addressed him, 'Whither art thou minded to go over the wide earth, thou who art an *only son*? Odysseus, your father, has died in a strange land'.[89] Hector's wife came to meet her husband, and with her was the maid-servant bearing in her bosom the tender boy, the *agapētos* of Hector.[90] Demosthenes speaks of Nikeratos as the *agapētos* son of Nikias.[91] All seem to refer to an 'only' son. The concept of contentment with, and acquiescence in, one's lot, making the best of it, is evident in classical Greek contexts, for instance, the least in a choice of evils.[92]

Describing the horrors of the famine in the Jewish war, Josephus has the phrase, 'it was *agapēton*', concerning the wretches who were deprived of the meagre food they had: 'it was *to be expected as something to be acquiesced in* that they were only robbed, and not also slain'.[93] This very phrase, *agapēton esti* (it is the only course, one must be content) is not rare in classical Greek. '*Agapēton* (we must be thankful),' says Plato, 'if someone shows us the way to virtue', and, '*Panu agapēton* (we must be very thankful)', says Xenophon, 'if only God refrains from destroying the innocent, and, '*Agapēton einai* (a man must be content)', says Demosthenes, 'to do his duty', and for Aristotle the phrase *agapēton* means, 'we must be content', 'we have no choice'.[94]

In the Biblical language there is a change. True, *agapētos* renders the Hebrew *yāḥîdh* (Gen 22[2,12,16]; Jer 6[26]; Am 8[10]; Zech 12[10]), that is, 'only', in contexts that refer to an only child, but the change appears when *agapētos* also renders the various Hebrew words which mean 'beloved': *dôdhî* (Isai 5[1]), *yaqqîr* (Jer 38 (31)[20]), and *yādhîdh* (especially in the psalms, 44 (45)[tit] 59 (60)[5] 83 (84)[1] 107 (108)[6] 126 (127)[2]). Further, *agapētos* seems to mean 'beloved' in those apocryphal books which have no extant Hebrew original (Ecclus 15[13]; Tob 3[10]S 10[13]B; Bar 4[16]; Sus 63) and in Isai 26[17] which also has no Hebrew equivalent. In later Greek versions, subsequent to the NT, *agapētos* exclusively means 'beloved', and at times the versions appear to be correcting the LXX by substituting *monogenēs*, as if they considered *agapētos* to be the wrong word where 'only' is meant.

We may guess that some earlier translators of the LXX[95] not only continued to follow secular precedent but also were guilty of confusion when they introduced *agapētos* into contexts calling for 'only', and that they muddled in fact two Hebrew words – *yādhîdh* (beloved) and *yāḥîdh* (only) – where one small stroke makes all the difference. It may be, moreover, that the requirements of some particular contexts where *yāḥîdh* is found demanded a word more affectionate in tone than *monogenēs*, and so the word *agapētos* came smoothly to mind as already the equivalent of the like-sounding *yādhîdh* – that is, if by then the Psalms were translated. Not the later versions alone, but also St. Paul is demurely correcting the LXX, for when he alludes to Gen 22[3] (in Ro 8[31]) he avoids the *agapētos* of the LXX in the phrase which means 'only son' and instead resorts to the word *idiou* (his own).

There is further evidence that for Christians the word *agapētos* was 'beloved'. In some Christian texts the plural *agapētoi* is used of the elect community, the Church, and is the equivalent of *adelphoi* (brethren): 1 Pet 2[11] 4[12]; T. Abr 104[5] (Christian addition). St. Peter's 'dearly beloved' are his Christian readers. Moreover, in the Diocletian persecution a Christian woman escaped in a party of gravediggers and her safe arrival at a Christian community is reported in a letter which her protector received from another priest, addressed to 'Apollo the presbyter, his beloved *(agapētos)* brother'.[96] Another Christian letter of about AD 346 addresses 'my master and beloved *(agapētos)* brother Abinnaeus'.[97] A century later a letter addresses 'my dear (*agapite*, mis-spelt) lord' who was a brother Christian.[98]

'Beloved' was then the current Christian meaning of the word, although the connotation may have been born of muddle between two like Hebrew words.

The word is closely associated not only with the term 'brethren', but it is synonymous with another term for Christians, viz. 'the elect'. St. Matthew, it should be noticed, substitutes the word *agapētos* when he is quoting the LXX of Isai 42[1], which has *eklektos* (Hebrew *beḥîrî*), strongly suggesting that for the first Christians 'Beloved' and 'Elect' were interchangeable terms, both titles of Messiah. Moreover, St. Luke sees no harm in substituting *eklelegmenos* (elect) for *agapētos* in the avowal at the Transfiguration (9[35]).[99]

LOVE (EARNEST DESIRE)

ἐπιπόθησις: ἐπιποθία: ἐπιπόθητος

The words, *epipothēsis, epipothia, epipothētos,* were probably coined in Biblical or Christian Greek, and they express the warm feelings which believers have for each other, like the Corinthians' 'earnest desire' *(epipothēsis)* towards St. Paul (2 Co 7[7,11]). Aquila (at Ezek 23[11]) uses *epipothēsis* to render 'lustfulness' *("ghābhâ),* perhaps because the Hebrew letters suggested *agapē* (love). Indeed, *epipothēsis* was much the same as *agapē* among Christians, and the Suidas lexicon defines *epipothia* as *agapē.*

Epipothia, our second word, also denotes a strong feeling among the brotherhood, expressing St. Paul's warm desire to visit the Romans (Ro 15[23]).

Our third word, the adjective *epipothētos,* occurs in the phrase, 'dearly beloved brethren, *earnestly longed for'* (Ph 4[1]). It will be a Christian coinage. 'Peace and concord is *earnestly longed for,'* writes St. Clement of Rome (1 Clem 65[1]), and another Father writes, 'The sight of you is *earnestly longed for'* (Barn 1[3]). A little later, however, Appian used it in a military context. 'In subsequent wars,' he writes, 'the treaties of Gracchus were often *longed for (epipothētos)'*.[100]

NOTES

[1] *Pax* 935.

[2] C. F. Burney, *The Aramaic Origin of the Fourth Gospel,* Clarendon 1922, p. 107.

[3] Ibid., p. 106.

[4] C. K. Barrett, *The Gospel according to St. John,* SPCK 1958, p. 147.

[5] Burney, op. cit., p. 108.

[6] J. Jeremias in Kittel *TWNT* I, p. 339.

[7] T. XII P. *Joseph* 19[18].

[8] A. Rose, *Bible et Vie Chrétienne* (Paris) 62 (1965), pp. 27–32.

[9] N. Hillyer, *Evangelical Quarterly* 39 (1967), p. 229.

[10] Ro 2[12, 14b] 3[20f.] 4[15], etc.

[11] S. Lyonnet, *Verbum Domini* (Rome) 41 (1963), pp. 238–42.

[12] S. Pancaro, *The Law in the Fourth Gospel,* Brill 1975, p. 514.

[13] C. E. B. Cranfield, *Scottish Journal of Theology,* 17 (1964), pp. 43–68.

[14] E. F. Kevan, *The Grace of Law. A Study in Puritan Theology,* Carey Kingsgate 1964, p. 253.

[15] B. H. Branscomb, *Jesus and the Law of Moses,* Hodder 1930, p. 280.

[16] E. F. Kevan, op. cit., p. 207.

[17] *Lives: Caesar* 10.

[18] P. Lond 1678.5, Preisandanz 4.2606, 2670 (editor: 'die freule').

[19] Philo *de Vita Mosis* 2.198.

[20] Diodorus Siculus I 14.

[21] Josephus *Bell. Jud.* VII viii 1 (Niese VII 264).

[22] P. Oxy I 129.7.

[23] *Legatio* 34[2]. See *Athenagoras: Legatio and De Resurrectione,* ed. W. R. Schoedel, Clarendon 1972, p. 82.

[24] H. Windisch in Kittel *TWNT* II, p. 908.

[25] Karl Hude, *Corpus Medicorum Graecorum,* II Leipzig, 1908, p. 162, line 10.

[26] Herodotus I 62, 95.

[27] Sophocles *Electra* 1509.

[28] Plato *Laws* 698A.

[29] Andocides *de Mysteriis* 142.

[30] A. Güemes, *Estudios Bíblicos* (Madrid) 22 (1963), pp. 219–42.

[31] P. *Aboth* III 5.

[32] Collect for Peace, B.C.P.

[33] D. Stanley, *Way* (London) 15 (1975), pp. 83–98.

[34] Aeschylus *Agamemnon* 878; Thucydides IV 20; Xenophon *Anabasis* V 7.27.

[35] Demosthenes XLIII 15, XLVI 19.

[36] E.g. P. Fay 106.15 (ii AD) – as in the gospels (e.g. Mt 8[2]).

[37] John Reid, *Expository Times* 15 (1903), p. 296.

[38] Burton, pp. 399–404. Burton made a possible exception of 'Lord and Christ' (Act 2[36]) which he agreed was original.

[39] R. G. Bratcher, *Expository Times* 64 (1952), p. 93.

[40] G. D. Kilpatrick, *Novum Testamentum* 19 (1977), pp. 285f.

[41] W. Foerster in Kittel *TWNT* III, p. 1054.

[42] Deissmann LAE, pp. 353ff.

[43] P. Tebt 284.6.

44 P. Oxy 110.2.

45 IG vol. XIV, 1124.

46 CIG 4897a. See W. Foerster in Kittel *TWNT* III, p. 1048.

47 R. H. Fuller, *The Foundations of New Testament Christology*, Lutterworth 1965, p. 88.

48 R. Bultmann, *Theology of the NT*, ET London, vol. I, 1952, pp. 124f.

49 W. Bousset, *Kyrios Christos* (FRLANT 4) Göttingen 3rd ed. 1935, pp. 75–104. On this see V. Taylor, *The Names of Jesus*, Macmillan 1953, pp. 47ff., and R. P. Martin, *Carmen Christi* CUP 1967, p. 243.

50 J. C. O'Neil, *Scottish J. of Theology*, 8 (1955), p. 174. See also his, *The Theology of Acts in its Historical Setting*, SPCK 1961, pp. 129ff.

51 Fuller, op. cit., p. 68.

52 O. Cullmann, *Les Premières Confessions de foi Chrétiennes*, Presses Universitaires de France, 2nd ed. 1948, pp. 13ff.; O. Cullmann, in *Revue d'histoire et de philosophie religieuses* (Strasbourg) 17 (1937) pp. 424–34. See also N. Hofer, *Theologische Quartalschrift* (Tübingen) 145 (1965), pp. 1–12.

53 C. K. Barrett, *The Gospel according to St. John*, SPCK 1958, p. 477.

54 CIG 4957.18 (AD 68). See Deissmann BS p. 217.

55 S. V. McCasland, *Journal of Biblical Literature*, 49 (1930), p. 68.

56 C. W. Dugmore, *Neotestamentica et Patristica*, 1962, pp. 272–81.

57 Origen PG VII 132C, etc.

58 *Historia Ecclesiastica* IX x 10.

59 Aristotle *Nicomachean Ethics* II 14; Diogenes Laertius VII i 67.

60 As on a second-century AD inscription, Dittenberger, 3rd ed., 1239.20. See also, for 'sickness', a first-century papyrus, *Ägyptische Urkunden*, Berlin 1895ff., II 588.4.

61 I. Smyrn 1² 5³ 7² 12²; I. Eph 18² 20¹; I. Magn 5² 11¹; I. Philad 9². Also Barn 6⁷.

62 *Mand.* IV 1.6, *Sim.* VI 5.5.

63 Quoted in Trench, p. 306.

64 C. K. Barrett, *The Gospel according to St. John*, SPCK 1955, p. 180.

65 C. Spicq, *Agape in the New Testament*, ET 1963, St. Louis and London, ii p.v.

66 A. Nygren, *Agape and Eros*, ET SPCK 1953, p. 48.

67 *Magna Moralia* 1208b, 26–32.

68 N. Snaith, *Expository Times* 70 (1958), p. 20.

69 A mere fragment of ii BC in the Berlin papyrus 9869 has the letters ΜΑΛΙΣΤΑ ΑΓΑΠΗΣ, and while it exemplifies the word it is unintelligible as to meaning: cf. *Berliner Klassikertexte* 2 (1905) 55. The rendering is somewhat uncertain in the second example, from Philodemus c. 60 BC: δι' ἀ[γ]άπης ἔ[ναρ] γοῦς (*Peri Parrēsias* col. 13a 3. A. Olivieri, Leipzig 1914, Teubner, p. 52.) A third instance has been adduced: A. Ceresa-Gestaldo argued that the word is restored in an inscription of 27 BC (*Rivista di Filologia* 31 (1953), pp. 347–56).

70 Two examples come from ii AD: P. Oxy 1380, 28 and 1380, 109. In the latter, 'agapē of the gods' is a cult-title of Isis given in the Egyptian town of Thomis according to an Isis-liturgy which has the various names of the goddess in various places. This is to follow the emendation of Grenfell-Hunt (agreed by C. H. Roberts), but Dr. Stephanie West emends 'agapē of the gods' (line 109) to 'agathēn thean', i.e. the Bona Dea (*Journal of Theological Studies* NS 18 (1967), p. 102), an idea rejected by R. E. Witt (*Journal of Theological Studies* NS 19 (1968), pp. 209–11). There is a third-century inscription (*Supplementum Epigraphicum Graecum*, ed. J. J. E. Hondius, 1923–38, VIII 1937, 548), and there is reputed to be an instance in a scholion on the *Tetrabiblos* of Ptolemaeus (Basel 1559, p. 52) of the same date, and there are other examples in H. Lietzmann's excursus after 1 Cor 13 in his commentary. Yet a further example

is brought out in a previous article of A. Ceresa-Gestaldo which discusses a new secular papyrus and a new secular inscription of iii AD.

[71] For the detailed evidence, see HDB 1963, p. 594.

[72] E.g. Aristeas 229 (*agapē* the gift of God), Ps. Sol 18[4] ('Thy *agapē* is towards the seed of Abraham'), Philo *Deus Immutabilis* 69 ('Moses has linked two other principles ... fear and *agapē*. ... All the exhortations in the Law refer to our either fearing or loving the Existent'), T. Gad 4[7] ('the spirit of *agapē* works together with the Law of God for salvation of men'), 5[2] ('Cleave to the *agapē* of God'), T. Abr 98[28] ('the greatness of Abraham's *agapē* to God').

[73] Porphyry *ad Marcellam* 24, ed. A. Nauck, *Porphyrii Opuscula*, Teubner 1886.

[74] Commentary on Song of Songs (Latin).

[75] *Stromateis* VI 9.72.

[76] Against Lightfoot's arguments, see C. Bigg, *The Christian Platonists of Alexandria*, Clarendon 1886, pp. viii–xii.

[77] Spicq, op. cit., vol. i, pp. 142f.

[78] Ibid., ii, pp. 306, 341, 383.

[79] In *Neotestamentica 6: Die Nuwe-Testamentiese Werkgemeenskap van Suid-Afrika*, Pretoria 1972, pp. 67–77.

[80] Sib. Orac. 8[402, 497] 5[265].

[81] J. B. Lightfoot, *Apostolic Fathers*, part II, vol. II, Macmillan 1889, p. 313.

[82] C. Bigg, op. cit., pp. 102–5.

[83] *Epistle* XXII 3–6.

[84] P. Geneva 14 (iv/v AD).

[85] C. C. Tarelli, *Journal of Theological Studies* NS 1 (1950), pp. 64f.

[86] C. H. Turner, *Journal of Theological Studies* 27 (1926), pp. 113–29, supported by A. Souter, ibid. 28 (1927), pp. 59f.

[87] Op. cit., p. 129.

[88] Op. cit., p. 117.

[89] Homer *Odyssey* II 365.

[90] Homer *Iliad* VI 401.

[91] *Midias* 165.

[92] Andocides, Teubner III 22.

[93] *Bell. Jud.* V x 3 (Niese V 438).

[94] Plato *Protagoras* 328B; Xenophon *Oeconomicus* VIII 16; Demosthenes XVIII 220; Aristotle *Metaphysics* 1076a 15.

[95] The confusion is confined to the translators of Genesis, Jeremiah, and the Minor Prophets. See HDB, 2nd ed. 1963, article BELOVED.

[96] P. Grenf. II 73, late iii AD.

[97] P. Brit. Mus. 417.

[98] P. Heid 6 (iv AD).

[99] J. A. Robinson in HDB vol. II, p. 501a.

[100] Appian *Ibērikē* 43, 179 (ii AD).

M

MARTYR

μάρτυς: μαρτύριον: μαρτυρία

From the general meaning of 'witness' in secular Greek the words have changed their direction in Christian use to mark the supreme witness of all, the testimony to Jesus which ends in martyrdom.

Secular Greek. *Martus* is a witness, or a record, as in the phrase, 'I call the gods as *witnesses*.'[1] *Martus* is frequent in Plato: 'In the law-courts,' he says, 'they bring a number of *witnesses*,'[2] but he has a less legal sense. 'For all these sayings they cite their poets as *witnesses*.'[3] Plato speaks of adducing the nature of beasts as evidence *(martus)*.[4] Xenophon refers to the physique and complexion of residents as clear 'witnesses' to the health of a locality.[5] *Martus* is one who speaks from personal experience about actions and persons, and from conviction about truths and views, *Marturion* and *marturia* are testimony or proof, in the same way.[6]

Christian Greek. An additional meaning developed for *martus*, giving the English language the word 'martyr' – one who dies witnessing. *Martus* is usually a martyr in that sense in the apostolic Fathers (e.g. M. Pol. 2[3] 14[2] 15[2] 16[2] 17[3] 19[1]), but to render *martus* by 'witness' in the peculiarly Christian sense of an inspired witness to Christian truth, not necessarily going to the full extent of the supreme sacrifice, would sometimes be more appropriate (as in I. Philad. 7[2]; 1 Clem 63[3]). The verb *marturō* (1 Clem 5[4]) certainly has the connotation of dying for the faith.

In the NT three passages of AV show the rendering 'martyr' for *martus*. 'Thy martyr, Stephen', 'the martyrs of Jesus', and 'my faithful martyr' Antipas, alike shed their blood (Act 22[20]; Rev 2[13] 17[6]). However, as Dr. Casey remarked, there is nothing to suggest that St. Stephen's death was an essential part of his being a *martus*. Like St. Paul he was an eye-witness to the risen Jesus, and the incidental fact that he died in consequence of his testimony made him no more and no less a *martus* than St. Paul.[7]

One specially Christian sense of *martus* is therefore the bearing witness to Jesus without necessarily paying the supreme sacrifice. 'Ye shall be *witnesses* of these things,' He promised (Lk 24[46ff.]). 'It is evident that the Apocalypse was written at a time when the consequences of such testifying were dangerous and often fatal.[8] The question is whether, according to Heb 12[1] we are surrounded in our Christian struggle by OT 'martyrs' or by OT 'witnesses'.

By some of those who have investigated the words closely, it is

272

urged that *marturion* and the verb *marturō* (to witness) have not yet in the Christian language arrived at the stage where they become equivalents of 'martyrdom'. However, *martus* is rather a different case, for death seems to be implied at Rev 1^5 3^{14} 17^6, although AV has 'witness' in the first two. But in Rev 11^3 *martus* does retain its forensic meaning of witness in a law-court (and probably also in 2^{13}, where AV has 'martyr'). Nevertheless, martyrological elements are present, for the Beast kills the two 'witnesses' who thus become martyrs, and Antipas was assuredly 'slain'. It is felt, then that *martus* is moving towards the meaning, 'martyr', and yet some think 'it is still questionable whether the martyrological understanding has become part of the dictionary definition of the word'.[9]

In 1 Ti 2^6 we have the second noun, *marturion*. It is apparently in apposition with *antilutron*, and Christ's death may be described therefore as a 'martyrdom'. The Apostle says that Christ gave Himself a 'ransom' for all, a *marturion* in times of His own choosing. Falconer insisted that 'here there is no reference in the word to the later meaning of martyrdom'.[10] St. Chrysostom, however, is not slow to see the connection which is inherent in the context. It is plain that what St. Paul refers to is a 'witness' which cannot be distinguished from 'martyrdom', for it involves death on others' behalf. In his seventh homily on the Pastorals St. Chrysostom writes, 'Undoubtedly Christ died even for the heathen, and you cannot bear to pray for them. Why then, you ask, did they not believe? Because they would not: but His part was done. His suffering was a *marturion*, he says; for He came, it is meant, to *bear witness* to the truth of the Father and was slain.'[11] The death of Jesus is the first instance of martyrdom in the later Christian sense. 'Here the death of Jesus is the testimony of which Paul is the herald, and Jesus offers the evidence by the sacrifice of His life.'[12]

Although *marturion* is not itself a peculiarly Biblical Word, yet the phrase, *eis marturion*, is a feature of Christian Greek applied in the following contexts: 'for a proof' that the leper was healed (Mt 8^4, etc.), persecution is 'for a testimony' against world-rulers (Mt 10^{18}, etc.), and 'for a proof' to the disciples (Lk 21^{13}). Gospel-preaching is 'for a testimony' to all nations (Mt 24^{14}), the dust is removed 'for a testimony' (Mt 10^{18}, etc.), Moses was faithful 'to testify' (Heb 3^5), and the fading of riches is 'for a testimony' against those that trust in them (Jas 5^3). In none of these contexts need *marturion* necessarily involve death, but neither do the contexts exclude death.

Marturia is a characteristically Johannine word – fourteen times in the gospel, seven in the epistles, and nine in the apocalypse, as against only seven times in the rest of the NT. Most times it is used in the secular sense – a record, report or testimony. In the gospel of St. John it has the 'normal Greek usage'[13] – to establish by one's testimony the fact alleged. But in Revelation it comes near to meaning 'martyrdom' sometimes, though not often. The Seer was in Patmos because of his *marturia* which he had borne to Jesus Christ (1[9]). In his vision he saw beneath the altar the souls of them that were slain for the *marturia* which they held (6[9]). The two Martyrs have a martyrdom *(marturia)* to finish (11[7]). They overcame the Devil by the blood of the Lamb and by the word of their *marturia* (12[11]). *Marturia* is a 'testimony' which inevitably has death as its reward (12[17] 19[10] 20[4]). In the final chapter of St. John the Beloved Disciple has a *marturia*, but there is clearly a play on the idea of 'martyrdom' for St. Peter's death is spoken of in the same context (21[19]).

If only by inference, these words and the phrase *(eis marturion)* have much to do with tribulation and at any time in the Christian life 'witness' may prove to be 'martyrdom'.

> *What? wearied out with half a life?*
> *Scar'd with this smooth unbloody strife?*
> *Think where thy coward hopes had flown*
> *Had heaven held out the martyr's crown.* – KEBLE

'Witness' varies with 'martyrdom' according to the time in which we live. From the first the words had signified Christian witness: public preaching, zeal, and the manifestation of the sanctified life. But when persecutions come our circumstances change and a more sensational and dangerous way of 'testifying', where death follows, becomes inevitable. These outward circumstances changed the meaning of the words from witness to martyr.

MEMORIAL SACRIFICE

ἀνάμνησις

Anamnēsis is a word which Plato uses for 'reminiscence': what we now remember, 'recollection'.[14] Socrates observed, 'When the soul has lost the memory of a perception and then regains it, we call everything of that kind *recollections*.'[15] In Josephus and the papyri[16] it is much the same – a reminder, a remembrance.

When, however, *anamnēsis* came into Biblical Greek it was used in a singular context, for the LXX at Lev 24[7] make it the equivalent of *'azkārâ*, which is a memorial offering. In this passage *anamnēsis/'azkārâ* is the incense which was burned upon the showbread, 'for a memorial, even an offering made by fire'. It is more than a memorial, it is a sacrifice. Indeed, it is difficult to see what relevance *anemnēsis* in the sense of 'act of remembrance or recalling', could have in the context.[17]

Another passage in which *anamnēsis* is used is Num 10[10] where it renders the Hebrew *zikkhārôn,* here meaning 'memorial'[18] – that your 'sacrifices' may be a 'memorial' before God – which elsewhere applies to the grain-offering of jealousy (Num 5[15,18,25]). The purpose of the 'memorial' sacrifice was not to remind the worshippers, but to bring certain things to the notice of God, 'a reminder on your behalf before your God' (Num 10[10]).

A third special context for *anamnēsis* is that in the psalms (37(38)[tit] 69(70)[tit]), where the word renders the Hiphil of *zkr* (commemoration and bringing to remembrance). The Hiphil is used further in Isai 66[3] in connection with *l'bhōnâ* (frankincense) in the sense of offering an *'azkārâ* (memorial sacrifice). A further instance of Hiphil may be Ps 42[5] MT, where *'azkirâ* has been read for the Qal: 'let me make my *'azkārâ* and pour out libation for my life'.[19] There is no reason at all, then, why the Hiphil of *zkr* may not have the same sacrificial sense in the titles to the psalms – psalms in connection with the memorial sacrifice – and it should be recalled that in these titles *anamnēsis* is the Greek rendering of the Hiphil of *zkr.*

The sacrificial connotation of *anamnēsis* may very well have passed from the LXX into Christian Greek, and AV is then inadequate with its plain word 'remembrance' (Lk 22[19]; 1 Co 11[24f.]; Heb 10[3]). The whole context of 1 Co 11[25] consists of sacrificial terms: the new Covenant in blood and the verb *poiō* with the meaning 'to sacrifice' (acquired from the LXX context, and illustrated in Mt 26[18]).[20] According to St. Matthew's and St. Mark's gospels, the Last Supper was part of a Passover which is in itself a sacrifice, and Dr. Kilpatrick reasoned that St. Luke too identified the Supper with Passover, taking an association with the Passover 'more seriously than any other New Testament writer'. He inferred from this that St. Luke regarded the occasion as sacrificial.[21]

Then the Lord's words of institution have new significance: 'This is My Body ... this do as a **memorial sacrifice** of Me' – that is, an objective memorial directed not to the faithful, much less to unbelievers, but a memorial for God Himself.[22] It is not necessarily, as Jeremias interprets the phrase, 'that God may remember Me'.[23] Not, of course, that God needs any reminder, either of Christ's offering for our sins or of Christ Himself.

Then, too, what the writer to Hebrews says is, that in those OT offerings there is a **memorial sacrifice** made for sins (10[3]).

In later Christian Greek *anamnēsis* is used of the Jewish

Passover sacrifice, the symbol of the lamb being the *anamnēsis*,[24] and St. Justin goes so far as to say that the fine flour sacrifice, offered on behalf of lepers (Lev 14[10]), was a type of the Bread of the Eucharist which Jesus Christ bade us offer for an *anamnēsis* of His suffering on behalf of us lepers (*Dial*. XLI 1). The Bread which Christ taught us to offer is an *anamnēsis* of His being made flesh and the Cup is an *anamnēsis* of His Blood (*Dial*. LXX 4). Later still, liturgical offerings in commemoration of the dead were referred to as an *anamnēsis*.[25]

Douglas Jones puts[26] the opposing case, while the statement of the case in favour of *anamnēsis* (in Biblical usage) as a ritual and liturgical term is made by Stephen Bedale, S.S.M.[27] A rewarding study of the subject is that by a member of the Taizé Community, Dr. Max Thurian, who argues that, 'when it celebrates the Eucharist, the Church places on the altar the signs of the sacrifice of Christ, the bread and the wine, His Body and His Blood, as Israel placed the shewbread on the golden table as a memorial before Yahweh'.[28] So the Church continually proclaims the sacrifice of Christ and on her altar shows forth that sacrifice before the Father.

Anamnēsis is not so much 'memory' or 'memorial' in the NT context. Dr. Kilpatrick supplies evidence that in the Greek Bible the corresponding verb, *anamimnēskomai*, frequently has the meaning 'to proclaim' (Ex 23[13]; Ps 44[18]vl; Am 6[10]vl), and he assumes that the noun *anamnēsis* has the meaning too. 'Do this to *proclaim* My death.'[29]

As the late Dean of York correctly observed, the Fathers of the Church in the sub-apostolic Age, the Ante-Nicene, and the Nicene Age, everywhere spoke of the Eucharist as a sacrifice and habitually employed sacrificial phraseology in its connection. If the Fathers were wrong, so was the whole Church from the time of St. Clement of Rome till the sixteenth century, and – which God forbid – the Holy Spirit was not guiding the disciples of Jesus into all the truth.[30]

William Bright combined the 'proclamation' idea with that of 'sacrifice':

> *And so we show Thy death, O Lord,*
> *Till Thou again appear,*
> *And feel when we approach Thy Board,*
> *We have an altar here.*

ἱλάσκομαι

In Biblical Greek *hilaskomai* is no longer the act of 'placating' One Who is angry and must be soothed, but it is the act of 'expiating' a sin, which is rather different, and of being 'merciful'.

Secular Greek. As far as possible a distinction must be made between the middle and passive voices of *hilaskomai*. The middle is apparently used in secular Greek and means 'placate', 'appease', or 'conciliate', whether the object be gods or mortals.

In Homer *hilaskomai* is invariably used of placating the gods by choral dance or other means.[31] In Herodotus it is to placate with money, and in Plutarch to placate wrath. Plato asks, 'How to placate and with what speech?'[32] The same usage of the middle is found in Philo, Josephus, and the Sibylline oracles, and the meaning is always the same. In the *Antiquities* Saul swears to 'placate' God by slaying his son Jonathan if need be, and Solomon prays, 'How can we *placate* Thee when Thou art angry?' The Sibyl counsels, 'Make propitiation to God ... *placate* the immortal God'.[33]

Biblical Greek. NT contexts are difficult, but the middle voice indicates 'expiate', 'make propitiation for', or 'cover' – with sin as the object – as when Christ is described as a merciful and faithful High Priest, 'expiating' the sins of the people,[34] which is rather different from 'placating' of a Person.

Moreover, if the passive voice is supposed, another new meaning has developed: not so much, 'to be placated' as 'to be merciful'. The publican cried, 'God be *merciful* to me' (Lk 18[13]). Neither 'placate' nor 'expiate' suits this context, for the publican brought nothing in the way of sacrifice. 'Be merciful', rather than, 'be placated', may indeed be its meaning in Heb 2[17]. The variant of Alexandrinus and 33 seems to reflect the inclination of an editor to understand *hilaskomai* as **be merciful to**, for these manuscripts read, 'to sins', in the dative *(hamartiais)*.

The new meaning arose in the LXX where the Lord is said to **be merciful** (Ex 32[14]) and where Naaman prays Him to **be merciful** to His servant (4 Km 5[18], where Alexandrinus has passive but Vaticanus has middle). The new meaning is continued in the psalms, God **being merciful** to our sins (77(78)[38] 78(79)[9]), and in Daniel's prayer to the Lord to **be merciful** (Dan Th 9[19]). It is a conspicuous change, and the verb's subject is no longer a human suppliant, as in secular instances, but One Who is supplicated. Very often the voice is now passive – indicating that He has been propitiated and His wrath turned away – and yet between middle

277

and passive the manuscripts vary, and the new Biblical meaning holds in both voices.

When the LXX would signify 'propitiate', they did not use *hilaskomai*, as secular authors did; *exhilaskomai* instead is the LXX's word. As Thackeray observed, *hilaskomai* in Biblical Greek has thus become a deponent verb, 'be propitious', 'be merciful', and the causative sense must now be expressed by prefixing *ex-*.[35] It does not mean that we may neglect the hint of propitiation in the new meaning, **be merciful;** indeed, God is merciful *because* His anger is averted, as the contexts make clear.[36]

Dr. C. H. Dodd most carefully showed that Hellenistic Judaism, as represented by the LXX, did not look upon the cultus as a means of pacifying God's displeasure, but rather a means of delivering man from sin, looking in the last resort to God Himself to perform that deliverance. He showed that the verb *hilaskomai* had a meaning which is quite strange to non-Biblical Greek.[37] The meaning, 'to be gracious', 'to have mercy', 'to forgive' *(hilaskomai, exhilaskomai)*, is a new usage unknown everywhere outside Biblical Greek and quite without pagan parallel.[38]

What are we to say, then, of the differences between AV and RV at Heb 2[17]? Did Christ make 'reconciliation' for our sins, as in our understanding of the new non-secular meaning of *hilaskomai?* Or is RV right in its correction of AV (i.e. 'propitiation', for AV's 'reconciliation')? Moffatt too thought not, for he has 'expiation' in his translation. RSV follows Moffatt, and NEB likewise. The British & Foreign Bible Society is correct in its note: 'The writer is not speaking here of propitiating. ... The central idea is that of forgiveness.'[39] See also 'Mercy-seat', 'Atonement'.

MERCY-SEAT

ἱλαστήριον

We base our rendering of *hilastērion* upon the 'mercy-seat' of Tyndale and the 'Gnadenstuhl' of Luther. We have to consider also the 'propitiation' of AV and RV and the 'propitiatory' of Wycliffe, as well as the 'expiation' of RSV.

Secular Greek. The adjective, *hilastērios*, meant placatory, propitiatory, offered in propitiation. By this, Wycliffe is right. The word is infrequent in secular authors, possibly absent altogether in the classical period, but Josephus reports that Herod, affrighted after sacrilegiously entering David's sepulchre, built a 'propitiatory' monument.[40] The adjective qualifies a variety of sacrifices in a papyrus of ii AD,[41] and a death in a Jewish book contemporary with

Jesus – the 'propitiatory' death of the Maccabaean martyrs (4 Mac 17[22]).

Hilastērion becomes a neuter noun, standing parallel to the votive offerings made to Athena.[42] The lexicon of Hesychius declares it to be synonymous with *katharsion,* an expiatory or purificatory offering.

Biblical Greek. The neuter form of the adjective *(hilastērion)* appears, as if *epithema* (covering) were to be understood, giving the meaning, 'a propitiatory covering', and indicating thereby the Hebrew *kapphōreth,*[43] the covering suspended over the Ark and forming what was conceived as the seat of the Lord's Throne, on which the High Priest sprinkled the blood of sacrifice on the day of Atonement and which was made of pure and solid gold. This covering was the Throne of Mercy.

It is to this that *hilastērion* refers at Heb 9[5], where it is but indirectly applied to Christ. Christians welcomed the LXX word which foreshadows Him Who is the centre of the personal hopes for mercy in every believer's heart and the divine Presence in the new Israel.[44] The writer to Hebrews is not alone in taking the LXX meaning of *hilastērion.* Writing of the Ark within the sanctuary, Philo explains that it was covered with a sort of lid, called in the sacred books *hilastērion,* a symbol of God's gracious power.[45]

Josephus avoids it, preferring *epithema* to indicate the Mercy-seat,[46] but the Testament of Solomon declares that the Queen of Sheba took stock of cherubim and seraphim overshadowing the *hilastērion.*[47]

The word occurs once more in the NT. God set forth Christ Jesus as *Hilastērion* through faith in His blood to declare His righteousness (Ro 3[25]). The debate is whether *hilastērion* in this text is adjective (expiatory, propitiatory), or masculine noun (an expiatory or propitiatory sacrifice) or, as in the LXX, a neuter noun (Mercy-seat). Old Latin versions afford a variety of renderings: *propitiationem* (means of propitiation), *propitiatiorem* (Propitiator), and *propitiatorium* (mercy-seat). St. Chrysostom understood it as 'expiatory sacrifice', Christ being the Fulfiller of all the animal offerings which foreshadowed Him.

Chrysostom's is a superb concept, and yet the interpretation which has the support of Origen, Theophylact and most Greek Fathers,[48] is irresistible. St. Paul revered the Greek Bible and cannot have missed the implication that upon Christ Jesus – Mercy-seat of purest gold – rests the Shᵉkhinâ glory, for He is at once Victim, Priest and Altar.

'You will find', said Origen impressively, 'that He Himself is Mercy-seat *(propitiatorium),* and Priest *(pontifex),* and Victim *(hostia).*'[49] Are we 'in the morass of subjectivity'?[50] It may be whimsical to plead[51] that the propitiation idea is quite misleading in the context suggesting that from sheer mercy God effects the remission of sins. Yet it is true that Christ provided the means by which God reconciled the world to Himself, becoming priest, victim, and altar as well.

The trouble with this polychrome figure of Priest, victim and place of sprinkling all at once, is that to many it seems harsh, confusing and impersonal. After all, the mercy-seat was but 'an inanimate piece of temple furniture' – more appropriately regarded as a type of the cross than as a type of Jesus.[52]

It must be admitted, too, that in the context of Ro 3 the wrath of God is upon man's sin, and the suggestion seems clearly to be that somehow in the death of Jesus God's wrath is propitiated.[53]

MINISTER OF CHRIST

ὑπηρέτης

Hupēretēs is a word which the Christians adopted to indicate a minister of the Gospel. Rarely it was used in a religious sense in pagan Greek. Commonly it was an underling or servant,[54] as sometimes in the LXX and NT (Jn 18[18]). In classical Greek, Hermes is the gods' *hupēretēs*.[55] It was said that the very 'servants' in every kind of employment were attached to Cyrus.[56] The word indicates an adjutant or staff-officer.[57]

Josephus had the ordinary secular meaning. Recording Herod's final cruelty he describes how men were delivered to the proper 'officers' to be put to death,[58] but more often he has it in the Jewish context, either of Moses or of other servants of God.[59] Later, it is found in pagan Greek with a religious sense, as attendant, 'serviteur' (Cumont), in the cult of Zeus-Helios-Mithras at Rome; these officers took part in consecrating offerings made to the god.[60] In effect, they were priests.

John Mark is described as *hupēretēs* of Barnabas and Saul on the first journey (Act 13[5]: Western text has the verb, replacing the noun). Does it signify that John Mark was a servant in the general sense of secular Greek? In the gospels and Acts, at least sometimes, *hupēretēs* indicates an officer of the synagogue (e.g. Lk 4[20]; Act 5[26]), and it is argued[61] that the term as applied to St. Mark has not the secular sense. It is a technical title, indicating the Jewish officer, the *ḥazzan*, which according to Beyer[62] was always and only rendered into Greek by *hupēretēs*. St. Mark, of course, did not minister in the synagogues, but it may be that he carried out other duties of the *ḥazzan*, like teaching outside the synagogue. St. Mark perhaps gave Christian instruction to converts who had been won by Barnabas and Saul on this journey. There may have been regular Christian ministers of this kind, for St. Luke had referred in his preface to 'hupēretai of the Word'. R. O. P. Taylor reminded us that the synagogue hupēretēs had to teach exclusively from memory and so had developed a prodigious ability to learn by heart.

A suggestion has been made, which brings the term into line with secular usage, for hupēretēs was sometimes a public official engaged in presenting or handling copies of a document.[63] On this basis it has been assumed[64] that John Mark had charge of documents concerned with early Christianity, and that his gospel was already written by this time, in some shape at least.

However, St. Paul starts a usage of hupēretēs which is new, denoting a Christian minister in its widest sense. The risen Christ made Paul a 'minister' and the ministry includes more than preaching the Gospel. The hupēretēs is a steward of the mysteries of God (1 Co 4[1]), indeed a 'minister' of the Word (Lk 1[2]). Brethren and sisters are to toil together as God's 'ministers' (I. Pol 6[1]), and deacons are 'ministers of the Church of God', not merely to deal with meats and drinks (I. Trall 2[3]). No one seems to know the meaning of 'the servants of the enemy' (Barn 16[4]) who are now building up the Temple that was destroyed when the Jews made war, except that it may be a reference to Isai 49[15-17], viewing Sion as the Church to be built up by Gentile 'ministers' of the Gospel.

MYSTERY, MYSTERIES

μυστήριον, μυστήρια

The word mustērion has an intricate history, of no small significance in the general development of language.

The pagan background. Josephus has the word to indicate a matter which sounds incredible, the life of Antipater being a 'mystery' of wickedness.[65] Among non-Biblical authors we come close to Christian use with the meaning, 'secret' or a 'secret doctrine' which was made known to the initiated. The word, usually found in the plural (mustēria), signifies in the fragments of Aristophanes the 'secret rite' of Demeter at Eleusis,[66] and in the speech of Andocides (Concerning the Mysteries) it once more refers to the Eleusinian Mysteries (I 10, 11). The 'mystery' was the rite rather than a doctrine, although it came to signify also the esoteric teaching about the rite. In the Hermetic literature mustērion is a secret disclosed by God – information, for instance, which concerns the origin of the human race[67] – and is close to the 'mystery' as understood in Biblical Greek.

The Bible background. In the LXX the word *mustērion* is generally confined to the book of Daniel, translating the Aramaic *rāz* (a secret), and to the Wisdom literature where wickedness is said to blind one to the 'mysteries of God' and where the mysteries concern divine Wisdom (Wis 2^{22} 6^{22}). Mysteries are also the solemn rites associated with idolatory, and that is the secular sense (Wis $14^{15,23}$). For Ben Sirach *mustērion* is a 'secret', a 'confidence' (Ecclus 22^{22} $27^{16f.,21}$).

In the OT version of Theodotion *mustērion* renders a different Hebrew word for 'secret' *(sôdh)*. Has Job heard the 'secret' of God (15^8)? The context assures us that *mustērion* has to do with the divine Wisdom. Like Wisdom, *mustērion* is a special bequest to those who fear the Lord (Ps $24(25)^{14}$).

> *Blest are the pure in heart*
> *For they shall see our God;*
> *The secret of the Lord is theirs. ...*

The 'revealing of heavenly Wisdom' is broadly the meaning in Christian Greek, with the added nuance of a disclosure which nearly concerns the kinship of Jew and Gentile and which is made in Christian days of grace. Among the *mustēria*, these secrets of the Lord, are those of the Kingdom which are perceived only by Christ's disciples (Mt 13^{11}; Mk 4^{11}; Lk 8^{10}). Then there is the 'mystery' of Israel's blindness for a time until salvation comes to all nations (Ro 11^{25}), an exposure of the fact that Gentiles are to be fellow-heirs with Jews in the Gospel's blessings (Ro 16^{25}). That is the *mustērion* touching the rich glory to come (literally: 'of glorious richness' (Col 1^{27})).

By a special revelation – most likely on the road to Damascus – St. Paul has been acquainted with the 'mystery' of Christ about the Gentiles and what they are to inherit (Eph $3^{3f.}$; Col 2^2). Indeed, the Gospel absorbs much of what the *mustērion* is about. The *mustērion* is a secret of the Lord, but it is a secret *about* the Lord, too. In the epistle to the Colossians the mystery is no less than Christ Himself, the Word of God. In each of the three passages where *mustērion* appears it is expressly so equated and in two of them it is further identified with the Word of God.[68] The preaching of the Word, the proclamation of the glorious Gospel, is the *koinōnia* (sharing) of the *mustērion* which had been kept secret since the world began (Eph 3^9; Ro 16^{25}). The 'mystery' is the preaching and its content. Inaccessible to man's cleverness, the secret of the Lord is the divine Wisdom which is now revealed in the powerful charismatic eloquence of St. Paul (1 Co 2⁷). He must boldly make known the *mustērion* of the Gospel (Eph 6¹⁹).

To speak with tongues is to reveal 'mysteries' in the Spirit (1 Co 14²); yet if we know all 'mysteries' and still exercise no Christian love we are nothing (13²). As a minister of the Church (Col 1²⁶), Paul must fulfil the Word of God which is the *mustērion* stifled from the beginning and now revealed. He prays for an opportunity to speak the *mustērion* of Christ which has placed him in bonds (Col 4³). Christian ministers are all stewards of the 'mysteries' (1 Co 4¹).

Again St. Paul reveals a secret of the Lord when he discloses that the eschatological Trump shall sound before the resurrection (1 Co 15⁵¹), and a still further mystery concerns the End when in God's good time all heavenly and earthly things are blended in Christ (Eph 1⁹). During these days a mystery of 'lawlessness' is already at work, still concealed, however, because the Restrainer is not yet removed (2 Th 2⁷).

Here, I think, we meet a further Christian meaning of the word, for it may signify a 'type' or 'figure' of Antichrist.[69] As we shall see, the word did become 'figure' and 'symbol' in Christian Greek.

Mustērion embraces the Christian faith and all the details of it. Deacons must hold the mystery of the faith in a pure conscience (1 Ti 3⁹), probably 'the secret counsel of God which is expressed in the Christian creed'.[70] The 'godly mystery' concerns incarnation, resurrection, ascension, Gospel preaching and the Kingdom of God (1 Ti 3¹⁶) – very like the rudiments of a creed. It extends to details: marriage in itself is a great 'mystery', for it is a figure of Christ's nearness to the Church (Eph 5³²). The book of Revelation is full of mysteries which concern detail, disclosing that the seven stars and candlesticks are the seven churches of Asia (1²⁰), and that the Woman in Purple symbolizes Babylon (17⁵), but it refers to the tremendous Gospel mystery, too (10⁷).

Later Christian development. The special meaning, a secret of the Lord, continues in the Fathers, particularly the epistle to Diognetus. God's design, once held in a 'mystery', tightly guarded by the elements, still cannot be learned from man. Yet we have been entrusted with mysteries which divine grace makes plain and which in our compassion we pass on to others.[71] What the Didache means by a *kosmikon* (worldly) mystery of the Church is not so plain. It may have been a revelation enacted by some worldly prophets who propagated their own ideas and failed to disclose the will of God (Did 11¹¹).

For St. Ignatius deacons are not ministers as such, but are 'deacons of the mysteries of Jesus Christ' (I. Trall 2³), and he discerns three mysteries which were wrought in the silence of God, unknown to the Prince of this world. They must be 'cried aloud' – they are the mysteries of Mary's virginity, of her Child-bearing, and of the death of the Lord (I. Eph 19[1]). There is also the resurrection – a mystery 'whereby we attain to belief' (I. Magn 9[2]).

The new sacramental meaning. The Mystery cults featured certain rites of a cryptic kind which they expounded to their initiates in terms of contemporary religious philosophies. While in earlier Greek the rite itself was the *mustērion,* now the philosophical interpretation of the esoteric rite is supposed to be the mystery. I would not claim that St. Paul himself used the term in this sense; he has it in its strictly Palestinian-Jewish meaning of a divine secret hitherto hidden but now revealed, or else shown to Israel but concealed from the rest of us. Once only, so Dr. Knox declared, does he use it in the secondary Hellenistic way of a rite with a 'mystical' meaning.[72] The exception which Knox had in mind was Eph 5[32], where 'the great mystery' was the rite of Holy Matrimony. The Vulgate renders St. Paul's words, 'Sacramentum hoc magnum est'. Perhaps this circumstance explains why marriage was later regarded as a 'sacrament'.

On occasion, therefore, the first Christians borrowed a term from the contemporary heathen Mystery religions. And why not? The Mystery cults assisted the spread of Christianity, and both religions brought something new into the world. Under the older paganism religion belonged largely to the governing classes and was an affair of the State. Both Mysteries and Church, however, cared for the individual and the poorer man. They satisfied his longings. They probably borrowed each other's techniques at times, until at last the Christian Gospel outlived its rivals.

Although the contents of the *mustērion* are very different in the Christian revelation, not so different was the meaning of the term itself – a sacrament or symbol. *Mustērion* in the NT, it is true, is not a secret rite which the initiates are pledged never to disclose[73] nor, except perhaps in Eph 5[32], worship of any kind. But with the Apologists we do come upon a sacramental interpretation. Hatch has shown that Justin Martyr connects the word with *sumbolon* (a symbolized action), with *tupos* (a type) and with *parabolē* (a similitude). St. Justin suggests that in all false religions the serpent was pictured as a great *sumbolon* and *mustērion* (*Apol.* I 27[4]). The *mustērion* of the Passover was a *tupos* of Christ (*Dial.* XL 1), and he says that many things uttered obscurely and in *parabolais* or *mustēriois* or in *sumbolois* were explained by the prophets (*Dial.* LXVIII 6). In a fragment of Melito, Isaac is said to be a *tupos* of Christ and an astonishing type too, for here one might see a strange *mustērion,* a son led by the father to be sacrificed.[74] It is obvious now what *mustērion* has become. It is interchangeable with *parabolē* and *sumbolon* and *tupos*. But I do not think we have to wait till the time of Justin: the new meaning of *mustērion* (type) is already present in the NT. Hatch would have us turn back from these texts to three passages, two written by the Seer and one by St. Paul, where we shall find 'the *symbol* of the seven stars' (Rev 1[20]), 'the *symbol* of the woman' (17[7]), and the great *symbol* of marriage explained as a type of Christ's union with the Church (Eph 5[32]). In each, *mustērion* could mean 'symbol'. With these three passages we may include 'the *mystery* of iniquity' (2 Th 2[7]) which Tirinius saw as the figure of antichrist's evil rule (see above). *Mustērion* in fact is already 'symbol'.

It is not after all so surprising an innovation that the Apologists made when they equated mystery and symbol. 'A secret purpose or counsel was intimated enigmatically by a symbolical representation in words, or in pictures, or in action.'[75] The secret of the Lord is often revealed in symbols for those with eyes to see. His 'mysteries' are displayed in symbols in the great book of nature where pure hearts may read God everywhere.

> *Two worlds are ours: 'tis only sin*
> *Forbids us to descry*
> *The mystic heaven and earth within,*
> *Plain as the sea and sky.*

Church Latin, as seen in Old Latin versions and the Vulgate, often expressed *mustērion* by the word *sacramentum,* thus charging the Latin word with fresh meaning – no longer a military oath but a 'sacrament', a symbolical act, a type, or a secret of God revealed. As early as the end of the second century, Tertullian applies *sacramentum* to the rites of Baptism and the Eucharist. Even earlier Pliny may have used *sacramentum* in this sense – no longer meaning an oath.[76]

The complex history of *mustērion* and its relation with *sacramentum,* provide an instance of Christianity's power over language. In modern Greek, the *Achranta Mustēria* (immaculate mysteries) are the Holy Communion and other sacraments.

NOTES

[1] Sophocles *Trachiniae* 1248. So Thucydides IV 87.
[2] *Gorgias* 471E.
[3] *Republic* 364C.
[4] *Laws* 836C.
[5] *Cyropaedia* I 6.16.
[6] Herodotus II 22; Thucydides I 33.

[7] Beginnings, part I, vol. V, p. 33.

[8] Casey, op. cit., p. 35.

[9] Dr. Allison A. Trites, *Novum Testamentum* 15 (1973), p. 80.

[10] R. Falconer, *The Pastoral Epistles*, Clarendon 1937, p. 128.

[11] Homilies on the Epistle of St. Paul, VII 2.

[12] Beginnings, part I, vol. V, p. 36.

[13] C. K. Barrett, *The Gospel according to St. John*, SPCK 1955, p. 133.

[14] *Phaedo* 72E, 92D.

[15] Plato *Philebus* 34C, plural.

[16] E.g. Dittenberger 929.10 b (ii BC).

[17] Stephen Bedale, S.S.M., *Theology* 56 (1953), p. 299.

[18] It had been better if LS had given the whole evidence from the OT, instead of Num 10^{10} alone, thus avoiding the stricture of G. B. Caird, *Journal of Theological Studies* NS 19 (1968), p. 458.

[19] BDB p. 271, referring to J. P. Peters in *Journal of Biblical Literature* 12 (1893), p. 58.

[20] Bedale, op. cit., p. 300.

[21] G. D. Kilpatrick in *Neues Testament und Kirche*, ed. Joachim Gnilka, Herder (Freiburg) 1974, pp. 429–31.

[22] E. H. Peters, *Catholic Biblical Quarterly*, 10 (1948), p. 248.

[23] To which W. C. van Unnik replied in *Nederlands Theologisch Tijdschrift* (Wageningen) 4 (1950), pp. 369–77.

[24] Methodius *Symposium* 9.1 (PG XVIII 180B).

[25] Serapion *Euchologium* 13.17 (iv AD), etc.

[26] *Journal of Theological Studies*, NS 6 (1955), pp. 183ff.

[27] *Theology* 59 (1953), pp. 298–301.

[28] M. Thurian, *The Eucharistic Memorial:* part 2 *The New Testament*, ET Lutterworth 1961, p. 36.

[29] G. D. Kilpatrick, *Liturgical Review* (Edinburgh) 5 (1975), p. 36.

[30] Alan Richardson, *An Introduction to the Theology of the New Testament*, SCM 1957, pp. 380f.

[31] Iliad I 147, 386, 472, *Odyssey* III 419, Hesiod *Works and Days*, Teubner 338 ('with drink-offerings and sacrifices to placate the gods'), Strabo IV 4.6.

[32] Herodotus VIII 112, Plutarch *Cato Minor* 61, Plato *Phaedrus* 95A.

[33] Philo *de Specialibus Legibus* I 116, Josephus *Ant. Jud.* VI 124 (VI 5), VIII 112 (VIII iv 3), *contra Apion* I 308 (I 34), Sib. Orac. $3^{625, 628}$.

[34] AV has a good paraphrase: 'to make reconciliation for sins' (Heb 2^{17}).

[35] H. St. J. Thackeray, *A Grammar of the OT in Greek*, CUP 1909, p. 271.

[36] Leon Morris, *The Apostolic Preaching of the Cross*, Tyndale 1955, p. 155; David Hill, *Greek Words with Hebrew Meanings*, CUP 1967, pp. 23ff.

[37] C. H. Dodd, *The Bible & the Greeks*, Hodder 1935, p. 93.

[38] Ibid., p. 89.

[39] BFBS, p. 523.

[40] *Ant. Jud.* XVI vii 1 (Niese XVI 182).

[41] P. Fay, p. 313, no. 337.

[42] Dio Chrysostom, *Orat.* xi 1 (see MM s.v.).

[43] *Kapphōreth* is rendered *hilastērion epithema* in Ex $25^{16(17)}$, but usually by *hilastērion* alone: Ex 25 (6 times) 31^7 35^{12} 38 (4 times); Lev 16 (6 times); Num 7^{89}. Even in Ex $25^{16(17)}$ *epithema* may be no part of the text.

[44] C. J. Vaughan, *St. Paul's Epistle to the Romans*, Macmillan 1893, p. 73.

[45] *Life of Moses* II 95.

[46] *Ant. Jud.* III vi 5 (III 135, 136).

[47] XXI 2 in the fifteenth-century Holkham Hall manuscript.

[48] So also F. Büchsel in Kittel *TWNT* III, p. 321f.

[49] Comm. on Romans 3, 8.

M

[50] Leon Morris, *New Testament Studies* 2 (1955), p. 39, who reasoned powerfully for the meaning, 'means of propitiation'.

[51] With W. J. Dalton, *Australian Biblical Review* 8 (1960), pp. 3–18.

[52] C. E. B. Cranfield, *Romans*, ICC T. & T. Clark 1975, p. 215.

[53] G. E. Ladd, *Expository Times* 68 (1957), p. 272.

[54] Herodotus III 63.

[55] Aeschylus *Prometheus Bound* 954.

[56] Xenophon *Anabasis* I 9.18.

[57] Xenophon *Cyropaedia* II 4.2.

[58] *Bell. Jud.* I xxxiii 4 (Niese I 655).

[59] *Ant. Jud.* III 14 (Niese III 16), *Bell. Jud.* II xv 4 (Niese II 321).

[60] F. Cumont, in *Revue de l'histoire de religions* (Paris) 1934, vol. 109, pp. 64f.

[61] R. O. P. Taylor, *Expository Times* 54 (1942), pp. 136–8.

[62] H. W. Beyer in Kittel *TWNT* II, p. 91.

[63] BGU 226, P. Oxy 1203, P. Lond 361, P. Tebt 434.

[64] B. T. Holmes, *Journal of Biblical Literature* 54 (1935), pp. 63–72.

[65] *Bell. Jud.* I xxiv 1 (Niese I 470).

[66] Aristophanes *Fragmenta* 479.

[67] W. Scott, *Corpus Hermeticum* Clarendon 1924, I 16, etc., II p. 46.

[68] C. L. Mitton compares it with St. Paul's earlier uses of 'mystery' and sees it as 'a new and remarkable development'. *Expository Times* 60 (1948), pp. 320f.

[69] J. Tirinius, S.J., *In universam S. Scripturam commentarius*, Turin 1893, pp. 715f. ('mysterium, id est, figura et symbolum illius Antichristianae iniquitatis').

[70] Edwin Hatch, *Essays in Biblical Greek*, Clarendon 1889, p. 59.

[71] Diog 4[6] 7[1f.] 8[10] 10[7] 11[2,5].

[72] W. L. Knox, *St. Paul and the Church of the Gentiles*, CUP 1939, pp. 183f.

[73] Armitage Robinson, p. 240.

[74] Hatch, op. cit., p. 60.

[75] Hatch, op. cit., p. 61.

[76] *Epistles* X xcvi.

N

THE NEW CREATION

κτίστης: κτίσμα: κτίσις: κτίζω

In contemporary secular Greek the meanings of this word-group were, broadly speaking, 'founder' *(ktistēs)*, 'colony' *(ktisma)*, 'foundation' or 'settling' *(ktisis)*, and 'to people' (the verb *ktizō*). On the whole, the notion was that of founding sects, cities, houses and games, of discovering and peopling a country or city,[1] of planting a grove, setting up an altar, establishing worship,[2] and only dubiously and rarely, of bringing into being from nothing.[3]

In the Greek of the Jews and the Bible, however, creation from nothing is a regular meaning.[4] Biblical translators and writers chose the *ktistēs* word-group in preference to more obvious alternatives, such as *dēmiourgos* and its derivatives which were consistently used by pagan writers to express their views on the formation of the world, as in Plato's Timaeus and then often in Neo-Platonism. *Ktizō* and its derivatives, on the other hand, are used in this sense for the first time in Jewish Greek.[5]

Moreover, a further aspect of the word-group is God's operation on the soul. We are His workmanship, **created** (pass. part. of *ktizō*) in Christ Jesus unto good works. Christ by His sacrifice has **created** one new man. We are to put on the new man who is **created** in righteousness and true holiness (Eph $2^{10,15}$ 4^{24}). In Biblical Greek then the concept is essentially that of *divine* creation, physical and spiritual.

Sometimes indeed we have the secular sense of *ktisis* (founding, settling), as when the tabernacle is said to be 'not of this *building*', and when there is a reference to 'every *ordinance* of man' (Heb 9^{11}; 1 Pet 2^{13}). However, the implication behind such passages is that *God* and not man has created the human authorities, and so *ktisis* is still divine creation.[6] The meaning in the NT is consistently the Biblical sense, the act of **creation** or a **creature** – whether it is God's creation of the world (Mk 10^6; Ro 1^{20}) or a creature of God by physical making, as when the whole *ktisis* of God is said to share in the Fall (Ro 8), or a creature by new spiritual birth (Mk 16^{15}? 2 Co 5^{17}). The NT picture of creation says Dr. Lampe, is anthropocentric in a new sense, different from the Hebrew picture where God in His dealing with man is fundamental, for in the NT the 'new man' in Christ is the centre of *ktisis*. Indeed, this word sometimes denotes merely 'man', as in the phrase, 'preaching the Gospel to every *creature*' (Mk 16^{15}; Col 1^{23}). The Church is the first fruits of the 'new humanity' inaugurated by the redemptive work of the Saviour.[7]

Ktisma too in Biblical Greek has the prevailing sacred meaning of **created world** or a **creature** of God.[8] It is scarcely different from *ktisis*.

Similarly, *ktistēs* in Biblical Greek is the Maker of all things.[9]

NOURISHING TEACHING

γάλα

The secular meaning of *gala* was 'milk', but it is conceived metaphorically in Christian Greek to mean wholesome Christian teaching.

St. Paul claims that he fed the Corinthian saints with simple teaching *(gala)* 'and not with meat' *(brōma)* which they were unable to bear (1 Co 3[2]). The *gala* is contrasted not only with *brōma*, but also with *sophia* and *gnōsis*. The writer to Hebrews complains that beloved brethren, instructed with 'elementary teaching' *(gala)*, are themselves unskilled at teaching others. His readers have become such as need *gala* – 'babes' (Heb 5[12f.]). *Gala* is in contrast with the *sterea trophē* and the *logos dikaiosunēs* which the author himself can afford (5[13ff.]), and which is for the 'perfect' *(teleioi)*. Anything more 'heavenly' may 'choke' them, as St. Ignatius protests (I. Trall 5[1]). The NT authors may have borrowed the idea of *gala* from Philo and the Stoics.

Epictetus has the verb *apogalaktisthēnai* (to be weaned), using it as an educational metaphor, meaning, 'no longer to cry for old wives' lamentations',[10] but to do something desperate to achieve peace and freedom. He has the verb again for the recollection of what we have heard from philosophers.[11] Philo has *galaktōdesin* (the milky food of infancy) when he refers to what nourishes the childhood of the soul as opposed to 'virtues' – the grown-up food.[12] He has also *galaktōdous*, saying that when we come to the land of Wisdom there awaits us a nature that need not be 'fed on milk'.[13]

St. Peter uses *gala* to the same effect, a nourishment for 'new-born babes', for recent initiates (1 Pet 2[2]). Selwyn observed, 'There is ample evidence ... that from the second century onwards milk and honey were administered to the newly baptized' (p. 155). He noted that the verse of St. Peter suggests how the rite might have arisen. It is not to say, however, that Christian Greek had completely abandoned the secular meaning, actual milk (as 1 Co 9[7]).

Reitzenstein sought to show[14] that *gala* was a regular term in the mysteries, but whether it was the Christians or the Mystery devotees who first made it a metaphor, we do not know. Sallustius, a fourth-century philosopher, undoubtedly applied the term to the Mysteries (quotation in MM), but much later.

For the Alexandrian alegorist, however, the 'milk' and honey of Canaan are types of Christian faith (Barn 6[17]). The Odes of Solomon carry the picture rather far. The author refers to catechumens but speaks in a Gnostic context: 'I fashioned their limbs and prepared my own breasts for them to drink my holy milk *(gala logikon)* and live thereby. ... The Son is the cup, and He who was milked is the Father, and the Holy Spirit milked Him' (e.g. 8[16f.] 19[1-4]). For the Gnostic the 'milk' was *gnōsis.*

St. Clement of Alexandria has Gnostics in mind,[15] and he too departs from the NT way of regarding *gala* for he no longer stresses, with St. Paul, St. Peter and the writer to Hebrews, the elementary nature of the *gala* – as fit only for 'babes', that is, for initiates. St. Clement dwells heavily upon its mature quality, 'the nourishing substance of *gala,* swelling out from breast of love'. He compares the milk and honey promised for the Sabbath rest. By some Church writers the Incarnation is conceived as the 'milking' of the Father; what was born of the Virgin's womb is as milk received by the faithful, that is Christ, for they feed upon the Logos (the Odist, followed by Irenaeus[16] and Clement).

St. Clement understands the Apostle to say, 'I have given you the instruction which nourishes to life eternal', but he is not correct in his understanding of the Apostle who, far from emphasizing the nourishing quality of *gala,* contrasts it with 'meat'. To Hort, also, the whole discussion of St. Clement was 'fanciful and confused' (p. 102). As to St. Peter, he urges his readers to 'desire' the *gala,* it is true, but let us recall that his readers are 'new-born babes', recent initiates, and that he ventures the hope that they will 'grow' out of it as they become 'built up'. Only the newly baptized are 'fed with abundant milk at the Church's bosom'.[17] There is some variance in what is meant by the symbol *gala.* In the NT it is elementary teaching but later, through Gnostic influence, was the 'food' which nourishes to life eternal.

NUMINOUS, SENSE OF

ἔκστασις: ἐξίστημι

From being 'distracted frenzy' the noun *ekstasis* and verb *existēmi* represent in Biblical Greek religious emotion, the experience of a powerful working and presence of God Himself.

By etymology *ekstasis* is a 'displacement, and medical men used the word for the dislocation of the joints.[18] The verb *existēmi*, too, is a displacing. Outside the Biblical literature it is used in the active voice transitively, both literally (to change) and metaphorically (to drive out of one's senses or to amaze), as indeed sometimes within the Bible (Lk 24[22]). It is found in the middle and passive intransitively with the meaning, to be displaced, to stand aside, to shrink from, to be distraught.

The nearest we come to the Christian extension may be that of frenzy and distraction of mind beyond the normal limits of self-control, brought on by an unpleasant emotion such as terror, astonishment, anger, or else induced by artificial stimulants.[19] However, the resemblance is more apparent than real, and Oepke justly observes that secondary Hellenistic influence on the technical meaning of the words is non-existent in the OT and only weak in the NT.[20]

The noun. In Christian Greek, on the other hand, *ekstasis* is a numinous involvement and entrancement. In the LXX *ekstasis* had rendered several words, notably *tardēmâ* (deep sleep) which God caused to fall upon Adam at the creation of woman (Gen 2[21]) and upon Abram at the vision of promised inheritance (Gen 15[12]). So out of traumatic experience comes this kind of joy. It renders also *ḥᵃrādhâ*, the sense of dread which came over Isaac when he realized that the inheritance had been misdirected (Gen 27[33]). The Hebrew word is a 'trembling of God', rendered in Greek by *ekstasis* and by the verb (1 Km 14[15]), for it accompanied the incredible bravery of Jonathan and his armour-bearer at Michmash. The feeling at that time was so transcendental that the earth was said to quake.

The spell occurs again at the fall of Tyre in the prophecy of Ezekiel (26[16]). It occurs in Daniel's vision of the Man with loins of gold, his face like lightning and his voice like a multitude's. Daniel's friends were struck with *ḥᵃrādhâ*, with sublime *ekstasis* (DanTh 10[7]), although they could see nothing.

Another transport which in Biblical Greek is described as 'the *ekstasis* of the Lord' is the Hebrew *mᵉhûmâ*, when God vexed the nations with adversity upon Israel's turning to Him in trouble. The tremendous experience came upon nations (2 Chr 15[5]) as well as individuals. In the prophecy of the End, looking for Christ's Coming, Zechariah foretells that 'divine *ekstasis*' shall visit the foes of Jerusalem (14[13]). Yet another emotion denoted by *ekstasis* is said to be divine, the Hebrew *pāḥadh* (awe). Saul exuded this sense of numinous (1 Km 11[7]), this 'ekstasis of the Lord'. The reforming zeal of Asa brought down the Lord's *ekstasis* (2 Chr 14[14]). His successor, Jehoshaphat, another of God's warriors, brought the sensation upon neighbouring rulers (17[10] 20[29]). So the Biblical use of *ekstasis* conveys the idea of extraordinary astonishment, alarm in no small measure, but never distracted or drunken frenzy as in secular Greek.

The same holds for the NT. Jairus's daughter is raised and the bystanders are smitten with wonderment (noun and verb are used), not a frenzy but an intense disquietude of mind (Mk 5^{42}). *Ekstasis* was the state of the women at the empty tomb. They were anything but frenzied; they were deeply in awe (Mk 16^8). St. Luke is clear that the *ekstasis* which seized all present at the healing of the palsied man was an infusion of awe (Lk 5^{26}), and it was that emotion which impelled the crowd at the Gate Beautiful (Act 3^{10}). St. Peter on the house-top was seized with it (10^{10} 11^5), and St. Paul was in an *ekstasis* when he visited the Temple (22^{17}).

The verb. The peculiar Biblical sense of the verb is the sense of astonishment mingled with fear (Bauer), a feeling brought on by miraculous or strange events. When Joseph entertained his brethren he induced this feeling in them (Gen 43^{33}). Boaz experienced it when he found a kinswoman lying at his feet (Ruth 3^8). Jesus induced it when He cast out devils (Mt 12^{23}), when as a Child He sat in the midst of the doctors (Lk 2^{47}). The multitude at Pentecost experienced it (Act 2^7). The Jews at Cornelius's house were moved by it when the Holy Spirit came upon Gentiles (Act 10^{45}). It excited the Christians at Mary's house who saw that Peter was out of prison (Act 12^{16}).

The instances are enough to show that the Church begins her distinctively Christian life on earth with a profound sense of *ekstasis,* of God's sublimity, majesty, glory, and transcendence – the Church is a Kingdom which is not of this world.

NOTES

[1] E.g. Polybius IX 1.4 (a city).

[2] W. Foerster in Kittel *TWNT* III, p. 1024.

[3] 'Creating' is poetic only (Aeschylus *Suppliants* 172, *Persae* 289, Sophocles *Oedipus Coloneus* 715, Euripides *Suppliants* 620).

[4] E.g. Josephus *Bell. Jud.* III 354 (Niese); Jdt 9^{12}; Ecclus 24^8 $36^{20(17)}$ 38^{34}; Wis 9^2 13^5; 2 Mac 1^{24} 7^{23} 13^{14}; 3 Mac 5^{11}.

[5] Foerster, op. cit., pp. 1022ff.

[6] Cf. H. Teichert, *Theologische Literazeitung* (Leipzig) 74 (1949), pp. 303f.

[7] G. W. H. Lampe, *Scottish Journal of Theology* 17 (1964), pp. 449–62.

[8] Wis 9^2 13^5 14^{11}; 3 Mac 5^{11}; 1 Ti 4^4; Jas 1^{18}; Rev 5^{13} 8^9; Diog 8^9; Hermas *Mand.* VIII 1, XII 4.3, *Vis.* III 9.2; T. Abr 112^8 117^{30}.

[9] 2 Km 22^{32}; Jdt 9^{12}; Ecclus 24^8; 2 Mac 1^{24} 7^{23}; 4 Mac 5^{25} 11^5; 1 Pet 4^{19}.

[10] *Discourses* book II xvi 39.

[11] Op. cit., II xxiv 9.

[12] *De Congressu Quaerendae Eruditionis Gratia* 19.

[13] *De Migratione* 29.
[14] R. Reitzenstein, *Die hellenistischen Mysterienreligionen*, Leipzig and Berlin 3rd ed. 1927, pp. 84, 159.
[15] *Paedogogus* I 124.
[16] *Haereses* iv 38.12 (PG VII 1105ff.).
[17] Poem on Easter, by Venantius Fortunatus, cited by J. H. Bernard, *Odes of Solomon*, CUP 1912 (Texts & Studies VIII no. 3), p. 67.
[18] Hippocrates *Peri Arthrōn Embolēs* 56.
[19] Aristotle *Categoriae* 10a 1; Plutarch *Solon* 8; Plotinus (Teubner) V.3.7, VI 9.11; Cornutus *de Natura Deorum* (Teubner) 30.
[20] A. Oepke in Kittel *TWNT* II, p. 448.

O

OFFENCE

1. σκανδαλίζω: σκάνδαλον

The two words, *skandalizō* and *skandalon,* and the noun *proskomma* (see below), all share the same translation in English versions – 'offence' or 'stumbling-block'. Both the noun *skandalon* and the verb *skandalizō* are still Biblical coinages despite the presence in secular Greek of *skandalēthron,* a 'stick' which sets a trap.

According to the lexicons of Hesychius and Photius (s.v.), the words *skandalon* and *skandalēthron* were synonyms. It can hardly be doubted, pronounced Moulton, that *skandalon* existed before *skandalēthron,* though it does not occur in literature.[1] We are not sure of that, but we can say that *skandalon* in a papyrus of the third century BC is nothing but a conjecture of the editor's.[2] If they are not unknown in contemporary secular Greek, at least the words *skandalon* and *skandalizō* are very rare indeed. Stählin observes that, at any rate, there is no intellectual or abstract extension of the meaning of *skandalon* outside the Jewish-Christian sphere.[3] It is another instance where the influence of the Bible is seen in secular language, for the vernacular of the eighth century provides examples of the Biblical meaning, 'offence'.[4]

So another Greek word has been modulated by the Christians' own exegesis. A look at the NT and patristic phenomena reveals that the meaning is two-fold, 'either to put someone off from becoming a believer or to cause a believer to fall away. The scandal of the Cross is an instance of the first meaning, to cause to apostatize an instance of the second.'[5] The second meaning then is the same as that of *proskomma* (see below). 'Stumbling-block' is a poor word, but the sense is right.

The words, *skandalizō, skandalon,* probably occur first in the Greek OT (the LXX) and indicate the act of overthrowing or causing to fall. 'Do not look at a virgin, lest you *stumble*', warns Ben Sirach (Ecclus 9⁵). 'Keep me back from every wicked woman that causeth the simple to *stumble*', prays King Solomon (Ps Sol 16⁷, i BC). The Law makes hypocrites to *stumble* (Ecclus 35(32)¹⁵), and the sinner's lips may *trip* one up (Ecclus 23⁸). The same word expresses the *overthrow* of countries (Dan LXX 11⁴¹), rendering the Hebrew *kshl* (Niphal). In Lev 19¹⁴; 1 Sam 25³¹, etc., the Hebrew *mikhshôl* (stumbling-block) may have suggested *skandalon* to the translators because of the similarity of sound in Hebrew and Greek.[6] At first in the LXX, and then in Aquila, Symmachus and

Theodotion, the noun *skandalon* is a *môqēsh,* a noose or snare (metaphorically, in Ps 69[22]; Ro 11[9] cit.), but it denotes also a person who is a *mikhshôl,* a stumbling-block, an occasion of offence, like the Canaanites who dwell among the Israelites, a thorn in their eyes (Josh 23[13]), and in Aquila's version of Isai 8[14]. The verb *skandalizō* is used in the Testament of Solomon concerning the tenth demon, Saphthorael, who was delighted to bring dissentions among men and 'cause them to stumble' (XVIII 17.1. Cf. D III 8).

The NT use of the two words 'is exclusively controlled by the thought and speech of the OT and Judaism'. The words are far away from Greek thought; not only do they occur hardly at all in Greek literature, but the Christian Fathers feel the need repeatedly to explain their new meaning.[7] In wielding the words, Christians doubtless had OT figures in mind: they were dwelling on earth among worldlings who ceaselessly drew them away from life in Christ. Their Lord had indicated that Peter was a **stumbling-block** of this kind (Mt 16[23]). Eye and hand and foot, our very closest members, cause us to relapse (Mt 5[29f.] 18[8f.]; Mk 9[43f.]). Stählin rejects the attempt of W. C. Allen[8] to show that 'snare' or 'trap' is the proper idea behind *skandalon* and *skandalizō* in LXX and NT, as 'künstlich und daher nicht überzeugend' (artificial and unconvincing).[9]

J. H. Moulton had started the idea in the *Expository Times,*[10] when he concluded, 'Since our purely Greek evidence is all for "trap", and a Hebrew word with this meaning accounts for the largest number of LXX occurrences of the noun, the question struck me whether *snare* might not be at least the normal meaning in NT'. Moulton confessed that if *skandalon* ever does mean 'stumbling-block', it will be through the influence of what he would call a mistranslation of *mikhshôl.* 'It will be a real "Biblical" sense, as due to a mistake which gained currency through appearing in the Bible. ... At a later time the NT use of the word gave birth to a new meaning in M.Gr. as the 'English *scandal*', and Moulton referred to his master, Thumb.[11] Stählin was not the first to be mistrustful of Archdeacon Allen's and Professor Moulton's attempts to interpret *skandalon* on the basic of secular usage. When Moffatt followed upon Moulton in the same periodical[12] he expressed his doubts and he urged the passion and intensity with which the words of Jesus hereabout are charged. 'I am afraid,' he said, 'that the rather conventional associations of the English words "offend" and "offence" have been partly responsible for the fact that many readers of the NT do not realize the tremendous severity of what Jesus said about "stumbling-blocks".' A *skandalon* in the Christian sense is something more than a snare or trap; it is more than contempt and dishonour, as Theophylact supposed. It is not simply the *hubris* (insult) of St. Chrysostom's interpretation. To be a *skandalon* is to achieve the moral ruin of another person. Better that a mill-stone were hanged about his neck than that he should *skandalizō* (offend) one of the little ones that believe in Jesus. The angels will gather the offenders out of the Kingdom and into the fire (Mt 18[6f.] 13[41]; Mk 9[42]; Lk 17[1f.]). 'It is a warning to all who teach Christianity, a warning not to add or omit, from any motive whatsoever, truths which are vital to the gospel. They will be held responsible for having induced others to take Christ less seriously than He meant.' It is a warning not to convey a wrong impression of the Gospel by word or deed, when our example and precept may prove the undoing of simpler souls of our circle.[13] Moffatt cited St. Paul's attitude. Receive the weak. Destroy him not. Let not this liberty of yours become a *proskomma* to the weak for whom Christ died. Lest I make my brother to stumble *(skandalizō)*!

The meaning is not a 'snare', but something more weighty, something more solemn. Woe to the man by whom the disciple falls away! 'It is morally certain that such pitfalls will be met with, in the course of life; yet that does not, in the judgment of Jesus, absolve the individual whose misconduct proves an obstacle to his neighbours. He may bring disaster on them, but he brings a worse disaster on himself.' So Dr. Moffatt interpreted.

We must add that Christ Himself and His cross fend many off from commitment while He draws others to Him (Mt 11[6] 13[57] 24[10] 26[31,33]; Mk 6[3] 14[27]; Lk 7[23]). Christ crucified is often a **stumbling-block,** an 'offence' (1 Co 1[23]; Gal 5[11]). He was a stone of *skandalon,* laid in Sion (Ro 9[33]), 'unto them which be disobedient ... a stone of **stumbling'** (1 Pet 2[8]).

The first Christians, however, were specially uneasy with the *skandalon* which caused them to slip back on their way to glory. They knew that many a 'little one' is made to **stumble,** many a 'weak' brother **offended.** The Christian who is richly endowed with faith and for whom all things are pure, easily excites a weak one to **stumble** (Ro 14[21]). St. Paul would have it avoided at all cost (1 Co 8[13]). 'Who is **offended** and I burn not?' (2 Co 11[29]). 'Let us not, therefore, judge one another any more; but judge this rather, that no man put a *proskomma* (stumbling-block) or a *skandalon* (an occasion to fall) in his brother's way' (Ro 14[13]). Love and respect for the 'weak' would prevent it. There is no *skandalon* in him who loves his brother (1 Jn 2[10]). So far from it being a light matter to set this offence afoot, the Apostle would have those who make divisions and *offences* noted and shunned (Ro 16[17]).

So, to stumble, to be offended, is to slide back from grace, to fall behind in the battle. I suspect that *skandalon* and *proskomma* do not much differ.

The apostolic Fathers apply *skandalizō*, the verb, to Christian backsliding. The Didache expects that many **will fall away** and be lost at the fiery trial in the eschatological days (16⁵). Hermas beseeches the Lord to give repentance to His servants **who had fallen away** (participle). He declares that the servant of God must comfort those who are oppressed in spirit and not cast aside those **who had fallen away** from faith.[14]

Later Fathers were at pains to clarify the concept of *skandalon*. 'I consider it necessary first of all,' says St. Basil, 'to know what "scandal" is. ... Now "scandal", as I am led to infer from Scripture, is everything that draws us away from true piety towards any form of defection, or introduces error, or fosters impiety; or, in general, everything which hinders us from observing God's command even unto death.'[15] Origen declared that *skandalon* was a word which Christians normally used of those who pervert simple folk who are easily seduced from sound doctrine,[16] and the verb *skandalizō* he defined as furnishing an occasion of sinning. A graver punishment is reserved for those who engage in this activity than for the sinners themselves.[17] One more instance is enough to show the gravity of *skandalizō* in the ancient Church. 'Quicunque scandalaverit,' explains St. Jerome, 'hoc intelligimus: qui dicto vel facto occasionem ruinae dederit'.[18] Both word and example are included, and *ruinae* is not too strong a word to mark the effect of this disastrous spell upon our fellows.

A happy suggestion from Dr. B. A. E. Osborne describes the relationship of the 'stumbling-block' to the Pauline concept of the 'flesh'.[19] Starting from the circumstance that stumbling-block (*mikhshôl* in Hebrew) is one of the seven names said by Joshua ben Levi (c. AD 250) to have been given to the evil *yêzer* (impulse),[20] he notes also that in first-century Palestinian Aramaic, *Kêphâ* has the meaning 'rock' (Greek *petra*) and that rabbi Simai (c. AD 200) compares the evil *yêzer* to a big rock protruding at crossroads, making men stumble,[21] – providing a play on St. Peter's name in the words of Jesus. Dr. Osborne suggests that the evil *yêzer* is understood as Satan, the 'stumbling-block' and the 'rock'.[22] We find then in the teaching of Jesus an interesting parallel with the distinction in rabbinical thought between the good and evil *yêzer* and that in Qumrân texts between the Spirit of Falsehood and the Spirit of Truth or Holiness, as well as in the Pauline distinction between 'thinking the thoughts of the Spirit' and 'thinking the thoughts of the flesh' (Ro 8⁵). Peter was a 'stumbling-block', he was addressed as 'Satan' and was charged with savouring the things of men, thinking the thoughts of the flesh, of the evil *yêzer* (Mt 16²³).

2. πρόσκομμα

In secular Greek *proskomma* meant a bruise, the result of stumbling. Apollo, it is said, would look ridiculous if he sat giving orders about chamber-pots and about deliverance from 'bruises on the shin'[23] – a silly jest.

The word has a specialized turn in Biblical Greek, a metaphor reserved for serious concepts like idolatry (Ex 23[33]) and covenanting with the heathen (34[12]). Gold is a *proskomma*, as is the excessive use of wine (Ecclus 34(31)[7,30]).

In Christian parlance *proskomma* bears the proper meaning which it shares with *skandalon,* that is, the overthrowing of a 'weak' brother in the race, casting a *proskomma* at his feet (Ro 14[13]). An instance arising in the church at Corinth was the *proskomma* occasioned by the member who sees no harm in dining at an idol's temple. An idol is nothing and no harm is done by going out to dinner; on the other hand, a 'weak' brother's conscience is hurt. 'Take heed lest ... this liberty of yours become a *proskomma* to them that are weak' (1 Co 8[9]). Pure as all things are to the brother of strong faith, yet if he eat 'with **offence** *(proskomma)*' it is 'evil' for him. 'Hast thou faith? Have it to thyself before God' (Ro 14[20ff.]).

Hermas advocates reverence in Christian behaviour, for there is no evil *proskomma* therein, but the steep and thorny crooked path has many *proskomata* (*Mand.* II 4).

OFFERING

προσφορά

Secular Greek. In Biblical Greek *prosphora* is a religious sacrifice, but occasionally it was a word of wide-ranging meanings derived from both the middle and passive senses of the verb *prospheromai* (e.g. 'take food' in the middle, 'be carried' in the passive). So, among meanings based on the middle, we find 'food' or the consumption of food. Aristotle mentions the '*consumption* of fluids',[24] and *prosphora* is the 'eats' in Plutarch's 'eats and drinks'.[25]

Among meanings which come from the passive sense we have 'anything added', an increase, a benefit (Sophocles), an application or a use. Plato reports[26] the Athenian stranger's remark to Megillus when he wittily likens hasty judgments to those who disparage cheese as soon as they hear of it, 'not having learnt its effects or the method of using it *(prosphora)*'! There is in Sophocles the phrase, 'It cannot be made worse,' which literally expressed is, 'There is no *prosphora* (increase, benefit)', and Theseus asks in the play, Oedipus Coloneus, 'When may we hope to reap the benefit *(prosphora)?*'[27] These comprehensive meanings become for Josephus more definite in the plural as the income or revenue accruing to Agrippa from Caesarea and Samaria.[28]

None of them occurs in the NT.

Biblical Greek. A novel emphasis arises from the use of *prosphora* to render *minḥâ* (Ps 39(40)[6]) and *pānîm* (3 Km 7[48]) in the LXX.[29] The word was adopted in Christian Greek in this sense, i.e. sacrificial offering, and was applied to the oblation once and for all of the body of Jesus who, by one *prosphora* perfected for ever them that are sanctified, so that there is no more *prosphora* for sin (Heb 10[10, 14, 18]). Christ has given Himself, a *prosphora* to God (Eph 5[2]). Just by reading secular authors we would have no idea what the word implied in such contexts.

As puzzling would be its figurative application by St. Paul to his collection of alms for the saints in Jerusalem (Act 24[17]), and its still more subtle application to the Gentiles who are Paul's *prosphora* to God (Ro 15[16]). St. Polycarp, tied and bound at the stake was a *prosphora* and a 'burnt' sacrifice (M Pol 14[1]). Delicate also and difficult to decipher are the words of St. Clement (1 Clem 36[1] 40[1, 4]). He may mean by *prosphora,* the prayers, thanksgivings, alms and oblations of the Christian.[30] Jesus Christ is said to be the High Priest of our 'offerings' which must be performed with care at appointed seasons.

For St. Irenaeus, *prosphora* is the offering of the Eucharist (PG VII 1253B). Still, in the Apostolic Constitutions, *prosphora* indicates the sacramental elements (PG I 8.13).

These then are the specialized and refined off-shoots of the new Biblical meaning, 'a liturgical offering made under the Law' – as in the LXX and in Act 21[26]; Heb 10[5, 8].

Josephus is the first to evince this meaning outside the Bible, for at the building of Zerobabel's Temple he reports the offering of 'sacrifices',[31] thus displaying in his writing examples of both the secular and Biblical usage of *prosphora*. Philo does not have the word in the Biblical sense. Derivatives of the Biblical meaning, i.e. various kinds of 'offering', appear in later Greek from the fifth century onward.[32] In Byzantine Greek *prosphora* sometimes signified a mass offered for the dead. In an arbitration of a family dispute (AD 567) the defendant excuses the vast sums that had been spent on the father's and the brother's funerals.[33]

ἀλλόφυλος : ἐθνικός : ἔθνος

King Solomon
Finisht and fixt the old religion.
When it grew loose, the Jews did hope in vain
By nailing Christ to fasten it again;
But to the Gentiles He bore Crosse and all,
Rending with earthquakes the partition-wall. – G. HERBERT

Christian teaching on the great question of Jew and Gentile relationship, is that by the Cross Jews and Gentiles are reconciled and both are admitted to all its benefits. The partition-wall is rent. The Gospel and all its blessings are borne to the Gentiles ...' to the Jew first and also to the Greek' (Ro 1^{16}). The three words, *allophulos, ethnikos* and *ethnos,* are applicable to Gentiles, but sometimes they refer to all who are outside the new People of God, outside the Christian Church.

The adjectives. The two adjectives, *allophulos* and *ethnikos,* had meant 'foreign' in secular Greek, an outsider from the point of view of the Roman empire or of Greek culture. In the Biblical language the words denote Gentile, an outsider from the viewpoint of Israel and the Church.

In Polybius *ethnikos* is applied to 'national' leagues, combinations of cities and states struggling for independence (XXX 13.6). It has the meaning of 'national' in Diodorus Siculus too, when he refers to permission to go home because of some 'national' business (XVIII 13).

Allophulos is more definitely 'foreign', especially seen from the position of Athens. Plato speaks of 'quarreling with *aliens*',[34] but according to Thucydides the Spartans regarded the Athenians as 'foreigners' (I 102), for all that they were Greeks.

The use of the words in the Bible and the Church introduces a new phase, 'non-Jewish', 'Gentile'. In the LXX *allophulos* in particular translated the Hebrew word for a Philistine which is especially frequent in the books of Kingdoms. It was extended to include all who were of non-Jewish religion and race. St. Peter in the house of Cornelius recalls that it was an unlawful thing for a Jew to keep company with 'one of another nation' (*allophulos* Act 10^{28}). The word recurs in the epistle to Diognetus where it means a Christian – an outsider in a quite different way (5^{7}).

The second adjective, *ethnikos,* is lacking in the LXX but emerges in a later Greek version to mean 'profane' (Lev 21^{7}). In the NT it is contrasted with the Christian brethren and comes to mean an unbeliever. 'Do not even the *ethnikoi* the same?' asks Jesus,[35] differentiating His own disciples. The *ethnikoi* use vain repetitions in prayer,[36] and have nothing in common with disciples. A brother who will not heed the local church is regarded as an unbeliever *(ethnikos)* and a publican (Mt 18[17]). When missionaries are said to accept no gifts from *ethnikoi*, the term will denote both Jewish and Gentile non-Christians (3 Jn 7).

Hermas in the sub-apostolic Church dubs certain friendships *ethnikos* – outside the Christian fellowship.[37] The derogatory sense which the word gained in later secular Greek,[38] a 'tax-collector', may owe something to the influence of the Bible. In modern Greek it is a national, a Gentile, and a heathen, combining both secular and Biblical meanings. The adverb, *ethnikōs*, 'after the Gentile manner', is a hapax of St. Paul describing Peter's conduct of eating with Gentiles when no Jews were present (Gal 2[14]), and it accords with the Biblical sense.

The noun. In secular Greek *ethnos* was 'barbarian'. It denoted a nation, a crowd. In the Bible, however, it is usually found in the plural *(ethnē)* and has become the Gentiles, translating the Hebrew *haggōîm* – a term to denote the non-Hebrew peoples as distinct from *'ām* which is specially associated with Israel. There are the LXX citations by Christians – St. Matthew's 'Galilee of the *ethnē*' and St. Paul's 'Rejoice, ye *ethnē* with His People' – plainly distinguishing the *ethnē* from the *laos* (Israel).[39]

Jesus makes the contrast with the People on two occasions, referring to things that the *ethnē* seek (Mt 6[32]) and forbidding His disciples to go into the way of the *ethnē* (Mt 10[5]). However, risen from the dead, He sends St. Paul to the *ethnē* (Act 26[17]; Gal 2[8]), for God is their God as well as Israel's (Ro 3[29]), and *ethnē* receive salvation in order that Israel may be spurred to jealousy (11[11]). St. Matthew too records the notable change in the instructions of Jesus after the resurrection. It is no longer, 'Go not to the *ethnē*,' but now it is, 'Make disciples of all the *ethnē*', the Gentiles (Mt 28[19]). It might be maintained that *ethnē* includes Israel, but an exhaustive survey of St. Matthew's use of the term[40] prompts the conclusion that the phrase, 'all the *ethnē*' excludes Israel.

Many have felt the seeming contradiction between the words of our Lord when He sent out His twelve disciples to the lost sheep of the house of Israel, telling them to avoid the way of the *ethnē*, and His instructions after the resurrection to visit the Gentiles. Some have gone so far as to suppose, with ingenuity, that within St. Matthew's community there were two contradictory missionary policies which the evangelist is trying to reconcile.[41]

In some circumstances it looks as if *ethnos*, in the singular, as well as *laos* is the Jewish people (Jn 11[50ff.]). Trench pointed out that *ethnē* (plural) was Gentiles but that *ethnos* (singular) 'has no such limitation' (p. 346). It is a name given to Jews by others and not intended dishonourably (Act 10²²). Indeed Israel is *ethnos hagion* (Ex 19⁶) and an *ethnos* rising from the midst of the *ethnē* (1 Clem 29). The highpriest's use of *ethnos* and *laos* has nevertheless caused some controversy. 'It is expedient that one man should die for the *laos* and that the whole *ethnos* perish not. ... He prophesied that Jesus should die for the *ethnos* and not for that *ethnos* only.' As R. H. Lightfoot insisted, for Caiaphas himself the change of word had no significance, whereas it had for St. John and the Christians, for whom 'the whole *ethnos*' was the total of mankind. 'The human race is to become one family as a result of the Lord's death.'⁴² Schanz, on the other hand, thought that in Jn 11⁵⁰ff. *ethnos* was the whole Jewish nation while *laos* was the theocratic People,⁴³ and this is near to the view of Pancaro,⁴⁴ who urged that *ethnos* is the Jewish nation and *laos* is Israel, the same distinction pervading the use of *aulē* and *poimnē* (10¹⁻⁵, ¹⁴ff.).

On some occasions, at any rate, the first Christians understood Israel by *ethnos*. 'He loveth our *nation*' (Lk 7⁵). Jesus is charged with perverting the 'nation' (23²). 'The *ethnos* of the Jews,' was on the lips of Cornelius' men (Act 10²²). Tertullus and Paul spoke of 'this nation' and 'my nation', the Jews (Act 24², ¹⁰, ¹⁷ 26⁴ 28¹⁹). It should be recollected that on each occasion St. Luke is reporting the speech either of persons who were not presumably acquainted with Biblical Greek or of Jews who were addressing such persons – excepting only St. Paul's speech before the Jews in Rome (Act 28¹⁹), and he might wish to preserve *laos* for the Church. He would then be giving the name *ethnos* to all outsiders, Jews included – which is just what Jesus was doing, when He sent His disciples to all the *ethnē* (Mt 28¹⁹), not to Gentiles only, despite what Hare and Harrington have to say concerning St. Matthew's use of the term.⁴⁵

K. L. Schmidt notes the curious fact that St. John's gospel does not use *ethnē* for the Gentiles and suggests that the reason is that in this gospel the Jews in their faithlessness are acquainted with the evil *kosmos* (world) are so are themselves to be considered as *ethnē*. Schmidt reminds us that this conception belongs to a line of thought common in the early Church and instances St. Paul classifying Jew and Gentile together from the standpoint of the Gospel.⁴⁶

Origen understood by *laos*, 'those of the circumcision', and by *ethnos* 'the rest'.⁴⁷ He was commenting on the speech of Caiaphas and was not using *laos* in the new Christian sense. See, 'God's People'.

In some Christian circles the racial significance of *ethnos*, whether Jewish or non-Jewish, is quite forgotten and the distinction from *laos* is placed elsewhere. The *laos* is now the Church and the *ethnē* are outsiders from the Church's point of view. The morals of Church members must be better than those of **outsiders** (1 Co 5[1]). The **outsiders** *(ethnē)* are carried away to dumb idols (12[2]), to sexual lusts, and they know not God (1 Th 4[5]). The **outsiders** *(ethnē)* speak evil of Christians, but Christians must set them a good example (1 Pet 2[12]). Their contributions are not acceptable (3 Jn 7, vl. for *ethnikōn*).

In Biblical Greek, whereas *laos* is the Jews, and then the Church, *ethnos* and *ethnē* may include Israel too, especially when the Jews are considered as outsiders to the new Israel, the Church.

OUTWARD PRETENCE

μόρφωσις

An old word has received a new passive sense (external shape) in place of its active meaning hitherto (a shaping).

In secular Greek *morphōsis* was a rare word, perhaps a Stoic term for 'education' (MM). Theophrastus, however, joins it with *schēmatismos* (configuration) in referring to the '*schēmatismos* and *morphōsis* (bringing into shape) of plants'.[48] The compound *diamorphōsis*, used by Plutarch,[49] concerns the 'shaping' of wood. Hence, its secular meaning is active, an intrinsic influence or vital impulse, working outwards. But the meaning fails to suit Christian contexts, where *morphōsis* is a soulless and dead shell revealing, as St. Chrysostom observes, only *schēma* (outward show), *tupos* (impression), and *hupokrisis* (playing a part).

St. Paul demonstrates that the Jew, for all his pretensions regarding the Law of Moses, had no more than the *morphōsis* (outward pretence) of knowledge and truth (Ro 2[20]). It is a shape received, not from within, but from the outside. Unlike the secular meaning, this is passive. Later, St. Paul foretells that heretics in the last times will have only the **outward pretence** of godliness (2 Ti 3[5]) – the *species* of piety (Vulgate, Claromontanus). Secular writers would no doubt have resorted to *morphōma*, for *morphōsis* had for them an active meaning. Ellicott observed that in the NT there is a tendency to replace the verbal nouns in -*ma* by the corresponding nouns in -*sis*.[50] The Jerusalem Bible has 'the outward appearance' of religion, Moffatt and RSV, 'form', and Knox and NEB, 'the outward form' of religion, and all point to the word's new meaning.

TO OVERCOME SPIRITUALLY
ὑπερνικάω

Tyndale translated, 'overcome strongly', but the AV rendering, 'are more than conquerors', which comes from the Geneva Bible, is expressive. *Hupernikō* is a rare and generally late word in secular Greek. It was not in extensive use when St. Paul introduced it to Christians.

The victory envisaged is spiritual – the believer's attainment of glory after his sufferings, his salvation fully wrought after faith's good fight. In all persecutions which he must endure, the saint is 'more than conqueror' through Him that loves him (Ro 8[37]).

In a recension of Theodotion's Daniel (6[3]), the young man is **preferred above** (*hupernikō*, passive) the princes, satraps, etc. Perhaps Daniel, by the time of this recension, was already seen as an allegory of the 'overcoming' Christian, victorious in faith's good fight.

There is a corresponding neologism in Christian Latin, *supervincimus* (Tertullian and Cyprian, on this passage).[51]

After quoting the former derogatory sense of the verb ('*nikān* is good, *hupernikān* is envy-provoking'), H. A. W. Meyer felt that in Ro 8[37] there was in the word 'a holy *arrogance of victory,* not selfish, but in the consciousness of the might of Christ'.[52] Beza observed that we *glory* in the Cross of Jesus. Sharing the death, we too are delivered to death, that the life of Jesus may be manifested in us.

NOTES

[1] *Expository Times* 26 (1914), p. 331.
[2] C. C. Edgar, *Catalogue Général des Antiquités Egyptiennes du Musée du Caire: Zenon Papyri,* L'Institut Français 1931, vol. IV, no. 59608, p. 58.
[3] G. Stählin in Kittel *TWNT* VII, p. 339.
[4] *Greek Papyri in the British Museum,* vol. IV *The Aphrodito Papyri,* ed. H. I. Bell, London 1910, p. 9, lines 26f. (papyrus 1338), p. 11, line 11 (papyrus 1339). See G. Stählin, *Skandalon. Untersuchungen zur Gesch. eines bibl. Begriffs* (Beitr. z. Förderung christl. Theologie, 2, XXIV), Gütersloh 1930, pp. 322, 361.
[5] G. D. Kilpatrick, *Journal of Theological Studies* NS 10 (1959), p. 129.
[6] G. Stählin in Kittel *TWNT* VII, p. 341.
[7] Stählin, op. cit., p. 343f.
[8] W. C. Allen, *St. Mark,* Rivington 1915, pp. 119f.
[9] *TWNT* VII, p. 341, n. 17.
[10] *Expository Times,* 26 (1914), pp. 331f.
[11] A. Thumb, *Die griechische Sprache im Zeitalter des Hellenismus,* Strassburg 1901, p. 123.
[12] James Moffatt, *Exp. Times* 26 (1914), pp. 407–9.

[13] Ibid., p. 409.

[14] Hermas *Vis.* IV 1.3, *Mand.* VIII 10.

[15] Basil *de Baptismo* book II, Q.10 (R.1).

[16] Origen *contra Celsum* V 64.

[17] Homily *in Num.* XXV §1. See *Origène: Homélies sur Nombres*, A. Méhat, Du Cerf (Paris) 1951, pp. 472f.

[18] Jerome in Matth 15[12].

[19] B. A. E. Osborne, *Novum Testamentum* 15 (1973), pp. 187–90.

[20] Op. cit., p. 189.

[21] *Pesikta* 165a.

[22] Op. cit., p. 190.

[23] Plutarch *Moralia* 1048C.

[24] *De Partibus Animalium* (ed. Bekker) 671a 13.

[25] Teubner 2.129E.

[26] *Laws* 638C.

[27] *Oedipus Coloneus* 1270, and 581 (OCT).

[28] *Ant. Jud.* XIX viii 2 (Niese XIX 352).

[29] Half-way to the Biblical meaning seems to be 'the act of offering' (Ecclus 46[16]).

[30] J. B. Lightfoot, *Apostolic Fathers*, part I, vol. II, note p. 135.

[31] *Ant. Jud.* XI iv 1 (Niese XI 77).

[32] C. Wessely, *Studien zur Paläographie und Papyrus-kunde*, Leipzig 1901, I, p. 7, line 27, a Christian text, see the editor's note, p. 6; A. Heisenberg and L. Wenger, *Byzantinische Papyri*, Teubner 1914, no. 8, line 23 (p. 98): 'meine heiligen Opfergaben' (a Christian text).

[33] *Greek Papyri in the British Museum*, ed. H. I. Bell, vol. V, London 1917, no. 1708, line 62 (p. 120).

[34] *Laws* 629D.

[35] Mt 5[47] in the best texts. Byzantine text however reads 'publicans'.

[36] Mt 6[7] but the Vatican MS and Curetonian Syriac version read 'hypocrites'.

[37] *Mand.* X i 4.

[38] A papyrus of AD 572 (P. Oxy I 126.13).

[39] Deut 32[43] in Ro 15[10]; Isai 9[1](8[23]) in Mt 4[15].

[40] D. R. A. Hare and D. J. Harrington, *Catholic Biblical Quarterly* 37 (1975), pp. 359–69.

[41] E. Käsemann, *Zeitschrift für Theologie und Kirche* (Tübingen) 57 (1960), p. 167.

[42] R. H. Lightfoot, *St. John's Gospel: a Commentary*, Clarendon 1956, in loc. 11[50].

[43] P. Schanz, *Kommentar über das Evangelium des hl. Johannes*, Tübingen 1885, p. 423.

[44] S. Pancaro, *New Testament Studies*, 21 (1975), pp. 396–405.

[45] See above, *Catholic Biblical Quarterly* 37 (1975).

[46] Kittel *TWNT* II, pp. 368f.

[47] *Die griechischen christlichen Schriftsteller der ersten drei Jahrhunderte* (Leipzig) 28 169f.

[48] *De Causis Plantarum* Teubner III 7.4.

[49] *Moralia* 1023C.

[50] C. J. Ellicott, *The Pastoral Epistles of St. Paul*, Longman 5th ed. 1883, p. 144.

[51] Sanday and Headlam, *Romans*, ICC, p. 222.

[52] H. A. W. Meyer, *Handbook to the Epistle to the Romans*, 5th ed. ET, T. & T. Clark, 1874, vol. II, p. 105.

P

παραβολή: παροιμία: παρρησία

All three words, *parabolē*, *paroimia* and *parrēsia*, in Christian Greek concern the teaching of Jesus, a method of His by which an aspect of revealed truth was temporarily veiled. In this sense they are quite new words.

Parable (*parabolē*). In secular Greek *parabolē* was an illustration or an analogy,[1] a comparison, a 'setting-aside', as the derivation indicates. One variety of life is placed in comparison with another.[2] Polybius speaks of things worthy of similitude, worth setting side by side (I 2.2). For Aristotle it means juxtaposition in the sense of analogy.[3] In the purely physical sense it is a travelling cheek by jowl, a running alongside, as of ships.[4]

In Biblical Greek *parabolē* becomes a by-word, a proverb (Ezek 18²), even in a derogatory sense (Ps 43(44)¹⁴), and it is used in the LXX to render *māshāl* (a maxim, symbol, by-word, similitude, riddle, wisdom-sentence). An instance of a *māshāl*, rendered by *parabolē*, is that in 1 Km 10¹²: 'Is Saul also among the prophets?' It was a saying understood by wise hearts (Pr 1⁶; Ecclus 3²⁹, etc.), like, 'Physician, heal thyself' (Lk 4²³) and, 'Can the blind lead the blind?' (6³⁹).

Much of our Lord's teaching is given in the synoptic gospels in the form of *māshāl/parabolē*, but some of His narratives are rather longer, and the story of the Sower, for instance, is a series of parables. Commenting on this way of teaching, Jesus said that the *parabolē* was for 'them that are without', confirming them in spiritual blindness (Mk 4¹¹ᶠ·), whereas He expounded the Sower to His own disciples – a parable concerning the mystery (q.v.) of the Kingdom, which, once hidden, is now disclosed to the Twelve.

Allegory (*paroimia*). According to Hesychius, the fifth-century lexicographer, *paroimia* was a way-side saying; in the lexicon of Suidas it is a 'hidden saying'. In classical Greek it was a 'digression',[5] but more often a maxim. Plato speaks of the fool in the 'adage'.[6] Clytemnestra puts faith in the 'proverb' that good news must come after bad.[7]

Where *parabolē* was not used to translate *māshāl*, the LXX and later versions usually had *paroimia* instead.[8] Both Greek words are interchangeable in the OT. Except St. John, however, who retains *paroimia* (10⁶ 16²⁵·²⁹), Christians prefer *parabolē* for the teaching of Jesus. St. John himself departs from the secular use of *paroimia* for, unlike 2 Pet 2²², he indicates thereby not so much a maxim or a

306

digression as a long discussion wherein figures and comparisons are extended. Of the allegory[9] of the Good Shepherd, with its series of metaphors, he writes, 'This *paroimia* spake Jesus unto them' (10[6]). A *paroimia* is more complex than a *parabolē*.

Nevertheless, in Christian Greek, the two words had this in common: both were means of veiling for a time an aspect of revealed truth. Mark 4 makes it clear that *parabolē* had this sense, but so also had *paroimia*. 'The time cometh when I shall no more speak to you in *paroimiai*, but I shall show you plainly' (Jn 16[25]). 'Thou speakest plainly, and speakest no *paroimia*' (16[29]).

Not in parables (*parrēsiā*). The adverb *parrēsiā* is formed from a noun which meant freedom, especially in speech. It is indeed a term which Christianity has borrowed from the secular language, only to invest it 'with a new and more glorious meaning'.[10] In Biblical Greek addition comes through LXX influence. There the noun renders *qôm^emîyôth* (uprightness, Lev 26[13]) and means 'boldness' (Wis 5[1]; Ecclus 25[25]AS; 1 Mac 4[18]) and 'openness' (Pr 1[20]). In rabbinical language the similar-sounding *pirsùm* meant publicity as opposed to privacy and secrecy, and *p^erās* was to publish, while *b^epharesyâ* was 'publicly'. In Biblical Greek the word is clearly under Semitic influence. His brethren urge Jesus to be more *parrēsiā* (non-parabolic), to behave more 'publicly' (Jn 7[4]), but He withdraws from public appearance among the Jews (11[54]: 'He behaved no longer *parrēsiā*'). When, however, he plainly declares, 'I leave the world and go to the Father', the disciples perceive that He is no longer speaking in parables and is now speaking *parrēsiā* (Jn 16[29]). The parabolic method was adopted in order to preserve the mystery (q.v.) which had always been hidden, but to speak *parrēsiā* is the very reverse of using a *parabolē* (parable) or a *paroimia* (allegory), as Jn 16[25] shows.

St. Paul glories in the *parrēsia* (publicity) of his preaching (2 Co 7[4]; Ph 1[20]), which is not esoteric but rather bold (Eph 3[12]; Phm 8; 1 Ti 3[13]). It has been demonstrated[11] that the *parrēsia* concept appears in NT Greek in contexts of threatening (Act 4[29]) which concern preaching of the Gospel publicly on a background of opposition'. In Macedonia, 'our flesh had no rest' (2 Co 7[4f.]) because for the Corinthians he experienced this *parrēsia*. The context of *parrēsia* is, 'whether by life or by death' (Ph 1[20]). It represents a speaking with authority and refers to the proving of holy Scripture (Act 2[29]); it is a heavenly gift which comes to simple and unprofessional men (Act 4[13]), with a public manifestation of spiritual power (Act 4[31]).

By the term the writer to Hebrews indicates the confidence with which Christians must persevere to the end (3[6]); they may boldly enter the veiled place and are in no sense outsiders (10[19]). St. John envisages a face-to-face encounter with Christ at His Coming (1 Jn 2²⁸) when mysteries and parables give place to *parrēsia* (publicity). The Apostle who affirmed that there was no fear in love mentions *parrēsia* a dozen times, extending it even to the day of Judgment (1 Jn 4¹⁷) and to the importunity of prayer (3²¹ 5¹⁴).

The meaning of *parrēsia* in Biblical Greek continues in the apostolic Fathers as 'plainness' and 'openness', e.g. 1 Clem 34¹; M Pol 10¹.

> What we have felt and seen,
> With confidence we tell,
> And publish to the sons of men
> The signs infallible. – C. WESLEY

PARADISE

παράδεισος

Paradeisos in the Christian vocabulary embraces both a temporary resting-place for the blessed departed and also their eternal abode in heaven itself. The Christian content of the word owes much to Jewish precedent.

In the LXX *paradeisos* renders the Hebrew *gan* (garden, orchard) and *pardēs* (park), while in secular Greek it has the same meaning.[12] It was originally a Persian word, *pairi-daêza,* coming into the Greek Bible by way of the Hebrew form, *pardēs.* In secular Greek it was first used by Xenophon in reference to the Persian aristocrasy, describing a great park *(paradeisos)* filled with wild beasts.[13]

Besides 'garden', Jewish Greek has the additional meaning, the temporary or permanent abode of the blessed departed. Indeed, among later Jews, *paradeisos* may no longer mean 'garden' at all, for which *kēpos* is now the word[14] – certainly always in the NT (Lk 13¹⁹; Jn 18¹,²⁶ 19⁴¹).

The Jews at the time of Jesus saw Paradise in various ways,[15] but two views in particular interest the Christian student. Sometimes Paradise was the *immediate* resting-place of the righteous elect after this life, to which Enoch was translated (1 Enoch 60⁸ 61¹²). At other times it was their *ultimate* resting-place, the third 'heaven' kept by three hundred bright angels, sweetly singing, a blessed place for eternal inheritance (2 Enoch 8, 9), all its occupants residing in joy and in infinite happiness (2 Enoch 42³), the 'many mansions' referred to by Jesus, prepared by God, 'very good dwellings', 'sweet houses' (2 Enoch 61³), a bright and incorruptible

Paradise continuing when all corruptible things have worn away (2 Enoch 65[10]), the Paradise of Delight (4 Ezra 7[36]), 'whose fruit endures incorruptible' (4 Ezra 7[123]).

Both views of Paradise are reflected in the NT. To be in Paradise with Jesus was promised to the dying Robber immediately upon death[16] (Lk 23[43]) and yet, following another Jewish precedent, St. Paul placed Paradise in the third 'heaven'[17] (2 Co 12[4]). The Seer of Patmos, like the author of the first part of a contemporary book (Enoch 1–36), apparently based his idea of Paradise upon the earthly Garden of Eden when he conceives it as a reward for the overcomer and as harbouring the Tree of Life. It is a *paradeisos* of righteousness (Greek Enoch 32[3]; Rev 2[7]). However, as in the promise of Jesus, when Enoch's Paradise is described in chapters 37–70, it is the abode of the departed righteous, a heavenly place and not an earthly bliss. There are therefore two rather different conceptions of Paradise in the book of Enoch, an earthly and a heavenly. Dr. Charles affirmed that Enoch's second Paradise (1 Enoch 37–70) 'is in fact identical with the division set apart in Sheol for righteous souls',[18] an immediate resting-place following upon death.

Indeed, all through apocalyptic literature Paradise is the present resting-place of the departed. Enoch's righteous forefathers dwell there (1 Enoch 70[4]; see Apoc. Mos. 37[5]), and the precious soul of Abraham was escorted by singing angels immediately at death to the dwellings of the righteous and holy, where is no toil nor grief nor mourning, only peace and exaltation and everlasting life (T. Abr XX A). The place is called Paradise (*paradeisos*). Enoch and Abel are there and they hold a judgment of good and wicked souls at death (T. Abr X B). As time went on, Paradise was thought to house only the righteous. Ungodly souls tended to be seen as inhabiting Sheol, although the older view that immediately after death both wicked and good go alike to Sheol for a time, did persist.

The idea of Paradise as an immediate and temporary resting-place from which souls wait to be delivered, may be implicit in a messianic song which has Christian associations (T. Levi 18). Here it is foretold of the New Priest that 'he shall open the gates of Paradise and shall remove the threatening sword against Man and shall give to the saints to eat from the Tree of Life'. Whether or not the passage is Christian, its apparent sentiments have made the deepest of impressions on believers' hopes. The Latin hymn proclaims of Christ,

> Thou hast opened Paradise
> And in Thee Thy saints shall rise;

and the hope is echoed by Wesley:

Death in vain forbids His rise,
Christ has opened Paradise.

But the idea is confused. Does Christ open Paradise to let man *in*, or to let him *out*?

Some early Christians, following the Jews, wrote rapturously of an earthly Paradise. 'Consecrate your minds within your breasts. ... He will raise up His Kingdom for all ages; ... to godly men He promised to open out the earth ... and the portals of the blessed and all joys.'[19] They conceived 'the portals of the blessed' as a very beautiful and fruitful garden *(paradeisos).* 'They who honour the true and everlasting God inherit life throughout the time of the coming Dispensation, dwelling in the fertile *Paradise,* feasting on sweet bread from the starry heaven.'[20]

Two distinct conceptions were associated: Paradise on earth and Paradise in heaven. The earthly Paradise is conceived in the book of Genesis: it was the Garden of Eden, full of pleasant trees around the Tree of Life and the Tree of Knowledge, watered by four rivers (Gen 2^{8-17}). The conception was developed in parts of the book of Enoch, where it was the garden of righteousness, having many beautiful trees, including the Tree of Wisdom, and it formed a third part of the north quarter of the world (1 Enoch 32^{3-6} 77^3). The other conception, the heavenly Paradise, features in parts of the same book: the patriarch Enoch was translated here, to the heavenly garden of Life where they sleep in heaven above, where the elect dwell aloft, where Enoch was raised on chariots of the Spirit (1 Enoch 60^8 61^{12} 70^3). So the primitively conceived Garden of Eden has been re-located in heaven. As some seers rendered the new conception of Paradise, it still retained features of the earthly – sweet smells, four streams, healthful fruit and the Tree of Life – where every place is blessed and is tended by bright singing angels. Indeed, in his highly coloured description (2 Enoch 8), the seer blends both notions, the Paradise on earth and the Paradise in heaven. The first should perhaps be seen as an allegory of the second, a type of the Reality.

The second reaches its supreme expression when the risen righteous, according to Pharisaic hopes, are seen to dwell among the heights of the invisible world. For this is called Paradise. Like to angels, and made equal to the stars in this idealized bliss, the risen righteous are in heaven where they are transformed from one beauty and loveliness to another, from one splendour of glory to a rapture even more intense. 'Ostendetur paradisus,' cries the seer (4 Ezra 7^{53}). 'And there shall be spread before them the extents of Paradise' (2 Bar 51^{11}). Paradise, once a place of waiting, has now become our final and eternal home. It is a 'world which does not die' (2 Bar 51³).

This was the Jewish heritage upon which St. Paul had entered. This was the glory he envisaged for sanctified children of God. 'We all ... are changed into the same image from one glory to another glory' (2 Co 3¹⁸). Since the apocalypse of Baruch, with its vision of the world invisible, in which time no longer withers and souls become like angels, transformed from 'beauty into loveliness, from light into glorious splendour' – since this bright vision is nearly contemporary with St. Paul, we cannot say that either is dependent upon the other. A little later comes the apocalypse of Ezra: '*Vobis enim apertus est paradisus!* To you Paradise is open! Planted is the Tree of Life, the future Dispensation is prepared, abundance is ready, the City is built and a Rest appointed' (4 Ezra 8⁵²). This glory does not await us immediately at death, but it belongs to the new age. It comes with the heavenly Sion.

St. Paul, richly inheriting the tradition which associates Paradise with heaven (2 Co 12⁴), ultimate and eschatological, seems to part company with our Lord for Whom Paradise is the immediate resting-place of the faithful at the moment of death. Nevertheless, St. Paul has other concepts like that of escaping from the body and being 'with' the Lord, of being 'with' Christ at departing (2 Co 5⁸; Ph 1²³), in which the word 'paradise', in the way Jesus used it, is trembling upon his lips but never uttered in this sense.

Moreover, the Christian Seer too seems to inherit a different tradition from our Lord's. For them both, Paradise truly is a resting-place, but whereas for Jesus it awaits the faithful at death, for the Seer Paradise is the new Sion, the reward of him that overcometh, not to be realized until after the Millennium, the final abode of God and His saints.²¹ The Tree of Life is now within the new Jerusalem (Rev 22¹⁴); it is in the Paradise of God (2⁷).

Can we not trace within the NT two distinct Jewish ideas concerning Paradise? The first, which Jesus shared (Lk 16²² 23⁴³), suggested that righteous persons like Lazarus and the penitent robber were transported away to bliss in Abraham's bosom by angels at the very moment of death, the second, which the Seer of Patmos shared, suggesting that perfect bliss is not attained until the City is built, until the consummation of all things, after the great Judgment when the Lord of Glory comes down again to earth at the general Resurrection and final Assize.²²

As combined in Christianity, the views are not logically at odds, for one is a temporary repose, a 'sleep' until the awakening of resurrection,²³ while the other is the final glory in heaven after the resurrection of the body. Of this last state Thomas Campion wrote:

Ever blooming are the joys of Heaven's high Paradise,
Cold age deafs not there our ears, nor vapour dims our eyes:
Glory there the sun outshines, whose beams the blessed only see;
O come quickly, glorious Lord, and raise my sprite to Thee.

At this point the Christian student will be induced to ponder just what takes place in the Paradise which is represented as being an interim state, and to wonder what part of him will 'sleep' in Paradise after death. A traditional belief of Christians has been that while the tired body lies in the tomb waiting to rise again, the soul rests in Paradise until soul and body are re-united on the great Easter Day,

> *But the soul in contemplation*
> *Utters earnest prayer and strong,*
> *Bursting at the Resurrection into song.*

St. Paul has inspired the traditional belief by his disclosure that here on earth, while we are 'in the body', we are absent from the Lord, and that at death our real selves ('we') are absent from the body and present with the Lord (2 Co 5$^{4-6}$). Here then is conceived an intermediate state in which the spirit and soul[24] of each one of us await re-union with the body at the final Easter Day. But neither St. Paul nor any other NT writer suggests that in Paradise, the interim state, we are in any *unconscious* condition. To that extent 'sleep' is not a word to describe it. St. Stephen is said to have 'fallen asleep' (Act 7^{60}), but 'falling asleep' may simply be a euphemism for dying, rather than a reference to his 'sleeping' in Paradise. In the same way, many of God's people are said to have arisen 'from sleep' at Christ's resurrection (Mt 27^{52}), but again the expression may be but a euphemism for death rather than an indication of their condition in an intermediate state. Whether or not the state in Paradise is called a 'sleep', at least the blessed dead are not in oblivion there: Paradise is rather a situation of happiness, 'with Christ ̄which is far better', and is compared to Abraham's bosom. Moreover, the dying Robber is encouraged to look forward to Paradise immediately as a conscious, happy posture, as the enjoyment of Christ's own presence.

Still, this is not an embodied state.[25] We wait for the Resurrection before being 'in the body', and in the mean time in Paradise we are with Christ but 'absent from the body'.

PARTNERSHIP IN SANCTIFICATION

1. συνεγείρω

In secular Greek *sunegeirō* meant 'to raise together' in a literal sense, to help in stirring up. 'Any pretext,' so it was said, 'is sufficient to *help to arouse* (active of *sunegeirō*) griefs and lamentations'.[26] It was used of an invalid 'reviving'.[27] These are generally its senses in the LXX.[28] However, in Christian Greek, it denotes the believer's experience of spiritual exaltation with Christ, for He has 'sanctified us together' (active of *sunegeirō*) and made us to sit in heavenly places in Christ Jesus (Eph 2[6]); in baptism we are 'sanctified together' with Him (passive of *sunegeirō*) through God Who raised Him (Col 2[12]) and, once 'sanctified together' (passive of *sunegeirō*), we are to seek those things that are above (Col 3[1]). 'Labour with one another,' cries St. Ignatius, 'struggle together, run together, suffer together, rest together, be sanctified together (passive of *sunegeirō*), as God's stewards.[29]

2. συνζωοποιέω

Sunzōopoiō is a coinage of Christian Greek, discovered nowhere else. It indicates an early stage in the attainment of sanctification, perhaps earlier than that indicated by *sunegeirō*. It is the newness of life which follows justification, as St. Paul makes clear when he sets both words together in a logical sequence. 'God ... even when we were dead in sins, hath quickened us together (*sunzōopoiō*) with Christ ... and hath sanctified us together (*sunegeirō*) and made us to sit together in heavenly places in Christ Jesus' (Eph 2[5f.]).

The sequence is confirmed by the word's situation elsewhere. 'You ... hath He quickened together *(sunzōopoiō)* with Him, having forgiven you all trespasses' – that is, immediately upon justification (Col 2[13]).

PARTNERSHIP WITH UNBELIEVERS

ἑτεροζυγέω

Leave then thy foolish ranges,
For none can thee secure
But One Who never changes,
Thy God, thy life, thy care. – HENRY VAUGHAN

Heterzugō is one of several new words expressing the Christian ideal of a separated life. Our verb is a coinage of Christian Greek, apparently with metaphorical meaning, 'to draw unequally' or 'to be yoked unequally'.

Although the verb is not found in secular Greek, the adjective *heterozugos* is, and it appears not to have anything to do with 'breeding' – rather with mixing the different sizes of yokes which harness beasts together. On the other hand, in the LXX (Lev 19[19]) the adjective indicates the cross-breeding of cattle which is forbidden to farmers. The same applies to Philo who refers to the mating of cattle 'with those of other species' *(heterzugois).*[30]

There comes to light, therefore, a new Christian meaning, 'miscegenation', interpreted spiritually of the intermarriage of believers with unbelievers. One might suppose that St. Paul intends to forbid a Christian to marry a non-Christian. 'Be not unequally yoked with unbelievers,' he says (2 Co 6[14]). But the context permits a wider view. What is forbidden may not be marriage alone, but any kind of partnership between Christians and the world. 'What communion hath light with darkness?' he goes on to say at once. 'And what concord hath Christ with Belial? ... Wherefore come out from among them, and be ye separate.'

The Christian view is a wider interpretation of *heterozugos*. It is to take the secular meaning of the adjective, i.e. unequally yoked together, and to give to it a metaphorical turn. It is not the OT meaning of *heterozugō* (to cross-breed), re-interpreted as mixed marriage.

PASTOR AND FLOCK

ποιμήν: ἀρχιποιμήν: ποίμνη: ποίμνιον

They are technical words for Christ, His bishops, and His Church.

Secular Greek. *Poimēn* was a herdsman in Homer, and after that usually a shepherd, often enough understood in the poetical sense as a pastor of people, like Agamemnon[31] and Cyrus,[32] or guide of inanimate things, like a stormy sky with its flock of clouds – described as 'a mad *shepherd* tearing his own flock'.[33] It was not a pastor or teacher in a religious sense until Biblical Greek made it so.

Archipoimēn, much rarer word, was a master-shepherd or chief herdsman.[34] Deissmann pointed out that this word is found on the mummy label of an Egyptian peasant of the Roman period (LAE 97ff.). However, its meaning is not religious; the peasant was a head-shepherd by trade, and so there can be no parallel with the Christian use of the word.

Poimnē, our third word, was a flock of sheep from the time of Homer, but Aeschylus brings Apollo from his temple brandishing bow and quiver to dismiss with this dramatic cry the guilty chorus who attend the matricide:

'Away! Graze other fields, you flock unshepherded!
No god loves such as you!'[35]

Plato's use is no less metaphorical, when he describes mankind as a 'two-footed flock'.[36] *Poimnion,* our final word, was diminuitive of *poimnē.*[37]

Christian Greek. These then are secular words for a shepherd and his flock of sheep, but in Christian Greek the terms apply to Christ Himself and to presbyter-bishops, with their 'flock', the Church. There was Christ's own precedent for the new use of the words (Jn 10[11, 14, 16]), a precedent readily followed with regard to Christ as *Poimēn* (shepherd) and *Archipoimēn* (chief-shepherd) (Heb 13[20]; 1 Pet 2[25] 5[4]). The adjective 'good' *(kalos)* applied to Him in the phrase, 'Good Shepherd', corresponds to the Hebrew *yāphê* in the rabbinical phrase applied to David,[38] the Shepherd Boy.

Christ is the *Poimēn* of the world-wide Catholic Church[39] (M. Pol. 19[2]), but *poimēn* is a Christian pastor, too (Eph 4[11]; I. Philad. 2[1]; I. Rom 9[1]). *Archipoimēn* is later a Christian bishop,[40] as well as pope, patriarch and metropolitan. Christians avoided the title, *Archiboukolos* (chief herder), which appears in the Dionysus Mysteries.

Poimnē in Christian Greek continues to enjoy its secular sense of a flock of sheep (Lk 2[8]; 1 Co 9[7]), but in Jn 10[16] it denotes the Church. Christ prophesies that there shall be one Church *(poimnē),* and the word is used in the context of divine election. Unbelief of the Jews is accounted for by their not belonging to Jesus' 'sheep', whom no man shall pluck away for they were 'given' to Him by the Father. 'What the Father has given to Me is greater than all things.' The reference is surely to divine predestination, the charge to accomplish the salvation of the elect, the weightiest ('greatest') of all things.[41]

Poimnion too is the Church (Lk 12[32]; Act 20[28f.]; 1 Pet 5[2f.]), which for St. Clement is the '*flock* of Christ' (1 Clem 16[1] 44[3] 54[2] 57[2]).

PATIENT ENDURANCE

1. μακροθυμία, μακροθυμέω

They are secular words, filled with a new Christian sense of hope and patience.

In secular Greek the meaning was perseverance rather than patience. The noun, *makrothumia,* though never listed by the Stoics as a virtue, is 'patience' occasionally,[42] a comparable quality with constancy,[43] applied by Josephus to the perseverance of the Jews despite their ill successes; and the verb *makrothumō* is 'to persevere'.[44]

In Biblical Greek, however, the words denote particularly a divine forbearance which the recipients should themselves emulate in facing their problems. The Letter of Aristeas may have the new meaning. 'By showing clemency *(makrothumia),*' said the envoy to the king, 'you will turn your people from evil' (p. 188).

J. Horst observes that *makrothumia* assumes a characteristic depth in the Bible,[45] but confesses that inevitably there enters the use of the word in later Judaism an element from secular thought to weaken it. He instances the case in the Letter of Aristeas which, though it has a pious ring, comes from quite a different world from that of the OT (p. 381). Complaisancy and mildness is no part of the *makrothumia* of God in the OT.

Makrothumia rendered the Hebrew *'erekh 'apphîm,* the divine forbearance of anger (Jer 15[15]), and in Jewish Greek it is the patient endurance which gives a happy issue under temptations (T XII P *Jos.* 2[7]). It is indeed one of the fruits of the Spirit (Gal 5[22]) and is a characteristically Christian quality (Eph 4[2]; Col 1[11]; 2 Ti 3[10]; Heb 6[12]; Jas 5[10]), whereas, so Trench reminded us (p. 185), the pagan term for long-suffering was *anexikakia.*

The verb, *makrothumō,* in Jewish works denoted the patient suffering of such inevitables as the wrath of God (Baruch 4[25]), or disease and poverty, and is the same thing as resignation to His will (Ecclus 2[4]). 'Ye that fear the Lord, wait for His mercy!' is the philosophy behind *makrothumō.* 'I shall not live for ever to *suffer patiently,*' mourns the resentful Job. 'Away! My life is empty!' (7[16] LXX).

The NT has verb as well as noun. God the King in the parable of the Debtors is entreated to **have leniency** (Mt 18[26, 29]). God **is patient** to us by granting time for repentance before the Day (2 Pet 3[9]). Christians too must **hold out patiently,** waiting for the Coming of our Lord (Jas 5[7f.]). Abraham **endured patiently** (Heb 6[15]). It is a mark of Christian love to **endure** (1 Co 13[4]).

Jesus assures His disciples that God **suffers patiently** His elect (Lk 18[7]). 'And shall not God avenge His own elect, which cry day and night unto Him, though He **bear long** with them?' (AV). I can see little evidence that *makrothumo* meant 'delay' (RSV, Bauer, following many commentators), though it is said that the best parallel for such a meaning is in Chrysostom.[46] But writing of the storm in the boat St. Chrysostom says that Jesus often suffered His disciples to fall into more grievous tempests of fortune, and 'bare long with them'.[47]

Indeed, the NT no longer employs the secular sense, 'to delay'.[48] However, many commentators have taken the meaning to be 'delay' or 'be slow to act' (in their defence).[49] Warfield cites for this Godet, Meyer and Plummer, and quotes Van Osterzee as declaring that, with *makrothumō*, 'it is not the idea of *forbearance* in general, but *delaying* of help that is to be adhered to'. He cites also Jülicher who, in turn, cited already for this meaning St. Clement of Alexandria and B. Weiss, Steinmeyer, Stockmayer, Weizäcker, Holzmann, Nösgen and Göbel. It is foolhardy to stand against so august a gathering. Riesenfeld[50] pointed to Ecclus 35[11-24] as an inspiration behind the whole passage and assumed that *makrothumō* is 'delay' (as if it were *bradunō*). But in the Sirach context *makrothumō* means rather 'be patient' than 'delay', although it balances *bradunō* in the first half of the same verse. The context is, 'The righteous Judge executes judgment. The Lord will not tarry *(bradunō)*, neither will He have mercy *(makrothumō)* upon them, until ... He requite vengeance' (Ecclus 35[19f.]). Ljungvik insisted that we take the whole Lukan context and the general meaning of the parable of the Unjust Judge into account: the point of the Lord's argument is, that if a wicked earthly judge cannot hold out against such a supplication as the widow's, how much less can God.[51] Ljungvik would render our Lord's words: 'Will not God avenge His elect who cry out night and day to Him, *but* will He *hold out against* them?' It is to give a new twist to *makrothumō* ('to hold out against', *aushalten gegenüber*) which is as doubtful as is the rendering of *kai* by 'but'.

Cranfield, more happily, I think, prefers to give to *makrothumō* the meaning, 'to be patient', but Cranfield understands it as patience 'with regard to' His elect, not patience *with* His elect. He sees the forbearance as directed towards their persecutors, delaying His retribution from motives of mercy.[52] So if the Coming of our Lord seems to delay, and the time appointed to be long, we are to recall that the interval is inserted by God's mercy and patience to allow both us and our persecutors alike time for repentance. There is a tension, truly, an earnest longing for His Coming, contained by thankfulness for a season of repentance and amendment of life.

Delling's interesting suggestion supposes an allegorizing relationship to exist between the 'widow' of the parable and the eschatological situation of God's elect when they fail to understand the delay in His Coming. God hears His own and helps them. He is forbearing towards them *(makrothumō)*, and they must be prepared.[53] Stählin developed Delling's thought by looking at the concept of 'widow' in OT and NT (*'almānâ* and *chēra*). Moreover, in antiquity, cities tended to be personified as women. There is Zion as an ornamented bride (Isai 49¹⁸), as a wife of youth for a small moment forsaken but with great mercies gathered (54⁶ᶠ·), as a virgin married to a young man, a bride rejoiced over (62⁵), as the Bride of the Lamb (Rev 19⁸; 22¹⁷). The parable teaches that God is bound to hear the prayers of His own and to save them. The messianic note, 'when the Son of Man comes' (verse 8), may indicate that the 'widow' is destined to be a 'bride' once more.⁵⁴ On such a background is the Lord's patience plainly seen.

The apostolic Fathers. The Lord Jesus taught *makrothumia* (1 Clem 13¹). We will please God by righteousness, truth, *makrothumia*, and holiness (1 Clem 62²). St. Clement's prayer for every elect soul is that he may have faith, fear, peace, *hupomonē* (patience), *makrothumia* (patient endurance), temperance, chastity and soberness (64). St. Ignatius too joins *makrothumia* with *hupomonē*, and he sees the Christian life as a contest in these virtues, as well as in faith and in admonition (I. Eph 3¹). He warns that in eschatological times we should fear the *makrothumia* of God (11¹).

A third Father to link the noun with *hupomonē* is the Alexandrian allegorist who declares that our belief has four allies: fear, *hupomonē*, continency and *makrothumia* (Barn 2²). Hermas links it with *tapeinophrosunē* (lowliness of mind): in the commandments there is nothing about the first place or about reputation but there is plenty concerning a man's *makrothumia* and *tapeinophrosunē* (*Sim.* VIII 7.6).

The verb *makrothumō* has the same meaning. Christian love **has patience** (1 Clem 49⁵). God **was forbearing** to us (Diogn 9²). We should **be forbearing** with one another, as God is with us (I. Pol 6²).

2. ὑπομονή, ὑπομένω

A new Christian sense of hope and patience has filled these words too.

The verb *hupomenō* in secular Greek was 'to stay behind',⁵⁵ 'to await',⁵⁶ to 'submit' to such things as servitude, to 'await' the festival, and to 'stand firm' in battle.⁵⁷ The noun *hupomonē* was a 'remaining behind',⁵⁸ 'endurance', whether of grief or war or death or toil.⁵⁹ Polybius refers literally to the sword's 'sustaining' of blows.⁶⁰ *Hupomonē* is expectancy of what is inevitable, but the concept of patience and hope again enters from the LXX, where *hupomenō* often renders the Piel of *qwh* (hope) and the noun *miqwê* (hope). David prays, 'Before Thee there is no *hupomonē/miqwê* (hope 1 Chr 29¹⁵). In Ezra's reforms there is *hupomonē/miqwê* (hope) for Israel (Ezra 10²) God is Israel's *hupomonē/miqwê* (Jer

318

14^8 17^{13}). The idea of expectancy is present: 'The Lord is good to them that call upon Him in *hupomonē*' (Ps Sol $2^{40(36)}$).

St. Paul has both *makrothumia* and *hupomonē* in the same context (Col 1^{11}). *Makrothumō,* according to St. Chrysostom, is the refraining from retaliation; *hupomenō* is patient endurance without power to retaliate. The former is exercised among believers, the latter among unbelievers. However, Trench (pp. 84, 187) observed that the use of the verb *(hupomenō)* in Heb $12^{2f.}$ is against the definition, insofar as Christ did have power to retaliate. Trench preferred the distinction that *makrothumia* is patience towards persons, *hupomonē* towards things; the latter may not therefore be applied as a characteristic of God whom all things obey and whom persons alone can resist, because they have free will. But I doubt whether this is the right distinction, for *hupomonē* is applied to the martyr Polycarp in respect of his patience toward persons, since he overcame 'the righteous ruler' by his *hupomonē* (M. Pol. 19^2). *Hupomonē* is especially the patient waiting for the End, for the Coming of Our Lord (I. Rom 10^3). St. Paul probably has the LXX rendering of *miqwê* (hope) in mind when he links *hupomonē* closely with 'hope in the Lord' (1 Th 1^3) and with waiting for Him in the eschatological sense (2 Th 3^5).

The time when 'the mark of the Beast' is received will be supremely the time of the *hupomonē* of the saints (Rev 13^{10} 14^{12}). 'The *hupomonē* of Jesus Christ' will not be His personal patience, but an instance of objective genitive: 'the **patient waiting** for Jesus Christ' (Rev 1^9).

Hupomonē then is an unruffled expectancy of God's salvation, to be fulfilled in the Coming of our Lord (1 Th $1^{2f.}$; Rev 1^9). The motives behind it are hope attaining perfection and salvation. For its exercise Christ is our model. It is founded upon Christian love (1 Co 13^7), enduring and suffering all, and it is of no avail without Christian love.[61]

The verb *hupomenō* in two instances, of the child Jesus and of Silas and Timothy (Lk 2^{43}; Act 17^{14}), retains its classical meaning, to 'tarry behind', but most of the time it demands a new Christian sense of **patient endurance** for Christ's sake, of enduring the eschatological sufferings before the End (Mt 10^{22} 24^{13}; Mk 13^{13}), of exercising patience in the Christian life (Ro 12^{12}), for the sake of the brethren (2 Ti 2^{10}), knowing that such suffering entitles us to reign with Christ at last (2 Ti 2^{12}). He **endured** the cross for us (Heb $12^{2f.}$), and we for Him must **endure** a great fight of affliction (Heb 10^{32}) and chastening (12^7). It is a blessed thing to **endure** trials (Jas 1^{12} 5^{11}). 'If when ye do well, and suffer for it, **ye take it patiently,** this is acceptable with God' (1 Pet 2^{20}). 'Endurance' is the way the Master went: should not the servant tread it still?

PEACE (IN CHRIST)

εἰρήνη

Eirēnē is an old word with a wealth of new Christian nuances.

Secular Greek. The word's extensive use is based on the concept of the cessation of strife, whether public or personal, absence of war and quarrelling. For instance, the Lydians and the Medes were anxious to make *eirēnē*, and Cyrus wished for *eirēnē* between the Armenians and Chaldeans.[62]

It was besides a treaty of peace, as when Plutarch referred to 'the terms of that notorious *eirēnē*'.[63] To 'carry peace to us' means not to wish to quarrel with us,[64] and laws are intended to leave men free to dwell in *eirēnē*.[65] It was a virtue in Greek eyes, personified from the beginning, along with Order and Justice.[66]

Biblical Greek. In the LXX, on the other hand, *eirēnē* was 'health' and 'well-being', in the sense of abatement of God's wrath, with spiritual security. Almost always it rendered *shālôm*, peace, welfare, prosperity – especially peace with God. 'Is it peace?' was a Hebrew salutation (Jdg 18[15]; 1 Km 17[22]; 4 Km 4[26]). Prince of Peace was Messiah's title. Through the LXX the Greek *eirēnē* and the Hebrew *shālôm* are closely related, and in Biblical Greek *eirēnē* may only be understood in the light of the association. 'Peace' is the gift of God in all the traditions of the OT – the exodus-tradition, the sapiental-tradition, and the messianic-apocalyptic-tradition. It is a gift and cannot be fought for. To try to obtain it by 'historical' action will end in establishing a false peace, a mere tranquillity.[67]

Christian Greek takes a step forward when *eirēnē* becomes personalized as no less than our Saviour Himself, who is our Peace, reconciling Jew with Gentile, and both with God (Eph 2[14]). *Eirēnē* is one of the fruits of the Spirit (Gal 5[22]) and occurs in the Christian phrase, 'Depart in peace' (Jas 2[16]).

Probably its most momentous use is in soteriology. After we have been justified by faith, says the Apostle, it is for us to take the next step. 'Let us have (i.e. enjoy or experience) *eirēnē* with God,' a point on the road to full salvation.[68]

The *eirēnē* which Jesus gives is 'not as the world gives'. Our world looks for 'peace' and is for ever speaking of it and assuming that political justice will effect it. Christian *eirēnē* is a gift from Jesus and has no connection with political aspiration. Christian *eirēnē* corresponds with nothing in the secular vocabulary. It is not even the *eirēnē* of the OT which, although it was a messianic gift, was linked with justice and was realized in an earthly political situation.[69]

Even within the NT it may be that St. Paul has a deeper

meaning still for *eirēnē*. For him it expresses the new relationship with God to replace former hostility. It pictures our 'access' to Him (Ro 5[1f.]). We were enemies and have been reconciled and saved (Ro 5[10]). It is not merely that Christ in His person 'abolished our enmity', for the context suggests something more sacrificial.[70] 'By the *blood* of Christ,' says St. Paul, 'you have been made nigh' (Eph 2[13]). It was 'in His flesh' that the enmity was abolished. In Eph 2[14] it is therefore possible that when St. Paul says, 'Christ our *eirēnē*,' he has in mind the Hebrew *shelem*, the peace-offering, which is sometimes rendered in the LXX by *eirēnikos*. True, the LXX avoided *eirēnē* when confronted with *shelem* and used *eirēnikos* instead.[71] Nevertheless, that is a word from the same stem. It is true that there is no recorded instance where *eirēnē* renders *shelem*, and even *eirēnikos* is not so common in the LXX as a rendering for *shelem*. Dr. Snaith would rather look at Isai 53[5] where the Servant is 'our peace' *(sh[e]lōmēnû)*, and he finds no connection with the sacrificial system of the Temple. He would rather trace behind St. Paul's use of *eirēnē* the idea of vicarious self-sacrifice.

At all events, with some slight peripheral adjustments, the Christian word *eirēnē* corresponds with the Hebrew *shālôm*.[72]

PATIENT IN TEACHING

ἀνεξίκακος

Anexikakos represents a divine and a Christian quality.

Secular Greek. The meaning of *anexikakos* had been 'enduring pain' (or evil), derived from the verb (to bear) and the noun (evil). It was a medical term.[73] A fragment of an extant treatise on therapeutics explains that the constitution of a patient must be considered, whether he is *en tois loipois anexikakos* ('generally of a good endurance'), whether able to bear the thirst, etc.[74]

Christian Greek. A moral and didactic connotation is added to the idea of patience. 'The servant of the Lord must not strive, but be gentle unto all men, apt to teach, *anexikakos*' (2 Ti 2[24]).

The noun, *anexikakia*, implied in the LXX the quality of patiently affirming a belief in face of mockery (Wis 2[19]). It is linked with *epieikeia* (reasonableness, gentleness). The picture is that of a relentless teacher who firmly overlooks the painful consequences of his affirmations.

Christians must have the quality of the *anexikakos*,[75] which is applied to the good bishop.[76] It is further a divine quality. In St. Cyril's commentary on Hosea he applies the adjective to the Lord, 'good by nature and *anexikakos,* longsuffering, of great tender-mercy, Master of all things'.[77]

PEOPLE OF GOD (THE CHURCH)
λαός

Laos is the Greek word from which our own 'laity' is ultimately derived. In the Biblical language it signified Israel and then the Christian Church.

Secular Greek. *Laos* was the 'people', like the citizens assembled in the *ekklēsia* (Aristophanes), or 'the much people' in the phrase of Plato, denoting the multitude, or the Attic 'people' (Aeschylus). *Laos* was a unit of men who are called by one name, like 'the whole *people* of Achaea'.[78] Homer has the plural for soldiers, for subjects and for common men in contrast with their leaders. Trench observed that it was a word of rarest use in Attic prose, and yet it occurs between one and two thousand times in the LXX (p. 345). In Biblical Greek, it becomes the special equivalent of 'Israel'.

'Thy salvation', said Simeon, 'which Thou hast prepared before the face of all *people*' (Lk 2[31]). Here we have *laoi* (plural) and the usual interpretation is 'Gentiles'. But that is firmly rejected by Dr. Kilpatrick[79] and others. Nowhere else, be it noted, does *laos* stand for Gentiles in Luke-Acts. We must therefore regard Simeon as greeting the salvation which God had prepared before 'all the tribes of Israel' – and not, 'all nations'.

Christian Greek. Because 'Israel' typified the Church, *laos* also is to be understood of the Church in the Christian vocabulary. When the death of Jesus is said to be 'for the *laos*' (Jn 11[50]) perhaps even then the term ought to be interpreted of the Church – for St. John the evangelist, not of course for Caiaphas, the speaker. For St. John, *laos* has 'a highly technical meaning',[80] since he distinguishes between Israelite/Israel and Jew (*Ioudaios*). 'Israelite' signifies for him a believer in Christ: I think that St. John saw Nathanael in this light, 'an Israelite indeed' (1[47]), and he recognized the Church when Jesus was hailed as 'King of Israel' by Nathanael and by the crowds who cried, 'Hosanna: Blessed is the King of Israel.' In each case the speaker did not realize what he was saying, but St. John does (1[49] 12[13]). The Church is the new Israel, a Jewish Christian concept.[81]

The case is altogether different with *Ioudaios,* which has no connection with the new Israel. When St. John has this word, he probably means, 'Judaean' – a Palestinian use of the term to distinguish the inhabitants of Judaea from those of Galilee, in contrast with the use of the term in the Dispersion to mean a Jew. As Lowe protests, to translate it 'Jew' is 'a constant excuse for antisemitism whose further existence cannot be permitted'.[82] In contrast to *laos*, the word *Ioudaios* is Judaism together with those official leaders who opposed Jesus, having their headquarters at Jerusalem. *Ioudaios* stands for the letter of the Law, for refusal of the claims of Jesus, for denial of our true King. The *Ioudaioi* are unworthy of being the *laos* of God. 'John's use of the title,' writes Dr. Kingsley Barrett, 'showed that he (like most Christian writers at and later than the end of the first century AD) was well aware of the existence of the Church as a distinct entity, different from and opposed by Judaism, which it claimed to have supplanted'.[83]

When contrasting *laos* and *Ioudaios* it is well to recall that St. John's gospel is anti-Judaean and not anti-Israelite. *Laos* is 'Israel', but 'Judaean' is something different. Israel and *laos* are now Christian terms. In St. John's gospel *laos* has a sense which rests on the supposition that the Christian community is none other than the People of God. Indeed, it is not Gentiles, or even Dispersion Jews who are the 'children of God that were scattered abroad' (11^{52}) and whom Jesus is going to gather together in one, but it is all, both Jew and Gentile, who shall be united into the new People of God through the death of Jesus.

At the council of Jerusalem St. Peter affirmed that God did visit the Gentiles to take out of them a *people* for His name (Act 15^{14}) – a clear understanding of *laos* as the Church. St. Peter transfers *laos* from the LXX context to a Christian one (Ex 19^5; Deut 14^2; 1 Pet 2^9), and not only St. John and St. Peter but St. Paul besides makes clear that *laos* is the Church. 'Ye are the Temple of the living God', he informs the assembly at Corinth. 'As God hath said ... They shall be my *laos*' (2 Co 6^{16}). Moreover, St. Paul has a new People in mind when he mentions those who were not God's *laos* but now are (Ro $9^{25f.}$). When he speaks of a peculiar *laos* he means the Church (Tit 2^{14}).

The writer to Hebrews, too, speaks of the Church at rest as 'the *laos* of God' (4^9), and the Seer of Patmos is speaking of the Church when he uses *laos* (Rev 18^4 21^3 sing. as vl. for *laoi*).

In the apostolic Fathers *laos* is both the old Israel (1 Clem $55^{5,6}$ 64) and the new (59^4). From the argument in 2 Clem 2^3 *laos* will be the Church – 'our *laos* which seems to be deserted by God'. The letter of Barnabas plays on both OT and NT meanings in $13^{1,2,6}$: 'let us see whether this *laos* or the former *laos* is the heir, and whether the covenant is for us or for them'. Sometimes the sense is that of the LXX (8^1 12^8 14^1 16^5), but *laos* is also the new People, the Church (3^6 5^7 7^5).

It is worth remarking that the Greek adjective *laïkos*, formed

323

from *laos,* came into Western languages to give us the word 'laity', and is a religious word in the sense that all members of the Church are *laïkoi* or laity, that is, the People of God.[84]

The first use of *laïkos* in Christian literature implies that the 'layman' is not the unprofessional man as in secular Greek, not the common man distinct from his leaders, but a member of the *laos* of God, the chosen People (1 Clem 40[5]). Then the word became secularized again and in our modern parlance means no more than 'unqualified', used of those who are not recognized members of a profession or sphere of knowledge. We must not suppose that that is its meaning within the Church context: the 'laity' are not outsiders in any way and Catholics as well as Protestants recognize this and regard the 'laity' as those who are bound 'by the layman's ordinances' (1 Clem 40[5]), having privileges and obligations. In the common language of today the evolution of the term illustrates sadly enough a decline in a Christian ideal. 'Ecclesiastic' and 'churchman', terms which should include all believers, now simply mean a 'cleric', while 'layman' is debased to mean an outsider.[85]

PERFECTION IN THE CHRISTIAN LIFE

1. τέλειος : τελειότης

Secular Greek. *Teleios* and *teleiotēs* have not even in the Mystery religions or among the Stoics the special meaning they were destined to find in the Bible and in the Church.

The adjective *teleios* meant 'without blemish' when it was used of sacrificial victims,[86] and sometimes 'full-grown'[87] in the sense of mature, as when Clytemnestra, having plotted with her lover, mourns the 'man' she murdered on his return from Troy. This 'mature man', great without a doubt, every inch a king, was Agamemnon – slain on the altar of Justice for the sake of 'striplings'.[88] He was an example of *teleios.*

Plato, too, used *teleios* of 'adult' human beings.[89] It will mean 'married', but more often 'accomplished'.[90] With the meaning, 'fulfilled', *teleios* described prayers and vows.[91] With the meaning, 'complete', it described numbers.[92] With the meaning, 'powerful to answer prayer', it is devoted to the gods, particularly to Zeus:

'O *perfect* Zeus, Zeus! Make my prayers perfect!'[93]

Aeschylus elsewhere employs the phrase, *teleion hupsiston Dia,* in the mouth of the priestess as she calls upon a list of gods and finally upon Zeus most High, 'mighty to answer prayer'.[94]

In secular Greek a child was *teleios* when he came 'of age'. A notification of what amounts to a summons for debt in AD 178 requested that a copy of the petition be sent to the debtor or, if she is deceased, to her heirs, 'being of age' *(teleioi)*.[95] *Teleios* also were 'mature' ladies, mistresses of their persons.[96] In a quite a distinct sense *teleios* is applied to a Theban mill, 'in good working order'.[97] Still, faultlessness and maturity are inherent meanings until in the Mysteries *teleios* became a technical term for an 'initiate' into secret rites. Though the term belongs to paganism, yet St. Paul echoed it in the first instance from Judaism, as Clemen conceded.[98]

Biblical Greek. In the Biblical language of the LXX the sense progresses in two ways, for *teleios* renders *tāmîm* (sound), used of sacrificial animals and also of moral integrity. In a context where separation from heathen abominations is urged, the Israelite is told, 'Thou shalt be *teleios* with the Lord thy God' (Deut 18[13]). The Passover lamb must be *tāmîm* (Ex 12[5]), but so must the Israelite. Noah was *tāmîm* (Gen 6[9]) and the Hebrew word indicates an 'upright' man (2 Km 22[26]). All are *teleios* in Biblical Greek. The moral development is yet more manifest when our word renders the Hebrew *shlm* stem, to indicate spiritual maturity: Solomon was urged to be *teleios* (1 Chr 28[9]) and he in turn exhorted the hearts of others to be *teleios* (3 Km 8[61]) when his own was not (11[4]), as Abijam's was not (15[3]). The heart of Asa was *teleios* (15[14]). True, the *teleioi* and the *manthanontes* are associated in the phrase, '*teachers* and scholars' (1 Chr 25[8] where there is no Hebrew). When there is Hebrew thinking behind it, *teleios* commonly indicates one who is in a right rapport with God and is obedient to God.

So, it is not so much in pagan associations as in LXX and Hebrew origins that we shall find the clue to the word's meaning in the NT.

Jesus spoke to His disciples and to the sorrowful young man, bidding them be 'perfect', in language which recalled the LXX meaning of *teleios*, that is, 'perfect in heart', 'obedient to God', 'committed to His service' (Mt 5[48] 19[21]). The writer to Hebrews urges Christians to go on to *teleiotēs* (perfection) and describes Jesus as *made perfect* through suffering (Heb 2[10] 6[1]). An OT sense of obedience is prominent.

The word *teleios* was part of the jargon of the Mysteries, as we have seen, and it indicated one who was effectually instructed and initiated, in contrast with novices,[99] but this is not quite the tune of St. Paul when he declares that all his preaching and exhortation and teaching had the resolve of presenting every man 'perfect' in Christ Jesus (Col 1[28]). St. Paul would not indicate by *teleios*, a mature or fully accepted member of the community, as the Mysteries meant it. His conception of *teleios* involves rather more than instruction, more than indoctrination in esoteric philosophy. In the context of *teleios* St. Paul mentions the enticing words which he shuns (Col 2⁴). Rather, for him, *teleios* involves a walk 'in Christ' and stedfastness of faith (2⁵ᶠ·).

Neither does St. John's use of the word recall the Mystery jargon. St. John's contribution is to see Christian love as a virtue which affords spiritual maturity and makes us 'perfect' (1 Jn 4¹², ¹⁸).

Probably the time has gone when scholars were easily persuaded that in very early days Hellenistic Christianity had been invested by such Gnostic motifs as the *teleios* man, and took for granted that when St. Paul spoke of the 'perfect man' coming to a knowledge of the Son of God (Eph 4¹³), he had hold of the Gnostic myth of the heavenly Man. Bultmann,¹⁰⁰ for one, assumed too eagerly that the borrowing was on the Christian side, when in reality the Gnostic myth of the heavenly Man was likely to have been reconstructed by scholars from the Hermetic writings which are somewhat later than the NT. Today it is more modish to suppose that neither Gnostic nor Christian borrowed from the other, but that both took something from a common background.¹⁰¹

In the Hermetic writings, accessible in the edition of W. Scott, a passage¹⁰² reports Hermes Trismegistos as explaining why God did not impart 'mind' to all men. 'Mind' is a prize for souls to win; it was sent down from heaven as a kind of laver. 'Those who dipped themselves in the bath of mind', he says, 'got a share of *gnosis* (the knowledge of God); they received mind, and so became complete *(teleioi)* men'. Initiates are contrasted with mindless men who admire what is not worth looking at and heed only bodily pleasure as if man was created for that. If one is to rise above it all and become *teleios* earthly and bodily things must be deplored. *Teleios* in the sense of a fully developed man who forsakes the things of earth to look at heaven, is near to the Christian use of the term. However, in Hermetic literature *teleios* sometimes carries the sense of an 'initiate' who has been consecrated by sacramental rites.¹⁰³ Indeed, the phrase of Hermes Trismegistos, 'dipped (or *baptized*) in mind', may itself indicate a sacramental initiation.¹⁰⁴ By contrast, St. Paul's use of the word is exclusively of holiness, moral excellence and proficiency in the Christian life. St. Paul is far from the Basilidians, for instance, who believed they were permitted to sin 'on account of *teleiotēs*'.¹⁰⁵ Different from St. Paul's is the language of the Mysteries, in which *teleios* is the superior man who is distinct from the rabble. It is therefore clear, as Kennedy concludes, that though we must not rule out the suggestion that the Mystery-atmosphere is to some extent present in St. Paul's words to the Colossians, as indeed Lightfoot allowed,¹⁰⁶ yet no conclusion may be drawn from it as to his personal attitude towards Mystery conceptions.¹⁰⁷

Teleios belongs to a circle of Mystery ideas, it is clear, but other aspects of the Christian *teleios* must not be ignored – that is, the meaning 'mature', showing no lack of spiritual progress, representing a stage of sacred knowledge well beyond a rudimentary attainment. *Pneumatikos* (spiritual, q.v.) is its equivalent in 1 Co 3[1ff.] and is there contrasted with 'babes'.

Kennedy moreover pointed to the persistent use of *teleios* in the later Stoics and in Philo for the culminating stage of a good life to which the philosopher is called to bestir himself.[108] Epictetus warns the *teleios* of the danger of making no progress and of remaining on ordinary levels. For Epictetus, as for Paul, *teleios* is the man who sets out on the right path and is still advancing.

Influenced probably by the use of the word in the Mysteries, early Christians used *teleios* of the baptized, as distinct from catechumens. Lightfoot instanced St. Justin Martyr and St. Clement.[109] Indeed, as he remarked, we may ascribe to its connection with the Mysteries the adoption of *teleios* by Gnostics of a later time to distinguish the possessors of *gnōsis* from the vulgar herd of believers. St. Paul employed this favourite Gnostic term to strike at the root of Gnostic ineptitude. He turned their word upside down. 'The language descriptive of the heathen mysteries is transferred by him to the Christian dispensation,' observed Lightfoot.[110] In this way St. Paul could the more effectively contrast the things signified. Every believer is *teleios*, for he knows the Gospel's most awful and profound secrets.

What it means is this. T. K. Abbott correctly defined the new Christian sense of *teleios* as 'maturity of faith and spiritual life'. The definition accommodates the LXX and Hebrew meaning – one who obeys the will of God and responds to Him, totally submitted, absolutely dependent, devoted to His service. It explains why Abraham's faith is specified by St. James as *teleios* – that is, wholeheartedly devoted to God, made sincere by deeds (Jas 2[22]). It explains St. Clement's description of Esther as 'perfect' in faith (1 Clem 55[6]).

In Christian parlance *teleios* goes with the word *peplērophorēmenos* which is a perfect passive participle of a verb meaning, 'to have full assurance' (q.v.), another special word of NT Greek (Col 4[12]). However, unlike full assurance, *teleiotēs* (perfection in the Christian life) is very much in the future in most of its references. 'Let us go on to it', urges the writer to Hebrews (6[1]).

As St. John said concerning the adjective *teleios*, namely that Christian love gives us spiritual maturity, makes us *teleioi*, so St. Paul says of *teleiotēs* that Christian love is its bond, its adhesive, to further the total Body, the Church, towards the 'perfection' of every single member, to final sanctification at Jesu's Coming, the blameless preservation till then of the integrated man, body, soul, and spirit (Col 3[14]; 1 Th 5[23]). The 'perfection' of the saints, which is yet to be achieved, is not promised before that day, but it is well assured. The *teleios* man, measuring up to the stature of Christ, no more a child distracted by worldly whim and fashion, shall be seen in every saint who overcomes, for he belongs to the developing Body (Eph 4[12ff.]). That which is *teleios* is ahead, it is to be (1 Co 13[10]). The fullness is to come. Let us go on to it. 'Let us become a temple, *perfect* unto God' (Barn 4[11]).

It is well known how John Wesley, to the end of his days, preached that **perfection** was attainable on earth. Perfection was for Wesley love of God and love of neighbour, a 'perfect' love received by faith and not an esoteric freedom from error or ignorance – freedom in the sense of reluctance to disclaim what we know of the will of God.

Sometimes indeed **perfection** is already attained before the Lord's Coming. 'We speak wisdom among the *teleioi*' (1 Co 2[6]). 'In understanding be *teleioi*' (14[20]) – not children. The Apostle refers to himself as *teleios*, having only just admitted, 'I count not myself to have apprehended ... I reach forth ... I press towards the mark' (Ph 3[13-15]). The writer to Hebrews speaks of 'them that are *teleioi*' (5[14]). St. James encourages his readers to be *teleioi* (1[4]) and the *teleios* man will have his tongue under control (3[2]). St. Ignatius declares, 'Ye are *perfect*' (I. Smyrn 11[3]).

We can be, and are, **perfect**! And yet that which is **perfect** is to come! We are *teleioi* here and now in an anticipatory sense, for the grace of God will surely not fail ultimately. However, not yet have we attained. For all that we possess the *aiōnios* life now, yet it is by definition *aiōnios* – it belongs to the future Dispensation. We are not yet in every sense saved, but we may be sure that sanctification is secure if we persevere to the end, when God shall crown all His faithful mercies.

St. Paul refers to the *teleion* will of God (Ro 12[2]). It is not so much that God's will is morally perfect (which goes without saying), but the adjective is active in sense, for the context concerns our not conforming to this world and our transformation by the mind's renewing – it means, the will of God is that we be sanctified, it means that His will concerns the believer's final glory. The *teleion* will of God is the 'perfecting' will of God.

Moral and spiritual perfection is included but is not necessarily the only element of *teleios*. In early Church writers the *teleioi* are the baptized, distinct from catechumens (Lightfoot). Later, the Lord's Supper is the *teleion*, and to 'come to the *teleion*' and to 'receive the *teleion*' is to partake of the Eucharist.[111] Some influence of Mystery jargon may be present and the Christian *teleios* may have been seen in some quarters as the recipient of esoteric knowledge, an innermost initiate of the Brotherhood.

Another element is the antitypal. The Reality is more 'perfect' than the type, at least as regards the two tabernacles (Heb 9[11]). The moral sense of the word which derives from the LXX, is not prominent in the passage, where the contrast lies between what is now, the earthly, and what is to come, the 'perfect' in a heavenly sense. Many may be faithful, but Christ is '*perfect* faithfulness' (I. Smyrn 10[2]). All *teleiotēs* (perfection) is heavenly and future, belonging to a new Dispensation. Love of any kind on earth is lovely, and yet it is at best a type. Christian love, on the other hand, has *teleiotēs* (perfection): it makes all the elect of God 'perfect' (1 Clem 49–50). St. Paul and St. John declared it (see above). *Teleiotēs* is 'unsurpassable' (1 Clem 53[5]). It is Wesley's love divine, all loves excelling – the antitypal, the perfect.

On one occasion in the NT *teleios* has the secular sense, 'without blemish' (Jas 1[17]) – 'every good and perfect gift' – but the phrase is not St. James' own, I suspect; it reads like a quotation from some Hellenistic source, a hexameter poetic line. Nevertheless, where St. James draws our attention to 'the *teleios* law of liberty' (1[25]), the context recalls Ro 12[2], the 'perfect' will of God which is our sanctification. The phrase refers to 'the law in the observation of which a man feels himself free'.[112] The 'perfect law' is the Christian way of life, leading to holiness at last. See, 'Law'.

2. κατάρτισις: καταρτισμός

In secular Greek *katartisis* had meant discipline and training,[113] and *katartismos* was both the 'setting' of a limb in medical writers and, elsewhere, the 'furnishing' or preparation of a chamber[114] and of an outer garment.[115]

In Christian Greek the words acquired a spiritual sense. When St. Paul desires the final *katartisis* of the Corinthian believers (2 Co 13[9]), 'it is the *growth* in holiness that is meant'.[116]

St. Paul looks ahead to the *katartismos* of the saints (Eph 4[12]), and in the passage the word concerns the increase of the Body, the Church, which reaches maturity at His Coming (1 Th 5[23]).

In both environments the words indicate the complete salvation of believers, their full sanctifying, their maturity, their change from glory into glory.

> *Finish then Thy new creation,*
> *Pure and spotless let us be;*
> *Let us see Thy great salvation*
> *Perfectly restored in Thee.* – C. WESLEY

PILGRIMAGE (EXILE IN THIS WORLD)

Onward we go, for still we hear them singing,
'Come, weary souls, for Jesus bids you come.'
And through the dark, its echoes sweetly ringing,
The music of the Gospel leads us home. – F. W. FABER

παροικία

The new word *paroikia* not only has profound Christian content but also contributed a word to subsequent secular language.

It is a coinage of Biblical Greek, found in the LXX first of all, once rendering the Hebrew word *gôlâ* (captivity, 2 Esd 8[35]), but usually rendering the *gûr* stem (sojourn).[117] It recurs in the free Greek books and means, a stay in exile or captivity.[118] *Paroikos* is a secular word for 'neighbouring', but later it replaces *metoikos* and means 'non-citizen', 'stranger', a resident alien having no civic rights. From this late sense the noun *paroikia* derives.

Philo has *paroikia* for the 'pilgrimage' of our real selves within the body.[119] It is any kind of living in a strange place. 'As fire in a threshing-floor ... so is the sojourning of the evil man among men' (Ps Sol 12[3]). The obscure expression, 'Precious in the sight of the *paroikia* was one life saved from among them' (Ps Sol 17[19]), may mean, 'Precious in the sight of the *Dispersion Jews* was one life saved from perils in Jerusalem.'

Of the two NT instances, one bears the LXX meaning, 'sojourners' in the land of Egypt (Act 13[17]), the other has a new Christian meaning, 'the time of your **exile in this world**' – which Christians must pass in fear (1 Pet 1[17]).

True it is that the brethren are exiles and strangers on earth, avoiding fleshly lusts (1 Pet 2[11]). They are born again, they live differently and, unlike the world's people they believe in one God, the Father of Jesus Christ, They appear foreign to their contemporaries but are not to isolate themselves for they must bring pagans to acknowledge God. To this end their witness to Him is apparent in their manner of life.[120] They have no continuing city. They seek one to come (Heb 13[14]).

They shall pass their time in fear. Obedience is a mark of their high calling. In 1 Pet 1[2] three prepositional phrases define respectively the source, the means and the goal of the brethren's election, which is according to *(kata)* God's foreknowledge, in *(en)* the sanctification of the Spirit, and leading to *(eis)* obedience.[121]

The watery deep we pass with Jesus in our view;
And through the howling wilderness
Our way pursue.

From the very beginning the life in Christ has appeared like a trek through a wilderness, and exhortations to have done with worldliness abound in the apostolic Fathers. 'Let us forsake our *paroikia* of this world' (2 Clem 5¹). The writer means, 'Let us be ready to die.' God's Church is said to 'sojourn' in Smyrna (the verb *paroikō*), and the author addresses himself 'to all the pilgrimages *(paroikiai)* of the holy Catholic Church in every place' (M. Pol. *intr.*). The churches everywhere are in exile. Eusebius speaks of the church 'sojourning' in Gortyna, together with other Cretan dioceses *(paroikiai)*.[122] The way is prepared for modern Greek where *paroikia* has become a colony, parish, or neighbourhood.

POLITICAL AGITATOR

1. βιαστής

Biastēs is a new word of uncertain meaning. It is formed from the verb *biazō* (to force). It is perhaps a coinage of Biblical Greek but it occurs as a scribal interpretation in Philo,[123] and with a medical sense of 'violent' in the second-century Aretaeus.[124]

It occurs at Mt 11¹² and in no other early Christian text.[125] Jesus remarks that 'from the days of John the Baptist until now the Kingdom of Heaven suffereth violence, and *biastai* take it by force'. The verse is obscure and perhaps is not concerned with *men* of violence but with demons. The struggle is that between God's Kingdom and Satan's. The divine kingdom will receive a violent onslaught of the Devil and his demons (the *biastai*) before it is finally victorious.[126] Schrenk proposes that *biastēs* is one who violently assaults the divine rule and robs those who come to it of its blessings.[127] However, the earlier submission of M'Neile had been that the meaning was probably political – the Kingdom had been 'violently snatched at' by agitators, as in AD 6. Even Jesus Himself was tempted to seek an earthly sovereignty.[128]

An analysis of the verbs *harpazō* and *biazō*, with cognates, in Josephus[129] suggests that they indicate a connection with illegal violence, used for forcing men's opinions against their better judgment. It is likely that our Lord's words (Mt 11¹²) are a strong condemnation of the political Pharisees who imagined that the Kingdom might be established by force of arms.

Political agitation is a form of worldliness from which believers must dissociate themselves.

331

2. ἀλλοτριεπίσκοπος

Allotriepiskopos is a further coinage of Christians, formed from existing words, and again the meaning can be determined only from the way it is used. No help comes from the LXX or profane Greek. The parallel cited by Deissmann, 'one who lusts after other people's things', is not by any means the same word in appearance *(allotriōn epithumētēs)*[130] nor does the context indicate that it is a synonym. The nearest secular parallel, which is *allotria episkopō,*[131] prompts the meaning of interference in the business of others (Selwyn, p. 225).

In the NT context, *allotriepiskopos* is some kind of civil offender (1 Pet 4[15]), a criminal in the same class as a 'murderer' and 'thief'. The Apostle warns believers against crimes for which they might well fall foul of the civil authorities: he instances murder, theft, 'crime', and then, like an apparent anticlimax, the offence of being an *allotriepiskopos.* The meaning, a 'busybody', is too mild for the context – an anticlimax – and Deissmann's alleged synonym ('covetous') is wholly irrelevant in the passage. Our word, however, is likely to refer to political agitation. A. Bischoff infers a revolutionary or traitor.[132] Beyer rejects the submission and notes that another suggestion is 'trustee' (i.e. one who fails as a trustee), another is 'defaulter'. Beyer himself suggests a 'calumniator' or 'informer' and notes that such men were liable to be punished at law, as St. Peter's context requires – not, however, till a later date, the days of Nerva and Trajan.[133] Trajan first made the offence of being a *delator* (informer) a criminal one.

A crime of a 'political agitator', however, was heinous in the eyes of the Church from her earliest days (Ro 13[1-7]; 1 Pet 2[13ff.]), and it would doubtless merit the attention of the civil power, just as St. Peter's homily indicates. Believers on the contrary were called to be aloof from politics, to have on earth no continuing city (Heb 13[14] etc.).

As the context changed, so the meaning of *allotriepiskopos* varied, and in the fifth century, the days of Epiphanius and the pseudo-Areopagite, other kinds of interference and usurpation are envisaged. Dionysius Areopagita refers to a bishop intruding into an alien sphere of office.[134]

A POSSESSION (AN INHERITANCE)

κατάσχεσις

In secular Greek *kataschesis* had meant a 'holding back' of the breath,[135] and 'holding back' is evidently the meaning in the Western text of Acts 20[16] (delay). In Biblical Greek, however, *kataschesis* acquired an additional and altogether distinct meaning, a **possession**. Once more, the OT accounts for the change.

The LXX has it for the Hebrew word *'aḥuzzâ* (possession), but very occasionally for *naḥ'lâ* (inheritance). Joseph gave his father and brethren a portion of land *(kataschesis = 'aḥuzzâ)* in Egypt (Gen 47[11]). God promised Jacob that He would give his seed the country of Canaan for an everlasting **possession** (Gen 48[4]). You can be said to sell some of your **possession** (Lev 25[25]). Often enough the Hebrew word, rendered by *kataschesis,* means 'landed property'.[136] In Gen 17[8], a text which St. Stephen has in mind (Act 7[45]), God promises all Canaan to Abram and his seed for a **possession** *(kataschesis = 'aḥuzzâ).* Field (p. 116) showed that the Hebrew word will not bear the meaning, the *act* of possessing or the *taking* of possession (which would be *yārash*), but a *having* in possession. It rather means 'a possession', 'an object possessed', and so we must understand the Vulgate *possessionem* and the AV *for a possession.*

It is the land of Canaan also in St. Stephen's speech (Act 7[45]) where Israel under Joshua is said to be brought into a **possession** of the Gentiles. AV makes it abstract possession,[137] mistakenly, I think. Better to have kept its rendering of Gen 17[8] 47[11], etc.

It was the material inheritance of the Davidic King, 'the uttermost parts of the earth for Thy possession' Ps 2[8] (cited in Act 13[33]D, 1 Clem 36[4]) where *'aḥuzzāth'khā* is synonymous with 'Thine inheritance' *(naḥ'lâ).*[138] I believe the meaning to be concrete too in T XII P (Benjamin) 10[4] where it is 'an everlasting possession', rather than, 'to possess everlastingly'. The thing possessed is also the meaning in Justin Martyr's reference to 'the other Joshua' (Jesus) Who will give us 'our possession for ever', i.e. eternal life *(Dial. CXIII 4).*[139] 'Act of possession' or 'taking of possession' would be most unnatural in St. Justin's argument, I believe.

POWERS

δυνάμεις

Singular. The singular *dunamis,* in the NT as in Greek generally, indicates ability, abundance, power, might, violence. In some secular writers the singular had also denoted a personalized spirit. It specifies Athena, the *dunamis* of Zeus.[140] It specifies Mēn Uranios, 'the great *dunamis* of the immortal God'.[141] In certain pagan movements there was a tendency to reach out in the direction of monotheism, and particularly in the text concerning Mēn we may see this tendency at work, representing the polytheistic gods as aspects or agencies of one supreme Being.[142] The title *dunamis* is not exclusively pagan. In Jewish rabbinical literature the Hebrew equivalent of *dunamis*, i.e. $g^e bh\hat{u}r\hat{a}$, is a quality of God, literally 'the Power' (*Sabb.* 87a, 88b. See Jastrow, p. 205). Moreover, to Caiaphas Jesus declares that he shall see the Son of Man sitting on the right hand of the 'Power' (*dunamis*): Mt 26[64]; Mk 14[62]. In the second-century Gnostic book, the gospel of Peter, 5[19], Jesus is reported as crying on the cross, 'My Power, Power, thou hast forsaken Me' (Hennecke I, p. 184). Perhaps the author was reading *'ēlî* (God) in the original of Ps 22[1], as Vaganay suggested.[143] The LXX so renders it once (Neh 5[5]). The similar-sounding Hebrew word, *ḥayil* or *ḥêl* (power), is rendered by *dunamis* in the LXX. In Biblical Greek *dunamis* is the power of the living personal God. In the Magical literature, which is a blend of Jewish and pagan ideas, *dunamis* is used of 'the great *Power* which is in heaven'.[144]

King Antiochus urged Eleazar to recant before he tortured him, 'Even if there be some *dunamis* (i.e. God) whose eye is upon this religion of yours, he will always pardon you for a transgression done under compulsion'. (4 Mac 5[13]). Simon in Samaria is 'the great *dunamis* of God' (Act 8[10]). The concept is Biblical enough.

Plural. In the plural, however, *dunameis* receives an additional meaning in Biblical Greek – angels, members of the hierarchy of heaven[145] to which belong Authorities, Dominions, Principalities and Thrones (q.v.). The plural already had the meaning, 'disembodied forces', for Philo stated that though God is one God He has around Him numberless *Powers* which arrest and protect created being and among them are the powers of chastisement.[146] Whatever Philo meant, St. Peter clearly intends the word to indicate habitants of heaven who were subject to Christ when He went to the right hand of God (1 Pet 3[22]), and St. Paul too classes the *dunameis* with angels in the phrase, 'Nor angels nor **powers** ... can separate us from the love of God' (Ro 8[38]). We are reminded of the parallelism of the psalm: 'Praise Him all ye angels: praise Him all ye **powers**' (147(148)[2]). In Biblical Greek *dunameis* are angels.

It is a question what the writer to Hebrews means by 'powers' when he says that initiated Christians 'have tasted ... the **powers** of the Dispensation to come' (6[5]). Does he mean the guardian angels, who were ministering spirits sent forth to tend the heirs of salvation? (Heb 1[14]). Is it their care that we have experienced when we 'tasted' the **powers** belonging to a different sphere?

'Angels' were intended by St. Athanasius when he spoke of 'heavenly *dunameis*',[147] but there is another meaning which is exclusive to Biblical and Jewish Greek, i.e. **stars.** The LXX rendered the Hebrew $s^e bh\hat{a}\hat{o}th$ by *dunameis* (Isai 34[4] sun, moon, stars – the 'host of heaven'), and *dunameis* seems to mean **stars** in predictions concerning our Master's Coming (Mt 24[29]; Mk 13[25]; Lk 21[26]). 'The **powers** of heaven shall be shaken.'

A further sense for both singular and plural appears in Christian Greek – a **miracle** (e.g. Mt 7[22]; Mk 6[2,5] 9[39]; Lk 10[13]; Act 2[22] 8[13]; 2 Co 12[12]), or **workers of miracles** (1 Co 12[29]) – for miracles are a manifestation of the potency of the living personal God.

See also 'Angels', 'Principalities', 'Authorities', 'Dominions', and 'Thrones'.

PRAISE

1. μεγαλωσύνη: μεγαλύνω

Not before the Bible was put into Greek did these words commonly mean 'praise'.

Secular Greek. *Megalōsunē* and *megalunō* convey the idea of greatness, majesty, and princely liberality. Outside the Bible the noun, *megalōsunē*, appears but rarely. One is not surprised at this, seeing that abstract nouns in *-sunē*, corresponding to Sanskrit *-tvaná*, which were once common in the Epic literary dialect, 'failed to catch on in normal Attic'. Professor Pearson declared that comparatively few survive in Attic, and a few (like *megalōsunē* and *agathōsunē*) are resuscitations in the Koine of an earlier type which was submerged in the Attic dialect.[148] In Jewish books, the Letter of Aristeas and the Testaments of the XII Patriarchs, *megalōsunē* is the 'greatness' of God's strength, and in the Greek Enoch it is luxurious grandeur.[149]

The verb *megalunō*, on the other hand, occurs in classical literature. Even so, the meaning on the whole is not that of Biblical Greek. The verb is used for 'making great' or 'greater', of making one's enemies greater, of exaggerating one's influence upon a man like Tissaphernes, or blowing up an affair out of all proportion.[150] What does Xenophon mean when he says that Socrates by 'making himself great' *(megalunō)* in the court brought envy upon himself? It is not likely that he means that Socrates 'praised' himself, for directly afterwards Xenophon uses *epainō* for praise (36). I think he means that Socrates showed himself to be 'great'.[151] Moreover, when Plutarch says that Cimon 'magnified' Lacedaemon to the Athenians, using *megalunō*, the meaning is that Cimon for his own purposes 'exaggerated' the renown of Sparta; that he painted Sparta as 'great' and Athens as small.[152] Again, the history of Diodorus Siculus explains that the god Osiris passed from the company of men into that of the gods, and that Isis and Hermes instituted mystic rites 'magnifying' *(megaluno)* the power of the god. The word is not 'praising', but 'exaggerating'.[153] Sometimes in poetry *megaluno* means 'praise'. 'Thou art glad', says Teiresias, 'when all Thebes doth *praise* the name of Pentheus'.[154]

Biblical Greek. Their incidence in the LXX has changed the direction of these words. The Hebrew stem which the Greek verb rendered was *gādhal* (Piel and Hiphil), signifying greatness but also, in certain contexts, praise. 'O *praise* the Lord with me!' and, 'I will *praise* Him with thanksgiving' (Ps 34[3] 69[30]). So when *megaluno* is introduced in the NT it usually signifies **praise,** the exceptions being Mt 23[5]; Lk 1[58]; 2 Co 10[15], and St. Mary sings, 'My soul doth *praise* the Lord' (Lk 1[46]). The people **praised** the apostles. The Jews heard the Gentiles speak with tongues and **praise** God (Act 5[13]; 10[46]). At Ephesus fear fell upon them all and the name of the Lord Jesus was **praised** (19[17]). St. Paul's hope is that Christ shall be **praised** in his body by life or death (Ph 1[20]). St. Clement affirms that all God's gifts are **praised** (1 Clem 32[3]).

In Biblical Greek the noun *megalōsunē,* too, means **praise,** but not so often as the verb. It is the majesty of Darius in the LXX (1 Esd 4[46]) and the Majesty on high in the NT, a circumlocution for God (Heb 1[3] 8[1]). However, it does form part of a doxology in which *doxa* and *megalōsunē* (praise) are assigned to Him, and in the Christian additions to the Testament of Abraham (118[26]C) it comes in another doxology where honour and *megalōsunē* are ascribed.[155] Doubtless, praise is the meaning in the LXX of Deut 32[3]: 'Ascribe *megalōsunē* unto our God'.

2. αἰνέω, αἴνεσις

A similar change is encountered with *aino* and *ainesis.*

The form of the verb in classical prose was *epaino,* but the simplex *aino* is sometimes found, where it has the colourless meaning of telling or speaking – at the most, celebrating, and not in a religious sense. In the Agamemnon Clytemnestra is bidden to 'tell' what she can (98), and is accused of 'celebrating' by her words the Fury's wrath (1482). 'Son of Tydeus', cried Odysseus, 'neither approve of *(ainee)* me nor blame me' (*Iliad* X 249). According to Herodotus, Evalcides had won crowns and been much 'commemorated' (aor. part.) by Simonides of Ceos (V 102).

The object of the verb is changed to dative in Biblical Greek through the parallel use of the Hebrew *l*[e].[156] When *aino* means 'to promise' it has the dative in classical Greek, e.g. 'the goddesses *promised to* me'.[157] Philoctetes says, 'What you *promised to* me'. ...[158]

The Biblical meaning of *ainō* (adoration of God), on the other hand, with this use of the dative, is adopted in the NT at Rev 19[5] ('Praise ye *to* our God') and Field pointed out that a secular writer would not have used the verb *ainō*, but rather, 'Give praise *(ainon)* – two words (p. 245).

The noun *ainesis*, apparently a coinage of Biblical Greek based on the verb, is specially frequent in the psalms (LXX), usually rendering *t^ehillâ* (adoration, renown, a public act of praise). Discussing the Leviticus laws, Philo says that under the head of the preservation-offering is embraced what is called the offering of *praise*.[159] *Ainesis* passed into the NT, apostolic Fathers and Apologists.

Both the noun and the verb with the religious meaning, **praise to God,** are almost exclusively Biblical,[160] and in the Bible and early Christian literature that is their sole meaning.[161]

3. ὁμολογέω : ἐξομολογέομαι : ἀνθομολογέομαι

Secular Greek. All three verbs, *homologō, exhomologoumai* and *anthomologoumai,* signify confession, profession and promise – not 'praise'.

Homologō is to agree or concede. Thucydides used it of words 'agreeing', with deeds (V 55). The term belongs to apprenticeship agreements.[162] It never has the new Biblical meaning of 'praise', despite Bauer's resort to Dio Chrysostom. The student who reads the Trojan Discourse for himself where Dio wishes 'to offer a defence of Homer by *conceding* that there is nothing unworthy in his fictions', will find no thought of 'praise' in the context.[163]

Exhomologoumai was to allow or concede, in respect of acknowledging a son, a liability, or something else,[164] – sin, in Biblical Greek. Outside the Bible it means 'admit' (especially faults), 'acknowledge', 'grant', but never 'extol'.[165]

Anthomologoumai (middle voice) is to make a mutual agreement[166] or to confess sins openly as did Rehoboam, shut up in Jerusalem.[167] The verb is to 'thank' in Plutarch when used in conjunction with *charin,* gratitude (i.e. to profess gratitude). Thus, 'it was the custom of those who obtained the consulship to profess thanks *(anthomologoumai charin).*[168]

Biblical Greek. All three verbs gain additional meaning in the Biblical language. Outside the Bible praise does not concern any of them, but in the Hiphil and Hithpael the Hebrew equivalent *(yādhâ)* has both meanings – to 'confess' sins and to 'praise' God. LXX influence is apparent. There the verbs based on the *homolog*-stem render *hll* (praise): 1 Chr 23[30]; 2 Chr 5[13] 23[12]; 1 Esd 4[60] 5[61]A.

In the NT accordingly *homologō* is found with the meaning **praise** (Heb 13[15]).

Although 'confess' is the rendering of AV of Ph 2[11] the sense of *exhomologoumai* would be improved if the phrase were rendered, 'every tongue shall **praise** because Jesus Christ is Lord'. Bauer sees a difference between the meaning of the verb when followed by *hoti* with a noun-clause (acknowledge, confess) and the meaning when the verb is followed by the dative (praise), e.g. Ro 14[11] (every tongue shall **praise** God).[169] Dr. Martin relies on Bauer at Ph 2[11] and accepts the interpretation, 'own' or 'recognize'.[170] But there is no reason why *hoti* may not be causal and, as Lightfoot long ago observed, the meaning of *exhomologoumai* here is praise or thanksgiving, for this secondary sense has in the LXX almost entirely supplanted the primary sense, especially in the very passage of Isaiah which St. Paul adapts.[171]

So too, if we are right, Jesus may be saying, as in Moffatt, Knox and RV mg, 'I **praise** Thee, O Father' (Mt 11[25]; Lk 10[21]).[172] So too the LXX quotations at Ro 14[11] 15[9] will be, 'I will **praise** Thee among the Gentiles and sing unto Thy name' (as RV, RSV, Moffatt, Jerusalem, NEB). When Philo uses the verb he too has the new meaning, 'thankfully **gives praise** to God', joining it with *eucharistikōs* (thankfully).[173]

The apostolic Fathers, however, retain the primary meaning, confession of sin,[174] although St. Clement adheres to the new: 'We **praise** Thee through the High Priest and Guardian of our souls' (1 Clem 61[3]). Michel points out that in Hennecke's edition of the NT apocrypha the translation, 'to confess sins', at 1 Clem 52[1] can hardly be right.[175] Hennecke and Lightfoot must be mistaken, for St. Clement is about to cite David's cry of praise – 'I will *praise* the name of God with a song!' (Ps 69[30]). Moreover, St. Clement again uses *exhomologoumai* in the new sense of Biblical Greek in the citations at 26[2] and 48[2]. The epistle of Barnabas too has it for **praise** in his citation at 6[16] – it is a parallel with *psallō*.

The same additional meaning now attaches to *anthomologoumai*. This verb renders the Hebrew *yādhâ* at Ps 78(79)[13]: 'we will give Thee **praise** for ever'. The Hebrew specifies the giving of thanks in ritual worship, but it is rendered by *exhomologoumai* in Gen 29[35]; 2 Km 22[50]; 3 Km 8[33,35] and on countless occasions. By the verb *anthomologoumai*, with its Hebrew heritage of thankful praise to God, St. Luke indicates Anna's joyful **thanksgiving** on seeing the infant Messiah (Lk 2[38]). It is more exact to say that Anna offered **praise,** as indeed Moffatt's translation and the Jerusalem Bible make clear.

There cannot be a better example of the incomparability of Biblical Greek than is afforded by the change of direction in the three words.

4. ἀρετή

Aretē is an accommodating term in secular Greek – any kind of excellence of the gods, of women, of glorious deeds. In pre-Christian papyri it indicates bodily prowess[176] and the richness of Crown land.[177]

Especially for the Stoics it specifies moral excellence, and so incidentally in the Bible where the singular renders *hôdh* (splendour, vigour: Hab 3³; Zach 6¹³). 'We suffer for our upbringing and our *virtue*,' say the Maccabaean martyrs (4 Mac 10¹⁰). Perhaps they meant, 'for our *praise*'.[178] In the plural the new meaning of **praise** appears in the NT, evidently through LXX influence, for the NT uses the plural *aretai* to render the Hebrew *tᵉhillâ* (praise, praiseworthy deeds). 'My glory will I not give to another, neither my **praise** to graven images' (Isa 42⁸). 'Let them give glory unto the Lord and declare His **praise** in the islands' (42¹²). 'They shall show forth My praise' (43²¹). 'I will mention the **praises** of the Lord' (63⁷). Without Hebrew equivalent it still means 'praise': Est 4¹⁷ (**praises** of vain idols), supported by Vulgate *laudent* – although in Wis 4¹ it retains the secular sense.

The indication of **praise** seems clearly to mark a new departure, but Deissmann alleged that *aretai* already signified 'manifestations of divine power', 'miracles'.[179] A papyrus of the fourth Christian century reads: 'that I may obtain the art of clairvoyance by the manifestations of divine power (plural of *aretē*)'.[180] Moreover, Deissmann (BS p. 96) reasoned that Josephus understood *aretē* in the sense of 'God's manifestation of His power'[181] when he described Antipas as impudently abusing the *aretē* of the Deity, ascribing it to God's power that he had been preserved hitherto. If Deissmann was right, Josephus used the word in two different senses, for but a few sentences earlier he had spoken of 'judging by *aretē*', where the word must indicate a moral standard – a normal secular meaning.[182] However that may be, and Deissmann's interpretation of Josephus is questionable, it would seem more probable that the new sense in Biblical Greek is to be explained by LXX influence and that it is likely to be **praise**, rather than manifestations of divine power.

To me it is clear that the earliest Christian language follows the LXX and that St. Peter writes, 'You showed forth the *praises* of Him who hath called you' (1 Pet 2⁹). In 2 Pet 1³ the co-ordination of *aretē* with *doxa* (glory) brings to mind Isai 42⁸, ¹² and suggests that the proper translation is, 'Him that hath called us to glory and *praise*'.[183] The sense in the other instance of *aretē* in this epistle is obscure: 'add to your faith *aretē*, and to *aretē* add knowledge' (1[5]). *Aretē* is one in a list of virtues, rather than virtue in general. It may be a relic of the secular usage, as in 2 Mac 6[31] 15[12]; Wis 4[1] (the 'virtue' which brings immortality).

The regular Stoic understanding of *aretē* may appear once in the NT (Ph 4[8], virtue). The truth is that, compared with the gifts of the Holy Ghost pagan 'virtue' is little worth and early Christians seldom speak of it. In Ph 4[8] *aretē* is placed alongside *epainos* (praise) and follow *euphēma* (praiseworthy) – 'whatsoever things are praiseworthy, if there be any *aretē*, if there be any praise'. In that environment the word surely takes on a new meaning, the meaning which it has in the canonical books of the OT.[184] The sense of *aretē* just here is that of *hôdh* and *t*ᵉ*hillâ*. We had best render St. Paul's words: 'If there be any *thanksgiving*, if there be any praise, think on these things'. I am discouraged to find no modern translator following Hatch's line.

Though *aretē* among the first Christians may have ceased to signify virtue, the meaning does return in Christian apologists, for St. Justin has *aretē* when he compares Christian morals with the absence of virtue in the immoral gods (*Apol.* VI 1), and the apostolic Father urges, 'Let us follow after *aretē* and give up vice' (2 Clem 10[1]).

PRAY (BESEECH)

ἐρωτάω

In several languages 'ask' has a two-fold meaning and may seek an answer to a request as well as a reply to a question. In the classical period of Greek, however, to ask a question is the only regular meaning of *erōtō*, the seeking of information. Thucydides has the word for '*putting the question,* "Are they pirates?" (I 5)'. In Thucydides the verb's participle is used substantivally as a 'question' (III 61). Sentries might 'challenge' and 'ask' the password.[185] Not until much later was the meaning, 'beseech' or 'intreat', introduced – as if the word were the same as *aitō*.

The LXX is the first witness to the expanded meaning, although the new sense of request soon passed into the secular language. It came into Biblical Greek because the Hebrew verb *shā'al* had the two meanings – to ask a question and to ask a request. 'O *pray* for the peace of Jerusalem' (Ps 121 (122)[6]). 'They *required of* us there a song' (Ps 136(137)[3]). '*Ask for* the old paths' (Jer 6[16]). Greeven observes[186] that the transition from 'ask a question' to 'beseech' is specially easy in the cultic sphere, because a question put to a god at an oracle is invariably accompanied by a sacrifice which will doubtless carry a gracious answer, not only supplying information but also granting the seeker his desired object. A question at the oracle invariably goes with prayer and worship, and an enquiry for information is a request besides for help.

Conceivably the extra meaning is due to Latin interaction, since *rogare* is both 'enquire' and 'request'. Indeed, also in French *demander* is both 'enquire' and 'request', as *domandare* is in Italian, as *aske* in Middle English and *ask* in modern English. But the additional meaning came into Jewish Greek no doubt by the same Hebrew influence as is found in the LXX. *Erōtō* appears in the phrase, 'They *asked for* terms of peace' (T. Jud. 9[7]). In the Greek Enoch *erōtō* must mean 'beseech' (13[4]), and Josephus mentions Joshua as 'interceding' with God.[187]

The new meaning is seen in popular Greek early enough. Almost contemporary with the birth of Jesus a man in Alexandria wrote to his wife, using *erōtō*. 'I *beg* you ... to take care of the little one,' he said.[188] The suggestion of Cremer and Thayer[189] that the Biblical meaning of *erōtō* is a Hebraism was resisted by Milligan[190] and truly there is ample precedent for it in non-literary secular Greek of the first century,[191] by whatever means it came to be there.

The first Christians seized on a meaning which abounds in the LXX but was found elsewhere, and they used it particularly of Christian prayer – after the pattern of Jesus when He said, 'I will *pray* the Father' (Jn 14[16] 17[15]). Trench, however, rejected the suggestion that the word was used for Christian prayer (pp. 136f.). Urging that *aitō*, rather than *erōtō*, was the Latin *peto*, the request or petition from an inferior, he nevertheless excepted 1 Jn 5[16] where *erōtō* is undoubtedly used for Christian prayer. Of the sin unto death, St. John writes, 'I do not say, he shall *pray* for it.' Moreover, there is no doubt that *erōtō* is used of inferiors who address Jesus in His earthly life. The Syro-phoenician woman *besought* Him, the Pharisee *besought* Him, the disciples *besought* Him, the nobleman *besought* Him (Mk 7[26]; Lk 7[36]; Mt 15[23]; Jn 4[47]). The Pharisees and Sadducees *besought* Him (*eperōtō* this time) for a sign from heaven (Mt 16[1]). There is nothing to be built upon any supposed distinction from *aitō*. Field urged that the distinction was 'perfectly groundless' (p. 102).

In the Fathers too it is Christian prayer. Hermas says, 'I *prayed* much to the Lord' (*Vis.* II 2.1).

1. δέησις

In secular Greek *deēsis* meant 'need' and indeed 'supplication'.[192] Aristotle has the expression, 'according to their *needs*'.[193] There is 'making supplications' in Isocrates (VIII 138), but these are rather overtures for peace than prayers. Nor is *deēsis* really 'entreaty' in Demosthenes (XXIX 4): 'I make a reasonable *request* of you, men of the jury – give us a fair hearing.' In Josephus *deēsis* is a written 'petition' to Titus.[194]

It is a 'petition' from a prisoner in a pre-Christian papyrus.[195] One may doubt whether entreaties to Aphrodite in Lucian are strictly prayers.[196] In a fourth-century petition to the Emperor *deēsis* is equated with *hikesia* (a supplication).[197] Plutarch falls within the epoch of Biblical influence and uses *deēsis* of prayers in sacred shrines.[198]

However, in Christian Greek *deēsis* occurs only with a special meaning of **prayer to God**. It may be true also of the LXX (except 1 Mac 11[49]) which is quoted by St. Peter: 'The eyes of the Lord are over the righteous and His ears are open unto their **prayer**' (1 Pet 3[12]).

Of the evangelists, *deēsis* appears only in Luke, the others preferring *proseuchē*, the pagan word. In the apostolic Fathers again *deēsis* is **prayer to God.** The young man in the Vision of Hermas enquired, 'Why do you ask constantly for revelations in your **prayer**?'[199]

Both *deēsis* and *proseuchē* were widely used among early Christians for private and public intercession and there is no apparent difference between the words except that *deēsis* is peculiarly Christian.

2. ἐπερώτημα

Eperōtēma was an enquiry or question. Anger is shown at an ironical 'question'.[200] *Eperōtēma* was besides a sanction given by a higher authority in response to a petition.[201] Another special meaning resembles the Latin *stipulatio* (covenant, agreement).[202] Although none of the secular meanings suit the Biblical contexts where the word occurs, Dr. Bo Reicke's arguments to the contrary (see below) must be studied.

The secular use of *eperōtēma*, resembling the Latin *stipulatio*, involves the asking of a formal question in a legal sense in order to make a contract in law (MM). The *stipulatio* would be a question of this kind: 'Do you consent?' But it is difficult to see that such a meaning helps us to understand 1 Pet 3[21]. On the contrary, the candidate for Baptism is not asked to put any questions. He has to answer them. In the second-century Western text of Act 8[37] there probably survives an instance of a very early version of a baptismal liturgy, which poses a question to the candidate.

Response: 'Here is water. I would be baptized.'
Versicle: 'Dost thou believe with all thy heart?'
Response: 'I believe that Jesus Christ is the Son of God.'

In any case, there is no analogy between Holy Baptism and legal proceedings.

Alford still thought that 'enquiry' was more suitable in 1 Pet 3[21]: 'the like figure whereunto even baptism doth also now save us (not the putting away of the filth of the flesh, but the enquiry *(eperōtēma)* of a good conscience after God) by the resurrection of Jesus Christ'.

Other proposals for understanding the difficult word have been 'answer' (AV) which makes better sense in the context, since Baptism is an answer rather than a question. Knox seems to me to be quite near to the AV with, 'the test which assures us of a good conscience before God'. Holy Baptism is our 'response' to the test. Some have felt that *eperōtēma* implies 'asking', and they are supported by the Vulgate's *interrogatio:* hence 'interrogation' (RV), and 'petition' for a good conscience towards God (Grimm, and Knox's footnote). NEB has 'appeal to God made by a good conscience', and RSV is closer to Grimm: 'an appeal to God for a good conscience'. The verb *erōtō,* to which our noun is cognate, has in Biblical Greek the meaning of praying (see, 'Pray (Beseech).'). Request or appeal seems to be Bauer's preference. He does, however, notice the support of Richards and Selwyn for the rendering, 'pledge',[203] which was supported as early as De Wette and Bishop C. Wordsworth with, 'pledge to maintain a good conscience', and now by the Jerusalem Bible's, 'the pledge made to God from a good conscience', followed by BFBS ('promise made to God').

In the LXX the word was an 'enquiry' at a shrine, giving support to the suggestion of Alford and the rest. Greeven[204] thinks that the LXX furnishes the meaning of *eperōtēma* in our Christian context, i.e. an oracular question addressed to God. Ben Sirach speaks of an enquiry *(eperōtēma)* by means of Urim (Ecclus 36(33)[3]S), and Hermas later was to use the word for a 'request' made to a false prophet (*Mand.* XI 2). Such a meaning is supported by the Bible's use of *eperōtēma* to render the Aramaic *sheʾēltâ* (Dan Th 4[14]). It may be that this, like the verb *erōtō,* is a Christian word for **prayer,** based on the LXX. In the context of 1 Pet 3²¹ Greeven would render, 'the *prayer* to God *for* a good conscience', a point which Moffatt had already seen when he rendered, 'the prayer for a clean conscience before God'.

Dr. Bo Reicke objects to the meaning 'prayer' as quite unthinkable linguistically, and prefers the meaning 'question' as in classical Greek.²⁰⁵ *Eperōtō* is a professional term, he notes, for asking the gods for advice, and so perhaps the noun has been transferred in meaning from 'question' to 'answer', 'resolution', 'declaration'²⁰⁶ – an oracular response. Probably 'declaration' is the meaning in Dan 4¹⁷⁽¹⁴⁾Th ('and a word from the holy ones is the [oracular] declaration') and Ecclus 36 (33)³S ('as reliable as a reply from Urim and Thummim'). He notes that the Swedish Translation of the Apocrypha, 1921, has taken Ecclus 36(33)³ in this way. He thinks that an official use of *eperōtēma* such as this, accords to a certain extent with the meaning *stipulatio* (agreement, contract), for a contract was made by oral questioning. The questions may have given their name *(eperōtēma)* to the whole proceeding. Bo Reicke would therefore translate, 'an *undertaking* to a loyal attitude of mind' (the genitive of *suneidēsis* is then an objective genitive, a genitive of the content). The questioning party in the agreement is God or the Church, the One administering Baptism. The answering party is the candidate, and perhaps a special act in the ritual is in mind, perhaps a 'statement' of belief. He gives interesting examples of features in early Baptism services which illustrate his case.

So although *eperōtēma* literally signifies a 'question', that meaning is not very natural in the context of Baptism, and in normal Greek *eperōtēma* does not mean a 'prayer'. But it does make sense to regard it as positive moral undertaking, Bo Reicke observed. Baptism saves, but not unconditionally, St. Peter would say.²⁰⁷

Bigg had already²⁰⁸ rejected the translation, 'prayer to God from [or "for"] a good conscience', and had connected God with 'save'. He had made, 'Baptism saves us in God', parallel to, 'in the Ark'. He had taken *eperōtēma* as an allusion to the baptismal 'question' or 'demand' for repentance and faith. Bigg was supported by Mr. Linton Smith²⁰⁹ who pointed to Ro 10¹⁰, where he alleged that St. Paul uses *homologō* of the candidate's 'answer'. He suggested that 'St. Peter and St. Paul supply in combination the two sides of an essential part of Baptism' – the *eperōtēma* and the *homologia*. He cited the phrase from slightly later papyri, *eperōtētheis homologō* ('being interrogated, I affirm').

The question of *eperōtēma*'s special meaning in the Christian context cannot be said to be closed.

βοάω

King James' version, consistently rendering *boō* as, 'to cry',
follows a leading sense in secular Greek. 'Every city *tells* of it', and,
'a sound *rings* in the ears'. Aeschylus so uses the word,[210] and
Euripides makes Medea 'shriek' her woes upon the traitor.[211] It is
the shouting of battle, for Cyrus was 'calling aloud' to Clearchus to
lead the army against the centre, and Croesus 'called out' for Cyrus
at the capture of Sardis.[212] Polycritus 'called out' to Themistocles
with bitter taunt,[213] and Messene 'called aloud' for his son.[214]

Biblical Greek has taken the word and changed it. The
corresponding verb in Hebrew is *ṣā'aq* (ask for supernatural help)
when, as so often in the narrative of Judges, the Israelites came to
the end of their own resources. *Sā'aq* is more than a physical cry, it
is an anguished petition of repentance. 'The children of Israel *cried*
unto the Lord because of the Midianites' (Jg 6[7]), and again because
of the Philistines and Ammonites (Jg 10[10]).

The LXX uses *boō* when it mentions Israel's failure to 'call' on
God with their heart (Hos 7[14], etc.). When the blood of Abel
'pleads' to God for righteous vengeance (Gen 4[10]) and when Moses
'cries' to God for help in his need (Ex 8[12(8)] 15[25] 17[4]; Num 12[13], etc.)
the Hebrew is *ṣā'aq* and the Greek *boō*. When the poor brother
'pleads' to God for social justice (Deut 15[9]), and when Samson
utters his last prayer (Jg 16[28]) the verb is *qārâ*, but the Greek is
boō.

In the NT therefore we are not surprised that *boō* is the appeal of
God's persecuted ones: 'Shall not God avenge His own elect which
pray in anguish day and night unto Him?' (Lk 18[7]).

It is public prayer in the apostolic Fathers (1 Clem 34[7]) – a sense
which brings us far from secular Greek.

PREDESTINATION
προορίζω

The verb, *proörizō*, first appears in Christian Greek. Not found
in the LXX, it is used later in the Testament of Solomon – not of
God's foreordaining but that of the Angel who decreed that the
three-headed Beast should suffer (12[3]).

The verb is seen as a variant reading in Demosthenes,[215] but that
does not significantly tell against the Christian coinage of the word,
or at least of its special usage. It may be St. Paul's own creation.

He uses it when discussing the deep counsels of God: 'whom He did foreknow, He also did predestinate to be conformed to the image of His Son that He might be the First-born of many brethren' (Ro 8²⁹). The predestination is to glory, to the restoration of the 'image' that was lost at the Fall. As Sanday and Headlam remind us, the Christian is to reflect one day the image of his Lord, passing through a gradual assimilation of mind and character to an assimilation of His *doxa* (glory), a coalescence with the splendour of His presence.[216]

St. Paul has the verb to explain that the Mystery which revealed the hidden Wisdom of God **had been predestinated** by Him before the dispensations, unknown to the princes of this world (1 Co 2⁷). Further, St. Paul declared that God **predestinated** believers to be His adopted children 'by the good pleasure of His will', to have an inheritance with Christ (Eph 1⁵,¹¹).

St. Paul was treating only very indirectly the question of individual salvation, much less the lot of unbelievers and the relation of predestination to free will. What he was, on the other hand, concerned with is the whole scheme of salvation and God's determination from the beginning to unite everything in Christ.[217] He boldly puts together apparently irreconcilable things – divine election, human responsibility and universal salvation – in one big paradox which to us is illogical, and he does confess that it is all past our finding out (Ro 11³³ᶠᶠ·), all beyond the limits of thought.[218]

Evidently, apart from the NT, *proörizō* in the early Church is confined to St. Ignatius, who writes to a church which is 'predestinated' for glory from eternity (I. Eph. *intr.*).

See 'Elect', 'Election'.

PRIDE

φυσίωσις

Phusiōsis, an old word with a new Christian meaning, is a physical 'oedema' in secular Greek, though it but rarely occurs – perhaps once only, and that in the physician Galen.[219] Christian Greek has the word in the plural (AV: 'swellings', Vulg: *'inflationes'*), and changes its meaning to a metaphorical swelling – a sin of which believers may be guilty, rated along with a proneness to controversy, jealousy, anger, backbiting and quarrelling:[220] the sin especially of heretics.[221]

In the singular it is used by Eusebius of the Novatians, 'who in their *pride* of mind styled themselves Puritans'.[222]

It is an arrogant self-righteousness – not quite the same as 'conceit' (RSV) or 'self-conceit' (Knox), or 'arrogance' (Moffatt, NEB), much less 'obstinacies' (Jerusalem Bible), but very near (2 Co 12^{20}).

PRIESTHOOD (OF ALL BELIEVERS)

ἱεράτευμα

Hierateuma is a new word in Biblical Greek (Bauer), with no vernacular examples (MM). It was coined from the corresponding verb. This word is rare, according to Schrenk, appearing only in Biblical and closely related writings.[223]

In the LXX there is the phrase (Ex 19^6 23^{22}), *basileion hierateuma* (a royal priesthood), and *hierateuma* refers also to the priesthood which God had restored (2 Mac 2^{17}). In the NT Christian believers are said to be 'an holy *priesthood*' and a 'royal *priesthood*' to offer the sacrifice of praise (1 Pet 2^{5,9}). Selwyn liked to think that believers were described as a priesthood because the Church is to the world what the Jewish priesthood was to the whole nation (p. 160).

The extent to which Christians have understood and applied the doctrine of 'the priesthood of all believers' is seen in the history of the Reformation, of Puritanism and of the Evangelical Revival.[224]

PRINCE (OF THIS WORLD)

ἄρχων

*The ancient Prince of Hell
Has risen with purpose fell.
On earth is not his fellow.*—LUTHER

Archōn had been a ruler in secular Greek – a 'ruler' of Sparta,[225] one of the Atridae,[226] a chief magistrate,[227] a consul or prefect,[228] even the 'captain' of a ship[229] – but its special reference in Biblical Greek is to a 'prince' of this *kosmos* (world) and of this *aiōn* (dispensation), one of the crucifiers of Christ who are destined to come to naught and to be judged (Jn 12^{31} 14^{30} 16^{11}; 1 Co 2^{6,8}). Are the *archontes* human or more than human? Are they men inspired by demons? Are they the rulers of our world, considered as closely linked with the spirit-powers, the demons, who are subject to God, yet hostile in disposition, as Cullmann suggests?[230]

A familiar view is to see them as demonic beings who rule the world, an interpretation which is at least as early as Tertullian and Origen. Dr. A. Wesley Carr, on the other hand conceives the *archōn* as a human ruler and can find no Gnostic hints behind the vague references in 1 Co 2[6ff]; concluding that the significance of these verses for identifying the Corinthian error is negligible.[231]

Archōn, however, is Beelzebub, the **prince** of devils, by whose power Jesus was supposed to cast out devils (Mt 9[34] 12[24]; Mk 3[22]; Lk 11[15]), and is the **prince** of the power of the air who is now at work in the unregenerate mass (Eph 2[2]). Apostolic Fathers sometimes use *archōn* for the **Prince** of the world,[232] and they link it closely with angels. They explain how God sent His Son, rather than angels or an *archōn* (Diog 7[2]) and couple the *archontes*, visible and invisible, with heavenly beings (I. Smyrn 6[1]). St. Justin speaks of **princes** in heaven, appointed by God, gate-keepers for the King of Glory at the Ascension (*Dial.* XXXVI 5). The '*archōn* of deceit', moreover, is a spiritual power who darkens minds (T. Sim 2[7], T. Jud 19[4]).

The Acts of Paul at the end of the second century mentions the unrighteous Prince who seeks to be God, enslaving all men as the End draws nigh to judgment (3 Co 3[11]). We are reminded of the Wicked One in St. Paul's expectation, deceitfully working before the day of Christ in them that perish (2 Th 2). In the Acts of John the *archōn* is joined with angels and evil forces (114), becoming one of the seven creative angels of Gnosticism. In the Epistle of Barnabas he is Satan (4[13]). By patient endurance the martyr Polycarp overcame the unrighteous *Archōn* and gained the crown of immortality (M. Pol 19[2]).

See 'World Ruler'.

PRINCIPALITIES

ἀρχαί

The secular meaning of *archai* (plural) was magistrates,[233] as in Lk 12[11], but in Biblical Greek it has become a technical term, often found in company with *exousiai* (Authorities), *dunameis* (Powers), *kuriotētes* (Dominions) and *thronoi* (Thrones), q.q.v., to signify one of the hierarchy of angels, evil or good, rendered 'Principalities' by AV.

Like the Powers, the Principalities are angelic forces whom the overcoming saint must confront (Eph 6[12]), but God made them (Col 1[16]) and now such powers are subject to Christ (1 Pet 3[22]). They can never hurt the believer who fights the good fight and overcomes in the battle for sanctification (Ro 8[38]). It is barely likely that when

St. Paul speaks to Titus of the *archai* (viz. Tit 3¹), he understands the term in the secular sense of civil governors. If he were writing secular Greek he would of course be saying, 'Put them in mind to be subject to *magistrates* and authorities', but in his peculiar parlance he is more probably saying, 'Put them in mind to be subject to Principalities *(archai)* and Powers *(exousiai)*' – the heavenly hierarchy.

When, however, Christian Greek has *archē* in the singular (1 Co 15²⁴; Col 2¹⁰; Eph 1²¹), it may signify sometimes the Principalities considered as a class in the hierarchy of Heaven or the collective status of an *archē* – something like 'principalitiship'. In the same way, *exousia, dunamis* and *kuriotēs* may be used in the singular in this sense. Justin Martyr avers that the Samaritans honoured Simon Magus above every Principality (sing.) and Authority and Power (*Dial.* CXX 6).

The Principalities appear in later Christian and heretical Gnostic literature.²³⁴ Origen once gave the list of angelic orders as follows: Archangels, Thrones *(thronoi)*, Dominions *(kuriotētes)*, Principalities *(archai)*, and superior Authorities *(exousiai)*.²³⁵ In another place he mentions Thrones, Dominions, Authorities, Principalities.²³⁶ St. Hippolytus has Principalities, Authorities, Angels,²³⁷ and the Apostolic Constitutions have Thrones, Dominions, Principalities, Authorities, Powers, and in another place Aeons *(aiōnes)*, Armies *(stratiai)*, Powers, Authorities, Principalities, Thrones, Archangels, Angels (vii 35, viii 12). In the fourth century St. Methodius mentions Principalities, Thrones, Authorities.²³⁸ It was left to St. Dionysius Areopagita (v AD) to make the most elaborate specification in the early Church. He gives Dominions, Powers, Authorities, Principalities and Archangels.²³⁹ He mentions also Angels, and Seraphim and Cherubim and divides the whole into three great hierarchies. His speculations were adopted and developed by the mediaeval Schoolmen (Albert the Great, Bonaventure, Duns Scotus, Aquinas).

Proceeding by guess from St. Paul's two lists, I suppose that the great orders range from the most exalted (Dominions and Thrones) down to the least (the Principalities and Powers) – assuming the ascending order in Eph 1²¹, the descending order in Col 1¹⁶.

See also, 'Angel', 'Authorities', 'Powers', 'Dominions', and 'Thrones'.

βεβηλόω

The verb *bebēlō* is a coinage of Biblical Greek, used in the LXX of Pentateuch and Prophets to render the Hebrew *hll* in the Piel (to pollute, defile). Much of the Jews' religion concerned the cleansing of the Sabbath and Temple from profanation. The NT uses the word of the Sabbath (Mt 12[5]) and of the Temple (Act 24[6]). Hermas and Justin use it of defiling God's name.[240]

We are not aware of any secular use before the third century (Heliodorus). The verb is derived from the adjective *bebēlos*, which had the sense of public, current, and well-trodden. According to MM, the adjective was a technical term of religion not used in the vernacular. Josephus, indeed, uses it for 'profane'.

PROMISCUITY
κοίται

Secular Greek. In the singular *koitē* was a bed, particularly a marriage bed (as Lk 11[7]; Heb 13[4]). The chorus in Medea speaks of 'that awful *koitē*', by which they mean death,[241] and in Alcestis *koitai* (plural) refers to that lady's bridal couch.[242] In the LXX, Reuben is accused of defiling his father's *koitē* (matrimonial bed), which is a translation of Hebrew *mishbābh* (Gen 49[4]); during the plague of darkness no one rose from his *koitē* (bed) for three days (Hebrew *tahath*, Ex 10[23]). *Koitē* is a bed of sickness (*mishbābh*, Ex 21[18]), as well as a bed for sleeping in (*mishbābh*, Lev 15[4]).[243]

Biblical Greek. A new departure is introduced by the phrase *koitē spermatos* (seed produced in intercourse), which is literally, 'bed of the sperm *(zerâ)*' – a phrase found often in Leviticus (e.g. 15[16]). Within this phrase *koitē* appears to signify sexual intercourse, and this is the turning-point in its history. It now has the signification of coitus, e.g. Wis 3[16] ('seed of unlawful *koitē*'), and that meaning passed into Christian Greek.

Koitai is found in the plural with the sense of illicit intimacy, and it is rated with rioting, drunkenness, wantonness, strife and envying (Ro 13[13]). The word does not have this meaning in contemporary vernacular, although coitus is expressed by *androkoitō*[244] and by *koimaomai*. But *koitē* derives its strong sexual association from the LXX.

In the Fathers believers are urged to afford hospitality but not as an opportunity for 'illegal intercourse' (Diog 5[7]) – *koitē* (singular).

St. Paul's expression, *koitēn echō* (lit. 'to have intercourse') means 'to conceive children' (AV Ro 9[10]), used of Rebecca conceiving by Isaac.

PROPHECY (AND FALSE PROPHECY)

προφητεία: προφήτης: προφητεύω: (μαντεύομαι)

The first three words, *prophēteia*, *prophētēs*, *prophēteuō*, indicate a charismatic gift of the Holy Ghost, but *manteuomai* indicates false prophecy.

Prophecy. In the secular language the first word, *prophēteia*, is a power of interpreting to others the will of the gods;[245] sometimes it is an oracular response,[246] sometimes the office of a *prophētēs*,[247] one who speaks for a god. A *prophētēs* (prophet) may be one who interprets Zeus's word and will,[248] but it must be acknowledged that already in Greek the word had acquired a religious sense of denoting an official at Egyptian temples, probably a priest.[249] It is doubtful whether early Christians were aware of the fact, but they would certainly know that *prophētēs* in the Greek Bible rendered the three Hebrew words for a prophet of the Lord: *hōzê*, *nābhî* and *rō'ê*, all interpreters of the Lord's will. The Hebrew *n*ᵉ*bhû'â* and *ḥāzôn* (interpretation) are rendered there by *prophēteia*.

The OT meaning of the words was accepted by Christians (Mt 13[14]; 2 Pet 1[20f.]). All through the gospels and Acts, *prophētēs* is a prophet in the Hebrew sense.

However, there appears for these words a new meaning indicating the peculiar phenomenon of Christian **prophecy** – a divine charismatic gift (Ro 12[6]; 1 Co 12[10]; 1 Th 5[20]). Like 'tongues', but unlike Christian love it will vanish away (1 Co 13[8]) and yet will edify the Church in the mean time (14[6,22]). The book of Revelation is a **prophecy** (Rev 1[3] 22[7,10,18f.]), and several **prophecies** seem to have concerned Timothy (1 Ti 1[18] 4[14]).

The *prophētēs* was a considerable minister, only just below the apostles on some lists (1 Co 12[28]; Eph 2[20] 3[5] 4[11]; Rev 18[20]). Jude and Silas were **prophets** (Act 15[32]), and Agabus also (Act 21[10]). The **prophet's** words were specially inspired and to some extent ecstatic (1 Co 14[29,32]). Gross martyrdom of **prophets** is expected some day (Rev 16[6] 18[24]).

The verb *prophēteuō* too had the special Christian sense. It involved a highly rated gift of the Spirit (1 Co 14[1]), ministering edification, exhortation and comfort (14[3]), a better charisma than 'tongues' (14[5]), to be coveted (14[39]) and exercised by the Martyrs at the End (Rev 11[3]). Like prayer, it is undertaken with the head

uncovered, only one brother speaking at a time (1 Co 11⁴ 14²⁴,³¹).
Women prophesy with the head covered, and presumably this
happened in the case of Philip's daughters who prophesied (Act
21⁹). As a special function **prophecy** soon disappeared in the early
Church. The Didache testifies to the existence of prophets as an
itinerant ministry in the Church of about AD 100–120. _The
Didache probably should not be taken as more than a reconstruction of primitive Church life (J. Armitage Robinson, R. H.
Conolly, etc.), but the gift can still be said to be at work in the
Church in every movement for renewal.²⁵⁰ Montanism gave **prophets** a prominent place, but Montanism was a revival rather than a
continuance of the apostolic ministry.

Soothsaying. The verb *manteuomai* in secular Greek was to utter
prophecy or divination. 'Are we to *prophesy* that the King is
dead?'²⁵¹ It was to give an oracle,²⁵² but also to consult an oracle.²⁵³
In Biblical Greek it is used exclusively of false prophets who keep
company with enchanters, witches, charmers, wizards and necro-
mancers (Deut 18¹⁰; 1 Km 28⁹), provoking the Lord to anger (4 Km
17¹⁷; Jer 34(27)⁹; Ezek 12²⁴ 13⁶,²³ 21²¹⁽²⁶⁾ 22²⁸). It sinks as low as
divining for money (Mic 3¹¹) and in the NT it is the activity of the
possessed damsel at Philippi (Act 16¹⁶). For Hermas it is a form of
idolatry: the double-minded 'practise soothsaying', like the heathen
(*Mand.* XI 4).

PROSELYTE

προσήλυτος

Proselutos was coined by Jews. It is found nowhere in Greek
outside Jewish circles.²⁵⁴ It renders in the LXX the Hebrew word
for 'stranger' *(gēr)*. But *gēr* in late Hebrew denoted a foreigner who
nevertheless had been admitted, or was seeking admission, to the
Jewish religion. The latter sense was attached to *proselutos* in the
Greek of Philo and the Christians (e.g. Mt 23¹⁵).

Such men are mentioned separately from Jews (Act 2¹⁰). One of
the Seven, Nicolas, was a *proselutos* of Antioch (Act 6⁵). They are
called *'sebomenoi* proselytes' (Act 13⁴³), differentiated again from
Jews. The adjective *sebomenoi* (fearers) suggests 'God-fearers',
whom some would identify with proselytes. God-fearers are mentioned as a class (Act 10²,²² 13¹⁶,²⁶ 16¹⁴ 18⁷), among whom were
Cornelius, Lydia and Justus, who may have differed from proselytes only in the degree of strictness with which they observed the
Jewish ordinances.

Though God-fearers were very often no more than political

sympathizers with the Jews, yet an examination of the literature of the rabbis, and of Josephus and others[255] shows that they were firm supporters of Judaism, mainly in the north-eastern Mediterranean, between ii BC and AD iii, without becoming members of the synagogue communities and without being circumcised. They lived within the Jewish ethos, but not strictly according to the stipulations of the Law and the traditions. They worshipped the true God, but were not necessarily monotheists and were indeed estimated as pagans. They were not regarded as Jews.[256]

Proselytes, on the other hand, were fully committed to Judaism, even to the extent of circumcision and the ritual purification of baptism,[257] although they were held in lower estimation than native Jews and might not in public prayer reckon the fathers of Israel as their own fathers (Bikkurim i 4).

PSALM (HYMN)

ψαλμός

Psalmos in secular Greek was first a 'plucking' of bowstrings[258] and then a 'striking' of musical strings. 'He heard the *psalmos* (twanging) of the shrill-toned lyre'.[259] In the phrase of Aeschylus, 'The *twanging* shrills'.[260]

In Biblical Greek, however, *psalmos* is a song with instrumental accompaniment. The 'sweet psalms of Israel' (2 Km 23[1]) are the Psalms of David. Our Lord refers to the Book of *Psalmoi* (Lk 20[42]), and in the Testament of Solomon *psalmos* is applied to 'the fiftieth *Psalm* which David sung' (D I).

In the earliest Church *psalmos* became a name for believers' songs of praise which graced the local gatherings along with other hymns, the *humnoi* and the spiritual *ōdai* (Eph 5[19]).[261] There may be remnants of early Christian song in the NT, e.g. a hymn of baptism (Eph 5[14]), a hymn of redemption (1 Ti 1[15]), a hymn of the Incarnation and Ascension (1 Ti 3[16]), a hymn of martyrdom (2 Ti 2[11-13]), and a hymn of salvation (Tit 3[4-7]). Referring to the oldest hymns Eusebius affirms that 'all the *psalmoi* and *ōdai* which were written by faithful brethren from the beginning sing of Christ as Logos of God and state tht He is God.[262] The Odes of Solomon are first- or second-century examples of Christian song which are of much the same character as the Psalms of David and were perhaps baptismal hymns.[263]

σκώληξ

The meaning of *skōlēx* in secular Greek was an earthworm,[264] a grub, a larva,[265] sometimes a worm in decayed matter, for Josephus speaks of worms breeding in superfluous manna gathered by the Israelites,[266] and St. Clement of a worm engendered in rotting flesh (1 Clem 25³). Only occasionally was it metaphorical, and then not in the Biblical sense – but of 'flatterers',[267] and other forms of wretchedness. In Lucian's *Vitarum Auctio* (Philosophies for Sale), 'Sceptic' deprecates himself as 'devoid of judgment and insensitive and, generally, no better than a *skōlēx*.' (27).

In the Biblical language it is a word signifying **future punishment** and renders *tôlēᵉâ* (Isai 66²⁴), the damnation of the wicked. It refers to the fate of the ungodly (Ecclus 7¹⁷) and to the day of Judgment (Jdth 16¹⁷). In the fire of hell 'their *skōlēx* dieth not' (Mk 9⁴⁸).

The same meaning is discovered in the Apocalypse of Peter (25) where it is said that sinners are cast into unresting torment 'and their *skōlēkes* (punishments) are as numerous as a dark cloud'.[268]

NOTES

[1] Isocrates XII 227.
[2] Plato *Philebus* 33B.
[3] *Topica* 104a 28.
[4] Polybius XV 2.13.
[5] Herodian II 61.
[6] *Symposium* 222B.
[7] Aeschylus *Agamemnon* 264. Same meaning, 'adage', in 2 Pet 2²².
[8] Aquila at Eccles 12⁹; Ezek 18³. Symmachus at 1 Km 24¹⁴; Ps 77(78)²; Ezek 12²².
[9] Jülicher, Loisy, and Heitmüller described it as 'allegory'; Lepin, Spitta and Weiss as nothing but a parable; Buzy, in a middle position, called it an 'allégorie parabolisante'. See J. Quasten, *Catholic Biblical Quarterly* 10 (1948), p. 8.
[10] R. M. Pope, *Expository Times* 21 (1909), p. 237.
[11] H. J. B. Combrink, *Nederduits Gereformeerde Teologiese Tydskrif* (Stellenbosch, R.S.A.) 16 (1975), pp. 56–63.
[12] Can 4¹³; Eccles 2⁵; Gen 2⁸ (Garden of Eden), etc. B. F. Grenfell, *Revenue Laws of Ptolemy Philadelphus*, Oxford 1896, 33.11 (iii BC), C. C. Edgar, *Zenon Papyri*, Cairo 1925, 33.3 (iii BC), OGI 90.15 (Rosetta Stone, 196 BC), *P Fay* 55.7 (AD ii), *P. Flind. Petr.* ii.xlvi b (200 BC), Josephus *Ant. Jud.* VII xiv 4 (Niese VII 347): the garden of King David, XII iv 11 (Niese XII 233): the gardens of Tyre, I i 3 (Niese I 37): the Garden of Eden.
[13] *Anabasis* I 2.7. See also II 4.14, *Cyropaedia* I 3.14, *Historia Graeca* IV 1.15, Plutarch *Artaxerxes* 25.
[14] J. Jeremias in Kittel *TWNT* V, pp. 763f.
[15] R. H. Charles, *Revelation*, ICC T. & T. Clark 1920, vol. II, pp. 160f.

[16] Another way of taking the promise is, perhaps, 'I say to thee today, "Thou shalt be with Me in Paradise".'

[17] As also by the authors of 2 Enoch 8³; Apoc. Mos. 37⁵ 41¹ᶠ.

[18] R. H. Charles, *The Book of Enoch*, Clarendon 1893, pp. 103, 155.

[19] Sib. Orac. III 767ff. (see R. H. Charles, *Apocrypha and Pseudepigrapha of the OT*, Clarendon 1913, vol. II, p. 392.

[20] Sib. Orac., fragments iii 46ff. (see Charles, op. cit., II, p. 378).

[21] E. Langton, *Good and Evil Spirits*, SPCK 1942, p. 289.

[22] 1 Enoch 25⁴; 4 Ezra 7³⁶. See also Strack-Billerbeck, *Kommentar zum Neuen Testament aus Talmud und Midrasch*, Munich 1922–8, II, pp. 264f., IV, p. 1119.

[23] For an excellent discussion of the term 'sleep' as the proper Biblical term for the intermediate state, see R. E. Bailey, *Zeitschrift für die Neutestamentliche Wissenschaft* 55 (1964), pp. 161–7 (Berlin).

[24] Only I do not think that St. Paul regarded the 'soul' as the real 'we'. That was rather the 'spirit'. See the article, 'Sensual'.

[25] For a contrary supposition, after very careful discussion, see D. E. H. Whiteley, *The Theology of St. Paul*, Blackwell, 1964, p. 269.

[26] Pseudo-Plutarch, *A Letter of Consolation to Apollonius* 30 (II 117C).

[27] Aristides *Orationes* 48 (24) 43 (i AD).

[28] Ex 23⁵; Isai 14⁹; 4 Mac 2¹⁴.

[29] I. Pol 6¹.

[30] *De Specialibus Legibus* IV 203.

[31] Homer *Iliad* II 243.

[32] Maximus of Tyre (ii AD), Teubner VI 7d.

[33] Aeschylus *Agamemnon* 657 (Vellacott).

[34] *Herodiani Technici Reliquiae*, ed. A. Lentz, Leipzig 1867ff., i 16.19; PSI 286.6; T. Judah 8¹; Symmachus 4 Km 3⁴.

[35] *Eumenides* 197 (Vellacott).

[36] *Politicus* 267C.

[38] Plato *Republic* 416A, etc.; T. Sol C x 52; T. Abr. B 107²C ¹¹C.

[38] C. K. Barrett, *The Gospel according to St. John*, SPCK 1955, p. 310.

[39] 'Christus est unicus pastor; ceteri vero eius vicem-gerentes', N. Cavatassi, C. P., *Verbum Domini* (Rome) 29 (1951), p. 285.

[40] Gregory Nazianzus, *Orationes* 16.4, etc.

[41] S. M. Reynolds, *Westminster Theological Journal*, 28 (1965), pp. 38–41.

[42] Menander 549 ('resignation' in accepting fate); Strabo V 4.10 (desperate 'resistance' in a siege); Aretas *Peri Aitiōn kai Sēmeiōn* (ed. K. Hude, *Corpus Medicorum Graecorum*, II Leipzig 1923) 1.1 (p. 36.12) – a doctor's 'perseverance' in treating stubborn disease).

[43] Josephus *Bell. Jud.* VI i 5 (Niese VI 37).

[44] Plutarch *Moralia* 593f. The phrase, 'Bear up!' appears in ii AD Astrampsuchus.

[45] Kittel *TWNT* IV, p. 378.

[46] A. Wifstrand, *New Testament Studies* 10 (1964), pp. 289–94.

[47] Homily XXVIII on St. Matthew (PG LVII 351). See *Library of the Fathers*, Rivington 1844, part II, p. 415.

[48] Horst, op. cit., pp. 382f.

[49] So B. B. Warfield, *Expository Times* 25 (1913), p. 71.

[50] H. Riesenfeld in *Festschrift* for Josef Schmid, Regensburg 1963, pp. 214ff.

[51] H. Ljungvik in *New Testament Studies* 10 (1964), pp. 289–94.

[52] C. E. B. Cranfield in *Scottish Journal of Theology* 16 (1963), pp. 297–301.

[53] G. Delling, *Zeitschrift für die NT Wissenschaft* (Berlin) 53 (1962), pp. 1–25.

[54] G. Stählin, *Jahrbuch für Antike und Christentum* 17 (1974), pp. 5–20.

[55] Thucydides V 14.

[56] Xenophon *Anabasis* IV 1.21.

[57] Thucydides I 8, V 50, III 108.

[58] Aristotle *Rhetorica* 1410a 4.

[59] Plato *Definitiones* 412C; Polybius IV 51.1; Plutarch *Pelopidas* I 8; Josephus *Ant. Jud.* II ii 1 (Niese II 7).

[60] Polybius XV 15.8.

[61] K. Wennemer, *Geist und Leben* (Würtzburg) 36 (1963), pp. 36–41.

[62] Herodotus I 74; Xenophon *Cyropaedia* III 2.12.

[63] *Cimon* (Teubner) XIII 4.

[64] Aristophanes *Birds* 386.

[65] Plato *Republic* 465B.

[66] Hesiod *Theogony* 902.

[67] J. V. Pixley, *Revista Bíblica* (Buenos Aires) 35 (1973), pp. 297–313.

[68] This noteworthy variant is in place of the received text, 'We have peace with God' (Ro 5[1]).

[69] R. Costa, *Nouvelle Revue Théologique* (Louvain) 95 (1973), pp. 622ff.

[70] F. D. Coggan, *Expository Times* 53 (1942), p. 242.

[71] Norman Snaith, *Expository Times* 53 (1942), pp. 325f.

[72] D. Gillett, *Themelios* (Leicester) 1 (1976), pp. 80–4.

[73] Herodotus Medicus, apud Oribasius V 30.7 (iv AD); Galen (ed. C. G. Kühn, Leipzig 1821ff., V 38); Themistius *Orationes* 15.190 (AD iv); Lucian *Judicium Vocalium* 9.

[74] P. Tebt. II 272.19 (a medical fragment, AD ii).

[75] Justin *Apol.* XVI 1; Athenagoras *Legatio* 34[2].

[76] Apostolic Constitutions II 57.1.

[77] *S. Cyrillus patriarcha Alexandrinus in XII Prophetas,* Ingelstadt 1607. In Oseam Commentarius, LXX column 203.

[78] Sophocles *Philoctetes* 1243.

[79] G. D. Kilpatrick in *Journal of Theological Studies* NS 16 (1965), p. 127.

[80] Severino Pancaro, *New Testament Studies* 16 (1970), p. 122.

[81] S. Pancaro, ibid., 21 (1975), pp. 396–405.

[82] Malcolm Lowe, *Novum Testamentum* 18 (1976), p. 130.

[83] C. K. Barrett, *The Gospel according to St. John,* SPCK 1955, p. 143.

[84] See the development of this important idea, in Hendrik Kraemer, *A Theology of the Laity,* Lutterworth, Hulsean Lectures, 1958.

[85] B. J. Kidd, *A History of the Church to AD 461,* Clarendon 1922, vol. i, p. 182, n. 4.

[86] Homer *Iliad* I 66.

[87] BGU IV 1067.12 (AD 101).

[88] Aeschylus *Agamemnon* 1504f.

[89] *Laws* 929C.

[90] Isocrates XII 32.

[91] Pindar *Fragmenta* 122.15.

[92] Aristophanes *Lysistrata* 104.

[93] Aeschylus *Agamemnon* 973.

[94] *Eumenides* 28.

[95] P. Oxy III 485.30.

[96] P. Oxy II 237, vii 15 (AD 186).

[97] P. Oxy II 278.4 (AD 17).

[98] C. Clemen, *Primitive Christianity and Its Non-Jewish Sources,* ET T. & T. Clark 1912, p. 233. This is also the thesis of P. J. Du Plessis, *The Idea of Perfection in the New Testament,* Kampen (Holland) 1959.

[99] See J. B. Lightfoot, *Colossians,* Macmillan 1875, in loc. 1[28], pp. 236f.

[100] R. Bultmann, *Theology of the New Testament* I 166f.

[101] C. H. Dodd, *The Interpretation of the Fourth Gospel,* CUP 1953, pp. 53f.

[102] *Corpus Hermeticum,* ed. W. Scott, Clarendon 1924, I, libellus IV 4, p. 150.

[103] R. Reitzenstein, *Die hellenistischen Mysterienreligionen*, 3rd ed. 1927, Leipzig and Berlin, p. 165.

[104] W. Bousset, *Kyrios Christos*, ET Abingdon 1970, p. 260, n. 58.

[105] Clement, *Stromateis* III 1.3.3.

[106] J. B. Lightfoot, *St. Paul's Epistles to the Colossians and to Philemon*, Macmillan 1975, pp. 236f.

[107] H. A. A. Kennedy, *St. Paul and the Mystery Religions*, Hodder 1914, pp. 130–5.

[108] Philo *Legum Allegoria*, iii 159; Epictetus *Enchiridion* 51.1f.

[109] Op. cit., p. 237. Justin *Dial.* 8, Clement *Hom.* iii 29.

[110] Op. cit., p. 237.

[111] Council of Ancyra (AD 314), canons 4, 5, 6, 9. See Bingham, *Antiquities* I, p. 43, and Lampe, *Patristic Lexicon*, Clarendon 1961, p. 138.

[112] J. H. Ropes, *St. James*, ICC T. & T. Clark 1916, p. 178.

[113] Plutarch *Alexander* 7.

[114] P. Tebt 33.12 (ii BC).

[115] P. Ryl 127.28 (i AD).

[116] A. Plummer, *2 Corinthians*, ICC T. & T. Clark 1915, p. 378.

[117] Ps 54(55)^{15} 118(119)^{54} 119(120)^{5}; Lam 2^{22}.

[118] 1 Esd 5^{7} (Jews in Babylon); Jdt 5^{9} (Hebrews at Haran); Ecclus *prol.* (the Dispersion) 16^{8} (the place where Lot sojourned); 3 Mac 7^{19} (journey).

[119] *De Confusione Linguarum* 80.

[120] C. Wolff, *Theologische Literaturzeitung* (Leipzig) 100 (1975), pp. 333–42.

[121] V. P. Furnish, *Perkins Journal* (Dallas) 28 (1975), pp. 1ff.

[122] Eusebius *Historia Ecclesiastica* IV 23.5.

[123] Philo *de Agricultura* 89 (XIX). See Moulton-Howard, *Grammar* II, p. 365.

[124] *Corpus Medicorum Graecorum* II, ed. K. Hude, Leipzig 1922, IV 12.12.

[125] Outside a citation of Matthew in Justin *Dial.* 51^{3}.

[126] A. Richardson, *An Introduction to the Theology of the NT*, SPCK 1958, p. 210.

[127] G. Schrenk in Kittel *TWNT* I, p. 613.

[128] A. H. M'Neile, *The Gospel according to St. Matthew*, Macmillan 1915, in loc. p. 155.

[129] E. Moore in *New Testament Studies* 21 (1975), pp. 519–43.

[130] BS, p. 224, n. 4.

[131] Epictetus *Enchiridion* (Teubner) III 22.97.

[132] *Zeitschrift für die Neutestamentliche Wissenschaft* (Berlin) 9 (1908), p. 171.

[133] H. W. Beyer in Kittel *TWNT* II, pp. 618, n. 16, 619.

[134] Epiphanius *Ancoratus* 12 (PG XLIII 37C), *Adversus Haereses* 66.85 (PG XLII 165B); Dionysius Areopagita *Epistle* 8, section 1 (PG III 1089C).

[135] Hippocrates *Peri diaitēs* 2.64.

[136] BDB s.v. p. 28.

[137] So also Bauer: 'when they took possession of', and Meyer: 'while the Gentiles were in the state of possession', *Critical and Exegetical Handbook to the Acts of the Apostles*, H. A. W. Meyer, ET T. & T. Clark 1877, p. 211.

[138] BDB s.v.

[139] So also St. Irenaeus *Adversus Haereses* I 18.3.

[140] Aelius Aristides (ii AD), ed. B. Keil, Weidmann, Berlin 1898, vol. II, p. 312, line 16 (Oratio XXXVII, 'Athena', §28.

[141] An inscription from Lydia. See W. M. Ramsay, *The Bearing of Recent Discovery on the Trustworthiness of the New Testament*, London 1914, p. 117. Also J. Keil and A. von Promerstein in *Dankschriften der Wiener Akademie* 54 (1911), p. 110.

[142] C. H. Dodd, *The Bible and the Greeks*, Hodder 1935, p. 17.

[143] L. Vaganay, *L'Évangile de Pierre*, Gabalda, Paris 1930, p. 255.

[144] Quoted by Deissmann, BS, p. 336, n. from Wessely.

[145] Just as the plural is used of members of the heavenly hierarchy, so the singular

P

in a collective sense indicated the order itself: Eph 1[21] 'all *archē, exousia,* and *dunamis* and *kuriotēs*'; 1 Co 15[24] 'all *archē* and *exousia* and *dunamis*' (i.e. the order of Powers).

[146] *De Confusione Linguarum* 171.
[147] P.G. XXV 100B.
[148] A. C. Pearson, *Verbal Scholarship and the Growth of Some Abstract Terms,* inaugural lecture, Cambridge 1922, pp. 18f.
[149] Aristeas 192, T. Levi 3[9] 18[8]; Enoch 101[3].
[150] All from Thucydides: V 98, VI 28, VIII 81.
[151] *Socrates' Defence* 32.
[152] *Cimon* XVI 3.
[153] I 20.6.
[154] Euripides *Bachanals* 320.
[155] A similar doxology is 1 Clem 20[12], etc. M. Pol 20[2] 21[1].
[156] So Jer 20[13], etc., where *ainō* (dative) renders *hillēl l^e*.
[157] As in Euripides *Alcestis* 2.
[158] Sophocles *Philoctetes* 1398.
[159] *De Specialibus Legibus* I 224.
[160] P. Mag Paris (ZP IV 1146) may be an exception: 'I praise thee, O god of gods'.
[161] Lk 2[13,20] 19[37] 24[53]; Act 2[47] 3[8f.]; Ro 15[11]; Heb 13[15]; Rev 19[5]; Barn 7[1]; Diog 2[7]; M. Pol 14; Justin *Dial.* 22[9f.] 73[3], etc., *Apol.* 13[1] 41[1]; Ath. 21[4], etc.
[162] P. Oxy II 275 (pp. 262ff.).
[163] *Eleventh or Trojan Discourse* §i 47. Cf. Bauer, ET (Arndt and Gingrich), p. xx.
[164] P. Oxy 1473.9 (iii AD), P. Hib 1.30.18 (iii BC).
[165] Michel in Kittel *TWNT* V, p. 203f.
[166] Demosthenes XXXIII 8; Polybius V 105.2; P. Tebt 21.6 (ii BC).
[167] Josephus *Ant. Jud.* VIII x 3. So Diodore and Polybius.
[168] Plutarch *Aemilius* 11.
[169] Confess (AV). Praise (RV mg, RSV, Moffatt, Jerusalem).
[170] R. P. Martin *Carmen Christi* CUP 1967, pp. 263f.
[171] J. B. Lightfoot, *St. Paul's Epistle to the Philippians,* Macmillan 4th ed. 1891, p. 115.
[172] E. Norden, *Agnostos Theos,* Leipzig 1913, pp. 277ff.
[173] *Legum Allegoria* I 80.
[174] E.g. Hermas *Vis.* III 1.5, I 1.3, III 1.6, *Mand.* X 3.2, *Sim.* IX 23.4, Didache 4[14].
[175] In Kittel *TWNT* V, p. 218, n. 51. So also Lightfoot's translation ('to confess unto Him'), *Apostolic Fathers,* part I, vol. II, p. 298.
[176] P. Hibeh I 15, 85ff. (c. 280 BC).
[177] P. Tebt I 5.165ff. (118 BC).
[178] Secular meaning also in Wis 4[1] 5[13] 8[7], etc. Hermas *Mand.* VI 2.3, XII 3.1. *Sim.* VI 1.4, VIII 10.3.
[179] As also in the Letter of Constantine, apud Eusebius *Vita Const.* 2.42. (PG XX. 1017C).
[180] P. Lond xlvi 418ff. (iv AD).
[181] *Ant. Jud.* VII 130.
[182] *Ant. Jud.* VII 124.
[183] As E. Hatch, *Essays in Biblical Greek,* Clarendon 1889, p. 41.
[184] E. Hatch, op. cit., p. 41.
[185] Aeneas Tacticus 22.12, 26.9 (Teubner): iv BC.
[186] Kittel *TWNT* II, p. 684.
[187] *Ant. Jud.* V i 14 (Niese V 42).
[188] P. Oxy IV, p. 243, no. 744.
[189] Cremer, p. 716; Thayer s.v.
[190] G. Milligan, *The New Testament Documents,* London 1913, p. 51.

358

[191] E.g. P. Oxy II 292.7 (c. AD 25), P. Ryl II 229.8 (AD 38). Dittenberger, 3rd ed. 705.56; 741.5.

[192] C. Wessely, *Corpus Papyrorum Hermopolitanorum*, Leipzig 1905, 6.1.

[193] *Politica* 1257a 23.

[194] *Bell. Jud.* VII v 2 (Niese VII 103). But Josephus does use it of prayer made to God: *C. Apion* II 197 (II 23).

[195] *The Flinders Petrie Papyri* I, p. 60, xix 1 (a), line 2 (ii BC).

[196] *Erotes* 19.

[197] OGI 569, 11.

[198] *Coriolanus* 30^2.

[199] Hermas *Vis.* III 10.7. Also I. Magn 7^1; P. Philip 7^2; 1 Clem 59^2; Barn 12^7.

[200] Herodotus VI 67.

[201] SIG 856.6 (ii AD).

[202] F. Preisigke, *Griechische Urkunden des ägyptischen Museums zu Kairo*, Strassburg 1911, 1.16 (ii AD).

[203] G. C. Richards, *Journal of Theological Studies* 32 (1931), p. 77; E. G. Selwyn, ad loc.; LS s.v. 3.

[204] Kittel *TWNT* II, pp. 685f.

[205] Thucydides III 53.2, 68.1.

[206] SIG 856, line 6 (ii AD).

[207] Bo Reicke, *The Disobedient Spirits and Christian Baptism*, Acta Seminarii Neotestamentici Upsaliensis, XIII, Munksgaard, Copenhagen 1946, pp. 182–5.

[208] C. C. Bigg, ICC, p. 165.

[209] *Expository Times* 24 (1912), pp. 46f.

[210] *Agamemnon* 1106, *Persae* 605.

[211] *Medea* 205.

[212] Xenophon *Anabasis* I 8.12, *Cyropaedia* VII 2.5.

[213] Herodotus VIII 92.

[214] Pindar *Pythian Ode* VI 36.

[215] *Demosthenis Orationes* II, pars II, ed. W. Rennie, Clarendon 1921, p. 876, line 14 (XXXI 4); FD read *proōrisato* for *prosōrisato*.

[216] W. Sanday, A. C. Headlam, *Romans*, ICC T. & T. Clark, 5th ed. 1902, p. 218.

[217] H.-M. Dion, *Recherches de Science Religieuse* (Paris) 53 (1965), pp. 5–43.

[218] G. B. Caird, *Expository Times* 68 (1957), pp. 324f.

[219] Galen 14.386 (plural).

[220] 2 Co 12^{20}, Chrysostom *Homily* 12.1 in 1 Corinthians.

[221] Clement of Alexandria *Paedagogus* 15 (PG VIII 269C).

[222] *Historia Ecclesiastica* VI 43.1.

[223] G. Schrenk in Kittel *TWNT* III, pp. 249–52.

[224] C. Eastwood, *The Priesthood of All Believers*, London 1960, p. 241.

[225] Herodotus VI 106.

[226] Sophocles *Ajax* 668.

[227] Thucydides I 126.

[228] Polybius I 39.1, VI 26.5.

[229] Herodotus V 33.

[230] O. Cullmann, *Christ and Time*, ET London, pp. 103ff., 191ff.

[231] A. W. Carr, *New Testament Studies* 23 (1977), pp. 20–35. See also Trevor Ling, *Expository Times* 68 (1956), p. 26.

[232] I. Smyrn 6^1; I. Tral 4^2; I. Rom 7^1; I. Eph 17^1 19^1; I. Philad 6^2; Diog 7^2.

[233] Thucydides V 47, VI 54, Aeschylus *Agamemnon* 124.

[234] Acta Thomae A 133. At a Gnostic Baptism: 'We name over thee the name of the mother of the ineffable mystery of the hidden Principalities and Powers.'

[235] *Libellus de Oratione* 17 fin (PG XI 472D).

[236] *Contra Celsum* iv 29 (PG XI 1069C).

[237] *Refutatio Omnium Haeresium* vi 19 (PG XVI 3. 3223B).

[238] *De Resurrectione Mortuorum* x (PG XVIII 277B).
[239] Pseudo-Dionysius *De Coelesti Hierachia* ch. IX ii (PG III 260A).
[240] *Sim.* VIII 6.2, etc. *Dial.* XLI 3, etc.
[241] Euripides *Medea* 151.
[242] Euripides *Alcestis* 249.
[243] As in T. Sol D II 11.
[244] BGU 1058.30 (i BC).
[245] Lucian *Alexander* 40.
[246] Heliodorus *Erotici,* ed. W. A. Hirschig, Paris 1856, 2.27 (iii AD).
[247] P. Tebt 6.34 (ii BC).
[248] Aeschylus *Eumenides* 19.
[249] P. Tebt 6.3 (ii BC), BU 149.3f. (Fayûm ii–iii AD), 488.3f (Fayûm ii AD), BS pp. 235f.
[250] B. van Leeuwen, *Tijdscrift voor Theologie* (Nijmegen) 5 (1965), pp. 174–92.
[251] Aeschylus *Agamemnon* 1367, cp. *Eumenides* 716.
[252] Demosthenes XVIII 253.
[253] Herodotus I 46, IV 172.
[254] K. G. Kuhn in Kittel *TWNT* VI, p. 728.
[255] F. Siegert, *Journal for the Study of Judaism* 4 (1973), pp. 109–64.
[256] H. L. Strack, P. Billerbeck, *Kommentar zum Neuen Testament aus Talmud und Midrash,* Munich 1922–8, vol. II, pp. 715–23.
[257] H. H. Rowley, *Hebrew Union College Annual* (Cincinnatti) 15 (1940), pp. 313ff.
[258] Euripides *Ion* 174.
[259] Pindar *Fragment* 125.
[260] Aeschylus *Fragment* 27 (57), line 7.
[261] For Christian hymns in the earliest centuries, see *Liturgiae Preces Hymni Christianorum e papyris collati,* ed. Carolus de Grande, Naples 1928, and Ruth E. Messenger, *Christian Hymns of the First Three Centuries,* Papers of the Hymn Society 9 (1942), pp. 1–27.
[262] *Historia Ecclesiastica* V xxviii 6.
[263] J. Rendel Harris, *An Early Christian Psalter,* London 1909.
[264] Homer *Iliad* XIII 654.
[265] Aristophanes *Wasps* 1111, *Fragments* 583.
[266] Theophrastus (iv BC) *Historia Plantarum* III 12.6; Josephus *Ant.Jud.* III i 6 (Niese III 30).
[267] Anaxilas (iv BC comedian) 33.1 (T. Kock, *Comicorum Atticorum Fragmenta,* Leipzig 1880ff., vol. ii).
[268] Ed. E. Preuschen, *Antilegomena: Die Reste der ausserkanonischen Evangelien und urchristlichen Ueberlieferungen,* Töpelmann, Giessen, 1901, p. 49, line 27.

Q

ζωοποιέω

Secular Greek. *Zōöpoiō* had much the same meaning as *zōögonō* (propagate, breed),[1] but sometimes it may mean, 'bring the dead to life'.[2] In the Hermetic literature the divine Kosmos is said to make all things alive,[3] and Diogenes Laertius declares that the sun 'gives life' to everything.[4] We find the meaning in the LXX and NT (4 Km 5[7]; Ro 4[17] 8[11]; 1 Pet 3[18]).

Christian Greek. But in addition there is a new symbolical meaning, to **sanctify** or make spiritually alive. Jesus 'quickeneth whom He will', an activity comparable to raising the dead (Jn 5[21]). Both St. Paul and his Master envisage a conflict between the *sarx* (the evil impulse)[5] and the Spirit. The *sarx* profits nothing and the Spirit 'quickens' (Jn 6[63]). Christ, the Last Adam, is a 'life-giving' Spirit (1 Co 15[45]). The Spirit is 'life-giving' (2 Co 3[6]). The word has clearly gained a new speciality of meaning. God is said to quicken (*zōöpoiō*) all things, in the Byzantine text[6] of 1 Ti 6[13]; the context is the good fight of faith, the profession before many witnesses, and the blameless life which yearns for the Coming of our Lord.

The language of the apostolic Fathers evinces the new meaning – God 'quickens' by the Holy Ghost and by Christ's suffering upon the Cross (Barn. 6[17] 7[2]). The Alexandrian Father alludes in this way to some of Israel's experiences which are a type of Christian salvation, the 'quickening' from the serpent's bite and the 'quickening' which Moses gave when he lifted up the serpent (Barn 12[5,7]). In Hermas there is a reference to Holy Baptism, a symbol of the new life of sanctification, when he refers to Christians rising through the water that they might be 'quickened', and the verb is *zōöpoiō*. In the 'quickening' they come to know the name of the Son of God (*Sim.* IX 16.2, IX 16.7).

A sanctifying experience is indicated when the writer to Diognetus twice uses the verb. Christians are persecuted, yet 'quickened'; punished, yet they rejoice 'as being *quickened*' (5[12,16]). They are, as it were, the soul within the unsanctified body of the world (6[1]).

Accende lumen sensibus
Infunde amorem cordibus,
Infirma nostri corporis
Virtute firmans perpeti. – ALBANUS MAURUS

NOTES

[1] Aristotle *Historia Animalium* 555 b 9; Diodorus Siculus (Teubner II 52).
[2] Lucian *Vera Historia* I 22 (the miracles of the moon).
[3] W. Scott, *Corpus Hermeticum*, Clarendon 1924, IX 6.
[4] VIII 27 (iii AD).
[5] See the article, 'Flesh'.
[6] The Neutral text (Vaticanus) has the verb *zōögonō*, and there God is seen as Creator. The text is superior, but the Byzantine reading makes better sense in the context.

R

REAL, ARCHETYPAL (MADE WITHOUT HANDS)

ἀχειροποίητος

Acheiropoiētos is a coinage of Christian typology, based on existing words, and appearing again about 200 AD (Pseudo-Callisthenes).

It was part of the charge against Jesus that He had threatened to 'destroy this temple' and build another **made without hands** (Mk 14[58]). If the accusation was truthful, Jesus may well have intended His resurrection body to be understood as the new temple, and St. Paul indicated our own resurrection body by a similar use of the new word. The apostle speaks analogically, comparing earthly bodies with the tabernacle of God in the desert, a figure of Heaven itself. The first tabernacle has already been done away, to give place to a better, and so shall these poor frames give place to a heavenly **acheiropoietic** body, eternal in the heavens (2 Co 5[1]).

Again, he speaks by analogy in Col 2[11]. Circumcision was a token of admission to the covenant of old, itself a figure of the New. Saints and faithful brethren, however, are circumcized with an **acheiropoietic** circumcision, which involved putting off the body of sins of the flesh (Col 2[11]).

The writer to Hebrews pressed another analogy, based on the more perfect tabernacle, which is not **cheiropoietic**, reasoning that Christ entered the archetypal sanctuary by shedding His own blood, which is contrasted with the blood of goats and calves, concluding that the old things are but figures (*antitupa*) of the real, the greater, and more perfect (9[11,24]).

So the old circumcision, performed with hands, and the old tabernacle, built with hands, are types of the Christian remission of sins and of the Heaven where Christ pleads the suppliant's cause before the Throne.

RECONCILE

ἀποκαταλλάσσω

Apokatallassō is a double compound, a coinage of Christian Greek, as I suppose, appearing nowhere else.[1] St. Paul speaks of Christ making peace between Jew and Gentile and **reconciling** two parties 'unto God in one body by the cross, having slain the enmity thereby' (Eph 2[16]). The distinction between two parties – 'you which were afar off', the Gentiles, and 'them which are nigh', the Jews – is a reference to Gentiles being called to the Church. In the parallel passage in Colossians the reconciling, which is by means of Christ, is first between God on the one side and all things in heaven and earth on the other (1^{20}), and next, between God and alienated paganism (1^{21}).

The Fathers echo the thought of St. Paul. The Areopagite declares that first, Christ reconciled us to Himself and then, by that means, we were reconciled to God.[2] 'We were reconciled in the Second Adam', affirms St. Irenaeus. 'With Him whom we offended in the first Adam through disobedience, we are reconciled in the Second Adam who was obedient unto death'.[3] The mediating part of Christ is prominent. The context in Irenaeus is that of restoring man's lost image, the likeness of God, by assimilating man to the invisible Father through the means of the visible Word.

RELIEF

ἄνεσις

Anesis had indicated in Greek any kind of relaxation, physical or mental, as indeed it still denotes St. Paul's physical release from prison or detention (Acts 24^{23}). For Plato *anesis* was the 'relaxing' of strings that had been drawn tight and it was the reverse of *spoudē* (haste);[4] it also meant 'indulgence' and 'licence',[5] and some early Christians used it in this way. The author of Barnabas speaks of 'indulgence' for the soul to walk with sinners (Barn 4^7). For Herodotus *anesis* was the 'abatement' of evils (V 28), while Polybius (I 66.10) coupled it with *scholē* (leisure). For Plutarch it was the remission of tribute (*Sertorius* 6), and *anesis pagōn* was a thaw in the ice (*Sertorius* 17). Plutarch contrasts it with *epitasis*, political 'tension' (*Lycurgus* 29). In Strabo *anesis* was the 'ebbing', the reverse of full tide (VII 2.1). Galen used it of the 'remission' of fever, the reverse of *paroxusmos* (VII 427). For Josephus *anesis* was 'rest' from physical hardship,[6] temporary 'rest' from toil upon a festival day,[7] and intermittent 'rest' for the land from ploughing and planting.[8] For Plotinus it indicated the remission of punishment (IV 3.24), and in a third-century inscription it was 'relief' from taxation.[9]

Among early Christians, however, *anesis* denoted also a very novel kind of 'relaxation'. It expressed 'relief' as the reversal of distress. They did not derive their special usage from the LXX where *anesis* means 'permission' (Ecclus 15^{20}), 'liberty' for a daughter (26^{10}), and 'freedom' to go and build up Jerusalem (1 Esd

4^{62}). Symmachus comes nearer to the new meaning with 'relief' from distress (Ex $8^{15(11)}$) and from tears (Lam 3^{49}). The Christian meaning, the reverse of *thlipsis* (spiritual affliction), is well illustrated in 2 Co 2^{13} where St. Paul had no 'relief' in his spirit, in 7^5 ('relief' from anxiety), 8^{13} (ease), 2 Th 1^7 ('relief' from trouble in the Day of Christ). Here it has special eschatological significance.[10]

Trench aptly contrasts the Christian use of *anapausis* (rest) which Jesus promises to the weary ones resorting to Him (Mt 11^{28f}) – the complete cessation of toil. When, on the other hand, St. Paul promises *anesis* in the Day of Christ he does not anticipate 'rest', as much as 'relief', a relaxation of tension and 'of the chords of endurance, now so tightly drawn, strained and stretched to the uttermost' (p. 140).

RENUNCIATION

ἀπέκδυσις: ἀπεκδύομαι

Both the noun, *apekdusis*, and the verb, *apekduomai*, are likely to be coinages of Christian Greek.

The noun (renunciation). St. Paul devised the word when he was urging us to 'discard' fleshly desires, and he affixed it to the notion of a spiritual circumcision ('made without hands') – St. Paul speaks in the context of Christ's circumcision understood symbolically. The removal of the flesh at the Last Adam's circumcision is a figure of the Cross and of the renunciation of carnality by the believer as part of the austere sanctification which is a spiritual circumcision (Col 2^{11}).

Nowhere in the LXX, apostolic Fathers or Apologists, does the noun occur. It was probably a logical formation from that other Christian coinage, *apekduomai*. It is absent from known texts except those which are dependent on Col $2^{13,15}$, until St. Gregory of Nyssa uses it for the discarding of the fleshly body at death,[11] and then disappears until the twelfth century.[12]

The verb (to Put Off). The verb *apekduomai* appears in one manuscript of Josephus. Again we probably have a coinage of St. Paul (Col 2^{15}), who applies it to the action of Christ in 'putting off' principalities and powers, making a show of them openly, triumphing over them in His cross – a difficult enough concept. His theme is elucidated later when he refers to 'the old man', and we see that the theme corresponds with the reasoning in Ro 6^6 (the old man crucified with Christ). We see that, like the noun, the sense of the verb correlates to sanctification. The justified believer must **renounce** such an insidious sin as lying because the old nature ('old man') is crucified with Christ (Col 3⁹). The obscure 2¹⁵ is now clearer: at Calvary the spiritual powers enslaving the believer are 'triumphed over' and 'spoiled'. They are put off like an abandoned vesture. They have no dominion over our regenerate nature.

As St. Paul exclaims elsewhere, the demonic powers – angels and astral deities[13] – are seeking to triumph over us but they cannot (Ro 8³³ᶠᶠ·). We have **put off** the old vesture if we have put on Christ and share His resurrection.

It should be observed that both words have double prefixes, *apo* and *ek*. The renunciation is a 'stripping right off,'[14] which is very emphatic.

RESPECT OF PERSONS

προσωπολημπτέω : προσωπολήμπτης : προσωπολημψία : ἀπροσωπολήμπτως

These words 'may be reckoned amongst the earliest definitely Christian words' (MM). *Prosōpolēmptō, prosōpolēmptēs, prosōpolēmpsia*, and *aprosōpolēmptōs* are formed from the Hebrew *pānîm* (face) and *nāśâ* (see). Some have attributed them to 'Palestinian Greek' (MM), and indeed they do not appear in the LXX.[15]

It is a sin 'to respect persons' (*prosōpolēmptō*), to make distinctions in the Christian fellowship based on wealth (Jas 2¹,⁹). God is no 'respector of persons' (*prosōpolēmptēs*), to Whom Jew and Gentile are both alike acceptable (Act 10³⁴), master or servant making no difference to His lack of *prosōpolēmpsia* (Ro 2¹¹; Eph 6⁹; Col 3²⁵). St. Polycarp's advice to presbyters is to avoid 'respect of persons' (ad Phil. 6¹).

God judges all men 'without respect of persons' (*aprosōpolēmptōs*), and yet believers will often give more regard to 'corruptible things as silver and gold', unmindful that the blood by which they were redeemed is far more precious (1 Pet 1¹⁷). St. Clement opens his letter to the Corinthians with an observation on their attitude to visitors, their magnificent disposition of hospitality: 'You did all things without respect of persons' (*aprosōpolēmptōs*). Christians are reminded that the Lord will judge the world in this scrupulously fair way (Barn. 4¹²).

Thackeray[16] found it interesting to note the three stages through which the Hebrew idiom finds its way into Greek: 'first the possible but unidiomatic version' (e.g. *thaumazō to prosōpon*), 'then the baldly literal' (e.g. *lambanō prosōpon*), 'then the new Greek words coined from the literal version' (e.g. *prosōpolēmptō*, etc.) in the NT).

RECOMPENCE

God's stern and loving reaction to His children in represented in Christian Greek by the following most solemn words.

1. ἀνταπόδομα: ἀνταπόδοσις

The former word, *antapodoma*, is a Bible coinage. The similar idea in the secular language is expressed by the latter word, *antapodosis*. Both words, however, in the Christian dialect, signify the reward for Christian service.

Antapodoma is closely connected with resurrection in the epistle of Barnabas.[17] 'He who walks in the ordinances of the Lord ... shall be glorified. ... For this reason there is a resurrection and there is an *antapodoma*'.

When Jesus used the word He intended **reward** by it (Lk 14[12]), not in the Christian sense but in the way the LXX uses it to render *shalmōnîm*, a public recompence or even a bribe (Isai 1[23]). St. Paul, however, finds a new meaning within the Biblical vocabulary, for he cites Ps 27(28)[4]: 'Let their table be ... an *antapodoma* (punishment) unto them', where the idea behind the Hebrew *gᵉmûl* is not reward but God's **punishment** of His people for their blindness (Ro 11[9]). The Apostle reminds the Roman believers, and us through them, that God's grace is not to be trifled with.

The other word, *antapodosis*, is found in the LXX and also in secular Greek, where it is a reprisal or repayment. St. Paul's use is novel – a **reward** for Christian service (Col 3[24]). The contrast between the two words is seen in the fact that *antapodoma* inclined rather to be **punishment** than reward, as confirmed in the later Christian Greek of Theodoret[18] and Marcus Eremita[19] in the fifth century.

2. ἀντιμισθία

Antimisthia is another solemn word with apparently the same meanings, frequent also in Church Greek. It was perhaps coined by St. Paul.

It is both **punishment** (Ro 1[26]) and **reward** (2 Co 6[13]). By derivation it would indicate a balance, a give-and-take, and St. Paul invites the Corinthians to feel for him, as he does for them.

Similarly in Romans it is the tit-for-tat of natural justice, men with men behaving unseemly and getting what they deserve.

The idea of an oblation to God in return for the grace we enjoy at His hands appears in Christian Greek. What *antimisthia* (return) shall we make to Jesus Christ, worthy of what he has given us? (2 Clem 1[3,5]). Let us give ourselves to God, offering Him an *antimisthia*, which is repentance from a sincere heart (9[7]). This is the *antimisthia* which we can pay to God, let us remain righteous (15[2]).

3. μισθαποδοσία

We have in *misthapodosia* yet another coinage of Christian Greek. It too has a good (Heb 10[35] 11[26]) and a bad sense (Heb 2[2]). It is the **recompense** for holding fast the faith. It is the reward of Moses and of Christians. But it is also the **punishment** of the Israelites' disobedience, which we too shall not escape if we neglect so great salvation.

A parallel Christian coinage is the *misthapodotēs*, the divine **Rewarder** (Heb 11[6]) who will recompence those who seek Him.

All these words represent the reaction of a loving God to His people, which may be both favourable and otherwise.

> Come, Lord, come Wisdom, Love and Power,
>> Open our ears to hear,
> Let us not miss th' accepted hour;
>> Save, Lord, by Love or Fear. – KEBLE.

REGRET

καταισχύνω: καταισχύνομαι

The NT sense of *kataischunō* and *kataischunomai*, as Bultmann observes,[20] is chiefly determined by that of the LXX and Judaism.

Secular Greek. The meanings are 'to put to shame' (*kataischunō*, active), 'to feel shame' (*kataischunomai*, middle), and 'to be ashamed' (*kataischunomai*, passive).

As early as Homer the active signified the bringing of disgrace upon a father's home and, by quarreling, the bringing of shame to a feast.[21] For Herodotus it means sullying the glorious achievements of the Persians (VII 53); for Plato, disgracing one's ancestors (*Laches* 187A); and for Demosthenes to 'dishonour' a man in the same way as to dishonour a woman (XLV 79).

However, in the middle voice it meant 'to feel shame' before the gods. 'Don't you *fear* the gods (i.e. feel shame before them) to speak thus?'[22]

In the passive, it was to be ashamed of what someone would think[23] or to be put to shame, like the Peloponnesians, by the courage of others.[24]

Biblical Greek. A change came about when the LXX used the verb to render the Hebrew *bôsh*, which means not only to be ashamed, but also to feel disappointed, that is, to 'regret', to be disillusioned. It expressed the disappointment felt in alliances with Egypt and with Assyria (Jer 2[36]), the disillusionment of Moab in Chemosh and of Israel in Bethel (Jer 31(48)[13]). Israel trusted in God and did not 'regret' it (Ps 21(22)[6(5)]). 'O my God, I trust in Thee: let me not *regret* it' (Ps 24(25)[2]). 'None that wait on God will *be disillusioned*' (3).

In the active voice, St. Paul affirms that hope does not 'make one regret' (Ro 5[4]); and in the passive, he affirms that believers shall not 'regret' their acts of faith (9[33]), quoting the LXX of Isai 28[16] (as also in Ro 10[11]), like St. Peter (1 Pet 2[6]): 'he that believeth on Him shall not *be made to regret it'*.

TO REJECT

μισέω

To 'hate' has been the secular meaning of the verb *misō* from the time of Homer, and sometimes the intended hatred is nasty – as bitter as that against a Tissaphernes who was slack in giving men their pay,[25] or hatred for a Menelaus after he sacrificed two children.[26] In secular authors the 'hatred' of the gods is prominently expressed, particularly by Aeschylus. *Misotheos* expresses how relentlessly the house of Atreus was 'loathed by the gods'.[27] And so *misō* may always infer, in any kind of Greek.

We should bear in mind, however, that in the Bible we are met with theological considerations of a novel kind, for the word is predicated of God Himself, whose nature is Love, the very reverse of all that *misō* had hitherto brought to mind. In the Bible *misō* renders the Hebrew verb *śānê*, which sometimes has a softened, and often quite different, sense – even when describing human relationships, let alone God's pitying attitude towards His children. In many an OT context *śānê* is not so much to hate bitterly as 'to love less', 'to regard indifferently', 'to despise'. This is specially true of the Wisdom-literature, where personal discipline and education is often the topic.

It is said to be brutish and fatal to 'hate' reproof (Pr 12[1] 15[10];

Ecclus 21[6]). The author has in mind the **rejection** rather than emotional hatred. The avaricious taker of bribes must learn to 'hate' gifts – in this new sense (Pr 15[27]): no one is expected to dislike gifts, but often they must be rejected. Fools do not 'hate' knowledge, in the secular sense of the verb, they simply **reject** it (Pr 1[22, 29]). It is not that a slanderer 'hates' those whom he ruins, but he does **despise** them (Pr 26[28]).

All this is made clear in the love for women. Jacob fails to be as greatly attracted to Leah as to Rachel (Gen 29[31]), but the emotion of 'hatred' in the secular sense is inappropriate in the word *misō*. The verb involves attitudes to a 'forsaken' wife (Isai 60[15]), and also to the less dear of two spouses (Deut 21[15f.]) and to an unsatisfactory wife (Deut 24[3]). The Hebrew behind *misō* in Isai 54[6] is *mā'as* (a young wife, 'rejected'). The feeling is seen as hate only when it is contrasted with a fervent love. God's attitude to Esau (Mal 1[3]), cited forthrightly by St. Paul from the LXX is expressed by *misō* in the Biblical sense (Ro 9[13]). 'Jacob have I loved, but Esau have I hated' (AV).

In Christian Greek the same is true of *misō* in lower relationships. It signifies **renunciation** rather than hatred. It is abnegation and is to be taken not psychologically and fanatically but 'pneumatisch' and 'christozentrich'.[28] A brother may never **reject** a brother (1 Jn 2[9, 11] 3[15] 4[20]). When the disciple faces the grim choice of severing earthly ties at God's bidding, it is not intended to convey that he 'hates' father and mother, as if *misō* had the accepted sense. He **loves** them **less** than his heavenly Master (Lk 14[26]). The ascetic is not said to hate the mammon which he has rejected and forsaken; he loves God more (Mt 6[24]; Lk 16[13]). The martyr is not said to hate the life surrendered for a greater love (Jn 12[25]). Nor should it be assumed that God hates (in the accepted sense of *misō*) the 'Esau' who has failed to respond to the Gospel. Hatred in the ordinary sense is forbidden to Christians, yet time and again they are told to 'hate' (*misō*). 'Hate evil to the last' (Barn, 19[11]). 'Hate' father and mother! We are told that God 'hates'! We speak a new language. The truth is, that rightly to understand the nuances of Biblical Greek vocabulary will illuminate a little the theology of divine Election, and at last bring home to us the greater love which Esau missed.

> *We barter life for pottage; sell true bliss*
> *For wealth or power, for pleasure or renown;*
> *Thus Esau-like, our Father's blessing miss,*
> *Then wash with fruitless tears our faded crown.* – KEBLE.

1. ἄφεσις

In secular Greek *aphesis* was a release of water,[29] decontrol of an engine,[30] dispensation from a bond,[31] remission of debts and money,[32] leave of absence,[33] even physical exhaustion,[34] and divorce.[35] Never, however, as in Christian Greek, forgiveness of sins.

For this Christ's blood was shed and from its benefit he who blasphemes against the Holy Ghost is excluded (Mt 26[28]; Mk 3[29]). In Christian Greek *aphesis* always has reference to the acquittal of sins which is through the blood of Jesus, as *aphesis* was through the blood of calves and goats in the previous dispensation (Mk 1[4]; Lk 1[77] 3[3] 24[47]; Act 2[38] 5[31] 10[43] 13[38] 26[18]; Eph 1[7]; Col 1[14]; Heb 9[22] 10[18]).

Although *aphesis* in the NT includes release from prison and repriving of captives, the context requires that the captives be understood as being in thrall to sin (Lk 4[18]). Never in the NT 'is forgiveness represented as the remission of penalties; what is remitted is sin'.[36] *Aphesis* is remission of sin.

Clearly for St. Clement *aphesis* is the forgiveness of sin. Speaking of Moses begging the forgiveness of his people's sin, he exclaims, 'The servant is bold with his Master; he asketh forgiveness (*aphesis*) for the multitude' (53[5])!

For St. Justin Martyr, 'remission' comes through repentance (*Dial.* CXLI 2), but he seems to agree with other Christian teachers[37] that *aphesis* has a close reference to baptism. 'You must take pains to recognize the way by which *remission* of your sins shall come to you. ... It is no other than this, that you should recognize this Christ and, washing yourselves in the laver ...' (*Dial.* XLIV 4). It is clear that the 'laver' is baptism (*Dial.* XIV 1).

2. πάρεσις

Like *aphesis*, *paresis* was in secular Greek a 'slackening', a 'dismissal', an allowing to escape.[38] Cremer observed, I believe mistakenly, that the meaning, actual, unconditional and full remission (of punishment) has secular precedent[39] and Deissmann (BS p. 266) endeavoured to pluck from a vernacular text of the Fayûm the meaning, remission (of debt). The papyrus, however, is post-Christian and besides, as Deissmann confessed, its diction is too concise and technical to be clear. Xenophon, nevertheless, used the verb for 'letting go' blunders unpunished.[40]

More typical of the secular meanings of the noun is that in

Hippocrates and Aretaeus, two medical writers, who used it for 'paralysis' and for haemaplegic conditions after a stroke.[41]

In Christian Greek *paresis* expresses a necessary part in the first stage of the process of salvation, as St. Paul sees it, i.e. initial forgiveness, what some understand by 'justification' – 'the *paresis* (forgiveness) of sins that are past, through the forbearance of God' (Ro 3[25]).

The Christian meaning of *paresis* is not a mere 'letting go unpunished'.[42] I think it more likely that Bultmann is right in seeing both *aphesis* and *paresis* as God's 'forgiveness'.[43] Many, however, assume that there is a difference, and the view that *paresis* is the passing over of sin is reflected, for instance, in Redlich's summary. 'In former days the sins of men had been passed over, and man had misunderstood God's forbearance, and there was a risk of men forgetting that He was a God of righteousness, but the hour had come when He must show how much He hated sin, as He did by the death of His Son'.[44]

To pass over unpunished is rather the secular meaning of *paresis* (e.g. Xenophon). Lightfoot observed that the distinction between *aphesis*, the revocation of punishment, and *paresis*, the suspension of punishment, is born out by classical usage. Secular Greek does observe the difference, but not so Christian Greek. St. Paul's idea of *paresis* is not a mere 'suspension' of punishment.

In a careful analysis Kümmel reasoned that St. Paul meant 'remission' and not 'passing over',[45] and claimed that 'it is not Paul's view that God has hitherto passed over sins'.[46] The question is whether in Christian Greek *paresis* is the same as *aphesis* (forgiveness, AV)[47] or whether it is a mere passing over of sin, as though ignoring its existence (AVmg, RV, RSV, Moffatt, Sanday and Headlam, Cranfield, etc.) – as in the pre-Christian epoch, the times of ignorance which God winked at (Act 17[30]).

This will not be St. Paul's meaning, for in fact God did not allow sins to go unpunished; every transgression and disobedience did receive a just recompense of reward (Heb 2[2]). Israel's sins were not 'passed over', to be sure, and indeed Israel received double for all her sins. St. Paul himself insists that the wrath of God is revealed from heaven against all ungodliness and unrighteousness of men (Ro 1[18]). C. Anderson Scott had a point: 'It is difficult to suppose that Paul could have written this passage if he had had vividly present to his mind the idea that God's failure to deal adequately with sin had created a problem with regard to his righteousness'.[48] Did St. Paul mean that *paresis* had reference to sins committed in previous epochs of history? At least Luther did not think so. He looked at the supposition that St. Paul meant by *paresis* the passing over of sins of the people of the past because of the satisfaction of

Christ that was to come, but Luther went on to say that it makes a better sentence if we read it to mean: By forgiving sins that *we have done* in the past God shows Himself as the justification of all.[49]

Paresis in a Christian context is no longer, I believe, simply the passing over or 'winking at' sins, as it was in its pagan environment. It is in the Pauline context, the vindication of God's 'forgiveness' of the past which the death of Christ established.

To return to the passage adduced by Cremer (p. 298) from Dionysius of Halicarnassus. Though Bultmann was correct, as far as the NT is concerned, in claiming that the sense of 'forgiveness' is carried by *aphesis* and *paresis* he was probably wrong, as Creed believed, to claim that this sense is attested in Dionysius.[50] J. M. Creed showed[51] that the passage of Dionysius, though habitually cited from Wettstein to Bultmann to show that *paresis* is the equivalent of *aphesis*, is on the contrary decisive for the conclusion that, in one case at least, *paresis* carries a different meaning from *aphesis*.[52] That is, as far as secular Greek is concerned. In the passage from Dionysius *paresis* is not, despite Cremer and the rest, the 'remission' of punishment. Coriolanus had not been condemned, he had not even been tried, and the expression, the Consuls 'failed to induce the tribunes to *drop the matter altogether (paresis)*' meant not that the tribunes should 'forgive' Coriolanus but rather that they should not bring him to trial at all and should 'let the whole matter drop' – should 'pass over' the whole thing. Creed urged that even Trench, who generally made a distinction between *paresis* and *aphesis*, was misled in supposing that the Dionysius passage proves that *paresis* equals *aphesis* (p. 110), and in fact the Dionysius passage 'falls into place with the general trend of Trench's argument'[53] – that St. Paul intended something different from *aphesis* by his choice of the word *paresis*. Indeed, Dionysius consistently uses *aphesis* and its verb when he expresses acquittal and release. Creed concluded that 'in the light of this evidence, taken as a whole', by which he meant the secular evidence, ' "passing over" not "remission" or "forgiveness" is likely to be the true meaning' of *paresis* in Ro 3[25]. Creed is correct in his assessment of the secular evidence.

However, the whole tenor of Christian theology, and St. Paul's in particular, so I believe, makes it clear that we cannot assume that secular precedent is any guide to the specialized Pauline meaning of theological words. In the Christian vocabulary both *aphesis* and *paresis* denote the forgiveness of sins. St. Paul must not be charged with saying that God overlooked, but did not forgive, the sins of His people in days gone by. Sins, though as scarlet, were as white as snow if God's people were willing and obedient. Such sins were not merely 'passed over'. If there was *paresis* of sins under the old

Covenant, there was *aphesis*, too (Heb 9[22]), accomplished by the shedding of blood. When, therefore, St. Paul uses a different word in Ro 3[25] he does not intend a difference of meaning.

REPENTANCE

μεταμέλομαι : μετανοέω : μετανοία

Repentance needs not fear the heaven's just rod,
It stays even thunder in the hand of God. – TH. CAMPION

The two verbs, *metamelomai* and *metanoō*, and the noun *metanoia*, represent in Biblical Greek a profounder attitude of contrition than the pagan ever knew.

Peccavi nimis cogitatione, verbo et opere; mea
culpa, mea ipsius culpa, mea maxima culpa.

Secular Greek. The verbs have the meanings, to regret, to have second thoughts, to change one's mind.

The first verb, *metamelomai*, is to realize that one's conduct is not what one intended. When Aristotle says that a man is not *metamelomenos* (regretful), he means that he has acted on purpose or deliberately.[54] The verb means to change one's feelings over policy or martial strategy. The Spartans 'thought better' of their foreign policy and instead of siding with Persia sought occasion of war with Artaxerxes.[55] It means to wish to go back upon an agreement.[56] The Byzantines became sufficiently alarmed about the war to have 'changed their feelings' on policy.[57] The secular verb comes nearest to the Christian meaning when it signifies 'remorse' after anger[58] or a murderer's regrets.[59]

The second verb *metanoō*, too, does not necessarily include a feeling of remorse. It is to have, literally, a new *nous* (mind) – to revise one's judgment or opinion.[60] Galba spent his whole time 'regretting' what he had done – presumably in writing to Verginius for help – and longing to lay down his burden of care.[61] Like the last, this verb amounts to a change of attitude about policy. 'When they could not see any Zealots to support them', reports Josephus, 'they were in doubt about the matter, and many of them *regretted* that they had come'.[62] So far from signifying 'repentance' from evil, *metanoō* in secular Greek might easily mean repentance of what is good.[63] It is actually to perceive something too late, the very reverse of *pronoō* and *probouleuomai* (to foresee).

The noun *metanoia* in the same way is nothing more deeply felt than the forsaking of a project,[64] an after-thought or a correction.[65]

'He who shall marry, comes to *metanoia*'.[66] *Metanoia* is despised as a *pathos* (feeling) by the Stoics, by Epictetus, Marcus Aurelius, and Arius Didymus, according to Michel.[67] Whereas *metameleia* (the noun from *metamelomai*) is the word belonging to general literature and philosophy, *metanoia* is the word of the Synagogue and of the Church. It corresponds to the Hebrew *tᵉshûbhâ*.[68] Behm reminds us that, both linguistically and materially, one searches in vain in the secular Greek world for the origins of the NT understanding of *metanoō* and *metanoia*.[69]

Biblical Greek. In the Greek OT, the noun *metameleia* expresses God's repentance, His *niḥûmîm* (Hos 11⁸). The verb *metamelomai* usually renders Niphal of the verb *nāḥam*: to be sorry for one's doings, as of Israel 'repenting' when they see war and wish to return to Egypt (Ex 13¹⁷), of God 'repenting' of His punishment, according to His mercy (Ps 105(106).⁴⁵ See also: 1 Chr 21¹⁵; Ps 109(110)⁴; Jer 20¹⁶), of God 'repenting' having made Saul king (1 Km 15³⁵), and rarely of being 'comforted' concerning an evil (Ezek 14²²). Once it renders *nāḥam*, to express the 'groaning'—of a sufferer (Pr 5¹¹). In the free Greek books, too, it retains the secular sense of changing the fancy (Wis 19²), or asking something back again (Eccles 33²⁰ (30²⁸)), or regretting having given a daughter in marriage (1 Mac 11¹⁰).

In the NT, however, there is the new and deeper meaning of turning from sin, although the writer to Hebrews is still very much under the influence of the LXX, quoting Ps 109(110)⁴ where God does not change His attitude (7²¹), and St. Paul has *metamelomai* for 'regret' (2 Co 7⁸). However, *metamelomai* is joined with 'belief' and is a reaction to the preaching of John the Baptist (Mt 21³²), and it is Judas's awful remorse (Mt 27³) – a turning from sin in both instances.

Metanoō, too, renders the Niphal of *nāḥam* (to repent of one's deed or of ill done to others). Often it is assumed that *metanoia-metanoō* corresponds to the Hebrew *shûbh* (turn), whereas regularly the underlying Hebrew is the Niphal *niḥam*.[70] Still it remains true that what the religious language of the OT expressed by *shûbh*, and what the theological terminology of the rabbis expressed by *tᵉshûbhâ*, etc., the NT and Jewish Greek expressed by *metanoō* and *metanoia*.[71] Often God is the subject of *metanoō*, but in the LXX of Jeremiah the verb is used of man's repenting of wickedness (8⁶ 38(31)¹⁹). The call to Simon the Sorcerer was to repent of his wickedness (Act 8²²), and *metanoō* is the regular word in the NT, especially in Revelation, for repenting from sin (2²¹ᶠ. 9²⁰ᶠ. 16¹¹), for repenting before believing the Gospel (Mk 1¹⁵) and repenting before Baptism (Act 2³⁸). The imminence of the Kingdom of God is a sufficient reason to repent (Mt 3² 4¹⁷). *Metanoō* is explained as a turning to God (Act 3^{19} 26^{20}). *Metanoō* is St. Luke's regular word for repentance from sin (Lk 10^{13} 11^{32} 13^{3,5} 15^{7,10} 16^{30} 17^{3f}).

Where the NT does distinguish between *metamelomai* and *metanoō*, its authors seem to be aware of a real distinction which secular Hellenistic writers too often efface.[72] St. Paul had sent to the Corinthians a severe letter and he says that he is not 'sorry' that he sent it. The sorrow he speaks of is not repentance from sin, and so he use *metamelomai*. When, however, a little later he refers to the Corinthians' 'repentance' leading to salvation he uses the other word, *metanoia* (2 Co 7$^{8-10}$). St. Paul may be aware of a distinction, which had become obsolete in contemporary Greek. Though both words in Christian Greek express repentance from sin, *metanoō-metanoia* is the characteristically Christian word for this aspect of repentance.

Metanoō is followed by *ek* or *apo* (from), which are appended perhaps because of the influence of the Hebrew expression, *shûbh min* (turn from): Act 8^{22}; Rev 2$^{21f.}$; 9$^{20f.}$; 16^{11}. It may be that the NT writers are following the example of the LXX phrase in Jer. 8^6 (*metanoō apo = niham 'al*).

The noun *metanoia* is repentance from sin in OT Greek, although there is no Hebrew equivalent. 'Thou overlookest the sins of men, in hope of their *repentance*' (Wis 11^{23}). 'Judging them mildly, Thou givest them a place of *repentance*' (12^{10}). 'Thou givest *repentance* when men have sinned' (12^{19}). 'Enoch was an example of *repentance* to all generations' (Ecclus 44^{16}). Always *metanoia* is a great virtue, used in the context of sin and judgment. And so in the Letter of Aristeas: 'If you exhibit clemency ... you will lead them to *repentance*' (188). It is a repentance from sin in the message of John the Baptist and in the preaching of the Gospel, where for Christians it is closely linked with faith (e.g. Act 20^{21}). God leads men to *metanoia* (Ro 2^4), and *metanoia* leads to salvation (2 Co 7^{10}).

It has been noted that the words for repentance are comparatively rarely used by St. Paul, but that is not to assume that the words were of no importance for him. Probably the ideas were already implicit in his conception of *pistis* (belief). Moreover, Cranfield suggests that repentance itself had been devalued by the tendency in Judaism to understand the concept legalistically.[73]

One early Christian book which deals fully with *metanoia* is the Shepherd of Hermas, in which are placed together both the NT preaching of conversion and the Judaized doctrine of penance. For this writer, Christianity is a religion of conversion. *Metanoia*, when sealed with Baptism, is the basic change which has made a sinner a Christian. The experience cannot be repeated and yet it may be renewed by a special revelation of the merciful God. There is, before the End, an eschatological 'opportunity for *metanoia*'. Hermas is allowed to be very Jewish when he sees asceticism and penal suffering as the fulfilment of *metanoia*. In this way he misunderstands Christian *metanoia*, according to Behm.[74] To be fair to Hermas, he cannot conceive repentance as leading to anything but good works. Sanctification must follow.

Once again, then, Jews and Christians have chosen ordinary pagan words which signified little more than a change of mind or attitude, and have made them bear a truth which lies at the very heart of the Gospel: God's forgiveness is for the repentant. To look for the meaning in secular Greek is vain. Secular meanings give altogether a wrong impression of Biblical penance and repentance.

Writers like de Quincey, Matthew Arnold and Percy Dearmer, seized on the secular meaning to support their protest against the Christian's obsession with repentance and sin.[75] The aim of these writers and many humanists is to eliminate the emotional and mystical element from associations of repentance and to substitute for conviction of sin the recognition by the 'sinner' that he has made a mistake, to see repentance as the unemotional and non-mystical admission of a failing, with consequent change of mind and will. We cannot think that this is what the words mean in a Christian vocabulary. They are more than touched with a little emotion. They rend the heart, passionately.

Except for Heb 7[21] – a citation of the Psalms – Christians never speak of God 'repenting', though the remark is frequent in the OT. Mr. Argyle has noted that in dealing with *nāḥam*, as it refers to God's change of heart, the LXX used a variety of words, usually seeking to soften the harshly anthropomorphic conception of God.[76] In addition to *metanoō* and *metamelomai*, the LXX uses at least six other verbs to express *nāḥam*. Indeed, 'repentance' expressed by *metanoō* words and by *metamelomai* is already becoming a specialized technical term for man's turning from sin, in Biblical Greek. This is 'a great advance upon the theology of the Old Testament, an advance which is seen to be foreshadowed in the LXX when it is compared with the Hebrew Old Testament'.

RESURRECTION

1. ἀνάστασις

In the secular language *anastasis* meant a rising up, a restoration, or an erection – of walls, for instance (Demosthenes

377

XX 72). The total novelty of the Christian meaning, 'resurrection from the dead', is correctly acknowledged.[77]

However, Lucian may be cited to the contrary when he mentioned the *anastasis* of Tyndareus which provoked Zeus' anger against Asclepius,[78] for this passage is often understood as a 'resurrection of Tyndareus from the dead'. It seems more likely to refer to his 'restoration' to the throne by means of Asclepius.

Neither is it quite 'resurrection' for Aeschylus in the line, 'There is no *anastasis* (setting up) of a man once he is dead'.[79] Most references are clear. In Herodotus it is the 'removing' of the Greeks from Ionia for safety (IX 106); in Thucydides, the 'moving off' of an army (VII 75); in Sophocles, the 'rising up' from sleep,[80] and 'overthrow' of Ilium in Aeschylus.[81] In a much later inscription, it was the 'setting up' of an icon.[82]

In the LXX it already indicated the resurrection of the dead (2 Mac 7[14] 12[43]). The NT applies it to the resurrection in which the Pharisees believed,[83] but in Christian Greek it specially denotes the resurrection of Jesus.[84] Besides that, it is the resurrection of Christians.[85] A 'first' resurrection of martyrs is distinguished from a second more general resurrection (Rev 20[5f.]).

Some have ways of their own to explain the two resurrections, and they cannot be said to be what the Seer intended. For instance, it is suggested[56] that the first resurrection refers to the experience of baptism and, understood in a certain sense, baptism is indeed a resurrection experience – the rising to new life with Christ. The second resurrection might then be interpreted literally, the resurrection of the body at the Coming of the Lord. 'Christ the first fruits; afterward they that are Christ's at His Coming' (1 Co 15[23]). Looked at from this ingenious standpoint we may say that the first resurrection is a personal salvation, the second resurrection a cosmic salvation, when all things at last are reconciled to Christ in the dispensation of the fulness of times, embracing all things in heaven and earth (Col 1[20]; Eph 1[10]).

No doubt there are two such separate experiences. The question is whether the Seer did not take the two resurrections literally. Did early believers expect two resurrections, with the reign of Christ intervening? St. Jerome seems to have had no strong belief in the Millennium.[87] St. Augustine was repelled by some of the wild excesses involved in it, and he interpreted the Seer's vision allegorically.[88] He saw the 'first resurrection' as our restoration from the death of sin and our call to the Christian life. He understood the reign of Christ and the saints to be fulfilled already by the historic Church carrying out its apostolate in this world. While he considered the possibility that the Thousand Years was to be the final period before the judgment, he preferred the view that it was the total duration of the Church on earth.[89]

As Dr. Charles showed,[90] early commentators on Revelation had not yet fallen into the spiritualizing method which emanated from Alexandria, by which every student saw in that book what he wished to find. So St. Justin, Tertullian, St. Irenaeus, St. Hippolytus and St. Victorinus all take *anastasis* literally – and not as a death to sin followed by a new birth to righteousness. Taking part in the 'first resurrection' are the martyrs who succumbed in the Great Tribulation. They reign with Christ on earth for a thousand years (Rev 5[10]). St. Paul, as well as the Seer, witnesses to the early Christian belief in a temporary messianic reign, although St. Paul leaves out the number of years. He is as earnest as the Seer, nevertheless. Before the End, he affirms, when Christ shall deliver the Kingdom to the Father, Christ must reign till He has put all enemies under His feet (1 Co 15[25]). Often there was uncertainty about the length of the reign on earth. It was four hundred years in a Jewish book which appeared about AD 120, and it preceded a general resurrection and final Day of Judgment (4 Ezra 7[28ff.]). Those who came at the number four hundred evidently relied on the prophecy made to Abram (Gen 15[13]). The thousand years is based on a Biblical estimate that one day is as a thousand years with God (2 Pet 3[8]) in Whose sight 'a thousand years are but as yesterday' (Ps 90[4]), coupled with the thought that as God made the world in six days He intended it to last for six, the last day being a sabbath of rest,[92] that is, the Millennium.

Insofar as we may construct a picture of their cosmic chronology, the first Christians understood it so. After six thousand years of world history, the Saviour was born, the Gospel was preached and there intervened an epoch of grace before the first *anastasis* and the beginning of the last thousand years. That is concluded with a second *anastasis* (a general resurrection) and a final day of Judgment, after which there is an end to the world, and there are new heavens and a new earth (Rev 20, 21). St. Irenaeus stressed that the salvation of man will be consummated at the Parousia (*adv. Haer.* V 20.1). Christ took our flesh in order to save it and His work is not complete until the resurrection in the totality of body, soul and spirit (V 14.1ff.). The first resurrection will be shared by the OT saints, with all the righteous dead. The wicked will not be raised till the end of the Millennium.[92]

Through Jewish and Christian influence the word became a technical term in Greek, so that in the third century Plotinus can speak of *anastasis* 'from the body' (III 6.6), and a Jew or Epicurean of the same century in Epimaneia can make a tomb on which are still inscribed the words, 'to the resurrection' (*eis a[na]stasin*). They seem to presuppose that the phrase was originally, 'looking to the resurrection', and the whole inscription on the Bomos may well be a sneer at Christian opinions, as the editor agrees: 'Forsitan ea, quae de resurrectione mortuorum sentiebant Christiani'.[93]

Leaving aside the cosmological aspect, the *anastasis* of Christ is seen as a figure of the believer's redeemed life, on its second level, the renewing of the mind, or sanctification. St. Paul draws out the analogy. 'If we have been planted together in the likeness of His death, we shall be also in the likeness of His *anastasis*' (Ro 6[5]). Wesley re-echoes it.

> *Made like Him, like Him we rise;*
> *Ours the cross, the grave, the skies.*

2. ἔγερσις

C. Kingsley Barrett reminds us that *anastasis* and the verb *anistanai* are not common in St. John's gospel. Apart from Jn 20[9] they are not used of Christ's resurrection. Instead we find the verb *egeirō*, which also designates the raising of men from the dead, but St. John stops short of using the noun *egersis*.[94]

The LXX follows the secular use, translating by *egersis* the Hebrew *qûm*, applied to the 'erection' of the Lord's House (1 Esd 5[62]), as to the 'setting up' of Hercules's temple in Josephus,[95] the 'setting up' of the watch (Jg 7[19]A), and a 'rising' to the feet (Ps 138(139)[2]).

In secular Greek *egersis* had signified 'waking' from sleep,[96] as in the epistle of Aristeas (160), and the 'awaking' of wrath,[97] 'recovery' from suffering,[98] as well as the 'erection' of walls.[99] But from recovery, rousing and erection, it may have changed its meaning in St. Matthew's Greek.

Altogether new is his use (27[53]) when he records that many bodies of the saints came out of their graves after Jesus' resurrection (*egersis*). Rather later, too, in the *Kerygma of Peter*[100] it indicates Jesus' resurrection. However, in these texts the word may be understood in the normal secular sense actively, 'after the raising of Him',[101] or (in Mt) after the raising of *them*, the saints. A fourth-century text, which is influenced by Christianity, has the phrase, 'the *egersis* of a dead body', which the editor renders, 'Erweckung eines Leichnams'. It is followed by an incantation for raising a corpse from death.[102]

At any rate, *egersis* is a rare word in Christian literature.

It has been suggested that at one time the death of Jesus was conceived as a direct apotheosis from the Cross to God, like the translation of Enoch and Elijah, bypassing a resurrection from the grave. It is thought that St. Matthew was not aware of the primitive Christian belief, but that verse 53 was corrected to conform to the idea. It may be that in this way a word (*egersis*) is used which signifies a 'raising up' (i.e. into heaven) and which was not at all the Christian word for 'resurrection'.

Although, as E. Schweizer says, the hypothesis is mere speculation and lacks supporting evidence,[103] nevertheless *egersis* may not be the Christian word for 'resurrection' and may only be, as in the secular language, the act of 'exalting' to a higher sphere.

REVELATION: SECOND COMING

ἀποκάλυψις

Apokalupsis is a direct revelation from God without human intermediacy – a directive of some kind, a vision perhaps, a charisma which some Christians have by direct will of the Holy Ghost, while the *apokalupsis* for which all Christians long and wait is the appearing of their Lord and their own 'manifestation' at that time.

Secular Greek. Here *apokalupsis* was the act of uncovering, of coming to the light, of ceasing to be hidden, like streams of water which come to the surface.[104] Further, it means human 'nakedness'. Roman fathers, so Plutarch says, were ashamed to uncover their 'nudity' by bathing in sight of their sons.[105]

Christian Greek. The LXX still has *apokalupsis* for nakedness and indecency, the Hebrew *'erwâ* (1 Km 20^{30}) and for the dis-closure of secrets (Ecclus 11^{27} 22^{22} $42^1(41^{33})$), but *apokalupsis* stands for something very different in the language of Christians. In Christian Greek it is the **manifestation** of divine truth and the **revelation** of our Lord at His glorious Coming for which we wait (1 Co 1^7; 2 Th 1^7; 1 Pet $1^{7,13}$ 4^{13}). In two contemporary visions in first-century Judaism, the appearing of Messiah is indicated by the same concept, but not by the Greek word: 'Revelabitur filius meus' and, 'Revelabitur principatus Messiae mei'.[106]

Apokalupsis appears in an eschatological context, where it is warned that the unbeliever's impenitent heart serves but to accumulate wrath in the day of *apokalupsis* wherein God's righteous judgment is exhibited (Ro 2^5) – a **revelation** which is called also an *epiphaneia* (2 Th 2^8), an Epiphany. The final and perfect stage of salvation is the transformation of all natural things, to be signalized by the spectacle (*apokalupsis*) of redeemed people accompanying Christ at His Coming (Ro 8^{19}). 'This revealing of the sons of God will be the signal for the great transformation'.[107]

Besides being eschatological, the context of *apokalupsis* is also that of the Church's charismatic ministry at the present time. The word is connected with 'visions' (2 Co 12[1]) and represents the kind of spiritual gift that might exalt its recipient (12[7]) – a gift of the Holy Ghost akin to that of wisdom (Eph 1[17]). **Revelation** is distinguished from 'tongues' and is rather to be compared with *gnōsis* (spiritual insight), with the gift of prophecy, and with *didachē* (the instruction of Christians). It is to be seen at work in the church meetings at Corinth, along with psalm-singing and 'tongues' (1 Co 14[6,26]; 2 Co 12[1,7]).

St. Paul received the Gospel by direct revelation (*apokalupsis*) – in contrast to human instrumentality (Gal 1[12]) – and he received the 'mystery' of the Gospel in the same way (Ro 16[25]; Eph 3[3]). The vision of St. John on Patmos, like the vision of Hermas (e.g. *Vis.* V tit.), was an *apokalupsis* (Rev 1[1]; Justin *Dial.* 81[4]). So was the divine directive which guided St. Paul's movements and led him to Jerusalem with Barnabas and Titus (Gal 2[2]). *Apokalupsis* was a **revelation** received by Pionius from the martyr Polycarp (M. Pol 22[4]). St. Justin Martyr refers it to the book of Joshua (*Dial.* 62[4]), to the divine **disclosure** to the Wise Men not to return to Herod (78[2]), and to St. Peter's insight that Jesus was the Son of God (100[3]).

REVERENCE (SENSE OF THE NUMINOUS)

φόβος: φοβέομαι

While the secular meaning of *phobos* and *phoboumai* remains in Biblical Greek, a new and religious sense has been added to it.

The noun *phobos* is panic, especially hurried flight (Homer). 'With us there arose a violent *panic* – where did the sound come from?'[108] Sometimes *phobos* means doubt or scruple.[109] It is not 'reverence' in secular language until well into the Christian period.[110] Characteristic meanings are illustrated by the following classical examples. 'The great *panic* at Sparta' (Thucydides III 54). 'The *terror* which the Greeks inspired in the barbarians'. 'They made a noise with their spears, causing *terror* in the horses'. 'As night advances, *panic* falls on the Greeks'. '*Terror* was instilled into the Greeks'. 'A *dread* of ever leading an army against him'.[111] '*Horror* grips me', wrote Aeschylus.[112]

Sometimes *phobos* is modified to deep concern: an '*anxiety* that I shall not persuade my mistress'.[113]

The verb *phobō* in the active was to put to flight (Homer), to terrify (classics). They 'put the wind up' Alcibiades.[114] 'They *scared* the Athenians with Tissaphernes, and Tissaphernes with the Athenians'.[115]

In the middle and passive *phoboumai*, the verb, was again to put to flight (Homer), but more often, to be seized with fear, whether of the gods above (Plato) or of demons (Aeschylus). 'I should *dread* to follow the guide that he might appoint.'[116] Sometimes it is a milder fear.[117]

The sense of fear, dread and panic, at least as far as it can be understood as 'anxiety', appears also in the Bible, the reverse of Christian love, the bondage of the old Law (Job 20[25]; Wis 18[17]; Ro 8[15]; 1 Jn 4[18]), the 'fear' of death (Heb 2[15]), the fear felt before Messiah comes (Lk 21[26]), and the fear of one's enemies (Jn 7[13] 19[38] 20[19]; 1 Co 2[3]; 1 Pet 3[14], etc.).

In Biblical Greek, however, the ingredient of panic and dread is lacking in most contexts. True, Herod 'feared' the multitude (Mt 14[5]), but **reverence** is now prominent. There was no reason why Herod should be afraid of John. More likely that he **reverenced** him (Mk 6[20]). Often when *phoboumai* indicates fear, it is godly fear, God's mercy is upon all those that **reverence** Him (Act 10[2]) and upon churches too (Act 9[31]). There was a well-defined class of 'God-reverencers' among the Jews (Act 13[16, 26]). *Phoboumai* appears in the context of worship and giving glory, of reverencing God and giving glory to Him. The song of the Lamb exhorts us to '*reverence* the Lord and glorify His name'. A reward shall be given 'to the saints and them that *reverence* Thy name' (Rev 14[7] 15[4] 11[18]). The gospel of Mark ends with the reverential awe of the women at the tomb. 'They *reverenced*!' (16[8]). We recall the mount of Transfiguration where the disciples fell down and **reverenced** (Mt 17[6]; Lk 9[34]).

We may claim that the noun as well as the verb indicates a sense of the numinous. It occurs in situations of tremendous awe. To have seen Christ walking on the water inspired it (Mt 14[26]). The Resurrection angel brought it with him (Mt 28[4]). The emotion is not terror, nor is it inconsistent with 'great joy' (Mt 28[8]). The panic in the boat was over and gone but still the disciples had *phobos*, for it was the numinous experience of being with the Lord of winds and sea, within the same boat (Mk 4[41]). It overcomes the priest at the altar when an angel appears beside him (Lk 1[12]). When a significant miracle is performed, the numinous emotion is present (Lk 1[65] 5[26] 7[16] 8[37]; Act 2[43] 5[5, 11] 19[17]; Rev 11[11]). Numinous atmosphere surrounded the shepherds whom the angels found (Lk 2[9]).

The wicked man has no *phobos*, no reverence for God (Ps 35[2] (36[1])). *Phobos* for the Lord is not an instinct of self-preservation, it is worship and must be taught. It is no natural motivation (Ps 33[12]

(34^{11})). It is not a feeling, such as fear, for it can be 'chosen' (Pr 1^{29}), while fear cannot. There is wisdom in **reverence** for God (T XII P *Levi* 13^7), and there cannot very appropriately be said to be wisdom in a feeling. *Phobos* cannot be involuntary, for not to have *phobos* for God is a sin (Ro 3^{18}; 1 Pet 2^{17}), and so it is rather pointless of AV to render it 'terror' after the manner of secular Greek (2 Co 5^{11}), unless AV understands by 'terror' a sense of the numinous, the quickening which the righteous man feels before the consuming fire of God's majesty. *Phobos* of the Lord accompanies the comfort which the Holy Ghost brings. It is not terror (Act 9^{31}), but *phobos* in its new realization may be said to be spontaneous and involuntary only insofar as the transcendental numinous experience is involuntary.

Reverence for God is a quality which makes holiness even more perfect (2 Co 7^1; 1 Pet 3^{15}). In the churches we submit to one another, and servants submit to their masters, in **reverence** for God (Eph 5^{21}; Col 3^{22}). Such an attitude cannot be understood in the secular sense. Rather, *phobos* depicts the devotion in which all our earthly pilgrimage is to be spent.[118]

'*Phobos* and patience are helpers of our faith' (Barn 2^2). We are to train children in **reverence** for God (Pol. ad Phil. 4^2). We are to receive God's oracles with **reverence** as true (1 Clem 19^1). Our whole lives, our whole service to God, is to be spent in **reverence** (1 Clem 51^2; Pol. ad Phil 2^1) St. Clement includes *phobos* in a list of Christian virtues, along with faith, peace, patience, self-control. Indeed, it cannot be separated from faith: **reverence** is the fundamental attitude of the believer who depends entirely on God.[119] With **reverence** he works out his salvation (Ph 2^{12}). With **reverence** and trembling the Corinthians received Titus (2 Co 7^{15}); **reverence** was a virtue of theirs (7^{11}) and Paul's (7^5).

But **reverence** is not directed to God alone. We owe it to rulers (Ro 13^7), to our husband (Eph 5^{33}; 1 Pet 3^2), and to our master (1 Pet 2^{18}; Eph 6^5), and to Church discipline (1 Ti 5^{20}; Jude 23).

These words are common in the apostolic Fathers but they are increasingly used in set formulae, like 'fear God', 'fear the Lord' (Barn $10^{10f.}$; 1 Clem 21^7 45^7, etc.). Reverence for the judgment of God is specially emphasized (I. Eph 11^1), as in Rev $18^{10, 15}$ where the Seer connects it with Babylon's torment.

One may argue that reverence as a sense for *phoboumai* is not peculiarly Biblical, being found in a secular papyrus as early as 99 BC, in which a civic official writes to the priests at Tebtunis: 'I revere (*phoboumai*) and worship your temple'.[120] Certainly it is a strong word for a secular writer to have used for 'revere', and it is not inconceivable that we see here something of the influence of the LXX.

See also 'Numinous, Sense of'.

NOTES

[1] So also Bauer (168) and F. Büchsel in Kittel *TWNT* 1, p. 259.

[2] Dionysius Areopagita *De Divinis* 11.5 (PG III 953B).

[3] *Haereses* V 16.2.

[4] *Republic* 349E; *Laws* 724A.

[5] Republic 561A; *Laws* 637C.

[6] Bell. Jud. III vii 33 (Niese III 319).

[7] *Ant. Jud.* III x 6 (Niese III 254).

[8] *Ant. Jud.* III xii 3 (Niese III 281).

[9] Dittenberger (2nd ed.) 533.16.

[10] R. Bultmann in Kittel *TWNT* s.v. He compares it with *anapsuxis* (refreshing) in Act 3[20].

[11] Gregory of Nyssa, *De Vita Macrinae* (PG XLVI 985A).

[12] Eustathius of Thessalonica, *Commentarius ad Homeri Iliadem ...*, ed. G. Stallbaum 1827, 91.28 (I 77); Th. Nägeli, *Der Wortschatz des Apostels Paulus*, Göttingen 1905, p. 50.

[13] See the article, 'Demons'.

[14] F. F. Bruce, *The Epistles to the Ephesians and Colossians*, Marshall 1957, p. 234.

[15] LXX instead renders the Hebrew idiom by *thaumazō* with *prosōpon*. H. St. J. Thackeray, *Old Testament Grammar*, CUP 1909, p. 43.

[16] Op. cit., p. 44.

[17] Barn 21[1]; Did 5[2].

[18] *Quaestiones in 2 Par.* I 597.

[19] *Opuscula* 4 (PG LXV 1013B).

[20] R. Bultmann in Kittel *TWNT* I, p. 189.

[21] *Odyssey* XXIV 508, XVI 293.

[22] Sophocles *Philoctetes* 1382.

[23] Thucydides VI 13.

[24] Isocrates IV 97.

[25] Thucydides VIII 83.

[26] Herodotus II 119.

[27] *Agamemnon* 1090.

[28] O. Michel in Kittel *TWNT* IV, p. 695.

[29] P. Petr xii 2 (iii BC), P. Flor 388.44 (iii AD). See Deissmann BS p. 99.

[30] Philo mechanicus, *Belopoeica* 58.24.

[31] Demosthenes XXXIII 3.

[32] C. Michel, *Recueil d'inscriptions grecques*, Brussels, 1900, 1340.13.7 (Cnidus, ii BC); B. Latyshev, *Inscriptiones* vol. i, Petersburg 2nd ed. 1916, 32 B 70 (Olbia iii BC).

[33] Aristotle *Politeia of the Athenians* (ed. Kenyon, OCT) 30.6.

[34] Hippocrates *Epidemiae* 3.6.

[35] Plutarch *Pompey* 42.

[36] V. Taylor, *Forgiveness and Reconciliation*, Macmillan 1946, 2nd ed., p. 3.

[37] Barn 11[1]; Irenaeus *adversus Haereses* I 21.2.

[38] Plutarch *Dio and Brutus*, 2.

[39] Cremer p. 298. On Dionysius of Halicarnassus see *Antiquitates Romanae*, Teubner VII 37.

[40] *De Equitum Magistro* VII 10.

[41] Hippocrates *Epidemiae* IV 45; Aretaeus *Healing of Chronic Diseases*, I 7.

[42] As in J. C. O'Neill, *Paul's Letter to Romans*, Penguin 1975, pp. 70-7; V. Taylor, *Expository Times* 50 (1938), pp. 295ff.; C. E. B. Cranfield, *Romans*, ICC T. & T. Clark 1975, p. 211.

[43] R. Bultmann in Kittel *TWNT* I, p. 508.

[44] E. B. Redlich, *The Forgiveness of Sins*, T. & T. Clark 1937, p. 110. See also Theodoret on Ro $3^{25f.}$ (3.44).

[45] W. G. Kümmel, *Journal for Theology and the Church* 3 (1967), pp. 1–13.

[46] Ibid., p. 9.

[47] For the meaning 'remission', see Origen, Comm. in Ro 3^8 (PG XIV 946B), and Cyril *Rom.* 3^{27} (p. 179.22) PG LXXIV 780C, *Arcadia et Marina* 5^2 98E.

[48] C. A. A. Scott, *Christianity according to St. Paul*, CUP 1927, p. 66.

[49] Martin Luther, *Lectures on Romans*, Library of Christian Classics, SCM 1951, p. 116.

[50] Kittel *TWNT* I, p. 507.

[51] Even so, Kümmel insists that Creed has not made his point, op. cit., pp. 3f.

[52] *Journal of Theological Studies*, NS 41 (1940), pp. 28ff.

[53] Op. cit., p. 30.

[54] *Nicomachean Ethics* 1110 b 23.

[55] Diodorus Siculus XV 9.

[56] Ibid. XIX 75.

[57] Polybius IV 50.6.

[58] Xenophon *Memorabilia* II 6.23.

[59] Xenophon *Cyropaedia* IV 6.5.

[60] *Cyropaedia* I 1.3.

[61] Plutarch *Galba* 6.

[62] *Bell Jud.* IV iv 5 (Niese IV 284).

[63] Plutarch *Septem Sapientum Convivium* 21.

[64] Polybius IV 66.7.

[65] Rutilius Lupus I 16 (ed. C. Halm, Leipzig 1863).

[66] Menander *Monostichoi* 91.

[67] O. Michel in Kittel *TWNT* IV, p. 630, n. 3.

[63] Michel, op. cit., p. 631.

[69] Behm in Kittel *TWNT* IV, p. 976.

[70] 1 Km 15^{29}; Am $7^{3,6}$; Joel 2^{13}; Jon $3^{9f.}$ 4^2; Zach 8^{14}; Jer 4^{28} $18^{8,10}$ $38(31)^{19}$. For discussion of this point, see A. Tosata, *Revista Bíblica* (Buenos Aires) 23 (1975), pp. 3–45.

[71] J. Behm in Kittel *TWNT* IV, p. 994.

[72] Michel gives examples from Philo and Josephus, *TWNT* IV, pp. 631ff.

[73] C. E. B. Cranfield, *Romans*, ICC T. & T. Clark, vol. I, 1975, p. 145.

[74] J. Behm in Kittel *TWNT* IV, pp. 1003f.

[75] F. P. Shippam, *Expository Times* 46 (1935), p. 279.

[76] A. E. Argyle, *Expository Times* 75 (1964), p. 367.

[77] MM, who give examples of non-Christian meaning in secular inscriptions.

[78] Lucian *De Saltatione* 45.

[79] *Eumenides* 648.

[80] *Philoctetes* 276.

[81] *Agamemnon* 589.

[82] *Sammlung* ..., ed. H. Collitz, Göttingen 1884ff., 3505.20 (Cnidus).

[83] Mt $22^{23,28,30f.}$; Mk $12^{18,23}$; Lk 14^{14} $20^{27,33,35f.}$; Jn 5^{29} 11^{24}; Act 23^8 $24^{15,21}$; Heb 11^{35}.

[84] Act 1^{23} 2^{31} $4^{2,33}$ $17^{18,32}$ 26^{23}; Ro 1^4 6^5; 1 Pet 1^3 3^{21}.

[85] 1 Co 15; 2 Ti 2^{18}; Heb 6^2.

[86] N. Shepherd *Westm. Theol. Jour.* 37 (1974), 34–43.

[87] *In Isai.* 18 (PL XXIV 627f.).

[88] *De Civ. Dei* XX 7.1.

[89] Ibid. XX 6.1; 7.2; 9.1.

[90] R. H. Charles, *Revelation*, ICC T. & T. Clark 1920, vol. 2, p. 185.

[91] *The Secrets of Enoch* (Slavonic) $33^{1f.}$. It is revealed to Enoch that the world's duration is 7000 years and that the coming of the next thousand marks the end of everything. 'Let the days be after the fashion of 7000'. The book lightens many dark passages of the NT. See Morfill p. xii. Its influence is shown in the Epistle of Barnabas ch. 15.

[92] See the article by A. Skevington Wood, *Evangelical Qu.* 41 (1969), pp. 30-41.

[93] *Inscriptiones Graecae ad Res Romanas pertinentes*, ed. R. Cagnat, Paris 1911-14, IV, p. 743.25; W. M. Ramsay, *Cities of Phrygia*, 1897, vol. i, part ii, pp. 386ff., n. 232.

[94] C. K. Barrett, *The Gospel according to St. John*, SPCK 1955, p. 329.

[95] *Ant. Jud.* VIII v 3 (Niese VIII 146). But this reference in Josephus is not to the erection of the temple of Hercules but to the feast of the resurrection of Hercules-Adonis (according to F. Abel, *Revue Biblique* 5 (1908), pp. 577f.).

[96] Hippocrates *Kōakai prognōsies*, 82. Waking personified in Empedocles 123.1, Philodemus *Volumina Rhetorica* (Teubner II 206S).

[97] Plato *Timaeus* 70 c 1, Aristotle *Nicomachean Ethics* 1116 b 30.

[98] Aretaeus *Peri Aitiōn* II 11.

[99] Herodian VIII 5.4.

[100] Paragraph 9 in Erwin Preuschen, *Antilegomena: Die Reste der auskanonischen Evangelien und urchristlichen Ueberlieferungen*, Giessen 1901, p. 54.

[101] A. Plummer, *An Exegetical Commentary on the Gospel according to St. Matthew*, Jas. Clarke, 2nd ed., n.d., p. 403, n. 1.

[102] Preisendanz II, p. 101 (13.277).

[103] E. Schweizer, *The Good News according to Matthew*, ET SPCK 1976, p. 516.

[104] Plutarch *de Aemilio* XIV 2.

[105] *Cato Maior* XX 5.

[106] 4 Ezra 13^{32}; Apoc. Bar.39^7 (Syriac).

[107] Sanday and Headlam, *Romans*, ICC T. & T. Clark, 5th ed. 1902, p. 207.

[108] Euripides *Hippolytus* 1204. Also 'panic' in Herodotus VII 10, etc.

[109] Plato *Phaedo* 101B.

[110] P. Oxy 1642.17 (iii AD), P. Lond 2.418.4 (iv AD).

[111] Xenophon *Anabasis* I 2.18, I 8.18, II 2.19, II 4.3, III 1.18, etc.

[112] *Agamemnon* 1243.

[113] Euripides *Medea* 184.

[114] Thucydides V 45.

[115] Thucydides VIII 82. So Euripides *Hippolytus* 572.

[116] Xenophon *Anabasis* I 3.17.

[117] Andocides IV 36, Thucydides I 95, IV 123, Euripides *Alcestis* 1057.

[118] *En phobō* (in fear) = 'reverently'; Selwyn on 1 Pet 1^{17} (p. 143).

[119] Kittel *TWNT* IX s.v.

[120] P. Tebt I 59.10.

S

SABBATH REST

O quanta qualia sunt illa sabbata. – ABELARD

1. κατάπαυσις

In secular Greek *katapausis* is the 'removing' of a man from office,[1] the 'putting down' of despots in the cities and the 'deposing' of Damaratus from his kingship,[2] and the 'ceasing' of Herod's government.[3]

In Biblical Greek it is no longer a putting to rest but **rest** itself, no longer a deposing but a **place of rest**.[4] In contributing to this development the LXX had rendered mainly the Hebrew *nôaḥ* stem. (1) *mᵉnûḥâ*, God's dwelling. It is Zion. 'This is My *rest* for ever; here will I dwell'. (Ps 131(132)[14]). It is the 'rest' in Canaan which 'you are not yet come to'. (Deut 12[9]; Ps 94(95)[11]). It is the sanctuary of God, a 'rest' for His people Israel (cf. Solomon's prayer at the dedication, 3 Km 8[56]). (2) *nûaḥ*, the 'resting' of the holy Ark (Num 10[36]). (3) *nôaḥ*, the 'resting place' of God and the Ark (2 Chr 6[41]). (4) *mānôaḥ*, the resting place of the Ark in the House of the Lord (1 Chr 6[31(16)]). It is the real presence of God with His people, and the people's 'rest' with God in Canaan.

St. Stephen quotes from Isai 66[1] when he refers to the Temple as the place of God's *mᵉnûḥâ* or 'rest' (Act 7[49]), and elsewhere in the NT *katapausis* is confined to Hebrews. There it is said to be reserved for believers and to be unattainable by faithless Jews (Heb 3[11,18], 4[3]). It is not the reward which comes from an initial act of believing but is the result of a faith which perseveres. 'Let us labour ... to enter into that *rest*, lest any man should fall after the same example of unbelief' (4[11]). We should fear lest we come short of the *katapausis* which has been promised us (4[1]).

Belief leads to **rest**, but the connection with the seventh day (Heb 4[4]) suggests that our rest is not yet fully attained, being reserved for the antitypal Sabbath – the final Dispensation, the Kingdom of God and Heaven to follow, i.e. the new Jerusalem (Rev 21). We must hold fast our profession and come boldly to the throne of grace to meet our need. The last stage of salvation must be striven for.

Quod et nos post opera, ideo bona valde quia Tu nobis ea donasti, sabbato vitae aeternae requiescamus in Te. – ST. AUGUSTINE.

2. σαββατισμός

Sabbatismos is a rare secular word,[5] and may even be a coinage of Christian Greek formed from *sabbaton*, a transliteration of Hebrew and Aramaic words (*shabbāth, sheᵇbhath*, etc.). It occurs in the same Christian context as *katapausis* and signifies an antitypal sabbath-rest for the people of God, a last reward obtainable by persevering faith (Heb. 4⁹).

The adjustment between *katapausis* and *sabbatismos* (4⁹) may well be expressive, but it is difficult to see any reason for the change. Perhaps the writer, by equating the words, wants to be sure of relating the concept of *katapausis* to the sabbath Dispensation without leaving any doubt, thus establishing the meaning of *katapausis* in Christian Greek.

Both *katapausis* and *sabbatismos* are the same concept as Paradise (q.v.) if we understand Paradise as a final resting place cognate with the Pauline concept of Glory (q.v.). About this time, our two words were combined in the Ezra apocalypse: 'To you is opened Paradise ... and a Rest (*requies*) is appointed' (4 Ezra 8⁵²).

SACRED SERVICE

λειτουργία

In Christian Greek the word indicates Christian service, seen especially in a sacrificial context, and there is some probability that it signifies the Eucharist.

Secular Greek. *Leitourgia* denoted the discharge of honorary civic office,[6] or any public work, as in the phrase, 'the officer over the *leitourgiai* (public works)'.[7] Sometimes it included a religious sense, service of the gods,[8] signifying in particular the Egyptian priesthood,[9]

Biblical Greek. Here the meaning is always religious. *Leitourgia* in the OT is limited to priestly and levitical ministration. In the LXX it renders chiefly the Hebrew *ʿᵃbhōdhâ* which signifies service of God, specially undertaken by priests and levites (e.g. Num 8²⁵; Lk 1²³; Heb 8⁶, 9²¹). In Christian Greek there is the additional meaning of brotherly beneficence operating in the local church, seen as a sacrifice to God. St. Paul speaks of himself being 'offered', as upon an altar (Ph 2¹⁷), and Epaphras as sacrificing almost his life to supply the Philippians' lack of *leitourgia* (2³⁰). He uses the word to indicate the almsgiving of Corinthian believers (2 Co 9¹²). St. Clement speaks of the *leitourgia* of each Christian apparently in the context of the Eucharist (41^1), and later in connection with the bishop's office ($44^{3,6}$).

The placing of the word *leitourgia* in the context of the Eucharist so early in Christian history naturally raises the question whether this term, having a strong sacrificial sense in Biblical Greek, does not figure in the same context in the NT. Is not St. Paul referring thereby to the offertory gifts at the Breaking of Bread (2 Co 9^{12})? What the Apostle may be saying is that *leitourgia* is not only almsgiving – 'not only supplieth the want of the saints' – but is also a contributory part (*perisseusousa*) of the Eucharist (*eucharistia*) of God. Christ has gotten a more excellent 'liturgy' than that of the old priests (Heb 8^6), and that liturgy may be the Eucharist. The verb *leitourgō* is used of the church at Antioch. It may well mean that 'when they were *offering the liturgy* to the Lord and fasting', the Holy Ghost made His will known (Act 13^2).[10]

SALVATION

THE WORDS, 'SAVE', 'SAVIOUR', 'SALVATION'.

Lord, Who hast form'd me out of mud,
    And hast redeem'd me through Thy bloud
    And sanctifi'd me to do good. – GEORGE HERBERT

The words are older than Christianity but in the Church's vocabulary they hold a special place, indicating a doctrine of Salvation which includes deliverance from spiritual malady. They relate solely with man's relationship to God, avoiding both the Jewish sense of earthly liberation and victory, and the secular sense of well-being, whether of body or mind. Salvation, in the Christian vocabulary, is accomplished by God alone, with no help from man.

Ross has analysed the Biblical concept[11] and has shown that the Christian environment made huge semantic contributions to the words. Ideas were brought over from the LXX, from general Hellenistic culture (demons and angels), from Stoic ethics, from secular philosophy (immortality). However, these pagan contributions had also Hebraic roots and the greatest influence by far came from the old Hebrew prophecies, the Psalms, and from the Maccabaean movement.[12] Our period was one of great ferment of thought and ideological adjustment. There was conflict with Judaism, with the imperial cult, with Gnosticism, and probably conflict within the Church herself. Everywhere there were healer cults, and a large number of healing legends and performances of resurrections.

TO SAVE
σώζω

Secular Greek. Among the meanings of the verb *sōzō* were healing, keeping, preserving from danger, and rescuing. The common expression, 'Be saved!' probably meant, 'Be well!'[13] A papyrus refers to a life 'saved' in sickness by the great god, Soenopaeus.[14]

The verb included recovery from famine[15] and rescue from danger at sea.[16] It included the preservation of inanimate things,[17] such as the State.[18] 'Our fighting the battle in the strait', writes Thucydides, extolling the wisdom of Themistocles, 'certainly *saved* the matter' (I 74).

It is to 'keep' a secret. In tragic drama Prometheus 'preserves' the fateful information which was told him by his mother, to be a bargaining counter with Zeus. He says, 'At all cost this must be kept secret, for by *preserving* it (*sōzō*), I will escape my bonds.'[19]

It is to 'recover' an opportunity. 'Men of Athens, in important transactions opportunities are often short-lived. Once surrendered, they cannot be *recovered*.'[20] It is used of 'preserving' documents in a temple.[21]

It is to 'keep' in mind, to remember. Plato debates whether a man with a bad memory should be enrolled among lovers of wisdom. 'He could not *keep* what he learned.'[22]

Christian Greek. Several of the senses are found in the NT, but to a small extent when compared with the Christian enrichment of the verb. *Sōzō* is an instance where a word of general character has been closely associated with the Church's doctrine of Salvation and has absorbed special meanings of deliverance from spiritual malady: even the old therapeutic sense was seen through Christian eyes as deliverance from spiritual powers. 'Your faith has *made you well*' (Mt 9[22]). To the Christian understanding, Jesus was saying, 'Your faith has saved you from the powers that enslaved your body'.

Sōzō in its new dress is conceived by NT writers in three distinct stages of accomplishment.[23]

1. A past experience of release, relating to the time when the Christian first believed. We are already saved. The experience has abiding results but, viewed initially, it may be described as forgiveness and remission of sin. From this standpoint it can be said, 'We *were* saved by hope' (Ro 8[24]) and '*have been* saved by grace' (Eph 2[5,8]) God *has* saved us, not according to our works of righteousness but according to His own purpose and grace and mercy (2 Ti 1[9]; Tit 3[5]). That is in the believer's retrospection.

2. There is however a present and prolonged experience, which can be called sanctification, involving the progressive deliverance of the believer from the 'old man', his former self. We are being saved. Daily, such as *should be* saved are added to the Church (Act 2^{47}) and they *are being* saved now (1 Co 1^{18}) by the preaching. The Gospel is more than an initial call to become a Christian, and salvation's second stage is to have Christ always in mind, a care not to have believed in vain (1 Co 15^2) and an endeavour to be a sweet savour of Him (2 Co 2^{15}). Believers are in the way of 'being saved' at the present time.

3. A future experience of salvation yet remains – the glorification at the peak of the ladder of holiness when 'he that endureth to the end shall be saved' (Mt 10^{22}). It is subsequent salvation, nearer than when we believed (Ro 13^{11}), and worked out with fear and trembling (Ph 2^{12}). Not utterly realized until Christ appears the second time (Heb 9^{28}), it will take in more than man's salvation. 'The whole creation groaneth and travaileth', and 'the creature itself also shall be delivered from the bondage of corruption' (Ro $8^{21f.}$).

Where very much more than our own salvation is at stake we would be perverse if we squeezed St. Paul's lavish words through an anthropocentric tourniquet and supposed that man is salvation's exclusive legatee.[24] The scope of redemption is vast.

St. Paul's christology is splendidly cosmic in extent. The Principalities and the Powers, with the *stoicheia* (see 'Demons') figure spectacularly in the discussion of the Christian's wrestling and of Christ's awesome triumph on the cross. The universe is hungry for redress and all the hidden powers in all the hidden places share the atonement which He gives. J. G. Gibbs concludes a critical survey of this field by demonstrating that St. Paul's 'cosmic Christology is congruent with other early Christian affirmations of Jesus' sovereignty over the creation, a sovereignty the redemptive purpose of which was not limited, neither for Paul nor for others, to justified persons or even to the Church as a whole, for the scope of the Lord's redemption is cosmic'.[25]

SAVIOUR

σωτήρ

Secular Greek. A *sōtēr* is a deliverer and a preserver from disease and physical ill, and yet the word had been used already by pagans in a moral and religious sense. Epicurus, philosopher and mentor, is 'our Saviour'.[26] Zeus is called Saviour, especially in his temples at harbours where thanksgiving was rendered for a safe voyage.[27] At banquets and drinking parties the third cup was toasted as a libation to 'Zeus *Sōtēr*' for a token of good fortune – hence the saying, 'Third time lucky', and the third cup became proverbially the *tritos sōtēr*, the third Saviour.[28] At the end of the play, Libation Bearers, the chorus declares that for the third time the tempest of the race has burst upon the royal house. 'And now a third, a Deliverer (*sōtēr*), has come – or shall I say a doom?' Orestes is overtaken by his mother's vengeance.[29]

Other gods were called Saviour – Apollo, Hermes, Asclepius – especially tutelary gods, and the heavenly Twins who empowered wind and waves. Ptolemy IV Philopator was hailed, 'O king, universal Saviour of all',[30] and the title was used of Euergetes I,[31] and often of Roman emperors and governors,[32] as is borne out by several inscriptions.[33]

There is no very early use of *sōtēr* for a god in anything like the Christian sense in the Mystery religions. The case cited by Bousset[34] where *sōtēr* applies to Serapis and Isis in the reign of Ptolemy IV does not, as Fuller indeed allows, really mean anything more than a favour received and does not involve a theological sense of salvation from death.[35]

The salvation brought by the *sōtēr*, whether it concerns gods or prominent men, extends no further than temporal help in this life, such as healing (Asclepius) or at best admission to the hereafter (Serapis and Isis), and falls short of the threefold implication of security in Jesus. Dr. Kingsley Barrett is convincing when he concludes that in part St. John's terminology and doctrine of salvation is drawn from Greek sources, but that 'he has behind him the Old Testament conception of, and hope for, salvation and the primitive Christian conviction that the hope was fulfilled in Jesus'.[36]

Christian Greek. The *Sōtēr* which is Christ the Lord, the only wise God, the Saviour of the world, raised up for Israel, Saviour of the Church and of all men, especially of those that believe, was sent by the Father.[37] The *Sōtēr* is said to be God (1 Ti 1[1], 2[3]; Tit 1[3], 2[10]) or 'the great God and our Saviour Jesus' (Tit 2[13]). St. Mary sang of 'God my Saviour', whether of her Son or the Triune Godhead. By *sōtēr* she intended no secular deliverer.

Commenting on Jn 3[17] Dr. Kingsley Barrett aptly says that no stress here is laid 'upon anything from which the world is saved; it is in fact saved from being itself.[38] From what then does He 'save' His people? From sins and from spiritual death and from all iniquity (Act 5[31]; 2 Ti 1[10]; Tit 2[13]) – with which there is no parallel in the word's secular usage. He is a Saviour not merely from what had gone before. We look for a *Sōtēr* from heaven, a Saviour at His appearing (Ph 3[20]; 2 Ti 1[10]). His security is continuous, His guiding,

His enlightenment, His strengthening, His comfort, lasts through every process of sanctification till glorification is seen in body, soul, and spirit. By the parallelism of Jn 3[16,17] it seems that the world's 'salvation' consists in having *aiōnios* life.

SALVATION

1. σωτηρία

Sōtēria has secular meanings of victory, deliverance, preservation, security and, in later post-Christian papyri, bodily health. In secular Greek *sōtēria* had moreover been 'a means of safety', a safe return, and a security or guarantee.

In the second century, a soldier named Apion writes home to his father, 'I thank the lord Serapis [a god] that when I was in danger at sea he saved me (*sōzō*). ... Write me a few lines about your health (*sōtēria*).[39] From this district of the Fayûm comes an illiterate letter of an anxious mother about her boy's bad foot. 'I went to Serapion', she writes, 'and asked about your health (*sōtēria*) and your children's. ... Write to me about your *sōtēria*.'[40]

In Christian usage an instance of the secular meaning of *sōtēria* survives in St. Luke's travel narrative – 'take some meat ... for your *health*' (Act 27[34]) – for in this part of Acts the author resorts to secularisms.[41] Elsewhere he adopts the OT view of *sōtēria*, based on the Hebrew *yᵉshû'â*, Israel's national deliverance (Lk 1[69,71,77]), particularly the escape from Egypt (Act 7[25]). *Sōtēria* is Noah's deliverance by means of the Ark (Heb 11[7]), but elsewhere in the NT *sōtēria* is predominantly used by St. Paul and is usually the Christian salvation.[42]

St. Paul sees it as a process culminating in glory after much suffering on earth. In the darkness of this world, mid rioting and drunkenness, chambering and wantonness, strife and envying, the pilgrim's night is far spent. His final bliss, his *sōtēria*, is nearer than when he committed himself (Ro 13[11]). Godly sorrow in the meantime is to be expected, ending in a *sōtēria* which will not disappoint him at last (2 Co 2[7]). Hope in all troubles centres in that full salvation to which he is appointed. For he is 'elect' and he is 'chosen' to obtain it, with eternal glory (1 Th 5[8f.]; 2 Ti 2[10]).

The way of reaching the haven is a process of sanctification, the second stage of *sōtēria*. Writing to the Corinthian saints, the *hagioi*, St. Paul reminds them that he is afflicted for their 'salvation', which is effectual if they endure the same sorrows as he, and are consoled by the same consolation (2 Co 1[6]). Believers are 'chosen' to it through sanctification of the Spirit (2 Th 2[13]). Quoting Isaiah he affirms that *now* is the day of *sōtēria* – the growth in holiness which is its second stage, achieved by grace. 'Receive not the grace of God in vain!' he warns (2 Co 6²).

St. Paul's appeal to holy Writ is no literary device. Knowledge of God's Word imparts a wisdom which accelerates ultimate *sōtēria* (2 Ti 3¹⁵).

Among their foes, in the loneliness and vulnerability of his absence, saints at Philippi have to work out their 'salvation' with fear and trembling (Ph 2¹²). Their foes are a token of their 'salvation', for the saints are sanctified through their sufferings for Christ, no less than the Apostle himself who humbly avers that his own afflictions and bonds, through their prayers for him, will turn to his *sōtēria*, as he daily is more sanctified (Ph 1¹⁹⁻²⁸).

When the Apostle recalls 'the Gospel of your *salvation*' (Eph 1¹³) for the Jew and then for the Gentile (Ro 1¹⁶), he cannot mean the initial call to repentance and faith, but affirms a divine succour leading all through life to a summit of glory. Belief of the heart sets justification going, the initial forgiveness and welcome, but belief of the heart does not suffice alone for ultimate *sōtēria*. That is achieved by 'confession with the mouth' (Ro 10¹⁰). There are three phases: justification, sanctification, glorification. Christians, said St. Augustine, must remember that faith alone without good works is not sufficient for salvation.[43]

One may be an heir of salvation and not yet a beneficiary, for there intervenes a season of confession or suffering in which angels minister (Heb 1¹⁴). The Captain of our salvation set the example by Himself being perfected on a sanctifying road of suffering, thus bringing many sons to salvation's true end (Heb 2¹⁰). Being perfected He became the Author of *aiōnios* salvation – a very lasting thing, belonging to the Age to come – unto all them that obey Him (5⁹). 'How shall we escape if we neglect so great *salvation*?' (2³).

The author's fearful warnings persist: the items that attend salvation, the tedious and difficult route to glory, will not be apostasy, and the putting of the Son of God to an open shame and the bearing of no better fruit than thorns and briars (6⁹). The truth is that good works are the fruits of faith, following after 'justification', and though they cannot put away our sins and though they endure the severity of God's judgment, are nevertheless pleasing to God in Christ and spring necessarily from a faith which is genuine. Indeed, as St. James vigorously affirms, the genuineness of faith may be known by good works, just as a tree is discerned by its fruit.[44] Only if we look for Christ, says the inspired writer, will His second Coming be 'unto salvation' (Heb. 9²⁸).

Today is St. Peter's 'last time', when salvation shall be revealed for those who are kept by the power of God through faith, having passed a weary pilgrimage of fiery trial 'for a season', to issue in rejoicing and glory, 'the end of your faith' (1 Pet. 1[5,9]).

The finality of *sōtēria*, the third stage, is confirmed in the song of heaven: 'Now is come salvation', that is, when the age of grace is done and after Michael's triumphant war (Rev 12[10]). It is indeed an *aiōnios* salvation (Heb 5[9]), a glorification in the Dispensation to follow. A great voice from heaven greets its coming. 'Alleluia, *sōtēria* and glory!' (Rev 19[1]).

2. σωτήριον

Sōtērion is a rarer word, the neuter of the adjective *sōtērios*, usually plural in secular Greek, signifying delivering and life-sustaining, as well as a thank-offering for deliverance. During a speech of Xenophon a man sneezed – lucky sign, especially as it came just as Xenophon uttered the word '*sōtēria*' (deliverance). As one man, the soldiers present all made obeisance to Zeus *Sōtēr* who had sent the omen, and Xenophon went on, 'I move, gentlemen, that we make a vow to sacrifice thank-offerings for deliverance (*sōtēria*, plural), to that god as soon as we reach a friendly land.'[45]

A little later the author uses the word *sōtērion* again. 'The preceding narrative', he says, 'has described ... how the Greeks ... paid the *sōtēria* (plural) which they had vowed to sacrifice ... when they should reach a friendly land.'[46]

Like *sōtēria*, however, it is a LXX word for the Hebrew *yᵉshû'â*, and in the NT two of the four instances concern Israel's Messiah and messianic Kingdom (Lk 2[30], 3[6]), and two concern Christian salvation (Act 28[28]; Eph 6[17]). As with *sōtēria* above, it is linked with practical faith, for it is a gift which must be 'taken', a weapon to be used in Christian warfare with watching and perseverance – 'take the helmet of *sōtērion*' (Eph 6[17]), or 'the helmet *as a means of salvation*'.[47] *Sōtērion* may be the noun of the instrument, the means of salvation (Ross's *nomen instrumenti*).

In Tit 2[11] the adjective *sōtērios* means, 'bringing salvation'.

SALVATION COMPLETE (AV. REDEMPTION)
ἀπολύτρωσις

Finish then Thy new creation,
Pure and spotless let us be,
Let us see Thy great salvation
Perfectly restored in Thee. – CH. WESLEY

In the Christian vocabulary *apolutrōsis* represents God's consummate salvation which embraces forgiveness, sanctification and glorification.

Secular Greek. The meaning of the rather rare word was either a holding up to hostage or deliverance by the payment of hostage. In Plutarch it is the holding to ransom of captive cities,[48] in Josephus the ransoming of prisoners,[49] in the Letter of Aristeas (12[33]) the ransom price for release of captives, while in Philo it is said that a boy who was a captive slave despaired of *apolutrōsis* (a ransom) and committed suicide.[50] The late Mr. E. K. Simpson noted two passages, in Menander and Strabo, which the lexicons have missed and in which, as elsewhere in literary Greek, a specific payment is expressed or implied.[51]

Biblical Greek. There is in the Bible a focus on the meaning, 'deliverance' as such. The payment of a ransom becomes less relevant, concern being less with the means than with the end. In a passage of Daniel where there is no extant Semitic original (4[30(33)]C) and where the concern is with Nebuchadnezzar's 'recovery' from his notorious affliction, and payment of ransom is beside the point, what is meant is only, 'The time of my *recovery* came'.

Neither in this passage, nor in the two places in the epistle to the Hebrews, are we likely to introduce a thought of ransoming unless we are engrossed with the secular use of *apolutrōsis*.

In Heb 9[15] the writer reasons from the old Covenant to the new and to Jesus who effects a deliverance (*apolutrōsis*) by taking away transgressions. The concept of death enters, not as a ransom paid, but to afford a play on the two meanings of the term *diathēkē* (will and covenant): where there is a will there must be a death.

The other passage is 11[35] which touches the martyrdom of the Maccabees: they were tortured, not accepting *apolutrōsis* (deliverance). In this instance the Greek word will not mean 'ransom'. No one was expected to offer payment on the martyrs' behalf, and their only hope, far from being a ransom, was recantation. It is pedantic to regard the recantation as itself a ransom![52]

In the rest of the NT, in St. Luke and St. Paul, the new meaning of *apolutrōsis* is manifest. Jesus warned that the Son of Man comes after certain signs at which His disciples may look up, for their *apolutrōsis* draws nigh (Lk 21[28]). What is intended by the term is evidently the final stage of salvation, their deliverance from sin's power, from suffering and death, their glorification at the Coming of the Lord, their fully restored communion with God.

St. Paul distinguishes justification, the initial moment of the gracious work, from the final stage. The forgiveness of our trespasses (Eph 1[7]) traces only the first moment but a little later St. Paul describes the effects of *apolutrōsis* when it gathers in one all things in Christ and we find our inheritance in Him (Eph 1[10]). St. Paul can state that justification is through the *apolutrōsis* because he is acknowledging forgiveness to be but one part of full salvation (Ro 3[24]). Indeed, *apolutrōsis* is equated explicitly with 'adoption' (q.v.), that is, the final and full reclamation of all created things (Ro 8[23]) which includes the *apolutrōsis* of 'this vile body', to make it resemble His glorious body. It is the perfecting climax in the work of grace; it is glorification.

St. Paul realises three stages: first, God's forgiveness; second, sanctification and growth in grace; third, glorification, to which the term *apolutrōsis* belongs (1 Co 1[30]). The stages are seen from a further angle as St. Paul opens his letter to the Ephesians: first, there is the choosing of us (verse 4); then the predestinating of us (verse 5); then, the acceptance of us (verse 6); and finally, the *apolutrōsis* (verse 7). The climax of all is reached in the Dispensation (oikonomia) to come (verse 10). After this rehearsing, he leaps to the passionate flight of ineffable oratory which occupies the first chapter of Ephesians, and St. Paul must presently go through the stages once more: predestination (verse 11), belief in Christ (verse 13), our being 'sealed' (verse 13), and our consummating *apolutrōsis* (verse 14). The last stage still more has to do with the Holy Spirit's power. By Him we are 'sealed unto the day of *apolutrōsis*' (Eph 4[30]). He moves to our rescue in the war with world, flesh and Devil; He intercedes with unutterable groanings until holiness and rehabilitation are complete, until beatification and all the gracious work be done and we share His throne (Ro 8). St. Paul was praying for the Colossians' increase in grace when he mentioned their *apolutrōsis* (Col 1[9-14]).

So, while the concept of a payment is inherent in the secular use of the word, its contexts in the Bible on the other hand are much wider. [53]

The ultimate triumph of the Cross was prefigured in the frequent appearance of a rod and tree in the OT. St. Justin Martyr offers the instance of Moses extending his rod over the sea when he was sent by God for the *apolutrōsis* of the people. The word for Justin bears much upon the Cross and upon deliverance, and there is no hint of ransom-payment (*Dial.* 86[1]).

SANCTIFICATION (SPIRITUAL RENEWING)
ἀνακαίνωσις: ἀνακαινόω

Anakainōsis, unlike the parallel word *palingenesia* (regeneration), does not appear in the secular language (Bauer). Neither the noun nor the verb *anakainō* have been traced earlier than St. Paul 'who might very well coin a word of this sort' (MM). Christians may have wished to have at hand a neutral term to express spiritual renewing, untainted by previous association, an indifferent vehicle of Christian thought.

After the earlier soteriological chapters of Romans St. Paul passes at chapter 12 to the effectual outflow of all this doctrine in the life of the believer and begins with the expression, 'Be ye transformed by the renewing (*anakainōsis*) of your mind' (12²). The Apostle envisages, not a new birth (*palingenesia*) – not a birth from above or anew (Jn 3³; 1 Jn 5⁴) – not a birth from God (*theogenesia*),[54] but rather the second stage in the process of a believer's salvation, the sanctification which follows regeneration and baptism. Much may be learned of *anakainōsis* by closely comparing it with *palingenesia*. When St. Paul writes to Titus, he puts side by side the two terms and the two stages which they represent: 'according to His mercy He saved us, by the washing of *palingenesia* (regeneration) and *anakainōsis* (subsequent renewing) of the Holy Ghost' (3⁵).

Palingenesia and *anakainōsis* are parallel terms, then, but there is a clear distinction. *Palingenesia* to the Stoic was the periodic re-animation of nature. For Philo[55] and St. Clement (1 Clem 9⁴) it was cosmological – revivification after the Flood. It has a national sense in Josephus.[56] It is equated with reincarnation (*metensōmatōsis*) in some Hellenistic writers.[57] For Dibelius[58] there is in Judaism no real analogy to the Christian use of *palingenesia*, and the thought-world of the Mysteries provides better parallels (see Bauer, s.v.). Dibelius points to: (1) Apuleius[59] in a later period, where the term is closely connected with the transfer of vital powers in the cult. (2) The so-called 'Mithras Liturgy' in the great Parisian magical papyrus[60] where, though the term does not occur, there is *genesis athanatos* (immortal birth) and the term *palingenomenos* (born again).

(3) The Hermetic secret discourse on Rebirth,[61] where Hermes explains *palingenesia* as the going forth into an immortal body, an experience of being born in the mind. Knowledge of God, which is a concept dear to St. John, is represented in the Discourse as bestowing eternal life and is a quality belonging to those who have passed through 'rebirth' from the dominion of body and flesh into

399

that of spirit and mind.[62] It should further be noted that in a passage of Philo,[63] *palingenesia* designates life after death, when 'we who are joined to the body ... shall be no more but shall go forward to our *re-birth*'. We do not know whether the discourse on Rebirth displays Christian influence or not, but it is one of the later *Hermetica* belonging to a period when Christianity was established in Egypt, and the Biblical influence may be explained by acquaintance with the LXX. Reitzenstein denied Christian influence. Scott acknowledged it as possible.The word *palingenesia* itself is pre-Christian (Philo, early Stoics), but Dodd went so far as to suppose that the impulse to use the figure of rebirth may have been partly due to Christian influence. He felt that in any case the figure conveyed to the Hermetist ideas which were already familiar to his school and 'not felt in any way as an alien intrusion'. The idea of re-birth will belong to the common background of thought – 'the kind of public which, as I take it, John had in view'.[64] There is probably no substantial borrowing on either side, the Hermetist's or St. John's.

Dibelius confessed that one ought not to under-estimate the differences between Hellenistic and Christian re-birth. For instance, in the Mithras Liturgy in the mystery described by Apuleius, the ecstasy of re-birth extends for a brief time (*pros oligon*), whereas for the Christian re-birth is a new and lasting life. The Christian context of *palingenesia* (Tit 3[5]) knows nothing of ecstasy but only lasting power. In Christian Greek the term represents an experience which is not solely available to certain individual mystics but is the fundamental event and lasting joy of all Christians.[65]

Palingenesia, then, will not be a uniquely Christian term, and even within the sacred vocabulary it has a wider reference than that of spiritual new birth, for in the report of our Lord's words (Mt 19[28]) it has an eschatological sense referring to the new messianic Age.

Besides *palingenesia* there is a further apparent synonym of *anakainō* in the word *anagennō*. The latter term again expresses man's regeneration. It is parallel with *palingenesia*, rather than with *anakainō/anakainōsis*. It is uncertain where St. Peter found the word. Büchsel doubts whether he took it from the Mysteries, even although the Mysteries may have influenced his language, and thinks it more likely that the term came from general usage. The point is that *anagennō* has acquired in the Christian vocabulary a new interpretation: it denotes a special bounty of regeneration which God has granted to Christians.[66]

Anakainōsis, on the other hand, is a uniquely Christian term and it comes near to the 'newness of life' which St. Paul declares to be the believer's portion after he has been justified and baptized (Ro 6⁴). The verb *anakainō* is twice used by the Apostle and in precisely this sense. The inward man, he declares, is 'renewed' day by day (2 Co 4¹⁶). The older we get the more our earthly faculties perish, and the closer we are to Life and Glory. Day by day a further step is taken on the road of sanctification. Another time he declares that the 'new man', which cannot wear out but only grows in stature, is 'renewed' in knowledge (*epignōsis*, consciousness of God and of spiritual truth) after the 'icon' of God who made us (Col 3¹⁰).

The pilgrim's journey is not taken far without constant aid of the Holy Ghost and let us ask God, in the nicely chosen words of the collect, to grant that 'we being regenerate (*palingenesia*), and made Thy children by adoption (*huiothesia*) and grace (*charis*), may daily be renewed (*anakainōsis*) by Thy Holy Spirit'. The Christmas collect makes proper use of Scriptural terms.

In his vision of the seven women Hermas enquired when the End should be, and was told, 'The *anakainōsis* (renewal) of your spirits is sufficient for you and for the saints' (*Vis.* III 8.9). St. Basil and other later writers understood the word to apply to the re-birth by the Holy Ghost in baptism,[67] but they scarcely maintain the helpful distinction that St. Paul makes when writing to Titus, 'the washing of regeneration (*palingenesia*) and renewing (*anakainōsis*) of the Holy Ghost' (3⁵).

Palingenesia comes first in the believer's experience, and then day by day *anakainōsis* follows.

SANCTITY

ἅγιος : ἁγιωσύνη : ἁγιότης

Hagios, hagiōsunē and *hagiotēs* are older words which in the Christian vocabulary represent the image of the 'sacred', that which is separated and consecrated to God alone.

Secular Greek. *Hagios* means 'devoted to the gods', with an application to a temple, devoted perhaps to Aphrodite,[68] or to oriental sanctuaries,[69] or to respected persons.[70] *Hagnos*, however, more usually expresses the idea in pagan Greek. The words become characteristically Christian, denoting the sanctity of God and the Church, of saints and of holy places. From the sixth century a complimentary address to bishops is, 'Your Holiness' (*hagiōsunē*).

Biblical Greek. *Hagios* translates most usually the Hebrew *qds* stem (setting apart, consecration). *Hagiōsunē* too translates this stem. 'Give thanks at the remembrance of His *holiness*' (Ps 29(30)⁴,

$96(97)^{12}$). Besides, it renders words for the 'splendour' and 'might' of God who is transcendent. Two phrases are, 'the majesty of the glory of the *splendour*' (*hôdh*) and, 'might and majesty' (*'ōz*) in Ps $144(145)^5$, $95(96)^6$.

In considering salvation at its progressive levels, Christians paid great heed to the notion of separation which is inherent in *qds*. It is noteworthy that they applied the adjective *hagios* equally to God, the 'Holy' Ghost, the Lord whose name is 'holy' (Lk 1^{49}), to the 'holy' Father (Jn 17^{11}), to Christ (Mk 1^{24}; Jn 6^{69}; Act 3^{14}, 4^{30}; Rev 3^7), and to the thrice-'holy' God Almighty (Rev 4^8) – even to angels (1 Th 3^{13}), to prophets (Lk 1^{70}), to John (Mk 6^{20}), to apostles (Eph 3^5). Christians saw their own sanctification as no less momentous: they too were *hagioi* (Act 9^{13}; Ro 1^7; Eph 1^4; Heb 6^{10}; Rev 5^8), and so too even their children (1 Co 7^{14}).

It is urged that so special an application of *hagios* is not exclusively Christian, being found in pagan religious use as a divine title on inscriptions of the first century AD (e.g. OGI 378.1), but a study of its Christian application in the texts will reveal that the concept of 'sacred' gained a very different meaning from what was current among pagans.

It is difficult to find a real distinction between the two words for sanctity, *hagiotēs* and *hagiōsunē*. The former is a rare word in the Bible but it refers to the saintliness of Christ which we are called upon to share (Heb 12^{10}), and it occurs as a variant reading, witnessed by Sinaiticus, Vaticanus and the Chester Beatty papyrus, at 2 Co 1^{12} where saintliness and sincerity are contrasted with 'fleshly wisdom'.[71] But *hagiōsunē* too represents the unblameable saintliness which was in Christ and which we must perfect in ourselves (Ro 1^4; 2 Co 7^1; 1 Th 3^{13}).

See also 'Consecration'.

SCRIBE

γραμματεύς : νομικός : νομοδιδάσκαλος

Within the Christian vocabulary all three words, *grammateus, nomikos* and *nomodidaskalos*, are used in the special Jewish sense of 'scribe'.

In classical Greek, 'the *grammateus* of the city' had been an official at Athens.[72] Demosthenes is contemptuous of a 'pestilent *official*' (XVIII 127), and Aeschylus refers to a 'wise *grammateus*', a scholar.[73] In the vernacular of ii BC the *grammateus* was a 'military officer'.[74]

It has this sense sometimes in the LXX (Jer 52^{25}; 1 Mac 5^{42}) and

Symmachus (Jg 5[14]; Jer 44(37)[15]), but the term is frequent in the gospels for a Jewish *sōphēr* (scribe). However, St. Luke uses the word in the classical sense to describe the official (the 'clerk') who procured order during the silversmiths' riot at Ephesus (Act 19[35]).

In secular Greek our second word, *nomikos*, had the adjectival meaning, 'relating to law' (as Tit 3[9]) and as a noun it had signified a lawyer or legal adviser.[75] Only in Biblical and Christian Greek do *grammateus* and *nomikos* indicate a doctor of Jewish law. Indeed, our third word, *nomodidaskalos*, is a coinage of Christian Greek (Bauer), the nearest secular word being the *nomodidaktēs* of Plutarch.

The teacher (doctor) of the Law was a Jewish scholar devoted to the Scriptures. Ezra was a *grammateus* skilled in the *Tôrâ* (1 Esd 8[3]). Eleazar, who was brought before Antiochus for torture, was a priest and a *nomikos* (4 Mac 5[4]). Although the term *grammateus* is frequent in the gospels, St. Luke has two alternative words, *nomikos* and *nomodidaskalos*, for the same idea. *Grammateus* is not found in the apostolic Fathers, but St. Paul has it in a derogatory sense, likening the learning of a *grammateus* to the wisdom of this dispensation which God has made foolish (1 Co 1[20]). Enoch is the '*grammateus* of righteousness' (T. Abr. 115[19]), for his task was to 'write' the deeds of each soul.

Both the *grammateus* and the *nomikos* are closely connected with the Pharisees (Mt 23[13]; Lk 7[30], 11[44, 45f, 52f], 14[3]) and the *grammateus* cannot well be distinguished from the *nomikos*.[76] St. Mark avoids *nomikos* and has *grammateus* for the Pharisee who plied Jesus with questions (12[28]), but Matthew and Luke have *nomikos* for the same individual (Mt 22[35]; Lk 10[25]). Zenas the *nomikos* appears in the early Church (Tit 3[13]), and some commentators have thought that he was a scribe in the OT sense (Chrysostom, Jerome), while others take the word generally of a lawyer. Was there such a thing as a Christian *grammateus*, 'instructed in the Kingdom of Heaven', along with the prophets and *sophoi* (wise men) who seem to be Christian missionaries, parallel to 'prophets and apostles' in St. Luke's version? (Mt 13[52], 23[34]). Our Lord's words as recorded by St. Matthew seem to fit better in the Jewish context of God's dealings with the Israelite nation.[77]

Our third term, *nomodidaskalos*, appears but three times, twice used by St. Luke for a scribe closely allied to the Pharisees (5[17]). He thus denotes Gamaliel (Act 5[34]). St. Paul however gives the *nomodidaskalos* a bad name. He is a heretic of some Jewish-Christian sect who failed to understand that Christian love is the goal of all the commandments and who was preoccupied with fables and genealogies (1 Ti 1[7]). The term 'failed to establish itself in New

Testament terminology',[78] whatever St. Paul may have understood by it.

THE SECOND COMING

1. παρουσία

Parousia is a special Christian term, not for the Last Day or a final Day of Judgment, but for the return of our Lord to earth, to the scene of His sufferings on our behalf.

Secular Greek. The general sense of *parousia* in Greek is both 'presence' and 'arrival'. 'The light of the house I deem to be the *presence* of its Lord.'[79] 'Would one of you announce our *arrival*?'[80] Dionysius of Halicarnassus (I 45) refers to the 'arrival' of Aeneas in Italy. The same meaning is often found in Biblical Greek – of the 'arrival' of Stephanas and Paul, of Titus, and of the Wicked One. *Parousia* is Paul's 'presence' as opposed to his absence.[81] In OT Greek *parousia* denoted the 'coming' of Judith (10^{18}), an army's 'approach' (2 Mac 8^{12}) and someone's 'presence' (3 Mac 3^{17}).

Examples from the secular papyri lead one to suppose that *parousia* has some innate reference to a royal visit during which certain prerogatives were exercised and taxes levied to furnish the royal personage with a crown.[82] Vernacular evidence, therefore, lends some point to St. Paul's use of *parousia*, for in one instance he seems to contrast the world's rulers with Christ in the sense that Christ gives, rather than takes, a diadem at His *parousia* – the crown of righteousness (2 Ti 4^8). It is an instance of secular influence contributing to a Christian word.

Another circumstance of the pagan *parousia*, the royal visit, was the dating of periods of time from it, and it lends considerable point to the implication that Christ's *parousia* will inaugurate a new *aiōn*, a new dispensation of time (2 Pet 3^{12f}).

Christian Greek. Like many another of the peculiar Christian terms, *parousia* is an instance where a pagan word was adopted for a special use. *Parousia* is now a cliché for the next Coming of our Lord. 'Second Coming' is not a term which is found literally in Scripture, although it expresses well enough the Christian sense of *parousia*. 'Thy *parousia*' is placed in conjunction with eschatological events (Mt 24^3) and the *parousia* of the Son of Man is said to be like lightning flashing (24^{27}), or like the days of Noah (^{37}), catastrophic (^{39}), accompanied by all His saints (1 Th 3^{13}). So, as early as St. Justin at least, it was obvious to Christians that they should give the qualification 'second' (*deuteron*) to the next *parousia* of our Lord (*Apol.* I 52).

The Second Coming is not precisely contemporary with the End of the world. Some, but not all, shall rise from the dead at His *parousia* – it marks no final resurrection, only that of the departed Christians (1 Th 4[16]). 'Then cometh the End', at a subsequent time, and not until the End is death destroyed (1 Co 15[23-26]). In the meantime we must suppose that people go on living and dying, even after the *parousia*. St. Paul envisaged that some of his own generation might still be alive when the Lord comes, for he uses 'we' (1 Th 4[15]) – as does St. John (1 Jn 2[28]). St. James believed that the momentous time was imminent and he called for patience (Jas 5[7f]). No one knows the time. In the intervening period all manner of indisciplined scoffers are expected to appear, making light of the *parousia* (2 Pet 3[4]). Further details about the Coming are given. St. Paul's own life is said to be set at a period in which 'the mystery of iniquity' was at work and in which a certain Restrainer was in force to modify the effects of wickedness. The Restrainer would one day go and the Wicked One would be revealed – that Man of Sin whom the Lord shall destroy with the brightness of His *parousia* (2 Th 2[8]). The Second Coming, then, is to be preceded immediately by an apostasy and by a régime of one who reigns with power and signs and lying wonders (2 Th 2[9ff]).

There is no alternative but to understand that the *parousia* of Christ takes place in two distinct phases, each separated from the other by an interval of time. The victorious revelation of Jesus in great power is evidently not the whole *parousia*, but it is the more dramatic aspect of it. The Lord Jesus is 'revealed from heaven', when He comes to end the régime of the Man of Sin (2 Th 1[8ff]), and He is said to be 'admired' by all believers and to be accompanied by 'all His saints' (1 Th 3[13]) – and 'all' must include those who have been removed from the earth 'to meet the Lord' at the *parousia* during the apostasy in the Man of Sin's régime (1 Th 4[17]). This will be a preliminary phase and seems to be quite secret. Nevertheless, in the culminating phase of the *parousia* these 'snatched away' saints shall 'accompany' the Lord, shall come *with* Him, not come to *meet* Him. Can it be that the Restrainer who at present holds the forces of wickedness at bay is the Church on earth? Nothing among the several alternatives that have been offered to explain the 'Restrainer' seems to me as probable as the Church, the 'salt' which has kept its savour, the City on the hill, the Light which shines in a dark world, the check to wickedness and the constraint against the rising tide of godlessness. What if the Church should be taken away, and what if that removal should coincide with the first, the secret, *parousia*? Then a darkness would fall upon mankind and the Man of Sin would be quite unrestrained for a time.

The public apparition of Christ, the bright *parousia*, comes after such a régime, after the first resurrection of all God's faithful departed, after the 'snatching away' (*harpagēsometha* 1 Th 4[17]) of the living saints to meet Him secretly at His Coming 'like a thief in the night'. The two phases of the *parousia* become clearer.

The NT itself makes a further distinction besides. The *parousia* of Christ is evidently not the *parousia* of the day of God, which is a later event altogether, when the elements and heaven itself shall be dissolved to make way for 'new heavens and a new earth' (2 Pet 3[12]; Rev 21[1]). Evidently the Second Coming, the *parousia* of Christ in both its phases, is a preliminary event before the End. It is not conceived as a final Day. It takes place in the ungodly times of the Man of Sin.

Sometimes there is said to be a difference between eschatology as conceived by the Seer of Patmos and that of Jesus and Paul. Some have demonstrated[83] the Seer's lack of concern with what is called 'sub-eschatology' or the events immediately preceding the *parousia*. It is urged that when St. John reports the words, 'Be thou faithful unto death, and I will give thee a crown of life' (Rev 2[10]), he presupposes that death alone gives entrance to the future life. The martyrs' intermediate state, it is believed, is consummated only at the general resurrection (6[9ff], 20[11-15]). However, despite such reasoning, there is little doubt that the notion of a transitional intermediate Kingdom (1 Co 15[24]; Rev 20[4]) is essential to the eschatological scheme present in both St. Paul's letters and in Revelation.[84]

Not all Christians have welcomed an interpretation like this. Teaching about an earthly Kingdom of Christ, unless it be a spiritual reign in the Church, was rejected in very early times. Origen allegorized the teaching. 'He must reign till He hath put all enemies under His feet', but the Apostle meant that Christ reigns in the heart of those who receive Him, instructing them until He has subjected them to the Father.[85] St. Augustine allegorized the whole book of Revelation. Christ's next Coming, he held, will not be before the final day of Judgment, so that until then His Coming is in the Church on earth. Thus, the Millennium began with Jesus, and the saints now reign with Him in the Church.[86] Nevertheless, great saints and doctors from early times shared a belief in the future Millennium, notably St. Justin Martyr, St. Irenaeus, Tertullian, and St. Hippolytus.

The apostolic Fathers speak of the intervening time that remains until His *parousia* (e.g. Hermas *Sim.* V 5.3), and they refer to a judgment in connection with the *parousia* (Diogn. 7[6]) – not a general Assize, for Christ shall come to be 'our' Judge, that is, a Coming that shall execute judgment upon all Christians. The 'proofs' of His *parousia* are the appearance of unconquered martyrs who are thrown to wild beasts. It is remarkable that, although the Didache closes with a prediction of Antichrist's reign and of our Lord's Second Coming on the clouds, nothing is said about the Reign. The author is content to leave matters there; the vision is stupendous enough. 'Then shall appear the signs of the truth: first a sign of spreading out in heaven, then of the trumpet sound, then the resurrection of the dead. But not of all the dead, but as it was said: "The Lord shall come and all the saints with Him." Then shall the world behold the Lord coming on the clouds of heaven' (Did. 15[6f]).

Eleusis is a word with a different meaning, for it indicates the first 'coming', which the prophets foretold, the 'coming' at Bethlehem of the Just One (Act 7[52]) – and so in the apostolic Fathers.[87] Christians seldom use *parousia* for that, and do not often confuse *parousia* with *eleusis*. Nevertheless, St. Justin Martyr has *parousia* for both comings,[88] and St. Clement of Alexandria almost always means the first Coming when he speaks of *parousia*. Later, however, the eschatological sense of *parousia* returns. In the West it was translated by the Latin *adventus*, while a third and even a fourth Advent were spoken of. The Church's holy season of Advent was associated with expectations of the Coming of our Lord.

It is the opinion of many, including Dr. Glasson,[89] that although the Parousia and the future Judgment held a firm place in Christian tradition by the end of the first century, yet they have a minor position in Christian hope. The great emphasis of early Christian thought is centred on One whose glory is present already and is now in our own day the Light of the world. God's deliverance is therefore not something to be hoped for but is offered here in Christ and can be a present possession. The incarnation has already brought in the Kingdom, the divine order. The Cross is already the magnet which draws all men. Dr. Glasson reminds us that Christ is with us all the time. He has said in a later book,[90] 'He is always the coming One ... and He still comes in the judgments and revivals of history. He comes into the hearts of those who receive Him'.

For all that, Christian hope is and always has been focussed upon the future.

In our days when we still look, after nearly two thousand years, for the fulfilment of this evocative word, *parousia*, which represents one of the primitive Church's dearest expectations – and are faced with fears of nuclear annihilation and with pressing questions about life on other planets – the teaching of the *parousia* ought not to be seen as irrelevant. God's judgment, in its vast spatial dimensions, together with all His grace in Jesus Christ, is still to be expected.[91] St. Irenaeus noticed that every prophecy relating to the first Coming has been vindicated by that event, and he was confident that those relating to the End will find fulfilment, too, though some of them be puzzling.[92] Countless numbers of believers still look forward.

Time appointed may be long but the promise must be sure;
Certainty shall make us strong; joyful patience can endure.

2. ἐπιφάνεια

Doubtless, the word *epiphaneia* is a secular term with religious significance among contemporary pagans and denotes 'any conspicuous intervention on the part of higher powers' (MM). The accession of the 'divine' emperor Claudius was described as an *epiphaneia*.[93] In the NT therefore it is not inappropriate to find the word used, not only of the first Coming of Christ (2 Ti 1[10]), but also to describe that bright Coming in which He triumphantly confronts the Man of Sin (2 Th 2[8]). The *epiphaneia* ends the reign of wickedness on earth and crowns the endeavours of the saints in hard times to keep His commandments without spot (1 Ti 6[14]). The *epiphaneia* marks the setting up of His Throne and the bestowing of crowns upon believers (2 Ti 4[1,8]). It is our blessed hope (Tit 2[13]). It is the same as the *apokalupsis*, for which God's people at Corinth were waiting. It is the spectacular second phase of the *parousia* (see above), reminding the Thessalonian believers and all of us, that we shall have 'rest' when the Lord Jesus is 'revealed' (2 Th 1[7]). We hope for the grace that shall be brought to us then (1 Pet 1[18]).

Crowns of righteousness are bestowed upon those who love His glorious appearing (*epiphaneia*) which has all the splendour typified by the Sh^{e}khînâ in the wilderness, the k^{e}bhôdh Yahweh, the Glory of the Lord.

Like *parousia*, then, *epiphaneia* is a pagan word, altered conspicuously in its surroundings of Christian hope, so as to become a neologism.

See 'Revelation', 'Resurrection'.

SELF-ASSERTION

φιλοπρωτεύω

The verb *philoprōteuō* is a Christian coinage from an existing adjective. Deissmann mistakenly relied on the first edition of Blass's *Grammatik* and supposed that it appears on a pagan inscription. Later he corrected his error.[94]

To 'love to have the preeminence' is anything but a Christian virtue. Self-assertion and ambition was the charge against an aggressive member – probably the leader – of the church of Gaius, named Diotrephes, who prated maliciously against the presbyter John and was inhospitable to brethren from other churches (3 Jn 9).

SENSUAL

ψυχικός

Psuchikos has a new pejorative meaning in Biblical Greek, extending to the animal side of our nature.

Secular Greek. In Aristotle, on the other hand, *psuchikos* means 'spiritual' and is contrasted with 'bodily'.[95] 'We must', he declared, 'make a distinction between *sōmatikai* pleasures (of the body), and *psuchikai* pleasures (of the higher nature).' The adjective is applied to the noblest part of man by Plutarch and it means, 'pertaining to life', being coupled with spirit or breath.[96] Similarly in Polybius (VIII 10.9): while *sōmatikē dunamis* is 'physical power', *psuchikē hormē* is contrasted with it as a higher kind of urge.

The author of 4 Maccabees follows secular use and writes, 'Of the desires, some are higher (*psuchikai*), some are physical (*sōmatikai*).'[97] Libellus IX of Hermes Trismegistus has a three-fold hierarchy, contrasting *sōma*, *psuchikē*, and *pneuma*, grading them as it were in the upward direction. He says that all things are in God and made by God, 'whether they be the things that put forth activity by means of their body (*sōma*) or things that effect movement by means of soul-stuff (*ousia psuchikē*), or things that generate life by means of vital breath (*pneuma*)'.[98] *Psuchikos* indicates something higher than a bodily faculty, although not the very highest, in this Hermetic text.

Biblical Greek. Outside Biblical literature before the period of Gnostics and Montanists, the meaning of *psuchikos* extends to the natural or animal aspect of man, the lower side which is contrasted by the first Christians with *pneumatikos* (spiritual). Early heretics of the antinomian type pushed St. Paul's words to an extreme and urged the truly 'spiritual' (*pneumatikos*) man not to enslave himself to moral precepts. Against the Valentinian heretics Irenaeus lays the charge, 'The most perfect among them do all forbidden things without fear. ... Slaves of all fleshly pleasures, they say that they give to the flesh the things of the flesh and to the spirit the things of the spirit.[99] Heretics borrowed from St. Paul the name of *psuchikoi* (unspiritual) and applied it to ordinary churchmen whom they supposed to be in bondage to moral precepts. The Gnostic Valentinians regarded their own sect, who alone possessed *gnōsis*, as *pneumatikoi*, and the Church they labelled *psuchikoi* (unspiritual),[100] the people who by faith and good works achieve no more than the middle realm of the Demiurge, the God of the OT who created the visible world.[101]

As to the Montanists, often did Tertullian[102] after he had embraced their tenets denominate them *pneumatici* (spiritual) and the Church *psychici* (animal), and St. Clement avers that the Montanists call all who do not hold the new prophecy *psuchikoi*.[103]

I have sought to show (see 'Soul') that *psuchē*, from which derives *psuchikos*, is not usually in the NT the highest part of man although there are instances where the secular Greek influence on the word's usage is evident. Hort is correct to say that we cannot without considerable exaggeration suppose that *psuchē* has in the NT a definitely depreciative sense. Yet there is no extravagance at all in supposing that the adjective *psuchikos*, from *psuchē*, has a very pejorative sense, nothing less than **sensual**.

Bible translators of all periods have fairly been at pains to display the new meaning of *psuchikos*, the Latin versions by *animalis*, Wycliffe by 'beastly', Cranmer by 'fleshly', and AV by 'sensual' and 'natural'. Recent translators no less: 'low creatures' (Moffatt), 'worldly people' (RSV), 'mere man with his natural gifts', 'natural' (Knox), 'sensual' (NEB), 'unspiritual' (Moffatt, RSV, Jerusalem, NEB), 'animal' (Knox, Jerusalem, NEB).

St. Paul related *psuchikos* to the unregenerate man who lacks discernment of the Spirit, who has not the mind of Christ (1 Co 2[14]) and he applies it to the earthly body which is laid in the tomb in contrast with the glorious body that shall emerge (1 Co 15[44]).

St. Jude relates *psuchikos;* to false teachers who break away from the Church's beliefs, being *psuchikoi* in the sense that, like the unbeliever, they are strangers to the Spirit of God (19).

Finally, St. James describes as *psuchikoi* the wisdom which is earthly and devilish (3[15]). There is nothing good about this adjective in Biblical Greek.

SEPARATION, THE LIFE OF

μεταμορφόομαι

An old verb has been newly harnessed to express an important aspect of the believer's life 'in Christ'. It means to live in a state of release from the world, on the Mount apart.

The meaning of *metamorphoumai* in secular Greek was, to be changed, transfigured or transformed – in outward appearance. It is to be changed to the shape of beasts, for instance,[104] or to the shape of Apollo,[105] or to the likeness of a fish.[106] The verb is by Lucian associated with the changing of shape due to practising magic.[107] Plutarch intends a physical change in the people when he refers to listlessness and fatuity seizing them 'as though they had *undergone a transformation* in Circe's house.[108]

In a magical and astrological text from the apocryphal books of Moses[109] of iii AD, a god is addressed: 'All things are subject to thee, whose true shape no god can see, who art *transformed* (our verb) into all things, invisible for evermore.' The references are to changes in outward appearance.

The verb applies to Christ's own transfiguration on the Mount when He manifested the glory of the Lord, 'apart by themselves' – in separation from the world (Mt 17[2]; Mk 9[2]), and the idea of disinvolvement brings us immediately to the new meaning.

In Christian Greek the verb is reserved for the transfiguration of the Lord and for the special manner of life to be adopted by sanctified disciples, the very reverse of worldliness.

Following the deeply doctrinal chapters in the epistle to the Romans, the argument turns at once to Christian behaviour and to the working out of theology in redeemed lives. As Emil Brunner says, the fruit grows from the sap of the tree; so this part of Romans grows out of what has been previously told us about God's mercy.[110] 'Be not conformed to this world: but be ye *transformed ...*' (Ro 12[1]). The change in the disciple occupies the ensuing chapters, involving new behaviour, sacrifices, and nonconformity with the world – with its standards, its values and its fashions – change into the image of Christ, from one glory to a more advanced glory, a final extrication depicted by the same verb, *metamorphoumai* (2 Co 3[18]).

> *O wondrous type, O vision fair*
> *Of glory that the Church shall share,*
> *Which Christ upon the mountain shows,*
> *Where brighter than the sun He glows!* – MEDIEVAL HYMN

See 'Glory'.

SIN

> *Who would know Sinne, let him repair*
> *Unto Mount Olivet; there shall he see*
> *A man so wrung with pains, that all his hair,*
> *His skinne, his garments bloudie be.*
> *Sinne is that presse and vice, which forceth pain*
> *To hunt his cruel food through ev'ry vein.* – GEORGE HERBERT

1. THE 'FAILURE' STEM

ἁμάρτημα, ἁμαρτία, ἁμαρτάνω, ἁμαρτωλός

Hamartēma, hamartia, hamartanō and *hamartōlos* are neologisms, old words with a new meaning in the Biblical vocabulary – any thought, word, or deed contrary to the eternal Law (St. Augustine).

Secular Greek. The meaning was a missing of the mark, a defaulting from a standard. At worst the words represented a feeling of guilt or a fault imputed. In several examples from Ptolemaic and imperial papyri,[111] *hamartēma* was a 'mistake', sometimes joined with *agnoēma* (ignorance), and except to one who was familiar with the Biblical dialect, the words all indicated failure to reach a goal, losing one's way, whether in fact or in metaphor.

As Trench observed (p. 228), touching the second word, *hamartia*, 'So far from having any ethical significance necessarily attaching to it, Aristotle sometimes withdraws it, almost if not altogether, from the region of right and wrong'. The word *hamartia* indicates a mistake, 'a fearful one, it may be, like that of Oedipus, but nothing more'. The verb *hamartanō*, our third word, signified the infringing of instructions laid down by a second-century Roman prefect.[112] *Hamartanō* for Plato was to err against the gods,[113] or to commit murder, or to act violently against parents,[114] and for Xenophon it extended to a strategical blunder in time of war. 'It is not at all strange for mortal man to *err*', confessed Cyrus.[115]

Biblical Greek. The meaning evolved considerably through association with the Hebrew concept of *ḥāṭâ* (to sin, to incur guilt before God, especially by violating His Law), as well as the Hebrew words *'āwôn* and *pesha'*. Christians inherited the Greek Scriptures and therewith new perceptions of words.

The noun *hamartēma* is not as prevalent as *hamartia* in the LXX and appears to indicate specific acts of disobedience to God, in contrast to sin considered in the abstract or specified as the act of sinning, which is *hamartia*. Christian Greek may have reproduced the particularity of the two words, for *hamartēma* appears when the reference is to 'all sins' excluding the 'eternal sin' (Mk 3[28f]), to 'sins that are past' (Ro 3[25]), and to 'every sin that a man doeth' (1 Co 6[18]),[116] whereas *hamartia* is the more inclusive term – not only sin in general, but acts of sin in particular, besides the action of sinning and its result, sinfulness. The difference between the words was nicely and categorically illustrated by Trench (p. 228) who called to mind St. Augustine's answer to the Pelagian claim that St. John Chrysostom had supported Pelagian views. Chrysostom had in fact insisted that infants were innocent only of *hamartēmata*, individual acts of sin, and were not free from *hamartia*, which was sin in general.

The distinction, however, is not invariable, as will be seen by considering two Christian Greek phrases, *ergazomai hamartian* (to commit a sin, Jas 2⁹) and *kratō tas hamartias* (to retain sins, Jn 20²³), in either of which, if we follow Trench, we might expect *hamartēma*. Burton's discussion of the difference[117] deserves attention: he concluded that whereas *hamartēma* is always an act of sin, *hamartia* may be either the committing of sin or a deed of sin. On the other hand, it is doubtful whether any delicate distinction will hold in the Testament of Abraham: the patriarch urges forgiveness for his sin (*hamartēma*), but a line or two later God replies, 'I forgive thee thy sin (*hamartia*)' 94²²,²⁷. The same thing is intended by either word. Is there any difference at all in Biblical Greek?

Hamartia may sometimes have the meaning, 'sin offering', in the Christian language, as in Lev 6²⁵ LXX. Ought we to understand Heb 9²⁸ as follows: 'So Christ was once offered to bring to the altar (*anapherō*) the *sin offerings* of many; and unto them that look for Him shall He appear the second time without a *sin offering* unto salvation'? On this supposition 1 Pet 2²⁴ might read: 'Who His own self brought to the altar (*anapherō*) our *sin offerings* in His own body on the tree'. It would relieve the problem, inherent in the normal rendering, how a sinless Man may be said with intelligibility to 'bear' the sins of others.[118]

The late Professor Dodd has reminded us that in the NT the use of *anomos* and *anomia* is notably restricted, and only in the first epistle of St. John is *hamartia* said to be *anomia*. 'The explicit equation of sin and lawlessness is quite in the spirit of the LXX, and is exceptional in the N.T.'[119] While *adikos, adikia* occur more often in the NT, yet usually they have their pagan Greek sense of 'injustice' or 'dishonesty'; and *asebeia, asebēs, asebō* are very occasional. By contrast, the *hamartia*-words occur in the NT more than 250 times. Dodd suggested that St. Paul's definition of sin leads to 'a profound and non-legalistic interpretation of the idea' – a falling short of the glory of God (Ro 3²³).[120]

2. THE 'DEBT' STEM

ὀφείλημα, ὀφείλω, ὀφειλέτης

The concept represented in secular Greek by *opheilēma, opheilō* and *opheiletēs* is that of debt but, through Aramaic influence, where the same word expressed both debt and injury, an additional meaning of 'offence' arises in Jewish Greek. The phrase, *hamartian opheilō*, does assuredly occur in a secular inscription of the imperial period,[121] but we must see that it means 'to owe a debt', for *hamartia* was a debt, and the phrase provides no evidence in itself that *opheilō* meant to sin.

Through Aramaic influence the transformation did occur in early Christian Greek and these three words came to include an affront to God. They may still mean 'debt' even so, for *opheilēma* renders *mashshā'â* (loan Deut. 24[10]) and indicates a debt of money in the free Greek books (1 Esd 3[20]; 1 Mac 15[8]), like the verb in Mt 18[24]. However, St. Paul (Ro 4[4]) argues that if we try to earn forgiveness as a reward we cannot look for grace and our only quittance will be reckoned an *opheilēma* (sin). Something more than 'debt' is meant. Attempting to earn forgiveness is tantamount to rejecting Christ's atoning death. So Article XIII of the Church of England affirms that good deeds 'done before the grace of Christ ... have the nature of sin.'

The *opheilēmata* for which we ask forgiveness in the Lord's Prayer are debts only in a very special sense, debts owing to God and therefore sins (Mt 6[12]). The unlucky eighteen beneath the tower of Siloam might conceivably have been sinners (*opheiletai*), but cannot conceivably have been debtors in the secular sense (Lk 13[4]).

So the words became regular Christian terms, not for debt and debtor, but for sin and sinner. St. Polycarp urged that we are all 'perpetrators of sin' (*opheiletai* of *hamartia*): Pol. ad Phil. 6[1].

3. THE 'TRESPASS' STEM

παράπτωμα

Another secular word has taken an ominous turn.

Secular Greek. *Paraptōma* was a 'blunder' or an error in judgment.[122] 'To abandon the habits of victors and to imitate those of the conquered ... was surely an incontestable *paraptōma* (error of judgment).'[123] In a more specialized way *paraptōma* might be a literary 'lapse',[124] or a defeat in battle, as when Antigonus, according to the historian, abandoned a source of revenue because of the *paraptōma* he had suffered.[125]

Biblical Greek. From the Bible there issues the ethical concept of a misdeed directed against God, rendered in AV by 'transgression' (e.g. Job 36[9]). The Hebrew is *pesha'* (rebellion against God). *Paraptōma* renders also *shᵉghî'â* (a sin of ignorance) and *'āwel* (injustice). *Paraptōma* often appears in Biblical Greek when it is intended to designate sins 'not of the deepest dye and the worst enormity', but 'the falling where one should have stood upright'.[126]

Paraptōma includes other men's trespasses against ourselves (Mt 6[14f]), and all offences against God provided the gravity is not prominent (Ro 4[25], 5[15f], 11[11f]; 2 Co 5[19]; Gal 6[1]; Eph 1[7], 2[1,5]; Col 2[13]). The emphasis is away from the sin in all these instances – upon the blessings of the last Adam, Gentile salvation, God's initiative in reconciliation, a sinner helped back to fellowship by the local church, new life and the riches of grace – rather than upon the heinous sin itself. Accordingly Field observed that two Syriac versions, Peshitta and Philoxenian, translated *paraptōma* by derivatives of the root, to 'stumble', and he suggested the meaning 'stumbling', a 'slip', a 'false step' (p. 160).

SIN OF INADVERTENCE

ἀγνόημα

Agnoēma is a variety of sin in Biblical Greek, somewhat different from the meaning hitherto conveyed by the word.

Secular Greek. *Agnoēma* was simply a want of information, a lack of sufficient observation, as when Theophrastus, a naturalist of the fourth century BC, represented certain statements about trees as a piece of 'ignorance'.[127]

It was 'oversight' and 'inadvertence',[128] and depicted an imperfect state of knowledge. The geographer Strabo, contemporary with Jesus, laments that what lies beyond Germany is not easy to say, and adds, 'The same *agnoēma* prevails in regard to the rest of the people on the north' (VII 2.4).

Biblical Greek. In the sacred language the word indicates more than 'ignorance'. It renders the Hebrew *mishgê*, the 'oversight' on the part of Joseph's brothers (Gen 43[12]) which incurred a feeling of guilt. The Hebrew root has the connotation of a sin committed in ignorance which nevertheless was no excuse for transgressing the Law (Lev 4[13]; Num 15[22]), and young bullocks must be offered to cover it.

Supposedly the same meaning occurs in an Egyptian decree, but in that text *agnoēma* suggests an oversight in a legal sense rather than any kind of moral failure.[129]

The writer to Hebrews follows the OT sense of *mishgê* when he discusses the entry of the high priest of old to the inner tabernacle once a year offering blood for his own and the people's *agnoēmata* (sins of ignorance): Heb. 9[7]. The *agnoēmata* were inadvertent but they were not mere errors, and blood must atone for them.

In the sub-apostolic age *agnoēma* included sins of the flesh. Hermas posed the question, 'How can the man who defiled his flesh be saved?' and the answer is that God may give him 'healing' for *agnoēmata*, if for the future he profanes neither the flesh nor the spirit. Hermas is directing his attention to a form of Gnosticism. The Church affirmed against the heretics that both flesh and spirit must be purified (Sim. V 7).

SINCERITY

εἰλικρινής, εἰλικρινία (-εια)

In secular Greek the words, 'pure' (*eilikrines*) and 'purity' (*eilikrinia*), signified the absence of alloy. 'Unadulterated' colour meant whiteness.[130] For Plato, unchanging truths were 'unalloyed',[131] and so also was divine beauty. It is 'unalloyed', not infected with the flesh and colour of humanity.[132] Plato does not particularly intend an ethical idea. It is not easy to exclude the moral meaning from all the uses of the words in Plato and post-Platonic Greek, but I think we need not quarrel with Trench when he said that the ethical use 'first makes itself distinctly felt in the NT; there are only approximations to it in classical Greek' (p. 302).

Nevertheless, Plato does ask what kind of thing is most closely related to truth, the pure and 'unadulterated' (*eilikrines*), or the violent and the great.[133] Perhaps the closest approximation to Christian use comes with Aristotle who compares 'pure' (*eilikrines*) and liberal amusement with 'bodily' pleasures.[134]

Christians apply the word to God, but in the book of Wisdom *eilikrines* has the secular sense of a 'pure' emanation of glory (7²⁵), by which the author means an undarkened ray of light, although he puts it all within the context of Wisdom reflecting the glory of the Almighty. The Christian historian Eusebius, too, applies the word to clean and 'pure' air, after the secular sense.[135] But St. Paul has an undoubtedly new emphasis when he teaches that a believer must be *eilikrines* and offenceless in face of Christ's judgment (Ph 1¹⁰). A Christian teacher seeks his readers' concentration, while he stirs up their 'sincere' minds (2 Pet 3¹).

Eilikrinia (sincerity) is the reverse of what is typified in holy Scripture by 'leaven' (1 Co 5⁸) and has to do with the gravity of the pilgrim walk – simplicity and godly 'probity' (2 Co 1¹²). It describes the preaching of Paul – 'as of *probity*, as of God' (2 Co 2¹⁷).

To some extent the ethical meaning passed into secular use. Two centuries later a civic official writes, according to a fragmentary papyrus, 'I am obliged to have recourse to your *probity*, begging you to. ...'[136]

THE SOUL

ψυχή

In holy Scripture both *psuchē* (soul) and *sarx* (flesh) tend to belong to man's lower faculties, contrary to the generally accepted view among Greek philosophers, while the Bible denotes the highest nature in man by the term *pneuma* (spirit).

In secular writers, as early as Homer, *psuchē* is both the 'life principle,' keeping the body alive, and also a conscious entity continuing after death. 'Diomedes, renowned spearman', sings Homer, 'took away their life and *soul*.'[137] 'This was the man', reports Herodotus, 'who had restored to the king his *psuchē* (life)' (III 130). 'The destructive wrath of Achilles', sighs Homer, 'sent to Hades many strong *souls* of heroes.'[138] Plato, for instance, exalts the 'soul' of man as undying.[139] And so too Xenophon. In the *Cyropaedia*, Cyrus speaks on the 'soul's' immortality. 'My sons, I have never convinced myself of this: that only as long as it is contained in a mortal body is the *soul* alive ... for I see that the *soul* endues mortal bodies with life. ... Neither can I convince myself of this', he adds, 'that the soul will want intelligence when it is separated from this unintelligent body' (VIII vii 19). The soul is divine. 'The winds are themselves invisible', says Xenophon once more. 'The *soul* of man, which partakes of the divine, reigns manifestly within us, yet is itself unseen.'[140]

Aristotle's use of *psuchē* denotes the principle of life or intelligence even in the lower animals, plants, and the universe.[141] The 'soul' is the actualization of a potentially living organism; all matter found in nature has a definite potentiality and some matter is capable of being vitalized as an organism. The specific form or actuality of this matter is vitality or 'soul'.[142] On the one hand, he ascribes existence to the *psuchē* not absolutely but only in relation to the body. On the other hand, he makes *nous* (mind) eternal and identifies it with *psuchē* in the sense that *nous* is *noētikē psuchē*.[143] Whereas Plato begins with ideas as real existences, Aristotle embarks from the fact of life. Plato therefore sees the soul as an entity, while Aristotle sees it as an actuality (*entelecheia*) of the body. For Plato the soul is pre-existent, for Aristotle it is no older than the body, for form cannot exist without matter. Aristotle then sees the soul not as immortal, seeking freedom from the body, but as having its own existence with the body and dying with it.

Aristotle did see *nous* (mind) as immortal in the sense of the universal *nous*; as individual *nous*, it perishes with the body.

Later Greek writers regarded the 'soul' as a kind of shade, departing from the body in death. Souls in living creatures, says Arius Didymus, cling to the universal soul, and the souls of the dead live on. The Stoics affirmed that the soul was immortal. Souls depart from us to Hades at death, wrote Cornutus, a Greek writer in the early Christian period.[144]

It has been observed that with Jewish Greek writers at Alexandria, especially Philo, and with the Greek OT, a change is seen in the usage of 'soul' which leads us on to the NT (F. C. Grant). Secular usages survive in so far as they were embedded also in the OT, but a shift appears when Philo seeks to express Hebrew religious ideas in Greek philosophical terms. Philo uses *pneuma*, *psuchē* and *sarx* in the way of the Greek OT. *Psuchē* for Philo, as for the Stoics, is still a divine spark, implanted in man by God, and yet he never says that the *psuchē* is caught in the tangle of human existence or that salvation involves escape from the body. He stands between Greek and Jew. For him, *psuchē* had a lower or irrational part, as well as a divine. Its essence was blood and it consisted of those features of consciousness which a man shares with the brutes, though it is true they are interpenetrated with mind. They do not always obey the mind's dictates, and *nous* (mind) is spoken of as being a god to the senses, as Moses was to Pharaoh. The senses are what Philo conceived to be lower manifestations of the *psuchē*, and sometimes they are so overpowering that he could speak of 'the death of the soul'. Yet, on the other hand, he could visualize the higher elements of consciousness in the *psuchē* as powerful enough to overcome the animal elements and he could speak then of *psuchē* as something infused from above and quite separable from animal life – a part of the divine nature. But for this aspect of the *psuchē* Philo sometimes substitutes the word *nous* (mind).[145] Indeed, he is a bridge between Greek and Jew, accepting the Greek where it does not conflict with the Hebrew. Philo leads the way towards a Biblical vocabulary.[146]

We must concede that in Biblical Greek *psuchē* still means 'physical life'. Herod sought the young Child's *psuchē* (Mt 2[20]) – an ordinary use of Greek – and the counsel to take no thought for the *psuchē* is probably a reference to the same idea (Mt 6[25]), as is also perhaps (but, I think, doubtfully) the counsel that he who finds his *psuchē* shall lose it (Mt 10[39], 16[25]; Mk 8[35]; Lk 9[24]). The contrast involved in the phrase, to save a *psuchē* or to kill (Mk 3[4]; Lk 6[9]), makes it clear that sometimes in the Bible secular usage survives. The Epistle of Barnabas quotes Ps 21 (22)[21(20)] – 'Spare my *psuchē* from the sword!' – which is clearly, 'Save my life!' (5[1]).

So the secular usage of *psuchē* is 'breath' (from *psuchō*, to breathe), the vital principle in a human being, as well as his immortal 'soul' – the part of him which survives physical death. However, alongside the conception of *psuchē* as life and breath, perhaps even superseding it, there appears in Biblical Greek the meaning, 'person'.[147] There are some instances of such an extension in secular Greek; in a papyrus of 13 BC the phrase, 'your *psuchē*', appears to mean only, 'you' (MM p. 699), reminding us of Lk 9[24f] (where *psuchē* will not therefore have the meaning of 'life'). Although doubtless *psuchē* in secular Greek is often the conscious self, as when 'the soul of Orestes' is neither more nor less than Orestes himself,[148] yet clearly the LXX and not Sophocles was the inspiration of the meaning ('person') for NT writers. In Lev 17[4] *psuchē* renders *'îsh* (man), but that was rare; more often it renders *nephesh*, as in Ezek 18[4]: 'All souls are mine ... the soul that sinneth, it shall die'. This was an extended use of *nephesh* to mean 'person'. 'Hear, and your *soul* shall live' (Isai 55[3]). 'How long dost Thou make us (*psuchē*) to doubt?' (Jn 10[24]). 'As you (your *psuchē*) prosper' (3 Jn 2). *Psuchē* has a reflexive meaning, like *nephesh* in Hebrew. The Son of Man gives Himself (His *psuchē*), a ransom for many (Mk 10[45]). 'I will say to my *psuchē*' – to myself (Lk 12[19]). 'I call God for a record upon my *psuchē* – upon myself (2 Co 1[23]). The Epistle of Barnabas speaks of humbling oneself (one's *psuchē*) by fasting, and of arrogance in oneself – in one's *psuchē* (Barn 3[1], 19[3]) 'Thou shalt not exalt thyself nor give boldness to thyself' – to thy *psuchē* (Did 3[9]).

It is not so much that *psuchē* has emptied its meaning[149] through Semitic influence, as that a new meaning has been annexed. Early Christian Greek follows the LXX, and though some of the usages of *psuchē* agree with those of secular Greek they are only those which agree also with the LXX – the life of man, his will and emotions, and above all, the man as a 'self'. If a man gains the whole world, only to lose his *psuchē*, it represents a loss of himself – not a part of him (Mt 16[26] etc.) When there was added to the Church about three thousand *psuchai*, whole men and women were added, not 'souls' (Act 2[41]). The fear, coming upon every *psuchē*, was upon every person (2[43]). Every *psuchē* (person) must be subject to the state (Ro 13[1]) – and so throughout the NT (Act 3[23]; Ro 2[9], 16[3]; 1 Co 15[45]; 1 Pet 3[20]; 2 Pet 2[14]; Rev 16[3]; Hermas *Sim.* IX18.5; 1 Clem 27[1], 61[3], 64) and Jewish Greek.[150] 'Every *soul* of men shall begin to call to his succour the mighty King'. (Sib. Orac. III 558). Consequently one may reason that 'salvation of souls' (1 Pet 1[9]) was in fact the saving of 'your life' in the fullest sense; the phrase is a Semitism, and the absence of the article may be a Semitism, too.[151]

Psuchē in Biblical Greek signifies what is characteristically human, the self, the material body having God's *rûaḥ* breathed into it. It is the personality, what we often call the Ego, especially with emotional emphasis. I stress the emotionl emphasis, because there are occasions in Hebrew, especially in the hypothetical document D of the Pentateuch, and in later writers influenced by it, when *nephesh* is linked with the heart (*lēbhābh*) in expressions such as, 'with all thy heart and with all thy soul' (Deut. 4^{29}, 6^5, 10^{12}, etc.). Even so, the emphasis is on the whole self, rather than an emotional faculty alone. When an Alexandrian lover speaks of fire burning in 'my heart' (*psuchē*), it is not the same thing (P. Grenf. I 1 i 9, ii BC), and a highly charged emotional and erotic feeling is intended. However, the sword was to pierce Mary's very self, not one part of her only (Lk 2^{35}). Mary's *psuchē*, far from being only her heart, was the human personality of Mary, her 'self' as the bearer of life – as one who had received the *pneuma* of God.

A man's *psuchē*, his Ego, is what Christians believe to be the subject of salvation. Hope is an anchor, not of the soul but of the very personality (Heb 6^{19}), and from our faith springs the salvation of our whole self, our personality, our *psuchē*, our Ego (Heb 10^{39}). When church elders watch for our *psuchē* they are interested in something more than one part of our make-up (Heb 13^{17}). The Word of God saves more than one part of the believer (Jas 1^{21}). If we convert a sinner, we save the 'whole man' (the *psuchē*) from death (Jas 5^{20}). St. Peter is concerned with the whole Ego when he exhorts, 'Purify your *souls*' (1 Pet 1^{22}). Lusts make war upon the whole self of a man, upon his *psuchē* (1 Pet 2^{11}). And Jesus invites me to repose upon Him the whole of my weary personality, the Ego, the entire Me (Mt 11^{29}). There was no nice carving of personality when He cried, 'My *soul* is sorrowful! My *soul* is troubled!' (Mt 26^{38}; Mk 14^{34}; Jn 12^{27}). It was not only His 'soul' in the Greek sense, or His life, or His spirit, that He gave upon the Cross. He gave His very self (*psuchē*) for the sheep (Jn 10^{11}). The Son of Man gave His *psuchē* a ransom for many (Mt 20^{28}; Mk 10^{45}). The apostolic Fathers understood *psuchē* in the same way: it is the 'person' who knows God (2 Clem 17^1). The sins which destroy the 'soul' are those which destroy the whole man – arrogance, adultery, magic (Barn. 20^1). We are to pity the 'soul' (the person) that is abased (Barn 3^5).

The Hebrew idea of *nephesh* (*psuchē*) is the human personality, the man himself, a living being, especially where the context is one of emotions or passions – like, 'My soul is sorrowful', 'My soul delights', and, 'Praise the Lord, O my soul'. It is man's essential character in all its wretchedness and need of God. 'My soul longeth after Thee, O God'. Indeed, medieval and modern Christianity, in exalting the soul as a separate faculty within us, is nearer perhaps

SOUL

to pagan Greece than to the Hebrews and to St. Paul.[152] In Greek philosophical writings the *psuchē* was often taken to be the most valuable part of man; it was immortal, pre-existent.

> The soul that rises with us, our life's Star,
> Hath had elsewhere its setting
> And cometh from afar;
> Not in entire forgetfulness,
> And not in utter nakedness,
> But trailing clouds of glory do we come
> From God who is our Home.

When the modern Christian echoes the Epistle of Barnabas (19[10]) in speaking of saving 'souls', that is well and good if he understands souls as complete individuals, and not in the usual secular sense. In the Biblical idiom the author of 2 Clement speaks of converting 'a perishing soul that it may be saved' (15[1]). But the soul is often conceived by Christians as if it were imprisoned in the body, as Plato conceived it, and is said by Christians to fly to God at death, in much the same way that Jesus gave up His *pneuma* (spirit) when he died. Sometimes we speak of being in the body and absent from God, as St. Paul did (2 Co 5[8]), but St. Paul never elsewhere spoke as if the 'soul' were our true entity, the part of us which soars aloft, or hovers over the body for three days after death, whatever later Judausm may have done under Greek influence.

By contrast, the traditional trichotomistic Hebrew conception of man as a unity of flesh (*bāśār*), animal and individual life (*nephesh*), and spirit or divine life which returns one day to God who gave it (*rûaḥ*), was inherited by the early Christians. St. Paul could refer to 'spirit and soul and body' as one whole to be preserved blameless till Jesus comes (1 Th 5[23]). In Heb 4[12] the Word of God is said to be powerful enough to divide *soul* from *spirit*, implying that there are these two elements in man, *nephesh* and *rûaḥ*, the natural and the divine, so unified that only the greatest Power in the universe can divide them. The Hebrews had no distinct word for 'body', existing apart from the soul, and soul itself may sometimes mean 'corpse' (Lev. 21[11]; Num 6[6], etc.). We are very far away from any thought of the soul's pre-existence; the *nephesh* has no priority, according to early Hebrew thought. The *nephesh* that God creates is a synthesis of two elements: the animal frame and the breath of God. The *psuchē* in the Bible is the whole sinful human self which needs salvation, a unity of flesh and spirit, one man in his total personality. The *psuchē* goes into Sheol at death (Ps 16[10] cited in Act 2[27,31]). It is the whole lustful man (Rev 18[14]). But nowhere in the Bible 'is there any suggestion of an

421

immortal soul which survives death'.[153] The word which is used to describe what lives after death is not *psuchē* but *pneuma* (spirit). The violent letters of protest which Cullmann received after his famous Ingersoll lecture on the Immortality of Man reveal how widespread is the mistake of attributing to primitive Christianity the Greek belief in the immortality of the soul.

Attacks upon Cullmann were based not on exegetical arguments but on prevalent philosophical and psychological sentiments.[154] Cullmann was right in accusing his critics of appealing to Socrates rather than to the Christian scriptures, Old and New.

The immortality of the soul exclusively, as distinct from resurrection of the whole man, is a secular idea. This is not to say that early Christians were precisely conscious of this, for they were not deliberately rejecting Greek ideas, and for them resurrection included immortality of the soul (which included the body) and the spirit. Jesus Himself may be considered to support the Greek idea when he speaks of God as able to kill the soul, but He evidently did not intend to separate it from the body but rather to separate God from those who can kill only the body (Mt 10^{28}). He meant that the latter cannot touch the individual's personality, the 'soul', which is indeed immortal unless God wills otherwise.

The early Christians, if St. Paul is any guide, exalted the 'spirit' (*pneuma*) and placed the 'soul' in the background – and this in spite of the secular precedent that might have influenced the Church. In their thoughts about man's personality the first Christians preserved a Biblical, a Hebrew tradition.

The Hebrews did not often conceive of a disembodied *nephesh* (soul). Man was flesh animated by *nephesh* in inseparable union. For most early Christians *psuchē* is just this, the Self or Ego. One OT passage does speak cryptically of 'those who dwell in houses of clay' (Job 4^{19}), which sounds like Greek influence at work, and a passage in Daniel speaks of the spirit 'in the midst of my body' (7^{15}), but generally man became a living *nephesh* when God breathed *rûaḥ* (spirit) into Him (Gen 7^{15}). It is the same with the animals: *psuchē* is used for the living 'creature' which the earth brought forth (Gen 1^{24}) – any animate thing, man or beast. Greek influence entered the Bible in the Wisdom of Solomon, where the virtuous 'soul' is said not to die (3^1). The sequel makes clear what is meant. Being virtuous, the 'soul' enters an undefiled body, it is pre-existent (8^{19}). Temporarily it is burdened by this tent of clay which is the body (9^{15}). The 'soul' goes to Hades at death (16^{14}): this may refer to the whole man, rather than a part of him, but the Greek influence which is probable makes it unlikely.

The early Christians mainly followed the non-Greek view. Burton has pointed out that whereas for Greek writers in general *psuché* conveyed the idea of life and mentality, *pneuma* was a term of substance, and while in the contemporary Hermetic literature *pneuma* is graded below *psuché*, yet in the NT *pneuma* is doubtlessly superior to *psuché*.[155] In the NT *psuché* is still, as in Greek generally, the seat of life, feeling, thought and will, but *pneuma* is now the seat of the mental and religious life of man. *Pneuma* is not used in secular Greek for an element of man's inner life, but *psuché* is. The fact that *pneuma* is given the supreme place is one of the indications that the Bible's view is distinctive from other psychology.[156] Only in the Greek OT and NT has the *pneuma* the sense of a spiritual being or refers to man in his higher reaches. 'Thus it is a good example of the language-building and enriching power of the Bible-religion'.[157] *Pneuma* and not *psuché* was to early Christians what later became known as the 'soul'. Later Christians were to conceive the 'soul', the *psuché*, as surrendered at death, but early Christians on the contrary spoke of Jesus as surrendering His *pneuma*. It is *pneuma* and not soul that reaches out to God, as St. Paul shows clearly. The Holy Spirit, he says, 'beareth witness with our *pneuma*, that we are the children of God' (Ro 8[16]). We have received from God the *pneuma*, in order that by it we might know the things that come from God (1 Co 2[12]). St. James too is referring to what many at a later date would call the soul when he declares that the body without the *pneuma* is dead (Jas 2[26]). However, there is sometimes a real blurring of the distinction between the two words in the NT. St. Mary sings, 'My *soul* doth magnify ...: my *spirit* hath rejoiced ...' (Lk 1[46]), and St. Paul cries, 'One *spirit* ... one *soul* ...' (Ph 1[27]), as if human personality were dualistic and not tripartite, and spirit and soul were synonymous as in some later Church thinking.

Secular precedent soon finds its way into the Church. One expects the apologist who writes to Diognetus to adopt something like the normal Greek view of the soul. He refers to it as 'immortal', in the manner of the Greeks. His beautiful simile wherein Christians appear as the 'soul' of the world is well known. He departs somewhat from the Biblical vocabulary when he says the soul is dispersed through all members of the body. 'The soul dwells in the body, but is not of the body.' He says that the flesh hates the soul (VI). St. Paul would refer to the 'spirit' (*pneuma*) in such a context.

The non-Biblical or Greek view is seen in Church history, even more forcefully, among those whose strong Platonist sympathies looked upon the pre-existent soul as confined in the body to punish it for the errors of its previous incorporeal state. Although Origen rejected the Platonic doctrine that souls migrate from body to body on this earth (metempsychosis), nevertheless he held to the soul's pre-existence. St. Jerome subscribed to it at one time and St. Augustine did not deny it. By the time of the Schoolmen, the soul had been defined in Aristotelian fashion as the 'form' of the body. It was held to be made for the body and to be incapable of final separation from it, though the soul has a separate existence for a while after death. St. Thomas held that each individual soul is a new creation, placed by God in its destined body; the soul is not material although, in an Aristotelian sense, it is the body's 'form'. According to this view, which is known as Creationism, our souls are not produced by our fathers' generative system, nor are transmitted from parents to children. A new soul is created for each new child. Protestants have tended not to follow St. Thomas, for they have preferred to view human personality, including the soul, as totally depraved and transmitted from our first parents. Their view is known as Traducianism. Adam's likeness and image were transmitted to his son, Seth (Gen. 5^3). So man is shapen in iniquity and his mother conceives him in sin (Ps 51^5); he is the child of wrath. No part of man, not even the soul, is exempt from the traditional curse, for his soul and his body came from the loins of his father. Levi is said to have paid tithes, to have been a whole man in fact, when he was yet in the loins of his father (Heb 7^{10}). This had not been St. Jerome's view, for he had held by such texts as, 'He fashioneth their hearts aright' (Ps 33^{15}) and, 'He formed the spirit of man within him' (Zach 12^1) – demonstrating that one part of man is granted to him sinless. The apologist, Lactantius, and St. Hilary who was a fourth-century convert from neo-Platonism, both defended Creationism. However, St. Augustine, although he never felt certain about the question,[158] thought that Creationism did not recognize sufficiently the transmission of man's sinful propensity.[159] He would like to have agreed with St. Jerome but found it difficult and wrote to him on the deep subject, 'God help me out of my ignorance by your means; and if not, may He give me grace to be content not to know.'[160]

Earlier than Augustine, Tertullian had held Traducian views. Although Tertullian had said that we Christians (*apud nos*) regard the human soul as springing from the breath of God and as being a special substance,[161] yet he also believed that soul and body come into existence simultaneously. 'As they are separated at the same moment through death, so they are united at the same moment through life.'[162] He declared that the soul came into existence at the moment of conception (§3). In sexual intercourse one feels that something is detached not only from the body but from the soul (§6), and eventually all men arose from the soul of Adam (*ex uno homine*, §9).[163] St. Gregory of Nyssa held similar views. 'The soul and the body have a similar beginning', St. Gregory said. 'The soul is present in what is being formed in the womb.'[164] Concerning the controversy bishop Westcott rightly observed that 'a mystery is indicated to us into which we can but see a little way, a final antithesis in our being'.[165] All the time we are dependent on the past; on the other hand, the future depends largely upon ourselves. That is the antithesis. Whereas our outward life is conditioned by our ancestry to a great extent, by our fathers after the flesh, yet we are much rather within the control of the Father of our spirits, and we stand in immediate and personal connection with God. 'Each man is at once an individual of a race and a new power in the evolution of the race. He is *born* (Traducianism), and also he is *created* (Creationism).'

Some Christian writers refer to the 'soul' as if it were the *pneuma* (spirit). In our own days, Hort[166] was one of the first to recognize that the modern religious estimate of the term 'soul', as the highest element in man, was founded on a misunderstanding of the NT. True, he added the caution that to suppose that *psuchē* has in the NT a definitely depreciatory sense was a considerable exaggeration. We have to concede that Greek secular vocabulary still lingers in some parts of the NT where the soul is a valuable and separate entity apart from a man's Ego. 'Thy *soul* is required of thee' (Lk 12[20]), sounds very like a reference to a separate entity, and *psuchē* has not always in the NT the pejorative sense of the fallen human personality, being sometimes identified with the *pneuma*, as we have seen in our survey. The NT vocabulary has still contributed something quite new, with its main emphasis upon the 'soul' as man in his entirety.

SOUND MIND (AV)

σωφρονισμός

In secular Greek *sōphronismos* invariably has an active and transitive sense, a making sober, an admonishing. Josephus says that a treatment was meted out, 'for *reducing to discipline*' after a tumult had been made.[167] Plutarch has the same active sense: 'for *admonishing* the others'.[168] He speaks of the *disciplining* of dogs and horses (*epi sōphronismō*)[169] and of conversing with young men 'for the purpose of *moral instruction*' (*epi sōphronismo*).[170] Plutarch alludes to affairs with casual women, *hetairai*, which are cut short by the *sōphronismoi* (chastening experiences) or *metanoiai* (second thoughts) of the young men.[171]

Clearly this is a different sense from that new intransitive sense which is found in Christian Greek. God has not given us the spirit of fear, St. Paul observed, but the spirit of power and of love and of a 'sound mind' (2 Ti 1⁷). The Revisers of 1881, aware of the secular sense of *sōphronismos* tried to retain it here and rendered 'discipline' in place of 'sound mind', as if the word indicated a faculty for correcting others. Alford too assumed the secular sense, 'admonition of others', arguing that Timothy was by nature timid, that he was liable to shrink from bold testimony.[172] Alford cited the secular writers, Plutarch and Appian.

There has evidently been a change of meaning, and the active sense of secular writers no longer applies in the NT. As Ellicott shrewdly observed on this verse, *sōphronismos* in secular writers 'usually has a transitive force ...; as however both the substantives with which it is connected are abstract and intransitive ... it seems on the whole best ... to give it either a purely intransitive ... or perhaps rather reflexive reference'.[173]

So then it is most likely that in Christian Greek *sōphronismos* has assumed all the intransitive and reflexive sense of **self-control**. That is very much what the King James version made of it, following the Vulgate's *sobrietas*. The 'sound mind' is a gift from God, allied to His other graces of spiritual power and love, to replace *deilia* (timidity). It involves self-discipline but not necessarily the power or taste to discipline others.

THE SPIRIT, SPIRITUALLY

πνεῦμα, πνευματικῶς

Secular Greek. Burton commodiously analysed the use of *pneuma* from Aeschylus onwards.[174] *Pneuma* was a blast of wind that fell upon the sea,[175] and it was the air breathed in,[176] or out, whether a fetid *pneuma* caused by certain diseases,[177] or the respiration which frequently interested Hippocrates, and the flatulence mentioned by Aristotle and Diogenes Laertius.[178]

In Menander, of the fourth century BC, *pneuma* is once a vague directive influence, a Luck which oversets all things, 'whether we call it divine *pneuma* or *nous* (intellect)'.[179]

Pneuma in secular Greek is neither the soul nor a spirit nor God, but by the time of Polybius it comes near to meaning the breath of life, and that may conceivably be due to Greek Biblical influence, even so early. A man may owe his *pneuma* (life) to the action of others, says Polybius (xxxi 10, 4).

At the arrival of Christianity *pneuma* was less often used in secular literature, if surviving examples are anything to go by.

Biblical Greek. In the LXX, however, it had rendered *rûaḥ*, the spirit of God and man, a good or an evil spirit, besides wind and breath. In Christian Greek the word had an extensive currency, and Burton found that NT usage is effectively influenced to a much greater extent by OT ideas than by secular writers. St. Paul's treatment, moreover, has peculiarities of its own, and *pneuma* is conspicuously superior to *psuchē*. In some Hermetic literature, almost contemporary, *pneuma* is on the other hand 'definitely graded below' *psuchē* in the scale of value.[180]

An allusion to the spiritual side of our nature, contrasted with the *sarx* (fleshly impulse), is conspicuous in very many of the contexts of *pneuma* and *pneumatikōs*. It is however, almost impossible to detect whether in these sentences St. Paul refers to the believer's own *pneuma* or to the Holy Ghost who takes part in the inner conflict between the old and the new man. Perhaps the question is off the point: the Holy Ghost is operative within the human spirit, coming to the believer's aid to open the way for glorification (Ro 8[16f]).

It cannot fairly be shirked that *pneuma* has become a new word, 'applied to new situations', and gradually acquiring 'new shades of meaning'.[181]

The adverb, *pneumatikōs*, clearly shares the new shade of meaning. 'We speak these things', St. Paul explains, 'not in the words which man's wisdom teaches, but in words which the Spirit teaches, judging spiritual things *spiritually*.[182] The natural man does not receive the things of the Spirit of God, for they are foolishness to him and he cannot know them, because they are *spiritually* discerned' (1 Co 2[13f]). Both times, *pneumatikōs* must mean, 'in a way which is contrary to the flesh', and the assumption is that Christians have at command a faculty denied to the 'natural' man, acting against the lowest impulse (the *sarx*), raising them to heights otherwise beyond them.

By this faculty within Himself, the risen Jesus was united with the Father *pneumatikōs*.[183] St. Ignatius exhorted us to abide in Jesus Christ in our flesh (*sarkikōs*) and in our spirit (*pneumatikōs*): ad Eph. 10[3]. So he counselled St. Polycarp to vindicate his office with all diligence both *sarkikē* and *pneumatikē* – with a heed that concerns both the lower and the higher nature (ad Pol. 1[2]).

Is this what *pneumatikōs* means for the Seer? 'Metaphorically' seems to be intended in the phrase, 'Jerusalem is called *pneumatikōs* Sodom and Egypt', but on the strength of St. Paul's use of *pneumatikōs* we might rather render, 'Jerusalem is Sodom and Egypt *to the believer's spiritual discernment*' (Rev 11[8]).

That is how St. Clement understands the adverb when he reminds the Corinthians that St. Paul's injunctions as to party spirit were given to them *pneumatikōs*, that is, to the very highest spiritual faculty they can command. He appears to mean that St. Paul was appealing to the human *pneuma* which in Christians is inspired and controlled by the divine *Pneuma*, the Holy Ghost (1 Clem 47[3]).

See 'Soul'.

SPIRITUAL EDIFICATION

οἰκοδομέω, ἐποικοδομέω, οἰκοδομή

The old words, *oikodomō, epoikodomō* and *oikodomē*, now have a spiritual meaning – no longer denoting material structure.

Secular Greek. The secular meanings of the verb *oikodomō* refer to construction, as perhaps the building of a house, but they are sometimes figurative. '*Build* ye upon that foundation still other works of love.'[184] 'He *raised* the Art', wrote Aristophanes.[185]

The compound verb *epoikodomō* is literally used of the Athenians building their walls;[186] it is to construct a brick wall.[187] The aorist passive participle denotes 'superstructure'.[188] The noun *oikodomē* is the act of building;[189] it is metaphorical in the NT alone,[190] and is always spiritual there. 'Ye are God's *building*' (1 Co 3[9]).

Biblical Greek. The sense is metaphorical in Biblical and Christian Greek, referring to the spiritual life of the saints or to the growth of religious character.

In the LXX, the verb *oikodomō* renders the Hebrew *bānâ* (to be established) and refers to the safety of Johanan (Jer 49(42)[10]), to the return of captives from Babylon (40(33)[7]) and to the future edification of Gentiles (Isai 54[14]).

The LXX expression, to 'build' someone, is important for the NT. It is the reverse of 'rooting up' and 'tearing down', and God may do either to Israel. He has set Jeremiah over the nations and over the kingdoms, to root out and to pull down, and to destroy, and to throw down, to build, and to plant' (Jer 1[10]). God promises to 'build' Israel and not to pull them down, to plant them, and not pluck them up (Jer 24[6], 38(31)[4], 40(33)[7]). 'Ye shall be built and I will raise up the decayed places', He promises. 'Thou shalt be built ... thy foundation shall be laid' (Isai 44[26, 28]). 'I will lay thy stones with fair colours, and lay thy foundations with fair sapphires' (Isai 54[11]). So although these words were in pagan use, and even occasionally in a metaphorical way, the Biblical vocabulary has made them specially its own.

The first Christians answered this direction and applied *(ep) oikodomō* to the **edification** of the churches of Palestine and of the

Ephesian elders by God's gracious word (Act 9³¹, 20³²). Christian love **edifies** the believer in a way that even spiritual perception (*gnōsis*) cannot (1 Co 8¹). *Oikodomō* is contrasted with mere legitimacy: 'all things are lawful, but all things **edify** not' (1 Co 10²³). There are two kinds of **edification** – of the believer and of the whole Church. The gift of tongues **edifies** the believer, prophecy the Church (14⁴·¹⁷). Believers should **edify** and comfort one another (1 Th 5¹¹). Here the verb is shown in a good light, but it has the bad sense of 'embolden' when a weak brother is said to become 'hardened' in conscience through the uncharitable conduct of those who profess to have *gnōsis* (1 Co 8¹⁰). Nevertheless, here the meaning may still be 'edify' – in a sarcastic sense – for the phrase may be an ironical quotation of a Corinthian expression.¹⁹¹

The verb *(ep)oikodomō* has special links with the Judgment-seat of Christ, denoting what the grace of God has done with a believer's life (1 Co 3¹⁰·¹²), whether or not the believer has **built spiritually** in precious material, meriting a reward at that tribunal. The Church is **spiritually built** on Jesus Christ, chief Corner Stone, and on apostles and prophets (Eph 2²⁰; Col 2⁷). It is composed of elect and precious living stones which are **spiritually built** upon a chief Corner Stone, (q.v. 1 Pet 2⁵). Instruction is a necessary part of **edification** and St. Jude exhorts Christians to pray in the Spirit, to **edify** themselves in their most holy faith – in correct belief and not in heresy (Jude 20). The Tower which will be quickly **built up** in the Visions of Hermas is symbolic of the Church (*Vis.* III 8.9).

Early Christians avoided the regular secular words, *oikodomia* and *oikodomēsis*, adopting instead the vulgar *oikodomē*; perhaps they sought an unusual means¹⁹² for expressing the unique concept of a mutual 'building-up' in faith (Ro 14¹⁹) and the bearing of burdens for weaker brethren (Ro 15²).

The 'edification' concept owes something to pagan influence, for *oikodomō* belongs to the established vocabulary of the Gnostics and the conformation of initiates into the building of life is a metaphor of Gnosticism. Laying a foundation is a common metaphor also in the Stoic diatribe. 'Do you not wish to make your beginning and your *foundation* firm? Whether your decision is sound to rear thereon the *structure* of your determination?'¹⁹³ 'But if you lay a rotting and crumbling *foundation* you cannot rear thereon even a small building.'¹⁹⁴

It is more likely that the OT was the real influence behind it, in spite of some Stoic influence in 1 Co 3¹⁰⁻¹⁵ and Gnostic influence in 2 Co 5¹, as Vielhauer concedes.¹⁹⁵ Although no doubt the Corinthians already knew the building metaphors which Paul was using, doubtless Paul himself derived them from the OT rather than contemporary philosophy. He was obsessed with the idea of God Himself building up in history His own people.

The whole Church is an *oikodomē* (Eph 2[21]) and believers are God's *oikodomē* (1 Co 3[9]). St. Paul has received authority for their *oikodomē*, certainly not for their humiliation (2 Co 10[8], 12[19], 13[10]).

Our 'spiritual standing' (*oikodomē*) in heaven, the result of faith, is, like the verb, associated with the Judgment-seat of Christ. 'We have a *building* of God ... eternal in the heavens', and it is our assurance that we shall not be ashamed at the Judgment-seat (2 Co 5[1,10]). The 'spiritual building up' (*oikodomē*) of the Body of Christ is entrusted to apostles and other missionaries (Eph 4[12,15]) but may be assisted by the converse of every believer, which ministers grace to the hearers (4[29]).

SPIRITUAL GIFT

χάρισμα

IN later secular Greek the verbal noun *charisma* was used in a similar way to *charis*, in the sense of favours bestowed.[196] In the Jewish Greek of Philo it was, like *charis*, the grace of God.[197] It is scarcely found at all in pagan writers and is not in Josephus.

In the fourth century AD Alciphron has it with the meaning, favour bestowed, but the word may very well be *charis*, which the Teubner text records in the apparatus.[198] The characteristic Ionic ending in *-ma* denoted the result of the action – the 'gift' is the result of favour – but the distinction is probably not applicable at our period of Greek, and *-ma* is favoured in the Koine.[199]

The occurrence of *charisma* in the LXX is uncertain,[200] but Theodotion uses it to translate *ḥesedh*, lovingkindness (Ps 30(31)[21].

In Christian Greek, on the other hand, it is a momentous Pauline word in a soteriological environment. *Charisma* has the special sense of a **gift of God's grace**. It is a blessing which may be imparted by one Christian to another (Ro 1[11]), and it is one of a diversity of 'gifts' bestowed by the Spirit – whether faith, the word of wisdom, the word of knowledge, power to heal, miracle-working, prophecy, discerning of spirits, tongues, interpretation of tongues (1 Co 12[4]). Any variety of charismatic ministry is a *charisma*. It is the reverse of an earned merit such as wages (Ro 6[23]), for it is Gof's free bounty, like the granting of salvation (Ro 5[15f], 6[23], 11[29]). Death is a penalty, but life is a 'gift', a *charisma*.

In the apostolic Fathers, as in the NT, *charisma* is one of those spiritual endowments of which the Church has no lack (I. Smyrn intr.). Believers are urged to pray that they may abound in every *charisma*, in every charismatic gift (I. Pol 2², I. Eph. 17²). St. Clement indicates that it is each member's portion in the Body of Christ,[201] as both St. Peter (1 Pet 4¹⁰) and St. Paul (Ro 12⁶; 1 Co 7⁷) indicated. Every one of us has *charismata*, different according to the grace of God, and we must minister them one to another. St. Justin uses the *charismata* as an argument against the Jews: the Jewish religion is bypassed because these great gifts have passed from Judaism to Christianity (Dial 88¹).

STIFF-NECKED

σκληροτράχηλος

Sklērotrachēlos is of Biblical Greek coinage. MM gave no vernacular instances and in the few literary examples it is but a physical disability. The word refers in the Bible to the arrogant in heart who are destined for divine punishment (Ecclus 16¹¹; Bar 2³⁰).

In Biblical Greek it means much the same as 'hardness of heart' (*sklērokardia*), q.v., and renders the Hebrew for 'stiff of neck', applied always to wickedness, *qᵉshê-'ōreph*,[202] and *maqshê-'ōreph*.[203] The Hebrew phrase, *qᵉshê-'ōreph* is characteristic of the Dead Sea Scrolls.

The word applied to disobedient Israel (so also 1 Clem 53³). By this word St. Stephen refers to his judges, adding that they are 'uncircumcized in heart and ears' (Act 7⁵¹).

SYNAGOGUE, CHRISTIAN MEETING

συναγωγή

In secular Greek *sunagōgē* denotes an assembly, a bringing together,[204] a collection (of writings),[205] but in Biblical Greek the word was used for the Jewish **synagogue**. Jesus foretold that believers would be brought for judgment into **synagogues** (Lk 12¹¹), and that is the regular usage of *sunagōgē* in the NT, especially frequent in the gospels and Acts.

In Christian Greek, however, a further specialization of the word has developed, for it is once in the NT used of a Christian local body. St. James (2²) envisages a rich man coming into the *sunagōgē* with a welcome. The context allows the meaning of 'congregation' or even 'place of assembly'[206] and certainly Christian Greek tended to keep the term *ekklēsia* for the Church as such.

Sunagōgē was an Ebionite term for the Church[207] and in

Christian Palestinian Aramaic the same word ($k^e n\hat{i}sht\hat{a}$) served both for 'synagogue' and 'church'.[208]

It must be said that *sunagōgē* is used not only for assemblies and synagogues of the Jews, but also for worship-meetings and meeting-places of Christians. It is even used by Christians of themselves, and in wider circles than Jewish Christian ones.

Except when the apostolic Fathers use the word in the old sense ('into its reservoirs'), 1 Clem 20[6], they use *sunagōgē* for Church, but they preserved the distinction from *ekklēsia*, reserving *sunagōgē* for the **meeting** of righteous men (Hermas, *Mand.* XI 9, 13, 14) – that is, Christian gatherings which are in effect the local church, as when St. Ignatius writes, 'Let the meetings be more numerous' (I. Pol 4[2]). Origen uses *sunagōgē* for 'church' and the Apostolic Constitutions have the two terms interchangeably – '*sunagōgē* of the Lord' and '*ekklēsia* of the Lord'.[209]

A Christian addition to the Testament of Benjamin (11[2f]) refers to 'synagogues' in a Christian sense – 'the synagogue of the Gentiles' – placing the word apparently in the context of St. Paul and indicating thereby St. Paul's predominantly Gentile churches. But the deliberate use of 'synagogue' for 'church' has probably the aim of introducing a Jewish colouring into the Christian additions in the book to disguise them.

NOTES

[1] As Collatinus, in Dio Cassius XLVI 49.
[2] Herodotus V 38, VI 67.
[3] Josephus *Ant. Jud.* XVII ii 4 (Niese XVII 43).
[4] Cf. the distinction made in LS s.v.
[5] 'Sabbaths' occurs in MSS of Plutarch *de Superstit.* 3, in a list of superstitious practices, but some prefer the reading, 'baptisms' (*Moralia* 166A).
[6] Andocides iv 42.
[7] Polybius III 93.4.
[8] Aristotle *Politica* 1330 a 13.
[9] Diodorus Siculus I 21.
[10] A. Richardson, *An Introduction to the Theology of the New Testament*, SCM 1958, p. 297.
[11] J. T. Ross, *The Concept of sōtēria in the New Testament*, Univ. of Chicago, 1947.
[12] Ibid., p. 352f.
[13] Plato *Crito* 44B.
[14] P. Tebt I 56.11 (ii BC).
[15] P. Tebt II 302.16 (AD 71).
[16] P. Oxy I 33 verso v 12 (c. AD 300).
[17] Homer *Odyssey* V 490, *Iliad* XVII 144.
[18] Herodotus VIII 34.
[19] Aeschylus *Prometheus Bound* 524.

[20] Demosthenes *de Falsa Legatione* 6.
[21] BGU 423.8 (ii AD).
[22] *Republic* 486C.
[23] C. J. Vaughan, *St. Paul's Epistle to the Romans*, Macmillan 1893, p. 106.
[24] A point made by M. Barth, *Journal of Ecumenical Studies* 1 (1964), pp. 58ff.
[25] J. G. Gibbs, *Biblica* 56 (1975), p. 29.
[26] Polystratus (*Epicuri et Epicureorum scripta in Herculanensibus Papyris servata*, ed. A. Vogliano, Berlin 1928, p. 80).
[27] E.g. Strabo IX 1.15.
[28] Plato *Republic* 583B, *Charmides* 167B, *Philebus* 66D, *Laws* 692A, 960C, *Epistles* vii 334D, 340A.
[29] Aeschylus *Choephori* 1073.
[30] P. Enteuxis 11.6 (iii BC), ed. O. Guéraud, Cairo 1931.
[31] P. Petr II 8 (1) B 1f. (c. 250 BC).
[32] E.g. P. Lond 1. 177.24 (i AD).
[33] Lily R. Taylor, *The Divinity of the Roman Emperor*, Middletown, Conn. 1931, pp. 267–83.
[34] W. Bousset, *Kyrios Christos*, p. 242.
[35] R. H. Fuller, *The Foundations of New Testament Christology*, Lutterworth 1965, p. 93.
[36] C. K. Barrett, *The Gospel according to St. John*, SPCK 1955, p. 204.
[37] Lk 2[11]; Jn 4[42]; Act 13[23]; Eph 5[23]; 1 Ti 4[10]; Tit 1[4], 2[13], 3[6]; 2 Pet 1[1,11], 2[20], 3[2,18]; Jude 25.
[38] C. K. Barret, *op. cit.*, p. 181.
[39] BGU II 423.13 (ii AD). See also P. Oxy 939.20 (iii AD).
[40] BGU II 380 b (iii AD).
[41] For a tentative explanation of the phenomenon of style, see *Studies in New Testament Language and Text*, ed. J. K. Elliott, Leiden 1976, p. 392, and also Moulton-Turner, *Grammar*, vol. iv, T. & T. Clark 1976, p. 61.
[42] Exceptions are few: *blessing* (Lk 19[9]; Act 4[12]), Jewish *salvation* (Jn 4[22]).
[43] *De Fide et Operibus* 21–6 (PL XL).
[44] See Article XII of the Church of England.
[45] Xenophon *Anabasis* III 2.9.
[46] Ibid. V 1.1.
[47] J. T. Ross, *The Conception of sōtēria in the New Testament*, Univ. of Chicago 1947, p. 256.
[48] *Pompey* 24.
[49] *Ant. Jud.* XII ii 3: 'ransom money' of more than 400 talents to release prisoners.
[50] *Quod Omnis Probus Liber Sit*, 114 (II 463).
[51] E. K. Simpson, *Words Worth Weighing*, Tyndale 1946, p. 9.
[52] Ibid., p. 8, n. 1.
[53] See the excellent discussion by David Hill, *Greek Words and Hebrew Meanings*, CUP 1967, pp. 73ff.
[54] Dionysius the Areopagite (Trench p. 62).
[55] *Life of Moses* II 65.
[56] *Ant. Jud.* XI 66 (Niese).
[57] E.g. Plutarch *de Iside et Osiride* 72.
[58] M. Dibelius and H. Conzelmann, *The Pastoral Epistles*, ET Fortress, Pa., 1912, pp. 148f.
[59] *Metamorphoses* 11.21 (ed. R. Helm 1907, p. 283).
[60] Preisendanz 4.499ff.
[61] W. Scott, *Corpus Hermeticum*, Clarendon 1924, libellus XIII 3.
[62] See C. H. Dodd, *Interpretation of the Fourth Gospel*, CUP 1953, pp. 49f.
[63] *De Cherubim* 114.
[64] C. H. Dodd, op. cit., p. 53, n. 1.

[65] Dibelius, op. cit., p. 150.

[66] F. Büchsel in Kittel *TWNT* I, p. 674.

[67] *De Baptismo* I 2.22, etc.

[68] Herodotus II 41, Xenophon *Historia Graeca* III 2.19.

[69] IG XII 694.14, Dittenberger 3rd ed. 768.16.

[70] Aristophanes *Birds* 522 ('once they treated you as mighty and *hagios*; now they treat you as knaves'). The adverb appears in Isocrates XI 25.

[71] However, the text of this difficult verse is clearer if we read *haplotēti* (simplicity) instead of *hagiotēti* (sanctity) with the Western text, as in AV. In favour of *haplotēti*, see G. D. Kilpatrick in *Journal of Theological Studies* 45 (1944), pp. 60–5. According to Miss Thrall 'the evidence remains finely-balanced', inclining towards *hagiotēti*. See J. K. Elliott, *Studies in New Testament Language and Text*, Brill, 1976, pp. 366–72.

[72] Thucydides VII 10.

[73] *Fragmenta* 358.

[74] P. Par 63 b (165 BC), P. Lond XXIII (158 BC). Deissmann BS p. 110.

[75] Philodemus *Volumina Rhetorica* (Teubner I 37.S), Plutarch *Cicero* 26.

[76] Dr. Kilpatrick argued that *nomikos* as a professional description is a term belonging to free Greek, while *grammateus* belongs to translation Greek. G. D. Kilpatrick, *Journal of Theological Studies* NS 1 (1950), pp. 56–60.

[77] A. H. M'Neile, *The Gospel according to St. Matthew*, Macmillan 1915, p. 339.

[78] G. D. Kilpatrick, op. cit., p. 57.

[79] Aeschylus *Persae* 169. So also Euripides *Alcestis* 606, Thycydides VI 86.

[80] Sophocles *Electra* 1104. So also Thucydides I 128.

[81] 1 Co 16^{17} (of Stephanas, etc.); 2 Co 10^{10} (of Paul); Ph 2^{12} (opp. of 'absence'); 2 Co 7^6 (of Titus); Ph 1^{26} ('my arrival'); 2 Th 2^9 (of the Wicked One).

[82] P. Petr II 39e 18 (iii BC), P. Par 26.i.18 (163 BC).

[83] S. Bartina, in 'La Escatología del Apocalipsis' in *Estudios Bíblicos* (Madrid) 21 (1962), pp. 297–310.

[84] W. B. Wallis, *Journal of the Evangelical Theological Society* (of Wheaton) 18 (1975), pp. 229–42.

[85] *On First Things* ii 1, iii 6.

[86] *Civitas Dei* xx 6f.

[87] 1 Clem 17^1; Pol ad Phil 6^3.

[88] E.g. *Apol.* I 52, *Dial.* XL.

[89] T. F. Glasson, *The Second Advent; the Origin of the New Testament Doctrine*, Epworth 1945. See especially pp. 211ff.

[90] *His Appearing and His Kingdom*, Epworth 1953, p. 201.

[91] See H. Greeven, *Kerygma und Dogma* (Göttingen) 10 (1964), p. 135.

[92] *Adversus Haereses* book V, ch. xxvi 2.

[93] *The Inscriptions of Cos*, ed. W. R. Paton and E. L. Hicks, Clarendon 1891, p. 391.

[94] BS p. 198, and his article in *Realencyclopädie*, acknowledged as an error in *Light From the Ancient East*, ET, Hodder 1927, p. 76, n. 1 (ET 1910, p. 70, n. 2).

[95] *Nicomachean Ethics* 1117 b 28 (III 10.2).

[96] II 1084E.

[97] 4 Mac 1^{32}, once thought to be by Josephus, now by a contemporary Egyptian Jew.

[98] Libellus IX 9. See W. Scott, *Corpus Hermeticum*, Clarendon vol. I 1924, p. 184.

[99] *Adversus Haereses* I vi 3.

[100] For the Gnostic material, see Preisandanz 4.524f. 510, 4.725, W. Scott, op. cit. I, p. 184.

[101] Irenaeus *adversus Haereses* I vi 2.

[102] E.g. in *de Ieiunio adversus Psuchicos*, and *adversus Marcionem* IV 22.

S

Clement of Alexandria *Stromateis* IV 13 (PG VIII 1300C).

104 Diodorus Siculus 4.81.

105 Philo II 559.

106 Athenaeus (Teubner) VIII 334C (ii-iii AD).

107 Lucian *Asinus* 11.

108 Plutarch *How to Tell a Flatterer* 52E.

109 *Papyri Graeci Musei Antiquarii Publici Lugduni Batavi*, ed. C. Leemans, Brill 1843, II, p. 87; papyrus W, pagina 2a.

110 *The Letter to the Romans: a Commentary*, Lutterworth 1959, in loc.

111 P. Oxy I 34 iii 13 (AD 127), P. Tebt I 5, 3 (118 BC), P. Par 63 xiii 2ff. (165 BC), BGU IV 1185.7 (i BC).

112 P. Oxy I 34 iii 4.

113 *Republic* 366A.

114 *Phaedo* 113E.

115 Xenophon *Cyropaedia* V 4.19.

116 An important variant has *hamartēma* at 2 Pet 1⁹ in place of *hamartia* in the accepted texts: 'purged from his old sins' – individual acts.

117 E. de W. Burton, pp. 436–43.

118 See C. Bigg, *1 and 2 Peter*, ICC, in loc. See under the entry, 'Bring to the altar'.

119 C. H. Dodd, *The Bible and the Greeks*, Hodder 1935, p. 80.

120 Ibid. pp. 76–81.

121 Deissmann BS p. 225.

122 Philodemus (i BC), *Herc.* 1251.14 (Teubner) in plural.

123 Polybius IX 10.6.

124 Longinus (iii AD) OCT 36.2.

125 Diodorus Siculus (i BC) XIX 100 (Teubner).

126 Trench, pp. 226, 232.

127 *Historia Plantarum* IX 4.8.

127 Gorgias, a sophist (v BC), *Helena* (ed. Blass) 19.

129 P. Tebt I 5.3 (118 BC). Moreover, in OGI 116.2, the reading and the meaning are anything but clear.

130 Plato *Philebus* 53A.

131 *Philebus* 59C.

132 *Symposium* 211E.

133 *Phaedo* 52D, 66A, 81C.

134 *Nicomachean Ethics* X vi 4.

135 *Praeparatio Evangelica* xv 15.4 (ed. E. H. Gifford, Clarendon 1903, vol. 2, p. 449).

136 P. Oxy X 1252 verso ii 38 (AD 288–95).

137 *Iliad* XI 334.

138 *Iliad* I 3.

139 *Phaedrus* 246A, *Republic* 608D, etc.

140 *Memorabilia* IV iii 14.

141 E. de W. Burton, *Spirit, Soul and Flesh*, Univ. of Chicago Historical and Linguistic Studies, second series, III 1918, p. 29.

142 Developed in book II of *de Anima*.

143 Burton, op. cit., p. 47.

144 See the citations in Burton, op. cit.

145 For an excellent discussion, see Edwin Hatch, *Essays in Biblical Greek*, Clarendon 1889, pp. 112–24.

146 F. C. Grant, *An Introduction to New Testament Thought*, Abingdon 1950, pp. 165f.

147 Or, 'Man in the prime of life': see G. Dautzenberg, *Biblische Zeitschrift* (Paderborn) 8 (1964), pp. 262–76.

148 Sophocles *Electra* 1127.

[149] J. H. Moulton *Grammar* I, p. 87.
[150] E.g. T. Abr 78^{22}, 97^{22}.
[151] G. Dautzenberg in *Biblische Zeitschrift*, op. cit.
[152] The theme of W. D. Stacey's book, *The Pauline View of Man*, Macmillan 1956.
[153] N. H. Snaith in *Interpretation* 1 (1947), p. 324.
[154] O. Cullmann, *Immortality of the Soul or Resurrection of the Body*, Epworth 1958, p. 6.
[155] Burton, p. 489.
[156] J. Laidlaw in HDB IV, p. 612.
[157] Ibid., p. 612.
[158] PL XXXII 587.
[159] *De Anima et Origine eius* i 10 (PL XLIV 500f).
[160] *Liber de Origine Animae Hominis* 27.
[161] *De Anima* 19.§2.
[162] Op. cit. 27.§2.
[163] *De Anima*, ed. J. H. Waszink, Meulenhoff (Amsterdam) 1947, pp. 26f., 38, 39.
[164] S. *Gregorii episcopi Nysseni de Anima et Resurrectione cum sorore sua Macrina Dialogus*, ed. J. G. Krabingerus, Lipsiae 1837, pp. 117ff. See also *The Fathers of the Church, 58. St. Gregory of Nyssa's Ascetical Works*, Catholic Univ. of America 1966, pp. 254f.
[165] B. F. Westcott, *The Epistle to the Hebrews*, Macmillan 1889, p. 179.
[166] Commentary on 1 Peter 2.11.
[167] Josephus *Bell. Jud.* II i 3 (Niese II 9), *Ant. Jud.*XVII ix 2 (Niese XVII 210).
[168] *Cato Maior* 5.
[169] *The Cleverness of Animals* 3 (Moralia 961D).
[170] *Table Talk*, 6.1 (Moralia 653C).
[171] Ibid. VII 3 (Moralia 712C).
[172] H. Alford, *New Testament*, vol. III, p. 370.
[173] C. J. Ellicott, *The Pastoral Epistles of St. Paul*, Longman 5th ed. 1883, p. 113.
[174] Burton, pp. 486–8.
[175] Herodotus VII 16.
[176] Euripides *Bacchae* 128; Aeschylus *Persae* 507.
[177] Thucydides II 49.
[178] Aristotle *Problemata* 948 b 25; Diogenes Laertius VI 94.
[179] Menander 482.3.
[180] Burton, p. 489.
[181] D. E. H. Whiteley, *The Theology of St. Paul*, Blackwell 1964, p. 42.
[182] Here Vaticanus and the important minuscule 33 read *pneumatikós*.
[183] I. Smyrn 3^3.
[184] Xenophon *Cyropaedia* VIII 7, 15.
[185] *Pax* 749.
[186] Thucydides VII 4.
[187] Xenophon *Anabasis* III 4.11.
[188] Plato *Laws* 793C.
[189] P. Cairo Zen. 499.93 (iii BC).
[190] It has the secular sense of physical construction in the LXX, and also in Aquila (Ezek 40), Symmachus (Ezek 40; Hab 2^{11}), and Theodotion (Ezek 11^1).
[191] Robertson and Plummer, *1 Corinthians*, ICC T. & T. Clark 2nd ed. 1914, p. 171.
[192] And a despised means, for *oikodomē* was a word rejected by fine literary writers, the Atticists.
[193] Arrian *Epictetus's Discourses* book II xv 8.
[194] Ibid. II xv 9.
[195] P. Vielhauer, *Oikodomē. Das Bild vom Bau in der christlichen Literatur vom Neuen Testament bis Clemens Alexandrinus*, Karlsruhe-Durlach 1940, p. 122.

[196] BGU 1044.4 (iv AD).

[197] *Legum Allegoria* III 78, but perhaps we should read *charis* instead.

[198] III 17.4, ed. M. A. Schepens, Teubner 1905, p. 78.

[199] Blass-Debrunner, *Grammatik des neutestamentlichen Griechisch*, Göttingen 8th ed. 1949, §109, 2, p. 52; E. Schwyzer, *Griechische Grammatik*, Munich 1953, vol. I, p. 128.

[200] One MS of Ecclus 7^{33} (AB have *charis*) 38^{30} B[1] (rest have *chrisma*).

[201] 1 Clem 38[1]; literally, 'he was appointed with his *charismatic gift*'.

[202] Ex 32^9 Sm Th, $33^{3,5}$, 34^9; Deut $9^{6,13}$.

[203] But emend to *miqq^{e}shê 'ōreph* in view of the LXX (Pr 29^1).

[204] Plato *Theaetetus* 150A; Polybius IV 7.6; Diogenes Laertius II 129.

[205] Dionysius of Halicarnassus II 27.

[206] L. Rost *Palästinajahrbuch* 29 (1933), pp. 54f.

[207] Epiphanius *adversus LXXX Haereses* XXX 18.

[208] J. H. Ropes, *James*, ICC T. & T. Clark 1954, p. 189.

[209] For the detailed evidence see W. Schrage in Kittel *TWNT* VII, p. 839.

T

TABERNACLE: FEAST OF TABERNACLES

σκηνή : ἐπισκηνόω : σκηνοπηγία

They have become Biblical words and, among Christians, words of typological and spiritual significance.

Secular Greek. The first word, *skēnē,* was a tent, and backcloth and other part of a theatrical stage, called also the 'tragic *skēnē*.[1] Actors in a play, as distinct from the chorus, may be referred to as, 'they from the *skēnē*'.[2] *Skēnē* is entertainment given in tents.[3] Josephus used the word of a shrewd trick or deception, such as John of Gischala used against Josephus himself.[4] At an Athenian public funeral the bones of the fallen were laid out in a *skēnē* which was specially erected.[5] It is true that *skēnē* might be used for a tent which served religious purposes: a chorus in Euripides confides that 'my lady's spouse hath stolen into the festal *tent* to offer sacrifice for welcoming and birth ... of this new son' (*Ion* 806), but the use of the word as a sort of shrine is not the same as the technical term *skēnē,* the Hebrew holy Tent. In the plural *skēnai* was a soldiers' camp.[6]

Our second word, *episkēnō,* was 'to be quartered', a rare word used in reference to soldiers,[7] and the noun *skēnopēgia,* our third word, which is literally the setting up of tents was used by Aristotle of the 'nest building' of swallows,[8] but is rare indeed outside Biblical and Jewish Greek.

Biblical Greek. All these words, by their consonants, reminded the translators of the Hebrew stem *skn* and may have influenced them in the choice of an equivalent. Mainly, the Hebrew word rendered by *skēnō* and *kataskēnō* is *shākhēn* (whence *sh^ekhînâ*).

From the Greek Bible *skēnē* gained the special connotation of the Mosaic 'Tabernacle', the holy Tent in the wilderness, and of God's 'dwelling' among His special people. 'Even to this day', He said, 'I have walked in a tent, in a *tabernacle (skēnē)*' (2 Km 7[6]). Among Christians *skēnē* has special significance: it applies not only to the earthly Tabernacle and Temple[9] (Act 7[44]; Heb 8[5] 9[3] 13[10]), but also to the archetype in heaven which is not made with hands (Lk 16[9]; Rev 13[6] 15[5] 21[3]) – and also to the three 'booths' mentioned at the Transfiguration (Mt 17[4]; Mk 9[5]; Lk 9[33]), a symbol of God's gracious Presence there.

The verb *episkēnō* (not in the LXX) has in its context the same significance, the Glory 'tabernacling' among men. The verb is applied to Christ, the Sh^ekhînâ Glory, 'tabernacling' upon the Apostle who finds most glory in the moment of supremest weakness

438

(2 Co 12⁹). There is also the simplex verb *skēnō* and the verb *kataskēnō*. The former is a contemporary Greek word for dwelling temporarily, the latter means to pitch one's tent, to dwell. But in Christian language they have the same special connotation of the *Shᵉkhînâ* once more, i.e. God's dwelling with men (esp. Jn 1¹⁴).

The popular pilgrim feast of Booths or Tabernacles was expressed by *heortē* (feast) with the adjective *skēnopēgia* in Josephus and the NT,[10] following the same precedent (Deut 16¹⁶ 31¹⁰; Zach 14¹⁶,¹⁸,¹⁹) which rendered the Hebrew *sukkâ* (booth) in the plural. Deissmann[11] drew attention to the verb, *skēnopēgeisthai*, which was used in an inscription in a religious sense 'in the world which spoke the language of the Septuagint'.

From this evidence Deissmann reached the conclusion that the LXX had chosen a secular noun, *skēnopēgia*, for the Jewish feast: in doing so, 'they brought it more into touch with the religious usages of the world around them. This is one more factor in the great adaptive process for which the Septuagint Bible stands in general in the history of religion' (ibid.). But it should be noted that so far *skēnopēgia* has not been discovered in reference to cultic festivals, and so we must be careful when we speak of the influence of Hellenistic terminology in the Diaspora.[12]

The feast has special significance in the life of Jesus, for at it He was pressed to manifest Himself before His hour (of great Glory) had come (Jn 7²). Some of His important discourses, on Living Water and Light, are related to two great features of the ritual of this feast – water pouring and light burning – together with the mighty healing of the man born blind. It is part of Christ's manifestation to the Church: the man is put out of the synagogue for confessing Jesus to be the Christ, and Jesus foretells that the disciples shall be expelled for the same reason. 'The things typified by the Jewish feasts, then, are fulfilled in Jesus and His Church.'[13]

TAUGHT OF GOD

Θεοδίδακτος

Theodidaktos is a coinage of Christian Greek not appearing in the LXX. St. Paul reminds believers that they are **taught to God** to have brotherly love (1 Th 4⁹). Presumably the teaching which is conceived as divine in origin was the teaching handed down in the supernaturally inspired Didache or Tradition. Christians are said to be **taught of God.** They must enquire what the Lord seeks from them and behave so that they may be found in the Book of Life on the day of Judgment (Barn 21⁶).

The Apologists made good use of the word. Speaking of his own conversion to Christ, Tatian says that his soul was **taught of God** when he rejected secular Greek writings. He discerned that they led to condemnation while the Christian Scriptures in which he trusted put an end to slavery and brought deliverance from tyrants.[14]

Another of the Apologists, Athenagoras, speaks similarly of the Scriptures, applying the word to their doctrines. He pleads with the cultural outsider. 'We can persuade you,' he says, rebutting the usual charge against the Christians, 'that you are not dealing with atheists precisely through the doctrines which we hold – doctrines which are not man-made but are ordained and **taught of God**'.[15]

Towards the end of the second century Theophilus of Antioch uses the word of the prophets. 'The men of God, possessed by a holy Spirit and becoming prophets and being instructed by God Himself, were **taught of God** and became holy and righteous.'[16]

TEACHER OF CHRISTIAN MORALS

καλοδιδάσκαλος

We would expect the word *Kalodidaskalos* to bear the meaning, 'teaching good things', had it been constructed in secular Greek. It is, however, a Christian hapax legomenon (Bauer), found only in the Pastoral epistles where the context requires the meaning, a teacher of morals, one who instructs in sobriety, domesticity, discretion, chastity, virtue and obedience, according to the accepted tradition of the Church – not necessarily in public capacity, for it is applied to 'aged women' (Tit 2³), who must observe silence in the assembled church, i.e. in the presence of brothers. As Ellicott correctly observes, referring to St. Chrysostom, 'not by public teaching but, as the context implies by its specifications, in domestic privacy'.[17]

The noun *kakodidaskalō,* formed on the same principle, is a secular word, 'to instruct in evil'.[18]

TEMPTATION

πειρασμός, πειράζω, ἐκπειράζω

To some extent the meaning of *peirasmos, peirazō* and *ekpeirazō* is foreshadowed in secular Greek, but in the Biblical language they carry much stronger moral connotations than the words, 'trial' and 'attempt' can suggest.

Secular Greek. The meanings were: experiment, attempt, make trial of. The noun *peirasmos* refers to a trial,[19] specifically on land and sea,[20] but it is an unusual word. The verb *peirazō* appears in Homer (to make trial of),[21] but just before and just after the NT was written it has the meaning, 'to attempt',[22] Lucian's character, Gout, declaring that each man 'tries' a different skill against him.[23] At the same time, however, *peirazō* has the rather different meaning, 'to be sorely tried', whether by scurvy of the gums,[24] by epilepsy,[25] or, in a philosopher of iii AD, by cataract on the eyes.[26] The nearest we come to the Biblical meaning, i.e. **temptation,** is in Apollonius of Rhodes, 'to seek to seduce'.[27] Otherwise *peirazō* and *peirasmos* never have the meaning of deliberate enslavement or enticement to sin. 'Seduction' is *peirasis.*

Biblical Greek. So in the Bible and in Christian Greek, *peirasmos* and *peirazō* were transformed into moral and religious trial or tribulation, as when God put Abraham to the test concerning Isaac (Gen 22[1]). In the LXX the Hebrew word *massâ* (a test, trial) is rendered by *peirasmos.* The Hebrew word *nissâ* (Piel) means to test or try a person in order to see which way he will act (Ex 16[4]; Jg 2[22] 3[4]) or whether his character is firm (Gen 22[1]; Ex 20[20]; Deut 7[19] 8[2-6] 13[3] 29[3]; 3 Km 10[1]). By this word men are said to 'prove' God when they doubt His character (Ex 17[2,7]; Nu 14[22]; Ps 106[14]): *peirasmos* is the provocation of God by the Israelites in the wilderness (Ex 17[7]; Heb 3[8]), the temptation of Jesus (Lk 22[28]), the tribulations which beset St. Paul on his travels (Act 20[19]; Gal 4[14]), and the 'trials' of our earthly pilgrimage which merit the crown at the end, fiery 'trials' indeed (Jas 1[2,12]; 1 Pet 1[6] 4[12]) out of which the Lord will deliver the godly (2 Pet 2[9]) and keep them from the supreme hour of 'trial' (Rev 3[10]). The new connotation of 'trial' as affliction or disaster, and therefore as 'chastisement', comes into Biblical Greek in the later books of the LXX.[28] 'Having been a little chastised they shall be greatly benefited, for God proved *(peirazō)* them and found them worthy of Himself' (Wis 3[5]). They were tried *(peirazō),* 'albeit in mercy chastised ...' (11[10]). So Ecclus 2[1]; Jdt 8[24f.].

'Persecution' is one very important meaning of *peirasmos* in Christian Greek, but the persecution should be understood to include temptation to sin.

Part of the persecutions of Jesus were His *peirasmoi* in the desert (Lk 4[13]). Those of the disciples, causing them to fall away, are forecast in the parable of the Sower (Lk 8[13]) and in the Lord's Prayer (Mt 6[13]; Lk 11[4]; Did 8[2]). Against these predicted *peirasmoi* the disciples must pray (Mt 26[41]; Mk 14[38]; Lk 22[40,46]). They may take comfort because their *peirasmoi* are such as are common to man and are not intolerable: God provides a way to escape (1 Co 10[13]). The rich, however, must expect to fall into them (1 Ti 6[9]).

'Lead us not into *peirasmos*'. To a large extent the clause in the Lord's Prayer is 'an unsolved problem'. In almost all traditions of Jesus' teaching the inevitability of suffering is evident and disciples are never on any other occasion bidden to pray for escape except in the one instance confronting us in the Lord's Prayer. Perhaps the key to understanding is to be found in the example of Jesus (Mk 14[36]) who demonstrated the legitimacy of praying to escape what seems inevitable, as long as there is the offer of obedience at the same time in the words, 'Thy will be done.'[29] On the other hand, as Jeremias observes,[30] the word *peirasmos* in the context does not indicate the small temptations of everyday life, but the last great Test, when the power of Antichrist is revealed, the *peirasmos* of believers at the hands of pseudo-prophets and *pseudochristoi*. In the Lord's Prayer then we ask that at the last we may not fall from grace. 'Lead us not into,' has rather the meaning, 'Let us not be overpowered by'. Jeremias compares the old Jewish evening prayer which Jesus may have known. It says, 'Do not lead me into the power of a sin, a temptation, a shame'. It is not that we ignore the small temptations of every day by making this petition. We overcome the smaller by concentrating on the larger. 'The Lord's Prayer,' says Jeremias, 'teaches us how to ask for the great things'.

The whole of our earthly way is one *peirasmos* upon another. Browning describes the succession of choice and probation all through life. You must not bar man 'from assuming earth to be a pupil's place', he urges. Man learns because he lives, and temptation comes only to be mastered and made to crouch beneath man's foot. 'Lead *us* not into temptation,' man cries, 'but lead temptations to us, by the head and hair, reluctant dragons, to us who dare to fight'. It would be otherwise if earth were our goal. Then would life be 'ghastly smooth', a sad obscure sequestered vale, and not 'the starting point of man'. Would we ever achieve the finishing-point, the prize, the glory, Heaven – were it not for one *peirasmos* after another?

The verb *peirazō* follows the same pattern as the noun: first, the putting of God or His Son to the test;[31] then the testing of disciples, including Abraham (Gen 22[1]; Heb 11[17]), the Maccabaean martyrs (Heb 11[37]), Philip (Jn 6[6]), false apostles (Rev 2[2]), and the church of Philadelphia (Rev 3[10]). *Peirazō* is used of the brethren's self-examination (2 Co 13[5]). In their trial they are helped by Jesus who Himself was 'tempted' (*peirazō* Heb 2[18] 4[15]).

Like the noun, the verb includes the meaning of temptation to sin, whether of believers tempted both by Satan and their own lust (Gal 6[1]; 1 Co 7[5]; 1 Th 3[5]; Jas 1[13f.]; Rev 2[10]; 2 Clem 18[2]), or of Jesus (Mt 4[1,3]; Mk 1[13]; Lk 4[2]).

The compound verb *ekpeirazō* – always in the NT used of testing

442

God or Christ (Mt 4[7]; Lk 4[12]; 10[25]; 1 Co 10[9]) – seems to be quite absent from secular Greek. There is *ekpeirō* (prove, induce), very similar, but what is said above on the differences between Biblical and secular Greek serves also to differentiate the Biblical *ekpeirazō* from the secular *ekpeirō*.

TERRIFIED

ἔκτρομος

Ektromos is not found in the LXX and the apostolic Fathers and, if it is the correct reading in the NT (Heb 12[21]), it is a Christian coinage which turns up later in a Jewish-Greek inscription from the necropolis of Hadrumetum in the third century:[32] 'I adjure thee by Him who ... causes the whole earth *to quake (ektromon).*'

The leaden tablet is a love-spell, a species of magic, in which the formulae by which the demon is adjured have been taken by the writer from the LXX. This line in particular (26f.) is reminiscent of Ps 103(104)[32] but the LXX, instead of *ektromon,* has the verb *tremein:* 'He looketh on the earth and it *trembleth*'.

Another work of a Greek-speaking Jew, acquainted with the Greek OT, may be the great Paris papyrus,[33] which has a similar formula of adjuration: 'I adjure thee, every demonic spirit, by Him who looks on the earth (cp. Ps 103) and makes its foundations to *tremble (ektromon)* and has made all things to come into being from nothing'.

Since *ektromos* is not in the LXX, how came it into these magical Jewish texts and into the D-text (supported by Sinaiticus) of Heb 12[21]? Christian coinage is the most probable explanation. The Christian context concerns the emotion of Moses at Mount Sinai when he was inspired by the encounter with God. 'I am full of fear,' he said. Whether or not Christians coined the word, I assume that it has affinities with the numinous term, *ekstasis.* See, 'Sense of the Numinous.'

TESTIFY BEFOREHAND

προμαρτύρομαι

Promarturomai, a Christian term, was a hapax until the appearance of two papyri of the eighth century. Subsequently it can be traced only in the fourteenth. For Christians, all that happened in the old dispensation was for their instruction, upon whom the ends of the dispensations had come, and St. Peter rejoices that by the OT prophets the Spirit of Christ 'testified beforehand of the sufferings of Christ' (1 Pet 1[11]).

See, 'Figure'.

TESTING

a. TRIAL

1. δοκιμή : δοκιμεῖον

The words dokimē and *dokimeion* were fairly rare in pagan use.

Dokimē cannot be traced earlier than St. Paul. It is used by the twelfth-century commentator on Homer, bishop Eustathius of Thessalonica, to indicate the 'trial' of gold by fire, and is almost exclusively Christian.[34] In Christian Greek *dokimē* corresponds to patience and is rendered 'experience' in Ro 5[4]AV, where the exercise of it is said to inspire hope. The *dokimē* may take the form of a test of obedience (2 Co 2[9]), a trial of affliction (8[2]), a ministration to the poverty of others (9[13]), much-needed severity towards friends (13[3]) or, in the case of Timothy, loyalty to a father in Christ (Ph 2[22]). In short *dokimē* is variously rendered **proof, experience, trial,** and is the seizing of each costly opportunity to test oneself in service to others.

The other word, *dokimeion* (sometimes spelt *dokimion*), appears in the better text of 1 Pet 1[7], meaning 'trial' – that is, the trial of the readers' faith. Plato has the word in the plural for 'instruments of testing', i.e. the veins of the body which he supposed to have the functions which we ascribe to the nerves.[35] It appears in Jas 1[3] (the *testing* of faith). Trench (p. 262) aptly explained that *dokimazō* in. secular Greek was the technical word for putting money to the *dokimē* (test) by the aid of the *dokimion* (the means of testing), while that which endures the test is *dokimos* (tried).

Deissmann suggested that *to dokimion* was a neuter adjective meaning 'standard' or 'genuine', applied to gold and other precious metals. It is, then, the substantival use of the adjective, and the translation of 1 Pet 1[7] will be, not 'the *testing* of your faith', but '*that which is genuine* in your faith'. Deissmann provided evidence of the adjective *dokimios* in secular Greek (BS pp. 259ff.), and I have endeavoured to show elsewhere the importance of his suggestion for the exegesis of Jas 1[3] and 1 Pet 1[7] – 'your faith when tested'.[36]

2. πύρωσις

The meaning of *purōsis* in secular Greek is a burning[37] – as in 1 Pet 4[12]; Rev 18[9,18] – an exposure to fire, as in cooking and boiling,[38] or destruction by fire.[39] It may be also a flame[40] or an inflammation.[41] It is then quite distinct from the **proving by fire** of Biblical Greek.

In the LXX *purōsis* is a furnace for gold (Pr 27[21]) and the blasting with which God had smitten His people (Amos 4[9]). And so in Symmachus (Jer 30(37)[13]).

St. Peter warns of the fiery trial which is to test Christians (1 Pet 4[12]). *Purōsis* is also the fiery trial which will be prominent at the End (Did 16[5]). The lexicon of Hesychius defines the word as 'trial by fire', the Christian usage having by then become general.

b. TRIED

δοκίμιος : δόκιμος

The first adjective, *dokimios*, is rare but, as we have seen, Deissmann discovered a secular example with the meaning, 'genuine', 'standard', and he applied it to the NT phrase, which thus reads, 'what is genuine in your faith' (1 Pet 1[7]). It seems to have the same meaning in the LXX: 'silver which from the earth is *genuine*' (Ps 11(12)[7]).

However, the second adjective, *dokimos*, had this meaning too in secular Greek – acceptable, trustworthy, approved. Neither *dokimios* nor *dokimos* are peculiarly Christian words, therefore. Still, they were filled with a new meaning by the context of the Lord's Coming.

All the words of this stem (see also, 'Trial') began in Christian Greek to signify approval at the judgment-seat of Christ, while at the same time not losing their secular and LXX association with the acceptability or testing of precious metals. In Gen 23[16], for instance, *dokimos* signified 'current' coinage, literally money that passes from hand to hand and is acceptable. The basic Hebrew verb is *'ābhar* (to pass). So also *dokimos* was 'best' or 'refined' metal.[42]

Dokimos passed into wide use among Christians, indicating fine metal that was 'approved', and denoting Apelles who was approved in Christ (Ro 16[10]). It was applied to every Christian who must stand his test before his fellow-men as well as before God (Ro 14[18]). The appearance of heresies will prove to be a testing for believers and will show up the true metal of those who are *dokimoi* (approved, 1 Co 11[19]).

The church of Smyrna affirmed that St. Polycarp's martyred bones were more refined *(dokimōtera)* than gold (M. Pol 18[1]). However, no Christian should boast of being *dokimos*, for it is the Lord who commends (2 Co 10[18]) and St. Paul would not appear *dokimos* in their sight (13[7]). Our sole concern is to show ourselves to God to be *dokimoi* (2 Ti 2[15]). As we have seen (under 'Trial'), the better text of 1 Pet 1[7] has the noun *dokimion*, although another text has the neuter of *dokimos* (what is approved, i.e. your faith).

We must study then to be *dokimos* at Christ's judgment-seat, where all Christians shall stand on the day that declares every man's work.

c. TO TEST

1. δοκιμάζω

Secular Greek. The verb *dokimazō* is the most used among words of this stem, and means to test, examine, approve, of both purple and gold in Isocrates (XII 39), and of wines in Aristotle.[43] It was to put a person to the test in Isocrates (II 50), to 'prove' friends in Xenophon,[44] and so it means to sanction and approve (Xenophon, Thucydides). It served for examining and admitting boys to the adolescent status of the *epheboi*.

Christian Greek. In the NT, however, *dokimazō* commonly appears in an eschatological context. The fiery tribulation is like the Refiner's fire, **trying** every man's work (1 Co 3[13]; 1 Pet 1[7]). As gold is **tried**, so must the disciple be (Hermas, *Vis.* IV 3.4). At the Table we proclaim the Lord's death until He come, and it behoves each participant to **examine** himself *(dokimazō)* so that he eats and drinks worthily (1 Co 11[28]).

The context of the verb in Hermas (*Sim.* VIII 2.5) is eschatological, the giving of crowns and palms. 'The Lord has **made trial of** you,' says the angel of repentance, 'and inscribed you among the number of us' (*Sim.* IX 24.4), while the Shepherd allegorizes, 'The Tower cannot be finished just yet, until the Lord of it come, and **test** the building in order that, if any of the stones be found decayed, He may change them, for the Tower is built according to His pleasure' (*Sim.* IX 5.2).

Moreover, in Christian Greek the verb expresses the Church's activity of **testing** by the Holy Spirit (e.g. 1 Clem 42[4]). As St. Paul had directed in the matter of prophesying, instructing the Church to **put** all things **to the test** *(dokimazō, 1 Th 5[21])*, so St. Clement directs that suitable ministers **be put to the test** (1 Clem 44[2] 47[4]), while Hermas and the Didache urge that true and false prophets be tested (*Mand.* 11[7,16]; Did. 11[11]). The Didache refers to bishops and deacons as **well tested** (passive, Did. 15). All is in accord with St. Paul's fundamental principle: he had urged the Church to **test** (*dokimazō*) suitable messengers to bring the Christian liberality to Jerusalem (1 Co 16[3]), and he had used the word for **approving** the believer's sincerity (2 Co 8[8,22]) and for **testing** hearts (1 Th 2[4]). So by this verb Hermas can speak of 'a devout soul tried and **tested**' (*Vis.* I 2.4).

It is not clear how the verb differs from *peirazō* (q.v.), especially when the words occur together: 'Examine *(peirazō)* yourselves, whether ye be in the faith; prove *(dokimazō)* your own selves' (2 Co 13[5]).

At all events *dokimazō* involves self-examination, for every believer must prove *(dokimazō)* his own work (Gal 6[4]), and as we remarked on *dokimē* (see A), the examination leads to Christian experience, '... proving what is acceptable unto the Lord', 'experiencing excellent things' (Eph 5[10]; Ph 1[10]), making proof of the virtue of our faith (1 Clem 1[2]).

2. πυρόω

Purō is to burn with fire in secular Greek and, in the passive (as in Eph 6[16]; 2 Pet 3[13]), to be influenced or excited (as in 1 Co 7[9]; 2 Co 11[29]).

In Biblical Greek the passive has the special meaning, to be refined, as if by fire, and so also in Philo. In the Christian apocalypse, the Alpha and Omega has feet like refined brass (Rev 1[15]). Fine gold is said to be refined in the fire (Rev 3[18]). In the letter of the Smyrnaeans the body of the martyr Polycarp is declared to be refined like silver or gold.[45]

TO THINK TOO HIGHLY OF ONESELF

φρεναπατάω ἑαυτόν

Phrenapatō heauton is literally 'to deceive oneself', and the phrase is a coinage of Christian Greek. *Phrenapatō* occurs nowhere previously as far as I know. It is St. Paul's expression (Gal 6[3]) for the spiritual pride to which a believer who forgets to pray for the pure and lowly heart may well be prone, the tendency to think himself something, so deceiving himself and forgetting the real spectacle that he makes – 'Not I, but the grace of God which is with me'. The noun *phrenapatēs* had already appeared in secular

447

Greek, to mean apparently a 'proud man': 'one who was once so *proud* that he denied the power of love' (Grenfell).[46]

THRONES

θρόνοι

The secular meaning of *thronos* was a seat, a chair of state, an oracular seat, a teacher's chair, and a judge's bench, but nowhere outside Jewish and Christian Greek does there occur its special meaning, denoting a status of the Jewish and Christian angelic hierarchy (see 'Authorities', 'Dominions', 'Principalities', 'Powers').

The Thrones (plural word, *thronoi*) were created by God, according to St. Paul (Col 1[16]), together with the other great orders of angels. They occupied the fourth heaven, and not the highest, according to some Jewish speculation.[47] However, Thrones are listed with Dominions, Principalities and Authorities, as residing with God Himself in the highest heaven, the seventh – according to one apocalyptic Jewish book.[48]

The Jewish thinking reappears in Gnosticism, for Throne (singular) appears as a special term for a certain status of angel.[49] The Slavonic version of the *Ascension of Isaiah* understands 'throne' in the secular sense in some places, i.e. the throne of God, but not so the Greek MS discovered by O. von Gebhardt. In this book are the words, 'Worship neither *Throne* nor angel which belongs to the six heavens' (7[21]), and the words, 'When I have raised thee to the seventh heaven ... thou shalt know that there is nothing hid from the *Thrones* and from those who dwell in the heavens and from the angels' (7[27]). Once more: 'It is He alone to Whose voice all the heavens and *Thrones* give answer ... the Lord of all those heavens and of those *Thrones*' (8[8f.]).

Though this section of the *Ascension of Isaiah* may be tinged with Gnosticism, still the orders of angels were part of normal Church tradition, and Origen mentions the *Thrones*, Powers, Authorities and Principalities[50] – in that order, which may mean that the *Thrones* were the very highest in the whole hierarchy. St. Dionysius Areopagita, the mystical theologian of the sixth century, mentions 'the holiest *Thrones*'.[51]

This then is a very high order of angels. It was fitly named, doubtless because of its distinct connection with the throne of God. Four and twenty elders (Rev 4[4]) sit upon 'seats' round about God's throne in heaven. Their 'seats' are lesser thrones, and upon their heads these angels have crowns of gold to suggest that their thrones too are royal emblems. The elders whom the Seer of Patmos beheld in his vision may therefore be attendant angels of this mighty order of Thrones.[52]

See also 'Angel', 'Authorities', 'Dominions', 'Powers', 'Principalities'.

TIME, THE GREAT DIVISIONS OF

a. A DISPENSATION

αἰών

Aiōn is in Greek a long space of time, but in the Bible it has specialized meanings.

Secular Greek. The noun *aiōn* indicated life, a season of life, a lifetime, a generation, an epoch, an age.

Philo used *aiōn* for the periods of one's life,[53] and for a long space of time.[54] It is as wide-ranging as the Latin *aevum* and, like it, has the meaning in the plural, 'eternity', e.g. in Plato and in Diodorus Siculus. The 'coming *aiōn*' means posterity,[55] and the phrase, *di'aiōnos,* which is literally 'through the *aiōn*', means 'continually'. When Menander wrote, 'It is an *aiōn*,' he meant it was a long time (536.5).

Biblical Greek. There are in the NT similar idiomatic phrases taken from the LXX, e.g. the frequent *eis ton aiōna* ('for ever': literally, 'into the *aiōn*') and *eis tous aiōnas tōn aiōnōn* ('for ever and ever': literally, 'into the aions of the aions'). *Aiōn* translated the Hebrew *'ōlām,* which had two broad applications – a past epoch ('the olden time') and a future ('eternity'), usually in a prepositional phrase. The use of the plural of *aiōn* in Biblical Greek in the expression, 'for ever', 'to eternity', is interesting. Cullmann considers that the speaking of eternity in the plural proves that it does not signify cessation of time or timelessness. He urges that 'eternity' *(aiōnes)* means rather endless time, an ongoing of time which is incomprehensible to our finite senses – it is the linking of an unlimited series of limited world-periods ('aeons'), whose succession only God is able to survey.[56]

But a peculiar meaning appears in Jewish and Christian Greek, and *aiōn* becomes one of the seven 'ages' or 'dispensations' which make up the world's history according to some contemporary Jewish thought. AV renders this new sense of *aiōn* by 'world', e.g. 'not only in this *world* but also in that which is to come' (Eph 1[21]). It is rarely that AV does less than justice to a new meaning, but

449

'world' is not so good for it has special associations. An apt equivalent is far to seek, however, without venturing upon the old-fashioned 'dispensation'.

Some Jews contemplated that for seven 'dispensations' *(aiōnes)* death is suffered to ravage the world[57] and that afterwards there would follow a general resurrection.[58] Assuming that a 'day' was reckoned as a thousand years (Ps 90[4]; 2 Pet 3[8]), then each 'hour' in apocalyptic represented approximately a hundred years, there being 'twelve hours' in the day (Jn 11[9]). One 'hour' of the *aiōn* is said to be a generation or a 'descent' of a hundred years (Apocalypse of Abraham 28) and the Ten Plagues of the future which shall distress the Gentile world were placed 'at the passing over of the twelfth hour' of the earth (ibid. 30) – that was, the end of the dispensation in which the author lived, c. AD 100.

According to an early Christian Father, the six days of creation mean 'that our Lord will make an end of everything in six thousand years, for a day with Him means a thousand years' (Barn 15[46]).

So a day signified, for some Jews, one of the seven periods *(aiōnes)* into which world-history was divided, and the six days of creation corresponded to the total endurance of all created things – six thousand years – the final *aiōn* being the reign of Messiah, yet to come.

Evidently, the author of the Secrets of Enoch, an Egyptian Jew early in the first Christian century, shared the belief that, as the world was created in six days, so it will endure for six ages each of a thousand years, the whole to be followed by a sabbath period of another thousand years to correspond with God's resting on the seventh day; that period was presumably Messiah's kingdom. Afterwards comes eternity (Slavonic, 32[2] 33[2]), its beginning marked apparently by the day of the great Judgment (50[4]). Our author's remarks may be the earliest evidence which testifies to a belief in what later became known as Chiliasm or Millennarianism.[59] The belief was widespread in the early Church: prominent adherents were the author of Barnabas, Papias, St. Justin Martyr, St. Irenaeus, St. Hippolytus, Tertullian. However, it was opposed by Origen, Dionysius, the Cappadocian Fathers, and St. Jerome and St. Augustine. It occurs in Rev 20[1-6]. Some opponents of Chiliasm sought to exclude that book from the canon of Scripture.

The seven days of creation are regarded in an eschatological way in the first-century Ezra-apocalypse, but with the observation that after the Messianic dispensation the world shall return to primitive silence in seven days, even as it was at the beginning (4 Ezra 7[30]).

Adam lived for nine hundred and thirty years (Gen 5[5]). The span of his life concurred with one *aiōn* but he died within the *aiōn*, and so for the author of Jubilees God's Word was fulfilled, 'In the *day* that thou eatest thereof thou shalt surely die' (Gen 2⁷). For this author, then, a 'day' is a thousand years (Jub 4³⁰). The first *aiōn* of the world was Adam's lifetime. The second *aiōn* may have been the period from Adam to Noah, the third the lifetime of Noah, nine hundred and forty years (Gen 9²⁹), the fourth may have led from Noah to Moses. The fifth dispensation, the Mosaic, may have been the time when the Law and Tabernacle were given. The author of the Apocalypse of Abraham, like the author of the apocalypse of Ezra, may have reckoned his own dispensation, the sixth, to have begun with the founding of Jerusalem by David (cf. 4 Ezra 10⁴⁶ᶠᶠ·) and ending with its destruction by Titus, or a little later.

A dispensation, then, would spell out twelve 'hours' of prophetic time, i.e. about twelve hundred years. The reckoning is confirmed by information from Josephus who discloses: 'From King David ... to this destruction under Titus, were one thousand, one hundred and seventy nine years'⁶⁰ – an *aiōn,* near enough. The author of the Abraham apocalypse may have written about twenty-one years later and felt himself to be on the brink of a new dispensation.

The seventh and 'great' and final *aiōn* was yet to come. It was expected to end in a general Judgment. 'From the days of the slaughter ... of the giants [i.e. the Creation] ... until ... the great Judgment in which the great *Aiōn* shall be consummated.'⁶¹ This 'great' period must be the reign of the Messiah, the sabbath rest corresponding to the seventh day of creation.

To some extent the Church adopted the Jewish divisions of time. The final form of the Testament of Abraham, with its seven *aiōnes,* was doubtless Christian, and St. John Damascene averred, 'There are said to be seven *aiōnes,* from the creation of heaven and earth to the common consummation of man and the resurrection'.⁶² Sometimes the number of dispensations was simplified to two: 'this *Aiōn*'⁶³ and 'the *Aiōn* to come', the former extending from creation to incarnation.⁶⁴

In the NT *aiōn* indicates not only this present period in which we live but also in a coming age of 'eternal' life which we strive to be worthy to obtain (Mt 12³²; Mk 10³⁰; Lk 16⁸ 18³⁰ 20³⁵). The life of the Coming Age is often described as 'eternal' life, but it must not be understood thereby that time and eternity are set in contrast, as if time was a quality of the present Age and 'eternity' was a quality of the future Age, as if the future Age involved 'timelessness'. As Cullmann points out, the Coming Age is limited in time on the one side (its beginning), but not on the other side. It begins with the events described by the Seer of Patmos, but for its end no limit is set.⁶⁵ The *aiōn* to come is not therefore 'eternity' as opposed to 'time', and we must free ourselves from the philosophical concepts, 'in time' and 'out of time'. It would, according to Cullmann, be misleading to translate the *aiōn* as 'eternity', for the *aiōn* is still a period of time. It is no less imprecise to render '*aiōnios* life' as 'eternal life'.

St. Paul contrasts 'this dispensation' with the 'coming dispensation' (Eph 1[21]) and frequently refers to 'this' or 'the present' *evil* dispensation (Ro 12[2]; 1 Co 1[20] 2[6,8] 3[18]; 2 Co 4[4]; Gal 1[4]; 1 Ti 6[17]; 2 Ti 4[10]; Tit 2[12]). According to St. Matthew (13[39f, 49] 24[3] 28[20]), Christ indicated that this present *aiōn* (AV 'world') would reach consummation at His Coming to judge. For St. Paul the present *aiōn* is a grim period to which this wicked 'set-up' *(kosmos)* belongs (Eph 2[2]). Its gods are the *archontes* and the Devil himself (1 Co 2[6]; 2 Co 4[4]). It has a pretentious wisdom which is arrogant and blind to the Gospel (1 Co 2[6ff.]).

The Christians were but following Jewish thought. The Ethiopic Enoch mentions the scorn which the righteous entertain for the present dispensation of unrighteousness (48[7]), and among the rabbis there is evidence of a belief that the present *'ôlām* will last for six thousand years followed by one thousand years of waste (R. Hash. 31a). They divided the *'ôlām* of falsehood (the present) from the *'ôlām* of truth (hereafter), and this *'ôlām* from the *'ôlām* to come.[66] The Jews would often confine their attention to two dispensations, the present and that to come (Isai 9[5] ASLC). The first-century apocalypse of Ezra states that 'the Most High has made this *saeculum* (dispensation) for many, but the *saeculum* to come, for the few' (4 Ezra 8[1]). 'Esau is the end of this *saeculum* and Jacob the beginning of the *saeculum* to come' (6[9]).[67]

But it seems to me that the early Christians may have introduced a variation in the two dispensations – a day of grace coming in between. Counteracting much contemporary exegesis, Prof. Doeve[68] questioned whether the early Christian expectation of a return of Jesus on short notice was as general as is claimed. Assuming that the Church was influenced by Jewish apocalyptic tendencies in her first generation, there would presumably have been a section of churchmen which accepted the division of history into much longer periods, as we have seen for instance in the book of Enoch. Such people would not expect the end of the *aiōn* very soon. However, it must be said that the Church probably did not expect long years ahead, for the period before the Parousia was not likely to be conceived as an *aiōn* at all, but rather as an indeterminate Day of Grace, interposed between two *aiōnes*, its length depending only on the mercy of God. Nevertheless, it remains true that the early Christians looked upon the intervening period as part of the present evil *aiōn* which also includes the wicked *kosmos* ('the *aiōn* of this *kosmos*', Eph 2[2]).

Some have urged that *kosmos* and *aiōn* are synonyms.[69] But in

Christian Greek *aiōn* is more than a synonym for *kosmos* (world). St. Paul does distinguish the terms *aiōn* and *kosmos* when he says that the present *aiōn* belongs to this *kosmos* (Eph 2²). Presumably, then, when contrasted with *aiōn* the term *kosmos* signifies an establishment of wickedness: 'according to the dispensation *(aiōn)* of this world *(kosmos)*'. It is true that the identification of *aiōn* and *kosmos* is found in the Hellenistic mysteries,[70] and in 4 Ezra 3⁹ *saeculum* which is otherwise an equivalent of *aiōn* is conceived spatially in the phrase, *habitantes saeculum*[71] – as if 'world' were a good translation of Latin *saeculum* and Greek *aiōn*.

Sometimes indeed *aiōn* seems to mean 'world' or 'universe' in a spatial and material sense. The writer to Hebrews may have used *aiōn* in this way when he declares that by the Son the *aiōnes* were made (1²) and that the *aiōnes* were framed by the Logos (11³). Such a meaning is not cited for secular writers in LS,[72] but it does occur in the LXX: 'the Lord ruleth the *world* for ever' (Ex 15¹⁸), the *world* is said to be 'explored' (Wis 13⁹), and light is given to it (Wis 18⁴). If that is the meaning of *aiōn* also in Heb 1² 11³ it is probably derived from the LXX. Burton felt that, 'This meaning is, perhaps, not established beyond all doubt, but it seems nearly certain that it must be assumed for Heb 1² and 11³' (Burton, p. 429). The Greek Fathers, including Chrysostom and Theodoret,[73] nevertheless understood *aiōnes* here as periods of time.

Doubtless, the meaning of *ʿôlām* too was spatial sometimes in Biblical Hebrew: the ungodly are said to prosper 'in the *world*' (Ps 72¹²), but the other instance is more doubtful, for to have the *world* in one's heart (Eccles 3¹¹) is too characteristically modern a conception and the text is probably in need of emendation. In later Hebrew *ʿôlām* means 'world': God is He who spoke and the world *(ʿôlām)* was (Mechilta 33b on Ex 14³¹). Among the rabbis from the first century AD *ʿolmâ* has the spatial sense of 'world'. Rabbis often say that God created the *ʿôlām*.[74] Thus, H. Sasse is not alone in supposing that the plural Greek word *aiōnes* shares the change of meaning that the Hebrew word experienced, and that in Heb 1² 11³ the meaning is 'worlds' or 'spheres' (Welträume).[75]

Long ago T. K. Cheyne, assuming that *aiōn* is used in this sense, acknowledged that by NT times the word *ʿôlām* too must have received the new meaning, 'world'.[76] He suggested that Persian stimulus had made the change possible and that in Heb 1² 11³ the author has in mind that the temporal sequence ('dispensation') is now conceived as the spatial theatre of the events taking place in the 'dispensation'. This was more or less the view of Bishop Westcott,[77] who took it that *aiōnes* had now come to mean, 'the sum of the "periods of time" including all that is manifested in and through them'. He instanced the same meaning in Wis 13⁹ (exploring the *world*), in Tob 13[6,10] (extol the King of the *universe*), and in 1 Ti 1[17] (now unto the King of the *universe*). *Aiōn* has not quite its sense of a period of time, a dispensation, but the conception is now the fuller one of a material creation as enfolded in time (Westcott, p. 353). These separate periods, with all the material creation they involve, form together one great 'universe', and that thought is taken up in Christian literature when St. Clement can speak of the Father, the God, and the King, of the 'universe' *(aiōnes):* 1 Clem 1[35,55,61]. It should be added that the Apocalypse of Peter has the same sense: 'where are all the righteous? Of what sort is the *aiōn* wherein they are (14)?' Moreover, St. Justin Martyr cited 1 Chr 16[28] and followed it with a doxology, 'Give glory to the Lord, the Father of the universe *(aiōnōn)*'.[78] AV may be right, after all, in its rendering, 'world'.

The background of thought surrounding *aiōn* may well be cosmological. Héring appears to take *aiōnes* (Heb 1[2]) as 'worlds' in the sense of the seven heavens. 'The Enoch literature ... recognizes seven superimposed worlds in the beyond, and it will be remembered that Paul speaks of a third heaven (2 Corinthians 12[2]). The notion that the Son created not only the visible world, but also the whole range of the others is not at all odd, as the Apostle Paul expressly says so.'[79] He refers to 1 Co 8[6] and Col 1[16] where St. Paul affirms that by Him were all things created in heaven and earth, visible and invisible, thrones, dominions, principalities and powers.

It may be that St. Justin, in his phrase, 'Father of the *aiōnes*', understood *aiōn* as an archangelic personification, after the fashion of Hellenistic syncretism and of the Gnostics. It may even be true also of the Slavonic Enoch and St. Ignatius,[80] and also of St. Paul when he lists the *aiōn* of this *kosmos* alongside the Prince of the power of the air (Eph 2[2]). We find a phrase like Justin's in both Judaism and early Christianity, namely, 'King of the *aiōnes*', which suggests that *aiōn* possesses personality (Tob 13[6,10]; 1 Ti 1[17]; 1 Clem 61[2]). Of course, one may assume that the genitive is adjectival and may render the phrase, 'eternal King', which is the way Sasse takes it, leaving open the question whether the meaning, 'King over the Ages', was subsequently introduced into the expression.[81] Yet St. Paul speaks of a secret hidden from the *aiōnes*, as if the latter were personal (Col 1[26]; Eph 3[9]). One cannot be sure that a personalized 'universe' is not meant here – AV's 'world'. Sasse is of opinion[82] that a personal *Aiōn* is alien to the NT, though he allows it perhaps at Eph 2[2], and certainly discounts it at Col 1[26]; Eph 2[7] 3[9] in spite of R. Reitzenstein[83] and later W. Bauer (50). Yet the personal *Aiōn* appears in St. Paul and St. Ignatius as well as in Jewish literature, as we have seen.

One cannot say how far Gnostic influence may be behind the

personalization, for it is 'not mere coincidence that the NT writings in which the doctrine of Christ as God's Agent in Creation is developed (viz. the Fourth Gospel, Colossians, and Hebrews) are those which are aimed at an incipient Gnosticism. It was in fact,' as Narborough observed, 'probably directly under the pressure of Gnostic tendencies that the belief was arrived at'.[84] The Gnostics adopted Jesus as one of the *aiōnes,* one of the angels who were the instruments of creation.

The Jewish Christian *Odes of Solomon,* which may show some Gnostic influence, speak of God as the Father of *aiōnes* (7[13]). They seem to be personal, and there are similar phrases in the magical papyri, such as, 'King and Lord of the *aiōnes*', and 'God of the *aiōnes*'.[85] The *Aiōn* of the magical papyri is remarkably personal; he is identified with the deity, Iaô. I find allusions to 'the great spirit of the immortal *Aiōn*',[86] to 'the Master of the whole, the *Aiōn* of the *aiōnes*', addressed as, 'You are the *Kosmokratōr.*' The editor renders another allusion as follows: '*Aiōn* rüttelt (an ihr), der Himmel wird bewegt, Kronos gerat in Furcht uber deine Vergewaltigung'.[88] This particular being is designated the *ploutodotēs* ('Reichtum spendender Aiôn, heiliger Guter Dämôn'),[89] and is called in Greek *aplanētos* ('nicht irrender Aiôn Iaô').[90]

It is clear that *Aiōn* was personalized early in the history of Greek religion, as the son of Kronos,[91] but the notion found a niche later in a certain type of Judaism, where God Himself was conceived as, 'Lord of lords and God of gods and King of the *aiōnes*' (Enoch 9[4]). Little wonder that there are allusions to the personal *Aiōn* in the NT itself. The Apostolic Constitutions go so far as to class such a being among the cherubim and seraphim and other angels (viii 12). As Dibelius observes, the phrases we have examined in the previous paragraph, like 'God of the *aiōnes*', are part of the 'cultic language of Greek-speaking Judaism',[92] doubtless very important for study of Christian beginnings.

b. BELONGING TO THE FUTURE DISPENSATION

αἰώνιος

If the noun *aiōn,* then, acquired new significance in Biblical Greek, so did the adjective, *aiōnios.*

Secular Greek. It had meant, 'lasting for an *aiōn* (a long period)'. In the near-contemporary historian, Diodorus Siculus, it means 'for ever' (I 63.5). On the other hand, Plotinus later on was to distinguish it from *aïdios* (everlasting).[93] Often, however, in secular writers as well as in the LXX (where it renders habitually the

Hebrew *'ôlām* in the sense of *perpetuus*) the meaning is that of the Latin *perpetuus*, 'everlasting'.

Christian Greek. The Christians clothed the word with a distinct accoutrement of thought, so I believe. Burton's view was different. *Aiōnios*, he said, had no associations with the two Ages, for the two Ages was a later concept.[94] I agree that *aiōnios* had been a secular word from Plato onwards, but I think it changed its meaning in Jewish and Biblical circles, just as the noun *aiōn* had done, and many other words.

After being the secular equivalent of *perpetuus* (everlasting) *aiōnios* acquired the different sense in the Christian language, 'belonging to the *'ôlām*'.[95] The dispensation intended in this special sense was that of the future, the Kingdom of Christ, the reign of Messiah. *Aiōnios* has a new meaning, and the '*aiōnios* Gospel' is not therefore in Christian language the 'everlasting Gospel'. Christians do not suppose that the Gospel lasts for ever. Rather, it is the Gospel of, or concerning, the Kingdom-age (Rev 14[6]).

Parallels have been adduced for a religious sense of *aiōnios* in the secular papyri, but these all have the secular meaning, *perpetuus*. In the instances of inscriptions, too, the meaning is always *perpetuus* (Deissmann BS p. 363), and this is rarely so in the NT, where almost always the context requires the sense, 'belonging to the Dispensation to come'. Unlike *aiōn*, the noun, which sometimes refers to the present dispensation (Mt 13[22]; Gal 1[4]; 1 Ti 6[17]), to which cares and riches belong and which is evil, the adjective *aiōnios* refers almost exclusively to that of the future. The invisible things are *aiōnios* and they belong to the future Dispensation (2 Co 4[18]). We read more than forty times of '*aiōnios* life', which is the life to come, though we may have the promise and foretaste of it now. The expression stands primarily for a quality of life. We read of habitations belonging to the Messianic Age – *aiōnios* habitations (Lk 16[9]; 2 Co 5[1]). We read of the Holy Spirit in that Age (Heb 9[14]), of that Age's covenant, its Gospel, its comfort, its atonement, its inheritance, and its punishment, its judgment and destruction, and its glory. Sometimes the context requires that *aiōnios* be understood objectively: thus, the Gospel, the covenant, the atonement, *concerning* the future dispensation.

In the instance of '*aiōnios* life', we find that it already had the new meaning in Enoch, as we are reminded by J. T. Forestell, C.S.B.,[96] for the life which is meant is not 'everlasting'; it lasts actually for seventy generations (10^5) or for 500 years (10^{10}). 'They hope to live an *aiōnios* life, and hope that each one of them will live five hundred years'. The expression '*aiōnios* life' appears in the OT, both in the LXX and Theodotion's version of Daniel (12[2]), and later Jews continued the idea in the rabbinic phrase, 'life of the Coming *'ôlām'*.

It is true, however, that on occasion *aiōnios* has reference to bygone ages. The Mystery was kept in silence in 'the times of previous dispensations' (*chronois aiōniois*, Ro 16[26]). God's grace was given to us 'before the times of previous dispensations' (*pro chronōn aiōniōn*, Tit 1[2]).

All the way through it is never feasible to understand *aiōnios* as 'everlasting', unless it be at Phm 15 ('that thou shouldest receive him *for ever*') and I. Pol 8[1] ('a *for-ever* memorable deed'). To denote the characteristic of everlastingness, there was a separate adjective in Christian Greek, *aïdios*, and when St. Ignatius would refer to life which lasted for ever he used *aïdios* (I. Eph 19[3]). St. Paul had the same recourse when he alluded to the 'undying' power of God (Ro 1[20]). So did St. Jude when he alluded to chains which never break (6).

Many have taken the meaning of *aiōnios* to be *perpetuus* when it qualifies the damnation which the unforgivable sin merits (Mk 3[29]). Rather the adjective qualifies a sin against the *aiōn* or Dispensation to come – the sin of being blind to the fact that the New Age has already begun to dawn in the eschatological miracles of Jesus. It is not a sin whose significance lasts for ever; there is no point in that. Likewise the guilty one is said to have no forgiveness *eis ton aiōna*, that is, in the coming Dispensation. Matthew's version of our Lord's words makes it clear. 'It shall not be forgiven him ... neither in this *Aiōn* nor in that to come' (Mt 12[32]).

c. BELONGING TO THIS DISPENSATION

πρόσκαιρος

The first Christians used *proskairos* to describe the age in which they were living.

The adjective cannot be said to be a coinage of Biblical Greek, when it occurs in Strabo and Dionysius of Halicarnassus, as well as Josephus, but as Moffatt[97] observed, it was nevertheless specially adopted by Christians into their vocabulary as a term to express an eschatological concept, the contrast with the adjective *aiōnios* (belonging to the Dispensation to come).

For secular writers it had the non-technical meaning of 'temporary', lasting only for a relatively short time.[98] Josephus refers to a 'temporary' inclination of fortune on a certain side in war,[99] and to the 'short' pleasure of lustful dalliance.[100] The same meaning appears in the gospels (Mt 13[21]; Mk 4[17]), concerning a 'short-lived' plant. Other secular meanings include 'occasional' or 'extra-ordinary' – of a festival,[101] and 'additional' – of taxes.[102]

The special Christian meaning, 'belonging to the present evil world', appears when St. Paul declares the things that are seen to be *proskairos,* as opposed to the future *aiōnios* (unseen) things (2 Co 4[18]). It appears when the writer to the Hebrews designated the pleasures of sin as *proskairos* and contrasts them with the future joys of the people of God (Heb 11[25]). It indicates the 'present' world in contrast to the world to come.[103] The writer to Diognetus (X 8) expresses admiration for the martyrs who endure for righteousness sake the *proskairos* fire of this world, contrasting it in a technical and eschatological sense with the *aiōnios* fire, the future punishment of the wicked which is referred to also in 4 Macc 12[12]; Mt 18[8] 25[41]; Jude 7. God told Abraham that His judgment was *proskairos* – designed for those living upon earth – and He distinguished Abraham's life in this world as *proskairos,* that is, 'temporal' (T. Abr 94[28]D, 77[15]).

'TONGUES', 'OTHER TONGUES', 'AN UNKNOWN TONGUE' (AV)

γλῶσσα, γλῶσσαι

There is no small contention over the precise meaning of this specialized word in the Christian vocabulary.

Secular Greek. *Glōssa* (plural, *glōssai*) signified physically the tongue and the act of talking, and also verbal messages which one entrusts to another.[104] It might be mere speech,[105] for *glōssa* is talking as opposed to thinking, or the metaphorical tongue as against the brain. Hippolytus confesses that he had taken an oath in ignorance of what it was about. 'My *glōssa* (voice) swore the oath, my thinking did not swear it.'[106] *Glōssa* might even be 'language', for Thucydides refers to the Doric *glōssa* (dialect).[107] In most literature, as well as Greek and English, the word for 'tongue' is also the word for 'language'. Tongue is *lingua* in Latin and Italian, *langue* in French, *lengua* in Spanish, *limba* in Rumanian, *tunga* in Old Norse, and *jazyk* in Russian.

Christian Greek. On the other hand, for Christians both singular and plural of *glōssa* might signify a special utterance of a peculiar kind, a competence which was a characteristic gift of the Holy Ghost, common in the Church's early days and promised by Christ Himself. 'They shall speak with (new) *tongues*' (Mk 16[17]). 'Tongues' was a prominent phenomenon at Corinth and probably elsewhere, confirming our Lord's promise.

Nothing resembling a trance, no psychic dissociation, can be traced in this charismatic gift, which was a marvel of an exclusively Christian kind, one of the many endowments of the Holy Ghost which the Church has received.[108] We may assume too hastily that the achievement of 'tongues' was a 'frenzied, inarticulate, incoherent, ecstatic speech',[109] recalling the corybantic cult of the Thracian Dionysus in Greek religion.[110] Still, the charge of drunkenness which was levelled at the participating Christians may have arisen because they gave the appearance of ecstasy. It should be noted that the current name is 'glossolalia' (from $gl\bar{o}ssa$ = tongue and $lalia$ = talking), which is no older than the nineteenth century and begs no questions.

The first manifestation was as early as Pentecost, when the appearance of $gl\bar{o}ssai$ (tongues) of fire is evidently symbolical, for $l^esh\bar{o}n$ '$\bar{e}sh$ (Isai 5[24]: tongue of fire) is the instrument of God's purging. However, it is the later versions of Aquila, Symmachus and Theodotion which render $l^esh\bar{o}n$ by $gl\bar{o}ssa$, and the LXX word, anthrax, turns the phrase into 'burning embers'. At the first manifestation, on the Day of Pentecost, the wind from heaven and the fiery nature of the visible tongues suggest the visionary or prophetic quality of the new supernatural gift. The apostles were filled with the Holy Ghost and spoke with other $gl\bar{o}ssai$ (languages?) in which they were understood by men of various nations. Did they speak therefore in foreign languages? Was the phenomenon in fact, not glossolalia but polyglossia? Origen[111] and other Church commentators[112] have supposed so. However, the answer cannot really be so simple, for subsequent expression of 'tongues' in the NT has nothing to do with preaching and everything to do with worship; besides, the contemporary Koine Greek itself would have been understood almost everywhere, making the new endowment superfluous on the day of Pentecost, supposing the endowment to have been merely a matter of communication.[113]

Arguments to the contrary have been advanced. Dr. R. H. Gundry made a convincing case for 'tongues' as miraculous utterance in human languages which were foreign to the speaker,[114] although Gundry stressed that it was not primarily the point of 'tongues' to be means of communication when communication might easily be achieved by Koine Greek, Aramaic, and perhaps by Hebrew. Then what was the point of 'tongues'? He suggested: 'The New Testament presents glossolalia primarily as a convincing miracle[115] – the miracle of speaking in an actual existent foreign language which one has not studied. The difficulty is that never except at Pentecost is a listener ever said to have recognized his own language, whether in the house of Cornelius or whether at

Ephesus or at Corinth. Surely his own language might have been identified by some bystander at one of these cosmopolitan places?

Dr. J. G. Davies had already shown that there is no reason why St. Paul should not have intended glossolalia as speaking in foreign languages, and that there is no conflict therefore with the record of its expression at Pentecost. St. Paul in 1 Co 14²¹ evidently quotes Isai 28¹¹ᶠ· ('with another tongue will he speak to this people'), and the reference is to the invading Assyrians whose unintelligible foreign language is to be a judgment on Israel. St. Paul reasons that glossolalia is a judgment on unbelievers. Moreover, of the twenty-one instances of the word for 'interpret' *(hermēneuō)* in the LXX and NT, outside 1 Co 12 and 14, eighteen have the primary meaning of translating a foreign language.¹¹⁶

After Pentecost the next enactment of 'tongues' was at the home of Cornelius (Act 10⁴⁶), a manifestation which St. Peter saw as parallel with the same occurrence at Pentecost: 'the Holy Ghost fell on them, as on us at the beginning' (Act 11¹⁵). At Pentecost, however, the tongues were understood by men of various nations without interpretation, and we do not find that feature mentioned at the house of Cornelius. There appears to be inconsistency.

The next recorded manifestation was at Ephesus (Act 19⁶) and again there is no indication that the gift involved speech in existent foreign languages, as was the case at Pentecost. Indeed, St. Paul affirms that this form of speech, this charisma of the Holy Ghost in the primitive Church, is not understood by human wisdom (1 Co 14²) – a strange way to speak of a foreign language. Then we may see the speaking with tongues at Pentecost as different from the tongues at Corinth. Whereas the one was multilingual and intelligible to all hearers, tongues at Corinth were inferior and different – perhaps nothing more than a carry-over from paganism.¹¹⁷

Fuller had adopted a radical way to explain the change, suggesting that St. Luke was mistaken in supposing that tongues was the ability to speak a foreign language, for 'by the time of *Acts* it was forgotten what tongues were: they had already died out'. On the ground that tongues were not encouraged in the early Church, Fuller made the assumption that tongues were misunderstood by St. Luke as a gift of speaking languages in his account of Pentecost.¹¹⁸

One other reflection may raise doubt whether tongues were normal speech in a foreign language. Even in secular technical Greek, *glōssai* might refer to obsolete or provincial or poetic phraseology which needed interpretation to be fully understood.¹¹⁹ It may be that the rare application of the word comes near to the Christian usage. So what was uttered in the various manifestations of tongues has been thought to be Aramaic terms like *Maranatha*,

Abba, and *Amen.* Still, jargon of that kind would have been intelligible anyway to Jews and Christians and would have needed no 'interpreter'. The need for him marks off tongues as understood by St. Paul from tongues as experienced at Pentecost. At Pentecost no interpreter was needed but later on an interpreter was essential. The explanation may be that as time went on, tongues became more and more involved with foreign terms which became more and more meaningless. According to some, the experience at Pentecost is best seen as an example of the Corinthian phenomenon – ecstatic glossolalia. The listeners on the day of Pentecost may have recognized occasional words in their own languages and dialects. C. G. Williams recalls that the magical papyri of the second and third centuries furnish a written analogy, providing a jumble of incoherent ejaculations interspersed with native and foreign titles of deities.[120] An interpretation would thus become increasingly desirable as the element of jargon became more prominent.

St. Paul insisted that unless the speaker with tongues be interpreted, he cannot edify the Church. St. Paul himself had exercised the gift but he would rather utter five words intelligibly than five thousand 'in a tongue'. Tongues must therefore be spoken by one brother at a time and each must be interpreted. Then will tongues be a 'sign' to unbelievers (1 Co 14[4ff., 13f., 18f., 22f., 26f., 39]). Interpretation must be sought by prayer (1 Co 14[13]).

St. Paul may indicate by *glōssa* a language of the Spirit, as opposed to a secular language, a medium that was sacred, miraculously devised and heavenly in origin, a means of communication between God and the angels (1 Co 13[1]), to which mortal man may attain when he engages in real prayer and is caught up to heaven (2 Co 12[2ff.]; 1 Co 14[2, 13]; Act 10[46] 2[11]). It originates in heaven (Acts 2[ff.]) and reveals the secrets of the world above. Such a view of 'tongues' meets all the facts as set out by St. Paul and St. Luke, and is also consistent with Hellenistic usage and syncretistic ways of thinking, and it is not damaging either to the links which exist between St. Paul and Jewish ideas. So argues Behm,[121] citing ch. 40 of the Ethiopic Enoch.

If tongues were not comprised of foreign languages, nor of peculiar heavenly speech, then presumably they were a dialect or variety of the Hellenistic Greek language. Tongues were intelligible to a wide circle of overseas visitors, like that assembled on the day of Pentecost. Tongues then may have been an early example, not yet carefully formulated, of the new dialect which we have called 'Christian Greek', a dialect heavily impregnated with Semitic constructions and vocabulary and not as yet generally understood, especially by 'unlearned and unbelievers' at the meetings in

Corinth, a language of the Holy Ghost, inaugurated at Pentecost but foreshadowed by the Semitic Greek of the OT.

One wonders whether tongues is the same phenomenon as that described by St. Paul as 'unspeakable groans' (Ro 8[26]),[122] for it too was an experience dominated by the Holy Ghost. 'We know not', says Paul. The Spirit takes full control. It is part of the deeper involvement of those who strive after sanctification and full salvation. The reaction is described in the course of that magnificent peroration where the Apostle declares that no harm can overtake God's elect, for whose glorious deliverance all things long and wait and whom nothing can sever from His love. The symptoms of this reaction may be the gift of tongues.

'Tongues' do not appear under that name in the apostolic Fathers and re-appear only with the heretic Montanus.[123] Eusebius quotes a treatise against Montanism which says that in Phrygia Montanus began to fall into frenzy and convulsions. He became ecstatic and began to speak strangely, prophesying contrary to the traditional custom. People thought he was devil-possessed. He could not be kept quiet. He stirred up two women and filled them with the 'bastard spirit' so that they uttered mad, absurd and irresponsible things. The Montanists were described as 'chattering prophets', falling into trances and trusting themselves to 'the spirit of deceit'.[124] The way of speaking which Eusebius notices is almost certainly intended to be the phenomenon of tongues,[125] for Montanism was an attempt to revert to the primitive fervour of the first Christians in order to counter Gnosticism and what seemed to be a growing secularization of the Church in the latter half of the second century.

The Montanists substituted ecstasy for *gnōsis* (knowledge) as a means of communion with God. They were revivalists as opposed to intellectualists. A specimen of the resurgent glossolalia is the remark of Montanus, 'I am come neither as angel nor ambassador but as God the Father'.[126] That is to say, Montanus was not speaking, but God the Father through his lips.

Nevertheless, the gift of tongues was not extinct in the time of St. Irenaeus.[127] He declares that St. Paul meant by 'perfect' those who spoke in all languages by the Spirit of God. He says that he heard of many brethren in the Church exercising prophetical powers and speaking in all kinds of languages through the Spirit, revealing the mysteries of God. It is claimed that the phenomenon often re-appears at times of revival. 'This morning', writes Thomas Walsh, a Methodist preacher, in his diary, 'the Lord gave me a language I know not of, raising my soul to Him in a wondrous manner'. The endowment has never dried up and there is a notable re-appearance in the twentieth-century Pentecostal Revival.[128]

'**Races.**' Already in OT Greek there was an idiosyncratic meaning of the plural *glōssai*, that is, 'races', of which no secular instances are known. 'I will gather all nations and *glōssai;* they shall come and see My glory' (Isai 66[18]). The Hebrew *lāshôn* is almost a synonym for 'race' in other passages where *glōssai* is the rendering (Zach 8[23]; Dan 3[7]). Sometimes there is no Hebrew (Jdt 3[8]).

The idiosyncrasy is revived in the Christian apocalypse where it is clear that *glōssa* is a nation or race in such phrases as 'every kindred and *glōssa*', 'people, nations and glōssai', 'kindreds, *glōssai* and nations' (Rev 5[9] 7[9] 10[11] 13[7] 14[6] 17[15]). It is a nation, considered as speaking its own language.

TONGUES, INTERPRETATION OF

διερμηνευτής, διερμηνεία

The words are evidently Christian inventions. *Diermēneutēs* (interpreter) re-appears in Byzantine Greek of the twelfth century,[129] apparently but once. Its occurrence in the NT is not certain, for Vaticanus reads the simplex, *hermēneutēs* (1 Co 14[28]). The second word, *diermēneia* (interpretation) is the charismatic gift without which tongues should not be exercised in the assembly (1 Co 12[10]AD*).

The verb *diermēneuō* belongs to a secular Greek (Polybius, etc.), unlike the nouns. Both nouns and verb refer in the NT to the charismatic gift of interpreting another charismatic gift, that of *glōssai* (q.v.). A brother may not exercise the latter gift in the assembly unless a *diermēneutēs* be present or unless he himself has the gift of interpretation *(diermēneia)*.

'TREE' (CROSS)

ξύλον

The meanings of *xulon* are wood, tree, staff. An ordinary tree is intended in Lk 23[31] (as also in 1 Clem 23[4]). The Tree of Life is often intended (Rev 2[7] 22[2, 14, 19]), and the Tree of Knowledge (Diog 12[2f.]). Fruits of a 'tree' are mentioned (Hermas *Sim.* 2[3] 4[4]), and the 'wood' from which things are made: 'we were worshipping stones and *wood*' (2 Clem 1[6]; Diog 2[2]; M. Pol 13[1]). It is the fruitful Tree which we Christians who are a Paradise of delight, raise up within us (Diog 12[1]).

In addition, secular writers sometimes use *xulon* for an

instrument of punishment, whether 'stocks',[130] 'gallows',[131] or 'impaling stake'.[132] For purposes of execution by hanging, 'tree' is perhaps the obvious instrument, and *xulon* need not be a technical term. From Aristophanes comes the line, 'If you fall, at least you will fall from a worthy tree *(xulon)*'. Hanging is in mind, and the scholiast quotes a proverb: 'If you must hang yourself, do it from a good *xulon*.'[133]

On the other hand the connection of punishment with *xulon* is comparatively rare in secular Greek and is more characteristic of Bible parlance[134] – the gibbet on which a Law-breaker was hanged (Deut 21[22f.]). 'Cursed is everyone that hangeth on a *xulon*,' is a Scripture quoted by St. Paul (Gal 3[13]); and so, for the earliest Christians, *xulon* became the Cross on which Jesus was hanged, as St. Peter says (Act 5[30] 10[39]; 1 Pet 2[24]). Men took Him down from the *xulon*, says Paul, when all that He came to do had been fulfilled (Act 13[29]). To call it *xulon* rather than *stauros* (cross) enhances the close connection with the Law, and the Church Father who speaks of the serpent on the *xulon* (Barn 12[7]) as a type of Christ, dwells on the *xulon* of Num 19[6] as 'the type of the cross' (Barn 8[1]).

This Father argues, 'It was necessary that He should suffer on a *xulon*' (5[17]). To hang upon a Tree, is the LXX equivalent of the Hebrew phrase in Deut 21[22] (to hang on the gibbet) which was the sequence to death by stoning, and the first Christians devoted the phrase to Christ's death. They understood the Roman form of capital punishment (by crucifixion) to be the equivalent of the Jewish penalty of stoning and hanging. So Wilcox, I think, is right to suppose against Barnabas Lindars that the phrase, to hang on the Tree, means more than, 'to be crucified'. The whole emphasis is clearly on the LXX phrase, especially shown by the word *xulon*.[135] Christ reigns from the Tree! *Abor decora ... ornata ... electa!* He was on the gibbet to pay the price for all Law-breaking.

TRUTH

ἀλήθεια

The apostles affirm that the Gospel is both 'the *alētheia* of God' (Ro 3[7] 15[8]) and 'the Word of *alētheia*' (Eph 1[13]; 2 Co 6[7]; Jas 1[18]); the martyr Polycarp states that St. Paul taught 'the Word of *alētheia*' carefully and surely (ad Phil. 3[2]). Christian writers insist that the Gospel is not to be weighed against the wisdom of this world, and so, whatever they meant by *alētheia* it was scarcely 'truth' in any secular sense.

The noun with its related adjectives (see 'True') is a leading example of the way Greek terms were bequeathed fresh meanings in Biblical settings. In this field we are debtors to the insight of Hermann Cremer[136] and of Gerhard Kittel,[137] and to Sir Edwyn Hoskyns who in 1931 instanced *alētheia* as a word which had subtly and finely modified its meaning by Biblical suggestion.[138]

In the vernacular Koine of the period it signified what the secular man of today might recognize as 'truth' – something genuine rather than counterfeit – without thinking particularly of an external standard or of acknowledging any absolute source of certification.

On the other hand, the Hebrew words which the LXX had so translated were *'emen* and *'aemûnâ,* and they involved moral potentialities and the idea of validation by the one true God, to such an extent that, according to Hebrew idiom, one could be said 'to walk in *alētheia*' and 'to do *alētheia*' (3 Km 2^4 3^6; 4 Km 20^3, etc.), in a way not understood by an unbiblicized Greek. When *alētheia* is found in the Bible its context, more often than not, is dominated by the image of the transcendent Deity. 'Truth' is among the highest qualities of God – with mercy, kindness, peace, and light (Gen 24^{27} 32^{10}; 2 Km 2^6 15^{20}; Ps $24(25)^{10}$ $39(40)^{11}$ $42(43)^3$). 'Truth' in the Bible involves behaviour and speech and their inspirations (Jg $9^{16, 19}$; 1 Km 12^{24}, etc.), something other than correctness of information. 'Truth' is conformity rather with basic and over-riding criteria in a real world where a supreme Being is the ultimate authority. The psalmist prays to be led in God's truth (Ps $24(25)^5$).

Until *alētheia, alēthinos* and *alēthēs* were matched with Hebrew roots, they had expressed such concepts as relatively 'genuine', contrasted with the counterfeit, regardless of the implication of unwavering standards. In the new setting *alētheia*, etc., had to serve also for ultimate Reality, for God's Truth, for the character of a God who is 'entirely worthy of man's trust, to be relied on in all their need.'[139]

It is only to be expected that during the course of exploitation in certain types of writing an abstract word will become so weighted with overtones of narrow association that subsequent users of the word in the same kind of circle understand it with quite a new meaning. It happened for the Jews in the case of many Greek words.

Jesus could say with OT antecedents in mind, 'I am the Truth' (Jn 14^6), but the citation of *alētheia* to Pilate (18^{37}) galled the Roman. He was aware of its secular function to denote a relative abstraction – whether 'truth' in contrast to a lie (from the time of Homer and the classics), or reality as opposed to appearance (the classics and the Koine), or truthfulness, dependability, uprightness, sincerity (the classics, Lucian and contemporary literary language).

465

And so Pilate, unversed in Hebrew literature, asked what it did mean!

To be sure, *alētheia* with the special meaning, absolute and transcendent Truth, is discovered outside the Bible, e.g. in Philo,[140] but Philo was a Jew. Plutarch was not, but in the passage where he uses *alētheia* apparently in an absolute sense,[141] he refers in point of fact to the gods and means correct information about them, as distinct from false propaganda.[142] This is not the sense of Philo who means nothing less than Judaism when he mentions the proselyte coming as a pilgrim to *alētheia*, to ultimate Truth.

Nearly everywhere in Christian Greek, *alētheia* is brought into close contact with the Gospel and very seldom signifies merely correct information, which is its secular sense – though of course it does so at times, especially in the phrase, 'of a truth' (Lk 4^{25}; 22^{59}; Act 4^{27} 10^{34}), and when the haemorrhage sufferer knelt down and confessed the 'truth' to Jesus (Mk 5^{33}), as when Paul promised the governor to keep to sober fact (Act 26^{25}), and when he himself counselled Christians to put away lying (Eph 4^{25}). The Biblical Greek phrase, 'I tell thee as God's truth', moreover, retains the secular meaning.[143]

Overwhelmingly in Christian Greek, *alētheia* is Truth not of this world, a mode of God Himself and of His Word. The *Truth* is in Jesus; He is full of grace and *Truth* (Eph 4^{21}; 2 Co 11^{10}; Jn $1^{14,17}$). It is in the Gospel (Gal 2^{14}; Col 1^5). When St. Peter wrote of 'obeying the *Truth*', his context requires, 'hearing the Gospel', as the preceding verses show.[144] There appears a direct copy of the OT formula, to 'do the Truth' (Jn 3^{21}; 1 Jn 1^6) which, with the similar mannerisms, 'speak Truth' (Mk 12^{32}; Jn 16^7; Ro 9^1; 2 Co 7^{14} 12^6; Eph 4^{25}; 1 Ti 2^7) and 'teach the Way of God in Truth' (Mt 22^{16}; Mk 12^{14}; Lk 20^{21}), looks like early Christian terminology for preaching the Gospel,[145] and there are many more phrases: to 'believe the Truth' (2 Thes $2^{13f.}$; 1 Ti 4^3), to 'bear witness to the Truth' (Jn 18^{37}), to 'know the Truth' (1 Ti 2^4; 2 Ti 3^7; 1 Jn 2^{21}), to 'acknowledge the Truth' (2 Ti 2^{25}; Tit 1^1), to 'receive the knowledge of the Truth' (Heb 10^{26}), to 'rejoice in the Truth' (1 Co 13^6). All the expressions seem to refer to Gospel preaching. One resists the Gospel, and that is to 'resist the Truth' (2 Ti 3^8), to turn one's ears from the Truth (2 Ti 4^4; Tit 1^{14}), to 'lie against the Truth' (Jas 3^{14}).

In a few instances, 'the Truth' indicates an assemblage of Christian doctrine, which St. Ignatius contrasted with heresy, for he wrote, 'Onesimus praises your orderly conduct in God, for that you all live according to Truth *(alētheia)* and that no heresy has a home among you'.[146] Such a sum of doctrine is wider than the Gospel. One may err from it (Jas 5^{19}) or one may walk in it (2 Jn 4, 3 Jn 3, 4), hold it (Ro 1^{18}), be established in 'the present Truth' (2 Pet 1^{12}), 'the Truth of God'[147] (Ro 1[25] 3[7] 15[8]) and 'the way of Truth' (2 Pet 2[2]).

Moreover, *alētheia* is something like an accepted body of doctrine in 1 Ti 3[15]; 2 Ti 2[15] and elsewhere, but always it is closely linked with the Father and Christ and, especially by St. John, with the Holy Ghost and holiness (Jn 4[23f.]; 14[17] 15[26] 16[13] 17[17,19]; Eph 4[24]). When St. John affirms that those who worship God must worship 'in spirit and in *truth*' (4[24]), he is probably echoing Ps 144[18] where the Hebrew had meant, 'with faithfulness' (i.e. loyalty). On the other hand, St. John may have understood the LXX version's *alētheia* in the Hellenistic sense as 'reality' contrasted with appearance,[148] thus nurturing a worship that is sincere and genuine as opposed to counterfeit or heretical worship. Similarly, when he reports Jesus as promising that 'the Spirit will guide you into all *Truth*' (16[3]), St. John echoes Ps 24(25)[5] where the Hebrew has, 'Cause me to walk in Thy *faithfulness*'. But here again, Dodd insisted, Christian Greek has allowed Hellenistic conceptions to colour the fundamentally Hebrew meaning of *alētheia*.

From 'faithfulness', then, the word changes to something like 'reality' – but only in the sense of an ultimate Reality which is God Himself, and that is certainly in keeping with Hebrew concepts.

Hellenistic philosophy has doubtless coloured the Christian meaning of *alētheia* but the Hebrew livery is still in evidence. Transcending both areas of influence, St. John affirms that the revelation of *alētheia* is intrinsically linked with the incarnate Word. Not only does the Word speak the Truth, but all Truth has its foundation in Him who reveals it. To know *alētheia* we must know the nature of Jesus,[149] and the gospel was written for this very purpose.

TRUE

1. ἀληθής

Very much the same may be said of *alēthēs*. Like the noun, the adjective is a LXX rendering of the Hebrew *'aᵉmeth* which, as we have seen, is a many-sided word, morally orientated. It is the dependable and loyal character, as in Neh 7[2] – 'a *faithful* man *(alēthēs)* who feared God above many' – and it often has special reference to reliability in the spoken word (Deut 13[14]) – 'Let them hear and say, It is truth' *(alēthēs)*: Isai 43[9]. The revelation to Daniel, and his vision, was true *(alēthēs):* Dan LXX 10[1], Th 8[26].

In secular Greek it had meant conformity to a standard, in the way that free-thinking men have always looked upon truth, no more than relative. 'A musical note is true or false according to its relation to another note.'[150] The word always has this significance in the contemporary papyri,[151] but in Biblical Greek the moral influence of *ᵃᵉmeth* has fostered the meaning, loyal and steadfast, as God is faithful. St. John and St. Paul affirm that God is *alēthēs* (Jn 3³³; Ro 3⁴), quite dependable. Christ is *alēthēs*, caring not for the person of man (Mt 22¹⁶; Mk 12¹⁴). 'True', in the same sense of absolute dependability, are the various witnesses and testimonies to God and Christ, with the records concerning them (Jn 5³¹ᶠ· 8¹³ᶠ·,¹⁶ᶠ· 21²⁴; Tit 1¹³; 3 Jn 12), the holy Scriptures.

2. ἀληθινός

Less common than the last in secular Greek, *alēthinos* meant truthful and genuine without reference to an unswerving absolute standard. Xenophon alludes to the 'genuine' army of Cyrus, in the sense that its officers were gentlemen not out for gain.[152] Demosthenes speaks of the duty of 'genuine' friends (IX 12), Plato of a 'genuine' passion for 'genuine' philosophy,[153] and Aristotle reasons that in practical science universal principles have a wide application whereas those covering a particular part of the field are more 'genuine' because they deal with facts.[154]

The LXX, however, used *alēthinos* to render *ᵃᵉmeth* when David exclaimed, 'O Lord, Thy words are *true*' (2 Km 7²⁸) and when the psalmist declared that the Lord's judgments are *true* and altogether righteous and that He is plenteous in *truth* (Ps 18(19)⁹ 85(86)¹⁵). The future Jerusalem, when God returns to her, shall be called an 'archetypal' city, a city of *truth* (Zach 8³). Moreover, *alēthinos* rendered the adverb *'amēn* in the divine title, 'God of Amen' (faithfulness) in Isai 25¹. The LXX had already crystallized *alēthinos* as a term for divine and heavenly reality.

In the NT it bespeaks several fundamentals which are everlastingly 'true' in the most absolute sense, archetypes of all other manifestations. It relates to the Light which is Christ (Jn 1⁹; 1 Jn 2⁸), to the Bread of heaven (Jn 6³²), and to the worship which the faithful offer (Jn 4²³), to the heavenly Tabernacle and to the worshipping heart (Heb 8² 10²²), and to the faithful Martyr (called Amen) who addressed the church of the Laodiceans (Rev 3¹⁴). It relates to matters of the most ultimate moment for patient believers – the prophecies revealed in heaven to the Seer concerning the consummation of all things (Rev 21⁵ 22⁶), and the affirmation of blood and water from the side of Christ (Jn 19³⁵).

Finally, *alēthinos* is the definition of God Himself, with all His oracles and ways and judgments (Jn 7²⁸ 17³; 1 Thes 1⁹; 1 Jn 5²⁰; Rev 3⁷ 6¹⁰ 15³ 19²,⁹,¹¹). In St. John's vocabulary, according to Dr.

Kingsley Barrett, it means 'real', 'genuine', 'authentic', being applied to Light, to heavenly Bread, to the Vine, and to God Himself. *Alēthēs,* on the other hand, tends rather to be 'veracious' (pp. 134f.).

For Justin Martyr, the old circumcision on the 'eighth' day was a type of the *alēthinos* circumcision, the 'archetypal' circumcision, which saved us because of Him who rose on the 'first' day of the week, and the 'first' day is called the 'eighth' (Dial. 41[4]), the eighth being the first day of another week. The word was used in Church Greek for all the spiritual realities as opposed to types and images and shadows.

TYPOLOGY (see 'Figure')

NOTES

[1] Xenophon *Cyropaedia* VI 1.54. Defined by Suidas, s.v., as a raised framework on which actors spoke the parts of gods.

[2] Aristotle *Problemata* 922b 17.

[3] Xenophon *Cyropaedia* II 3.1, al.

[4] *Bell. Jud.* II xxi 2.

[5] Thucydides II 34.

[6] Xenophon *Anabasis* III 5.7.

[7] Polybius IV 72.1.

[8] *Historia Animalium* 612b 22.

[9] For *skēnē* including Temple, see G. A. Barton's argument in *Journal of Biblical Literature* 57 (1938), pp. 197–201 (on use in Hebrews).

[10] Also in the contemporary Jewish inscription, CIG III 5361.1.

[11] G. A. Deissmann, *Light from the Ancient East,* ET Hodder 1910, pp. 116f.

[12] W. Michaelis, in Kittel *TWNT* VII, p. 393, n. 10.

[13] Aileen Guilding, *The Fourth Gospel and Jewish Worship,* Clarendon 1960, p. 52.

[14] *Oratio ad Graecos* 29. See *Texte und Untersuchungen zur Geschichte der Altchristlichen Literatur,* O. von Gebhardt and A. Harnack, vol. 4, Leipzig 1888, p. 30, line 11.

[15] *Athenagoras,* ed. W. R. Schoedel, Clarendon 1972, *Legatio* 11.1 (pp. 22f.).

[16] *Ad Autolycum* II 9. See *Theophilus of Antioch,* ed. R. M. Grant, Clarendon 1970, p. 38.

[17] C. J. Ellicott, *The Pastoral Epistles of St. Paul,* Longman 5th ed. 1883, p. 193.

[18] Sextus Empiricus *adversus Mathematicos* (ii AD) 2.42.

[19] The medical writer, Dioscorides (i AD), *de Materia Medica* I, praef. 5.

[20] Cyranides (ii AD), C. E. Ruelle, *Les Lapidaires grecs,* Paris 1898, p. 40.

[21] *Odyssey* XVI 319, XXIII 114.

[22] Polybius II 6.9 ('to attempt to retaliate').

[23] Lucian *Tragodopodagra,* 149.

[24] Strabo XVI 4, 24.

[25] Cyranides, Ruelle, op. cit., p. 47.

[26] Alexander Aphrodisiensis, *Problemata,* ed. Idder, Berlin 1841, 2.54.

[27] OCT III 10 (iii BC).

[28] E. Hatch, *Essays in Biblical Greek,* Clarendon 1889, pp. 71f.

[29] C. F. D. Moule, *Reformed Theological Review* 33 (1974), pp. 65–75.

[30] J. Jeremias, *Expository Times* 71 (1960), p. 146.

[31] Ex 17^2; Mt 16^1 19^3 22^{18,35}; Mk 8^{11} 10^2 12^{15}; Lk 11^{16}; Jn 8^6; Act 5^9 15^{10}; 1 Co 10^9; Heb 3^9.

[32] Deissmann BS p. 290; A. Audollent, *Defixionum Tabellae quotquot innoterunt,* Paris 1904, 271.26.

[33] K. Preisandanz, *Die griechische Zauberpapyri,* Teubner, Stuttgart, I, 2nd ed. 1973, p. 172 (4.3076).

[34] It occurs also in an interpolation in Dioscorides (time of Hadrian), *de Materia Medica* IV 184.

[35] *Timaeus* 65C. Plutarch *Moralia* 230B: 'a sure *means of testing*' a man.

[36] *Grammatical Insights,* T. & T. Clark, 1965, pp. 168f.

[37] Theophrastus *Historia Plantarum* (Loeb 5.9.1) iii BC.

[38] Aristotle *Problemata* 928a 24; Theophrastus op. cit., 7.7.2; Aristotle *Metereologica* 380b 28.

[39] Josephus *Ant. Jud.* I xi 4.

[40] Aristotle *Metereologica* 369b 6.

[41] Of the stomach, Dioscorides (i AD) *de Materia Medica* 2.124.

[42] 3 Km 10^{18} (Hiphil *pzz*, to be refined); 2 Chr 9^{17} (*tāhôr*, pure); 1 Chr 28^{18} 29^4 (Pual *zqq*, refined).

[43] *Nicomachean Ethics* 1118 a 28.

[44] *Memorabilia* II 6.1.

[45] M. Pol 15^2.

[46] P. Grenf I 1, 10 (ii BC). See *An Alexandrian Erotic Fragment,* ed. B. F. Grenfell, Clarendon 1896, pp. 2, 4 (papyrus I, col. 1, line 10).

[47] T. XII P. Levi 3^8.

[48] Slavonic *Secrets of Enoch* 20^1.

[49] *Ascension of Isaiah* 7^{14,21,27} 8^8 11^{25} (Ethiopic version); *Greek Legend* ii 12, 18.

[50] *Contra Celsum* iv 29 (PG XI 1069C).

[51] PG III 200D.

[52] Otto Schmitz in Kittel *TWNT* III, p. 167.

[53] *De Ebrietate* 195 (47), *de Sobrietate* 24 (5), *de Abrahamo* 271 (46).

[54] *De Cherubim* 2 (1), *Quod Deus Sit Immutabilis* 2 (1).

[55] Demosthenes XVIII 199.

[56] O. Cullmann, *Christ and Time,* ET SCM 1962, p. 46.

[57] T. Abr 101^{18}.

[58] T. Abr 112^3; Apocalypse of Abraham 28.

[59] R. H. Charles, *Eschatology Hebrew and Christian,* Black 2nd ed. 1913, p. 315.

[60] *Bell. Jud.* VI x 1.

[61] Greek Enoch XVI 1 (Syncellus).

[62] *De Fide Orthodoxa* 2.

[63] I. Eph proem.; Hom. Clem. 3^{19}; I. Rom 6^1; Hermas *Sim.* 3^2; I. Eph 17^1 (ruled by David); Enoch 99^{14}; Did 16^4.

[64] Eusebius *de Theophania* 6.

[65] O. Cullmann, *Christ and Time,* 3rd ed. ET SCM 1962, pp. 47f.

[66] Jastrow, pp. 1052, 1084; E. Schürer, *History* ..., ET Div. II, vol. II, pp. 177ff.

[67] Cp. 4 Ezra 4^{2,27} 7$^{12,29ff.,47,112f.}$ 8$^{1f.,52}$.

[68] J. W. Doeve, *Nederlands Theologisch Tijdschrift* (Wageningen) 17 (1962), pp. 32–8.

[69] A. Richardson, *An Introduction to the Theology of the NT,* SCM 1958, p. 208.

[70] Dittenberger 3rd ed. 1125.8 (an inscription of 73 BC, from Eleusis).

[71] H. Sasse in Kittel *TWNT* I, p. 204.

[72] But Bauer gives Hippocrates *Epistolae* 17.34, Maximus of Tyre 11.5e.

[73] See e.g. *Theodoreti Commentarius in omnes B. Pauli Epistolas*, Rivington 1870, part II, p. 136.

[74] Rabbinical examples of '*ôlāmîm* in this sense are given in Strack-Billerbeck III 671f.

[75] H. Sasse, op. cit., p. 204.

[76] *Encyclopaedia Biblica*, col. 1147.

[77] B. F. Westcott, *The Epistle to the Hebrews*, Macmillan 1889, p. 8.

[78] *Apol.* I 41².

[79] Jean Héring, *The Epistle to the Hebrews*, ET Epworth 1970, p. 4.

[80] Enoch 9⁴ 25f.; I. Eph 19².

[81] H. Sasse in Kittel *TWNT* I, p. 201. So also E. Stauffer, *Die Theologie des Neuen Testaments*, 4th ed. Kohlhammer, Stuttgart 1948, p. 59.

[82] Kittel *TWNT* I, p. 208.

[83] *Iranisches Erlösungsmysterium*, Bonn a. Rh. 1921, 86 A3, 235f.

[84] F. V. D. Narborough, *The Epistle to the Hebrews*, Clarendon Bible 1930, p. 82.

[85] P. Mag. Leid. V 7.36 (Preisendanz II 12, p. 75).

[86] Preisendanz I, p. 90 (4.520).

[87] Preisendanz I, p. 140 (4.2198).

[88] Preisendanz I, p. 144 (4.2315).

[89] Preisendanz I, p. 176 (4.3170).

[90] Preisendanz I, p. 196 (5.468).

[91] Euripides *The Children of Hercules* 900 (chorus).

[92] M. Dibelius and Hans Conzelmann, *Pastoral Epistles*, ET Fortress, Pa. 1972, p. 30.

[93] Teubner 1883, III 7.3 (iii AD).

[94] Burton, p. 432.

[95] Mt 18⁸ 25⁴⁶; Mk 3²⁹; 2 Th 1⁹ 2¹⁶; Heb 6² 9¹²,¹⁵ 13²⁰; Rev 14⁶; 2 Th 2¹⁰.

[96] *The Word of the Cross*, Rome 1974 (Analecta Biblica), p. 114n.

[97] J. Moffatt, *Hebrews*, ICC T. & T. Clark 1924, p. 180.

[98] Strabo VII 3.11, Dio Cassius *Fgm* 46.1, Dionysius of Halicarnassus, *Ars Rhetorica* VII 4.6, Plotinus IV 8.8.

[99] *Bell. Jud.* V ii 2 (Niese V 66).

[100] *Ant. Jud.* II iv 4 (Niese II 51).

[101] IG (vol. ii, editio minor, ed. J. Kirchner, part i, fascicle ii (1916), 1368.44.

[102] P. Lond 3.979.19 (iv AD), P. Masp 168.36 (vi AD).

[103] Pseudo-Clementine Homilies, ii 15.

[104] Thucydides VII 10.

[105] Aeschylus *Agamemnon* 813; Sophocles *Electra* 596.

[106] Euripides *Hippolytus* 612.

[107] III 112, as in Act 2¹¹.

[108] D. M. Smith, *Interpretation* 28 (1974), pp. 307–20.

[109] Ira J. Martin, *Journal of Biblical Literature* 63 (1964), p. 127.

[110] Aristophanes *Ranae* 357.

[111] Comm. on Rom 1¹³.

[112] Chrysostom *Homilies* 35.3 in 1 Corinthians.

[113] HDB II, p. 795.

[114] *Journal of Theological Studies* NS 17 (1966), pp. 299–307.

[115] Ibid., p. 303.

[116] *Journal of Theological Studies* NS 3 (1952), pp. 228–31.

[117] J. Painter, *Journal of Theology for Southern Africa* 7 (1974), pp. 50–60.

[118] R. H. Fuller, *American Church Quarterly* 3 (1963), p. 168. See also Beginnings I, p. 323.

[119] Aristotle *Rhetorica* 1410 b 12, *Poetica* 1457 b 4.

[120] *Religion* (Lancaster) 5 (1975), pp. 16–32.

[121] J. Behm, Kittel *TWNT*, pp. 725f.

[122] A view favoured by W. J. Hollenweger, *The Pentecostals*, London 1972, pp. 342f., and by E. Käsemann, *Perspectives on Paul*, London 1971, pp. 122–37, *An die Römer* HNT Tübingen 1974, pp. 229–31.

[123] C. L. Rogers, *Bibliotheca Sacra* (Dallas) 122 (1965), pp. 134–43.

[124] Eusebius *Historia Ecclesiastica* V xvi 7–14.

[125] M. Barnett, *The Living Flame*, Epworth 1953, p. 119.

[126] Epiphanius *adversus Haereses* xlviii 11 (PG XLI 872D).

[127] *Adversus Haereses* V 6.1.

[128] As recorded, for instance, by Michael Harper, in *As at the Beginning*, Hodder 1965.

[129] Archbishop Eustathius of Thessalonica, *Commentarius in Iliadem*, ed. G. Stallbaum 1827, p. 89.7. He seems to equate the word with *huperboleus* (interpreter).

[130] Herodotus IX 37, VI 75; Aristophanes *Knights* 367: Demosthenes XVIII 129.

[131] As in LXX, *Appendix Proverbiorum* 2.67, ed. E. L. von Leutsch and F. G. Schneidewin, *Paroemiographi* i, pp. 379–467.

[132] Alexis (iv BC) 222.10.

[133] Aristophanes *Frogs* 736.

[134] As to whether St. Peter and St. Paul found the LXX as we know it, as the underlying text-form of Deut $21^{22f.}$, see the interesting conclusions of M. Wilcox, *Journal of Biblical Literature* 96 (1977), pp. 85–99.

[135] *Journal of Biblical Literature* 96 (1977), p. 85.

[136] H. Cremer, *Biblico-Theological Lexicon of New Testament Greek*, ET 4th ed. T. & T. Clark 1895 and 1962.

[137] G. Kittel *TWNT*.

[138] E. Hoskyns and N. Davey, *The Riddle of the New Testament*, Faber 1931, chapter 1.

[139] C. H. Dodd, *The Bible and the Greeks*, Hodder 1935, pp. 72–5.

[140] *De Specialibus Legibus* iv 178.

[141] *De Iside et Osiride* 2.

[142] The rest of Bauer's examples are all either Jewish or Christian, s.v.

[143] T. Abr 102^{24}. See also 83^{22} 97^{28} 98^6 100^{20} 111^{29}.

[144] 1 Pet 1^{22}. See Selwyn p. 149. Same phrase in Ro 2^8; Gal 3^1 5^7.

[145] Of course, 'to do the Truth' had not this meaning in the LXX where it indicates a quality of faithfulness and steadfastness (Gen 47^{29}; Josh 2^{14}; 2 Km 15^{20}; Neh 9^{33}).

[146] Ad Eph 6^2; also Hermas *Mand.* 3^4 11^4.

[147] C. H. Dodd thought that Paul meant 'the *reality* of God', contrasted with the unreality of idols: *The Bible and the Greeks*, p. 74.

[148] So C. H. Dodd, ibid., p. 74.

[149] J. Blank, *Biblische Zeitschrift* (Paderborn) 7 (1963), pp. 164–73.

[150] Hoskyns and Davey, *Riddle of the New Testament*, Faber 1931, p. 27.

[151] MM s.v.

[152] *Anabasis* I 9.17.

[153] *Republic* 499C.

[154] *Nicomachean Ethics* 1107 a 31.

U
UNBELIEF (AGNOSTICISM)
ἀγνωσία

Agnōsia for Christians has become more than the 'ignorance' implied in secular usage and is nearer to 'unbelief'.

Secular Greek. *Agnōsia* had been a rare word, close in meaning to *hamartia* (mistake) and *agnoia* (ignorance), denoting a 'lack of knowledge'. The *agnōsia* (ignorance) and *hamartia* (blundering) of bad pilots had lost a ship.[1] 'What division', asks Plato, 'can we imagine more complete than that which separates *gnōsis* (knowledge) and *agnōsia* (ignorance)?'[2] It is the reverse of *gnōsis*, as prominently seen in the Hermetic literature. It may be complete inattention to what is transpiring. During the revolution of the four hundred at Athens, the people were demoralized by their *agnōsia* of one another – a lack of communication,[3] like the 'ignorance' of Antiochus Epiphanes when he did not know what was going on (3 Mac 5^{27}). The messenger tells Medea of her daughter's death in these words: 'In *agnōsia* of all, her poor father suddenly falls upon her corpse'.[4]

Another meaning was anonymity or obscurity. Plato says that no man is to be barred by the *agnōsia* (obscurity) of his parentage,[5] and someone declares, 'I shall never associate, I shall *recognize* no one *(agnōsia)*, and shall scorn everyone!'[6] – where it is lack of personal acquaintance, utter detachment.

Biblical Greek. In the Bible *agnōsia* gets a new sense, for it translates the Hebrew for lack of sapience (*beli-dha'ath*: without understanding), as when Job multiplied his words without wisdom (Job 35^{16}). In Wis 13^1 it denotes ignorance of God, the kind of foolishness to which the psalmist alludes, which is atheism. In assessing St. Paul's use of *agnōsia* we must recall that his acquaintance with the book of Wisdom is 'unquestionable'.[7]

A Christian addition to the Testament of Levi (18^9) which identifies the New Priest with Christ, refers to the Gentiles being multiplied in 'knowledge' during His priesthood and being enlightened by His grace which brings sin to an end. We are therefore ready to find that for St. Paul *agnōsia* and lack of belief are not far apart.

St. Paul speaks of his own 'ignorance' and 'unbelief' *(apistia)* before his conversion, although in this instance he uses the cognate verb *agnoō* instead of the noun (1 Ti 1^{13}). He upbraids some of the gifted Corinthians for their *agnōsia*, for their lack of real belief. 'Some have *agnōsia* of God: I speak this to your shame' (1 Co 15^{34}), and St. Peter leaves no doubt that he intends atheism or agnosticism by the term. 'With well-doing,' he says, 'ye may put to silence the *agnōsia* of foolish men', thus recalling the psalmist's 'foolish' body who made the assumption that there was no God. Moreover, St. Peter declares these foolish men to be the heathen who 'speak against you as evil doers' (1 Pet 2[12,15]).

The new Biblical meaning is not so much ignorance, then, as lack of belief and St. Clement insists that God has called the believer 'from agnōsia (atheism) to knowledge' (1 Clem 59[2]). The context is concerned with heresy and paganism. Denial of Christ's divinity is *agnōsia*.[8]

In the jargon of the Mystery religions, *agnōsia* denotes a lack of religious experience, which accords well with the new meaning of the word in Biblical Greek. 'Hearken, ye folk, men born of earth, who have given yourselves up to drunkenness and sleep in your *ignorance* of God; awake to soberness.' The masses are urged to repent and rid themselves of darkness.[9] *Agnōsia* was the greatest of all evils in man, whose soul is penned up in the body; such 'agnosticism' inhibits man's soul from finding anchor in salvation's haven; it sweeps the soul away.[10]

Agnōsia is the soul's vice, so the Mysteries taught. 'Such a soul is tossed about among the passions which the body breeds; it carries the body as a burden, instead of ruling it.' He who has *gnōsis* is divine and good and pious. In fact, *agnōsia* is slavery to bodily appetites. It is not so much ignorance of God as estrangement from Him.[11] Much of this corresponds with the Christian content of the word.

Hort makes a distinction as follows: *agnōsia* is not so much *ignorantia*, the absence of knowledge but is rather the equivalent of the Latin word *ignoratio*, the failure to absorb knowledge[12] – as applied in Biblical Greek, it is smug and insensitive agnosticism. It is the sentiment, 'I do not know, and I will not give Him the benefit of any doubt'. It is the view that God's existence is an unattested thesis, whether the view is held by the Logical Positivist, the modern philosophical non-theist, or the Dialectical Materialist, the Communist. It is the resolve to regard as meaningless any assertions about God which are not capable of empirical verification.

UNBELIEF (HARDNESS OF HEART)

σκληροκαρδία

The compound *sklērokardia* was coined in Biblical idiom through close rendering in the LXX and Philo[13] of a Hebrew phrase, *'orlath lēbhābh,* literally 'the foreskin of the heart', figuratively 'stubbornness' (Ecclus 16¹⁰), 'lack of repentance' (Jer 4⁴), and 'disobedience' of God (Deut 10¹⁶).

In the gospels *sklērokardia* denotes Israelite disobedience in the days of Moses (Mt 19⁸; Mk 10⁵), but later on in Christian Greek it is lack of saving faith in Jesus: according to the revelation to Hermas, the end of the rejected 'stones' is to have no place at all unless they repent, no salvation because of their *sklērokardia*.[14] In the longer ending of Mark, which is probably an example of Church Greek in the second century, the word is joined with *apistia* (unbelief) to denote lack of faith in the resurrection on the part of the eleven apostles (Mk 16¹⁴).

According to Christian vocabulary, therefore, belief is a matter of *kardia,* of inclination, and not of reason. 'I cannot believe,' is often pleaded, but what is more likely to be true is, 'Lord, I believe! Help Thou mine unbelief'. To believe, is to wish to believe. 'To believe in God,' said Unamuno, 'is, before all, and above all, to wish that there may be a God'.[15] Belief is not the logic of the mind, it is a thing of the heart. It is the reverse of *sklērokardia,* it is a tenderness of feeling. The heart leads us to God and its hardness keeps us away. Our wills set in motion what our reasoning never can, for the heart opens the faculty of comprehension, and without the desire to understand there is no understanding.

'Rise, clasp My hand, and come!' the Hound of Heaven cries to the responsive soul.

UNBELIEF (SPIRITUAL DARKNESS)

σκοτία, σκότος, σκοτίζω

The special Christian meaning of these three old words is spiritual, rather than material, darkness.

Secular Greek. *Skotia,* the first, is a word meaning gloom,[16] but the more widespread second word, *skotos,* is gloom, too, the darkness of the night and of death, of the nether world, the womb, and the darkness of blindness. It is moreover the blackness of vertigo, of obscurity, of ignorance, and of the dark shadows in a picture. The verb *skotizō,* our third word, has some of the same range of meaning. Secular senses appear in the gospels and in Acts (2²⁰ 13¹¹).

Christian Greek. The unenlightenment of the mind is a rare meaning in secular Greek.[17] **Spiritual darkness** seems to be a specially Christian use. The LXX on the whole still has the secular meaning, but *skotos* in Isai 9² 42⁷ (quoted at Mt 4¹⁶; Lk 1⁷⁹) may be interpreted in a spiritual sense. Doubtless Jesus intends the spiritual sense (*skotos* Mt 6²³; Lk 11³⁵ 22⁵³), and his 'outer *skotos*' which is reserved for unbelieving Jews (Mt 8¹² 22¹³ 25³⁰) may be a spiritual experience. In God is no *skotia* at all (1 Jn 1⁵); in Jesus *skotia* has fled (1 Jn 2⁸).

When the Word became flesh, light shone in *skotia*. Those who follow Jesus shall not walk in *skotia* (Jn 1⁵ 8¹² 12³⁵,⁴⁶; 1 Jn 2⁹,¹¹). This too is spiritual but how is it different from the *skotos* which men preferred when light came into the world (Jn 3¹⁹), from the *skotos* in which Christians must not walk (1 Jn 1⁶)? It is difficult to believe that the first Christians did not differentiate in some way between *skotia* and *skotos*. All we can say is that *skotia* is a word beloved by St. John, but *skotos* is the word of St. Paul and St. Peter.

The gospel-preaching of St. Paul and of all evangelists turns Gentiles from *skotos* to light (Act 26¹⁸), for unregenerate Gentiles are in *skotos* (Ro 2¹⁹) and their works are *skotos* (Ro 13¹²; Eph 5¹¹). Their foolish minds are **spiritually darkened** (passive of *skotizō* Ro 1²¹). Probably *skotos* (2 Co 4⁶) is a reference to Gen 1³ (the physical creation which brought light from darkness) but it is applied spiritually. *Skotos* (Heb 12¹⁸) has an OT reference, as also *skotizō* (to blind, Ro 11¹⁰) in a quotation.

Skotos is the darkness of unbelief (2 Co 6¹⁴; Eph 5⁸). It is a realm opposed to God's rule. With its spiritual rulers we have to wrestle (Eph 6¹²), and from its power we have been delivered (Col 1¹³; 1 Th 5⁵; 1 Pet 2⁹). It is the ultimate destiny of false teaching within the Church (2 Pet 2¹⁷; Jude 13).

The apostolic Fathers use the verb, *skotizō*, to the same purpose: 'We are *darkened* in our understanding by vain desires' (2 Clem 19²). By whom is this darkening done? As in Romans, it is part of the mystery of predestination. A Jewish, or Jewish Christian, book seems to be reminiscent of St. Paul when it declares,[18] 'So perisheth every young man, *darkening* his mind from the truth'.

UNBELIEVING (NON-CHRISTIAN)

ἄπιστος

In Christian Greek *apistos* denotes the infidel world outside our fellowship.

In the wider language the word had both a passive and active meaning. Passively, it was 'not to be trusted', like the Ionians who were 'mistrusted' by Xerxes,[19] like the plighted troth 'mistrusted' by both Greeks and barbarians,[20] and the confidence which is 'untrustworthy'.[21]

Passive also is the meaning, 'incredible', for Herodotus reports that at a council meeting words were uttered which, to some Greeks seemed 'unbelievable'.[22] The word has the same meaning when Hermes Trismegistos says, 'To those who have it in mind, what I have said is credible *(pista);* to those who do not, it is incredible *(apista).*'[23]

In the active sense, it is true, we come nearer to the Christian meaning. Herodotus notes that men are more 'mistrustful' of ears than of eyes (I 8) Demosthenes speaks of someone 'mistrustful' of Philip (XIX 27). In the Apology, Socrates addressed his leading accuser. 'You are even *mistrustful* of yourself, Miletus' (26 E). Actively too it means disobedient. Antigone feels no shame to be an 'unsubmissive' rebel against the state.[24]

Some of the secular senses recur in the NT – the passive 'incredible' (Act 26[8]) and the active 'suspicious', 'mistrustful', which may be the meaning in the LXX (Pr 17[6] 28[25]; Isai 17[10]) although we cannot be sure, for there is no Hebrew original to guide us. However, Jesus is styling His generation 'mistrustful' (Mt 17[17]; Mk 9[19]; Lk 9[41]) and Thomas 'mistrustful' (Jn 20[27]) – which is a secular sense of the word. Philo too has an active sense, when he declares that a man is *apistos* (i.e. in God) if he fails to believe that good gifts are bestowed on the worthy.[25] A not uncommon sense from the time of Homer,[26] is the passive, the reverse of 'faithful', i.e. not to be trusted, and it looks at first as if this is the meaning in our Lord's parable (Lk 12[46]) where the wicked servant is set among the 'unfaithful' (although AV renders it, 'unbelievers' – the Christian sense of the word), for in 12[42] the word is contrasted with *pistos* which in the context, applied to a steward, is likely to mean 'faithful'.

It still remains true that in the NT the common meaning of *apistos* is different from any of the previous meanings. It looks very much as if it bore the special sense, 'unbeliever', i.e. a non-Christian. AV indeed may be quite correct even in its rendering of Lk 12[46] ('unbelievers'), for the whole passage is parallel to that in Mt 24. Where St. Luke has *apistos* St. Matthew (24[51]) has *hupokritēs,*[27] which may well mean 'unbeliever' in the Christian language. Moreover, the *apistoi* who give heed to Jewish fables and turn from the truth are not Christians (Tit 1[15]). Likewise, the *apistoi* who have their part in the second death, the awful lake of fire and brimstone, must be unbelievers (Rev 21[8]). They cannot be within the fellowship of the Body.

As previously stated, the meaning of *apistos* in the LXX is doubtful, for there is no Hebrew original to guide us, and Dr. J. M.

Ford[28] may well be right that in Isai 17[10] *apistoi* stands for unworthy Israelites. The party strifes at Corinth may have included disputes between Pharisaic brotherhoods, and it is suggested that the Pharisaic terminology was the origin of the Christian term *apistos,* which is therefore the Pharisaic *'ām hā-'āreṣ* (People of the Land), a contrast with *adelphos (haber).* Certainly, *apistos* is put in contrast with the term *adelphos,* 'brother' (1 Co 6[6] 7[12–15]). *Apistos* may in the first place have been a term which the Jewish Christian would apply to a non-Christian, an outsider, or, at any rate, the *apistoi* will be people without the Christian fellowship (1 Co 10[27]), bidding Christians to one of their feasts. They will be outsiders who chance to attend a Christian meeting (14[22ff.]), those to whom the glorious Gospel has not yet shined (2 Co 4[4]), with whom no believer *(pistos)* should become unequally yoked (6[14f.]). To be worse than *apistos* is to be contemptible (1 Ti 5[8]). The *apistoi,* however, are not altogether to be shunned – one might as well leave the world – but fellowship with their unfruitful works must be avoided. Christ can have no concord with Belial, nor the *pistos* (believer) with the *apistos* (outsider).

Church Fathers see *apistos* as an unbeliever in contrast with Christ's disciples, the elect (I. Magn 5[2]; Diog 11[2]; M. Pol 16[1]), sometimes indicating the Docetists in contrast with catholics (I. Tral 10[1]; I. Smyrn 2), sometimes indicating the Jews.[29] At the Judgment **unbelievers** shall see Christ's glory (2 Clem 17[5]). In the same way *apistia* in Christian Greek is often 'unbelief' – all who are outside the Church (Ro 11[20, 23]; 1 Ti 1[13]).[30] The new meaning of *apistos* is eventually seen in modern Greek.

See, 'Faith'.

UNCORRUPTNESS

ἀφθορία

The noun, *aphthoria,* is a Christian coinage, although the adjective, *aphthoros* (chaste, incorrupt), occurs in secular Greek. 'Uncorruptness', the rendering of AV, is based on an inferior Greek text (*aphtharsia,* q.v.), but it is nevertheless the correct rendering of *aphthoria.*

LXX has *aphthoria* to render the Hebrew *shiddhāphôn* (a blight of crops), but the Alexandrian reading is probably an error for the *aphoria* (blight) which Vaticanus reads (Hag 2[18(17)]). It may be the Christians who coined the word, *aphthoria,* and not the LXX translators.

For Christians, however, *aphthoria* has the metaphorical

meaning of spiritual purity and uncorruptness in doctrine (Tit 2⁷). Titus must in all things present himself as a pattern in his teaching, exhibiting **spiritual** purity.

Later on, in Church Greek, the word denotes 'celibacy'[31] and the virginal 'purity' of the Holy Mother.[32]

UNFEIGNED

ἀνυπόκριτος

The word *anupokritos* cannot be certainly declared a coinage of Biblical Greek, though its Biblical meaning is new. It is used by Democritus Phalereus, whose date is now put at 270 BC (Grube). In his book on Style (*de Elocutione* 194) the meaning of Democritus is, however, 'unemotional' and, in discussing the reading aloud of a certain phrase of Menander, he contrasts *anupokritos* with 'histrionic'. Grube observes that Demetrius needs a negative of *hupokritos* (histrionic), 'and he coins one, a perfectly normal formation, no more significant than if we write un-histrionic. *It is not found again in this sense.* The later meaning "sincere", "guileless", is irrelevant here.'[33] That is the new Biblical sense.

As Grube correctly observes, there has been a change of meaning. The Bible uses it, not for 'un-histrionic', but for the impartiality of justice (Wis 5¹⁸). God's commandment is *anupokritos* (Wis 18¹⁶). Among Christians it refers to the 'unaffectedness' of Christian love (Ro 12⁹; 2 Co 6⁶; 1 Pet 1²²) and to the 'purity' of faith (1 Ti 1⁵; 2 Ti 1⁵) as well as the 'straightforwardness' of divine Wisdom (Jas 3¹⁷).

'UNLEARNED' (AV)

ἀγράμματος

In Christian Greek this word does not involve illiteracy. Nevertheless, its secular meaning had been 'ignorant' and 'illiterate' when applied to people; with animals and sounds it tended to mean 'inarticulate'. Epicurus declared of a certain philosopher, that he gave the 'illiterate' the impression that he said something new.[34] This is the meaning given by Plato – people so ignorant that they know only the names and no more, concerning great people, and so lowbrow that even the plague does not carry them off.[35] The *agrammatos* is the unintentional blunderer in reading and writing.[36]

Commonly in the contemporary papyri the word stood for a person who could not spell even his own name and must have a proxy to sign on his behalf.[37] It has been argued that therefore the apostles (Act 4[13]) are hailed as 'illiterate', unable to read or write, and not merely unversed in Jewish learning (MM). That is the outcome of insisting that there are no new Christian meanings for old words. But as early as Philo, signs of the new meaning appear. 'The laws of music, of grammar, of art in general, do not put the unmusical, the *non-literary*, the inartistic in general on equal footing in discussion with the musical, the literary and the artistic.'[38] Here the word should be rendered, 'non-literary', in order to balance with 'unmusical' and 'inartistic'. The true contrast is with the 'grammarian', the professional expert in words.

The NT context is against the classical meaning. When the rulers, elders and scribes saw the boldness of Peter and John and perceived that they were *agrammatoi* and *idiōtai* they marvelled. The wonderment of the rulers had no relevance to Peter and John's ability to read and write, but the marvel to the rulers was that, being 'rabbinically unlearned', and 'unprofessional', Peter and John could quote holy Scripture effectively. In the sentence, *agrammatos* is linked with *idiōtēs*, which is an unprofessional man, a layman, an average person without distinction. One is a layman without being illiterate. The Jerusalem Bible happily unites the two words thus: 'uneducated laymen'.

'The Lord opened unto me', said George Fox, 'that being bred at Oxford or Cambridge, was not enough to fit and qualify men to be ministers of Christ.' There is of course a wide difference between illiteracy on the one hand and the lack of an approved or fashionable education on the other. The early Christians were confessedly not wise 'after the flesh' and were the foolish things of the world lacking temporal distinction. Yet who, reading the literature of the NT, will dismiss the apostles as illiterate? True, they were strangers to the learning of this world, to secular scholarship and words to no profit, to vain babblings, foolish questions, erudition which is never able to come to the knowledge of the truth. But Timothy was commended for his youthful learning in the holy Scriptures.

According to the Apostolic Constitutions (II 1.2), being *agrammatos* does not necessarily disqualify from the bishop's office. The bishop may be 'unlearned', but he must himself possess and seek in others a higher kind of study. The bishop must still enquire of ordinands, 'Will you be diligent in Prayers, and in reading of the holy Scriptures, and in such studies as help to the knowledge of the same, laying aside the study of the world and the flesh?' *(Ordinal, B.C.P.).*

It would be wrong to assume, from this description of Peter and John, that the study of Hebrew and Greek is not of the first importance today. The Gospel has come to us in the sacred languages, and we shall not preserve it aright without them. It was Luther's belief that if we let the sacred languages go we shall lose the Gospel. The languages are, as he pointed out, the sheath in which the sword of the Spirit in encased, the box in which the jewel is carried, the cupboard where the food is kept.[39]

UNSEARCHABLE

1. ἀνεξιχνίαστος

Anexichniastos is a creation of the Bible to express the truth that God and His ways transcend human thought.

Like the LXX verb, *exichniazō,* our adjective was formed probably from the classical verb *exichneuō* (to track out). That verb occurs when Zeus aimed with his bow and found the target with unerring precision, so that the chorus of Aeschylus uses the verb metaphorically: 'This we can *clearly trace out.*'[40]

Our adjective, however, was borrowed by St. Paul from the LXX of Job and was re-echoed in the early Fathers (MM). It had rendered the Hebrew *'ên ḥēqer,*[41] and is restricted to God Whose actions are 'great' and incomprehensible.

In the NT it refers to God's ways which are **past finding out** (Ro 11[33]) and to the **unsearchable** riches of Christ (Eph 3[8]). How can you preach them, marvelled Theodoret, if they are 'past searching out?' St. Clement applied the word to the **inscrutable** depths of the abyss (1 Clem 20[5]), but it is used of God's workmanship once more in the letter to Diognetus (9[5]) or of God by St. Chrysostom.

'We call Him,' said St. Chrysostom, 'the inexpressible, the unthinkable God, the invisible, the inapprehensible, who quells the power of human speech and transcends the grasp of mortal thought, *anexichniastos* (inscrutable) to the angels, unbeheld by the Seraphim, unimagined by the Cherubim, invisible to Principalities, Authorities, and Powers, and to all creation'.[42]

> Stronger His Love than death or hell;
> Its riches are unsearchable.
>> The first-born sons of light
> Desire in vain its depth to see;
> They cannot reach the mystery,
>> The length and breadth and height. (C. WESLEY)

Meecham admitted that it was 'perhaps a "biblical" word, though formed on classical precedents'.[43]

2. ἀνεξεραύνητος

Anexeraunētos is a rare secular word, having the meaning 'inscrutable' in a fragment of Heracleitus[44] and in Dio Cassius.[45] Elsewhere it is exclusively Biblical and ecclesiastical.[46] Symmachus used it of the 'unsearchable' heart of kings (Pr 25³)[47] St. Paul has it for the 'unsearchable' judgments of God (Ro 11³³).

UNSPEAKABLE

Quod omnino sit Deus, non esse quaerendum:
quia nec inveniri possit nec enarrari. – LACTANTIUS

1. ἀνεκδιήγητος

Anekdiēgētos is a coinage of Biblical Greek based on the existing verb, *ekdiēgoumai*. 'What tongue can recite?' is an expression which St. Paul might have coined but it appears as a variant reading in the letter of Aristeas (99 BT), where it refers to an 'indescribable wonder'.

St. Paul thanks God for His gift **beyond expression** (2 Co 9¹⁵), which St. Chrysostom explains as the gift of God's own Son. St. Clement has the word three times: he states that love exalts to **unspeakable** heights (49⁴), and he refers to God's **unspeakable** might (61¹) and to the **unspeakable** statutes of nether regions, that is, the laws of nature (20⁵). St. Justin has it three times: he says that Christ's ancestral descent through a Virgin **cannot be declared,** by which he means that no mere human being is of such an origin.[48] Theophilus of Antioch speaks of God as **ineffable** in His goodness.[49] The word is used in Christian Greek to indicate the attribute and activity of God, particularly the Incarnation, the Holy Ghost, and the ways of grace and salvation. All are 'indescribable'.

2. ἀνεκλάλητος

Aneklalētos may have been coined in Christian Greek, from the verb *eklalō,* but it is found in the contemporary Dioscorides, for 'not capable of expression or calculation',[50] and in the Hermetic texts.

St. Peter refers to believers' **ineffable** joy in Christ even though they have not seen Him (1 Pet 1⁸), and St. Ignatius describes the light of the nativity Star as **inexpressible** because it manifested one

482

of three great mysteries – that of Mary's Child-bearing (I. Eph 19²).

The meaning, **ineffable,** is found in secular Greek occasionally, usually later than the NT.[51]

UNSPOTTED

ἄσπιλος

It is a word signifying Christian perfection. In secular Greek *aspilos* was applied to stones,[52] to a horse,[53] and to the two 'pure white cocks', which were sacrificed, one to the sun and one to the moon.[54] The offertory of a white cock, which was *aspilos*, is a common feature in magical texts.[55]

It has no moral content in these texts, even in the prayer, 'to be kept *aspilos* from every danger'.[56] But a new meaning appears when Symmachus uses the word in the phrase, 'the heavens are not *aspilos* in His sight' (Job 15¹⁵).

In the NT the word is applied to Christ and to Christians who have reached a high degree of extrication from the world; especially in later Christian ages it was interpreted as virginity,[57] particularly that of the Blessed Virgin.[58]

Christ is the *aspilos* Lamb of God, 'the wholly righteous and only *aspilos* One, who is free from any sin'.[59] The epithet is extended to a believer who has reached a high sphere of detachment – what St. James calls 'true religion' – and keeps himself *aspilos* from the world (1²⁷). The man of God must witness a good confession, like that of Jesus before Pilate, and must be *aspilos* and unrebukable until the Coming of our Lord (1 Ti 6¹⁴). The eschatological significance appears again in 2 Pet 3¹⁴: those who look for new heavens and a new earth ought to be found of Him in peace, *aspiloi* and blameless.

The apostolic Fathers invariably apply the word to believers in whom the Spirit dwells (Hermas *Sim.* V 6.7) and who have been elected by God to eternal life (Hermas *Vis.* IV 3.5). Christians who keep the seal of baptism *aspiloi*, obtain eternal life (2 Clem 8⁶). The concept implies a freedom from sin, such as will most splendidly come when God finishes His new creation, when we enter into His glory, when we see His great salvation perfectly realized, when we take our place in heaven at last.

UNSTABLE

ἀστήρικτος

Astēriktos occurs rarely in secular Greek, and the Christian meaning of unstable does not figure there until the second century AD,[60] when we find the phrase, '*unstable* in calculation'.[61] To be *astēriktos* is to be like water, unable to keep still.[62] It is to be unsupported by a staff.[63] By etymology it means, 'without a *stērigx* (staff)'.

If it was not a Christian coinage, at least it was a rare word which was adopted by Christians to describe two varieties of believer, the simple soul who is an easy prey to heretical teachers (2 Pet 2[14]), and the unlearned teacher himself wresting the scriptures of St. Paul to his own destruction (3[16]).

NOTES

[1] Hippocrates, *Concerning Ancient Medicine* 9.
[2] *Sophista* 267B.
[3] Thucydides VIII 66.
[4] Euripides *Medea* 1204.
[5] *Menexenus* 238D.
[6] Lucian *Timon* 42.
[7] HDB IV, pp. 930f.
[8] Athanasius *De Decretis Nicenae Synodi* 17.
[9] W. Scott, *Corpus Hermeticum* I, libellus I 27.
[10] Ibid. I vii 1.
[11] Ibid. I x 8, 9.
[12] F. J. A. Hort, *1 Peter I 1–II 17*, Macmillan 1898, p. 144.
[13] *De Specialibus Legibus* I 305: ' "Circumcize the *hardness of your hearts*," he said' (cit.).
[14] *Vis.* III 7.6.
[15] Miguel de Unamuno, *The Tragic Sense of Life*, Dover (NY) T 257, p. 114, and Collins Fontana 1962, pp. 122, 127. See the whole discussion.
[16] Apollonius of Rhodes IV. 1698 (iii BC).
[17] But see Demosthenes XIX 226, Plato *Laws* 864C.
[18] T. XII P. Reuben 3[8] (cp. Ro 1[21]; Eph 4[18]).
[19] Herodotus VIII 22.
[20] Xenophon *Anabasis* II 4.7.
[21] Thucydides I 120.
[22] Herodotus III 80.
[23] W. Scott, *Corpus Hermeticum*, vol. I, p. 186 (libellus ix 10).
[24] Aeschylus *Seven against Thebes* 876, 1035.
[25] *Legum Allegoria* iii 164.
[26] *Iliad* III 106.
[27] R. Bultmann *TWNT*, VI, p. 205, n. 234.
[28] *Journal of Theological Studies* NS 17 (1966), p. 73.
[29] Athanasius *de Incarnatione* xviii 2.

[30] Bultmann in *TWNT* VI, p. 205.
[31] Basil of Caesarea *Sermones ascetici* 1.1. (PG XXXI 872B).
[32] Gregory of Nyssa *In diem Natalem Christi* (PG XLVI 1128B).
[33] G. M. A. Grube, *A Greek Critic: Demetrius on Style,* Toronto 1961, p. 147. Italics are mine.
[34] Plutarch *Adversus Colotem* 26.
[35] *Critias* 109D, *Timaeus* 23A.
[36] Xenophon *Memorabilia* IV 2.20.
[37] BGU 118. ii 17; 152.6 (both ii AD).
[38] *Quod Omnis Probus Liber Sit* 51.
[39] Weimar edition (ed. J. C. F. Knaake, etc.) 1883ff. xv 38.
[40] *Agamemnon* 368. Cf. R. E. Thomas *Expository Times* 39 (1928), p. 283.
[41] Literally, 'there is no searching'. Job 5^9 9^{10} 34^{24}.
[42] PG XLVIII 721.
[43] H. G. Meecham, *The Epistle to Diognetus,* Manchester 1949, p. 130.
[44] 18 (Diels I 81.17).
[45] 69.14 (ii–iii BC): 'the number of those who perished by famine ... as *past finding out*'.
[46] Dionysius Areopagita *de Divinis* I 2; Andrew of Crete (viii AD) *Oratio* 6; John V of Jerusalem *contra Iconoclastes* 7; John Damascene *de Fide Orthodoxa* IV 13.
[47] And perhaps of the human heart, Jer 17^9.
[48] Dial. 43^3 76^2; Apol. 51^1.
[49] *Ad Autolycum* I 3 (PG VI 1028C).
[50] *Peri Euperistōn*, praef. (ed. M. Wellmann, Berlin 1914) i AD.
[51] Eunapius *Vitae Sophistarum* (ed. J. F. Boissonade 1841, p. 486B) iv–v AD; Aristophanes of Byzantium *Epitome* (ed. S. P. Lambros 1885, 26.10) ii BC; Emperor Julian *Orationes* 5.158 d iv AD.
[52] IG II 5, 1054 c, 4 (Eleusis c. 300 BC).
[58] Herodian V 6.7.
[54] Preisendanz I, p. 72 ('zwei ungefleckte Hähne'); *Abraxas* ed. A. Dieterich, Leiden 1891, ix. 26f.
[55] Preisendanz II 26 (two white cocks), III 693 (one white cock), XIII 370 (a white cock, *aspilon:* 'fleckenlosen').
[56] Preisendanz XII 260; *Papyrus Magica Musei Lugdunensis Batavi,* ed. A. Dieterich 1888, viii 11ff.
[57] Gregory of Nazianzus *Carminum Libri Duo* 1.2.1.658 (PG XXXVII 572).
[58] P. Grenf II cxiii 1 (an eighth- or ninth-century deacon's litany of the Coptic rite, commemorating the Virgin).
[59] Justin *Dial.* CX 6.
[60] Longinus II 2 (iii AD), Galen *de Usu Partium* II 15.
[61] Vettius Valens 242.3 (ii AD).
[62] Nonnus *Dionysiaca* 10.14 (Teubner).
[63] *Anthologia Palatina*, ed. F. Dübner, Paris 1864, 6.203.

V

VAIN REPETITIONS

βατταλογέω

The verb *battalogō* (to use vain repetitions) is a coinage of Christian Greek. *Battalogōs* was a derisory onomatopoeic name for Demosthenes,[1] who was a stammerer in early life. The verb appears in the Lives of Aesop (Bauer) but very doubtfully. The incidence in Simplicius of the sixth century is due to the influence of Christian Greek (Cremer p. 765).

It may be a transliteration of the Aramaic *baṭṭālâ* (vanity) or the Hebrew *baṭâ* (to speak rashly, to babble).[2]

It expresses our Lord's counsel to avoid insincerity in prayer (Mt 6[7]; Lk 11[2]D).

In an Aramaic papyrus from Qumrân *b*ᵉ*ṭēl* occurs, with the meaning 'to be void', together with *rîq*, the word from which 'Raka' may be derived, and the whole phrase is rendered by Benoit, Milik and de Vaux, the editors, *invalide et sans effet légal*. 'In other words, says Jesus, we are no longer to use prayers hitherto used by Gentiles and which are no longer of effect because they have been superseded by the manner of prayer which He was now teaching them.'[3]

THE VICTORIOUS LIFE OF HEAVEN

ζωή, ζωογονέω

The general meaning of *zōē* in Greek is sometimes found also in the NT.[4] It was life or existence, contrasted with death. Pindar puts both together, death and *zōē*.[5] It was one's living, one's substance, or property (Homer) – a livelihood[6] – and it was a 'way of life', like that of the Amazons, a *zōē* of hunting and plunder.[7]

In Biblical Greek, however, *zōē* is understood eschatologically as an inheritance in the Kingdom of God or as an equivalent of holiness and of the passage to final salvation. It is one of many instances where a secular word of no special connotation has been taken over into Christian Greek to express a characteristic idea. Christians would not be aware that in certain pagan circles it was already a religious term, since OT concepts were the first to come to mind.

'The words of this *zōē*,' must be no less than the Gospel itself (Act 5[20]). 'Holding forth the word of *zōē*,' is surely the preaching of

486

the Gospel (Ph 2[16]), for evangelism points the way to *zōē*, i.e. salvation. So, too, repentance may be said to lead to *zōē* (Act 11[18]), for the promise of the Gospel is that repentance issues in salvation. *Zōē* then has no longer any relation to its secular sense. It is not the duration of life, a way of living, a livelihood, or any kind of property. 'Justification of *zōē*', is a Christian phrase marking God's redeeming work on the sinner's behalf (justification), which leads to his full salvation. In Christ 'is *zōē*' (Jn 1[4]).

Among Christian terms that have been discovered in the Qumrân texts, it is perhaps strange that we do not as yet find any technical term for 'eternal life' in the Christian sense – the life belonging to the *aiōn* to come – nor does the idea itself find any particular emphasis.[8] There is of course the phrase *ḥayyê neṣaḥ* (endless life),[9] which Black thinks is almost certainly intended to mean a life without any cessation by death, but which is a life like that of the angels and which is contrasted with the fire of the dark regions.[10] It cannot be compared with the *zōē* which is in Christ.

In the NT *zōē* is nothing less than salvation, and when it is qualified by the epithet *aiōnios* (belonging to the Age to come), its fullness and finality is to the fore – as also in the expressions, 'newness of *zōē*' (Ro 6[4]), and 'the crown of *zōē*' (Jas 1[12]; Rev 2[10]), and the sanctifying 'water of *zōē*' (Rev 21[6]).

The sanctified believer, the overcomer, will find his name written in the Book of *zōē* Rev 3[5]) – salvation's register, recording those who have passed from death to 'life' (Jn 5[24]). Salvation is our new *zōē*, not ours in its fullness until we are saved by His *zōē* when we are risen with Him (Ro 5[10]).

In Christian Greek *zōē* is evidently a short way of denoting the ultimate stage in our pilgrimage to holiness, indeed the believer's glorification. The way to *zōē* is narrow and hard, and disciples must bestir themselves (Mt 7[14] 18[8f.] 19[17]; Mk 9[43ff.]).

What then is meant by the Tree of *Zōē*? It grew in the midst of Eden and it shall grow in heaven, with healing leaves and miraculous fruit for *anakainōsis* (see 'Spiritual Renewing') beside the sanctifying River (Rev 22[2]). The Tree has much to do with full salvation, as also has the Bread of *zōē*, Christ our heavenly food (Jn 6[48]). To have *zōē* is to overcome finally, to master the flesh and to inherit all things. To have *zōē* is to be spiritually minded (Ro 8[6]). At the end, all persevering believers shall be 'heirs together of the grace of *zōē*' (1 Pet 3[7]). The word has quite transformed itself.

The verb, *zōögonō*, was in secular Greek to propagate or engender, but in the Bible it comes within the influence of the Hebrew verb *ḥyh* and now means 'to preserve alive' – no longer to bring forth young,[11] or in the passive to be gendered as one element is gendered from another.[12] 'The Lord maketh alive!' cried Hannah

(1 Km 2⁶). 'He who is prepared to lose his *psuchē* (self),' cried Jesus, 'shall *preserve his life*' (Lk 17³³). In the Greek of the Christians, the verb is particularly to bestow what they understood by *zōē*. According to the best texts of 1 Ti 6¹³, God 'gives' this kind of *zōē*, and the initiative in our achieving full salvation lies entirely with God. We must use our best endeavours, but *zōē* is not simply a reward for effort. It is still the gift of God's grace and part of His plan of salvation.

VIGILANCE (SPIRITUAL ALERTNESS)

ἀγρυπνία: ἀγρυπνέω

In the language of the Bible and the Church, the noun *agrupnia* and the verb *agrupnō* denote the concept of 'carefulness'. Readers are advised that the editor's abbreviating work calls for 'vigilance' (2 Mac 2²⁶). The noun in Sirach and the Wisdom of Solomon is metaphorical.[13] However, in secular Greek the words had denoted sleeplessness in the literal sense, wakefulness in a crisis,[14] insomnia through a pain of the head.[15]

The themes of watchfulness and rousing from sleep in a spiritual, and not a natural sense are appropriate in Christian teaching. Elect and justified, the brethren are nonetheless always to be alert, since this world's night is far spent and it is high time to don the armour of light (Ro 3¹¹ᶠᶠ·). Using the verb *agrupnō* and looking to the End, their Lord had counselled watchfulness and prayer to stand worthily before the Son of Man in the last persecution (Mk 13³³; Lk 21³⁶). *Agrupnō* meant perseverance, constant prayer for one another (Eph 6¹⁸). An overseer or bishop has the special duty to 'watch' for souls (Heb 13¹⁷) and the noun *agrupnia* is one of a list of harassments a minister of God may expect, along with hunger, corporal punishment and detention (2 Co 6⁵). St. Paul 'glories' in this form of austerity. To be 'in *watchings* often' was inseparable from the care of all the churches (11²⁷). The apostolic Father assures his readers of his *agrupnia* (watchfulness) for them, particularizing members of 'the way of darkness' as those who '*watch* not to the fear of God' *(agrupnō).*[16]

In late Church Greek *agrupnō* is to keep a vigil, to pass a sleepless night in asceticism, and to be spiritually vigilant,[17] while *agrupnia* is a vigil, an ascetic exercise, spiritual alertness and vigilance.[18]

The late Mr. Bishop reminded us of a Palestinian institution, the practice of spending the night in talk around a fire, and he suggested that St. Paul resorted to the practice at Troas, wherein

Eutyches met his accident, and that often besides St. Paul would use the watches of the night to talk of Christ. In the prison at Philippi he was singing hymns at midnight, and Christians of Bithynia in Pliny's time were singing hymns 'before daylight'.[19] So, then, the *agrupnia* was perhaps part of the missionary technique and the word denotes, not insomnia, but the voluntary assumption of a 'wakeful' night.

NOTES

[1] Aeschines (Teubner 1896) 2.99 (adv. Timarch. 51).
[2] Moulton-Howard, *Grammar* II, p. 272; DCG II 499b, 790a.
[3] Canon F. Bussby, *Expository Times* 76 (1964), p. 26.
[4] Lk 1^{75} 16^{25}; Act 8^{33} 17^{25}; 1 Co 15^{19}.
[5] *Nemean Odes* IX 29.
[6] Herodotus VIII 105.
[7] Herodotus IV 112.
[8] J. C. Coetzee, *Neotestamentica 6: Die Nuwe-Testamentiese Werkgemeenskap van Suid-Afrika*, Pretoria 1972, pp. 48–66.
[9] 1 QS iv 6ff.
[10] M. Black, *The Scrolls and Christian Origins*, Nelson 1961, p. 139.
[11] Plutarch II 494C.
[12] Vettius Valens 162.17.
[13] Ecclus prol. $38^{26ff, 30}$; Wis 6^{15}.
[14] Plutarch *Moralia* 337B.
[15] Dittenberger 4th ed. 1960, vol. 3, 1169.50 (iii BC).
[16] Barn 20^2 21^7; Cp. Did. 5^2 ('vigilant for good').
[17] E.g. *Apostolic Constitutions* 7.18.2.
[18] E.g. Chrysostom *Homily* on Gen 3^5 (4.19E).
[19] E. F. F. Bishop, *Evangelical Quarterly* 37 (1965), pp. 29–31.

W

WAIT FOR

ἀπεκδέχομαι

The verb *apekdechomai* was coined in Christian Greek and was set in an eschatological context, implying eager longing for the second Coming of our Lord. The whole created universe 'waits for' its deliverance (Ro 8[19]), believers 'long for' complete salvation (8[23, 25]) and the Lord's Coming (1 Co 1[7]; Ph 3[20]; Heb 9[28]). They 'patiently wait for' the hope which justification holds out (Gal 5[5]).

However, the word occurs in later Jewish Christian literature in a way which is not eschatological,[1] as well as once in St. Peter's language (1 Pet 3[20]). It is not often found outside the NT and Christian literature. It appears in some secular writers of our period in a different sense, meaning 'to draw a conclusion', a wrong conclusion,[2] or 'to await'.[3] In the eschatological sense dear to St. Paul it is a distinctive usage, 'expectation' of the End.[4] In this special sense the word belongs to Jewish and Church Greek,[5] occurring again in St. Clement of Alexandria, St. Basil and St. Gregory of Nyssa,[6] as well as the Testament of Abraham and the Acts of Paul.

'WAY'

ὁδός

Hodos is a word which received much attention in the Bible and among Christians. In Greek it indicated a road or journey, and it often had a metaphorical application, a 'manner' or method, like 'the *path* where wisdom leads' or 'the oracular *road*', i.e. the way of divination,[7] '*ways* of telling a story',[8] and 'the Athenians' *path* of injustice'.[9] In contemporary Greek *hodos* might represent the doctrine of a philosophical school. 'Can you name me a man', asks Lycinius, 'who has tried every *path* in philosophy?'[10] Nevertheless, the metaphorical usage in Biblical Greek is influenced by Hebrew idiom. The Biblical *hodos* indicates a course of conduct or thinking, especially a moral or immoral 'way' of life, after the manner of the Hebrew *derekh*.

Dr. J. A. Kleist pointed out that two streams meet in the Greek of the NT – the Hellenistic and the Palestinian. The Syrian Koine was modified by the vernacular Aramaic of the people who used the Koine, and later on Hebraisms came in by the Greek OT, but we must concede that 'the workings of the human mind are essentially the same everywhere',[11] and therefore some idioms which are Semitic were duplicated by the same idiom in Koine Greek. The 'way' metaphor is so spontaneous that men of different nationalities would hit on it independently. One cannot be sure whether the bilingual Christians were consciously translating a Semitic idiom into Greek or whether they were using a current Greek expression known to them from the Koine. It happened so often that we may suppose this variety of Greek to have already absorbed many idioms like this.

The first Christians were quickly accustomed to the word in its new dress. Barnabas and Saul spoke of all nations walking in their own 'ways' (Act 14[16]) and accused Elymas of perverting the right 'ways' of the Lord by his mischief (Act 13[10]). The same OT sense is present in St. Peter's quotation from David to the effect that God made known the 'ways' of life (Act 2[28]) and is present also in St. Paul's awful indictment, 'None have known the ways of peace' (Ro 3[17]). 'Just and true are Thy *ways*', sing the overcomers, 'Thou King of the aeons' (Rev 15[3]) – a usage of *hodos* which is reminiscent of Deut 32[4] LXX. The 'ways' of God are past finding out (Ro 11[33]) and Christians speak of the preaching of the Gospel as the 'way' of salvation (Act 16[17]). Reminiscent too of LXX usage is the description of John coming in the 'way' of righteousness (Mt 21[32]) and of Jesus teaching the 'way' of God in truth (Mt 22[16]; Mk 12[14]; Lk 20[21]). St. Paul follows the Bible usage when he refers to his own conduct as 'my *ways* which be in Christ' (1 Co 4[17]), and refers to Christian love as 'a very excellent *way*' (1 Co 12[31]). St. James begins his letter by declaring a doubting Christian to be 'unstable in all his *ways*' and ends by likening the conversion of sinners to a turning from the errors of their 'ways' (Jas 1[8], 5[20]). *Hodos* is a course of conduct.

Another new usage of *hodos* is seen when it denotes the Christian religion itself. Both new meanings appear together (2 Pet 2[15]) where heretics are said to have forsaken the right *hodos*, the Christian faith, and to have erred in the *hodos* (LXX sense) of Balaam.[12] Saul was off to Damascus to fetch 'any of this *hodos*', that is, any Christians, and the 'way' in Act 18[26] is not so much the LXX word as the new Christian term, and so with the *hodos* which many at Corinth slandered and of which Felix had no better information than that it was a sect of the Nazarenes (19[9,23] 24[22]). *Hodos* is the Faith, is Christianity itself.

As Michaelis pointed out,[13] there are two standpoints from which to view *hodos*, Hebrew and Hellenistic. In Hellenistic thought, the 'way' to God or to happiness and immortality is conceived as less momentous than the attainment of the goal itself. In Hebrew thought, on the other hand, the 'way' itself was intrinsically important and was governed throughout by God's own laws. It was the 'commanded walk'. A reviewer of the Wörterbuch article,[14] while owning that the antithesis is not absolute, confessed that as a broad characterization it was illuminating, and he applied the point made by Michaelis to the passage where Jesus gently corrects Thomas (Jn 14[4], shorter text). The disciples' thoughts were, perhaps unconsciously, Hellenistic, conceiving that the attainment of the goal was paramount. 'We can't know the goal', says Thomas, 'for we do not know the way.' But Jesus remonstrates that disciples need not know the goal so long as they know the 'Way', which is Jesus Himself.

Following Hebrew syntax,[15] where *derekh* (way) functions as a preposition, the accusative *hodon* (way) is used prepositionally in Biblical Greek with *thalassēs* to form the phrase, 'by the sea' (Mt 4[15]). The expression is absent in the LXX, but St. Matthew takes it from Theodotion's version of Isai 9[1f.].

WILES

μεθοδεία (-αι)

Methodeia is a word for heretical deception which is based ultimately on Satan's twisted cunning. It resembles *planē*. See 'Deceit'.

Methodeia and the plural, *methodeiai*, are a coinage in Christian Greek (Ephesians), made from the late verb *methodeuō* (to prevent, deceive) which in the LXX came to mean to slander (2 Km 19[27(28)]) and, in Aquila, to lie in wait (Ex 21[13]).

It appears in papyri of the fifth and sixth centuries,[16] with however only the non-Biblical sense of 'method'. In the NT it is used of the **trickery** of heretics, their cunning craftiness (Eph 4[14] singular), and also of the **wiles** of the Devil (Eph 6[11f.], p[46]). The lexicon of Suidas gives both senses: 'skills or treacheries'.

WILL-WORSHIP (AV)

ἐθελοθρησκία

Ethelothrēskia is not a secular word, although it is defined by the lexicographer Hesychius, nor does it occur elsewhere in Biblical Greek. St. Paul seems to have coined it (MM) from existing words when he wished to describe the nature of certain Pelagian-like heretics who had 'indeed a show of wisdom in *will-worship*, and humility, and neglecting of the body' (Col 2[22]).

Some renderings of the Latin versions – *religio, observatio, simulatio religionis* – miss the point, according to K. L. Schmidt;[17] *ethelothrēskia* is a piety which fails to maintain the true object of worship and in place of Christ selects its own objects. The prefix *ethelo-* (will) implies the concept of free choice and says nothing of the object of the worship. The meaning is therefore **free worship** or **uncontrolled worship**, rather than 'worship of free will'. It is what the Geneva Bible (1560) sets down as 'voluntarie religion', and in the margin, 'Such as men have chosen according to their own fantasie', and not as Jeremy Taylor, 'will-worshipper'.[18]

WITHOUT GOD

ἄθεος

The secular meaning of *atheos*, as in Plato,[19] was an 'atheist', one who, like Socrates for instance, denies that the official gods exist, or else as in Pindar,[20] and Philo,[21] 'ungodly', or as in Sophocles,[22] 'abandoned by the gods'.

The sense of ungodly or godless seems to lie in the upbraiding of Apollo by the chorus in Eumenides (151), because he had succoured the matricide Orestes: 'Shame, son of Zeus ..., thou hast ridden down aged divinities by showing respect to thy suppliant, a *godless* man and cruel to a parent'. This is not the sense of Christian Greek (*not knowing the true God*, a parallel to 'without Christ', Eph 2[12]), but indicates rather, one who has offended ancient and official divinities.

St. Ignatius applies it to the heretical Docetists (I. Trall. 10[1]) and St. Hippolytus to Marcion's heresy.[23] With this word St. Ignatius chides his readers: 'Even the *atheoi* (those who know not the true God) respect our bishop' (I. Trall. 3[2]). He supplies a definition of the word when he adds, 'I mean, *apistoi* (unbelievers)' – a strange epithet for the Docetists, and the sense is that of 'non-believers' in the real humanity of Jesus – not Plato's meaning, nor that of the proconsul who endeavoured to force Polycarp to subscribe by saying, 'Away with the *atheoi*', at the last.[24]

Christians were denounced in secular Greek as *atheoi* (atheists) because they had no shrines nor visible images of deity. Justin Martyr confessed that Christians were indeed *atheoi* (atheists) as far as the immoral gods of paganism were concerned (*Apol.* I 6.1), but the Apologists on the whole tended to resent the charge. 'Poets and philosophers have not been voted *atheists* for asking about

God', protested Athenagoras (5¹). 'Plato is not an *atheist* for conceiving of one God, nor are we *atheists* who acknowledge that He is God Who framed all things by the Logos' (6³).

This is the secular meaning of *atheos*, deployed in a discussion with pagans. St. Polycarp, however, could cheerfully cry, 'Away with the *atheists*', for he brought into play the Christian sense as he waved his hand towards a crowd of heathen, those who knew not God. The incident provides a specimen of the difference between the secular and the Christian interpretation of the word.

THE WORD

λόγος

It is fruitless to look in secular Greek for the meaning of this important Christian word in its most signal occurrences, though secular Greek will help us in less weighty contexts.

Secular Greek. The secular meanings were wide and various. *Logos* was reckoning or computation, like that of the king who would take 'account' (*logos*) with his servants (Mt 18²³). It was a banking account or treasurer's ledger and, metaphorically, a penalty, or the account one must give of oneself.

Leaders in the local church watch for souls as those that must give a *logos* (Heb 13¹⁷), and so *logos* was a kind of concern. 'All things are naked to the eyes of Him with Whom we have concern' (*logos*: Heb 4¹³). It was, moreover, a measure. 'No church communicated with me to the extent of giving and receiving' (Ph 4¹⁵). An item might be of no *logos* (account) or value.²⁵

Logos was besides the relation, the correspondence, the proportion of one subject to another. Herodotus, for instance, speaks of 'inverse *proportion* or *ratio*' (*logos*).²⁶ Nearer to its peculiar Christian use, is the secular reference of *logos* as an explanation, a ground, a plea or a pretext. Plato asks, 'On what *logos* (ground)?'²⁷ and Xenophon, 'For what *logos* (reason)?'²⁸ So, in the writing of St. Luke, Peter asks, 'For what *logos* have you sent for me?' (Act 10²⁹), and Gallio remonstrates, 'If it were a *logos* of wrong or wicked lewdness, I would bear with you' (18¹⁴). So it is a legal ground of action, and the town clerk protests, 'If the craftsmen have a *logos* against any man, the law is open' (19³⁸). This is the kind of context to be found in secular Greek.

Logos was for Aristotle, moreover, a proposition in logic.²⁹ Among the Stoics it became philosophical – a generative principle existing in all organisms, causing them to reach their destiny, the *spermatikos logos*, the generative life-imparting principle.³⁰ For

494

Plato it was the life-force bringing the world to birth. While Plato believed that the archetypal pattern of eternal nature was timeless, without beginning, he held that the copy of it exists in time and is continually changing. 'Wherefore as a consequence of this agency (*logos*) on the part of God ... the planets came into existence ... for determining time'.[31]

The secular meanings are not yet exhausted. *Logos* was also reasoning, reflection, and mental debate.[32] Aristotle refers to 'the inward *logos* which is in the soul',[33] and Stoics contrasted the inner *endiathetos logos* with the *prophorikos logos*,[34] the former being the reasoning which only potentially shapes the world, the latter that which has realized itself.

Moreover, *logos* was a narrative, a story, a 'treatise' (Act 1[1]). It is speech, talk, expression by words, like the 'saying' which went abroad among the brethren (Jn 21[23]), and the 'utterance' in which the brethren were rich (1 Co 1[5]). It is too a particular 'word': Jesus cast out the spirits with His *logos* (Mt 8[16]). It is subject-matter, like that momentous topic discussed by the apostles and elders (Act 15[6]). So in the common usage of Greek *logos* has become a convenient term for describing any kind of self-expression and it does not follow that St. John, in writing his Prologue, had any special knowledge of Stoicism, Platonism, or other philosophy.[35]

Christian Greek. In the NT *logos* acquires two underived senses. (1) Supremely it denotes Christ Himself, the eternal 'Word', who is uncreated and is co-creator of God's world, very God, the potent life-imparter and the illuminator of the night, incarnate as Jesus (Jn 1[1,14]; 1 Jn 1[1]; Rev 19[13]). In the language of St. John, *logos* describes God 'in the process of self-communication'. *Logos* is a creative Word of God, declaring His nature and creating a life in which divine power circulates. He is not just the archetypal Man like the *Logos* in Philo. His relation with man is soteriological. Men who receive the incarnate Logos are born of God, they belong to a new humanity represented by the Logos. This is 'not a Platonic relationship of type and antitype', but a human relationship since the Word became flesh.[36] In that sense *logos* is a term avoided by all NT writers save St. John, but the new meaning is so original that it has added the special word 'Logos' to every language.

Much has been debated on the name *Logos* as divinely deployed. St. John may have known the writings of Philo, the Jew of Alexandria who had written of *logos* about thirteen hundred times and who tried to put together Hebrew and Stoic conceptions. Philo identified *Logos* with the holy Wisdom of Proverbs and the apocrypha. He conceived *Logos* as a divine Person, a living Principle a personalized instrument by which God fashions and governs the world,[37] what he calls the 'Helmsman of the universe'.[38]

However, St. John's gospel is Jewish enough in tone to suggest that it is nourished much more sufficiently by the OT than by Philo or by any Hermetic distillation. St. John's concept of the *Logos* has been shown to differ essentially from that in Stoicism, Philo, and Gnosticism.[39] Scholars once thought that St. John was influenced by the current expression, 'the *memra* (word) of the Lord' in the Aramaic paraphrases of the OT which were made for the Palestinian synagogues. But *memra* was not an intermediary or a real being at all.[40] It was rather an attempt to avoid saying that God is directly involved with the world. It is doubtful whether St. John was influenced by the Targum.

Divine creative energy, as expressed in the prologue, recalls vividly the first chapter of Genesis, particularly it preoccupation with 'light'. St. John has in mind the Hebrew *dābhār*, rendered *logos* in the LXX. In Psalm 33 the spoken *dābhār* of God is said to be causal and by its instrumentality were the heavens made. In Wis 18[15] *Logos* had already been personalized as 'Thine all-powerful Word' who leaped from heaven 'down from the royal throne'. This scripture probably influenced not only St. John but Philo too, and perhaps the Hermetic writer.[41]

St. John's specific contribution was to declare that the divine co-Creator became incarnate: 'the *Logos* became *sarx*'. The concept of the *Logos* illuminating all men is not merely intellectual, for the light is the Truth by which men believe and are born spiritually. The light brings salvation, only in and through the *sarx* of Jesus Christ.[42]

(2) That is not all, for *logos* in the NT denotes the sacred message which concerns God's saving grace and which God Himself has confirmed by miracles in Christian history (Mk 16[20]). It is in this second Christian sense of the word that 'ministers of the *logos*' are preachers of the Gospel (Lk 1[2]), and in which hearing of the *logos* is said to lead to saving 'belief' (Act 4[4]). So also the scattered church of Jerusalem preached the *logos*, the Gospel (Act 8[4]), and those who heard it received the Holy Ghost (10[44]). In the Gentile mission field, the *logos* (Gospel) was received (17[11]).

Preaching the *logos* is none other than preaching the Gospel (2 Ti 4[2]), and very likely we would do better to take *logos* alone (without, 'of the Lord') in Act 19[20], understanding that the Gospel prevailed by 'the might of the Lord'.[43]

Christ was the *Logos* and He preached the *logos*. He was the Sower and the Seed (Mk 2[2] 4[14]). The synoptic evangelists seem reluctant to name Jesus explicitly as the Word, as St. John does, but they make the fact clear enough, and for them Jesus is the one in Whom the *logos* (the Gospel) 'decisively encounters mankind'.[44]

'Christ *was* the Word *and* spake it' (QUEEN ELIZABETH I).

λογικός

There is a new Christian meaning for the old adjective, *logikos*.
Secular Greek. Broadly it had two meanings, one derived from *logos* (speech) and the other from *logos* (reason). Under the first come such expressions as *logikē phantasia* (phantasy expressed in speech) and *agōnes logikoi* (contests in eloquence),[45] while under the second came the meanings, intellectual,[46] dialectical,[47] logical,[48] and rational.[49]

The adjective, *logikos*, is found twice in the NT, once used by St. Paul (Ro 12¹) and once by St. Peter (1 Pet 2²). St. Paul urges that the offering of our bodies as a living sacrifice is our 'reasonable' (AV) service, and St. Peter urges converts as new-born babes to desire the 'milk *of the word*' (AV) so as to grow thereby. Bengel understood *logikon* as 'of the Word'. Other commentators preferred meanings which accord better with secular Greek: 'rational' (Hort, de Wette, C. Wordsworth) or 'spiritual' (Huther, Alford, RV).[50]

Dr. Moule observes that *logikos* is used in a sense found, for example, in the Hermetica to designate what belonged to the realm of words or concepts rather than to that of matter. He would therefore understand, not 'rational' (Hort) but 'immaterial', almost 'spiritual'.[51]

Hort had pointed out that every Latin version has either *rationabile* or *rationale* and had urged the rendering, 'the food which nourishes reason', that is, which calms down passion and appetite.[52]

Christian Greek. Despite Hort's weighty plea that *logikos* cannot mean 'belonging to the Word', I still hold this meaning to be a special creation of St. Peter's language. As Bigg protested,[53] it is no more difficult to derive the adjective from *logos* (Word of God) than to derive it, as Hort did, from *logos* (reason). One hesitates to claim that St. Paul had the same meaning (Ro 12¹) but, in Bigg's words once more, 'the usage of St. Paul can never be compared with that of St. Peter without great caution and reserve' (p. 126). What, then, does St. Paul say? Your reasonable service? or, your service of the Word? or, your service as laid down by the Word?

And what does Eusebius mean? He mentions a letter of the bishop of Corinth which imparted to a Christian lady the nourishment described as *logikē*. Is this the nourishment of the Word?[54]

THE WORLD: WORLDLY: WORLD-RULER

κόσμος, κοσμικός, κοσμοκράτωρ

The words, *kosmos, kosmikos* and *kosmokratōr*, are old words but they find in Christianity a new sense, marking the essentially evil sphere in which our lot is cast.

Secular Greek. 1. *Kosmos* was 'order' as against chaos (Homer, Herodotus, Aeschylus). Thucydides wrote concerning a battle, 'There was no *kosmos* in anything that was done, so that the Peloponnesians saw the confusion' (III 77). *Kosmos* was also 'discipline',[55] and especially 'government'. *Kosmos* is the term used in the two expressions, 'to change the *constitution*' and, 'under the oligarchical *constitution*'.[56]

It is an 'ornament' in the sense of adornment,[57] particularly the feminine kind.[58] It is used, especially in the plural, of ornaments worn on the body.[59] *Kosmos* has this sense in the NT when St. Peter disparages the outward adornment of ladies (1 Pet 3³).

It is 'honour' or 'credit', as in the tag of Sophocles: 'Woman, to women silence brings credit' (*Ajax* 293). Sometimes it is a 'ruler'.[60] *Kosmos* is the universe, or world-order, in general (Act 17²⁴). Heracleitus pronounced, 'No one, divine or human, made this *kosmos*; but it always was, is, and will be, fire' (30). Aristotle linked together *kosmos* and *ouranos* (heaven) as being the constitution of everything.[61]

In later secular Greek, however, *kosmos* becomes the inhabited earth,[62] as we shall find sometimes in the NT, and Nero is described as lord of the whole *kosmos*.[63] Not until the Christians do we find a new meaning, the world at enmity with God, estranged from Him by sin.

2. *Kosmikos* is an adjective meaning, 'of the world' or, 'of the universe'. The *kosmikē diataxis* was the arrangement of the universe.[64] Again the NT has brought a fresh meaning, 'earthly' or 'worldly' or 'secular', in contrast with the sphere of God's rule, while in Church Greek we find the meaning 'secular,' 'non-clerical'.[65]

3. *Kosmokratōr* was in secular Greek a 'ruler of the world', an epithet of Uranos and Zeus,[66] applied also to the emperors.[67] It then became an astrological term, one of the seven planets controlling the state of man.[68] Iamblichus refers to the *kosmokratores* who control the elements (*stoicheia*) beneath the moon.[69]

Christian Greek. 1. *Kosmos.* Those are not the new Christian meanings, though *kosmos* will sometimes still stand for the inhabited earth,[70] and for ornament (1 Pet 3³). Even in Jn 1¹⁰, 'the world made through the Word is a world capable of knowing, or of

498

reprehensibly not knowing, its Maker'.[71] The characteristic meaning in Christian Greek is a bad sense of worldly affairs. 'The world', says Sasse, 'is the summary (*Inbegriff*) of unredeemed creation'. *Kosmos* is now a convertible term with 'darkness'. The *kosmos* rejects light, is perverse and deceitful.[72] This is the *kosmos* that those gain who lose their souls (Mt 16[26]; Lk 9[25]; Mk 8[36]) and whose fashion is passing away (1 Co 7[31]), which consists of the lusts of the flesh, of the eyes, and the pride of life (1 Jn 2[16]). The Biblical view of *kosmos* is conspicuous in the Johannine writings where St. Paul's seed-thoughts are developed and the terminology becomes firm and positive.[73] In St. John's gospel, says Dr. Barrett, 'the emphasis lies on the distinction between the 'world', and the disciples (representing the Church), who are chosen out of it'.[74]

Kosmos frankly is the godless rout (1 Jn 4[5]) who hate the children of God and whose works are evil; they can neither know nor receive the Holy Ghost and afford no peace to the disciples (Jn 7[7] 14[17,27] 15[18] 17[14]). Their wisdom brings no knowledge of God (1 Co 1[21]). Their values are not His (1 Co 1[21-28]). A believer will keep well away from them (Jas 1[27]), for to be their friend is to be an enemy of God (Jas 4[4]), and He will judge the *kosmos* (Jn 12[31]). A gap opens between such people and Christ's disciples who are not of the *kosmos* and are 'called out' of it (Jn 15[19]). They are in it because it is the place of their tribulation (Jn 16[33]); yet they are dead to all of it, and all of it is dead to them (Gal 6[14]). If they love it, the love of God is not in them (1 Jn 2[15]), for the whole *kosmos* lies in the embrace of the wicked one (1 Jn 5[19]). St. Ignatius is as forthright as St. John. 'Do not speak of Jesus Christ and also desire the *kosmos*' (I. Rom. 7[1]). It is a good thing, judges St. Polycarp, to refrain from lusts in the *kosmos* (Pol. Phil. 5[3]).

When the *kosmos* is redeemed it will cease to be *kosmos*. The reconciled and redeemed world is no longer *kosmos* nor 'this dispensation', but is the Kingdom of God, the coming Dispensation, 'the new heavens and the new earth'.[75]

The Christian view of the *kosmos*, therefore, hardly resembles that of the Stoics. Epictetus thought that a man gains freedom by turning away from the world and receding into himself. We too are delivered from a world which is passing away (1 Co 7[31]) and in the meanwhile we are to have no affection for it (1 Jn 2[15ff.]), but the Christian's deliverance is outside himself. The ground of a Christian's liberty from the world is not just that the world itself is passing away but that our Lord is now spiritually present and is coming again. To this extent St. Paul is said to differ from the apocalyptists, for he teaches that the fullness of time has arrived and Christ is even now Lord.[76] There can be no doubt, however, that St. John and St. Paul see the *kosmos* as dangerous and to be avoided. It lies all around the Christians,[77] and they must shine as lights within it (Ph 2[15]). Their attitude may not be the negation of the world, nor even contempt for it, but their faith has overcome it.[78]

In Christian history there have been differences in believers' attitudes to the world. What is called 'other-worldliness' has been a fine ideal among certain groups and sects, both Catholic and Protestant. How to renounce the world has been the chief care of many. They see that their citizenship is in heaven and that earthly politics have no importance there. Their Lord's Kingdom is not of this world and He gave His disciples no encouragement to involve themselves in its affairs.

We have been reminded lately, on the other hand, that we live in a period when this *aiōn* and the *aiōn* to come overlap, and that we are in two dispensations at once. We are therefore burdened with the problems of both. According to Dr. Vidler, for instance,[79] we may not lay aside our present responsibilities, for we do not live entirely within the *aiōn* to come. We need both the Law and the Gospel at this moment. The Law, which includes besides the Torah the law of Nature, together with moral obligation and social duty, is God's communication of His will for us now. We are not to forget, either, the Law of Christ which is summarized in the Sermon on the Mount. For Vidler, therefore, the question of world-renunciation is not a very easy one. The truth, however, may be that the highest law, Christ's teaching on the Mount, is itself an imperative call to world-renunciation: to leave all and follow Him at this present time.

2. *Kosmikos*. Christian Greek reserves the adjective for mundane lusts (Tit 2[12]; 2 Clem 17[3]), for an inferior temporal sanctuary (Heb 9[1]), for 'worldly' tortures (M. Pol. 2[3]) and 'worldly' goods which we ought not to desire (2 Clem 5[6]). When a Christian prophet is said to enact a 'worldly' mystery the sense is clearly bad and will imply that some prophets were making revelations by human wisdom rather than surrendering themselves to the divine influence (Did. 11[11]).

3. *Kosmokratōr*. In Christian Greek the word becomes a 'ruler of this wicked world', a tyrant of this darkness (Eph 6[12]), an evil spiritual being placed immediately after the *archai* and the *exousiai* in the angel hierarchy. 'We wrestle ... against Principalities, against Powers, against the *kosmokratores*, against spiritual wickedness in high places'. They are called 'rulers of the world' in order to emphasize the terrifying power of their influence and the efficiency of their plans, and so to undermine the seriousness of the believer's struggle because we have to contend with devilish foes.[80] *Kosmokratōr* was a term for Satan among some Gnostics. The Acts

of John was a second-century work which the Manichaean heretics elevated as Scripture and substituted in place of our Acts of the Apostles. In this book 'the Prince of the world' (*kosmokratōr*) is clearly Satan (23). However, in the more orthodox Acts of Philip the *kosmokratores* appear in the plural in connection with the 'evil Dragon that opposeth us', i.e. Satan (144). In the Testament of Solomon, a medley of Jewish folklore, magic formulae, and demonology, wherein Christ is pictured as Conqueror of demons, the demons are known as *kosmokratores* (8^2).

All three words get a deeply evil sense in Biblical and Jewish Greek, especially among Christians. They represent a world which is overrun by Satan and his agents, separated from God and hostile to Him. The deadly weapon against the *kosmos* is faith.

THE WORLD TO COME

ἡ οἰκουμένη (ἡ μέλλουσα)

Elsewhere in the NT, as in Greek generally, *oikoumenē* was the inhabited earth[81] or the Greek or Roman world.[82] In Heb 2^5, however, the word *oikoumenē*, here qualified by the participle *mellousa* (coming), is almost synonymous with *aiōn* and indicates the future or eschatological dispensation (q.v.). The coming dispensation is said not to be subjected to any angel, but to the Son.

Thus, *oikoumenē* may well have a new Christian use as a near equivalent of *aiōn*, with the proviso that *oikoumenē* will lay more stress than *aiōn* on the inhabitants of the dispensation to come.

Further light is thrown on the Christian meaning of *oikoumenē* from the context of the word in the LXX of Ps 95(96)[9-11] ('the world shall be established') where it is not this present world that is intended,[83] but the dispensation to come.

The context of *oikoumenē* in Heb 1^6 2^5 concerns enthronement (crowning with glory and honour and the sitting-down on the right hand of the Majesty on high). So the bringing of the First-Begotten into the *oikoumenē* in Heb 1^6 refers to the Coming of our Lord and the inauguration of the future dispensation.[84] The bringing of the First-Begotten 'into the world' (AV) has no direct reference to Christ's birth at Bethlehem. The Ascension of Isaiah represents the angels as pouring out their rapture to Christ as He ascends through the successive heavens in which they live ($11^{23f.}$). It is a good comment on the words of the Seer, 'When He shall bring the First-Begotten into the Age to Come, all the angels of God shall worship Him'. The argument of 10^5 is no parallel ('when He cometh into the world'), for there the word for 'world' is *kosmos* and has a different meaning. The bringing of the First-Begotten into the *oikoumenē* (1^6) must look forward to events in the future, regarded as fulfilled at a time as yet undetermined.[85]

WORLDLINESS

ματαιότης, ματαιόομαι

The verb *mataioumai* occurs in the second-century Herodian,[86] and the noun *mataiotēs* in the second-century Pollux (VI 134) and Sextus Empiricus,[87] and in Philodemus[88] and Philo of i BC. Philo will not have a story accepted on mere hearsay, for he believes that hearing is a faculty inferior to sight and full of *mataiotēs*,[89] by which he must mean 'deceptiveness' or 'false appearance'.

If it were not for these instances, we would assume that the words were formations within the Biblical language based on the adjective *mataios* (ineffective), which is the reverse of *teleios* (mature).

The noun *mataiotēs* appears in the LXX, usually to render *hebhel* (vapour, vanity), especially in Ecclesiastes, but several times in the Psalms.[90] The forsaking of the Lord in order to follow superstitious vanities (*mataiotēs*) is the way this 'vaporous' activity is manifested and 'every man living is altogether vanity (*mataiotēs*)', the children of men being lighter than *mataiotēs* itself. Such idolatry turned to Israel's trouble when as a punishment God consumed their ways in *mataiotēs*.

The quality is a dense foolishness in Biblical Greek, contrasted with trust in God; it shows itself as reliance on oppression and robbery, and on worldly riches; as amassing of wealth for legatees to squander; it is associated with all the terrors that materialism brings, and shows man at his lowest, bereft of God. In Christian language it is a feature of the Gentile world and of all unregenerate creation (Ro 8^{20}; Eph 4^{17}). It is linked with 'the lusts of the flesh' and is distinctive of certain heretics (2 Pet 2^{18}).

The verb *mataioumai* expresses failure to glorify God, the darkening of foolish hearts who revel in arrogant wisdom (Ro 1^{21}) – it is, in short, to be worldly.

The whole concept is worldliness, with emphasis on its ultimate transitory nature – to be escaped by all means (Barn. 4^{10}), castigated by Polycarp as 'the foolishness of the crowd', the falsity of the multitude, and contrasted with God's Word and with watching, fasting and praying (ad Phil. 7^2).

It is a Christian word insofar as the contemporary meaning is superseded by one of profounder significance.

ὀργή

In Greek *orgē* was a natural impulse or mood,[91] usually anger. There are, for instance, the phrases, 'to use anger', which is to be in a passion,[92] 'to be visited with anger',[93] and the phrase, 'quick to anger'.[94]

Biblical Greek affords a fresh angle, involving the reaction of the divine nature to our sin. Some passages are found in which secular writers have *orgē* in the sense of divine 'wrath', like the wrath of Zeus.[95] Indeed, all peoples have been aware of wrathful deities so nervously that one may explain every cult of the ancient world, and perhaps of ours too, as an elaborate bid to soften their anger.[96] The Biblical notion may be seen in that secular passage where the great soldier Titus confessed that God had shown His 'wrath' by allowing him to take Jerusalem, and on that account Titus declined an official crown.[97] While in the general range of Greek it is a rare and contingent meaning, in the Biblical dialect God's emotive reaction to man's disobedience and stupidity is regularly expressed anthropomorphically by this word which translates most often the Hebrew *'aph*, usually divine anger (nearly one hundred times), but also *ḥārôn* (burning anger) and *ḥēmâ* (wrath), and sometimes *qeṣeph* (wrath of God) and *'ebhrâ* (rage, fury). In its Hebrew setting, *orgē* denotes anger experienced from the bottom of one's heart and may not always be explained as an impersonal working out of the consequences of breaking divine laws. Whiteley quotes Ex 4[14] (the Lord being enraged with *orgē*) and insists 'that all scholars are in agreement about this matter. But, though only one quotation has been made, it must be remembered that there are many others'.[98] The LXX does not studiously set *thumos* apart from *orgē*, which is indeed 'anger' personally experienced.

The NT *orgē* refers often enough to God's wrath, but once or twice the secular sense of human vexation is retained (Ro 12[19]; Eph 4[31]; Col 3[8]; 1 Ti 2[8]; Jas 1[19f.]) – in contrast to thirty instances of the Biblical sense. Incidentally in one conspicuous example where human vexation is pictured, the word *parorgismos* is substituted – 'Let not the sun go down upon your *parorgismos*' (Eph 4[26]). The avoidance of *orgē* is remarkable in view of the close parallel in Plutarch (*Moralia* 488 B, C) which nevertheless has *orgē*. It is the famous passage forbidding one to wage a battle when impelled by emotions arising from *orgē*. It was said that if the Pythagoreans were led by it into any recrimination, they would not let the sun go down before they had joined right hands over the quarrel. St. Paul may deliberately in this passage of his have turned to another word

503

for human anger. He may have seen *orgē* as characteristically divine.

The word's context in the NT is nearly always eschatological,[99] although as Richardson pointed out, 'its hidden workings are already present and active in the world'.[200] The beginnings of the final drama of the End are even now being enacted in the world, and its details – including God's wrath – are discernible to the eyes of faith.[101] *Orgē* is usually 'the *wrath* to come' (Mt 3^7; Lk 3^7; 1 Th 1^{10}), the '*wrath* against this People' in the last days (Lk 21^{23}), or the 'wrath' of the Day of Judgment (Ro 2^5). *Orgē* is contrasted with the mercy of God which at last leads to eternal life (Jn 3^{36}), and *orgē* is palpably associated with events at the End. Thus, 'the *wrath* of the Lamb' is said to belong to the great Day of His *wrath* (Rev $6^{16f.}$). At the End worshippers of the Beast shall drink of 'the wine of the *wrath* of God' (Rev 14^{10}). Concurrently the nations shall be angry but a fiercer wrath, God's *orgē*, shall have come (Rev 11^{18}), and spiritual Babylon shall receive the cup of the wine of the fierceness and 'wrath' of Almighty God (Rev 19^{15}). 'These are the last times', recalls St. Ignatius. 'Let us fear the *orgē* which is to come' (I. Eph. 11^1).

The wrath of God, warns St. Paul, is upon unregenerate mankind (Ro 2^8; Eph 2^3) and is in despite of His justifying action (Ro 1^{18}, 5^9) and of salvation (1 Th 5^9), but is directed against believers too if they share the sins of this evil time. God's wrath is on 'the children of disobedience' (Eph 5^6; Col 3^6). All men, believers or no, who fail in duty to the civil power experience it (Ro $13^{4f.}$). The disciple who fails to forgive his brother from his heart, warned Jesus, provokes it (Mt 18^{34}). Here the word is the verb (*orgizomai*) from the same stem, 'to be angry'. So might the heavenly Father do unto us, Jesus warns. We pray in the Litany, even as Christians, 'Be not angry with us for ever'.

One may insist that *orgē* in Jewish and Christian Greek applies not personally and directly to God, that *orgē* is not God's own anger but is sin's consequences working themselves out by some remorseless divine law. Should I, or a nation, embark upon a certain course, then the sure consequences may be expected to follow, as night the day. This inevitability, it is said, is not the expression of a feeling or an attitude in God.

Indeed, Dr. C. H. Dodd noted that the verb *orgizomai* (to be angry) is never used in the Bible with God as subject. Dodd found that the actual subject is always avoided by means of recourse to 'awkward paraphrases',[102] and so he thought of *orgē* rather as an impersonal quality, *effectus* rather than *affectus*. The 'wrath' is often spoken of, without mention of God's name, as if it were an independently working power. 'Wrath' is the objective and determined consequences of sin working themselves out inexorably in my life or on the stage of history, an ineluctable process of cause and effect in a moral universe.[103] Some have gone further and urged that the consequences are not God's personal dealings with us at all but they take place rather within the sphere of law, while God's own relations with us are confined to the sphere of love.[104]

So deterministic a view, as it seems to me, exaggerates a rigid principle of cause and effect. It attracts because it is logical. It exalts the sovereignty of Nature. It puts emphasis upon the immanence of God, allowing less weight to His transcendence and to His overruling Providence which orders all things, even His wrath. But to press the necessary legacy of breaking Nature's laws, both moral and physical, may be to forget the smiling Face behind the frowning Providence of God.

Certainly, the Law displays His wrath conspicuously. It is upon Gentiles (1 Th 2[16]), but not only upon them, for the Jew who transgresses finds that the Law works wrath (Ro 4[15]). Indeed, God sware not to the Gentiles in His wrath so much as to Israel (Heb 3[11] 4[3]; Ps 94(95)[11]). Nevertheless, though Dr. Hanson's is an attractive and comfortable view, I shrink from conceding that it is the Biblical meaning of *orgē*. It accords with modern sentiment to take the personal sting out of it. 'It is hard to see why God, who hates sin, should impose upon those who have sinned the penalty of committing further sin'.[105] Much is hard to see, but it is what St. Paul seems to say (Ro 1[18-32]), for his words suggest very strongly that one penalty of sin is that further sin is committed. It is not that God is vindictive, for 'vindictive' is a highly wrought and inconclusive word. It is too easy to assail the Bible by appealing to transitory sentiment.

A weakness of Hanson's great book is that the powerful arguments from the Bible, as put forward by Dr. Leon Morris,[106] might have received more weight. As Prof. Moule gently protested,[107] Morris is not so much as mentioned in this book on 'wrath'.

The Biblical meaning of *orgē* is distinct from the secular sense of the word, and yet I would not go as far as to suppose that personal feeling has been removed from it.

NOTES

[1] T. Abr 96[23]; Acta Pauli ch. III.
[2] Aratus *Phaenomena* I 7.7 (c. 300 BC).
[3] Sextus Empiricus *adversus Mathematicos* II 73 (ii AD); Heliodorus *Aethiopica* II 35 (iii AD).

[4] W. Grundmann *TWNT* II, p. 55.

[5] *New Testament Studies* 1 (1955), p. 223.

[6] Clement *Stromateis* 1.1, 2.12; Basil *de Fide* 2; Gregory of Nyssa *contra Eunomium* 4.

[7] Aeschylus *Eumenides* 989, *Agamemnon* 1154.

[8] Herodotus I 95.

[9] Thucydides III 64.

[10] Lucian *Hermotimus* 46.

[11] *Catholic Biblical Quarterly* 8 (1946), p. 193.

[12] Jude 11 has 'the *way* of Cain'.

[13] In Kittel *TWNT* V, pp. 42–65.

[14] C. H. Dodd in *Journal of Theological Studies* NS (1954), p. 246.

[15] A. H. M'Neile, *The Gospel according to St. Matthew*, Macmillan 1955, p. 44.

[16] P. Oxy 136.18, 24; 1134.9, etc.

[17] Kittel *TWNT* III, p. 159, n. 23.

[18] HDB IV, p. 923a.

[19] *Apology* 26C.

[20] *Pythian Ode* 4.162.

[21] *Legum Allegoria* 1.49.

[22] *Oedipus Tyrannus* 661.

[23] *Refutatio Omnium Haeresium* 7.31 (PG XVI 385C).

[24] *Martyrdom of Polycarp* 9^2.

[25] Herodotus I 120.

[26] I 134.

[27] *Republic* 366B.

[28] *Historia Graeca* II 2.19.

[29] *Analytica Priora* (ed. Bekker) 24 a 16.

[30] Zeno Citieus (iv BC), *Stoicorum Veterum Fragmenta*, ed. H. von Arnim, Leipzig 1903, 1.28.

[31] *Timaeus* 38C.

[32] Plato Theaetetus 189E. In *Timaeus* 71D: '*logos* and understanding' are said to be in abeyance.

[33] *Politica* 76 b 25.

[34] Von Arnim, *Stoicorum*, op. cit., vol. II, p. 43.

[35] C. K. Barrett, *The Gospel according to St. John*, SPCK 1955, p. 127.

[36] This is excellently expounded by Dr. Kingsley Barrett, op. cit., pp. 61f.

[37] *Legum Allegoria* ii.

[38] *De Migratione Abrahami* 6.

[39] K. Wennemer, *Scholastik* (Freiburg) 38 (1963), pp. 1–17.

[40] H. A. Wolfson, *Philo*, Harvard 1948, vol. I, p. 278.

[41] *Logos* is named 'Son of God' in *Corpus Hermeticum* (Scott) I.6.

[42] F.-M. Braun, *Revue Thomiste* (Paris) 64 (1964), pp. 341–63.

[43] A. W. Argyle rightly: *Expository Times* 75 (1964), p. 151.

[44] G. Frost, *Scottish Journal of Theology* 16 (1963), p. 194.

[45] Plutarch *Coriolanus* 38; Dionysius of Halicarnassus *de Compositione Verborum* 11; von Arnim, *Stoicorum Veterum Fragmenta*, Leipzig 1903, 2.61; Philostratus *Vitae Sophistarum* 1.22.1.

[46] Aristotle *Nicomachean Ethics* 1108 b 9.

[47] Diogenes Laertius 3.58; Aristotle *Metaphysica* 1080 a 10.

[48] Aristotle *Rhetorica* 1355 a 13.

[49] The Stoics (e.g. Epictetus, Teubner 3.1.26) and Philo often, Eusebius *HE* I 2.19.

[50] Supported by the author of T. Levi 3^6 who like Paul spiritualizes the Jewish sacrifices, asserting that the angels offer to God in praise a *logikon* and bloodless offering. Origen seems to say the same of Raphael's offering on Tobit's behalf, a

logikēn hierourgian (de Orat. 11*).* The Hermetic writings have *logikē thusia* (spiritual sacrifice), which Philo opposes to animal sacrifices (*Spec. Leg.* I 277).

[51] C. F. D. Moule, *Journal of Theological Studies,* NS 1 (1950), pp. 34f.

[52] F. J. A. Hort, *The First Epistle of St. Peter,* Macmillan 1898, p. 101.

[53] C. Bigg, *St. Peter and St. Jude,* ICC T. & T. Clark, 2nd ed. 1902, p. 126.

[54] *Historia Ecclesiastica* IV 23.13.

[55] Demosthenes XVIII 216.

[56] Thucydides IV 76, VIII 72.

[57] Herodotus V 92.

[58] Plato *Republic* 373C.

[59] Aeschylus *Agamemnon* 1271; Isocrates II 32.

[60] Aristotle *Politica* 1272 a 6.

[61] *De Caelo* 280 a 21. Also Diogenes Laertius VIII 48, Xenophon *Memorabilia* I 1.11.

[62] OGI 458.40 (9 BC).

[63] SIG 814.31.

[64] Plutarch II 119ff.

[65] Justinian, the Christian emperor, *Novellae* 123.1.2.

[66] Orphic Hymns, ed. by E. Abel, Leipzig 1885, 4.3; *Notizie degli Scavi,* serie V, 1912, 323.

[67] *Inscriptiones Atticae ...,* ed. A. Kirchhoff 1873, 14.926.

[68] *Catalogus Codicum Astrologorum,* ed. F. Cumont, etc., Brussels 1898, vol. VI, p. 68; Vettius Valens 171.6. See W. L. Knox, *St. Paul and the Church of the Gentiles,* CUP 1939, p. 104.

[69] *De Mysteriis* 2.3. Perhaps we have traces of Iranian influence here.

[70] Mt 26[13]; Mk 14[9], etc.; Jn 3[16] (the inhabited earth which God loves) 21[35].

[72] C. K. Barrett, *The Gospel according to St. John,* SPCK 1955, p. 135.

[72] See the exposition of 'le péche du monde selon saint Jean', by F.-M. Braun, *Revue Thomiste* 65 (1965), pp. 181ff. H. Sasse in Kittel *TWNT* III 894.

[73] Sasse, op. cit., pp. 895f.

[74] Barrett, op. cit., p. 365.

[75] Sasse, op. cit., p. 893.

[76] W. Schrage, *Zeitschrift für Theologie und Kirche* (Tübingen) 61 (1964) pp. 125–54.

[77] Some commentators interpret *kosmos* differently here – including 'mankind', 'universe', and even 'sky'.

[78] Sasse, op. cit., p. 896.

[79] A. R. Vidler, *Christian Belief and This World,* SCM 1956, passim.

[80] W. Michaelis in Kittel *TWNT* III, p. 913.

[82] Aristotle *Meteorologica* 362 b 26 – as in Act 19[27]; Lk 4[5]; Rev 12[9] (Alford).

[82] Demosthenes VII 35, Herodotus IV 110, P. Oxy 1021.5 (i AD) – as in Lk 2[1]; Act 11[28].

[83] A. Vanhoye, *Biblica* 45 (1964), pp. 248-53.

[84] G. Johnston, *New Testament Studies* 10 (1964), p. 354.

[85] B. F. Westcott, *The Epistle to the Hebrews,* Macmillan 1889, p. 22 (*hotan* with aorist subjunctive, see Moulton-Turner III, p. 112).

[86] *Herodiani Technici reliquiae,* ed. A. Lentz, Leipzig 1867, I, p. 453, 13.

[87] Meaning 'idle talk'. *Adversus Mathematicos* (Teubner I 278) ii AD.

[88] *Volumina Rhetorica* (Teubner II.26 S).

[89] *De Confusione Linguarum* 141.

[90] Ps 30(31)[6(7)], 38(39)[5(6)], 61(62)[9], 77(78)[33], 143(144)[4] and 35 times in Eccles.

[91] Hesiod *Opera et Dies* 304, Herodotus VI 128, Thucydides I 140.

[92] Herodotus VI 85.

[93] Demosthenes XXI 175.

[94] Herodotus I 73.

[95] Dittenberger 3rd ed., 1237.5.

[96] H. Kleinknecht in Kittel *TWNT* V, p. 384.

[97] Philostratus *Vita Apollonii* VI 29.

[98] D. E. H. Whiteley, *The Theology of St. Paul*, Blackwell 1964, p. 64.

[99] J. Y. Campbell showed that St. Paul took over from Judaism the objective and eschatological conception of the wrath of God and that he uses the terms *wrath of God*, and *wrath*, articular and inarticular, without distinction in meaning, just as the LXX does. *Expository Times* 50 (1938), p. 232.

[100] Alan Richardson, *An Introduction to the Theology of the New Testament*, SCM 1958, p. 76.

[101] Ibid., p. 75.

[102] *Journal of Theological Studies*, NS 5 (1954), p. 248.

[103] C. H. Dodd, *The Epistle to the Romans*, Moffatt commentary, Hodder 1952, p. 23.

[104] See the argument behind A. T. Hanson, *The Wrath of the Lamb*, SPCK 1957.

[105] Whiteley, op. cit., p. 61.

[106] E.g. *The Apostolic Preaching of the Cross*, London 1955.

[107] C. F. D. Moule, *Expository Times* 69 (1958), p. 138.

Index of Christian Words

510

511

512